McFarland Classics

Adir. *The Great Clowns of American Television*

Anderson. *Science Fiction Films of the Seventies*

Archer. *Willis O'Brien*

Benson. *Vintage Science Fiction Films, 1896–1949*

Bernardoni. *The New Hollywood*

Broughton. *Producers on Producing*

Byrge & Miller. *The Screwball Comedy Films*

Chesher. *"The End": Closing Lines...*

Cline. *In the Nick of Time*

Cline. *Serials-ly Speaking*

Darby & Du Bois. *American Film Music*

Derry. *The Suspense Thriller*

Douglas. *The Early Days of Radio Broadcasting*

Drew. *D.W. Griffith's* Intolerance

Ellrod. *Hollywood Greats of the Golden Years*

Erickson. *Religious Radio and Television in the U.S., 1921–1991*

Erickson. *Syndicated Television*

Fernett. *American Film Studios*

Frasier. *Russ Meyer—The Life and Films*

Fury. *Kings of the Jungle*

Galbraith. *Motor City Marquees*

Harris. *Children's Live-Action Musical Films*

Harris. *Film and Television Composers*

Hayes. *The Republic Chapterplays*

Hayes. *3-D Movies*

Hayes. *Trick Cinematography*

Hill. *Raymond Burr*

Hogan. *Dark Romance*

Holland. *B Western Actors Encyclopedia*

Holston. *Starlett*

Horner. *Bad at the Bijou*

Jarlett. *Robert Ryan*

Kinnard. *Horror in Silent Films*

Kinshasa. *The Man from Scottsboro*

Langman & Gold. *Comedy Quotes from the Movies*

Levine. *The 247 Best Movie Scenes in Film History*

McGee. *Beyond Ballyhoo*

McGee. *The Rock & Roll Movie Encyclopedia of the 1950s*

McGee. *Roger Corman*

McGhee. *John Wayne*

Mank. *Hollywood Cauldron: Thirteen Horror Films*

Martin. *The Allied Artists Checklist*

Nollen. *The Boys: ...Laurel and Hardy*

Nowlan. *Cinema Sequels and Remakes, 1903–1987*

Okuda. *The Monogram Checklist*

Okuda & Watz. *The Columbia Comedy Shorts*

Parish. *Prison Pictures from Hollywood*

Pitts. *Western Movies*

Quarles. *Down and Dirty: Hollywood's Exploitation Filmmakers*

Selby. *Dark City: The Film Noir*

Sigoloff. *The Films of the Seventies*

Slide. *Nitrate Won't Wait*

Smith, L. *Famous Hollywood Locations*

Smith, R.D. *Ronald Colman, Gentleman of the Cinema*

Sturcken. *Live Television*

Tropp. *Images of Fear*

Tuska. *The Vanishing Legion: ...Mascot Pictures*

Von Gunden. *Alec Guinness*

Von Gunden. *Flights of Fancy*

Warren. *Keep Watching the Skies!*

Watson. *Television Horror Movie Hosts*

Watz. *Wheeler & Woolsey*

Weaver. *Poverty Row HORRORS!*

Weaver. *Double Feature Creature Attack*

Weaver. *Return of the B Science Fiction and Horror Heroes*

West. *Television Westerns*

Poverty Row
HORRORS!

Monogram, PRC and Republic
Horror Films of the Forties

by Tom Weaver

Research Associates:
Michael Brunas *and* John Brunas

McFarland & Company, Inc., Publishers
Jefferson, North Carolina, and London

The present work is a reprint of the library bound edition of Poverty Row HORRORS! Monogram, PRC and Republic Horror Films of the Forties, first published in 1993. McFarland Classics is an imprint of McFarland & Company, Inc., Publishers, Jefferson, North Carolina, who also published the original edition.

Library of Congress Cataloguing-in-Publication Data

Weaver, Tom, 1958–
    Poverty row horrors! : Monogram, PRC and Republic horror films of the forties / by Tom Weaver ; research associates, Michael Brunas and John Brunas.
      p. cm.
    Filmography: p.
    Includes bibliographical references and index.
    ISBN 0-7864-0798-0 (paperback : 50# alkaline paper) ∞
    1. Horror films—United States—History and criticism.
I. Brunas, Michael. II. Brunas, John. III. Title.
PN1995.9.H6W38   1999
791.43'616—dc20   92-50324 CIP

British Library Cataloguing-in-Publication data are available

Front cover: From the film poster for the 1944 release of Monogram Pictures' *Voodoo Man* (PHOTOFEST)

Frontispiece: Poverty Row's most prominent prisoner, Bela Lugosi starred in a nine-film Monogram horror series and also top-lined one of PRC's low budget chillers.

Manufactured in the United States of America

McFarland & Company, Inc., Publishers
  Box 611, Jefferson, North Carolina 28640
  www.mcfarlandpub.com

DEDICATED TO

Dr. James Brewster
Dr. Lorenzo Cameron
Dr. Max Von Altermann

Table of Contents

Introduction   ix

Boys of the City (Monogram, 1940)   1

The Ape (Monogram, 1940)   5

The Devil Bat (PRC, 1940)   14

Invisible Ghost (Monogram, 1941)   26

King of the Zombies (Monogram, 1941)   35

Spooks Run Wild (Monogram, 1941)   45

Black Dragons (Monogram, 1942)   52

The Corpse Vanishes (Monogram, 1942)   63

The Mad Monster (PRC, 1942)   74

Bowery at Midnight (Monogram, 1942)   84

Dead Men Walk (PRC, 1943)   93

The Ape Man (Monogram, 1943)   102

Ghosts on the Loose (Monogram, 1943)   114

Revenge of the Zombies (Monogram, 1943)   121

Voodoo Man (Monogram, 1944)   129

The Monster Maker (PRC, 1944)   141

The Lady and the Monster (Republic, 1944)   151

Return of the Ape Man (Monogram, 1944)   164

The Girl Who Dared (Republic, 1944)   174

Bluebeard (PRC, 1944)   177

Crazy Knights (Monogram, 1944)   191

Fog Island (PRC, 1945)   195

The Phantom Speaks (Republic, 1945)   204

The Vampire's Ghost (Republic, 1945)   211

Strangler of the Swamp (PRC, 1945)   219

The Face of Marble (Monogram, 1946)   228

The Flying Serpent (PRC, 1946)   236

Devil Bat's Daughter (PRC, 1946)   246

The Catman of Paris (Republic, 1946)   253

Valley of the Zombies (Republic, 1946)   261

Spook Busters (Monogram, 1946)   269

Appendix I
   The Music of Poverty Row (by Bill Littman)   275

Appendix II
   Exclusions, Borderline Inclusions,
   a Few Late '40s Films   278

Appendix III
   Filmographies of 35 Actors and Actresses   288

Appendix IV
   The Experts Rank Lugosi's Monogram Films   356

Index   361

Introduction

The "Poverty Row" horror films of the 1940s. It's difficult to think of a group of movies that are as popular with fans and yet at the same time are as widely bad-mouthed. Black sheep in the family of vintage horror pictures, they seem to attract only the most pejorative of adjectives, yet rare is the dyed-in-the-wool horror fan who hasn't seen just about every last one of them – repeatedly. They sell well on prerecorded videotape and turn up regularly on television. Original 16mm prints of these titles sell for premium prices, and related memorabilia (posters, lobby cards, and so on) often go for astronomical amounts. But they must be the proverbial "films we love to hate," because on the printed pages of horror film books and genre-related magazines, they obstinately remain "wretched," "abysmal," "execrable," and the people who made them are "hacks" and "no-talents." In a funny switch on the old adage, many fans just won't put their mouth where their money is.

Pretend it's 1944 and you want to kill an hour or two at the movies; you're in the mood for horror. Universal always *used* to be a reliable brand name but now, with just an exception here and there, their horror pictures are almost unspeakably bad. This year's crop of losers includes the dismal Inner Sanctum mysteries *Dead Man's Eyes* and *Weird Woman,* the haunted house comedies *Murder in the Blue Room* and *Ghost Catchers,* the umpteenth Invisible Man film and the Technicolor *The Climax,* another stinker; the studio's Sherlock Holmes mysteries are better and scarier than any of these. RKO, too, made some real classics in the past but all they're offering this year is *The Curse of the Cat People,* a gentle Val Lewton fantasy. Columbia's trying to follow in Lewton's footsteps with pictures like *Cry of the Werewolf* and *The Soul of a Monster,* movies that keep the monsters off-screen entirely while unheard-of actors stand around making speeches. MGM – *The Canterville Ghost?* Paramount – *The Man in Half Moon Street?* Those won't cut the ice either.

You're forced to cross over to the "wrong" side of the cinematic tracks, to go down to what came to be called Poverty Row. There, Lugosi hams up a storm in the lively, entertaining *Return of the Ape Man.* Ralph Morgan is doing some Grade–A acting in the Grade–Z *The Monster Maker.* John Carradine turns in one of his greatest performances (and cult director

Edgar G. Ulmer does one of his better jobs) on the stylish *Bluebeard,* "the kind of picture any company, or any producer, would like to release . . . a class product from start to finish" (*The Hollywood Reporter*). Even Republic, an action oriented studio unsuited to making horror pictures, has pulled all the budget stops on *The Lady and the Monster,* the first film treatment of *Donovan's Brain* by Curt Siodmak.

No one likes to admit it, but in the midst of the '40s horror film cycle, Poverty Row movies were sometimes among the best bets in town.

Of course, none of this is meant to imply that the average Poverty Row movie (or even an *above* average one) is good enough to wipe the shoes of '40s classics like *The Lodger* or *The Uninvited* (to name the two fine 1944 thrillers that were purposefully left out of the above scenario); the average Monogram, PRC or Republic chiller isn't even up to the level of striking major studio B films like *Son of Dracula, The Monster and the Girl* or *Dr. Renault's Secret.* (*And,* truth be told, words like "wretched," "abysmal" and "no-talents" turn up more than just occasionally in some of the appraisals in this book you're now holding.)

But the fact that these sloppily written, ultracheap, rapidly made Poverty Row movies still hold a loyal audience 50 years later means that they had to have a certain *something,* regardless of the fact that mainly they *were* made by people that the word "hacks" seems to describe quite well. What *is* that *something* that keeps us coming back?

Is it their casts? Horror stars like Lugosi, Carradine, George Zucco, Glenn Strange, Lionel Atwill and–once, just once–Boris Karloff? Is it the unintended humor that often crops up amidst the horror? (Or should that be the *horror* that crops up amidst all the unintended *humor?*) Maybe the fascination of seeing what *auteur* directors like Ulmer and Joseph H. Lewis can concoct with their backs against the wall budget- and time-wise? The "camp" value? Could it be the offbrand monsters–ape men, potbellied zombies, devil bats and flying reptiles soaring down piano wire? Or perhaps just sweet empty-headed nostalgia for the old-fashioned horror pictures we enjoyed in simpler days?

It's certainly an evasive *something,* one that most writers can't be bothered to try and nail down. One that perhaps *I've* missed pinpointing, too. So in addition to (or maybe in lieu *of*) that long awaited explanation, this book examines the 31 horror movies made by Monogram, PRC and Republic in the period between 1940 (the first year that one of them made an outright horror film) and 1946 (the year the '40s horror cycle ended). "Pick-up" films–movies made by other people, then sold to these distributors for release–are excluded. (These pick-ups, plus an assortment of other films

Opposite: **Almost without exception, the Poverty Row horror films of the 1930s were a dreary and antiquated lot. One of the dullest of the dull was Academy Pictures' *Revolt of the Zombies* (1936).**

with horrific sounding titles but no real horror content, are discussed in Appendix II.) Many of the people (directors, writers, actors, others) involved in Poverty Row horror filmmaking get brief biographical writeups within the chapters of movies on which they worked. Complete filmographies of 35 actors and actresses familiar to fans of low budget horrors, from John Abbott to George Zucco, are featured in Appendix III. It's everything you never needed to know about Poverty Row horrors, and more.

Too many studio histories of Monogram, PRC and Republic have been written for a recap here to be necessary, but let's take a quick overview of the horror film output of each studio.

Monogram was certainly the most prolific purveyor of horror films among the trio of studios here surveyed. Monogram's horrors have gotten more attention than PRC's or Republic's mostly on the strength of the fact that nine of their chillers featured "camp"/"cult" (take your pick) icon Bela Lugosi. This by itself sets Monogram above the other two in the eyes of many fans, even though Bela was generally the only real attraction *in* these films. Monogram wouldn't hesitate for a moment to play up *Black Dragons, Bowery at Midnight* or *Ghosts on the Loose* as horror movies, but in pictures like these and others, the horror content (except for Lugosi) was actually scant, sometimes nonexistent; for 60-odd minutes, Lugosi carried the whole damn show on his back, which is heaven for his fans, but pretty rough sledding for horror buffs not quite susceptible to that elusive Lugosi "magic." Legendary Hollywood skinflint Sam Katzman produced these nine pictures under his Banner Productions logo.

Other Monogram producers weren't fortunate enough to get Lugosi into their pictures; Lindsley Parsons tried twice, tentatively lining up Bela for both *King of the Zombies* and *Revenge of the Zombies* but then ending up recasting both times. Parsons' zombie films put the accent on humor as well as horror; black comedian Mantan Moreland, featured in both, stole the show in *King* and tried again (less successfully) in *Revenge*. Petty larceny, to be sure, but Moreland's comedy relief was a decided cut above the lame humor in the Lugosi films; Vince Barnett (seen in Lugosi's *The Corpse Vanishes* and *Bowery at Midnight*) was more jinx than hijinks, and the East Side Kids, who worked twice with Poor Bela, were no better. By the time the Lugosi series was wrapping up with *Voodoo Man*, the "funny" stuff was being entrusted to John Carradine.

The unfortunate part about the Monogram horror films is that in some ways, a number of them came awfully close to being halfway decent; all they needed was a bit more production polish, and a good writer to fiddle with the scripts and the dialogue. Monogram's horror scripts were notoriously bad, but somewhere in them – buried in incoherent dialogue and goofy plot twists – were often ideas that had a good bit of unrealized potential. *The Corpse Vanishes*, for instance, pioneered the horror subgenre of a wacky doctor kidnapping young women in order to restore youth/beauty/life/what-

Celebrated Tinseltown tightwad Sam Katzman was probably responsible for more low budget '40s horror films than any other Hollywood producer.

ever to *his* elderly/ugly/dead/whatever wife. *Black Dragons* is so poorly written it almost doesn't make sense, but the kernel idea was good enough that it seems likely that television's *The Outer Limits* ripped it off for one of their best early episodes. *Invisible Ghost* and *Voodoo Man* both had the makings of respectable B fright films early on, but again the scripts just got out of hand. You wonder why Monogram never put in that *little* extra bit of effort (script- *and* production-wise) that might have made all the difference. But it's also important to remember that during this early– to mid–'40s period, the average Monogram movie made the company a profit of $1,932.12, a minuscule dividend that left little room for tinkering and fine tuning.

PRC made its pictures for so little money that the company had to be the butt of jokes even at places like Monogram and Republic. But when it came to their horror pictures, PRC had more going for them than Monogram did. For one thing, they rarely skimped on the horror content; while

Monogram felt that Lugosi alone would keep aficionados entertained for an hour, PRC had their bogeymen (Lugosi once, but usually George Zucco) backed up by an assortment of monsters: The Devil Bat, the Flying Serpent, a werewolf (in *The Mad Monster*), a vampire (*Dead Men Walk*) and even an acromegaly victim that easily out-uglied Universal's much-vaunted Rondo Hatton (a heavily made-up Ralph Morgan, in *The Monster Maker*). Monogram came up with a monster now and again (*The Ape Man* and *Return of the Ape Man*), but generally their pictures were pretty tame stuff next to PRC's far grislier (and livelier) lineup.

Also, all of Monogram's horror movies have become the subject of ridicule down through the years, while two of PRC's have courted quite a bit of respectability: *Bluebeard* and *Strangler of the Swamp*. Actually, these two films really aren't all that hot on the entertainment level; they're better as *subjects of study* for cinema "students" than as crowd-pleasing fun for the average horror fan. But the fact remains that these two PRCs have gone down in some movie books as B movie gems; in these same record books, Monogram's batting average is an easy-to-remember .000.

Republic was the MGM of Poverty Row. Their B Westerns and serials were fast-paced, often well-directed, and boasted some of the best stuntwork and special effects in the picture industry. And when Republic set out to make a "prestige" picture, the results weren't the overly long, overproduced Bs Monogram and PRC came up with when *they* were in expansive moods; the feathers in Republic's cap include such classics (or near classics, or cult classics) as Welles' *Macbeth* (1948), Ford's *Rio Grande* (1950) and *The Quiet Man* (1952), Nicholas Ray's *Johnny Guitar* (1954) and others.

Republic's forte was the action-filled outdoor film; in the claustrophobic, atmospheric world of horror, Republic's team of moviemakers were strangers. It seems likely that they knew this themselves, as they steered clear of the genre in the mid-'30s and early '40s, when the popularity of horror films was at or near its height. But by 1944 they had decided to dip their toe into those dark waters, beginning with their top-budgeted adaptation of Curt Siodmak's bestselling science fiction novel *Donovan's Brain*. Republic's film version, retitled *The Lady and the Monster*, was well produced and got some excellent notices, but lacked many of the qualities that audiences expected and wanted from their horror films.

Horror quickly became the province of the studio's lower echelon producers, who put many of the same actors they used in their Western and action films into the horrors. Chases and fistfights, *de rigeuer* in the average Republic picture, were featured in the horrors as well. Established horror stars like Lugosi, Zucco, Carradine and Atwill never turned up in a Republic. The Republic horror films—*The Vampire's Ghost, The Catman of Paris,* etc.—were expensive looking productions compared to the dirt poor Monograms and PRCs, but then and now they remain films that horror buffs are usually only too happy to ignore; Republic (like everybody else) stopped making them in 1946. But even in the '50s, when horror and science fiction had made a big comeback and Allied Artists (the later incarnation of Monogram) was churning them out a mile a minute, Republic was still warily avoiding the genre. The Republic double bill of *The Unearthly* and *Beginning of the End* (1957) – both pick-up films – was soon followed by the closing of the company's doors.

The Poverty Row studios also had a Roger Corman–esque knack for finding and employing future star talents at an early stage of their careers. Universal's '40s thrillers starred all the top horror personalities of that era, but were otherwise cast with B players, and were generally written and directed by less-than-illustrious craftsmen. Poverty Row's casts not only featured the *same* horror greats but also boasted the up-and-coming likes of Ava Gardner, Yolande Donlan, Vera Ralston, Gale Storm, and Blake Edwards (not to mention future Academy Award–winning writer Ned Young); their directors were often cultish figures like Ulmer, Lewis, Frank Wisbar and Steve Sekely; Carl Foreman (*Champion, High Noon, The Bridge on the River Kwai*), who wrote *Spooks Run Wild*, was under contract to Huntz Hall(!); and Leigh Brackett (*The Big Sleep, Rio Bravo, The Empire Strikes Back*) wrote *The Vampire's Ghost*.

These films also employed rising horror stars Elizabeth Russell and Glenn Strange before the larger studios' horror films did; future Oscar winners John Alton and Eugen Schufftan photographed; *King of the Zombies* received an Oscar nomination for Best Musical Score; and the Bowery Boys' haunted-house pictures were the unmistakable basis for the megahit *Ghostbusters* (1984). Again, nobody's saying that these Poverty Row films compare with the best horror stuff coming from Universal in the '40s, but by one of those weird coincidences, Poverty Row's all-spit-and-no-polish horrors had perhaps the more noteworthy array of personnel and accomplishments.

Lots of people helped out in the preparation of *Poverty Row Horrors!*, doing all the little things that go into a book of this sort: locating tapes or 16mm prints, sharing stills and information, making corrections and suggestions. Prominent among them are Edward Bernds, Tom Johnson, Carl Del Vecchio, Sam Sherman, Terry Frost, Mary Runser, Albert Glasser, Curt Siodmak, Ruth Brunas, Bruce Goldstein, Tony Timpone (*Fangoria*), Louise Currie, Elizabeth Russell, Nell O'Day, Herb Strock, Howard W. Koch, Robert Clarke, Alex Gordon, Scott MacQueen, George Feltenstein, everyone who took part in the Bela Lugosi Poll, Yolande Donlan, Gene O'Donnell; Zap, Blaze and Ice; Dave McDonnell (*Starlog*), Greg Mank, Eddie Bracken, Robert Shayne, Gary Svehla and the whole FANEX crowd, Martin Kosleck and Steve Swires.

Extra big thank-you's go to:

Don Leifert, whose articles on Poverty Row horror films in *Filmfax* included pithy analyses as well as entertaining and informative chats with some of these movies' stars; these were a great starting point, and Don went out of his way to encourage and facilitate the writing of *Poverty Row Horrors!* right from Day One;

Maurice Terenzio, an avid Lugosi fan, who not only provided stills but also interesting production tidbits and insights;

The crack staff at Manhattan's Lincoln Center Library for the Performing Arts, who never commented on my taste in films as I submitted endless requests for files like *Return of the Ape Man, The Ghost Creeps* and *Devil Bat's Daughter* (well, *almost* never);

Bill Littman, for penning an excellent article on the music makers of Poverty Row (see Appendix I);

Mark Martucci–having access to his overwhelming collection of horror and SF videotapes has been making *my* job a snap for years;

John Cocchi, one of the world's *numero uno* film experts (and a helluva nice guy), who double-checked, amended and augmented my filmographies to the point where he deserves, and gets, co-credit for the chapter;

Jack Dukesbery, another inveterate credits-watcher, who did the same thing;

And my frequent co-conspirators in all this nonsense, Michael and John Brunas, who couldn't be baited into collaborating with me on this book (Lord knows I tried), but whose suggestions and input were invaluable every step of the way. (Mike, in fact, did do some writing, on the *Fog Island* chapter – that one's practically *all* his doing – and on *Bluebeard.*) Their influence can be found on just about every page of this book, so if you read anything in here that you don't like, feel free to let them know about it.

Tom Weaver
Fall 1992

Note: The films are listed in chronological order of release but are discussed in the order in which they were made, which leads to some funny juxtapositions (i.e., the chapter on the last Monogram film Bela Lugosi worked on *Voodoo Man* appears *before* the chapter on his next-to-last, *Return of the Ape Man*).

Boys of the City
(Monogram, 1940)

Released July 15. 63 minutes. Also known as *The Ghost Creeps*. Produced by Sam Katzman (Four Bells Pictures, Inc.). Directed by Joseph H. Lewis. Original Story and Screenplay: William Lively. Production Manager: E. W. Rote. Assistant Directors: Robert Ray and Arthur Hammond. Photography: Robert Cline, A.S.C. Harvey Gould, A.S.C. Settings: Fred Preble. Film Editor: Carl Pierson. Sound Technician: Glen Glenn.

Cast: Bobby Jordan (Danny Dolan), Leo Gorcey (Muggs), Hally [Hal E.] Chester (Buster), Frankie Burke (Skinny), Vince Barnett (Simp), Inna Gest (Louise Mason), David O'Brien (Knuckles Dolan), Sunshine Sammy [Morrison] (Scruno), Minerva Urecal (Agnes), Dennis Moore (Giles), Donald Haines (Peewee), David Gorcey (Ike), Eugene Francis (Algy), Forrest Taylor (Judge Malcolm Parker), Alden [Stephen] Chase (Jim Harrison), Jerry Mandy (Cook), George Humbert (Tony), Jack Edwards.

"PINT-SIZED KILLERS GO FOR A VACATION IN THE COUNTRY . . . in a haunted house!"

"Tough guys of the tenements with a chip on their shoulders wind up with hayseed in their hair . . . when they tangle with a killer in a haunted house!" — ad lines

Film historians turn up their noses at the group, but the East Side Kids (a.k.a. the Dead End Kids, *and* the Little Tough Guys, *and* the Bowery Boys) kept movie audiences entertained for over 20 years. Most of their comedies pitted them against ordinary adversaries, but there were also regular forays into horror (*Spooks Run Wild, Ghosts on the Loose, Master Minds, Ghost Chasers*), science fiction (*Junior G–Men, Junior "G" Men of the Air, The Bowery Boys Meet the Monsters*) and even fantasy (*Bowery to Bagdad, Hold That Hypnotist, Up in Smoke*). There was no pretense to art, no anxious waiting for the Envelope on Oscar night, just a lot of good-natured hooliganism, lowbrow shtik and mangling of the English language.

Monogram's second East Side Kids entry (and the first to feature Bobby Jordan and Leo Gorcey), *Boys of the City* isn't much of a film, by any stretch of the imagination, but it's still a few pegs above most of their other horror comedies. Gearing himself up for the Big Time, director Joseph H. Lewis gives this minor quickie an interesting look and even manages to work up a bit of mild suspense. Lewis was biding his time at Monogram, PRC and

1

Universal during this early-'40s period before making his move to the Columbia B unit in the mid-'40s. There he directed stylish B's like *My Name Is Julia Ross* (1945) and *So Dark the Night* (1946) as well as the shaky-A *The Undercover Man* (1949), films that finally attracted a bit of attention from the critical community; the 1949 *Gun Crazy*, a Bonnie and Clyde–style sleeper, remains his claim to fame. In the 1960s, after Lewis had dropped from films and gone into television, he was "rediscovered" by the *auteur* faction of film scholarship which had also rushed to embrace Edgar Ulmer and several of Lewis' other Poverty Row compatriots. This latter-day adulation of Lewis was partially deserved (as deserved as Ulmer's, at any rate!), and the long-retired Lewis continues to enjoy his *auteur* rep to the present day.

Sweltering in midsummer heat, the East Side Kids crack open a fire hydrant, get into a brawl with a street vendor and find themselves collared by the cops. Knuckles Dolan (David O'Brien), a one-time gangster who has taken the gang under his now virtuous wing, convinces the judge to allow him to take the boys out of their slum environment, up into the Adirondacks. Knuckles had been sentenced to die for a murder he did not commit, and then exonerated at the last minute. (Actor O'Brien and his Dolan character are carryovers from the series opener *East Side Kids,* also 1940).

Meanwhile, Malcolm Parker (Forrest Taylor), a crooked judge about to go on trial on bribery charges, is receiving death threats from the gangsters he's preparing to double-cross. Accompanied by his pretty ward Louise (Inna Gest), his righthand man Giles (Dennis Moore) and his bumbling bodyguard Simp (Vince Barnett), Parker flees from the city toward his home in Briarcliff Manor.

The Judge's car breaks down on a lonely upstate road and Giles flags down Knuckles and the Kids, imposing on them for a ride to Briarcliff Manor. Parker's home is a gloomy castle-like dwelling complete with graveyard – and even a mysterious figure skulking in the shadows. Anxious to be surrounded by as many people as possible, the nervous Judge invites Knuckles and the Kids to spend the night. Parker's housekeeper Agnes (Minerva Urecal) has a personality that matches the house; apparently mad, she talks of Parker's dead wife Lenora as though she still inhabits the house.

The usual stuff follows. Agnes goes around giving everybody the creeps; a shadowy figure drags Louise into a secret passageway and knocks her out; the Kids see a ghostly woman in a shroud; doing balletic leaps in the graveyard; Judge Parker is attacked in his room and strangled to death by an unseen assailant.

Giles is convinced that Knuckles is the killer – Parker was the judge who had sentenced him to die – and holds him at gunpoint. The Kids overpower Giles and Simp, keeping them trussed up in a bedroom while a search for the real killer and the missing Louise gets underway. Louise is found unconscious in the passageway and a stranger is captured, but he turns out to be Jim Harrison (Stephen Chase), a government man who came to keep an

eye on the judge. The killer stalks Louise a second time, but Knuckles arrives on the scene and the killer is revealed as Simp, Parker's bodyguard;
he's actually Johnny Harris, triggerman for the mob that was gunning for
Parker. Agnes admits that she dressed up as the ghost in order to scare
away the Kids (she hated the evil Judge Parker and was planning to kill him
herself), and even bakes a cake for the Kids in an upbeat finis.

It's practically impossible to build an atmosphere of suspense in an East
Side Kids or Bowery Boys picture, with that throng of street urchins always
around hurling one-liners or mugging shamelessly, but Joseph Lewis does
what he can and actually manages one fairly effective scene. Louise is in the
library of the "haunted" house when the frozen-faced Agnes appears
mysteriously in the room. Frightened, Louise turns her back to her, but
Agnes comes up from behind and begins to caress Louise's arm.

> You have such nice . . . soft . . . white skin. Lenora had white skin like
> that – until it became yellowed and shrivelled. What a pity, pretty lady,
> if *your* skin should lose its whiteness. . . . Strange things happen when
> the moon is full, and Lenora cannot rest. . . !

Building up her nerve, Louise finally spins around to confront Agnes –
and finds the room completely empty. (The situation and dialogue are too
similar to a scene in James Whale's *The Old Dark House* [1932] to safely
chalk up to coincidence.) The sequence is not a hackles-raiser, but it's creepy
enough to stand out in a picture like this; Monogram "remade" the scene
(this time with Luana Walters and Elizabeth Russell) two years later in *The
Corpse Vanishes.*

Supporting performances in *Boys of the City* meet or exceed the
minimal demands of the material. Vince Barnett is less irritating than
usual, and his climactic unmasking is nicely staged and acted. David
O'Brien, Dennis Moore and Forrest Taylor are all strictly business. Alden
Chase, who plays the F.B.I. man, is recognizably *Stephen* Chase, the doctor
who gets devoured by *The Blob* (1958). Ingenue Inna Gest (a.k.a. Ina Guest)
made a handful of films in the '40s before apparently dropping out of the
business; she died of hepatitis on New Year's Day, 1965, a youthful 43.

Minerva Urecal is in good form as the "mad" Agnes, and director Lewis
even graces the saturnine actress with a striking low-angle closeup. A
favorite among fans of cheapo horror films, Urecal enjoyed a long career in
motion pictures, playing some of her biggest parts in *Boys of the City, The
Corpse Vanishes, The Ape Man* and *Crazy Knights,* all Monograms. Born in
Eureka, California – the town from which she derived her surname – Minerva
Urecal (*née* Holzer) was of Scottish ancestry, a nationality she seldom if ever
played on the screen. She entered films from radio, where she enacted the
role of the dynamic Italian housewife Mrs. Pasquale on a show called *Sunday Night Hi-Jinks,* and appeared in hundreds of movies beginning around

1933. The poor man's Hope Emerson, glowering, hawk-nosed Urecal was usually seen as a noisy fishwife, a hard-hearted landlady, or (as in *Boys of the City*) a spooky domestic. In the 1950s she was a regular on the television series *The RCA Victor Show, The Ray Milland Show* and *Peter Gunn* (replacing Hope Emerson!) and even starred in a series of her own, *The Adventures of Tugboat Annie.** She died of a heart attack in a Glendale, California, hospital in 1966, at age 70.

Of course it's the East Side Kids who dominate the picture in their usual rambunctious style. Frankie Burke, who plays Skinny, was a James Cagney lookalike who had played Cagney as a youth in the classic *Angels with Dirty Faces* (1938); Hally Chester (Buster) later became producer Hal E. Chester and remains best known to horror–science fiction fans for *The Beast from 20,000 Fathoms* (1953) and *Curse of the Demon* (1958).

Monogram publicity made much of the Kids' boisterous on-the-set hijinks in their early films; as the Dead End Kids, they would knock over set walls, put water in the director's chair and slow production with their pranks. Edward Bernds, sound man on two of the low budget Columbia Westerns Joseph H. Lewis ground out in 1940, wonders how Lewis was able to maintain any control at all on the *Boys of the City* set.

> On those two Westerns, I never saw such poor discipline on the set – the crew had no respect at all for Lewis, and I thought he was ticketed for a very quick exit. He was not able to enforce any kind of discipline; it was brutal, and as a wishful director myself, I deplored this situation. The rumor was that Lewis had volunteered to direct these pictures at editor's salary – he had been a film editor. That was one of the things the crew resented, the fact that he came in and underbid [director] Sam Nelson – everybody liked Sam. So Lewis had no control at all and I mentally consigned him to oblivion; the guy couldn't survive if he wasn't able to maintain some kind of authority or presence on the set. But I was wrong – he *did* survive as a director, and did very well. (A hell of a lot better than *I* did *[laughs]!*)
>
> The other thing I recall is that they all disliked Lewis' artsy-fartsy photography. I remember one prop man, disgusted, saying, "There's a god-damn wagon wheel in every foreground!"

Lewis goes artsy-fartsy in *Boys of the City*, too: shooting from inside the fireplace, dollying his camera "through" walls, giving far more attention to the composition of shots and the arrangement of people and props than any of the hack Monogram directors. This attention to detail greatly enhances the visuals in *Boys of the City*, but the mood of tension Lewis almost succeeds in achieving is dispelled every time an East Side Kid opens his mouth.

---

*Tugboat Annie's *pilot episode cost upwards of $130,000, making it the most expensive pilot to that time. The subsequent 39 episodes were shot in Canada, where the show was a big hit; in the United States it was far less successful.*

The basic plot of *Boys of the City* was echoed a year later in *Spooks Run Wild*, and it was semi-remade four years later as *Crazy Knights*. The directors of *Spooks Run Wild* and *Crazy Knights* were (respectively) Phil Rosen and William Beaudine, who give these later films the type of slapdash, why-care? treatment Lewis went beyond the call of duty to rise above. Lewis directed two more East Side Kids films (*That Gang of Mine*, 1940, and *Pride of the Bowery*, 1941) before moving on to slightly worthier projects.

It could only have irked Lewis to find the critics ignoring or belittling his initiatives. The reviewer for *The New York Herald Tribune* scoffed, "Secret panels, eerie faces and spooky passageways are the stock in trade of this photoplay, but they are over-used props and fail to lift the film out of mediocrity." *Variety*'s Wood hated *Boys of the City* and everybody connected with it. Categorizing it as "a weak runoff," Wood raled on, "Reels are crammed full with faults in photography, direction, story and emoting. . . . Except for Dave O'Brien, the [supporting players are] woefully inadequate."

The New York World Telegraph wrote that "The Globe Theater's younger element. . .howled with delight. The others just howled." Elsie Finn of *The Philadelphia Record* chalked it up as "naive nonsense. . . . The Dead End Kids – or what's left of them – are assembled for this rehash which wavers between slapstick and old-fashioned mustache twirling draymer." A terse reviewer for *The New York Daily Mirror* called it "poor spook stuff." *The New York Times*, the last people in the world you'd expect to find reviewing a picture like this, sniffed, "[The East Side Kids] are a tough lot in their own domain, but put them in a spooky old mansion . . . and they turn out to be just a pack of whimpering, scared kids. For shame! . . . The boys are wasting their time on this sort of hocus-pocus entertainment(?). . . ." (In the Northeast, the film was released as *The Ghost Creeps*.)

Boys of the City is almost beyond criticism: Either you like the East Side Kids or you hate 'em, and nothing else that goes on in their pictures will sway you. It remains, however, one of their better horror comedies, with Joseph H. Lewis giving the film as professional a look as possible under the low budget circumstances.

The Ape
(Monogram, 1940)

Released September 30. 61 minutes. Associate Producer: William Lackey. Produced by Scott R. Dunlap. Directed by William Nigh. Screenplay: Kurt [Curt] Siodmak and Richard Carroll. Adaptation: Kurt [Curt] Siodmak. Suggested from the play by Adam Hull Shirk. Director of Photography: Harry Neumann. Film Editor: Russell Schoengarth. Musical Director: Edward Kay. Assistant Director: Allen Wood. Tech-

nical Director: E. R. Hickson. Production Manager: C. J. Bigelow. Recording Engi-
neer: Karl Zint. Makeup: Gordon Bau.
    Cast: Boris Karloff (Dr. Bernard Adrian), Maris Wrixon (Frances Clifford), Gene
O'Donnell (Danny Foster), Dorothy Vaughan (Mrs. Clifford), Gertrude W. Hoffman
(Jane), Henry Hall (Sheriff Jeff Holliday), Selmer Jackson (Dr. McNulty), Jack Ken-
nedy (Tomlin), Jessie Arnold (Mrs. Brill), George Cleveland (Circus Boss), I. Stanford
Jolley (Circus Trainer), Donald Kerr (Townsman), Ray Corrigan (Nabu, the Ape),
Philo McCullough.

> **"They always give the Academy Awards to the wrong**
> **people. They should have gone to the people who worked**
> **at the budget studios, because they managed to trans-**
> **cend the limitations of the budget." — Maris Wrixon**

    Boris Karloff's one excursion into Monogram horror, *The Ape,* is a ludi-
crous but not unwatchable 61 minutes of "sinister science" melodramatics.
It isn't a *good* film in any useful sense of that word, but it's entertaining in
its unabashed silliness and, perhaps for the last time, Karloff gives a sincere
performance in a C–grade picture.
    Like Bela Lugosi, Karloff must have heaved a sigh of relief when the
mid–'30s blackout on horror films was lifted, but Dear Boris didn't endure
the type of dark days Poor Bela did. The studios simply tossed Lugosi aside
like a sucked orange; Karloff rated better treatment in their eyes and they
sought to alter his screen persona so that he could continue to work. He was
characteristic without being terrifying in 20th Century–Fox's *Charlie Chan
at the Opera* (1936), but Universal changed his image totally for *Night Key*
(1937), casting him as a dotty, myopic old inventor just a few shades shy of
outright comic relief. Universal announced in the fall of 1936 that they
would transform their one-time horror star into a detective character or a
G–man, politician or *any* role other than a horror one.
    Curiously, it was not Universal but lowly Monogram that found (what
they considered) the right detective role for Karloff: James Lee Wong, the
Oriental sleuth popularized by Hugh Wiley's *Collier's* magazine stories.
Karloff must have known this wasn't what his fans were interested in seeing, but Monogram's money was as green as anybody else's and so ahead he
forged, turning out five of these turkeys over the next two years.* The films
were numbingly dull and Karloff had to feel like a horse's ass in his slant-
eyed makeup, but at least he wasn't losing his house to the mortgage company the way Lugosi did.
    Fortunately for Karloff *and* Lugosi, horror did make a comeback, and

---

*Mr. Wong, Detective *(1938),* The Mystery of Mr. Wong *(1939),* Mr. Wong in Chinatown
(1939), The Fatal Hour *(shooting title:* Mr. Wong at Headquarters; *1940) and* Doomed to
Die *(shooting title:* Shadow Over Chinatown; *1940).*

the two of them were paired in Universal's overblown *Son of Frankenstein*
(1939) as well as in the (far) less elaborate *Black Friday* (1940). Karloff, in
the meantime, was also off picking up fast money via the Columbia B unit,
appearing in what's come to be known as the "Mad Doctor" series. (Karloff
had nine films out in 1940 alone.) With horror flicks back in style, Monogram
knew that they were now wasting Karloff's talents (and, more importantly,
the Karloff *name*) in the Wong series. Chinese actor Keye Luke, Number
One son in Fox's Charlie Chan series, was recruited to play Wong in the
series' final film (*Phantom of Chinatown*, 1940) while Karloff was diverted
to the all-out horror entry *The Ape*.

On July 9, 1940, Curt Siodmak was hired to pen a screenplay for this,
Karloff's new Monogram vehicle, which the studio told the Hollywood
dailies would carry a top budget for the company. Together with co-writer
Richard Carroll, Siodmak conceived for Karloff a character very much in
the style of one of his Columbia "Mad Doctors." In *The Ape*, he's Dr. Bernard
Adrian, a much-hated small town physician seeking a cure for some undis-
closed form of paralysis (polio, we assume; it isn't specified). There was
much room for pathos in the character: Dr. Adrian had lost his wife and
daughter to the disease years before, and now dedicates all his energies to
curing an afflicted local girl (Maris Wrixon). But the script essentially makes
the bespectacled, walrus-mustached medico a Jekyll and Hyde character:
warm and paternal and selflessly dedicated to mankind, when he isn't out
clawing people to death in his homemade gorilla suit.

The credits roll to the tune of rollicking circus music and with background art of tigers, horses, clowns and an ape who looks like he's smiling.
After chasing away some kids who were throwing rocks at his house,* Dr.
Adrian strolls next door to visit a paralysis victim, pretty young Frances
Clifford (Maris Wrixon), and her elderly mother (Dorothy Vaughan). Adrian
presents Frances with a jewelry case as the wheelchair-bound girl objects
that it isn't her birthday.

> ADRIAN: This is a make-believe party, just as you're my make-believe
> daughter.
> FRANCES: Was she *very* like me?
> ADRIAN: She'd have been just 18 today. She was to have worn that.
> I couldn't save her and I couldn't save her mother. I hadn't the
> weapons to fight the disease that killed them. But I have now! Or at least
> I've got a knowledge of them. Ten years it's taken me. Frances, *you*
> *are going to walk again!*

---

*At no point do we find out why Dr. Adrian is hated by the people of Red Creek. We're told
that he arrived there years before during a "paralysis epidemic," and ostensibly the
townsfolk resent him because he wasn't able to keep the incurable disease in check; a small
minority feels that he used a few of his patients as guinea pigs. Other than that, their aversion centers (vaguely) around the fact that he "experiments too much."

Monogram's maiden voyage into all-out horror, *The Ape,* boasted a sincere Boris Karloff performance but was spoiled by a mixed-up script.

Adrian insists that Frances visit the circus which has just arrived in Red Creek, and that night she and her boyfriend, local mechanic Danny Foster (Gene O'Donnell), take in the show, which includes animals, clowns and (most impressively) a trapeze act in slow motion. After the performance, one of the circus bosses (George Cleveland) catches a trainer (I. Stanford Jolley) abusing Nabu, the ape (Ray Corrigan); two years before, the primate had killed the trainer's equally abusive father. Like father, like son, like an idiot, the trainer backs up into Nabu's clutches and the beast begins to throttle him. The trainer's fallen cigarette starts a fire as the ape bursts from its cage and breaks the trainer's back with a judo flip. The Big Top burns to the ground as Nabu makes his escape.

The mauled trainer is rushed to Adrian's, but the wacky sawbones is less interested in saving his life than in extracting his spinal fluid, with which he intends somehow to cure Frances. The next day, as a posse hunts for the gallivanting ape, Adrian calls on the Cliffords and gives Frances the spinal injection. Within 24 hours Frances claims to have sensation in her lower limbs, and Adrian is ecstatic – so ecstatic, in fact, that he clumsily allows the vial containing the rest of the trainer's spinal fluid to roll off a table and shatter on the floor. Adrian is devastated.

Nabu kills one of the posse members and later bursts through a window and into Adrian's house. Blinding the great beast with a faceful of chemicals, Adrian drives a knife into its back, killing it. He fails to notify the local sheriff (Henry Hall) about the incident, however, for a daring plan has begun to hatch in his mind. Adrian skins Nabu (off-screen, of course) and dons the pelt, stealing out into the night and murdering one of the locals. He divests the body of its spinal fluid, injecting it into Frances, who is now able to move one of her feet. During another nocturnal romp in his ape suit, Adrian is spotted by a group of boys and one of them shoots him with his .22 caliber rifle. Wounded, but not seriously, Adrian is well enough to field questions directed at him by the suspicious sheriff, who can't figure out why bloodhounds keep leading the posse to Adrian's house.

With Frances at the point where she needs only one more injection, Adrian climbs into the ape skin once again, attacking one of the posse members – and getting knifed in the process. Staggering home, the "ape" is spotted by Frances, whose screams bring the sheriff and his men a-running. Adrian is shot, collapsing on his own front stoop. The sheriff's men pull the scientist out of his ape's clothing, and Adrian's last sight before dying is of Frances rising from her wheelchair and walking toward him.

It probably goes without saying that *The Ape* did not live up to Monogram's initial promise of a big-budget production. All circus footage (the troupe's arrival in Red Creek, the big top acts, the fire scene) is obviously taken from an earlier film, possibly a silent; even the shots of Dr. Adrian leaving and returning to his house in his ape guise are repeated. But no one really expected Monogram to lay out big bucks to make a movie like *The*

Ape; it was just the sort of hype on which publicity departments and Hollywood trade papers thrived.

Withal, *The Ape* is still a small cut above many of the other Poverty Row horror films of the '40s. It's not as much fun as a deliriously inane Bela Lugosi film like *The Corpse Vanishes*, or as stylish as something like Edgar Ulmer's *Bluebeard*, or as well produced as *The Lady and the Monster*; but nevertheless it manages to stand just slightly above some of the other low budget horror pictures of its day, mostly on the strength of the Karloff presence. In Monogram fashion, the plot doesn't really make even a grain of sense, but it was Good Enough–Good Enough, in fact, for them to revamp this unwieldy blend of mad doctor, cranky ape and cure-all spinal injections into *The Ape Man* three years later.

One of the most schizophrenic characters in filmdom, Dr. Adrian paradoxically rebounds between kindly father-figure and cold-blooded killer. The film doesn't make it clear whether Adrian could have saved the life of the mauled circus trainer; while the man is still clinging to life, Adrian tells him, "I'm going to write you into medical history–and I'm going to keep a promise" (his promise to Frances), indicating that Adrian is about to kill his own helpless patient. The first (and only) man that Adrian slays in his ape-guise is a character that had been laboriously established as a stone-hearted moneylender, so apparently screenwriters Siodmak and Carroll hoped that by having Adrian kill someone who "deserved" to die, he would remain in the good graces of the audience. ("You gotta give that ape credit. He only picks out the ornery cusses," one of the townsmen remarks.) But later in the picture, Adrian tries to wring the neck of a mild comedy relief character, which effectively negates his previous "public service" killing; the script doesn't bother to try to reconcile the two sides of the character. Like Karloff's Dr. Kravaal (*The Man with Nine Lives*, 1940) and Dr. Sovac (*Black Friday*), his Dr. Adrian in *The Ape* becomes so contemptibly ruthless that his climactic death seems well-deserved, and can be viewed without an ounce of the compassion that we extend to Karloff characters in "Mad Doctor" movies like *Before I Hang* (1940) and *The Devil Commands* (1941).

Enacting his part in a serious and straightforward manner, Karloff effortlessly rises above the low level of his material; it's the type of performance that in later years he no longer bothered to give when a picture was (in *his* opinion) "beneath" him. It's funny to find him so sincere in a nothing film like *The Ape*, and in a few other nothing films of the period, when he's so phony and exaggeratedly sinister in much better-made pictures like *Black Friday*, *The Climax* and *House of Frankenstein* (both 1944)–all Universals, interestingly. (He's even *worse* in the British *Juggernaut* [1936], again playing a murdering doctor seeking a paralysis cure.)

There's even a standout moment for Karloff in *The Ape*, in a scene with supporting player Selmer Jackson. Jackson, playing the representative of a foundation that had booted renegade experimenter Dr. Adrian out years before, has now become convinced that Adrian was on the right track all along. Pumping Adrian's hand, he sheepishly asks, "May I notify the Foundation that you've come back to us?" In one of the few closeups in *The Ape*, Karloff's face takes on a look of amusement, then delight, then–as he remembers the lengths he went to in order to effect the cure–total dismay. "Too late...," he whispers ruefully. A tepid and poorly thought-out movie, *The Ape* is bolstered immeasurably by the Karloff presence; without him, the film would have almost no entertainment value at all.

Supporting roles in *The Ape* didn't leave the actors much room for "artistic expression." Maris Wrixon, on loanout from Warner Bros., is pretty and demure as the crippled Frances; the scene where Karloff exhorts her to rise from her wheelchair is probably her best moment in the film, although it certainly doesn't compare with the classic Stand! Walk! scenes in Karloff's later *The Body Snatcher* (1945). (Wrixon ran up against an ape again in PRC's *White Pongo*, 1945.) Gene O'Donnell, playing her mechanic-suitor Danny, can't begin to overcome the deficiencies in the script. He plugs away earnestly, but the character is a thick skulled buttinski who continues to resent Dr. Adrian even after Frances is on the road to recovery. Danny doesn't trust what he can't understand, and he practically comes out and says that he'd rather Frances remain a cripple than have her cured by Adrian through a process that *he* cannot grasp in his Jiffy-Lube brain. Henry Hall, a familiar face in low budget films, makes for a likable no-nonsense sheriff. And Ray Corrigan, the serial and low budget Western star, gets some more mileage out of his trusty ape suit playing Nabu.

Maris Wrixon, interviewed by Don Leifert, had fond memories of Karloff and mixed emotions about Monogram:

> I received the script a day or two before shooting began. Working at Monogram was like living in a poor apartment. It was like being in a foxhole. The dressing rooms always felt cold. But I admired the professionalism. [Director William Nigh] had worked at Metro before coming to Monogram. He was very good. ...I rather liked my role in the picture; it was very sensitive and believable. I remember that Karloff was always saying something funny to me when the cameras weren't rolling. He was an elegant, well-educated man, and he was considerate of others.

Gene O'Donnell, who fell victim to Bela Lugosi later that same year in PRC's *The Devil Bat*, concurs. Describing himself as "seven years older than God," the garrulous O'Donnell recently reminisced:

> It was a marvelous experience doing *The Ape*. William Nigh was at one time a very important director, and he was quite a guy. We were out socializing one night, getting a little smashed in some bar, and William Nigh said to me, "You know, you could be another Henry Fonda." I

thought to myself, "The booze has really got him," but the next morning when we all got together to nurse our hangovers, he said, "I was a little drunk when I said you could be a Henry Fonda, but I really think you could." And I never forgot that. He was a wonderful guy. And Boris Karloff was just a dream to work with, an absolute dream. He was cooperative and meticulous and he told wonderful stories on the set. He told me I was good in the picture. (By the way, a friend of mine was on the vice squad in Los Angeles, and one time he arrested a number of prostitutes. He asked them who the best "swordsman" in Hollywood was, and they answered, "Why, Boris Karloff, without a doubt!")

You started a Monogram picture on a Monday and you wound up Saturday night come hell or high water. And if anything went wrong, you were told not to worry about it, they'd cut around it. These Poverty Row studios didn't have much money, and so they were very frugal and awful careful about what they did. You want to know how much I got for *The Ape*? A hundred and twenty-five dollars, man! And I'll tell you something else about those Monogram pictures: They made a lot of money in England and Australia. They *loved* our pictures, and nobody ever really figured out why!

A respectable figure during silent days, William Nigh was among the league of directors knocked down a number of pegs after talkies came in. A native of Berlin, Wisconsin, Nigh began his film career in 1911 as an actor, then went on to direct comedy shorts and eventually silent features (many of which he also wrote). In addition to directing Karloff in the five *Mr. Wong* films and *The Ape*, Nigh directed Chaney, Sr., in Metro's *Mr. Wu* (1927) and Lugosi in Monogram's *The Mysterious Mr. Wong* (1935) and *Black Dragons*; he also helmed Universal's *The Strange Case of Dr. Rx* (1942), a trite horror-mystery replete with hooded villain and ferocious ape (Ray Corrigan again). Nigh died in 1955.

The Ape was "officially" a remake of an earlier Monogram film, *The House of Mystery* (1934), *also* directed by William Nigh, which in turn was based on a play by Adam Hull Shirk. The two pictures are completely dissimilar except for the plot gimmick of a character disguising himself as an ape. (The gimmick turned up again, perhaps most notoriously, in 20th Century–Fox's 3-D *Gorilla at Large*, 1954.) "Whether it was *The Ape* or *The Climax* or *I Walked with a Zombie* [1943], I never used the original material. I used my own stories," Curt Siodmak avers. "In *The Ape*, Karloff played a scientist who discovers that fluid taken from the human spine can be used to cure a crippled girl. That was an idea which *I* had."

The Ape went into production on Tuesday, August 6, 1940, and according to Maris Wrixon, was finished in a week (Karloff's next film, RKO's *You'll Find Out*, began shooting on August 8). By the end of September *The Ape* was in theaters, where critics like *Variety*'s Art, knives at the ready, were waiting to pounce: "*The Ape* is a Boris Karloff starrer, presumed at the outset to be a thriller, but it misses by a considerable margin. Ultimate

Hollywood's greatest "swordsman"? Boris Karloff as the demented Dr. Adrian in *The Ape.*

weight of the flick as a suspenser is nil, and most of the footage is extremely boring." The *New York Times'* reviewer wrote, "Perhaps if you are under 12 or just like to be frightened and try very hard, *The Ape* will scare daylights out of you. Otherwise, we think this newest growl-and-glower epic is apt to seem merely quaint. . . . Karloff, both in his gruesome disguise and in mufti, is properly baleful, and most of the other actors cast dark looks in mufti, is properly baleful, and most of the other actors cast dark looks about in the best 1912 style of acting. . .[From] where we sat we couldn't count half-a-dozen goose pimples in the house."

Other reviewers, like the *New York Daily News'* woman-on-the-aisle Kate Cameron and the *New York Post's* Irene Thirer, were less critical. Cameron opined that "the story doesn't bear scrutiny at close range, but it does get over some good horror effects." Thirer gave the film a rating of FAIR on the *Post's* Movie Meter, summing it up as "not awfully exciting. . . . William Nigh, who used to have a hand in the old Lon Chaney chillers, directed this one rather tamely." The Legion of Decency gave the film a B (adults only) rating, citing its tendency "to present as permissible murders committed for scientific purpose."

A reviewer for *The Hollywood Reporter*, wrote, "The higher production quality which has marked recent Monogram productions is again manifest in this last of the Boris Karloff series, which is well-made, interesting and notable for excellent performances. . . .Karloff gives an excellent portrayal . . . under-playing nicely to good effect." Equally bowled over, England's *Kinematograph Weekly* dubbed *The Ape* "first class thriller fiction. Boris Karloff . . . acts with conviction and sincerity."

A bit more down-to-earth, Phil Hardy (*The Encyclopedia of Horror Movies*) put it down as "agreeably dotty . . . but distressingly tacky." Michael Weldon (*The Psychotronic Encyclopedia of Film*) called *The Ape* "probably the silliest movie of Karloff's entire career. . . . He kills an escaped circus gorilla, skins it [and] goes after more spines. What a brilliant idea! Nobody would notice a gorilla killing people. And you thought only Bela Lugosi made movies this dumb." *The Motion Picture Guide* cut right to the heart of the problem: *"The Ape* never finds the right groove, veering between odd thriller and ridiculous mad scientist tale."

The Devil Bat
(PRC, 1940)

Released December 13. 68 minutes. Also known as *Killer Bats*. Associate Producer: Guy V. Thayer, Jr. Executive Producer: Sigmund Neufeld. Produced by Jack Gallagher. Directed by Jean Yarborough [Yarbrough]. Screenplay: John Thomas Neville. Original Story: George Bricker. Director of Photography: Arthur Martinelli. Sound Engineer: Farrell Redd. Art Director: Paul Palmentola. Musical Director: David Chudnow. Production Manager: Melville De Lay. Film Editor: Holbrook N. Todd.

Cast: Bela Lugosi (Dr. Paul Carruthers), Suzanne Kaaren (Mary Heath), Dave O'Brien (Johnny Layton), Guy Usher (Henry Morton), Yolande Mallott [Donlan] (Maxine), Donald Kerr ("One-Shot" McGuire), Edward Mortimer (Martin Heath), Gene O'Donnell (Don Morton), Alan Baldwin (Tommy Heath), John Ellis (Roy Heath), Arthur Q. Bryan (Joe McGinty), Hal Price (Police Chief Wilkins), John Davidson (Prof. Percival Garland Raines), Wally Rairdon (Walter King).

"A madman laughed as innocent men struggled against
a monster hideous and cruel!! See *Devil Bat* but beware!"

"P.R.C. Pictures are SHOWMEN'S PICTURES!!!!
They're 'Pictures for Showmen, Made by Showmen' and
Devil Bat is the best picture P.R.C. has yet produced!"—
PRC ad lines

The banner year for motion pictures was 1939, also the beginning of a
long overdue comeback for horror star Bela Lugosi. All but unemployable
in Hollywood during the industry's self imposed two-year ban on horror
(1937–38), He began the year working as one of the stars of Universal's *Son
of Frankenstein*: Looking, acting and sounding nothing like his usual self,
Lugosi gave one of his best-ever performances as the scruffy, broken-necked
Ygor, friend to the Frankenstein Monster (Boris Karloff). *Son of Frankenstein* clicked at the box office, and horror was officially back in vogue.

No one in Hollywood could have been happier about it than Lugosi, a
forgotten man during the horror moratorium. His phone that never rang
during that period now buzzed with offers. In February 1939, he replaced
Peter Lorre (sick with pneumonia) in Fox's *The Gorilla*, opposite the Ritz
Brothers. Universal announced that they were preparing a "different type
of serial" for him, one which would include a few jolts of chills without too
much horror. (One of their objectives, Universal told the Hollywood trade
dailies, was to start to move Lugosi *away* from the horror rut in which he
had been typed.) In April he was in England, playing the lead in producer
John Argyle's *The Dark Eyes of London* (*The Human Monster*), and he
returned to the States just two days before production began on his
"different type of serial," Universal's dullsville *The Phantom Creeps*.

In June he was signed for Metro's *Ninotchka* and in November, after
returning from a series of radio guest shots in New York, he appeared in
RKO's *The Saint's Double Trouble*. (They were to be Bela's last straight film
roles.) In December, as Lugosi was preparing for Universal's *Black Friday*,
John Argyle was attempting to lure him back to England for a *second*
British starring feature. During this same year, various studios announced
that he was up for the leads in *The Hunchback of Notre Dame* (as
Quasimodo), *The Return of Doctor X* (a.k.a. *The Doctor's Secret*) and *The In-
visible Man Returns*. It had been a good year for the relieved and grateful
Lugosi, who probably looked ahead with renewed confidence to the 1940s.

In 1940, however, Lugosi got a slightly better idea of what the future
would hold: Horror films would be his niche from then on—exclusively—and
many of the better roles would continue to go to Karloff. Lugosi would still
be getting the crumbs. And in the early '40s, "the crumbs" meant Poverty
Row: Monogram and PRC.

On Saturday, October 19, 1940, Lugosi signed with Sigmund Neufeld to
play the top role in the PRC producer's upcoming production *The Devil Bat*,

PRC may have been an even *poorer* cousin to some of the other studios on Poverty Row, but they still managed to turn out one of Bela Lugosi's better low-budget films, *The Devil Bat.*

which began shooting nine days later. The cost of production was undoubtedly dirt-cheap and the film shot in record time, but at least at a humble fledgling studio like PRC, someone like Lugosi was as much of a star as Clark Gable was at MGM. PRC's publicity department blurbs couldn't have been bad for his ego, either:

> Bela Lugosi is a real name – take advantage of this fact, and plug him all along the line. You've made money with him consistently and unless your town suffers an earthquake or an attack from Mars, he'll help you make money in *Devil Bat*.

The Devil Bat is set in Heathville, a small village which loves Paul Carruthers (Lugosi). But beneath his genial exterior, Dr. Carruthers seethes with hatred. Years earlier, he had sold his formula for a greaseless cold cream to local businessmen Henry Morton (Guy Usher) and Martin Heath (Edward Mortimer); using the cold cream as a base (no pun intended), they have built up a cosmetics company that now nets a profit of over $1,000,000 a year. The mad Carruthers has decided to take revenge, and the film opens in his hillside laboratory as he uses a weird array of electrical equipment to enlarge an ordinary bat to eagle-sized proportions. Carruthers had already trained the mammal to react violently to a certain scent. "Now, if you detect the fragrance in the night – ven you're fully avake – you vill *strike!*" he gloats.

Heath telephones to invite Carruthers to his magnificent estate (Heathhaven) that night; he and Morton are planning to surprise Carruthers with a bonus check for $5,000. Carruthers, absorbed in his bat work, forgets all about the engagement, so Roy Heath (John Ellis), Martin's son, drives up to his laboratory and presents him with this token of the firm's appreciation. Carruthers isn't much impressed with the gesture ("a bone, tossed to a faithful dog!" he thinks to himself via the soundtrack), and presents Roy with a bottle of a "new shaving lotion" which Roy obligingly daubs on his throat then and there. Of course, it's the fragrance that Carruthers' Devil Bat detests. After Roy has left, Carruthers unleashes the bat through an attic window, and it catches up with Roy just as he arrives home. The vicious Devil Bat severs Roy's jugular vein and gets away unobserved.

The Chicago Daily Register dispatches star reporter Johnny Layton (Dave O'Brien) and photographer "One-Shot" McGuire (Donald Kerr) to Heathville to cover the grisly story. Police Chief Wilkins (Hal Price) shows Layton a picture of Roy's torn-out throat – the lawman has figured out that the beak and talons of a bird were responsible – and tells him that the hair of a mouse was found on Roy's coat. Layton quickly figures out that the killing was the work of an oversized bat and, after interviewing Mary Heath (Suzanne Kaaren), he and "One-Shot" stand watch in the gardens at Heathhaven. Meanwhile, Carruthers has invited *another* Heath, brother Tommy (Alan Baldwin), up to his house, encouraging *him* to slap on a bit of the new "after-shave"; and again the Devil Bat comes swooping out of the sky, this time ending Tommy's life. Layton shoots at the bat, but it gets away. Layton has a tough time convincing his boss, city editor Joe McGinty (Arthur Q. Bryan), to run the fantastic story, but McGinty finally relents and the Devil Bat makes headlines. Below the account is a front-page story titled PERICLES THE GREAT ATHENIAN SPEAKS, all about the famous Greek statesman (ca. 495–429 B.C.), apparently *another* story McGinty's been squelching awhile. Meanwhile, back in Heathville, Don Morton (Gene O'Donnell), Henry Morton's son, becomes victim #3.

Layton finds a bottle of the mysterious "after-shave" in Don's bathroom and shows it to Chief Wilkins; the stuff smells just like the Devil Bat victims do. Layton has begun to suspect Carruthers but Wilkins doesn't agree; *he* thinks the killer might be a disgruntled factory employee. (Does Wilkins really think a Devil Bat works at the factory?) Layton and Wilkins interrogate Carruthers, but the amiable doctor fields their questions easily. As Layton leaves, Carruthers presents *him* with a bottle of the after-shave; but Layton gives it to "One-Shot." That night the bat goes after "One-Shot," but Layton is quick enough on the draw to fill the bat with lead and save his photographer's life. (A news story about the death of the Devil Bat lists the hero as *Henry* instead of *Johnny* Layton.)

Carruthers, however, is undeterred; back in his lab, he uses his electrical apparatus to enlarge a second bat. Later he gives a bottle of the after-shave to Henry Morton, who (after applying it) gently chides Carruthers for selling out years before:

> You shouldn't have demanded all cash, Doc. You should have ridden along with *us* – then *you'd* be rich, too. Well, but then you've had a lot of *fun* in your laboratory, with your experiments, dreaming up something new. You're a dreamer, Doc. Too much money is *bad* for dreamers!

Carruthers, annoyed by Morton's innocent (but still insensitive) comments, carelessly drops a hint that he's behind the Devil Bat killings. Morton drives to Heath-haven, intending to warn Heath and Chief Wilkins but Carruthers has already released the new Devil Bat; the flying beast mows Morton down before he can divulge what he's learned.

Carruthers plants a bottle of his formula on Mary Heath's dressing table; the girl mistakes it for a new perfume and tries it out before she goes to bed. The Devil Bat attacks, but can't get in through the window. Layton still suspects Carruthers and searches the doctor's house, finding in his lab and attic all the evidence he needs. Not letting on that he's solved the case, Layton lets Carruthers "convince" him to try out the after-shave, then invites the doctor to share his all-night vigil; Carruthers, eager to eye-witness a bat attack, accepts. But in the Heath-haven gardens, Layton suddenly

The Devil Bat has done its customarily neat and bloodless job of ripping out its victim's throat. Left to right, standing: Edward Mortimer, Suzanne Kaaren, Guy Usher, Alan Baldwin, Yolande Donlan and Gene O'Donnell; squatting, Bela Lugosi; ten toes up, John Ellis.

douses Carruthers with the after-shave just before the bat arrives on the scene. Chief Wilkins shoots at the bat and in the confusion, Carruthers gets away; when he stumbles upon Mary, he tries to lure the unsuspecting girl back to his house. But the Devil Bat comes screeching unexpectedly out of the skies, attacking and killing Carruthers. Just as the bat is about to strike down Mary, Layton and Chief Wilkins arrive and kill the giant marauder with bullets.

   The Devil Bat easily sizes up as one of Bela Lugosi's best low-budget films; it's almost indisputably better than any of his Monogram movies. The storyline is colorfully lurid, the title creature is a rather exotic movie monster, the bat attacks are well-staged and Lugosi is amusingly intense as the mad doctor. While the Devil Bat murders become a bit redundant in their set-up and staging, the film is a pioneer of the type of "murder-a-reel" plot that became the backbone of the horror film industry a generation later.

   As in other Lugosi films like *The Raven* (1935), *Black Dragons* and others, the plot of *The Devil Bat* revolves around a fairly standard device: Bela's been wronged (or at least *thinks* that he has), and he's out to even the score. *Devil Bat*, like *Son of Frankenstein*, finds him using a monster to eliminate his perceived enemies. Unfortunately, the Devil Bat's no Frankenstein's Monster; once the audience has seen one killing, they've seen 'em all. Two of the Devil Bat attacks take place entirely off camera, sort of an unspoken admission on the part of the filmmakers that they had tipped their hand and shown all their cards rather prematurely.

Like most of the PRC horrors, *The Devil Bat* plunges headlong into the plot: The film opens as Lugosi enlarges one of his bats, then (to let *us* know what's going on) floridly describes his evil plans *to* the bat(!). PRC's films often began at the point of creation of the monster (*The Devil Bat, The Mad Monster*), or with the monster already in existence (*Dead Men Walk, Strangler of the Swamp, The Flying Serpent*). Most would probably find this a lazy or juvenile device, but there's something to be said for movies that know just what their audiences want, that skip all the worn-out yap and jump right into the meat of their stories. By its halfway point, the werewolf in *The Mad Monster* is already hip-deep in murder and mayhem; at the halfway point in Universal's *The Wolf Man*, Lon Chaney has yet to show even a trace of five o'clock shadow. This is not to say that *The Mad Monster* is a better movie than *The Wolf Man*, but just that some studios made horror films that had a lot of buildup while the folks at PRC, who liked zip in their pictures, relied more on action.

The Devil Bat is no less fantastic than any of Bela Lugosi's other horror assignments, but pressbook writers worked overtime trying to sell readers on the fact that "this *could* happen." According to publicity, George Bricker*, who wrote the original story, majored in botany at school and was especially interested in the work of Luther Burbank. "If, says Bricker, flowers can be cultivated and new varieties brought forth, if by breeding animals can be made tougher and stronger, then why couldn't somebody develop the bat to tremendous proportions by scientific breeding?" Bricker's story angle of a scent attracting the Devil Bat was defended by pointing out that bees are attracted to flowers not only by their bright colors but also by the odors. It might all be tommyrot but it sure *sounds* half-right, and it's a nice touch that PRC bothered to try to make their absurd film seem a bit less unlikely. No such effort went into Lugosi's Monogram films; not only were *their* screenwriters unconcerned about plausibility, half the time they didn't even seem to care if their storylines could even be followed!

Mostly *The Devil Bat* is well-paced, but there *are* scenes where it spins its wheels. Except for gobbling up some running time, there's not much point to the scenes where Dave O'Brien and Donald Kerr rig up a phony Devil Bat for photographic purposes; it betrays them as a pair of irresponsible journalists, and also leads up to even *duller* scenes of O'Brien feuding with his boss (and spatting with Suzanne Kaaren) over the failed de-

---

The prolific Bricker wrote fiction, TV and radio scripts in addition to being a screenwriter (his movie career began in 1935). He died of a heart attack on January 22, 1955, in Hollywood. His other horror credits include Sh! The Octopus (1938), Pillow of Death (1945), She-Wolf of London, House of Horrors and The Brute Man (all 1946).

ception. Every bat murder is followed by a barrage of headlines and lengthy opening paragraphs, none telling us anything we didn't already know. After going to the trouble of getting off to a jack-rabbit start, *The Devil Bat* allows itself to sputter and stall. (Apparently *Devil Bat* was meant to be even *longer*, and was cut prior to release: In the opening credits, Billy Griffith is credited with playing the role of "Coroner," but no coroner turns up in the film. There *is* a coroner scene in *The Devil Bat's* remake, *The Flying Serpent*.)

Lifelike characters are also in short supply. Dr. Carruthers, consumed by his desire for revenge, is a stereotypic movie madman, just as the wisecracking reporter-photographer combination lives up to all our expectations of triteness. The Heath and Morton families are all but wiped out by the Devil Bat, but no one ever seems overly upset; the two tycoons even brush aside Chief Wilkins' offer of police protection, as though the lawman is overreacting to the string of gory murders. Finding Layton and "One-Shot" staked out in the garden waiting to catch the killer, Tommy Heath gently mocks them, nonchalantly heading off to bed while complete strangers risk their lives to catch his brother's murderer. The ritzy Heaths get a condescending laugh out of "One-Shot's" announcement that he's engaged to marry Maxine (Yolande Donlan) the maid, treating these blue-collar types like lower life forms.

But there's also plenty that's just right about *The Devil Bat*, starting with Lugosi's performance. Lugosi brings color and his own distinct personality to the clichéd part; *The Devil Bat* (and all the ultra-low-budget pictures that preceded or followed it) might be Grade Z stuff, but Lugosi seldom skimped on the evil leers, melodramatic delivery or wicked intensity that these roles required. Was it good acting? That's another story, but in a film like *The Devil Bat*, Bela's is just what the (mad) doctor ordered.

Lugosi's delivery of parting lines to his victims has become one of the main highlights of *The Devil Bat*. Early on, after tricking Roy (John Ellis) into applying the after-shave, Lugosi's Carruthers responds to Roy's "Good night, doctor," with a wan smile, a small sigh of pleasure and a deliciously delivered "Good*bye*, R-r-r-roy...!" Throughout the picture, he bids characters farewell with these flowery "good*byes*"; in fact, it becomes a running gag. Just in case anyone is missing the joke, he even tosses in other lines pregnant with hidden meaning:

> [*As Tommy rubs on the lotion:*] I don't think you'll ever use anything else...!
> [*When Morton frets about the future of the cosmetics industry:*] You can believe me, Henry: *You* don't have to vorry.

As always, Bela delivers these lines with his own unique brand of dead-pan foreboding. On or off the cob, it's pure corn, but it's the kind of material Lugosi facilely worked wonders with. Oddly, no one ever catches Lugosi's cruel implication or the decidedly diabolic glint in his eyes; it's as if no one's really listening to him. When Guy Usher mocks Lugosi's decision to sell his formula for $10,000 rather than becoming a partner in the company, Lugosi's response is unmistakably venomous:

> *For-r-r-mula!* That's but child's play for a great scientist! Your brain is too feeble to conceive what *I* have accomplished in the realm of science!

Lugosi gives it all the passion he's got, squeezing every last ounce of potential out of the trite lines, his eyebrows arching and dropping like crazy, sitting threateningly on the edge of his chair. Usher, half-listening, takes it all to mean that Lugosi has made a new lab discovery that he's anxious to share. Poor Bela!

Gene O'Donnell, who played the ill-fated Don Morton, recalls *The Devil Bat* well: "Oh, that *was* a campy one *[laughs]*!" O'Donnell had appeared opposite Boris Karloff earlier in the year, in Monogram's *The Ape*, and remembers "a *lot* of differences" between the two leading horror stars:

> Lugosi was a nice guy but he was on drugs – he was *always* on drugs! The less he had to say, the happier he was. In *Dracula* he only had about four lines *[laughs]*, and he said that was the way he liked it! He didn't like lines, but he was a good actor and he had a lot of presence.

Other actors in *The Devil Bat* weren't as adept as Lugosi in coping with the far-out situations and sometimes inane dialogue, but all come off well enough. Dave O'Brien, who with Wallace Ford was one of Lugosi's most frequent screen adversaries, is agreeably all-business as the glib "yellow journalist"; even his sidekick Donald Kerr, who does everything but wear a COMIC RELIEF signboard, is less bothersome than the run-of-the-reel movie dolt. Pretty Suzanne Kaaren, later the real-life wife of actor Sidney Blackmer, is okay in the usual do-nothing ingenue role; on television's *The Joe Franklin Show*, she once proudly showed off still after still from *The Devil Bat*. Gene O'Donnell, Alan Baldwin and John Ellis are merely bat fodder; Edward Mortimer (Mr. Heath) was a silent film director; Arthur Q. Bryan, O'Brien's acerbic boss, was the voice of Elmer Fudd in the old Warner Bros. cartoons. Yolande Mallott [Donlan], who played Maxine the maid, was a Jersey City–born actress who became a hit on the London stage playing the dumb blonde in *Born Yesterday* (1947); this led to numerous other roles in British stage and screen productions. She's back in the U.S. today, and has long been married to cult science fiction director Val Guest.

Donlan recalls *The Devil Bat* with a bit of a gasp:

> Oh, my God! I don't own that one on video; I wasn't even interested in it *then!* I wasn't interested in being in a picture of that kind at that time; I was terribly snobbish *[laughs]*! It was quick and it was fast; they were out to get the money as quickly as possible. It was one of those kind of pictures, a potboiler.

The jig's just about up for Poor Bela as he wrestles with Dave O'Brien in the climax of *The Devil Bat.*

Bela Lugosi was very polite, very pleasant, and he had an eye for the ladies – in fact, he was a bit of a flirt. It was rather fun having Bela Lugosi, "The Spook," being a bit of a flirt *[laughs]*!

Lugosi's *real* co-star, of course, is the Devil Bat itself, which swoops along on wires to the accompaniment of a long sustained scream. (At some points, when it banks, it appears to be on the end of a fishing line.) For a low-budget production such as *The Devil Bat*, the result is effective; the spectacle of the giant flying beast power-diving down to overwhelm its victims probably had more than a few hearts up in people's throats in 1940. Many shots of the Devil Bat are intercut with footage of a *real* bat; again, the effect could be better, but it ain't bad.

The Devil Bat must have been a big moneymaker for PRC to remake the thing twice. The first retread, *The Mad Monster*, was a well-disguised revamping, but the basic plot (a mad scientist creates a monster for the express purpose of destroying his enemies; the monster turns on *him* at the end) was unmistakable. *The Flying Serpent*, featuring another airborne messenger of doom, was a more recognizable reworking of *The Devil Bat* story; in that one, the killer was Quetzalcoatl, a winged reptile. George Zucco played the madman in both of these follow-up productions. A dull sequel to *The Devil Bat, Devil Bat's Daughter*, gave the late Carruthers a daughter (Rosemary LaPlanche) who gets it into her head that she's a vampire. At the picture's end, not only is she rid of her delusion but Carruthers himself is absolved from blame for the original Devil Bat killings. One hopes that no theater ever double-billed the two films.

The Devil Bat was a fairly auspicious horror movie debut for director Jean Yarbrough; his luck with genre films didn't hold out. Born at the turn of the century in Marianna, Arkansas, he started out in films during the silent days as a prop man and built up to assistant-directing and finally to directing. He refereed more than his share of Bowery Boys and Abbott and Costello movies (also working in Bud and Lou's television show) as well as dozens of undistinguished B potboilers, horror films and comedies. In the horror bracket his other credits include *King of the Zombies* and *House of Horrors* (1946), which aren't bad, and *She-Wolf of London, The Brute Man* (1946), *The Creeper* (1948), *Master Minds* (1949) and *Hillbillys in a Haunted House* (1967), which are. He died in 1975.

PRC pushed *The Devil Bat* like crazy, coming up with gruesome ad lines by the carload ("The horror-man creates a mate and torture is their child!!") and above all capitalizing on the Lugosi name:

> *Devil Bat* is horror! It's the kind of a picture that fits Lugosi's personality perfectly. He hasn't had a role such as this in a decade and the time is ripe to cash in on his tremendous box-office pull. You can dare your community to see *Devil Bat* for it will freeze the marrow in their bones. They'll gasp, they'll shake, they'll turn livid...

According to another PRC "scoop," "Bela Lugosi says that for sheer dramatic tension and unadulterated horror, *Devil Bat* far outshines *Dracula*." (There may be more truth to that statement than traditionalist horror fans will want to admit!) Tips to exhibitors included using bright colored cardboard to make silver-dollar sized amulets reading THIS AMULET PROTECTS ME FROM THE "DEVIL BAT"; making their own Devil Bat out of cardboard or stuffed burlap and stretching it across theater lobbies; and displaying a collection of bats in the lobby(!). Other tag lines, like "More terrifying than bombing by night—more thrills than a three alarm fire!!" are interesting allusions to the coming war.

Lugosi probably was pleased himself with the results on *The Devil Bat*; it was a good, juicy part, and PRC bent over backwards playing him up big. In November, just as *The Devil Bat* was wrapping, there was talk of a follow-up to the Kay Kyser-Karloff-Lugosi-Lorre comedy/thriller *You'll Find Out* (RKO, 1940), again with these four stars, but nothing came of these plans; and in February 1941 Lugosi was back down in the supporting ranks, playing a sinister-looking gardener in Universal's inane *The Black Cat*. Possibly Lugosi still held out some hope for a future as a horror star at that studio, but that wasn't to be. Around this time, the actor who *would* fill that slot at Universal was at MGM, making his first appearance on the lot where his father became famous: Lon Chaney, Jr., was working in *Billy the Kid* (and occupying Chaney, Sr.'s old dressing room). Once Chaney, Jr., hit it big at Universal with *The Wolf Man*, Lugosi's chances of regaining his position as head man of horror went from slim to none.

Naka's ineptly-written *Variety* review of *The Devil Bat* was brief enough to reprint here in its entirety:

> This is pretty terrible.
> With Bela Lugosi as the star, and the crazed scientist bent on avenging what he believes has been an unjust deprivation of the wealth accumulated by the cosmetic manufacturers for whom he works, *The Devil Bat* hardly can pass muster on even the most lowly dual situations.
> Acting, directing, photography – all poor.

Modern fan-writers would disagree; some of them dote on *The Devil Bat*, and even the Lugosi buffs who disdain his low-budget films (as though Lugosi did much of anything else!) aren't too tough on it. *Psychotronic* marvelled over the film, calling it "a wonderfully ridiculous chiller." Don Leifert wrote in *Filmfax*, "*The Devil Bat* rambles from director Jean Yarbrough's leisurely pacing. The film is saved, however, by a vintage Lugosi performance. Whether discussing scientific theories with one of his creations or presenting shaving lotion to his victims, the Hungarian horror star is a delight to watch."

Denis Gifford (*A Pictorial History of Horror Movies*) seemed to consider Lugosi a bit miscast: "His Dracula tones and suspect sneer hardly fitted the role of 'kindly physician, Paul Carruthers.' In the rushed world of the B-picture there was seldom time for a re-write." A two-star review in Leonard Maltin's *Movies on TV* rated it "fairly entertaining." Richard Bojarski (*The Films of Bela Lugosi*) wrote, "Despite the drab sets and poor special effects, the plot's premise was potentially interesting. . . Lugosi managed a credible, brooding performance." Lugosiphile *extraordinaire* Arthur Lennig pointed out some of the production's flaws in *The Count*, but summed up with, "For all its drawbacks, the film is kind of fun." Leslie Halliwell called it "horror comic hokum from the bottom of the barrel" but William K. Everson (*More Classics of the Horror Film*) disagreed, writing *The Devil Bat* up as "a most commendable effort." Don Willis commented, "One moment Lugosi approaches comic genius; the next he's embarrassing. . . . His performance is an involved mixture of the good, the bad, the pathetic and the admirable – it might be his career in miniature." For a cheap little film it had its moments, most of them pure Lugosi." Even Phil Hardy, who scowls his way through hundreds of writeups in *The Encyclopedia of Horror Movies*, admitted *The Devil Bat* was "sufficiently bad as to be rather enjoyable."

Invisible Ghost
(Monogram, 1941)

Released April 25. 64 minutes. Associate Producer: Pete Mayer. Produced by Sam Katzman (Banner Pictures Corporation). Directed by Joseph H. Lewis. Story and Screenplay: Helen Martin and Al Martin. Photographers: Marcel Le Picard and Harvey Gould. Film Editor: Robert Golden. Production Manager: Ed W. Rote. Assistant Directors: Edward M. Saeta and Harry Slott. Settings: Fred Preble. Musical Directors: Lange & Porter, A.S.C.A.P. Recording: Glen Glenn.

Cast: Bela Lugosi (Charles Kessler), Polly Ann Young (Virginia Kessler), John McGuire (Ralph Dickson/Paul Dickson), Clarence Muse (Evans), Terry Walker (Cecile Mannix), Betty Compson (Mrs. Kessler), Ernie Adams (Jules Mason), George Pembroke (Police Lt. Williams), Ottola Nesmith (Mrs. Mason), Fred Kelsey (Ryan), Jack Mulhall (Tim), Robert Strange (Coroner Kirby).

> **"When Karloff turned down a script from the smaller studios, there was always Lugosi. 'Eck-sss-ellent!' he would invariably exclaim as he went about his, and their, fiendish work, happy to take the money and lope."** — Denis Gifford, *A Pictorial History of Horror Movies*

Virtually an outcast in Hollywood during the two-year 1930s ban on horror films, Bela Lugosi had cause to celebrate when the chillers came back in style in 1939. In 1941, things began to look even brighter; Boris Karloff headed East to New York to star in Broadway's *Arsenic and Old Lace*. Horror had come back and Karloff had gone away! It was a combination of events that Lugosi had to have taken as a good omen.

He went after the lead in Universal's *The Wolf Man* (1941), not realizing that the film and the role had been expressly tailored for Lon Chaney, Jr., who became to Lugosi in the '40s what Karloff had been in the '30s. Universal lined up Chaney for one starring role after another: the Wolf Man, the Frankenstein Monster, the Mummy and even Count Dracula, a bit of casting that had Poor Bela fuming. Occasionally Lugosi would turn up in a supporting role in one of Lon's movies (*The Wolf Man, The Ghost of Frankenstein*, 1942), or in other minor Universals (*The Black Cat*, 1941, *Night Monster*, 1942). But any hopes he might have had of becoming the studio's top horror man were dashed—again.

The year 1941 found Lugosi allying himself with Monogram Pictures. Lugosi had worked for Monogram once in the '30s, playing the title role in *The Mysterious Mr. Wong*, which was shot at RKO-Pathé in September, 1934. Lugosi's English film *The Dark Eyes of London*, luridly retitled *The Human Monster*, had also been distributed stateside by Monogram, in 1940. Between 1941 and 194, Lugosi turned up in nine of Monogram producer

Sam Katzman's minor horror productions: *Spooks Run Wild, The Corpse Vanishes, Black Dragons, Bowery at Midnight, Ghosts on the Loose, The Ape Man, Return of the Ape Man, Voodoo Man*, and – The Film That Started It All – *Invisible Ghost*. Better to reign in Hell than serve in Heaven, John Milton wrote in *Paradise Lost*, and Lugosi evidently took that philosophy to heart. But at least at Monogram Lugosi could once again be a star, a consolation that must have been good for the proud and aloof Hungarian actor's much-battered ego.

Titled *Murder by the Stars* in initial press announcements, later called *Phantom Monster* and produced under the shooting title *The Phantom Killer, Invisible Ghost* commenced shooting on March 20, 1941 (Lugosi was fresh from the sets of Universal's *The Black Cat*). Bela had been set for the lead more than a month in advance of that date but in typical Monogram fashion most of the supporting players – Clarence Muse, Betty Compson, Ernie Adams, George Pembroke, Fred Kelsey and Jack Mulhall – were signed only a day before production began.

Charles Kessler (Bela Lugosi), a wealthy philanthropist, lives with the painful knowledge that his wife ran off with their best friend years before. Once a year, on their wedding anniversary, a special dinner is prepared by Evans (Clarence Muse), Kessler's understanding black butler. The mild-mannered Kessler addresses his wife's empty dining room chair as though she were there as Evans serves the meal to "both" of them. (The other 364 days, characters assert, Kessler is "normal." Right.) Kessler's daughter Virginia (Polly Ann Young) has a boyfriend, Ralph (John McGuire), a young engineer who shows up unexpectedly that night and catches a glimpse of the unnerving.

After Virginia and Ralph have gone off for a drive, Jules (Ernie Adams), Kessler's gardener, steals a bagful of food from the kitchen and sneaks off to the nearby garden house. Descending through a trap door, he presents the food to a haggard older woman – Mrs. Kessler (Betty Compson). Years before, when she had fled with her lover, their car crashed and the lover was killed. Mrs. Kessler's mind and memory have been affected by the accident, and Jules has been keeping her hidden in the garden house ever since. Jules hasn't got the heart to tell Kessler, feeling that it would kill him to see his adored wife in her present condition.

Virginia and Ralph return from their drive, and after Virginia has gone into the house, the departing Ralph is confronted by Cecile (Terry Walker), the Kesslers' maid. Ralph and Cecile had been shacked up for a time, and Cecile doesn't intend to allow him to dump her for Virginia. Ralph threatens her and leaves. Unobserved, Evans the butler has overheard the full conversation.

After the rest of the household has retired, Kessler senses a presence outside the house, and in a daze he wanders over to a second-story window. Mrs. Kessler, strolling around the grounds, is below, and the two stare

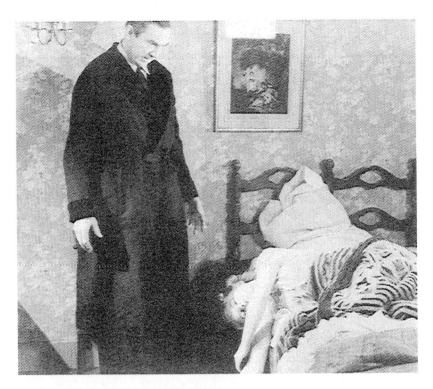

Joseph H. Lewis' direction made the most of the murder of the maid (Terry Walker) in *Invisible Ghost* with Bela Lugosi (left).

fixedly at one another. ("I'm afraid to come home," the simple-minded Mrs. K. murmurs to herself. "He'd kill me. He'd kill *any*body.") Slipping into a strange trance, Kessler sleepwalks into the servants' part of the house and steals into Cecile's room. As the frightened maid cringes in bed, Kessler removes his robe, advances menacingly, drapes it over her head and shoulders and strangles her. The next morning, when her body is found, Kessler has no memory of having committed the crime and is as shocked as everyone else.

Police Lt. Williams (George Pembroke) is baffled. Cecile's murder is the latest in a series of killings to occur within the Kessler household (Kessler committed them all), but there have never been any fingerprints or a motive. Until now. When Evans describes what he overheard between Ralph and Cecile the night before, Lt. Williams arrests the young man. A web of circumstantial evidence tightens around Ralph, and his trial ends with a verdict of guilty. Despite Kessler's plea to the governor for clemency, the innocent Ralph walks the last mile.

The Kessler home is shaken once again a short time later when Ralph appears at the door. Only it *isn't* Ralph, it's his twin brother Paul (also John

McGuire), just returned from South America and newly apprised of Ralph's execution. Sympathetic toward the young lookalike, Kessler invites him to stay at the house. Late that night, Kessler spots his footloose wife saunter- ing around the yard again and slips into another one of his trances. Jules the gardener, pulling one of his midnight raids on the icebox, is his newest victim. The police come and go again.

In a ridiculous scene, Jules' wife (Ottola Nesmith) visits the coroner's office while Kessler is there, asking for one last look at her husband (doesn't she intend to go to his wake?). Kirby the coroner (Robert Strange) accedes, showing her into the next room where Jules' body lies. The wife shrieks – Jules *isn't* dead (just almost). Kessler presses him for the name of his at- tacker, but Jules dies before he can utter Kessler's name.

The film becomes mired in repetition. During a fierce nighttime rain- storm, Mrs. Kessler shows her face again (framed in a rain-streaked win- dow), prompting the spellbound Kessler to wander to Virginia's room. But before Kessler can bring himself to kill the sleeping girl, a flash of lightning momentarily snaps him out of the deadly trance.

In the a.m., a hallway portrait of Mrs. Kessler is found to have been slashed during the night. Worried that the killer may have struck again, Kessler searches the house for the newly-hired cook Marie, who's nowhere to be found – until she strolls in from an early morning shopping expedition. But later the dead body of Ryan (Fred Kelsey), a detective who had been staking out the house, is found behind a curtain.

A false clue points to Evans as a possible suspect, and a psychiatrist is summoned to the house that night to give the black butler a sanity test. Mrs. Kessler, fending for herself in this new post–Jules age, filches a bone from the icebox but is caught in the act by cops who escort her upstairs – and into Kessler's presence. Falling into his usual stupor, Kessler begins to sleep- walk the halls as Paul, Lt. Williams, Evans and the psychiatrist follow quietly. Suddenly he spins on his heel and seizes Lt. Williams by the throat. For no reason whatsoever, Mrs. Kessler keels over dead and Kessler becomes himself again, relaxing his death-grip around the policeman's neck.

Shocked and horrified by the realization that he himself is the killer, Kessler regains his composure and as he pauses beneath his wife's portrait, he mutters, "I knew you'd come back. Nothing can part us now, my dar- lingk." Police lead him away, presumably to be tried and executed.

Featuring all the physical requirements of an okay thriller, *Invisible Ghost* is deflated and nearly sunk by its dreadful script. Poorly constructed and illogical to the point of exasperation, it vitiates the best efforts of direc- tor and cast. (Scripts like these became the hallmark of the Monogram hor- ror films.) Numerous murders have been committed in the Kessler home, but no one seems upset about them, no one locks their doors and no one even talks about them except after one has just been discovered. This weird murder house would be talked about nationwide (*à la* the Amityville home)

A victim of spells of madness, Bela Lugosi slashes a portrait of wife Betty Compson in *Invisible Ghost.* The film was Lugosi's first in a nine-film series for Monogram Pictures.

in real life, but in the film, Lugosi is able to hire locals who've never *heard* of the place. The police don't even stake out the house, just casually drop by after each murder like tired men checking out a report of a barking dog.

There isn't an ounce of potential in the script, but the film is at least partially salvaged by imaginative touches brought to it by director Joseph H. Lewis. Unlike the typical Monogram hack who viewed the studio as their last stop, Lewis looked on it as only a First Step, and he loads the film with mildly interesting camera moves, lighting effects, editing tricks and the like. As with Lewis' earlier *Boys of the City*, they're the sort of flourishes that would be taken entirely for granted in any major film, but in a Monogram like *Invisible Ghost* these little whiffs of filmic style stand out like beacons. The camera, often immobile in low budget pictures, dollies and swoops around regularly, and there are many high- and low-angle shots; it even passes through walls as characters troop from one room to another. Two scenes are photographed in mirrors, alternating subjective shots are used in the scene where Kessler stalks the maid, and the camera occasionally shoots from inside the blazing fireplace. Two photographers, Marcel Le Picard and Harvey Gould, were employed on *Invisible Ghost*, though only Le Picard receives credit in the film's pressbook.

Lewis brings all his talent to bear the first time Kessler spots his wife (from a second-story window) in the film. High-angle over-Lugosi's-shoulder shots of the wife, extreme closeups, selective focus and spooky lighting are tricks of the filmmakers' trade that Lewis employs in making this short scene the highlight of the film. Unfortunately, Lewis goes to the well far too often: The first confrontation scene is effective, the second one less so, the third tiresome, and by the fourth time the scene has become almost funny through repetition.

Pacing is sometimes sacrificed for the buildup of suspense – a mistake, as the "suspenseful" scenes are redundantly written and staged. Much footage is spent watching the entranced Lugosi pussyfoot around the house, but after the first time it's done, all viewers can think about is that nothing is happening. The languorous pace makes the film seem far longer than its actual 64 minutes.

There's genuine confusion about the strange power Mrs. Kessler holds over her husband. According to the pressbook, she casts a spell over Kessler, implying that she is some sort of witch or hypnotist, yet in the film she's just a simple-minded victim of amnesia with no such powers. But then at the end there *is* a supernatural touch: when Mrs. Kessler inexplicably falls dead to the floor, Kessler is released from the spell, as though her control had expired with her death. Contrary to the film's meaningless title, she's neither invisible nor a ghost. (If she had been invisible, Kessler wouldn't have had a problem!) And can anyone explain why the film's credits are shown over background artwork of the shadow of an ape, while the credits of Monogram's *The Ape* feature artwork of circus clowns?

It also doesn't seem possible that Ralph Dickson could be found guilty of the maid's murder in a household known for frequent murders; that Kessler should be the only person ever to spot Mrs. Kessler, who prowls around the house constantly; or that the dead gardener should perk up again in the coroner's office. When the script comes up with an identical twin brother for the executed Ralph, the film starts to become almost *surreal*; it's an inane touch that stands out boldly, even amidst the film's other stupidities. Though it's a murder drama devoid of monsters or science fiction ingredients, *Invisible Ghost* is the most far-out of the Lugosi Monogram films; it's easier to believe that a real-life accident of science could create *The Ape Man* than that everyday people could behave the way they do in *Invisible Ghost*. (The absurd plot was echoed four years later in the mild Universal Inner Sanctum mystery *Pillow of Death*.)

Al Martin was a prolific hack screenwriter whose career dated back to the days of silents, when he wrote subtitles for an average of 200 pictures annually for ten years. Among the dozens of films he penned during the sound era are several forays into horror and science fiction (*The Rogues Tavern, Trapped by Television, Invisible Ghost, The Mad Doctor of Market Street* and *Invasion of the Saucer Men*), all of them linked by the same low level of quality. Writing his last feature in 1958 (the Bowery Boys' *In the Money*, another gem), Martin turned his "talents" to television. He died in 1971.

The role of Charles Kessler was an acting "stretch" for Bela Lugosi and he does a decent job, turning in a performance which has long been a favorite among Lugosi fans. Kessler's a warm-hearted philanthropist as well as a loving family man; the picture never lets us forget this, establishing it early and then underscoring it continually. There's hardly a trace of the customary Lugosi hamming, nor any of Lugosi's unwanted habit of imbuing sympathetic roles with an occasional touch of chill. The performance is proof that Lugosi could have passed muster in a "straight" (nonhorror) picture – although by 1941, the only way Lugosi was getting into a straight picture was by buying a ticket.

He's not as frightening as anticipated in his "mad" scenes, staggering unsteadily around like a wind-up sleepwalker. The scene where he steals into the maid's room and begins to disrobe is unintentionally funny; the act of partially undressing (not to mention the hundred-watt gleam in Lugosi's eyes) gives the impression that murder's the *last* thing on his mind as he creeps up on the cowering young beauty. (The actress, Terry Walker, falls victim to Bela again in *Voodoo Man.*)

Victims of the awful script, most of the supporting players flounder but struggle valiantly to appear sincere. Polly Ann Young has so little to do that she fails to make any impression; she'd worked in a Lugosi film before, a bit in Bela's *Murders in the Rue Morgue* (1932). John McGuire, a former featured contract player at Fox and RKO, is adequate in his dual role assignment, although McGuire provides no shadings of character to differentiate between the two brothers. The year before, he played a similar role in RKO's *Stranger on the Third Floor* (a young newspaperman wrongly arrested and accused of murder). A former silent screen beauty, the fortyish Betty Compson (who starred in the lost film *The Miracle Man* [1919] opposite Lon Chaney and in *The Great Gabbo* [1929] with Erich von Stroheim) has the unflattering minor role of Lugosi's haggard, bird-witted wife. (According to the *Invisible Ghost* pressbook, Compson studied various mental cases at a Los Angeles asylum in preparation for her role!)

Clarence Muse, one of the best black character actors of his day, rises above the material playing the faithful butler, although he too is let down by an inconsistent script; in an early scene he grouses at the gardener for gossiping about the murders, but later he can't wait to be the one to taunt the new cook with the news. A onetime minstrel singer and vaudevillian, Muse enjoyed a long career in films, with horror fans probably remembering him best for his minute role as the coach driver in Lugosi's *White Zombie* (1932). Monogram's publicity mill suggested that showmen with houses in all-black neighborhoods boost their grosses by co-starring Muse with Lugosi on their theater marquees.

For the first several reels *Invisible Ghost* is free of the unintentional laughs that mark many low-budget horror films, but toward the end they suddenly start coming hot and heavy. Kessler's staring contests with his wife become comical, as does the dialogue. When Lt. Williams begins to suspect Evans the butler, Virginia snaps, "You're just trying to make a case," like there's something wrong with that. After the painting of Mrs. Kessler is slashed, Paul comments, "Without doubt, the murderer is insane. The picture tells us that," as though the series of killings alone left room for doubt. Best of all is Paul's interrogation of the psychiatrist ("Is it possible, Doctor, for a man to be normal, say for two or three months at a time, then go completely insane for an hour or two?") and the doctor's casual response ("Yes, quite common!"). Comical music is heard as Kessler wanders the halls for the last time, and when he seizes Lt. Williams by the throat, everyone just stands around and watches with vague interest.

Coproducer of Lugosi's Monogram series, Sam Katzman was the legendary Hollywood character whose name is now synonymous with mini-budgets and lightning-fast schedules; he produced scores of films, but today is probably best remembered for his horror and science fiction films and serials. Born in New York, he started in films at age 13 at the old Fox Film studios in Fort Lee, New Jersey; there he carried mail, film and props for $9 a week. He worked his way up from prop boy to assistant director and began his producing career in the early '30s. His first picture, *His Private Secretary* (1933) with John Wayne, was made for $9600, of which $2500 was cash and the rest deferred payments. (Wayne earned $150 a week.) Katzman said he wrote the picture himself (the credits don't bear him out) and put it together in six days.

For years Katzman thrived on this sort of movies-on-a shoestring activity; while he worked in most every genre, the movies themselves were just about always aimed at "the cap-gun set" (small kids) or teenagers. In a 1952 interview, "Jungle Sam" (his nickname) bragged that he never spent more than half a million on a picture (no kidding!), and that he never produced a film that lost money. By this time, of course, his Monogram/Lugosi days were already behind him; he was now at Columbia where he specialized in serials (including the *Supermans*), *Jungle Jim* films, miniswashbucklers, rock-'n'-rollers, etc. Working under his Clover Films banner, he produced such '50s SF flickers as *Creature with the Atom Brain*, *The Giant Claw* and the stop-motion favorites *Earth vs. the Flying Saucers* and *It Came from Beneath the Sea*; occasionally he'd even produce a horror film which, as often as not, had some of the flavor of his old Monogram shockers (*The Man Who Turned to Stone*, *Zombies of Mora Tau*). In 1958, he announced his plans to "sweeten" his teen-aimed pictures: no more gangster *or* science fiction subjects. "In the future I'll concentrate on showing the good side of the teenagers. All that other stuff has been knocked from my schedule ... I've simply turned over a new leaf."

Interviewed again in the mid–'60s, Katzman admitted that he'd lost count of the number of pictures he'd ground out but guessed that it might be as high as 1200. In the '60s, he was busy at MGM, where he even produced a few of the notorious Elvis Presley movies; Katzman paid the King $1,000,000 to star in *Harem Scarum* (1965). (A million dollars was undoubtedly much more money than had gone into the entire Lugosi series.) The patron saint of Hollywood tightwads, producer of some of the great "guilty pleasure" films of all time, Sam Katzman died August 4, 1973.

Monogram's publicists flirted with the limits of the law in advising exhibitors how to ballyhoo *Invisible Ghost*. One suggestion called for theater owners to dress a tall, well-built man completely in black (suit, hat, shoes, gloves and even mask), arm him with a coil of rope as well as either a dagger or a prop revolver, and send him out to wander the streets and stare down passersby. "If you get a smart ballyhooer, he can really do a job . . . tapping unsuspecting people on the back, looking into stores, parked cars, etc." Running off batteries or reduced regular current, an Electric Nerve Tester was a black box with handles and a sign reading,

TEST YOUR NERVES BEFORE SEEING **INVISIBLE GHOST**. Don't take a chance. If you can't stand a test like this, imagine what'll happen when you get a REAL SHOCK from the most terrifying show of the season!

Gripped by theater lobby gawkers, the box would deliver a slight electric shock – potentially fatal to people with heart problems. (Details, details!) Yet another stunt called for a skeleton (borrowed from a local clinic, hospital or high school) to be suspended on fine piano wire and swung across darkened theaters between features. (The Electric Nerve Tester and skeleton gimmicks call to mind producer William Castle's Percepto and Emergo promotions for his '50s films *The Tingler* and *House on Haunted Hill*.)

Except for the fact that Joseph Lewis' direction was invariably slighted, *Invisible Ghost* received the reviews it deserved. According to the *Motion Picture Exhibitor*, "The story is complicated and unbelievable." The *Hollywood Reporter* critiqued it on April 11 (only days after production wrapped up!), with the reviewer – evidently a visitor to our planet – stating, "The original by Helen and Al Martin is sound, their screenplay fairly consistent." Registering a **FAIR** rating on *The New York Post's* Movie Meter, it was dismissed as a picture that "trots out the usual Lugosi tricks. [But] these time-tested ingredients don't quite click, partly because of the over-complex plot, partly because the timing, essential to the buildup of suspense in a horror/drama, is imperfect." *The New York Daily News'* one-star review read, "The only real horror engendered by the film is in the necessity of sitting it through, for the sake of the record. The film is a ghastly bore that has been assembled, quickie fashion, in a series of closeups. . . . Bela Lugosi is not at his best [and] Polly Ann Young and John McGuire are ineffective under Joseph Lewis' inadequate dircction."

Lee Mortimer of the *New York Daily Mirror* called it "a hunk of ectoplasm gone haywire at the crossroads of the world. . . . It's unethical to spill the solution of a mystery picture, but we wouldn't know anyway. We had folded our shroud and floated forth long before the ghost was laid." *Variety*'s reviewer Hobe called the film "one of the feeblest pictures of the season. . . . Without going into details of the film's innumerable faults, call the story, characters, dialogue, score, lighting, photography and direction all terrible." *The New York Times* looked down its nose as well: "The motivation is as wild as the wind and the performances are as incredibly amateurish as *Invisible Ghost* is silly." "A little monstrosity," wrote Donald Kirkley of *The Baltimore Sun.* "Bizarre antics are staged in the most wooden manner possible, and the players behave as if they wish that they and not the ghost were invisible."

Invisible Ghost has long been a minor favorite among horror fans because it furnishes Bela Lugosi with the rare and welcome opportunity to play a kindly, paternal role. This, and the nice visual lift Lewis' direction gives the film, compensate slightly for the sheer stupidity of the script and its many dreary passages. Lugosi's Monogram debut isn't one of his most entertaining low-budget films, but on a different level it remains one of the most interesting.

Say what you want about Monogram, but at least Lugosi was finding a variety of roles and vehicles there: A "sympathetic killer" in a chiller (*Invisible Ghost*), tongue-in-cheek mystery figure in a comedy (*Spooks Run Wild*), tragic hero of a war propaganda thriller (*Black Dragons*) and a two-faced criminal in a gangster melodrama (*Bowery at Midnight*). Compare these roles to the stereotypic Big Bad Wolf parts he was playing everywhere else, almost without exception; what studio other than Monogram gave him the chance to stretch his acting muscles this way? He may not have stretched them too terribly *far*, and the Monogram films themselves were never anything to write home about, but at least Monogram recognized that he could play more than one type of role, and appear in more than one type of horror film.

King of the Zombies
(Monogram, 1941)

Released May 14. 67 minutes. Produced by Lindsley Parsons. Directed by Jean Yarbrough. Screenplay: Edmond Kelso. Director of Photography: Mack Stengler,

A.S.C. Musical Score and Direction: Edward Kay. Production Manager: Mack Wright. Film Editor: Richard Currier. Settings: Dave Milton. Sound Directors: William Fox and Glen Rominger. Art Director: Charles Clague.

Cast: Dick Purcell (James "Mac" McCarthy), Joan Woodbury (Barbara Winslow), Mantan Moreland (Jefferson Jackson), Henry Victor (Dr. Miklos Sangre), John Archer (Bill Summers), Patricia Stacey (Madame Alyce Sangre), Guy Usher (Admiral Wainwright), Marguerite Whitten (Samantha), Leigh Whipper (Momba), Madame Sul-Te-Wan (Tahama), Lawrence Criner (Dr. Couillie), Jimmy Davis (Lazarus).

> "Of all the 'B' monsters, the zombie was favourite. The walking dead looked pretty much like the walking quick, particularly if you used the less expressive, hence less expensive actors. Besides, a zombie cannot talk and that was another saving: the union scale was lower for a non-speaking part!" — Denis Gifford, *A Pictorial History of Horror Movies*

> "Make no mistake about it. Director Jean Yarbrough is a man of tact and finesse. He proved this while instructing Dick Purcell, Joan Woodbury and Mantan Moreland how to act for a scene in Monogram's *King of the Zombies*.
>
> "'Now, when you see this "dead man" rise from the coffin, recoil and blanch with fear—you know, turn pale,' Yarbrough ordered.
>
> "Moreland, a gentleman of color from Alabama, remonstrated, 'Mistah Yarbrough, that is a little difficult for me.' The director pondered a second, then said, 'Okeh, Mantan—you just sort of blanch darkly.'" — *King of the Zombies* pressbook

Say whatever you want about the old Monogram horror films, but never make the mistake of saying they were unimaginative. If anything, there was often too *much* imagination lavished on some of their films (*Black Dragons, Bowery at Midnight, King of the Zombies*, more), which combined themes that few other studios would have dreamed of pairing in a motion picture. The seriocomic *King of the Zombies* is a good early example of mismatched plot elements shoehorned into a single package: zombies, Nazis, hypnotism, an attempted soul-transference of the switched-sex kind, adventure, and scene upon scene of comic relief of the sort that's labelled racist today. Early plans even called for the zombies to *sing* in the picture. (And some people say these Monogram movies couldn't possibly have been any worse!)

King of the Zombies was the first of several '40s horror films that mixed monsters and members of the Third Reich. *Zombies* was filmed in the spring of 1941, months before America entered the war against the Axis powers, so the film treads a bit lightly. While the villain is not called a Nazi, his accent and bearing are Teutonic, his radio broadcasts are in German and his goals (coercing military secrets from a kidnapped admiral) nefarious. (The pressbook calls him "a secret agent for a European government.") After the December 7 Day of Infamy, filmmakers tossed subtlety to the winds of war. Later '40s horror films that featured Germans or Japanese amongst its monsters (or *as* its monsters) were *Revenge of the Zombies, Ghosts on the Loose, Black Dragons* (all Monogram), *The Gorilla Man, The Mysterious Doctor* (both Warner Bros., 1943) and *Invisible Agent* (Universal, 1942). The dirty rats also figure, less prominently, into the plots of MGM's *The Canterville Ghost* (1944), Columbia's *The Return of the Vampire* (1943) and RKO's *The Brighton Strangler* (1945).

Oddly, it was not only the renewed popularity of horror films that prompted *King of the Zombies*, but also the then-current box office success of Westerns with a tongue-in-cheek approach. Their profitability was noted by Monogram producer Lindsley Parsons, who announced in the Hollywood trade papers in January, 1941, that he would try this semihumorous treatment with *King of the Zombies*. (Common sense dictates that another, probably more direct inspiration had to have been Bob Hope's recent hit horror/comedy *The Ghost Breakers*, which also featured a zombie–Noble Johnson; the *King of the Zombies* pressbook instructs exhibitors to sell *King* along the same lines as *Ghost*.) Initial announcements of *King of the Zombies* stated that Bela Lugosi had been signed to play the lead and that Howard Bretherton would direct. These early press blurbs also promised that the zombies in the film would belt out a little ditty titled "The Grave Diggers' Song."

But by March, when *King of the Zombies* was ready to go under the hot lights, Lugosi had either bowed out or been sidetracked by another project. (Lugosi did film *Invisible Ghost* for Monogram in March, although that production was wrapped up in plenty of time for Bela to conceivably have done both films.) Now minus an actor to play the title character, Monogram busily dickered with Peter Lorre, but by the time filming got underway on March 31, character actor Henry Victor was enacting the villainous lead: Miklos Sangre, zombie-master of a mysterious Caribbean island. Initially proposed director Bretherton also fell by the wayside, replaced by reliable hack Jean Yarbrough.

The plot: A small plane bound for the Bahamas, blown off course by a storm and low on fuel, is lost somewhere over the ocean between Cuba and Puerto Rico. Aboard are pilot James "Mac" McCarthy (Dick Purcell), Bill Summers (John Archer) and Bill's black valet Jefferson Jackson (Mantan Moreland). Mac overhears a radio message (spoken in German) coming in so strongly that the transmitter must be directly below. Descending below cloud level, the three men spot an island and deliberately crash-land the plane in dense jungle.

Mac, Bill and Jeff awaken outside the plane wreckage to find themselves

STRANGER THAN YOU'VE EVER DREAMED!

A beautiful girl enslaved by the soulless master of voodooism! Compelled to serve in his illicit rites...used as *human bait* to lure other victims for his evil cult!

WEIRDEST THRILLS EVER FILMED!

MONOGRAM PICTURES presents

"KING OF THE ZOMBIES"

With DICK PURCELL · JOAN WOODBURY · MANTAN MORELAND · HENRY VICTOR

Produced by LINDSLEY PARSONS · Directed by JEAN YARBROUGH

Screenplay by EDMUND KELSO

in a desolate graveyard. To the sound of distant drums, they tramp through the underbrush and make their way to a dark mansion where they are greeted by the suave Dr. Sangre (Victor). Sangre invites Mac and Bill to remain in the house as his guests until the next boat arrives in a fortnight. As the pressbook points out, "There is an air of tension and 'black magic' about Sangre's huge stone house."

The doctor ushers the two men to their rooms but insists that Jeff stay in the servants' quarters (Sangre tells Mac and Bill that he cannot "set a bad example for the other servants"). Momba (Leigh Whipper), Sangre's cadaverous black butler, escorts Jeff to the servants' quarters, where Jeff flirts with Samantha (Marguerite Whitten), the pretty black cook, and pokes fun at the ancient Tahama (Madame Sul-Te-Wan), another colored domestic:

> JEFF: Who's that, Methuselah? . . . I know a museum that would give you a fortune just to have her under glass.
> SAMANTHA: What's a museum?
> JEFF: That's where they keep dead things.
> SAMANTHA: Oh, like here.

When a pair of zombies enters the kitchen, the frightened Jeff flees in panic, rushing to Mac and Bill's room to warn them. Sangre leads Mac, Bill and Jeff back to the kitchen, where zombies are conspicuous by their absence. Mac and Bill scoff at Jeff's ridiculous-sounding story.

Dr. Sangre introduces Mac and Bill to his wife Alyce (Patricia Stacey), who suffers from a "strange malady" which gives her the appearance of a sleepwalker. He also presents them to Barbara Winslow (Joan Woodbury), whom he introduces as his niece. "By marriage," Barbara adds reflexively, giving us a pretty good idea what she thinks of Uncle Miklos.

Returned to the kitchen, Jeff is warned by Samantha to be in bed before midnight:

> SAMANTHA: It's [the zombies'] feedin' time—and they likes dark meat!
> JEFF: *Dark* meat! You don't have to play no second chorus for me to find out who *that* means!

Once more Jeff is accosted by zombies, escaping with his life, only to have his story again dismissed by Mac and Bill. (Mac: "Ah, the crack-up must have given him a concussion. You'll be all right in the morning, Jeff.") Sleeping in Mac and Bill's room, Jeff awakens to see Madame Sangre enter the room through a secret panel, stand over the sleeping Mac and Bill, and then silently return whence she came.

Searching the house, Bill catches Barbara reading a book on hypnotism; she tells him she thinks that her aunt has been hypnotized into her present somnambulistic state. Mac and Jeff are attacked by a zombie (Jimmy Davis) who kayoes Mac before fleeing. The next day, after discovering that the radio in their wrecked plane has been dismantled, Mac decides to secretly search the house again. Elsewhere, acting on Sangre's orders, voodoo priestess Tahama continues to chant her spells over the unconscious Admiral Wainwright (Guy Usher) in hopes that under her power, he will spill to Sangre what he knows about Canal Zone fortifications.

Sangre quietly abducts Jeff through the secret panel and uses hypnotism to put the valet into a zombie-like state ("Move over, boys," Jeff deadpans as he joins a lineup of zombies, "I'm one of the gang now.") Mac, long-missing, turns up in a deep trance and is put to bed by Bill and Sangre. Dr. Coullie (Lawrence Criner), a native doctor, examines him promptly and declares that Mac has been dead since morning(!). Adhering to what he claims is local custom, Sangre orders the body buried immediately.

Startled to find Jeff among the zombie workers, Samantha seasons his meal with salt, which brings him out from under Sangre's influence. Jeff and Bill explore the hidden passage and discover the body of Madame Sangre, killed by her husband for trying to betray him to Mac and Bill (her secret panel visit).

In the secret ceremonial room in the bowels of the house, in a rite attended by a gang of natives and Sangre's zombie corps (which now includes Mac), Sangre and Tahama are working to transfer the soul of Admiral Wainwright into the body of the kidnapped and entranced Barbara. When Bill disrupts the ceremony, Sangre orders his zombie bodyguards to attack him. But Mac, despite his zombie state, manages to recognize Bill, and now leads the zombies against Sangre. Backing away in terror, Sangre pumps three bullets into Mac without effect before tumbling backwards into a fiery pit. (The film's pressbook, and therefore possibly an early draft of the script, called for Mac *and* Sangre to tumble into the flames.)

Barbara and the Admiral are rescued, and join Bill and Jeff in awaiting a Coast Guard rescue. Wainwright explains that Madame Sangre had been involved in an earlier attempt at a Rite of Transmigration, but broke under the strain and fell into her zombie state. We're even told that Mac – who had died, was buried, became a zombie, and then was shot three times at point-blank range – has started on the road to recovery.

Some horror film fans – the ones that take the genre, and themselves, too seriously – generally regard Monogram's two zombie films, *King of the Zombies* and *Revenge of the Zombies*, as the nadir of the zombie/voodoo subgenre. Ask them to name better films and they will cite the old-fashioned Lugosi vehicle *White Zombie* (1932), the genteel Val Lewton excursion *I Walked with a Zombie* (1943) and maybe Hammer's *The Plague of the Zombies* (1966). (All of which *are* better than the Monograms.) But outside of these three films – none of which is a full-fledged classic – most zombie movies have little or nothing to offer.

Among the best known, *Revolt of the Zombies* (1936), hailing from horror's so-called "Golden Age," is not only crude, but an excruciating bore. *Zombies on Broadway* (1945), an RKO comedy with a pair of Abbott and Costello wannabees, is strictly bush-league, although Bela Lugosi's presence lifts the film slightly out of the rut. Among the '50s/'60s low-budgeters, *Zombies of Mora Tau* (1957) is minor but entertaining, *Voodoo Island* (1957) with Boris Karloff is minor but *not* entertaining. Things like *Teenage Zombies* (1958), *I Eat Your Skin* (1964) and *Snake People* (1968, with Karloff again) are such sheer trash it took years for them to escape. The cheesy foreign films (e.g., *War of the Zombies*, 1965) are never up to snuff; the new school of gory zombie epic is not only beneath consideration, but beneath contempt. (This rundown eliminates science fiction and non-voodoo zombie movies like the excellent *Night of the Living Dead*, 1968, and its league of imitators.) It's a sad comment on the zombie's screen career that one of the very few films in which the monster was effectively presented was Bob Hope's *The Ghost Breakers*.

None of this is meant to imply that *King of the Zombies* is a better film than people have given it credit for; just that, in the zombie category, the pickings are so appallingly slim that it ought not to be taken completely for granted. It's a comedy as much as it is a horror film, due to the ubiquitous Mantan Moreland, and for a film of this type, it still plays fairly amusingly.

The horror scenes are another story entirely. *King of the Zombies* advertised itself as a straight horror thriller, but the comedy of Moreland remains front and center even throughout the zombies' footage. In fact, except for the finale, Moreland dominates every zombie scene in the film. The zombies (all black, until Dick Purcell joins them) are an eerier bunch than the desegregated group seen in the later *Revenge of the Zombies*, but just as ineffective in action. Stone-faced, their gaze directed up toward the ceiling, they march around like wind-up dolls, and even Mantan Moreland is nimble enough to escape from the very clutches of a pair of them. One of the zombies (Jimmy Davis) manages to knock Purcell down in a fight, but even this one then flees before the job is done. The impression the film gives is that all they ever do is wander around outside the kitchen waiting to be fed. (Samantha the cook implies that they're flesh-eaters, which fits in nicely with the zombie's post–*Night of the Living Dead* screen image.)

It also doesn't help that the film does a remarkably poor job of introducing its main characters. The leads, Mac, Jeff and Bill, are thrust upon us as though *King of the Zombies* were the umpteenth installment of a long-running series with these three stars. There's a fleeting mention of weather equipment aboard their plane, and a vague implication that Bill might be setting up a weather bureau at a new navy base; that's all we ever find out about them. Are Mac and Bill old friends, or did they meet just before the film opened? Jeff talks about Bill's "government mission," and Sangre suspects that Bill and Mac are secret service men, but none of this is ever

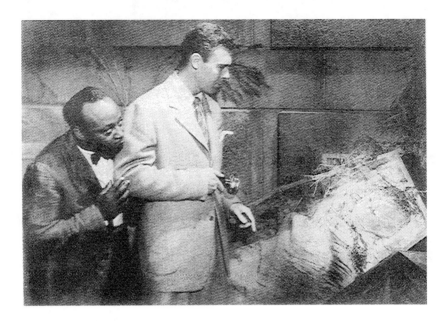

Mantan Moreland, John Archer and dusty mummy in a creepy tableau (not featured in the film). (From *King of the Zombies*.)

confirmed, nor does it seem likely. Indeed, the only definite thing about this very *indefinite* relationship is the fact that, even though Sangre gives each of the two men a room of their own, we find them sleeping together not only in the same room, but in the same bed!

Dick Purcell (Mac) didn't deserve his top billing – he's missing from too much of the picture – and John Archer (Bill) deserved better than fifth. Archer's character is the more likable of the two, thinking reasonably and getting things done while Purcell, playing a pugnacious Irish hothead, requires constant restraint. Archer would later turn up opposite Bela Lugosi in *Bowery at Midnight*, and in science fiction's *Destination Moon* (1950) and *She Devil* (1957); he's the father of actress Anne Archer, (*Fatal Attraction, Narrow Margin*).

Dick Purcell entered films after stage experience, worked at Warner Bros. throughout the late '30s, and then found himself demoted to studios like Monogram, where he made films like *Mystery of the 13th Guest* (1943) and *Phantom Killer* (1942), again opposite Moreland and Joan Woodbury. In his best-known role, Purcell talked tough-as-nails (but his sagging belly made him slightly comical) as the costumed star of the Republic serial *Captain America* (1944), battling the minions of arch-villain Lionel Atwill through 15 action-heavy episodes. Five months later, Purcell suffered a heart attack after playing a round of golf at the Riviera Country Club in Los Angeles and died at age 35.

Joan Woodbury employs a slight accent as Barbara, Dr. Sangre's reluctant niece; pretty and a not-bad actress, Woodbury appeared several times in horror and SF films, from *Bride of Frankenstein* (as the miniature queen) in 1935 to *The Time Travelers* in 1964. She died in 1989.

The real focal point of *King of the Zombies*, however, is black comedian Mantan Moreland. As much the "king of the zombies" as Victor (once Moreland joins the zombies' ranks, he immediately takes charge), the actor seems to appear in just about every scene, doing his patented shtick ("scared" jokes, self-deprecating ethnic jokes) in his own inimitable fashion:

> *[Admiring himself in a mirror:]* "The tropics sure gives a man a color."
> *[Learning that their plane is going to crash:]* "I knowed I wasn't cut out to be no blackbird!"
> *[Acting frightened:]* "If it was in me, I sure would be pale now!"
> *[Advised, during his zombie phase, that zombies can't talk:]* "Can I help it 'cause I'm loquacious?"
> *[Hearing voodoo drums:]* "It ain't Gene Krupa!"

Perhaps it's his self- spoofing manner, but Moreland comes off far better today than any of the obnoxious comedians (Vince Barnett, Nat Pendleton and Shemp Howard, for instance) that inflicted their particular brand of "look-how-stupid-*I*-can-be!" humor on '40s horror films. More than just milking the stereotype the way that human props like Willie Best did, Moreland is actually funny as the scared Jeff; seemingly every reviewer to cover *King of the Zombies*, both upon its original release and then down through the years, has singled out Moreland's comic relief for unqualified praise: "The real star of this outstanding example of inept wartime horror is comedian Mantan Moreland" – Michael Weldon, *The Psychotronic Encyclopedia of Film*. "Ridiculous chiller saved by Moreland's comedy relief" – Leonard Maltin's *TV Movies and Video Guide*. "For once, with Moreland doing his usual but excellent scared black servant act, the comic relief is welcome" – Phil Hardy, *The Encyclopedia of Horror Movies*. "Thanks to Moreland's witty asides, this is probably Monogram's best horror movie" – Don Willis, *Horror and Science Fiction Films*. "A good example of a routine film being turned into a better one through the efforts of its most talented performer" – John Cocchi, *Second Feature: The Best of the "B" Films*.

It's a performance Moreland wasn't able to top (or even match) two years later in *King of the Zombies*' semiremake, *Revenge of the Zombies*.

Henry Victor is also highly effective as the voodoo-happy foreign agent; as perceptively pointed out by Don Leifert in *Filmfax*, "His European accent and aquiline nose add up to a Lugosi-like presence throughout the picture." But unlike Lugosi, who would undoubtedly have played it like Mr. Spooky, Victor gives a crisp and assured performance (while at the same time occasionally going for, and getting, a well-placed laugh). An ardent student of the black arts (and closet Nazi), his secluded home filled with skulls and voodoo artifacts, garbed in cloak and ceremonial mask during the Rites of Transmigration, Sangre was a mildly unique character, and Victor makes the most of the opportunity.

Born in turn-of-the-century London, Victor was raised in Germany and began acting in pictures while still in his teens. His genre credits include the British *She, The Picture of Dorian Gray* (both 1916) and *The Living Dead* (1936), and in America, Tod Browning's *Freaks* (1932), as the ruthless strongman Hercules. When Germany began to be perceived as a threat to world peace, he was typecast as Gestapo types in such films as *Confessions of a Nazi Spy* (1939), *The Mortal Storm* (1940), *To Be or Not to Be, Sherlock Holmes and the Secret Weapon* and *Desperate Journey* (all 1942). On May 15, 1945, at age 52, he died in Hollywood of a cerebral hemorrhage which was the reported aftermath of an injury sustained while playing in a picture 20 years before.

Like Victor, Leigh Whipper (playing Momba, Sangre's eerie black butler) was a better grade of actor than one generally found playing supporting roles in Poverty Row horrors. Whipper knew from age 6, in 1882, that he wanted to be an actor, although one doubts that his early plans ever included *King of the Zombies*. After graduation from Harvard Law School, he decided instead to become an actor, going on to enjoy a rather distinguished career on stage and on the screen. The "human toothpick" (his own self-description) made his earliest pictures in Fort Lee, New Jersey, in the pre–Hollywood days, was the first black member of Actors Equity, co-founded the Negro Actors Guild in 1920, and appeared on Broadway and in films (most notably in *Of Mice and Men*, 1939, a reprise of his stage role, and *The Ox-Bow Incident*, 1943). The actor who blazed the trail for other Negro actors wrote his own obituary in 1970 and revised it on several occasions prior to his death at Harlem Hospital in 1975, at age 98.

Edmond Kelso's hodgepodge script for *King of the Zombies* is a curious blend of the innovative (the interesting Nazi/necromancer character), the humorous (Mantan Moreland's genuinely funny dialogue) and the ludicrous (just about everything else). Doing what was probably the best job possible under the low-budget circumstances, Jean Yarbrough's direction keeps the plot (and his players) on the go, for the most part; Yarbrough was aided by Mack Stengler's sometimes mobile camerawork, which is slightly better than the Poverty Row norm. The plane crash in the opening scene, achieved with a miniature plane and a not-bad jungle set, is also well done; this may have been lifted from an earlier picture.

In an impressive "first" (and simultaneous "last"!) for Monogram horror films, Edward Kay's music score was nominated for an Academy Award, and Kay went up against fellow nominees Bernard Herrmann (*Citizen Kane* and *All That Money Can Buy*), Alfred Newman (*How Green Was My Valley*),

Max Steiner (*Sergeant York*) and Franz Waxman (*Suspicion*) in the 1941 Oscar sweepstakes. Kay's score is a dismal arrangement that no one would ever have thought twice about had it not been Oscar-nominated; you have to suspect that there may be more to this story than meets the eye – and that we'll ever know. According to horror music aficionado Bill Littman:

> The *King of the Zombies* main theme consists, not too surprisingly, of the entire orchestra (probably all ten of them) beating out a jazzy imitation of voodoo drums. This three-note "motif" hammers away during various frenzied moments in the picture and climaxes with the orchestra joined by a native chorus yelling a chant that sounds suspiciously like "Eddie loves those cocoa beans. Zombies! I like cocoa, I like cocoa," etc.* Well, I don't know how much "Eddie" Kay liked those cocoa beans, but that was one heck of an ear-grabbing tune. The rest of the music vacillated between low-key "misteriosos" for the horror scenes and "wok-wok" muted trumpets for any sequence showing Mantan Moreland rolling his eyes in fear. Although the overall score was more completely developed than most other scores by Kay, that still isn't saying a whole heck of a lot.

To the surprise of probably no one, Kay didn't get the Award; it went to Bernard Herrmann for *All That Money Can Buy*.

Tips to exhibitors included ordering and distributing amulets with the inscription, "Let evil spirits beware! This charm protects me from the 'King of the Zombies.'" Theater owners whose houses were located in black neighborhoods were exhorted to play *King of the Zombies* up big: "Plant [photos] of Mantan Moreland and his new sepia sweetie Marguerite Whitten in all negro publications. . . . Do everything possible to start them coming, for once they see the show, the word-of-mouth will be sensational."

For all the nasty things that are written and said about it (much of it true!), *King of the Zombies* is actually one of the best of the many minor zombie movies, an atoll of mediocrity in a sea of awful films.

Spooks Run Wild
(Monogram, 1941)

Released October 24. 62 minutes. Associate Producer: Pete Mayer. Produced by Sam Katzman (Banner Pictures Corporation). Directed by Phil Rosen. Original Story and Screenplay: Carl Foreman and Charles R. Marion. Additional Dialogue: Jack

Could this be the promised "The Grave Diggers' Song"?

Henley. Assistant Director: Art Hammond. Production Manager: Ed W. Rote. Photography: Marcel Le Picard, A.S.C. Film Editor: Robert Golden. Settings: Fred Preble. Recording: Glen Glenn. Musical Directors: Lange & Porter, A.S.C.A.P.

Cast: Bela Lugosi (Nardo), Leo Gorcey (Muggs McGinnis), Bobby Jordan (Danny), Huntz Hall (Glimpy), Sunshine Sammy Morrison (Scruno), David O'Brien (Jeff Dixon), Dorothy Short (Linda Mason), David Gorcey (Peewee), Donald Haines (Skinny), Dennis Moore (Dr. Von Grosch), P. J. Kelley (Lem Harvey), Angelo Rossitto (Luigi), Guy Wilkerson (Jim, the Constable), Rosemary Portia (Margie), Joe Kirk (Man in Camp Office), Pat Costello (Bus Driver), Jack Carr.

> **"I wouldn't have believed it possible! Here we had all the trappings which made the original *Dracula* such a strange, eerie drama—the cobwebs, the bats, the dank cellars, the coffins, the menacing shadows—and yet the whole thing has become one long roar of laughter. Though I must remain just as serious as before, I found that I could hardly keep my face straight!"—Bela Lugosi, "quoted" in *Spooks Run Wild* pressbook**

If working with an up-and-coming director like Joseph H. Lewis on *Invisible Ghost* gave Bela Lugosi any illusions about the kind of films he would be making for Sam Katzman at Monogram, all such false notions were rudely dispelled three months later when the actor reported to the studio for *Spooks Run Wild*. A horror spoof, it teamed Lugosi with Monogram's reigning kings of comedy, the East Side Kids, for 62 minutes of raucous, knockabout antics.

Those lovable East Side Kids are rounded up by city cops and delivered to Jeff Dixon (David O'Brien), a budding lawyer who has arranged for the unwilling hooligans to spend two weeks in the country at a camp for underprivileged kids. (O'Brien isn't playing the same character he did in *East Side Kids* and *Boys of the City* even though the two roles are almost exactly alike.) When their bus arrives in upstate Hillside, Muggs (Leo Gorcey), Danny (Bobby Jordan) and Glimpy (Huntz Hall) saunter into a sweet shop where the pretty Margie (Rosemary Portia) works as a waitress. Muggs and his friends flirt with the girl before running to catch the departing bus.

That night, local yokel Lem Harvey (P. J. Kelley) has strange visitors at his service station: the mysterious-looking Nardo (Bela Lugosi) and his dwarf attendant Luigi (Angelo Rossitto). Nardo, who is driving a car with a trailer loaded with three coffins, asks for directions to the deserted Billings estate, and Harvey points it out near the top of nearby Billings Mountain. Harvey is certain that Nardo is the Monster, a homicidal maniac police have reported to be in the vicinity. After Nardo and Luigi drive off, a second car pulls in and Harvey recognizes the driver as Dr. Von Grosch (Dennis Moore), a known monster-hunter. Harvey assumes that Von Grosch is on Nardo's trail and tells him where Nardo is headed.

Nardo and Luigi visit Hillside Cemetery, as dogs bay in the distance. ("The city of the dead," Nardo intones. "Do they, too, hear the howling of the frightened dogs? Heh-heh-heh-heh-heh!") Nardo and Luigi pay their respects at one of the graves but they are spotted by a watchman who (without provocation) fires a shotgun at them. Nardo and Luigi mysteriously vanish right before the watchman's eyes.

At the boys' camp, Muggs tries to sneak off for a late date with Margie, but the rest of his gang—Danny, Glimpy, Scruno (Sunshine Sammy Morrison), Peewee (David Gorcey) and Skinny (Donald Haines)—catch on and tag along. Taking a shortcut through the cemetery, they are seen by the watchman, who proves once again what a trigger-happy moron he is. Peewee is hit and the rest of the gang drags him away to safety.

The boys bring the unconscious Peewee to the dark and cobwebby Billings house, and Nardo offers to treat his wounds. As Peewee sleeps, Nardo invites the rest of the gang to spend the night and they reluctantly agree. Later, Peewee rises as though in a trance and starts sleepwalking around the house. Scruno believes that Peewee has been turned into a zombie, but the no-nonsense Muggs is unimpressed: "Zombie or no zombie, we're gonna find Peewee and get him outta this spider's paradise, see?"

Muggs and his gang find one of Nardo's books, presumably *Dracula* (Muggs reads aloud, "In the night he prowls about seeking new victims, and in the daytime he sleeps in a coffin"), and they convince themselves that Nardo is the Monster. After an altercation with Nardo and Luigi they begin to search the house for the missing Peewee. Conventional haunted house hijinks follow, all from the "You first," "No, *you* first" school of screen "humor."

Linda (Dorothy Short), Jeff's girlfriend and the camp nurse, has become annoyed at him for not going out to search for the missing gang and has begun scouring the woods herself. She meets Dr. Von Grosch on the road, and he convinces her to accompany him to the Billings estate.

Frustrated by their failure to find the sleepwalking Peewee, the fast-talking Muggs decides to get tough with Nardo:

> MUGGS: Remember in that book what it said about the Monster? You can only scare him with two things, silver bullets and blessed iron. We ain't got neither, so there's only one thing we can do and that's to get tough, plenty tough, see? What do we do with the fellas back home when they step outta line?
> GLIMPY: Knock 'em out!
> MUGGS: Exactly! That's what we're gonna do with that vulture and the little termite that hangs out with him. Get it?

Using a sheet and a skull, the boys impersonate a ghost and frighten Nardo, who runs off howling. Bonked on the head by the thrown skull, Nardo is knocked out and then trussed up by the boys. Resuming their search of the house, they find Peewee snug in his own bed, cheerful and healthy and with no memory of the night's events.

Von Grosch and Linda steal into the house and start snooping around just as a posse hunting for the Monster arrives and surrounds the place. Showing his hand, Von Grosch – the Monster – advances menacingly on Linda in a locked attic room, and the girl's terrified screams bring Jeff, the Kids and the posse running. Unable to gain access to the room, Muggs climbs over the roof and in through a window, tackling the killer. Linda is saved and Von Grosch is led away in cuffs. In a short final scene, the amiable Nardo – a stage magician who had come to the house with his assistant Luigi to practice new routines – puts on a show for Muggs' gang, Jeff, Linda and the locals.

The Cleveland Press' Jack Warfel was right on the money when he wrote in his *Spooks Run Wild* review, "If anyone had asked us to think hard and name the most objectionable cast for any one picture, our unhesitating answer would have been, 'Bela Lugosi and the Dead End Kids.'" At Monogram the tenement terrors were called the East Side Kids, but it hardly mattered: their shenanigans were the same whether the studio was Monogram, Universal (where they were called the Little Tough Guys) or Allied Artists (the Bowery Boys). Strictly an acquired taste, the gang's lowbrow shtick varied little in these early cheapies: rough-and-tumble escapades, hardboiled posturing, silly malapropisms and dese-dem-and-dose delivery.

In Richard Bojarski's *The Films of Bela Lugosi*, Huntz Hall (Glimpy) reminisced about meeting Lugosi on the set of *Spooks Run Wild*:

> I decided to go over to his dressing room and say "hello." I knocked on the door and introduced myself. Bela was extremely cordial and we spent some time talking together. "Well, Mr. Lugosi, what do you think of the East Side Kids?" I asked. Lugosi raised his eyebrows theatrically and said: "Scum!" But Bela was only kidding. [He] took his work very seriously and did not like to clown around on the set. But Bela had a great sense of humor! He loved to laugh, but not to be laughed at. That would make him more angry than anything!

Interviewed by Tony Timpone in *Fangoria*, diminutive Angelo Rossitto (Luigi) also had fond memories of working with Lugosi:

> Bela Lugosi once told me that he wanted me in all of his pictures. And he gave Sam Katzman instructions to put me in them. Lugosi told me, "Angelo, you are my greatest free advertisement. When they see you they've got to say to themselves, 'There's the little guy who works with the monster.'" He even told his son, the lawyer, to come and visit me after he died. Lugosi was a sweetheart of a guy and he loved me.

Lugosi's just a red herring in *Spooks Run Wild*, although you'd never suspect it from this posed shot. Left to right, Angelo Rossitto, Lugosi, Dorothy Short and, about to throw a very awkward punch, Dave O'Brien.

Katzman had a role for me in *Spooks Run Wild* and that is when Lugosi decided that he wanted me in all his films. On that film we just dashed from room to room with the East Side Kids chasing me. We had a great time with it.

Sounds like everyone had fun making *Spooks Run Wild*, but for the humorless Lugosi "purists" and viewers not weaned on the East Side Kids' brand of humor, the film is 62 minutes of mighty rough sledding. It has more of a rushed look than any of Lugosi's other Monograms and the writing is particularly slapdash, with more loose ends than spooks running wild.

All the usual "haunted house" bromides are trundled out and staged in desultory fashion. Spiders dangle, suits of armor topple, people disappear into "magic" cabinets and a tobacco can slides along a table in the self-propelled style of Abbott and Costello's famous moving candle. Muggs and his gang split up and roam the long, shadowy corridors, spouting their lame one-liners (many of which sound ad-libbed).

Fans of the East Side Kids thrive on this sort of scaredy-cat antics, done in the gang's inimitable style, but to the uninitiated the scenes seem endless.

The late Phil Rosen, a director whose career went back to silent days and (supposedly) better pictures, does a sloppy job here. *Spooks Run Wild* is filled with scenes that go nowhere and mismatched insert shots, and it has an overall look of drabness which detracts from the fun. The first scene in the movie (Dave O'Brien corrals the Kids) is awkwardly and abruptly staged, looking like something that was quickly added as an afterthought; much of what follows is done in the same crude fashion. Rosen did a far better job on *Mystery of Marie Roget* (1942), a slick borderline-horror Universal B, and even on Monogram's *Return of the Ape Man*.

There's nothing for Lugosi to do but appear foolish as he goes through his clichéd paces; it's so embarrassing to find him in this juvenile film that whatever "Lugosi magic" the actor brings to the role is wasted. Much of what he does in *Spooks Run Wild* doesn't even make sense, not even after the revelation that he is an illusionist and not a monster. (How, for instance, does he manage to melt into thin air at the cemetery?)

Lugosi lays it on thick to keep the finger of suspicion directed at himself. He looms over the unconscious David Gorcey with a hammy expression of anticipatory delight, as though he's about to bite him on the neck; later, after he realizes that the Kids have been reading *Dracula*, he heaves the volume aside angrily and with all the menace he can muster in his voice intones, "Luigi – our guests *must not leave the house!*" They're such obvious cheats that they become irritating, especially on a second viewing. Lugosi's last-reel exposure as a mere magician is reminiscent of the similar cheat ending of *Mark of the Vampire* (1935), just another in Lugosi's long (*long*) line of red-herring roles. At least Lugosi is spared the ignominy of being knocked down by Leo Gorcey: a double takes his place in the fight scene. The double turns up again when Bela gets beamed with the skull, although Lugosi takes the fall himself this second time.

Obviously one of the film's writers had vivid memories of Lugosi's *Dracula*, as *Spooks Run Wild* accurately apes several aspects of that classic Universal production. Immaculately dressed in tuxedo and cape, and travelling with a shipment of coffins, Nardo is obviously supposed to make us think of Dracula; he even has a slavey (Luigi), and a Van Helsing-styled vampire-hunter (Von Grosch) on his trail. Some of Lugosi's dialogue, like his reference to the howling dogs, has also been glommed from *Dracula*. Apparently Monogram felt they might be infringing on Universal territory, and to throw off the Universal legal eagles the word *vampire* is never used in the film (although it's obvious a vampire is just what the East Side Kids think Nardo is). Confusion results when the film's killer is called the Monster (or the Monster Killer) while dialogue references make it plain that this fiend is "only" a sex maniac.

The East Side Kids are their old dependable selves; Leo Gorcey and Huntz Hall are best at what they do. Sunshine Sammy Morrison, the one black East Side Kid, mugs it up nicely and his friends' mild racist jibes roll right off his back. The Kids charge around and try to outshout one another, occasionally fight amongst themselves and ad-lib like mad. Lugosi, who didn't like to cope with ad-libbers, generally ignores them, although he seems to be doing a bit of improvising himself in the final scene.

Most of the other people in the film don't have much to do. Dave O'Brien, who plays Jeff, was a former song-and-dance man who had a long and varied career in pictures: as a bit player, stuntman, serial and B-action star and later as a comedy writer and director. No one explains why O'Brien's character in *Spooks Run Wild* is bothering with the East Side Kids; they don't want to *go* to camp and he doesn't want to *bring* them, but that's where they all end up anyway. O'Brien's real-life wife Dorothy Short plays Linda in the film; the two of them became acquainted on the set of MGM's *Student Tour* (1934) and subsequently appeared in several pictures together, playing sweethearts, man and wife, brother and sister or (in *Reefer Madness*, 1936) heroine and villain. Short is pretty, but like Polly Ann Young in *Invisible Ghost*, she has such a minuscule role that whether she's a good actress or not is anybody's guess.

Dennis Moore, in pince-nez, phony beard and mustache, looks greatly embarrassed but plays Von Grosch completely straight. (Moore replaced George Pembroke; the pressbook mistakenly credited Pembroke with the role, as did most contemporary reviews. The error is being perpetuated to this very day.) Moore is actually menacing in his final scene, removing his glasses and stalking the leading lady as full-bodied chase music from Columbia's *The Black Room* (1935) unexpectedly replaces the dinky Lange and Porter score on the soundtrack. Dennis (*Smoky*) Moore to legions to Western fans (he costarred in dozens), Moore was also a familiar face to fantasy film buffs. He was the hero of Universal's *The Mummy's Curse* (1944) and turned up regularly in serials at Universal, Republic and Columbia; he was in both Universal's last serial (*The Mysterious Mr. M*) and the two last-ever serials (Columbia's *Blazing the Overland Trail* and *Perils of the Wilderness*). He died in 1964.

Carl Foreman had a stellar career as a screenwriter (*Home of the Brave, Champion, The Men, Cyrano de Bergerac, High Noon, The Bridge on the River Kwai, The Guns of Navarone*) waiting ahead of him when he and Charles Marion ground out the story and screenplay for *Spooks Run Wild* in 1941. (According to *The Films of Bela Lugosi*, Foreman received $25 for the original story and $200 for collaborating on the script.) Foreman and Marion finished their script (titled *Trail of the Vampire*) before the end of May 1941, and cameras rolled in late June.

Again, the Monogram pressbook enticed exhibitors to flaunt the law in their promotion of the film. Theater owners were encouraged to dress a tall man and a bunch of kids as ghosts and turn them loose with instructions to run wild in the community's busiest sections—chase each other, invade stores, hotel lobbies, etc. (The tall man's costume should read BELA

LUGOSI, the youngsters' EAST SIDE KIDS, and the smallest tyke should
be lettered with the film title and theater name.) A really *smart* exhibitor
could send a jalopy around town driven by a man in a ghost costume and
with a passenger spook in the back seat. The passenger should give vent to
loud, sepulchral laughter, wave a revolver and shoot off blanks any time the
car stops; the driver should try to create traffic tie-ups. The title of the film
should adorn the side of the car. Imagine this car, and this activity, in (say)
South Central Los Angeles these days.

Contemporary reviews were quite lenient, some even complimentary.
The New York Daily News wrote that "all the old claptrap of the mystery
film is used to provoke laughs and excited squeals from the audience" and
Variety dubbed the film "okay supporting fodder.... This hokey, though
evenly balanced, mixture of chills and comedy should prove a winner with
the juvenile trade in particular. All the familiar tricks and situations of the
haunted house formula ... have been employed advantageously through
good use of comedy effects. The Dead End Kids [sic], despite stereo routines, hang up a pretty good laugh score." *The Hollywood Reporter* commented, "*Spooks Run Wild* has a lot of knockabout comedy and laugh lines
to balance the hodgepodge story. In its bracket it is good filmfare and will
satisfy its audience.... Lugosi's performance and the background provide
a field day for the capers of the youngsters and the laughs come thick and
fast when they go into action." The *Chicago Herald-American* review was
good enough for Monogram to quote from it in their pressbook: "This spook
show is rather special.... There's not a bad actor in the cast, nor a dull moment. There's fast, funny dialogue, knowing direction and sincerity of playing." *The New York Times*, to no one's surprise, was somewhat less bowled-
over, dubbing *Spooks* "less horror than horrible."

A mélange of spookhouse clichés and roughhouse comedy, *Spooks Run
Wild* is a shameless attempt to exploit Lugosi's Dracula image in a witless
farce. Foisting the East Side Kids on Lugosi was an unforgivable move on
Monogram's part, but from a standpoint of drawing an audience, the
strategy was remarkably sound. Angelo Rossitto told Tony Timpone in
Fangoria that the film brought in $2,000,000, and a repeat encounter be-
tween Lugosi and the kids–*Ghosts on the Loose*–was inevitable.

Black Dragons
(Monogram, 1942)

Released March 6. 61 minutes. Associate Producer: Barney A. Sarecky. Produced by Sam Katzman and Jack Dietz (Banner Pictures Corporation). Directed by

William Nigh. Original Story and Screenplay: Harvey Gates. Photography: Art Reed. Film Editor: Carl Pierson. Production Manager: Ed W. Rote. Assistant Directors: Arthur Hammond and Gerald Schnitzer. Art Director: David Milton. Sound Engineer: Glen Glenn. Musical Directors: Lange & Porter, A.S.C.A.P.

Cast: Bela Lugosi (Dr. Melcher/Monsieur Colomb), Joan Barclay (Alice Saunders), George Pembroke (Dr. Bill Saunders), Clayton Moore (Dick Martin), Robert Frazer (Amos Hanlin), Edward Peil, Sr. (Ryder), Robert Fiske (Philip Wallace), Irving Mitchell (John Van Dyke), Kenneth Harlan (Colton), Max Hoffman, Jr. (Kerney), Frank Melton (F.B.I. Man), Joseph Eggenton (Stevens, the Butler), I. Stanford Jolley (The Dragon), Bernard Gorcey (Cabby).

> **"For over fifty years the Black Dragon Society has held Japan in a grip of such terror that not even the so-called 'Son of Heaven,' the Emperor, is immune to it. In fact, the Black Dragons openly boast they are above the Emperor and can at any time overrule his edicts. It has ruled by virtue of the kind of men admitted to the Society, their single-minded fanaticism and their deadly efficiency as assassins. For over fifty years the Black Dragon Society has made Japanese history, and every chapter of it was written in the blood of men, women and children of other lands."** — historian Joseph Gollomb

> **"I defy moviegoers not to gasp when they see *Black Dragons*. Never have I worked in a story so startling or so blood-chillingly shocking. See it if you dare...!"** — Bela Lugosi, "quoted" on *Black Dragons* poster

It's the morning of December the *8th*, 1941, and shock waves emanating from the shattered naval base at Pearl Harbor, Hawaii, have touched every city in America—including Hollywood. News of the attack has galvanized the movie capital's studios, majors and minors alike, and film execs are scrambling to make switches in scripts and on many films already in production.

At Warner Bros., Harry and Jack Warner attempt throughout the day and early evening to effect the evacuation of WB employees in the Philippines. 20th Century–Fox sees a number of its trucks requisitioned by the Army. RKO is placed on a "No Visitors" basis and extra men are added to the studio police force. Paramount has to arrange for special permission to fly planes over Sonora for bombing scenes on *For Whom the Bell Tolls* while special broadcasts advise local residents that the planes are *not* Japanese. Paramount also bars its 30 Japanese employees (28 of them janitors) from the lot.

The smaller Hollywood outfits are quick to jump on the patriotic bandwagon, and their low-rent films are lighting up the screens of neighborhood theaters almost before the last of the bombed ships had settled on the bottom of Pearl Harbor. Sam Katzman wasn't about to be left out. Katzman and his Banner Productions staff (moved out of their headquarters at the Chadwick Studio on Sunset and Gower on November 12, 1941, and now snugly ensconsed on the Monogram lot) began hatching plans to shoehorn war elements into Bela Lugosi's upcoming chiller.

It took a lot of thinking (not all of it sound) to combine the Lugosi menace and the Jap threat into a single horror production, but if there was a studio where it could be done, it was Monogram. Writer Harvey Gates sat down at his typewriter, hurriedly melding these disparate elements into the studio's newest screenplay. Japanese agents transformed by plastic surgery into Occidental industrialists, a mad Nazi medico with the ability to vanish from moving taxis and even a monster found their way into Gates' screenplay. As plotty and convoluted as it is vague and confused, *Black Dragons* remains a minor landmark in the history of incoherent cinema.

A dinner party is in progress at the Washington, D.C., home of physician Bill Saunders (George Pembroke), where business leaders, bankers and lawyers schmooze about the War; classified information is being bandied about like back-fence gossip. This is followed by a montage of destruction: a sinking ship, a burning building, an exploding bridge and an oil well derrick engulged in flames (most of the clips are of silent vintage). The movie now returns to Dr. Saunders' party, after most of the guests have left. The "respectable" Saunders and his five remaining guests – businessmen Hanlin (Robert Frazer), Ryder (Edward Peil, Sr.), Wallace (Robert Fiske), Van Dyke (Irving Mitchell) and Kerney (Max Hoffman, Jr.) – are fifth columnists working for the Japanese, and they've already used the information they gathered to strike at the U.S.: All of the depicted acts of sabotage were apparently committed even before the party broke up. (Fast workers, those Japs!)

Congratulating one another on their night's work, the businessmen are interrupted by the entrance of the butler (Joseph Eggenton), who informs Dr. Saunders that a visitor wishes to see him on an urgent matter. Saunders has a private consultation with the stranger, Monsieur Colomb (Bela Lugosi), who acts so – so – *Lugosian*, that Saunders knows he's up to no good. Colomb jabs Saunders with a hypodermic needle as the physician howls in terror, but by the time the five guests burst into the room, Dr. Saunders and Colomb are both sitting convivially and Saunders is speaking in a mechanical monotone. (The audience – but not the guests – knows that Saunders is now under the power of Colomb's serum.) Hanlin, Ryder, Wallace and Van Dyke leave, but Kerney sticks around to spy on the suspicious-acting Saunders through a window. Kerney finally leaves, hopping a cab where he finds the mysterious Colomb already seated. When Colomb calls him by name, Kerney asks how he knew it. "Would you rather be called *Toko Nitobi?*" Colomb intones threateningly. When the cab arrives at its destination, the driver finds the back seat empty. Kerney's dead body is found by a cop on the steps of the deserted Japanese Embassy.

Suspecting a national threat, the F.B.I. assigns one of its new agents, Dick Martin (Clayton Moore), to do a bit of undercover work in and around Dr. Saunders' house. Martin can't get an audience with Saunders, who is sick and confined to his bedroom, according to the butler. Not even Saunders' niece Alice (Joan Barclay), just arrived home after years abroad, can get in to see her uncle. Encountering Monsieur Colomb in an upstairs hallway (he introduces himself as "a very old friend" of her uncle's), she gets spooked and runs downstairs into Dick's arms. Dick flirts obnoxiously with Alice before he leaves.

Wallace arrives at the house later and becomes suspicious when he, too, is told that Saunders cannot have visitors. (Saunders is still in Colomb's power; his face is kept hidden from the camera.) Wallace sneaks back into the house through a window and is searching it when he is caught and overpowered by Colomb. Colomb puts Wallace under his uncanny influence as well, and returns him to his hotel room, and there strangles him.

Strange goings-on continue at the Saunders home: Alice, sleeping with all her clothes on, is awoken and terrified by a misshapen shadow, charges downstairs and collides with Colomb. The butler searches for the shadow-visitor as Colomb and Alice converse:

> COLOMB: When a young woman's nerves commence to give way, it is time she sought refuge in a strong man's arms.
> ALICE *(flirtatiously)*: I just ran into yours.
> COLOMB: Mine might be dangerous...

Ryder and Van Dyke arrive at the house and Ryder, going upstairs alone, talks with Dr. Saunders through the closed bedroom door, telling him that Van Dyke is ready to crack. Saunders, acting on Colomb's instructions, orders Van Dyke's elimination.

Ryder lures Van Dyke into the cellar and the two men manage somehow to shoot and kill each other. Colomb, watching from hiding, is pleased by what transpires. The bodies are later found on the steps of the Japanese Embassy.

By now enough has happened in and around the Saunders house that government men stake it out; when Colomb leaves in a cab, they pursue it and pull it over. Colomb has vanished from the back of the car.

Dick Martin, his boss (Kenneth Harlan), Alice and other Federal men converge at Saunders' house, with Hanlin brought along as bait for the killer. Saunders, finally "out" from under Colomb's influence, leaves his bedroom and stumbles downstairs, a black hood wrapped around his head. In the confusion, Colomb is able to steal into the room and overpower Hanlin, dragging him off. In the fight Hanlin is killed and Colomb catches a bullet. The G-men capture Colomb.

Saunders, his hooded face hidden, tells a fantastic story (in flashbacks).

An unlikely duo: comic Bernard Gorcey (father of Bowery Boys Leo and David) shares the screen with Bela Lugosi in *Black Dragons.*

He and his five fellow fifth columnists were actually Japanese – members of the sinister Black Dragon Society. In Japan, a German plastic surgeon, Dr. Melcher (Lugosi), gave them the faces of American business leaders who had died (or were killed) abroad. (Wouldn't someone notice their now-yellow skin?) The Society then imprisoned Melcher so there could be no possibility of betrayal. Melcher changed his own features slightly, escaped and has been killing off his remodeled patients under the guise of Monsieur Colomb.

His story concluded, the hysterical Saunders tears off his hood to reveal a face of horror – Melcher/Colomb has turned him into a monster. "And you must go on *living!*" Melcher/Colomb cackles as he topples to the floor, dying from his bullet wound.

Making a movie about Japan's Black Dragon Society was a far better idea than putting Bela Lugosi into it. Founded in 1901, this organization of murderous fanatics – properly known as the Kokuryukai, or Amur River Association, popularly mistranslated as "Black Dragon Society" – was dedicated to the idea of conquest by war. Members of the rightist society concealed their identity even from one another, appearing at meetings and in public in costumes consisting of a voluminous overcoat, a broad-brimmed hat which fit far down over the head, and a long, black, curling beard made of dyed silk.

In 1904 the activities of the secret society resulted in the Russo-Japanese War. Thereafter the jingoistic Dragons embarked on a campaign of assassination, resulting in the murder of successive prime ministers who had signed naval limitation treaties in Washington and London, and of various other public officials or prominent citizens who opposed or criticized the activities of the Society. In most cases the killers, after dispatching their victims, committed suicide on the spot. The most brazen exploit of the Black Dragons took place in Tokyo on February 26, 1936, when 3,000 soldiers (splitting up into bands of 60) seized all government offices, police stations and cable, radio and telephone headquarters, and set up machine guns at all important street intersections in the city. Several weeks prior to December 7, 1941, an American radio station broadcast an account of the activities of the Black Dragons and reported that the terrorist organization had decreed a surprise war against Britain and the U.S., to be launched on August 26. The narrator went on to explain (this broadcast was later than August 26) that events on the German front had caused a postponement and that plans for the attack on America had been reset for November 26. On that date, the same narrator returned to the air to announce that the Dragons had again changed their plans and would attack early in December. Few people lent any credence to the warning – prior to December 7.

A tough film to dislike – but an even tougher one to defend – *Black Dragons* went into production on Thursday, January 22, 1942, as *The Yellow Menace*. (United Artists had registered that title after the War began but Sam Katzman had a five-month head start on the registration list.) Hurried onto the sound stages to take advantage of the timeliness of its theme, *Black Dragons* had a hectic production with dialogue being rewritten daily. It is by far the most confusing of the Monogram horror films.

Although only one writer (Harvey Gates) is credited, the screenplay would seem the work of several writers (none of whom knew what the others were doing). For instance: After Kerney is killed, he's called a murder victim in newspaper headlines and his identity is unknown to the authorities. When a clue points to the Saunders house, F.B.I. boss Colton dispatches Dick Martin there to try to ascertain the murdered man's identity. Colton also tells him to work undercover and to concentrate on Alice, Saunders' niece. When Martin gets to the house, not only does he flash his badge (blowing his cover) and call Alice the daughter rather than the niece of Dr. Saunders, he also inexplicably now knows that Kerney was the name of the victim! The murdered Kerney is also referred to at one point as a possible suicide; and when Ryder and Van Dyke talk about his death, they mention the cause as heart failure!

A confused script and choppy editing are the downfall of *Black Dragons*, but the film compensates in little ways. Fast-paced, it averages better than a murder a reel, and the way-out plot is appealing in a looney sort of way. It's a great "time capsule" film, with the "feel" of the early World War II years captured in what can only be called Monogram fashion. And, of course, it's got Bela Lugosi strutting his stuff for the umpteenth time, loading his menacing lines (and even many of his nonmenacing ones) with all the frosty foreboding his legion of fans could ever want.

Bela Lugosi had kept busy in the months between *Spooks Run Wild* and *Black Dragons*, appearing as the lycanthropic gypsy in Universal's *The Wolf Man* (1941) and then reprising his Ygor role in the same studio's *The Ghost of Frankenstein* (1942). By the early '40s it had to be pretty obvious that his bag of thespic tricks was severely limited, although once in a great while there'd be a pleasant surprise like his sympathetic playing in *Invisible Ghost* or (much later) the heartfelt soliloquy in *Bride of the Monster* (1956). Lugosi's Colomb in *Black Dragons* is mostly a stock performance, but there is a half-hearted stab at making him a sympathetic figure and even to imply that the leading lady is romantically interested in him. Unfortunately, writer Gates can't decide whether he wants Colomb to be a creep or a ladies' man, so he just makes him both. When Alice first encounters Colomb, she ends up fleeing in terror; in a voice dripping with sarcasm, she indicates Colomb and says to Dick, "Handsome devil, isn't he?" When Dick agrees with her derogatory assessment, she suddenly takes the opposite tack: "Oh, I don't know. Make it a moonlight night and a park bench — might be exciting!"

Even though Melcher/Colomb is motivated by a desire for personal revenge, the fact that his victims are saboteurs makes him a hero of sorts, and Lugosi does evoke more sympathy than he ordinarily would in a more conventional Monogram thriller. But as usual, Bela's character sustains the expected verbal slings and arrows of supporting characters. Before Colomb has done anything of a menacing nature, Dick says how he'd "hate to meet *him* in a dark alley" and Kerney mentions that Colomb (placidly seated in an armchair and minding his own damn business) "looks crazy."

Black Dragons also marks Lugosi's second and last time playing two entirely different characters in the same film (the first was *Murder by Television*, 1935). Chucked into a cell by the Black Dragon agents, the bearded Dr.

The first '40s horror film with a wartime milieu, Monogram's *Black Dragons* started production only a month and a half after Jap bombs fell on Pearl Harbor.

Melcher finds himself in the company of a weary wretch who resembles him
(it's Lugosi without the beard). Melcher somehow switches identities with
the poor noodge (performing plastic surgery right there in that grimy cell,
we have to assume), and gets away.

The rest of the characters are barely sketched, and the actors involved
must struggle just to keep their heads above water. Joan Barclay, a
Minneapolis-born actress/model with a long history of Western cheapies
(not to mention the 1936 Lugosi serial *Shadow of Chinatown*), does an okay
job as "Alice Saunders," who in the end turns out to be another of Colton's
operatives and not the girl she's pretended to be throughout the movie. The
role wasn't designed to bring out any outstanding acting, and maybe neither
was Joan Barclay. Clayton Moore, still several years away from his
lucrative run on television's *The Lone Ranger*, is an obnoxious and in-
efficient investigator, but at least Moore gets less clunker lines than most
of his fellow players. George Pembroke, Robert Frazer, Edward Peil, Sr.,
Robert Fiske and Max Hoffman, Jr., are all more than adequate as the
undercover saboteurs; Irving Mitchell, the sixth fifth columnist, is an
embarrassment.

It's sad to see the fortysomething Frazer, who played the tragic Beau-
mont in Lugosi's *White Zombie* (1932), looking old beyond his years in the
supporting role of Hanlin; you'd almost believe he was the *father* of the
Robert Frazer who was in *White Zombie* only ten years before. A native of
Worcester, Massachusetts, Frazer cut a dashing figure in his earliest screen
days and played characters like Robin Hood and Rob Roy (not to mention
Jesus Christ!) in pictures from the early teens. Cutting a paunchy, middle-
aged figure in B (and Z) films from the '30s and '40s, Frazer's list of horror
film appearances includes *The Vampire Bat* (1933) and *Condemned to Live*
(1935), and also a slew of serials like *The Clutching Hand* (1936), *Dick Tracy
vs. Crime, Inc.* (1941), *Captain America* and *The Tiger Woman* (both 1944).
Frazer died August 17, 1944, at St. Vincent's Hospital, age 50.

I. Stanford Jolley, who plays the pidgin–English speaking Dragon in
the flashback sequences, is actually made up to look like Mitsuru Toyama,
real-life head of the Black Dragon Society (Toyama was 92 and still going
strong in 1942 when *Black Dragons* was being made). Reminiscing about the
movie in *The Films of Bela Lugosi*, Jolley told author Richard Bojarski, "It
was a real challenge doing this Japanese character – I had to go through a
two-and-one-half-hour makeup session each day of shooting for a complete
change of features, plus creating a full beard." Jolley also told Bojarski that
he and Lugosi didn't get on well at all, nor did Lugosi get along smoothly
with any of his other co-workers.

Clayton Moore disagrees. He told *Filmfax*'s Don Leifert, "Lugosi seemed
like a nice man. He was very courteous, but he generally stayed to himself working on his lines." Asked about the film in general, Moore went on,
"We shot awfully fast. Things were written off-the-cuff. [William Nigh]

was always willing to change the script. But overall, Monogram was a very pleasant place to work. The actors received the respect they deserved there."

William Nigh's direction seldom rises above the sloppy script, reflecting the haste and stringency of production. The one scene where Nigh scores is the climactic flashback sequence; done with far more style than any other scene in the film, it almost looks like something that's been lifted from another movie. But like the players in the film, Nigh just doesn't have a chance to shine; the film's spare production values and wildly improbable plot stacked the deck against him even before cameras rolled, and Nigh is unable to keep the film's complications out of snarls.

Lugosi's next Monogram film *The Corpse Vanishes* holds the record for Most Absurd Dialogue in a Non–Ed Wood Bela Lugosi Movie, but *Black Dragons* is in there pitching for that coveted honor. It ranges from the silly . . . :

> COLOMB *(reacting to news that four of Saunders' five party guests have died in a 24 hour period)*: Heh! Possible coincidence!

. . . to the forced and unreal . . . :

> ALICE: You sound like a man of destiny.
> COLOMB: One must not flirt . . . with one's destiny.
> ALICE: With the world in the condition it is today, aren't we all flirting with destiny?

. . . to the utterly inane . . . :

> ALICE: I heard a strange noise, like a body falling.
> COLOMB: Oh, I was stumbling, I was awkward.
> ALICE: Yes, but there were – *gurgling* sounds!
> COLOMB: Oh, I was humming!

There are also plenty of gaffes and low-budget shortcuts for the Golden Turkey crowd to get off on (dig the "car" that follows Kerney's cab, or the lettering on the side of Hanlin's plane). But boo-boos like these are part of the charm of the Poverty Row films, and their fans wouldn't have it any other way.

Monogram publicists encouraged exhibitors to play up the fact that Dr. Yu-shan Han, a visiting lecturer on history on the Los Angeles campus of the University of California, had recently expressed his opinion that the Black Dragon was currently operating in Southern California. Republic also tackled the Black Dragon theme in 1942, pitting Rod Cameron against the terrorists in the serial *G-Men vs. the Black Dragon*. The accent was (of course) on action throughout the serial's 15 chapters, with an extremely mild element of sci-fi/horror rearing its head in Chapter 1 when a Black Dragon leader (Nino Pipitone) is smuggled into the U.S. in suspended animation – and in the guise of a mummy.

Reviews for *Black Dragons* were what you'd expect. According to *The Hollywood Reporter*, "any child wearing a Halloween mask can cause a more instantaneous and legitimate scare than *Black Dragons* manages to evoke." *Variety* called the film "probably the most incredible of the film productions which has come out of Hollywood since the outbreak of the war. Imposed on a whodunit with horror furbelows is a denouement that baffles all logic, science and respect for the average picturegoer's intelligence." Wanda Hale of *The New York Daily News* sensed that *Black Dragons* was "something Monogram ran up hurriedly, with little thought, in order to be among the first in Hollywood to get Japanese deviltry on the screen." *The New York Evening Post*'s Archer Winsten wrote, "The picture can be listed as a feeble attempt to publicize ill feelings between Japs and Germans. All it does, though, is put unwary Americans to sleep."

Echoes of *Black Dragons* have reverberated in some mighty curious places. The second episode of television's *The Outer Limits*, titled "The Hundred Days of the Dragon," was about an insidious Oriental plot to replace politician Sidney Blackmer (a shoo-in in the upcoming presidential race) with a Chinese agent who's been made Blackmer's exact double through the advanced science of "molecular plasticity." When "Blackmer" makes it into the White House, the next step is to replace his cabinet and leaders of industry, labor and the media with lookalike Chinese agents. Often described as having been inspired by *The Manchurian Candidate* (1962), "Hundred Days" owes a more considerable debt to *Black Dragons*; this is clinched in the episode's final scene where "Blackmer" is exposed and another character maliciously deforms his pliable face, permanently turning him into a monster.

· The other oddball place to find *Black Dragons* crop up was in the plot of the novel *Never Cross a Vampire* (St. Martin's Press, 1980), fifth in author Stuart Kaminsky's series of Toby Peters mysteries. Peters, a poor man's Philip Marlowe working in 1940s Los Angeles, is hired by Bela Lugosi to investigate a series of death threats; one day Peters goes to the Monogram studios to consult with his client. The conversation is interrupted when Lugosi is told to be ready for the next take in a few minutes. "'We have to work quickly. Time is money. I am the most expensive part of this film and it is a modest expense.'" When Peters asks what the picture is about, Lugosi shakes his head and smiles sadly. "'A very timely epic written last week and not yet finished. It's called *The Black Dragon* [sic]. . . . It goes on. I look in the mirror in the morning and I say to myself, "Can it be that you once played Cyrano and Romeo?" Always it is the same. When a film company is in the red, they come to me and say, "Okay, so we make a horror film." And so that is what we do, what I always do. And I do my best. That is the trick. . . . Always play it seriously no matter what the material. And always talk slowly so you will have more screen time.'"

Black Dragons wraps up an uneven balance of horror, mystery and flag-waving into a grim but not entirely disagreeable package. Having wartime Washington as the setting for a horror thriller is an intriguing and offbeat touch, and the film's fanciful depiction of the real-life Black Dragon Society also adds to the fun. It's easy (and probably wise) to dismiss the script as junk, but the basic premise is actually imaginative and full of potential (although it would take the talented crew of *The Outer Limits* rather than a schlub like Sam Katzman to prove it).

A topical espionage film with the added spice of pseudoscience and chiller ingredients, *Black Dragons* is one of Bela Lugosi's more entertainingly offbeat Monograms.

The Corpse Vanishes
(Monogram, 1942)

Released May 8. 63 minutes. Associate Producer: Barney A. Sarecky. Produced by Sam Katzman and Jack Dietz (Banner Productions). Directed by Wallace Fox. Screenplay: Harvey Gates. Original Story: Sam Robins and Gerald Schnitzer. Production Manager: Ed W. Rote. Assistant Director: Arthur Hammond. Photography: Art Reed. Film Editor: Robert Golden. Art Director: David Milton. Sound Engineer: Glen Glenn. Musical Directors: Lange and Porter, A.S.C.A.P.

Cast: Bela Lugosi (Dr. Lorenz), Luana Walters (Patricia Hunter), Tris [Tristram] Coffin (Dr. Foster), Elizabeth Russell (Countess Lorenz), Minerva Urecal (Fagah), Angelo [Rossitto] (Toby), Joan Barclay (Alice Wentworth), Kenneth Harlan (Mr. Keenan), Gwen Kenyon (Peggy Woods), Vince Barnett (Sandy), Frank Moran (Angel), George Eldredge (Mike), Gladys Faye, Pat Costello.

"**A dull murder mystery with all the cliches that usually accompany a second grade story of this kind**"—*Variety*

"**Horror to make your hair stand on end**"—Monogram publicity

When it comes to matrimony, some guys just don't have any luck. Take Bela Lugosi, for example. In *The Black Cat* his wife left him for a satanist. In *Invisible Ghost* he married a woman who haunted him and drove him to murder. In *Voodoo Man* his wife turned into a zombie. And then in 1955 he went and married Hope!

Poor Bela's got wife trouble again in *The Corpse Vanishes*, fourth in the line of Lugosi/Monogram horror films; Sam Katzman and Jack Dietz had no intention of letting him stray too far from his Mr. Dracula niche. In *The Corpse Vanishes*, he plays Dr. Lorenz, horticulturalist and kidnapper of young brides, a stereotypic heavy role requiring no acting stretch whatsoever. Although Lugosi seems more at-home here than he was as the Nazi medico in *Black Dragons*, his mad scientist performances would soon fall into a familiar pattern.

The Corpse Vanishes went into production on Friday the 13th of March, 1942; many of its principal roles had been cast only days before. The film reunited Lugosi with the leading ladies of his 1936 serial *Shadow of Chinatown*, Luana Walters and Joan Barclay (Barclay had played the lead in *Black Dragons* several weeks earlier). The screenplay by Harvey Gates was no improvement over his confused work on *Black Dragons*, but *Corpse Vanishes* is far more enjoyable; for all the wrong reasons, it may in some ways be the best film Lugosi made for Monogram. Finally coming through in the clutch, the multi-untalented Gates wrote a script that uncannily foreshadows Lugosi's notorious Ed Wood films, complete with hokey premise, zany plot twists and unreal behavior. *The Corpse Vanishes* is one of Poverty Row's most entertaining horror films of the '40s.

Standing at the altar alongside her husband-to-be, a young bride suddenly swoons and falls to the floor in mid-ceremony. "Shall I telephone for the ambulance?" the Reverend asks. "No," responds a doctor. "The undertaker. She's dead." As the body is being toted off and the grim scene begins to fade, one of the bridesmaids (center screen) breaks into a big grin.

A morgue wagon arrives and the girl's body is loaded into the back, where a mysterious man, Prof. Lorenz (Bela Lugosi), is beaming with delight. After the wagon has left, a second morgue wagon – the *real* one – shows up. This is the fourth time in recent months that a bride has died on the altar and had her body filched. (Fooled you once, shame on them; fooled you *four* times, shame on *you!*) Girl society reporter Pat Hunter (Luana Walters), covering the wedding for her paper *The Chronicle*, is happy as a lottery winner. "It's sensational! Another kidnaping of a dead bride! What a story!" she merrily babbles to her photographer-sidekick Sandy (Vince Barnett). A montage of newspaper headlines follows, including the classic **CORPSE THIEF BELIEVED CRANK.**

Bride-to-be Alice Wentworth (Joan Barclay) and her mother appear at the office of the District Attorney, who promises to provide police protection at Alice's upcoming wedding. But as the ceremony is about to get underway, Alice receives an orchid which she assumes her fiancé has sent. Wearing the flower at the altar, Alice, too, drops and dies. Sandy shoves a camera in the corpse's face and snaps a shot ("I just got the picture of the month!").

Profiting from past mistakes, a two-man police motorcycle escort accompanies Alice's morgue wagon. But the two officers are decoyed away

Bela (Mr. Dracula) Lugosi and Elizabeth (The Houri of Horror) Russell search for new victims amidst the wedding announcements. (From *The Corpse Vanishes.)*

when they spot a car in flames and rush to investigate. Seizing their opportunity, the body snatchers appear, carry Alice from the morgue wagon into their own and speed away.

The wagon arrives at a desolate mansion, pulling into a candlelit garage where an odd threesome – the hatchet-faced Fagah (Minerva Urecal) and her two sons, the dwarf Toby (Angelo Rossitto) and the hulking Angel (Frank Moran) – are waiting. "My little family! You're all so very faithful!" Lorenz murmurs with almost-paternal pride. Alice's body is hustled into a dark laboratory (the pressbook calls it the "Grotto of Horror") where Lorenz's eightyish wife, the Countess (Elizabeth Russell), is waiting, racked by sobs. Using a hypodermic needle, Lorenz extracts a fluid from Alice's neck, mixes it with a chemical and now injects the compound into the Countess, who becomes youthful. "You're beautiful. And I shall always keep you that way," Lorenz promises her. (The fact that Lorenz targets brides naively implies that only the bodily fluids of virgins will achieve the desired effect. But why brides, why not girls who are completely unattached?)

Meanwhile, the deadly orchid has fallen into cub reporter Pat's hands; rightly sensing that the flower is a lead, she takes it to a horticulturalist who tells her that the orchid was originally hybridized by the European scientist

Prof. Lorenz, now a resident of nearby Brookdale. Determined to interview Lorenz, Pat travels to Brookdale by train; the local cab driver is so afraid of the mysterious Dr. Lorenz that he tells her flat out that he won't drive her to his place. Lorenz's henchman Mike (George Eldredge) arrives at the depot to pick up a coffin-sized box for Lorenz, but he, too, refuses to drive the girl to Lorenz's house.

Pat hides in the back of Mike's truck but, halfway home, he spots her and tosses her off, leaving her stranded on a desolate stretch of road. Dr. Foster (Tristram Coffin), a young physician on his way to Lorenz's house, spots her and gives her a lift. Foster has been trying to help Lorenz find a cure for the Countess, although he (Foster) knows nothing of Lorenz's extracurricular body-snatching activities.

When Dr. Foster and Pat arrive at the Lorenz home, the Countess takes an instant dislike to Pat. "No one asked you to come here. You're not welcome!" she spits, slapping Pat across the face. (Elizabeth Russell doesn't seem to bother pulling her punch, apparently whacking Luana Walters right in the chops.) As a fierce storm rises, Lorenz invites Pat and Foster to spend the night.

Late that night, Lorenz enters Pat's room through a secret panel, stands over the slumbering girl menacingly, then goes into Foster's room and hypnotizes him in his sleep(!). The simple-minded Angel uses the secret passageway to creep into Pat's room and strokes her hair. Pat awakens with a scream, frightening Angel away. Rushing from room to room looking for help, Pat finds Lorenz and the Countess sleeping in coffins. She wakes up Dr. Foster and tells him what happened, but he is inclined to believe that Pat has had a nightmare. Lorenz, who secretly overhears the conversation, decides he must kill the imbecilic Angel.

Pat finds the secret panel and follows it to a basement crypt where the bodies of the missing brides are hidden; she watches from hiding as Lorenz corners and strangles Angel. Overcome, she faints, and wakes up the next morning in her own bed. Lorenz and Foster tell her that her whole ordeal was a dream; Pat is half-convinced that they're right, not even bothering to check for the secret panel. Foster doesn't remember the events of the night before because he was under Lorenz's hypnotic power at the time.

But Foster's suspicions have now been aroused, and as he drops Pat at the train station he decides to do a bit of snooping himself. Foster later turns up at the *Chronicle* office, where he and Pat tell their stories to Keenan (Kenneth Harlan), the editor. Pat convinces Keenan to hire an actress and stage a phony wedding which will really be a police trap for Lorenz.

At the wedding, the police are waiting to spring, but Lorenz somehow catches on and instead of going after the "bride" (Gwen Kenyon), kidnaps Pat instead. A policeman sees Lorenz carrying Pat out of the chapel, and his gunshots strike and kill little Toby. Rushing home, Lorenz is about to operate on Pat when Fagah, distraught over the deaths of her sons, goes mad and stabs Lorenz with a dagger. Lorenz chokes Fagah furiously and then, weak from loss of blood, collapses and dies. Pat and the Countess wrestle, and the Countess is thrown to the floor. With her last ounce of strength, the dying Fagah stabs and kills the Countess, too. The former brides, not dead after all, are restored to health.

It's a small miracle that the Golden Turkey crowd hasn't gotten around to *The Corpse Vanishes*, because it presages their beloved Ed Wood films strikingly. Harvey Gates' screenplay doesn't reach the dizzying heights of ludicrousness of *Glen or Glenda?* (1953) or *Plan 9 from Outer Space* (1959), but it isn't far from the mark; the just slightly off-center way his characters behave and react to situations has the inimitable Wood style stamped all over it. Luana Walters' pushy and callous reporter has a soul sister in Loretta King of *Bride of the Monster* (1956). The exasperated editor (Kenneth Harlan) is a forerunner of Harvey B. Dunn (*Bride of the Monster*) and John Carpenter (*Night of the Ghouls*, 1959), sitting around his office complaining while flunkies do his leg work. The grotto laboratory resembles the one in *Bride*. Lugosi is – well, Lugosi. Only the angora sweater is missing.

Gates' forced and foolish dialogue simply reeks of Wood. Informed by Pat that Prof. Lorenz and the Countess sleep in coffins, Foster observes, "We often find it difficult to explain the peculiarities of some people," and Lorenz himself later makes a plea for tolerance – all redolent of *Glen or Glenda?*'s have-you-hugged-your-transvestite-today? sermonizing. There's even an instance of Wood's brand of redundant, roundabout dialogue, as the two motorcycle cops eye the burning car ("Maybe it isn't a gag! Maybe it's a decoy!" "Maybe you're right!"). And, just as Wood turns up in most of his own movies, Sam Katzman (or his twin!) is an extra in a newspaper office scene.

Buried in this mess is one scene that might have been creepy if it had been done right. As Pat putters around in her bedroom at the Lorenz house, the Countess unexpectedly appears from nowhere, surprising Pat by coming up behind her. "You are beautiful . . . so young!" the Countess purrs. "Such lovely skin. Some time you, too, will be a br-r-ride, *hmmm?*" Frightened, Pat rushes to the door, where she momentarily looks back – to find the room empty. With some style and imagination, the scene might have stood out slightly, as it did when Joseph H. Lewis directed a quite-similar confrontation in *Boys of the City*. But with a director like Wallace Fox in charge, the room is overlit, the scene is done in prosaic long shots and the effect is lost; Elizabeth Russell's performance doesn't help, either. ("We took [the Monogram horror pictures] seriously since we didn't know they would come out comical," Angelo Rossitto told Tony Timpone.)

An attractive yet sinister-looking brunette, Elizabeth Russell was a natural for creepy roles; in the summer of '42 she began her long association with Val Lewton by playing a memorable bit in the RKO producer's *Cat People*. Over the course of the next four years, through Lewton's pictures (*The*

Seventh Victim, The Curse of the Cat People and *Bedlam*), not to mention Universal's *Weird Woman*, Russell attained an industry reputation as a sort of female Bela Lugosi; the Hollywood trades dubbed her the Houri of Horror. And, as with Lugosi, this typecasting doomed her, because once horror films were out, so was Elizabeth Russell.

Russell barely remembers *The Corpse Vanishes* today, a merciful lapse of memory: she's the center of some of the film's best unintentionally funny scenes. Russell adopts an accent, perhaps to match Lugosi's, but it sounds more Puerto Rican than Hungarian. Writhing hammily as Lugosi prepares to operate on one of the brides, Russell bawls, "Better dead than *ag-o-neeeeee* like *deese!*" Later, when Angelo Rossitto touches her hand, she bellows at him, calling him a "*gor*-goyle" as Lugosi, playing "Ave Maria" on the organ, smiles approvingly.

Saving the best for last, however, Russell gets the film's biggest laugh in the finale. Lugosi, dying from the knife wound, is trying to inject Luana Walters; he's gasping, gulping, his eyes are bulging and he's weaving around like mad (the entire finale is underscored by Keystone Cop–style music). Watching his gyrations with mild interest, Russell finally comes out with a matter-of-fact, "Your hand *eez* unsteady." The performance is probably Russell's worst.

The supporting cast is the usual mixed bag. No comedian could hope to match the laugh count chalked up by Bela Lugosi in pictures like these, but Vince Barnett indulges in that exercise in futility. Barnett was a screen comic from the early days of talkies right up until his death in 1977, but you could count the movies where he was actually funny on the fingers of one hand. Brimming with obnoxious one-liners, and snapping closeup flashbulb pictures of dead brides as the families grieve, Barnett here is even more taxing than usual.

Frank Moran, later to play the Neanderthal in *Return of the Ape Man*, is perfectly cast as the dim-witted Angel; like Lugosi and Russell, he comes off funny rather than scary. His eyes lit by a boyish gleam, and sporting one of the civilized world's worst haircuts, the goonish, apelike Moran was born for the part. Whether stroking the hair of the cataleptic brides, reacting with mild indifference to Bela Lugosi's cat o'nine tails or stalking Luana Walters with a turkey leg hanging out of his mouth, Moran plays it to the hilt.

Only the most twisted casting director would dream of hiring brute Moran and diminutive Angelo Rossitto to play brothers, but it's yet another touch of weirdness that suits the tone of *The Corpse Vanishes*; Rossitto (billed simply as Angelo in the film's credits) gets into the spirit of things quite nicely as well. (After playing his character as though he were a mute for half the movie, Rossitto suddenly starts talking in the second half.)

Born in Omaha, Nebraska, the 34-inch Rossitto moved to Hollywood in the mid–20s, dropping his plans for a career in the legal profession when

John Barrymore ("He and I were drinking buddies," Rossitto told Tony Timpone) helped him secure jobs on the stage and in silent films. To supplement his acting income, Rossitto operated a newsstand. ("If it wasn't for my newsstand I would have never made a living out here."). He doubled for Shirley Temple, ran for mayor of Los Angeles in 1941, delivered newspapers to Patton during World War II and cofounded the Little People of America Association, an organization designed to help diminutive performers find work.

Hard-to-miss, Rossitto has shown up in dozens of fantasy, science fiction and horror films, starting with *Seven Footprints to Satan* and *The Mysterious Island* (both 1929) and working right up to such films as *Mad Max Beyond Thunderdome* (1985) and *The Offspring* (1987). In between he's been seen in *Freaks* (1932), *Babes in Toyland* (1934), *The Spider Woman* (1944), *Scared to Death* (1947), *The Magic Sword* (1962) and more. Almost as typecast as Bela Lugosi, he generally played a dwarf.

Asked about his days at Monogram by Tony Timpone, Rossitto reminisced,

> Things were very cheap. We worked 54 hours a week and six days a week. They were struggling most of the time. . . . Anytime Sam Katzman wanted me for a picture, he would come by my newsstand at Hollywood and Wilcox and say, "I got a picture for you and you start work next week." He was a wheeler-dealer with the studio but not with us.

Rossitto is one of those lucky(?) actors who's managed to scare up a contingent of "fans" through his campy performances in bad movies. In fact, he got occasional jobs in recent years because of B movie buffs-cum-filmmakers that remembered him from movies like *The Corpse Vanishes*; for instance, producer Sam Sherman:

> For the part of Grazbo the dwarf in *Dracula vs. Frankenstein* [1971], the only person I could think of was Angelo Rossitto, because I thought so much of him from the Monogram Lugosi pictures. [Director] Al Adamson had already lined up Lon Chaney, Jr., and J. Carrol Naish for the picture; Jerry Rosen, the agent Al got Chaney and Naish from, also had a dwarf as a client. But I said to Al, "No, I want Angelo Rossitto, there's nobody else you can use in the picture." Al said, "Where can I get in touch with him?" and I said, "I don't think he's acted in years, but he has a newsstand on Hollywood Boulevard." Al said, "How am I gonna *find* him?!!" I said, "Please."
> Al went out on Hollywood Boulevard, walking up and down for two weeks, looking for Angelo Rossitto. No Angelo Rossitto. Finally he said to me, "I can't find him! I refuse to spend another day wandering around like an idiot on Hollywood Boulevard, looking for your man! We've got to go with Jerry Rosen's dwarf" – and at that point, I had to agree. Who's Rosen's dwarf? Angelo Rossitto *[laughs]*!

"Rosen's dwarf" died of complications from surgery, September 21, 1991. Lugosi plays Dr. Lorenz straight down the middle, with little of the uniquely Lugosian passion that marked some of his other mad doctor roles (*Murders in the Rue Morgue, The Raven, Bride of the Monster*). Even so, he seizes what few opportunities he can to overact. It's the script's fault, not his, that he's called upon to stand, threateningly and for absolutely no reason, over the bedside of Tristram Coffin, but the silly faces he makes are pure Lugosi.

A shot of Bela in the morgue wagon coffin, looking stunned, eyes wide, is invariably greeted with chortles. By the time the film is wrapping up, and Lugosi is chasing Minerva Urecal 'round and 'round the operating table in a scene out of a Three Stooges comedy, viewers caught up in the fun are usually weak from laughter. Lugosi would play the same type of role quite differently two years later in *Voodoo Man*.

Even though Lugosi is playing a nutty doctor here, *Corpse Vanishes* (like *Spooks Run Wild*) seeks to capitalize on his Dracula image, showing the actor nestled in a coffin (twice) and using hypnosis on a victim. The frightened cab driver who refuses to drive Luana Walters to Lugosi's house is a takeoff on Michael Visaroff's innkeeper character in the original *Dracula* (1931). These elements don't make the least bit of sense when examined under the bare bulb of cold logic, but are the kind of clichéd, good-natured touches that make the Monogram films as much fun as they are. Bela buffs give *Corpse Vanishes* a low mark because Lugosi has a limited amount of dialogue: 51 lines, according to one Lugosi expert. (He has almost exactly the same amount in *Dracula*, give or take, but apparently That's Okay with the Lugosi clique – now as always, a tough-to-figure bunch.)

Playing a character with more gall than brains, Luana Walters loses our sympathy in the opening scene when she's tickled pink by the death of the first bride. A poor man's Lois Lane, Walters' cub reporter character allows herself to be convinced, time and again, that every clue she uncovers is a figment of her imagination, and her editor's exasperation with her seems a perfectly natural reaction. Walters was reduced to bit parts by the late '40s (*Mighty Joe Young*, for instance); in the 1950s Alex Gordon, a lifelong fan of vintage films, tracked down Walters (then working in a drugstore) and gave her some additional minor roles in his AIP productions of *Girls in Prison* and *The She-Creature* (both 1956).

Tristram (billed as Tris) Coffin is saddled with a thankless role as well as most of the film's sillier lines. Coffin had a sinister look that worked against him whenever he played heroic roles, and the scenes where this middle-aged character actor starts making moves on Luana Walters are

Opposite: **Dying from a policeman's bullet, diminutive Angelo Rossitto is looking to the wrong person for help. From the climax of Bela Lugosi's** *The Corpse Vanishes.*

Hats off to Bela! Lugosi and would-be funnyman Vince Barnett in a forced gag shot for *The Corpse Vanishes.*

mildly embarrassing. Asked about the movie and Lugosi in *Filmfax*, the veteran player told Don Leifert,

> Bela Lugosi was a very unusual man who kept to himself a great deal. He had a great talent. In *The Corpse Vanishes*, Lugosi and Elizabeth Russell were required to sleep in caskets instead of beds. When we shot the sequence where she was supposed to get in the casket, she refused to get in it. She was fearful of it, you know. Eventually, they had to use a double.

Again, as with *Black Dragons*, the basic premise of *The Corpse Vanishes* would crop up in better-made pictures; it would in fact become a minor staple of horror and SF films, with the mad scientist/villain claiming a series of female victims in his quest to restore his wife's youth or beauty, or to revive her from the living dead. (*The Ape* pivoted around a similar device; *Corpse* polished it to a shine.) Lugosi had another crack at it in *Voodoo Man*, putting his faith in black magic rather than science; Basil Rathbone gave it a go in *The Black Sleep* (1956). A wife with a bad case of the uglies prompted Nazi surgeon Rudolph Anders to experiment on pretty island girls in *She Demons* (1958) while a scientist's burn-faced daughter was at the center of

Elizabeth Russell (second from right) has just delivered a sock to Luana Walters' jaw as Tristram Coffin and Bela Lugosi look on. (From *The Corpse Vanishes.*)

the plot of the French-made *The Horror Chamber of Dr. Faustus* (1962). Other variations on the theme include *Atom Age Vampire* (1960), *The Brain That Wouldn't Die* (1961), *Corruption* (1968), *Mansion of the Doomed* (1977) and *Faceless* (1988).

For British release, the film's title was changed to the milder *The Case of the Missing Brides.* Oddly, the 1943 Monogram release *Revenge of the Zombies* was later subjected to a title switch in Britain – to *The Corpse Vanished!* In the same trivial vein, the poster for *The Corpse Vanishes*, which features Lugosi and Joan Barclay, can be seen on display outside a theater in Lugosi's very next Monogram picture, *Bowery at Midnight.*

Variety's Eddy wrote about *The Corpse Vanishes*, "On the end of double bills it might interest youngsters, but it insults the average intelligence. . . . Lugosi does most of his acting with his eyes [and] Luana Walters is pretty, but not a good actress." Critic Archer Winsten of *The New York Post* agreed: "Mr. Lugosi smirks and menaces in his best style, but the game is familiar." An unfavorable *Hollywood Reporter* review was headlined "Horror Story Too Fantastically Told," and went on to complain, "There must be a market for such product or [Monogram] wouldn't grind it out. . . . Luana Walters does her best as the girl reporter, but our first four sights of the leering Lugosi are unconsciously funny. Tristram Coffin is a standard leading man with an unfortunate name for a shocker." The Legion of Decency pegged *Corpse* with their B (adults only) rating, citing "excessive gruesomeness and morbidness."

Don Willis wrote, "Bela and his friends are really the supporting players, and Luana Walters and Tris Coffin the stars, of a dull framing story." Phil Hardy tagged it "a lamentably shoddy piece of work." Richard Bojarski (*The Films of Bela Lugosi*) wrote, "Lugosi played his role in an entertaining, if not credible fashion." Leonard Maltin rated it "a cut above the average low-grade thrillers Lugosi made for Katzman," and Lugosi fan Michael Weldon (*Psychotronic*) called it "a must." But *The Count's* Arthur Lennig remained disgruntled: "It combines a dull mystery with unconvincing science, while expecting the mere presence of Lugosi to evoke fear with no help from story, dialogue, or direction."

Picky, picky. An unintentional comedy gem, *The Corpse Vanishes* remains a highwater mark in the Monogram horror film series.

The Mad Monster
(PRC, 1942)

Released May 15. 77 minutes. Produced by Sigmund Neufeld. Directed by Sam Newfield. Original Screenplay: Fred Myton. Director of Photography: Jack Greenhalgh, A.S.C. Sound Engineer: Hans Weeren. Music: David Chudnow. Art Director: Fred Preble. Makeup Artist: Harry Ross. Film Editor: Holbrook N. Todd. Assistant Director: Melville De Lay. Production Manager: Bert Sternbach. Special Effects: Gene Stone.

Cast: Johnny Downs (Tom Gregory), George Zucco (Dr. Lorenzo Cameron), Anne Nagel (Lenora Cameron), Glenn Strange (Petro), Sarah Padden (Grandmother), Gordon Demain (Prof. Fitzgerald), Mae Busch (Susan), Reginald Barlow (Prof. Warwick), Robert Strange (Prof. Blaine), Henry Hall (Country Doctor), Edward Cassidy (Father), Eddie Holden (Jed Harper), John Elliott (Prof. Hatfield), Charles Whitaker (Policeman), Gil Patric (Lieutenant Detective).

> "You're aware, of course, that this country is at war. That our armed forces are locked in combat with a savage horde who fight with fanatical fury. Well, that fanatical fury will avail them nothing when I place my new serum at the disposal of the War Department. Just picture, gentlemen, an army of wolf men! Fearless! Raging! Every man is a snarling *animal!"*—Dr. Lorenzo Cameron (George Zucco)

The first *patriotic* mad scientist to stand up and be counted (for *our* side, that is!), Dr. Lorenzo Cameron's man-into-beast experiments, gung-ho wartime enthusiasm and lust for revenge advance the comic-book plot of

The Mad Monster, one of Poverty Row's rare excursions into werewolfry. Shot in March of 1942, while Universal's *The Wolf Man* was pulling horror fans into theaters in record numbers, *Mad Monster* was clearly inspired by the Universal release. (So clearly, in fact, that perhaps PRC felt it wise to keep the nature of its central fiend *out* of their title, as did another werewolf film, Fox's *The Undying Monster*, five months down the pike.) In standard PRC fashion, *The Mad Monster* is crude and stark, and cost only a small fraction of the amount that was spent on Universal's well-produced and comparatively star-studded *Wolf Man*. This once, however, the air of economy that permeates the film could almost be mistaken for creepy atmosphere.

The Mad Monster wastes no time getting underway. After the opening credits fade, we find ourselves in the secret basement lab of Dr. Cameron (George Zucco) as he extracts blood from the leg of a caged wolf. Cameron's handyman and experimental subject Petro (Glenn Strange), a halfwit, is strapped to a nearby couch. Cameron injects Petro with his special serum, and just over three minutes into the movie, we get our first man-into-wolf transformation as Petro grows hair and fangs and takes on the vicious attitude of a wild beast.

Cameron is exultant as he watches the transition; his now-proven theories about the transfusion of blood between different species had been labeled "mad," and got him booted off the staff of a big-city university. Unfortunately, Cameron quite clearly *is* mad. As the werewolf-Petro strains at his bonds, Cameron crosses to a table and begins to ramble on as though listeners were present. One by one, we see the professors who humiliated him materialize in the empty chairs—transparent figments of Cameron's fevered imagination. For the benefit of his ghostly "guests," he re-states his ultimate goal of putting an army of wolf men into wartime uniforms:

> My serum will make it possible to unloose millions of such animal men. Men who are governed by one collective thought, the animal lust to kill, without regard for personal safety. . . . Such an army will sweep everything before it!

The "professors" continue to scoff, and one of them quite sensibly asks Cameron how millions of bestial wolf men will be rounded up after each battle; stuck for an answer, Cameron barks that he's heard enough of their "imbecilic mouthings." (Poor Cameron—even in his *own daydreams*, he can't win an argument!) These professors had publicly ridiculed Cameron, forcing him to move from the city to the swampy suburb of Ashton, and now revenge is the nutty professor's foremost desire. He administers an antidote which restores Petro to normalcy, and convinces the dullard that he was just asleep and *dreaming* that he had become a wild animal.

Cameron's daughter Lenora (Anne Nagel) hates the country life; she

Wolf and man-wolf: Glenn Strange (in Harry Ross makeup) and four-legged friend (*au natural*) in a publicity pose for *The Mad Monster.*

misses the city, and most of all her beau, newspaperman Tom Gregory (top-billed Johnny Downs). Cameron won't tell her the first thing about what he does in the lab, so she tries to wheedle some information out of Petro. Petro is about to tell her what little he can when Cameron arrives on the scene and breaks up their *tête-à-tête.*

That night, Cameron once again injects Petro with the wolf serum, only this time the professor purposely allows the wolf man to escape from the house. Harper (Eddie Holden), a farmer, spots the werewolf roaming around in the misty swamps and shoots him with both barrels of his shotgun, which has no effect. Harper high-tails it to the nearby home of another farmer (Edward Cassidy) and describes his terrifying experience ("I dunno whether it was a man, a beast – or ol' Satan his-self!"). As Holden tells his tale, the werewolf creeps into the house through their little girl's bedroom window and murders the child. Returning to Cameron's, the lycanthrope is again restored to normalcy.

In the city, Tom Gregory pays a late-night call on his friend Prof. Blaine (Robert Strange), one of the academics Cameron has marked for death. Tom has heard about the child murdered by an animal that walks on its hind legs, and needs an "angle" with which he can turn the news story into a Sunday feature. What kind of angle? Blaine wants to know.

TOM: The possibility of the survival in the depths of the swamp of some of those overgrown lizards that used to be head men on Earth. I understand they traveled around on their hind legs, and made our present-day public enemies look like horticultural specimens!

Blaine is amused, but won't stoop to lending his name to Tom's wacky story.

Cameron puts his schemes of revenge into motion. Later that night, he and Petro arrive uninvited at Blaine's, Cameron claiming that he's proven his theories. Through a clever ploy, he arranges for *Blaine* to agree to inject Petro at midnight sharp while he (Cameron) is supposedly running an emergency errand. Cameron actually goes to the home of *another* of his former colleagues, Prof. Fitzgerald (Gordon Demain), providing himself with an alibi. While Cameron is with Fitzgerald, Blaine injects Petro and is promptly killed by the werewolf Petro becomes.

But not everything goes Cameron's way: Back home in Ashton, Petro becomes a werewolf without benefit of injection and prowls around outside the house; Tom almost becomes a victim when he innocently comes a-calling. Cameron re-captures him and is preparing to shoot his now-unpredictable werewolf-accomplice, but reconsiders at the last instant: "No – I couldn't disappoint Prof. Fitzgerald!"

Tom, lost in the woods after leaving the Camerons, winds up spending the night at the home of the farmer whose child was murdered. The next morning, after another local is found dead, the subject of conversation naturally turns to the swamp killer. Grandmother (Sarah Padden) insists the fiend is a werewolf:

> GRANDMOTHER: You can't kill him no way, except by a silver *boo-let*.
> TOM: I can't see myself giving *that* story to the city editor! [Like Tom's "dinosaur" angle was better!]

Cameron invites Prof. Fitzgerald to his home on the pretext of discussing some new theories, but when Cameron raves about being able to control evolution, the usual name-calling session ensues:

> CAMERON: I can inject into your veins a substance that will give you the strength of ten men. Or, following the line of evolution, how would you like a pair of *donkey's* ears? Hah hah! That'd go *well* with your type of mentality!

As Fitzgerald is leaving, Cameron imposes on him to give Petro a lift into the city. Cameron injects Petro before the handyman leaves, and during the ride, Petro transforms and attacks Fitzgerald. The car crashes off the road.

Johnny Downs and Glenn Strange look ready to square off in a posed shot from *The Mad Monster*. The damsel is Anne Nagel.

The injured and unconscious Fitzgerald is rescued by a posse led by Tom and the farmers, and he is brought to the Cameron house, where he dies. The werewolf has let himself back into the house; Lenora stumbles across the secret entrance to her father's lab, and the beast comes after her. As a violent electrical storm rages outside and a bolt of lightning starts a fire inside the house, the werewolf attacks Cameron, choking him to death. The fire spreads quickly, forcing Tom and Lenora out of the house. The pair watch helplessly as a blazing ceiling crumbles, crushing the werewolf and the body of Prof. Cameron.

The Mad Monster is one of the few Poverty Row horror films of the '40s to feature a "conventional," Universal-style monster (a wolf man); perhaps because Universal could depict vampires/werewolves/etc. so much better, PRC and Monogram tended to come up with their *own* custom-made

monsters (devil bats, flying serpents, ape men and so on), or to just let Bela
Lugosi carry the ball alone. With *Mad Monster*, PRC strays into what you
might call Universal territory, and the results, while wholly unspectacular,
are interesting.

The *Mad Monster* shares with umpteen other Poverty Row horror films
a rural, backwoodsy milieu, but in this one the remote locale actually
becomes an eerie backdrop for the story. Films like *The Ape, Revenge of the
Zombies* and *Dead Men Walk* never capitalized on their similar settings;
their stories just happened to be placed in "the sticks." But in *Mad Monster*,
the ominous mists, dead trees, vines and hanging moss provide a dismal ambience which adds to the grim flavor of the film. *Mad Monster*, in fact, rivals
the much-touted *Strangler of the Swamp* for spooky atmosphere.

Although you don't see a thing, the scene where werewolf Strange
murders the little girl is the one thing about *The Mad Monster* that people
remember even if they forget everything else about the film. The werewolf
silently lifts her bedroom window and peers in as the lone child plays with
her toy ball; seconds later, from the *next* room, we see the ball bouncing in
as her mother (perennial Laurel and Hardy foil Mae Busch) instantly senses
that something is amiss. Monsters generally don't mess with children, even
in today's blood-drenched, anything-goes horror thrillers, but after the long
respite that followed the Monster's (Karloff) murder of Little Maria (Marilyn
Harris) in *Frankenstein* (1931), *The Mad Monster* brought infanticide back
into vogue (*another* proud moment for Poverty Row!). Other older horror
or suspense films where young 'uns buy the farm include *The Leopard Man*
(1943), *The Brute Man* (1946), *Robot Monster* (1953), *X the Unknown* (1956)
and *4D Man* (1959). Perhaps not wishing to be outdone by PRC's "Petro,"
Universal's Wolf Man (Lon Chaney) murdered teenage girls in each of his
first two sequels, *Frankenstein Meets the Wolf Man* (1943) and *House of
Frankenstein* (1944).

Glenn Strange's performance as the werewolf is another great asset to
The Mad Monster, but his scenes as the dull-witted Petro are almost embarrassing. Strange told Don Glut that Lon Chaney, Jr., had in fact kidded him
about this performance: "Lon Chaney said to me, 'What are you trying to
do? Lennie in *Of Mice and Men*?' And I said, 'Well, I haven't seen the thing.'
Then, of course, Broderick Crawford did it on the stage before Lon, the
same way. There's just one way to do a Lennie, and that's just a big 'Da. . . .
Da. . . .' You can't do it any other way."

That's arguable; Strange's simpering, singsong delivery becomes more
than annoying – he sounds, in fact, like a male Edith Bunker – and most of
his dialogue is lousy (*that* part of it isn't Strange's fault). But as the
werewolf, Strange is excellent, exuding ferocity the same way he did as
Frankenstein's Monster in the later Universal films *House of Frankenstein*
(1944), *House of Dracula* (1945) and *Abbott and Costello Meet Frankenstein*
(1948). Strange was *far* from the best actor to play the Monster – not that

any real acting on Strange's part was called for in those three films – but the actor's sheer physical presence (6'4", 218 lbs.) and powerful physique made his Monster one-of-a-kind.

These same characteristics are also on display in *The Mad Monster*, making Strange's a far more imposing and frightening werewolf than those seen in better-made films like *The Return of the Vampire* (1943) or *The Undying Monster*. He's victimized, however, by the wardrobe department (if there even *was* such a thing at penny-pinching PRC!), spending most of the picture in tight-fitting overalls and a goofy-looking hat; dressed like this, his werewolf looks like something left over from a *Hee Haw* Halloween skit. And except for the fangs, he's practically a dead ringer for famed Western sidekick "Gabby" Hayes. The fact that Strange is able to come off so well regardless is further proof of the actor's unique talent for playing monstrous roles.

Strange's lap-dissolve transformation into the werewolf isn't half-bad, although it doesn't begin to compare with John P. Fulton's outstanding special effects as seen in Universal's Wolf Man series (just as makeup man Harry Ross' hillbilly-werewolf is kid's stuff next to Jack P. Pierce's classic design). Still, it's one of the most ambitious special effects attempted by any of the films in this book; even Republic, which had a crack effects team, allowed *one* lap dissolve to suffice when their werecat transformed into Douglass Dumbrille at the end of *The Catman of Paris*.

George Zucco's flair for villainous and mad scientist assignments obviously made him a favorite of the PRC front office, and the English-born actor became a fixture in their horror films the way Bela Lugosi did at Monogram. Over the next few years, Zucco returned to the PRC fold for *Dead Men Walk*, *Fog Island* and *The Flying Serpent*, not to mention the studio's mystery/comedy *The Black Raven* (1943), which found him teamed with Glenn Strange again. Only in *Dead Men Walk*, however, is he as gleefully wicked and hammy as he is in *The Mad Monster*. From the very beginning of the film, where he fervidly gloats over the revenge he plans to take on the faculty professors who prompted his resignation, Zucco plays the role for all its worth and never lets up.

Zucco, a slightly haughty, off-putting actor, is somewhat harder to warm up to than genre icons like Karloff and Lugosi; somehow he's also not as colorful or as much fun as lesser lights like Lionel Atwill or John Carradine. But he *always* seemed to be giving these horror films, even the measliest of them, his best shot, which is more than can be said for some of these others (especially Karloff and Carradine). Turning Glenn Strange into a werewolf in *Mad Monster* seems an almost natural extension of Zucco's current activities at other studios: For Paramount, he transplanted the brain of a man (Phillip Terry) into an ape (Charles Gemora) in *The Monster and the Girl* (1941), and at Fox he turned a gorilla into a man (J. Carrol Naish) who became *Dr. Renault's Secret* (1942).

With Anne (*Black Friday, Man Made Monster*) Nagel and Glenn (Frankenstein's Monster) Strange on hand, PRC's werewolf tale *The Mad Monster* had a bit of the feel of a Universal thriller.

A former member of the "Our Gang" troupe, Johnny Downs is likable as the newspaperman/hero, although a bit too boyish and out of his league in the dramatic clinches; his idiotic theory that a dinosaur is at large brands him a nincompoop from his first appearance on. Pros like Robert Strange, Mae Busch, Henry Hall and Edward Cassidy all make the most of their brief appearances. Reginald Barlow, one of the two professors Zucco never gets to sic Strange on, was the villager killed by the Monster (Boris Karloff) in the flooded mill at the beginning of *Bride of Frankenstein* (1935).

Anne Nagel, a much put-upon leading lady in the Universal horror films *Black Friday* (1940) and *Man Made Monster* (1941), knew the ropes by now, and knits her pretty brow most convincingly as the first whiffs of trouble brew. *Mad Monster* is a mildly unique horror film in that the heroine (Nagel) is actually the daughter of the villain (Zucco); usually, being their niece would be the closest a heroine would come to having a blood tie to the baddie. Frightened by the look in Glenn Strange's eyes in one scene, she sputters, "He was possessed by a demon!", a very strange observation to come from the offspring of a no-nonsense scientist like Zucco.

Like (too) many actresses, Anne Nagel appears to have had one of those fairly miserable lives that might have made for a movie in itself. The

Boston-born daughter of a Technicolor expert, she appeared in niteries before making her film bow in 1933, became a Warners contract actress and married actor Ross Alexander in 1936. But Alexander, a homosexual who hated his "gay" side, was obsessed with Bette Davis, even though she had no use for him; all Alexander ever got out of *that* one-sided relationship was a black eye from Davis' husband. Nagel would leave him every time she found love notes to Davis around the house, but according to the newspapers she became hysterical when her butler brought her the news of Alexander's 1937 rifle-in-the-mouth suicide.

In 1941, after moving over to Universal, she married Air Force officer James H. Keenan, but more toil and trouble lay ahead. She slipped several rungs down the Hollywood ladder (*The Mad Monster*, for instance!), and in 1947 she sued Hollywood physician and surgeon Dr. Franklyn Thorpe (former husband of Mary Astor) for $350,000 claiming he sterilized her without her knowledge during an appendectomy operation performed in 1936, when she was still Mrs. Alexander. In 1951 she sued for divorce from Keenan, charging that hubby had unraveled her knitting, kicked in the front of her radio and gave away her cocker spaniel. Later telling *his* side of the story, Keenan claimed that Nagel embarrassed him by drinking to excess and that he "only looked out for her well-being by reason of the fact that she had no funds" after she was released from a hospital for alcoholism. Nagel died July 6, 1966, at Sunray North Convalescent Home in Hollywood, which she entered after cancer surgery on June 5. She was just 53.

Most every other plot element in *The Mad Monster* had been rather thoroughly tested in scads of earlier films. The basic story is a combination of *The Wolf Man* and PRC's own *The Devil Bat*, with Zucco subbing for Lugosi as the wacky doctor, and a werewolf rather than the flying mammal serving as the crazed scientist's instrument of vengeance. (PRC recycled this idea a second time for *The Flying Serpent*, again with Zucco.)

Even some of the (small) stylistic touches, like the way Zucco's strangulation-death is seen as a shadow cast upon a wall, were already rapidly hurtling toward clichedom. Zucco maintaining control over wolf man Strange with a whip hearkened back to the lash-cracking Charles Laughton in *Island of Lost Souls* (1933), and would be used again by Lugosi in *The Ape Man.*

Tired clichés to the cynical, these hoary touches are, again, just part of the charm of Poverty Row films. *The Mad Monster* trundles them all out so enthusiastically, and everyone seems so starved for approval, that it becomes one of those uniquely bad films that is difficult to dislike. At 77 minutes, it's by far one of the longest Poverty Row films of the '40s; only Republic's much-touted "A-picture" *The Lady and the Monster* is longer. A decent musical score might have made all the difference between a (very) minor cheapo classic and the oft-maligned B film that *Mad Monster* has become, but composer David Chudnow fails to meet the challenge, even leaving scenes that cry out for musical accompaniment completely unscored. Composer Albert Glasser, who allowed Chudnow to act as his agent for a time in the '40s, remembers those days well:

> I did about three or four scores for David Chudnow – for $300, then $325, then $350. I did a Cisco Kid picture called *In Old New Mexico* [1945] and the producers were so impressed that they called me in for another one. They said, "What did we pay you last time?" I said I got $350. They said, "Wait a minute! We paid $3,000 for that!" I said, "You paid Chudnow *$3,000?* He gave me $350!" They said, "Oh, that son of a bitch!"

The Mad Monster began shooting at the Chadwick Studios on Thursday, March 19, 1942, and was released in June. In uptight England, however, the film was banned by the British censor until the mid-50s, when it finally came out with the "X" Certificate (Adults Only) rating. Additionally, English theaters which played the film were called upon to exhibit a written notice:

> The public would be quite mistaken to think that any personal characteristics could be passed on by blood transfusion. Animal blood is never used for transfusions in the treatment of disease.

Promotion stunts this time around included a Gum Giveaway. A popular brand of chewing gum would be handed out on downtown streets together with a circular that read,

> This picture is a shocker. Can you take it? Suggestions for nervous patrons who see *The Mad Monster*: If you're chilled by horror, bring a hot water bottle for your feet. If you're subject to shock, bring someone you like, and hold hands. If you're nervous, bring this piece of gum and chew it. Keep warm feet, a cool head, hold hands and chew – and remember, it's only a movie.

The Hollywood Reporter's man-on-the-aisle saw beyond the film's dirt-cheap physical mounting and gave it a (*too!*) good review: "By the simple expedient of using competent and personable actors, PRC has turned out a thriller-diller that can stand up with the best of such product on the market. *The Mad Monster* pursues a premise no less fantastic than others of its ilk, but the playing is persuasive enough to make the idea thoroughly acceptable.... Sam Newfield directed it suspensefully. The settings are well done, as is the photography.... Glenn Strange gives top grade presence to the bewildered monster, wearing a terrifying wolfish makeup. George Zucco lends fine authority to his role of the scientist, and Anne Nagel brings poised beauty to the relatively unimportant daughter assignment."

"This picture is a childish, almost naive attempt to inject horror," complained *Variety*'s Eddy, "and its situations, rather than being tense, are ludicrous. Leftover dialog and warmed-over situations of this nature are strung together. . . . George Zucco does a creditable job as the scientist, and Anne Nagel is satisfactory as his daughter. Johnny Downs is miscast as the reporter, but Glenn Strange is properly horrible as the beast-man. Others lend generally satisfactory support. All are handicapped by childish situations, inane dialog and generally misty camerawork."

Lately, pans have been *The Mad Monster*'s lot. *Psychotronic* called it "a pretty funny no-budget film." Maltin's *Movies on TV* gave it a miserly star and a half: "Dull, low-budget mad-scientist thriller drags heavy feet for unintended laughs. Zucco effortlessly steals show." Even the still-pubescent Joe Dante raked it over the coals in *Famous Monsters of Filmland*, cataloguing it as one of his "fifty worst horror films ever made": "*Mad Monster* was the first horror film I ever saw and as such it terrified me. I was 5 and for a first horror film it packed a wallop – at the time. I recently saw it again – oh, brother! George Zucco, Anne Nagel and Johnny Downs were awful and so was the plot." Don Leifert in *Filmfax* thought George Zucco was the best thing about *Mad Monster*: "The moment he appeared on screen, complete with wavering eyes and delusions of grandeur, it was evident that he was a prime candidate for a strait-jacket. [*The Mad Monster*] features Zucco's least restrained performance in a horror film." William K. Everson (*More Classics of the Horror Film*) classed *The Mad Monster* (as well as Zucco's next PRC horror film *Dead Men Walk*) as "a disaster."

Bowery at Midnight
(Monogram, 1942)

Released October 30. 61 minutes. Associate Producer: Barney A. Sarecky. Produced by Sam Katzman and Jack Dietz (Banner Productions). Directed by Wallace Fox. Original Story and Screenplay: Gerald Schnitzer. Assistant Director: Arthur Hammond. Musical Director: Edward Kay. Photography: Mack Stengler. Film Editor: Carl Pierson. Art Director: Dave Milton. Sound Engineer: Glen Glenn.

Cast: Bela Lugosi (Prof. Frederick Brenner/"Karl Wagner"), John Archer (Richard Dennison), Wanda McKay (Judy Malvern), Tom Neal (Frankie Mills), Vince Barnett (Charley), Anna Hope (Mrs. Brenner), John Berkes (Fingers Dolan), J. Farrell MacDonald (Police Capt. Mitchell), Dave O'Brien (Pete Crawford), Lucille Vance (Mrs. Malvern), Lew Kelly (Doc Brooks), Wheeler Oakman (Stratton), Ray Miller (Big Man), George Eldredge (Detective Thompson), Pat Costello, Ralph Littlefield (Tramps), Eddie Kane (Police Chief), Bernard Gorcey (Tailor), Snub Pollard.

"Bela Lugosi adds another dual role to his film record in
Bowery at Midnight, new Monogram horror tale....
While Lugosi does not resort to make-up of any kind, he
manages to portray a dignified college professor by day,
and is the leader of a vicious gang of criminals by night.
The well known histrionic skill of this actor enables him
to make the transition with ease, giving both characters
all necessary realism." — *Bowery at Midnight* pressbook

Audiences might have felt gypped by its meager horror content, but at
least they got two Bela Lugosis for the price of one in *Bowery at Midnight,*
the halfway point in Monogram's nine-film Lugosi series. In the daylight,
Lugosi's Prof. Frederick Brenner is a famous psychologist, university professor and solicitous husband. At night, however, he adopts the identity of
"Karl Wagner," operator of a slum soup kitchen and secret mastermind of
a brutal series of combination murder/robberies. At any other studio, this
would be enough plot for a 61 minute picture, but not at Monogram: To spice
things up a bit more, they mixed in a nutty drug-addicted doctor with a
secret cellar full of zombies. This allowed them to advertise what was essentially a gangster picture as a horror film.

In the months between *The Corpse Vanishes* and *Bowery at Midnight,*
Lugosi had paid a visit to Universal to appear as the butler in *Night Monster*
(1942). The role was a smallish one but at least he got top billing, a rarity
for him at Universal (this was the second and last time; Lugosi made 16
features there). *Night Monster* was a very good horror-whodunit, well-made
and imaginative. Most Lugosi fans, however, don't like it. Taking time out
from tirelessly complaining about their man's entrapment in the horror
field, they moan about the fact that he's only a red herring in the film, and
not the monster. (With fans like these, Lugosi has never needed enemies.)

The months between *Corpse* and *Bowery* also found Monogram busy lining up several new titles for Bela. On April 17, 1942, as *Corpse* was gearing
for release, Monogram announced that Lugosi had been signed for two additional Sam Katzman–Jack Dietz films for the 1942–3 schedule, *Night of Horror* and *Torment.* Weeks later, these titles were conspicuous by their
absence from a published list of upcoming Monogram films, a lineup which
now included the Bela-bound *Bowery at Midnight* and *The Gorilla Strikes*
(The Ape Man). After spending several weeks in New York, Katzman
returned to Hollywood early in July and, together with Dietz, immediately
began preparing *Bowery at Midnight,* which went into production on Monday, August 3.

The film begins with a bang, as Fingers Dolan (John Berkes), a convicted safecracker, escapes from prison with the bullets of jailhouse guards
practically whizzing past his ears. Wandering around the Bowery section of
New York City, he overhears two vagrants, Charley (Vince Barnett) and

the Big Man (Ray Miller), discussing the Friendly Mission, a soup kitchen ("You can get some swell soup there, and no questions asked!"). Dolan follows the pair to the Mission, where the manager, Karl Wagner (Lugosi), warmly greets them:

> WAGNER *(magnanimously)*: Here you vill find food for your body, as vell as comfort for your troubled mind!
> CHARLEY *(unimpressed)*: Yeah, but could I have some soup?

Wagner seems to recognize Dolan, and lures him into his office on the pretext of offering him a cigar. There, Wagner calls Dolan by his real name, startling the escaped con. One of Wagner's confederates, Stratton (Wheeler Oakman), now enters through a secret panel; a friend of Dolan's, his presence reassures the fugitive as Wagner offers him a chance to "join our little partnership":

> DOLAN: You mean you'll lay out a job . . . case the place . . . and I tune the dial?
> WAGNER: The language is rather picturesque, but the meaning is perfect!

The threesome breaks into the Atlas Jewelry Company, Dolan cracks the safe and Wagner cleans it out. Wagner then takes both men by surprise by ordering Stratton to kill Dolan. Stratton is reluctant – Dolan's done nothing to deserve it – but finally pulls the trigger. (Leaving a dead accomplice at the scene of every crime is a habit of Wagner's.)

Back at the Mission, the shaken Stratton tells Doc Brooks (Lew Kelly), the janitor (and a drug addict), that he intends someday to follow Wagner and see what he does during the daytime. Doc, once a great doctor, now a derelict, warns, "A couple of men tried that before you and now they're buried." Wagner has watched and overheard the entire conversation on a small closed-circuit television in his office.

At this point we get a glimpse of Lugosi at home in his other identity, that of Prof. Brenner. In a cozy (i.e., dull) little domestic scene, he presents his lonely wife (Anna Hope) with an expensive necklace and dotes over her unctuously. Later, in his classroom at the university, one of his students, wealthy Richard Dennison (John Archer), just happens to talk all about the symptoms of paranoia. Of course, this scene is meant to subtly get across to us that paranoia is the mental condition driving Brenner/Wagner on in his homicidal double life.

Now the film takes an action break, as Frankie Mills (Tom Neal), a dangerous criminal, shoots it out with a pair of cops on the tenement streets. Police Sgt. Pete Crawford (Dave O'Brien) chases Mills, but the gun-crazy hood gets away after being grazed by a bullet. Mills ends up at the

A reissue poster for Monogram's crime/horror epic *Bowery at Midnight*. The rogues' gallery is comprised (clockwise from top) of Bela Lugosi, Wanda McKay, John Berkes, Tom Neal, Lew Kelly and Vince Barnett.

Mission, where Judy Malvern (Wanda McKay), a social worker, bandages his wound. When the police arrive, Wagner allows Mills to hide in his private office while he sends the cops away. Wagner now offers Mills a chance to join his criminal organization; Mills happily follows Wagner's first order, which is to kill Stratton. Doc lugs Stratton's body into yet another(!) secret room filled with the graves of the men that Wagner has had killed. After Wagner and Mills have left, the crazy Doc gets out his medical bag and begins to work over the dead body of Stratton.

Judy Malvern and Richard Dennison are in love, but argue over Judy's insistence on working every night at the Mission. ("Judy, I–I want you to give up that silly job. Saving humanity–it's ridiculous!") The next day in class, Dennison talks to Brenner about his upcoming term paper. Dennison has switched from an essay on what a man thinks just before he dies–talk about a paper that'd be a bitch to research!–to one on the psychology of the underprivileged.

Wagner and Mills, joined by Charley the transient, are about to pull a daylight heist. High on a rooftop, Charley thinks he's going to cover Mills' getaway, but he's really up there so that Wagner can toss him off in order to create a diversion in the street below. While crowds and cops encircle Charley's lifeless body, Mills easily robs a jewelry store.

Dennison goes undercover to get background material for his term paper, buying a cheap suit and dining at the Mission; there he recognizes Wagner as Brenner. Wagner/Brenner leads the student downstairs to the secret basement, taunts the bewildered boy a bit, and then orders Mills to shoot and kill him. (Now Dennison *knows* what a man thinks just before he dies, and it's the *writing* that'd be a bitch!)

Pete Crawford (now a plainclothes detective) realizes that Wagner and Brenner are one and the same when he sees a photograph of Wagner in Brenner's apartment. After killing his wife for cooperating with the police, Wagner flees back to the Mission, where he finds that Judy has browbeaten poor Doc into taking her on a tour of the secret rooms. He orders Mills to shoot her, but the gunman balks at killing a woman. Attempting to escape, Mills is killed by police bullets while Wagner retreats into his indoor graveyard. Doc opens a trapdoor in the floor and tells Wagner to hide in the sub-cellar–which is filled with walking dead men, Wagner's victims, brought back to life by Doc! Crawford and other cops watch with mild interest as the "zombies"–including Richard Dennison–close in on their killer.

Bowery at Midnight is just one more catchpenny melodrama in the Monogram Lugosi series, but its approach is significantly different from the rest of Bela's Monogram films. Whereas the emphasis in the other pictures was on horror or mystery (*or*, in the cases of the Lugosi/East Side Kids films, horror/comedy), *Bowery at Midnight* is basically a crime movie. In fact, there's *so* little horror in the film that Monogram's publicists were hard-pressed to find horror touches, and played up stuff which in fact is not there.

Much is made in the pressbook about Lugosi's adroit playing of the "Jekyll-and-Hyde" role of Brenner/Wagner. But we never truly get the impression that Lugosi's Brenner is a split personality: he's just a college professor who moonlights as a crook. At one point we find Brenner tossing in his sleep, tormented by a nightmare, a pointless scene except to imply that the Brenner half isn't aware of what the Wagner side of him is doing. But later in the picture, when detectives show up at the university, Brenner knows enough about Wagner to immediately get the hell out of there. "Karl Wagner" isn't his Mr. Hyde; it's his alias. (The pressbook also tries to pass off the characters played by Tom Neal and Lew Kelly as Lugosi's fellow bogeymen; Kelly's meek janitor is repeatedly referred to as a "maniac doctor.")

Lugosi's not bad in *Bowery at Midnight*, although someone should have told him he was only playing two parts, not four: He's open and personable as the soup kitchen major domo, dark and serious as the criminal, doting as the husband, stiff and pompous (in pince-nez, no less!) as the university professor. As usual, he livens up the picture just with his presence and with some of the little things he does, like the amusing way he beams paternally at Fingers Dolan (John Berkes) as the little man quietly sucks on his Havana cigar, and his persistance in mangling the English language 21 years after he got off the boat ("The police is looking for someone"). Lugosi was almost never a great actor, but he was also almost never an uninteresting one.

John Archer, hero of Monogram's *King of the Zombies* the year before, struggles with the role of the snotty Richard. He looks too damn old to still be going to school, talks about the skid-row characters with repugnance, and in person treats them condescendingly. In an embarrassing scene, Lucille Vance, the actress playing his sweetheart's mother, starts coming on to him. Tom Neal, playing Frankie Mills, sleepwalks through his role as the baby-faced killer; Neal's underplaying makes the character a bore. Vince Barnett (Charley) refrains from making a fool of himself, for a change; after the way he almost ruined *The Corpse Vanishes*, it's hugely gratifying to watch Lugosi toss him off the roof. Dave O'Brien, unjustly buried near the bottom of the castlist, does his customary good job as the young detective. Pat Costello (Lou's lookalike brother) and Bernard Gorcey, both unbilled, have funny bits.

Wanda McKay, in her first of three Poverty Row horror films, plays a character that seems more schizophrenic than Lugosi's. The Florence Nightingale of the flophouse, she showers attention upon the ungrateful riffraff at the Mission while allowing her relationship with boyfriend Richard to suffer; moments after spurning his offer of marriage (out of spite), she falsely teases him that there might be Another Man in her life. Later informed that Richard has vanished in that dangerous section of

Bela Lugosi tries out his charm on a classroom full of Monogram starlets. Publicity shot for the entertainingly preposterous *Bowery at Midnight.*

town, she brushes off the news, again out of spite ("Dozens of men every night have been missing for years. Nobody gets excited over *them!*"). Reassuring Richard's frantic mother, she comes across as stupidly naive ("I just wanted to tell you not to worry about Richard. He was doing research in the Bowery last night. Nothing could *possibly* happen to him down *there!*"). Working with what the screenwriter has given her, McKay comes across as a silly little brat.

A few notes on Wanda McKay: Born Dorothy Ellen Quackenbush on June 22, 1923, in either Fort Worth, Texas, or Portland, Oregon (sources differ), she trained for a business career before working as a model in New York City. She won a bathing beauty contest in Kansas City, and in Birmingham, Alabama, she won the Miss American Aviation title, which led to an association with TWA. The official hostess for TWA, she was "spotted" during a visit to a movie set, and made her screen debut in Paramount's *$1,000 a Touchdown* (1939) with big-mouths Martha Raye and Joe E. Brown.

McKay played small parts in many subsequent Paramount films, co-starred in cheap "oaters" at Monogram, Columbia and PRC, and took on Hollywood's baddest bogeymen not only in the *Bowery at Midnight* but also in *The Black Raven* (1943), *The Monster Maker* and *Voodoo Man*. When film offers dwindled she worked on early television (*The Lone Ranger, The Cisco Kid, The Range Rider*), but as of the mid–'50s, her career seems to have pooped out altogether. At last report (1952), she was collaborating with her brother in designing and building Hollywood homes as a business, and working with her brother and father in breeding and marketing rabbits. Like a lot of leading ladies who have dressed up B horror films, McKay wasn't that great as an actress but she was pretty and was always in there pitching. (Often that's enough.)

The *Bowery at Midnight* screenplay (written by Gerald Schnitzer, assistant director of *Black Dragons*) doesn't insult the intelligence the way some of the other Monograms do, but it still leaves plenty of loose ends. Why do felons continue to work for Wagner, knowing full well he's a fickle madman that arbitrarily kills accomplices? What the hell is in Doc Brooks' little medical bag that enables him to bring back life to the dead? Why do the revived "dead men" in Brooks' secret pit act like zombies (Richard Dennison is his old self again in the fadeout scene)? And why don't the police try to save Wagner from the zombies, instead of just watching from only a few feet away as they gang up on him? ("Well, that takes care of the professor!" Detective Crawford smirks, almost before the zombies have even laid a hand on Wagner.) Less importantly, why is there a map of Australia on Wagner's wall, a skull in his private office and a portrait of Mary Shelley in Judy's living room?

You learn, after watching a number of these Monogram films, that there isn't much point in trying to figure these things out; you just have to play along, pick up on what you can, and ignore the rest. *Bowery at Midnight,* for all its lapses of logic, is easy to enjoy; there's even an in-joke moment when the poster for *The Corpse Vanishes* (prominently featuring Lugosi and Joan Barclay) is plainly visible outside a movie theater during a street scene. (Later, one from the East Side Kids' *Mr. Wise Guy,* 1942, can be spotted.) And Gerald Schnitzer's dialogue, like this exchange between Wagner and gunmen Mills and Stratton, can only be described as priceless:

> MILLS *(indicating the mousy Doc Brooks)*: What's the matter with him?
> WAGNER: He's afraid of you – naturally.
> MILLS: That's the way I like it. *(walking menacingly toward Stratton)* What are *you* afraid of?
> STRATTON *(nervously)*: Don't get gay, kid, just because you're handy with the heater!

With *Bowery at Midnight* "in the can," Lugosi left on Sunday, August 23, by train for Chicago, where he starred in a revival of his famed stage success *Dracula* at the Cohan Grand Theatre. (Lugosi was slated for an indefinite run in the play, although his contract with its producers provided for the continuation of his Monogram features with leaves of absence from the stage production.) The opening of the play and the release date of *Bowery at Midnight* were planned to coincide, and Bela was scheduled to make appearances at Windy City movie houses exhibiting this newest horror vehicle. Dubbing Lugosi their Triple-Threat Terrorist, the *Bowery at*

Midnight pressbook played up his simultaneous *Bowery at Midnight*/stage *Dracula*/personal appearances "coup." "With Boris Karloff confining his talents to stage work, the A-1 Horror Man of the films is now Bela Lugosi," the pressbook proclaimed – a statement that Karloff fans (not to mention Lon Chaney, Jr.!) might have cared to dispute. Another Lugosi film opening at about the same time was a featurized version of Bela's Republic serial *S O S Coast Guard*, shot during the '30s horror ban. In it he played the villainous Boroff, a character name which fans have always suspected may have been a contraction of Boris Karloff.

Lugosi fans got an unexpected treat in 1982 if they caught the first episode of NBC's *Late Night with David Letterman*. The A.M. comedy show began with Letterman regular Larry (Bud) Melman looming up from out of the shadows and going into a paraphrase of Edward Van Sloan's opening speech from *Frankenstein* (1931), warning viewers of the "horrifying" events to follow. At the end of the show, Letterman introduced Steve Fessler, "a guy from Brooklyn who for some reason has committed to memory all the dialogue of the two-and-a-half hour classic B film *Bowery at Midnight* starring Bela Lugosi." Fessler came out and launched into a rapid-fire recitation of *Bowery*'s dialogue, playing all the characters, as a smattering of nervous titters rose from the mostly unreceptive audience. The show ended with Fessler still prattling on.

Critics like *Variety*'s Fran couldn't find it in their hearts to say many nice things about Lugosi's newest Monogrammer: "*Bowery at Midnight* is a prime example of how to ruin what might be a fair thriller. Over-writing is the major fault. The basic idea is good enough by 'B' standards, production is fine, cast is good, the direction drags, but the story dissipates by moving through too many by-paths. . . . Cast is okay, with the best chores being turned in by John Berkes, as a cracksman, Ray Miller, as a Bowery bum, and Lugosi." *The Brooklyn Eagle*'s Jane Corby advised her readers that *Bowery* "sure has a corner on terror. Don't go to see it unless you've had your vitamin pills. . . . Not since his portrayal of *Dracula* has Bela Lugosi appeared in finer fettle. He is unforgettable. . . ." *The Hollywood Reporter* also paid it a back-handed compliment or two: "Horror fans will find an offering that should be to their liking in *Bowery at Midnight*. . . . As a fantastic chiller-diller it has its points of popularity and Bela Lugosi in the starring role under capable direction by Wallace Fox. The results are not too good, or too bad for the following that enjoys being frightened."

More recent reviews have been mixed; several modern-day writers consider *Bowery* a semiremake of Lugosi's British film *The Dark Eyes of London*. Judging *Bowery* for its horror content rather than as the gangster picture it is, Arthur Lennig wrote in his Lugosi biography *The Count*, "Most audiences found the film mild and by no means terrifying. It had more plot than characterization, more incident than mood, more explicitness than suggestion." Richard Bojarski (*The Films of Bela Lugosi*) had his qualms, but still seems to have liked it; he wrote, "Worthy of mention was an ending hair-raising enough to give Val Lewton's fright films a run for their money." "The pointlessly convoluted plot seems an end in itself," wrote Don Willis, "as if the mere convolutions were an achievement."

Fangoria's Dr. Cyclops called it "a unique item of B-movie history for two reasons: one, it is a Sam Katzman movie that is watchable, and, two, it is a low-budget Bela Lugosi vehicle that does not embarrass the great horror star and instead actually allows him to perform with a dignified menace." According to Phil Hardy, "[T]his is a distinct cut above the average of Lugosi's later films. . . . It may not make too much sense, but it does have flashes of imagination." *Psychotronic* put it all in a nutshell: "Although it's considered one of the better Monogram films, nobody seems to quite understand the plot."

In standard Monogram fashion, the many questions that viewers might ask themselves about *Bowery at Midnight*'s garbled plot remain stubbornly un-answerable, but the fun is in the not-bad cast, lively pace, seedy flavor and unintentionally humorous moments.

Dead Men Walk
(PRC, 1943)

Released February 14. 63 minutes. Produced by Sigmund Neufeld. Directed by Sam Newfield. Original Screenplay: Fred Myton. Director of Photography: Jack Greenhalgh. Sound Engineer: Hans Weeren. Music: Leo Erdody. Musical Supervisor: David Chudnow. Film Editor: Holbrook N. Todd. Makeup: Harry Ross. Set Designer: Fred Preble. Assistant Director: Melville De Lay. Production Manager: Bert Sternbach.

Cast: George Zucco (Dr. Lloyd Clayton/Dr. Elwyn Clayton), Mary Carlisle (Gayle Clayton), Ned Young (Dr. David Bently), Dwight Frye (Zolarr), Fern Emmett (Kate), Robert Strange (Wilkins), Hal Price (Sheriff), Sam Flint (Minister), Al "Fuzzy" St. John (Villager), Forrest Taylor (The Devil).

> "You creatures of the light—how can you say with absolute certainly what does or does not dwell within the limitless ocean of the night? Are the dark-enshrouded legions of evil naught but figments of the imagination because you in your puny conceit say they cannot exist?"—The Devil (Forrest Taylor)

The most economical of movie monster characters, the vampire requires no elaborate makeup, outlandish rubber suit or costly special effects to achieve. But in the 1940s, Poverty Row, oddly, avoided vampires almost scrupulously. There was talk of them in *Spooks Run Wild* and *Devil Bat's Daughter*, but nary a trace of one in the films. Republic tentatively took the plunge in 1945 with *The Vampire's Ghost*, but they hedged their bet by making it a completely unconventional bloodsucker (John Abbott) who sipped tea and tramped around in Africa's equatorial sun. Ian Keith played a character with vampiric traits in a Republic film of 1946, but there were no dialogue references to vampires and the film was misleadingly titled *Valley of the Zombies*!

It remained for lowly PRC to finally put the vampire on the Poverty Row map with *Dead Men Walk*, an unimaginative thriller starring George Zucco. Even here, though, the vampire does not conform entirely to the legend (the popular Universal-Dracula legend, at any rate). Like Armand Tesla, undead protagonist of Columbia's *The Return of the Vampire* (1943), Elwyn Clayton (Zucco) does not become a bloodsucker through the bite of another, but returns as one after death as a result of his obsession with occult powers. In life, Elwyn had made a hypnotic subject of his niece Gayle (Mary Carlisle), plotting to indoctrinate her into his dark domain. But Elwyn's righteous doctor-brother Lloyd (also Zucco) confronted the madman at the edge of a precipice and, after a fight, pitched his sinister sibling over the brink to his death.

All of this transpired prior to the outset of *Dead Men Walk*, which opens at Elwyn's funeral in a small, obviously Midwestern town. Elwyn's send-off

Above: **A bit tacky even by PRC's standards, the cheap and dullish** *Dead Men Walk* **lacked the grisly verve of other PRC horror productions.**

has gotten a better turnout than the average mad fiend gets, but when the Minister (Sam Flint) asks if the assembled "mourners" would like a last look at the departed, only Lloyd steps forward. As he peers into the box, we get our first glimpse of Elwyn and see that the two are twins. Kate (Fern Emmett), a spinster-ish old woman, wanders into the church and declares that Elwyn was servant of the Devil. Kate's granddaughter was murdered by Elwyn, and Kate's mind has been affected by the tragedy.

Later, outside the vault where Elwyn has now been interred, Lloyd chats with niece Gayle and her boyfriend Dr. David Bently (Ned Young).

> LLOYD: I believe he hated me all his life. After he returned from India, Elwyn was like a man obsessed by a demon. Nothing was sacred to him. He had nothing but contempt for all that decent men hold dear. His mind became a black and evil thing, probing into perverted knowledge of ancient sorcery and demonology.
> DAVID: He must have been insane.
> LLOYD *(defensively)*: We are all quick to call insane any mentality that deviates from the conventional!

Later, Lloyd goes to Elwyn's dark and cluttered house, gathers up some of the sorceror's blasphemous books and papers and burns them in the fireplace. Zolarr (Dwight Frye), Elwyn's hunchbacked servant, catches Lloyd in the act and tries to stop him, but Lloyd hurls him to the floor three-quarters of the way across the room with hardly a touch. "You'll pray for death before you die!" Zolarr growls.

That night, Zolarr uses a cart to wheel Elwyn's coffin out of the crypt and trundle it to an abandoned cemetery nearby. Opening the box reveals a torn and crumpled inside-lid lining and, more impressively, a living-dead Elwyn who rises from the tattered casket. A vampire in death, Elwyn claims his first victim (a young girl asleep in her bedroom) that very night. (Like all incidental victims in vampire films, the girl fails to conform to legend and return as a vampire.)

The next night Elwyn materializes in Lloyd's study and confronts his bewildered brother.

> LLOYD *(muttering to himself in disbelief)*: There was no sign of life in Elwyn's body when it was placed in the vault!
> ELWYN: You'll know that I'm no intangible figment of your imagination when you feel the weight of my hatred. Your life will be a torment. I'll strip you of everything you hold dear before I drag you down to a sordid death.

(A split-screen is utilized at one point in the scene, but mostly the Lloyd-Elwyn confrontations are just an alternating series of medium shots of each Zucco. An over-the-shoulder double is also used.)

Lloyd empties a cheap, misfiring prop gun into the vampire, who laughs and disappears into thin air. Explaining the incident to Gayle and David, who hurry onto the scene, Lloyd alibis that he saw a shadow which he thought might be a burglar. (Holy itchy trigger-finger!)

Elwyn begins a systematic attack on Gayle, lightly feeding on the sleeping girl's blood each night. Lloyd fails to make the connection and begins to treat her for anemia. Gayle complains of nightmares in which she imagines a bat-like creature hovering above her bed (Elwyn is never seen in bat-form). Naturally, these scenes have their full share of the clichéd dialogue ("Where did you get those marks on your neck?") we're all sick to death of hearing. After giving the ailing girl a transfusion, Lloyd sees Elwyn through the window, floating in mid-air outside Gayle's second-story bedroom.

Lloyd isn't sure if Elwyn really exists or if he himself is going crackers, but he finally confides to David that he thinks he has seen his dead brother. When he asks David to accompany him to Elwyn's vault and destroy the body, David is reluctant ("I'd feel like a fool – or worse!"), but goes anyway. The coffin, of course, is gone, but David still isn't buying Lloyd's story.

In the film's most awkwardly staged scene, David tells the Sheriff (Hal Price) that he suspects Lloyd of somehow draining Gayle's blood in an effort to inherit the girl's money. The two men converse while standing just inside the door of the church on a Sunday morning, and remain rooted in the spot even though the gang of extras entering behind them must now squeeze past. One white-bearded extra enters twice.

The simple-minded Kate unexpectedly drops in on Gayle and gives her a cross to wear around her neck at night to avert the vampire's attack. When Lloyd finds Kate in the house, she tells him he must find and destroy Elwyn's body with fire (another departure from the vampire myth). That night, Elwyn steals into Gayle's room once again but the cross on the sleeping girl's throat thwarts the vampire.

David, still convinced that Lloyd is responsible, finally lays into him, promising to kill him if Gayle dies. Lloyd understands David's agitation and invites him to stand vigil in Gayle's room all night, taking most of the wind out of the indignant young doctor's sails. Zolarr, dispatched to the house by Elwyn to relieve Gayle of the cross, is chased downstairs by David. Cornered by Lloyd and David, he remains tight-lipped and quickly manages to get away. To David's shock and amazement, Elwyn materializes in the room, makes another of his stock threatening speeches and vanishes.

The next day, snoopy old Kate finds Elwyn's coffin, with the vampire resting in it, in a vault in the abandoned cemetery. After pausing to make an ill-timed speech, she leaves the vault just as Zolarr is arriving. Zolarr chases her into the woods and breaks her neck (off-screen). That night, fearing that the cemetery will be searched, he transports the coffin to Elwyn's house.

Split-screen shot (notice the dividing line) as vampire George Zucco points an accusing finger at his toupeed twin brother (also Zucco). (From *Dead Men Walk*.)

Capitalizing on local gossip that Lloyd is Kate's killer, Elwyn frames Lloyd by murdering a man on the edge of town and allowing himself to be seen by one of the locals, Wilkins (Robert Strange). Wilkins organizes a mob and storms into Lloyd's house; Lloyd isn't there, so they harass David.

Lloyd, in the meantime, has made a timely decision to search Elwyn's house for clues. Zolarr attacks him when he enters, and in the struggle a heavy pedestal falls on the hunchback, pinning him to the floor. Elwyn enters the fray, physically attacking Lloyd and knocking over a burning candle in the process. Draperies catch fire and soon the two men (and the helpless Zolarr) are surrounded by flames. Lloyd is weakening in Elwyn's iron grip until the first rays of morning sunlight shine through a window, rendering the vampire helpless. As David and the mob watch from outside through a barred window, Elwyn collapses to the floor, the flaming ceiling caves in and all three men are killed.

Drab and ordinary, *Dead Men Walk* is a small-time PRC potboiler utilizing all the stock and static plot elements of the low-budget vampire film. Directed along the lines of least resistance, it has even more of a dashed-off look than most of the other PRC horror films.

There's little that's original in *Dead Men Walk*. The film has a short precredits sequence, a rarity at the time (actor Forrest Taylor, superimposed over a fireplace into which a book titled *History of Vampires* has been tossed, dishes out some spook-talk), but thematically and stylistically it follows the well-traveled low-budget paths. The screenplay is, in fact, a disguised retread of Universal's *Dracula* (1931). Elwyn is Dracula, preying on Gayle (Mina). Lloyd embodies both Prof. Van Helsing and Dr. Seward; Gayle's fiancé David, the John Harker counterpart, remains stubbornly unconvinced about vampires and just gets in the way. Zolarr, of course, is Renfield, a parallel underlined by the fact that Dwight Frye played both roles. Fred Myton, the writer of *Dead Men Walk*, churned out scripts by the bushel-full between 1917 and 1951, mostly Westerns, including the all-black oater *Harlem on the Prairie* and the freakish midget Western *The Terror of Tiny Town* (both 1938). His less-than-illustrious name also graces the writing credits of *The Mad Monster, The Black Raven* (1943) and *Nabonga* (1944).

What the film does have going for it is George Zucco, whose hamming gives color to the role of the undead Elwyn Clayton. Leering, his voice dripping with sadistic satisfaction, spouting the overwritten dialogue with relish, Zucco is delightfully old-fashioned and unrestrained in his melodramatic acting. Zucco is less effective as brother Lloyd, purposefully underplaying the role; Lloyd at least has more hair, thanks to a toupee that looks pretty good on Zucco. The premise of a vampire at large in an American small town is appealing (turning up the same year in Universal's *Son of Dracula* and 15 years later in *The Return of Dracula*), but both Zuccos seem entirely out of place within this setting. Staunch Briton Lloyd and worldly vampire Elwyn are like fish out of water in a Middle American milieu replete with cracker-barrel hicks and bearded, Amish-looking extras.

Most of the other characters are barely sketched, and fall prey to all the usual clichés and formula predicaments. Gimlet-eyed Ned Young joins the procession of ho-hum (4-F?) leading men in PRC's horror films, playing his perfunctory role with conviction but little personality. Horror fans probably remember him better as the boozy Leon, assistant to maimed sculptor Vincent Price, in Warners' 3-D *House of Wax* (1953). That same year, 1953, Young (who was by then an actor/film writer) was placed on the Hollywood blacklist for refusing to testify before a Congressional committee as to his alleged knowledge of Commie activity in Hollywood. Blackballed, he went to work as a bartender and then, a few years later, used the pseudonym Nathan E. Douglas to write a script "on spec." The resulting picture — Stanley Kramer's *The Defiant Ones* (1958) — won "Douglas" and collaborator Harold Jacob Smith an Academy Award. The "Douglas"/Smith screenplay for Kramer's *Inherit the Wind* (1960) was also Oscar-nominated. Young died of a heart attack in 1968.

Pretty Mary Carlisle swoons and looks frightened, as expected of a heroine caught up in this type of melodramatic folderol. Earlier seen in the futuristic fantasy *Men Must Fight* (1933) as well as in *One Frightened Night*

(1935) and *Beware Spooks* (1939), she harbors no illusions about having worked at PRC. Talking to Don Leifert in *Filmfax*, she recounted that

> There was little time for lighting and rehearsing. Everything was different [from working in an A picture]. On an A picture, a designer designs the wardrobe. At PRC, we'd go to wardrobe and pick out something that had already been worn two or three times on other pictures. It was the difference between buying a diamond at Tiffany's or a little unknown place; it was the difference between a Rolls-Royce and a Ford. We'd shoot a picture at PRC in anywhere from ten days to two weeks. They were quickie B's.

Carlisle went on to say that George Zucco could not have been a nicer man. *Dead Men Walk* was her final film.

Most of the supporting performances are lacking, with spinster-type Fern Emmett as the addled Kate probably coming off the worst. Bringing to bear all the vampire lore she picked up when she appeared in Majestic's *The Vampire Bat* (1933), Emmett's is the one character with a sense of what's going on, but the other characters regard her as a pest. Robert Strange, a seedy, citified actor with scores of credits (including horror films *The Walking Dead*, 1936, and *The Mad Monster* and serials *Adventures of Captain Marvel*, 1941, and *Perils of Nyoka*, 1942) is badly miscast as a cantankerous rube in a comically crumpled hat. (The film's credits list him as playing Harper, but in the film he's called Wilkins.) Al "Fuzzy" St. John, a silent screen buffoon-cum-B Western sidekick, has a hammy and unfunny bit as one of the frightened townsmen.

The real surprise in *Dead Men Walk* is finding how greatly aged Dwight Frye looks as the humpbacked Zolarr: the tired and bloated Frye is a far cry from the baby-faced gangster and goon characters he played in '30s films. Plugging away day and night during wartime (by day as an actor, at night as a graveyard-shift tool designer at the Douglas Aircraft plant in Los Angeles), Frye kept from his family the knowledge that he suffered several mild heart attacks at the plant; an ardent Christian Scientist, he refused to see a doctor. By November, 1943, seven months after the release of *Dead Men Walk*, he was dead.

(Through what seems like divine intervention, Hollywood was never without a ghoulish Frye-type for their horror films. Frye ruled the graveyard roost from 1930 until his death in 1943, when the pockmarked, emaciated Skelton Knaggs made his horror debut in Val Lewton's *The Ghost Ship*. Knaggs turned up in many horror films between 1943 and his death [cirrhosis of the liver] in 1955 – the year Reggie Nalder had his first prominent role, as the assassin in Hitchcock's *The Man Who Knew Too Much*. Nalder carried the baton until his recent death. Next?)

Frye gives his all to the demeaning hunchback role in *Dead Men Walk*,

It looks like curtains for leading lady Mary Carlisle as the demented Dwight Frye
closes in on her in a publicity photo from *Dead Men Walk* (a.k.a. *Creature of the
Devil*). Frye, not in good health, looks awful for a man of 43.

his next-to-last horror film (only *Frankenstein Meets the Wolf Man* followed,
with Frye in a bit). Dressed like a cat burglar, his hair combed into an unflattering widow's peak, he spews his vitriolic dialogue with aplomb and
trundles Elwyn's coffin around like the professional grave-robber that (in
the movies) he was. As usual for Frye, it isn't much of a performance, but
seeing him reprising his Renfield role (replete with a Fritz-type humped
back) brings back cozy nostalgic memories of *Dracula* and *Frankenstein*.
Interviewed by John Antosiewicz and Charlie Rizzo in *Midnight Marquee*,
Dwight Frye, Jr., provided a handful of Frye, Sr., anecdotes, revealing
(none too surprisingly) that his father was unhappy with the way his career
had developed.

> There was in the latter years of his life a lot of discouragement. He'd
> gotten, unfortunately, into this mold of playing horror characters with
> lots of makeup or playing Nazis during the War or playing gangsters
> in the mid–1930s. He got typed and not until just before he died did he
> have the possibility of breaking out of type. . . . The unfortunate and
> ironic thing was that when he was in New York originally from 1922 to

1928, he was a big star on the stage playing musicals, comedies and all kinds of light stuff. The moment he went to California that all stopped and he never got the chance to do that sort of thing again.

Throughout the interview Frye, Jr., not a horror or even a film fan, continued to express surprise that anybody would remember or care about his dad. Like many of the PRC directors, Sam Newfield was mindful only of watching the clock and keeping costs low. Newfield does establish a dark, unhealthy atmosphere, but he fails to extract the full measure of suspense from scenes. The film's few action sequences are badly handled. Kate's murder could have been done with some style, but all we get to see is Kate running into the woods and Zolarr, trotting like he has a load in his pants, hurrying after her as the screen fades to black. Lloyd's hand-to-hand battle with Zolarr is intercut with shots of Wilkins and the mob languidly pacing around Lloyd's house. Even the climactic fight between Lloyd and Elwyn is poorly staged, with Zucco and a bald-wigged double, locked in "battle," lazily rocking from side to side in unison amidst the flames.

Continuity, that B-picture bugaboo, is once again sacrificed on the low-budget altar. In the transfusion scene, Lloyd's eyeglasses appear and disappear from his nose from shot to shot. One bearded extra enters the church twice during David's conversation with the sheriff. Elwyn's coffin is a half-couch in some scenes and a full-open in others. And the same footage of Zolarr wheeling Elwyn's coffin around is shown twice, once normally and the other time "flipped" left-for-right.

There are minor compensations for fans with soft spots for these cheaper films. Both Elwyn Clayton and the Devil, seen in that precredits bit, are eerily lit to good effect, and Jack Greenhalgh's lensing is persuasive in lending a gray dankness to Fred Preble's sets. There are a few nice subjective shots of Elwyn and a similar shot of Zolarr during his fight with Lloyd. A full quota of laughable dialogue is also helpful in getting the non-discriminating viewer through the picture.

Overall, however, *Dead Men Walk* lacks momentum and potent shock value. Scenes end when the dialogue runs out, and the film takes its time fading to black as the speakers now stand nervously about. Even at 63 minutes, the film is padded, like the useless footage that's spent watching Lloyd search the abandoned cemetery *after* Zolarr has carted the coffin away. Leo Erdody's music is the usual tuneless collection of dreary motifs, frequently not in concert with the level of action being seen on the screen.

Dead Men Walk was filmed in a six day stretch that began Friday, September 11, 1942, and was released five months later; unfavorable reviews were soon forthcoming. According to *Variety*'s Rose, the film "fails to ring the bell as a horror story. Its suspenseful moments are few and far between; the direction mediocre and the acting ditto. . . . Script offered several possibilities, which, however, were not realized, due chiefly to direc-

tor Sam Newfield's failure to inject proper punch and excitement in development of yarn." The *Motion Picture Exhibitor* wrote it up as "one of the best
vampire pictures since *Dracula.*" Wanda Hale of *The New York Daily News*
gave the film two stars, writing that, "If *Dead Men Walk* is a horror film,
it has a deficiency in its blood-curdling capacity.... It won't frighten you;
the distance between the sinister aspects is too long to create holding
suspense."

Even the usually lenient *Hollywood Reporter* took the gloves off. In a
review titled *"Dead Men Walk* Bad Even for Horror Film," an unnamed
critic grumbled, "Well, if there must be horror pictures – and there seems
no escaping them – here is a dilly. Almost everything about it is horrible, including the direction, production, story, dialogue, etc., etc. . . . George Zucco
was obviously unhappy about the whole thing. Mary Carlisle, blessed with
the only legitimate lines in the piece, stands out brightly. The rest is pretty
much a ham holiday. . . . The photographer had an easy time. All he had to
do was turn out the lights and start his cameras. The electricity bill for set
lighting was practically nil. So is the whole affair."

More recently, *Fangoria's* Dr. Cyclops wrote, "The movie's story doesn't
offer any surprises, but director Newfield managed a couple of spooky
touches while cranking out the picture in record time, and Zucco and Frye
give it their all." *The Phantom's Ultimate Video Guide* joshed, "It's Mondo
Zucco time as George gets to portray twin brothers. . . . The movie's typical
but fun." "Only one dead man walks," John Cocchi correctly points out in
Second Feature: The Best of the "B" Films, adding that the film was a "good
reworking of an old tale, and one of PRC's best." One man's treasure is
another man's trash: *Photon's* Ron Borst scoffed, "PRC's only attempt at
making a vampire film is a disastrous flop." An uncharacteristically terse
William K. Everson also wrote it off as "a disaster." Don Willis chimed in,
"A leading candidate for dullest vampire movie of the Forties."

Coasting on the presence of horror stars George Zucco and Dwight
Frye in principal roles, *Dead Men Walk* is a small-time vampire film, too
familiar to generate the proper interest, too slack to achieve the desired
effects. Zucco gets highway mileage out of his deep-dyed villainous role and
the film gives us one last look at poor, dying Dwight Frye in his accustomed
graveyard milieu, but these are doubtful charms for the uninitiated. *Dead
Men Walk* is hackneyed and obvious.

The Ape Man
(Monogram, 1943)

Released March 19. 64 minutes. Associate Producer: Barney A. Sarecky. Produced by Sam Katzman and Jack Dietz (Banner Productions). Directed by William

THE APE MAN   103

Beaudine. Screenplay: Barney A. Sarecky. Original Story ("They Creep in the
Dark"): Karl Brown. Director of Photography: Mack Stengler. Assistant Director:
Arthur Hammond. Film Editor: Carl Pierson. Art Director: David Milton. Sound:
Glen Glenn. Musical Director: Edward Kay.
    Cast: Bela Lugosi (Dr. James Brewster), Louise Currie (Billie Mason), Wallace
Ford (Jeff Carter), Henry Hall (Dr. George Randall), Minerva Urecal (Agatha
Brewster), Emil Van Horn (The Ape), J. Farrell MacDonald (Police Captain),
Wheeler Oakman (Brady), Ralph Littlefield (Zippo), Jack Mulhall (Reporter), Charles
Jordan (O'Toole), George Kirby (Townsend, the Butler), Charles Hall (Barney, the
Photographer), Ray Miller (Detective), Sunshine Sammy Morrison (Office Boy).

"Bela Lugosi seemed to enjoy doing this kind of work,
or I don't know whether he'd have done it; I think he was
a fine actor. But once you start playing those kinds of
roles, I suppose you're kind of stuck with it. Also, he did
definitely have a heavy accent, but the kinds of parts he
played, he didn't *need* to speak perfect English.
(Sometimes he didn't need to *speak!*) But he was an interesting man and certainly did a brilliant job on *The
Ape Man*. He took it so seriously, he really wanted it to
be believable, and I think it definitely was. His wife was
around, too, and she was a very lovely, educated lady. It
all seemed so strange, that they had such a wonderful
marriage and nice home life, and here he was portray-
ing mad scientists and voodoo men and apes!" — Louise
Currie

"Those who scream easily when a sliding panel moves
aside, and when a gent arrayed in an ape's fur coat carries off the heroine, will probably find this just their dish
of horror gruel. Others will concede it to be hilarious
burlesque. Producers of the venture probably had a few
doubts themselves, for they've spotted a nitwit character who roams through the piece and, at the finale, faces
the camera, admits the idea is nuts and reveals himself
as the 'author.'" — *The Hollywood Reporter*.

    Boris Karloff always used to call him Poor Bela, and nobody ever needed
to ask why. Sometimes Bela Lugosi just couldn't win for losing, and
everyone knew it. Put yourself in his penny loafers during the winter of
1942–43, while on the set of *The Ape Man*. You've only just finished playing
the Frankenstein Monster in *Frankenstein Meets the Wolf Man*. That's a
character you had refused to play in 1931; it was a mute character, and
beneath you—then. But just last month you were reduced to playing the
same damn thing. (You can console yourself, though: At least in this new
Frankenstein picture, *your* Monster gets to *talk!*)

Now you're covered with crepe hair and running around cheap Monogram sets alongside a guy in a gorilla suit. A few miles to the north, Universal is about to shoot the sequel to *Dracula* (1931), a follow-up you've waited
a dozen years for them to get around to. *Son of Dracula* is starting in about
three weeks and, oh, by the way, you're not going to be in it. They didn't
even ask you. . .

The folks at Monogram never forget you: On November 4, 1942, Sam
Katzman and Jack Dietz proudly proclaimed in the trades that the next film
in their continuing Lugosi/Monogram series would be entitled *The Gorilla
Strikes*. (Without wishing to hint at cause and effect, the very next day, on
the set of *Frankenstein Meets the Wolf Man*, Lugosi collapsed!*) On December 16, it was announced in the pages of *The Hollywood Reporter* that
Lugosi's costars in the ape opus (by now already retitled *The Ape Man*)
would be Wallace Ford and Amelita Ward. Production got underway that
same day; but it was Louise Currie and not Ward who shrieked and swooned
in Lugosi's hairy clutches. (Coincidentally, Universal's initial Ape Woman
film, *Captive Wild Woman*, with John Carradine and Acquanetta, was in
production at exactly the same time as *The Ape Man*. Amelita Ward, the
initially announced leading lady of *The Ape Man*, didn't get off scot-free;
she ended up in Universal's third Ape Woman film, *The Jungle Captive*,
1945.)

The script of *The Ape Man*, penned by associate producer Barney
Sarecky, took several plot elements from the earlier Monogram film *The
Ape*. *The Ape* had Boris Karloff as a nutty country doctor who donned the
pelt of an escaped circus ape, killing locals and siphoning off their spinal
fluid; this he injected into a crippled girl (Maris Wrixon) hoping to cure her
paralysis. In *The Ape Man*, Lugosi is Dr. James Brewster, a famous gland
expert experimenting with the spinal fluid of an ape. Aided by his colleague
Dr. George Randall (Henry Hall, the sheriff in *The Ape*), Brewster made an
astounding discovery which prompted him to inject himself with the ape's
spinal fluid. What the hoped-for results would have been, we're never told;
what happens is that Brewster becomes covered with hair, and takes on the
stance, walk and (occasionally) the feral instincts of a gorilla. (The simian
makeup, and the performance, are a bit remindful of Lugosi's earlier ape-
man portrayal in Paramount's *Island of Lost Souls*, 1933.) When Brewster
gets it into his hairy head that the spinal fluid of humans will cure him, the
fun begins.

The film opens at a busy city pier at dawn. Agatha Brewster (Minerva
Urecal), James' sister and a noted expert on ghosts, is returning from

---

It just wasn't a good day on the Frankenstein Meets the Wolf Man *set in general. Aside
from Lugosi's collapse, which was probably brought on by exhaustion (the Frankenstein
makeup and accessories that the actor was toting around weighed 35 lbs.), a coach ran over
the foot of actress Maria Ouspenskaya, fracturing her ankle.*

Poster art for Monogram's *The Ape Man*. Notice Louise Currie's Little Black Sambo broach.

Europe by boat in response to an urgent cable from Dr. Randall: James has vanished. Meeting her at the boat, Randall explains that his cable didn't tell the whole story:

> RANDALL: Agatha, Jim isn't lost, except to *this* world. He's hidden away at Springdale, in the old mansion. He'd be better off in the family cemetery plot...

Randall drives Agatha to the mansion, and together they pass through a secret doorway hidden behind a fireplace and descend into the basement laboratory. There, Randall opens a sliding wall panel, revealing the barred door of a cell in which an ape (Emil Van Horn) and a man are sleeping. The man, wakened from his nap, is James Brewster; his face (and, we assume, his entire body, underneath his clothes) are covered with hair, his posture stooped and ape-like. ("Oh, you poor boy," Urecal gasps at the sixtyish Lugosi.) Nobody feels sorrier about all this than Brewster, who bellyaches bitterly ("What a mess I made of things..."). He tells Agatha that he locks himself in the cage with the simian when he fears that his animal instincts are taking over his mind. Later, alone with her, he mentions that spinal fluid taken from a living human might counteract the ape fluid injection and return him to normalcy, but that Dr. Randall has obstinately refused to cooperate in that experiment. Agatha confronts Randall, who explains that to take a person's spinal fluid would cause their instant death.

Jeff Carter (Wallace Ford), ace newspaper reporter, and his new photographer Billie Mason (Louise Currie) arrive at the Brewster house to get a story on ghost-hunter Agatha's recent tour of haunted castles in Europe. Approaching the house, they hear the screams of Brewster's ape emanating from the cellar lab. Agatha grants them an interview, and talks about the personality traits of ghosts. When Billie takes a photograph of Agatha, Dr. Brewster, surreptitiously peering through a window into the room, is also captured on film.

Later, Brewster's brutal animal instincts come to the fore. After tossing some beakers around the lab, he releases his simian pal from its cell and the two steal out of the house. Arriving at Dr. Randall's home, Brewster climbs in through a window and argues with his former friend. A dumb detective (Ray Miller) arrives at the house, and Randall confers with him in private. Seizing the opportunity, Brewster rings for Randall's butler (George Kirby). (The butler looks a little like Alfred Hitchcock, the closest thing to a touch of class in the picture.) When the butler enters, Brewster accosts him, forcing the unsuspecting servant to walk backwards into the waiting arms of the ape. The butler is quietly strangled and Brewster uses a hypodermic needle to draw off the dead man's spinal fluid.

Brewster returns home grinning ear to ear and shows the little bottle of spinal fluid to Agatha, commanding her to call Randall and "tell him he's wanted–in *sur-ger-eee!*" When the angry Randall arrives and refuses to help, Agatha pulls a gun and forces him to inject her brother with the spinal fluid. Apparently cured, Brewster manages to straighten up and walk naturally. (The hair doesn't vanish from his face and hands, but this doesn't seem to bother him.)

Incidentally, a comedy relief character, Zippo (Ralph Littlefield), has been turning up at odd moments and imparting tips and little bits of information to Jeff Carter: He was at the boat, and now he's hanging around outside the Brewster house, watching everything that goes on through a ground-level laboratory window.

After Randall leaves, Brewster finds that the cure was only temporary when he suddenly returns to his hunched-over posture. Together with the ape, Brewster goes into the sleeping city and begins a murder spree, attacking a milkman, a store owner and a girl in her bed. When another young woman walks in the direction of the waiting-in-ambush ape man, Zippo appears, turns her around and hustles her the opposite way.

Triumphantly returning to his lab with a larger bottle of spinal fluid, Brewster exults that repeated dosages will surely effect a cure, but Dr. Randall, contacted by phone, adamantly refuses to come over and administer the injections. Furious, Brewster hurries to Randall's and begins to throttle the startled scientist, who finally agrees. But when Brewster relaxes his grip, Randall seizes the bottle of spinal fluid and dashes it to the floor. Outraged, Brewster attacks him a second time and chokes him to death. Brewster gets away while Agatha and the police arrive almost simultaneously; Agatha is taken in for questioning.

Throughout the film, Jeff and Billie have suspected that odd things are going on in the Brewster house. When Brewster's hairy, snooping face shows up in the photograph that Billie took, Jeff decides to sneak out to the house and do a bit of undercover investigating. Billie gets the same idea, and the two are slinking around the shadowy mansion at the same time. Billie doesn't know that the second skulker is Jeff (she also doesn't know that it isn't someone who lives there!) and she knocks out the lurking figure with an urn. Brewster seizes her and carries the unconscious girl down through the opening fireplace and into his lab, where he intends to extract her spinal fluid. But Billie revives and a fight ensues. Billie accidentally pulls a lever which opens the door to the ape's cage, and the ape surges forth angrily, attacking Brewster. The ape breaks its master's back and then lopes murderously after Billie. But at the last possible moment, Jeff and some newly-arrived policemen force Agatha to open the secret fireplace. Billie rushes through to safety and the rampaging ape is shot to death by the lawmen.

Leaving the house, Jeff and Billie find Zippo sitting in Jeff's convertible. Jeff, at the end of his patience, finally asks him who he is, and Zippo replies casually, *"Me?* Oh, I'm the author of the story." Then he turns to face the camera — "Screwy idea, wasn't it?" — as he rolls up the car window, upon which is written THE END.

The Ape Man is frequently cited as being Bela Lugosi's most demeaning film role, which might be true. (It's also often called the worst of *all* his films, which couldn't be more *un*true.) It's actually one of Lugosi's livelier and most entertaining Monograms, even though the Jekyll-and-Hyde plot is embarrassingly flimsy and characters barely sketched.

It might not have been dignified work for Lugosi, but at least the aging character star (just turned 60) was earning money and keeping busy, and probably just glad for the steady employment. Of course it's he who has to

Bela Lugosi, the actor too proud to wear the monster makeup in *Frankenstein* (1931), looks like he's ready to cry in this portrait shot from *The Ape Man.*

carry the film almost single-handedly, alternating between playing a whiner and a mad killer. Lugosi's Dr. Brewster is more than a little irritating in his kvetching moods: complaining, moaning, raising and dropping his arms to his sides in helpless exasperation. Unspeakably selfish, he'd rather kill a half dozen or so people than to endure a lifetime of poor posture; surely the application of a razor would get rid of all that unwanted hair faster than spinal fluid injections would. Even when Dr. Randall calmly tries to talk some sense into him, Brewster remains arrogant and bloodthirsty:

> RANDALL: Do you realize what you're asking me to do? Murder!
> BREWSTER: Ooh, call it vot you like!

A nervy, self-involved jerk, Brewster loses our sympathy after only a few minutes on screen. (Lugosi lurches around in a side-to-side manner, apparently trying to approximate the gait of an ape, but he looks more like a penguin. The tailcoat he wears even adds to that penguiny effect.)

The Ape Man expects its audience to believe that the killer Brewster is a sort of Mr. Hyde, acting on those "animal instincts" that Brewster keeps fretting about; perhaps the idea was to create a Larry Talbot-type character. (Like Talbot, Brewster on one occasion asks to be locked up so that he cannot harm anyone.) But again, as with *Bowery at Midnight*, the dichotomy isn't there. Even when Brewster is supposedly "himself," he's constantly talking murder, or at least counting upon getting the spinal fluid which he knows can only be procured at the cost of human life. (Scenes of Lugosi "shooting up" make for grim viewing, in light of later real-life developments.) But at least when Brewster is in these spiteful, selfish moods, Lugosi gets to chew the scenery a bit, spouting the dialogue with relish and doing all the dramatically bombastic little bits of business which make him Bela Lugosi. His menace and presence in these scenes enhance the film, raising it from the level of a tawdry potboiler to the slightly higher level of a tawdry potboiler with camp and star values.

Lugosi will always have his detractors, but it's tough to imagine who would have filled the bill in movies like *The Ape Man* if Lugosi hadn't been around to do them. Even when he's not at his best, he gives these quickies a great deal of color; the roles are tailor-made for his sinister personality, and few other actors had what it takes to elevate these measly pictures the way Lugosi did. The world of low-budget horror films became a much poorer place once they didn't have Poor Bela to kick around anymore.

Emil Van Horn is another one of those "actors," like Charles Gemora or Steve Calvert, whose name calls to mind the image of an ape or a monster rather than a human face. Van Horn hops and growls and flails in the best movie-ape tradition; Lugosi even talks to him in a whispered gobbledygook language in a scene or two, reminiscent of his *tête-à-têtes* with Erik the ape (Gemora) in *Murders in the Rue Morgue* (1932). Van Horn and his pretty-good ape suit are also seen in *Never Give a Sucker an Even Break*, *Keep 'Em Flying* (both 1941), *Ice-Capades Revue* (1942), *Sleepy Lagoon* (1943) and in the Republic serial *Perils of Nyoka* (1942), where he played Satan, the chained and perpetually outraged pet of the villainess Vultura (Lorna Gray). (Pulling down $300 a week for *Nyoka*, Van Horn was the serial's second highest-paid player, taking a back seat only to $350-a-week stuntman Dave Sharpe.)

According to the late Calvin Beck's book *Scream Queens*, Van Horn and his hairy costume had a beauty-and-the-beast night club act until the costume was stolen, leading to unemployment and an eviction from his apartment in Pensacola, Florida. After that, according to Beck, "he took to living in the streets in New Orleans' French Quarter while doing bit roles

in films shot on location in New Orleans, such as *Hotel"* (1967). Van Horn
shuffled off life's stage in the late '60s at New Orleans Charity Hospital.
Minerva Urecal tries to milk some sympathy out of the character of the
eccentric ghost-hunter Agatha. (Somebody should have changed her
character name when they found out Lugosi couldn't pronounce it!) The actress wrings her hands and frets constantly over Lugosi's misfortune, but
her silence to the police makes her an accomplice in Lugosi's murder spree,
and equally guilty for his poorly motivated crimes. Her "big moment" in the
picture is when she makes her speech about ghosts –

> AGATHA: Most spirits are honest, gentle and kind. . . . But a few are evil.
> And having been wicked in life, are wicked in death, and only haunt
> the scenes of desperate crimes, revelling in *murder!*

– but Urecal is hammy in the scene, which is poorly lit and photographed;
in fact, it's hard to tell if the filmmakers meant for it to be creepy or funny.
What it is, is dull. Scenes of Lugosi (stooped over in his tatty tailcoat) and
Urecal (middle-aged, dumpy) bickering in the lab might easily be mistaken
at a quick glance for a Groucho Marx picture with Margaret Dumont.

Neither Wallace Ford nor Louise Currie get to do much acting; almost
all of their dialogue is directed at each other. It isn't a relationship, just a
succession of wisecracks, as Currie taunts Ford about his age and Ford
belittles her for being a woman. Neither of them says a word to Lugosi at
any point. The very attractive Currie appeared three times with Lugosi, in
The Ape Man and *Voodoo Man* as well as playing an unbilled but highly visible part in RKO's *You'll Find Out* (1940); most of her fans remember her
best for her serial appearances, *Adventures of Captain Marvel* (1941) and
The Masked Marvel (1943). Long-retired from the picture business, she
looks back on the hectic pace of B movies like *The Ape Man* with great
fondness:

> I did several films at Monogram, and the people in charge paid me quite
> a compliment – they told me, "You are the Katharine Hepburn of
> Monogram." Which I felt was very flattering! But it *was* a really low-
> budget studio – in fact, I remember that I wore my own clothes in all my
> Monogram movies, because they really didn't have what you'd call a
> wardrobe department the way all the larger studios did. If they had sup-
> plied my clothes for these pictures, they would have been so terrible!

One of Lugosi's most frequent on-screen antagonists, Wallace Ford ran
up against Bela not only in *The Ape Man* but also in *Night of Terror* (1933)
and *The Mysterious Mr. Wong* (1935); additionally, he was a hero in Tod
Browning's *Freaks* (1932), *The Mummy's Hand* (1940), *The Mummy's Tomb*
(1942) and some spooky B mysteries. Born in 1898 in England (his real name

was Samuel Jones), he was abandoned by his destitute mom and wound up at a boys' home in Canada. There he was adopted by a woman who lived with her husband and son near Ingelow, Manitoba. "They didn't want to adopt a child, they wanted a slave – a child slave," he later commented. "One that they could abuse and beat and keep as ignorant as a pig."

Doing farm labor from dawn to dusk, and with the occasional flogging tossed in for variety, he met an itinerant farm worker named Wallace Ford, well-educated but a born hobo. When Jones tired of farm life he ran away, working an assortment of odd jobs and re-encountering the "gentleman bum" Ford. They worked together in Iowa at all kinds of jobs (harvesters, dish washers, etc.) until Ford learned that his mother was dying in Sioux City. The two jumped a freight train but during the journey Ford fell between the wheels and was killed. Jones continued on to the home of his friend's mother, who had passed away already anyway. Jones decided to adopt his dead friend's name.

Acting-wise, he started in stock, debuted on Broadway in 1919 and began appearing in films in the early talkie era. In the mid–'30s he went back to his native England to make some films, and in 1936 he found his natural mother living in an old circus wagon along the Thames, married to a blind matchseller(!). Returning to the States, Ford appeared again on Broadway (as George in *Of Mice and Men*), made scads more movies and even plenty of television (he was a regular on *The Deputy* in 1959–60; Henry Fonda narrated and occasionally appeared on the NBC series). Wallace Ford died of heart disease on June 11, 1966. (After he died, his young nephew contacted *Famous Monsters* and told Forrest Ackerman that Ford often read *FM* and was disappointed that he wasn't mentioned more often.) According to Louise Currie, "Wallace Ford was very nice, a very special man to work with. He was an actor who had been around and working a lot longer than I had, but he was very helpful and cooperative. He made things easy and fun."

As usual in a William Beaudine picture, the players seem to be completely on their own. Photographically, there is one clever moment (easy to miss) when Lugosi is carrying Louise Currie down into the lab: The panning camera passes and briefly photographs them through a giant beaker which distorts their image. (In the '50s, this little visual trick was run into the ground by SF director Nathan Juran.) The budget on *The Ape Man* was so scant that even simple rear-projection was apparently beyond the filmmakers' means. To keep costs low in a scene of Ford and Currie driving, the camera hovers above the hood of Ford's convertible and shoots down at the players as they talk. The inclusion of the Zippo character gives us a pretty good idea what the Monogram screenwriters thought of the film (and of its audience).

A few writers have conjectured that the *Ape Man* story might have initially been intended for Boris Karloff during his Columbia "Mad Doctor"

To Bela Lugosi (center) and Emil Van Horn, Monogram producer Jack Dietz (left) looks funny. Behind-the-scenes monkey business from *The Ape Man.*

series. The original story of *The Ape Man* was written by Karl Brown, who penned the Columbia Karloffs *The Man They Could Not Hang* (1939) and *The Man with Nine Lives* (1940); he even cowrote the original story of *Before I Hang* (1940). Also, the Ape Man's character name, James Brewster, seems to be a takeoff on Karloff's *Arsenic and Old Lace* stage role of Jonathan Brewster (what an inappropriate character name for Lugosi!). The evidence is pretty flimsy and the whole theory easy to write off, but they *are* odd coincidences.

Like Lugosi himself, the string of characters he played never profited from past mistakes; they should have known not to monkey with apes. In *Murders in the Rue Morgue*, Lugosi's Dr. Mirakle kept an ape which he talked to, and utilized it to kill people the way he does in *The Ape Man*. But this ape, too, got fed up with Lugosi's hamming and broke his back without much provocation. A human but ape-like henchman (Wilfred Walter) in *The Human Monster* (1940) chucked him into quicksand; a Neanderthal ape man (Frank Moran) gave his backbone yet another working-over in *Return of the Ape Man*. More apes (Art Miles and Steve Calvert, respectively) figured into *The Gorilla* (1939) and *Bela Lugosi Meets a Brooklyn Gorilla* (1952); Lugosi even got outsmarted and knocked out by a plain ol' monkey in *Zombies on*

Broadway (1945). In fact, just about the only horror film where Lugosi didn't die at the end, *Island of Lost Souls*, is the one where he *was* a gorilla! The critics had a field day picking apart *The Ape Man*. *Variety* opined, "*The Ape Man* [is] good for laughs which aren't in the script.... Bela Lugosi, rigged out in a shaggy beard and formal morning attire, ambling like an ape and sharing a cage with a gorilla, scares nobody.... Lugosi seems somewhat bewildered and bemused by his role and acts accordingly. As for Wallace Ford and Louise Currie, they offer outmoded impersonations of the fourth estate ... Direction n.g." *The Daily News* contributed this wreath: "Monogram's writer didn't have to wipe the dust from Bela Lugosi's *Ape Man*; he had to rake the mould off." *The Hollywood Reporter* had an understandably patronizing attitude toward its star, writing, "Bela Lugosi, in a 'horrible' makeup, gives another of the performances that addicts of the gruesome expect of him and applaud."

More recent appraisals have been mixed, with open-minded fans getting a bang out of the film's ineptness and Bela boosters seeing it as a personal affront to The Great Lugosi. Predictably, it apppealed hugely to *Psychotronic* ("An unbeatable combination: Beaudine and Lugosi! ... Great stuff!"); just as predictably, Lugosi biographer Arthur Lennig was appalled, calling the film "abominable.... Lugosi is simply lost in the stupidity of it all." *The New York Times*, of all places, reviewed it when it came out on video: "This unscary Lugosi horror vehicle is probably of interest only to the kind of fans who wear Dracula capes to bed at night.... Despite Lugosi's inappropriately passionate performance, the movie isn't quite campy enough to be entertaining."

Don Leifert (*Filmfax*) wrote that Lugosi "fared well considering the script limitations and the uninspired direction of William Beaudine.... Considering all that was working against him, Lugosi played the role like the seasoned professional that he was." Dr. Cyclops, *Fangoria*'s video maven, agreed: "He is compelled to mope around in a slouched monkey-walk, and wear a makeup of long hair and a beard which is supposed to give you the idea that he is part simian. Somehow, Lugosi manages to get by with a certain amount of style." According to Phil Hardy, "As directed by 'One-Shot' Beaudine, staged in cardboard sets, and overacted by all concerned with an element of self-mockery that doesn't quite make the grade, it is almost worthy of the Theatre of the Absurd." The humorless Leslie Halliwell branded *The Ape Man* "cheap rubbish shot in a couple of corners and offering no thrill whatever." (In Halliwell's England, the film was released as *Lock Your Doors*.)

At least one person was frightened by *The Ape Man*, according to Louise Currie:

> After *The Ape Man* was finished, I did go to see a preview and I took my son with me—and he told me in later years that it scared him so

much! He was six or seven when he saw *The Ape Man* and he had dreams for many years, of the ape capturing his mother! Of course, I couldn't imagine that he'd have that kind of reaction – I was right there with him as he was watching it, so obviously the ape didn't "get" me. But he vividly remembered the ape chasing his mother, and it left him with terrible dreams that had him waking up screaming for years!

Crudely dashed together and maladroitly plotted, *The Ape Man* does represent a low ebb in Lugosi's career, but its notorious reputation grows partly from the fact that it's one of the most enjoyable and popular of Lugosi's many bad films. Lugosi made many films (and serials) that were far worse than *The Ape Man*, no one but the staunchest Lugosi devotee subjects himself to such unwatchable dreck as *Murder by Television* (1935), *Shadow of Chinatown* (1936), *Scared to Death* (1947) and *Glen or Glenda?* (1953). Filled with incident and unintentional humor, *The Ape Man* has attracted horror buffs, general film fans, the "camp" crowd, worst-films festival organizers and public domain videotape peddlers by the carload. It's a Golden Turkey of the most beloved kind.

Ghosts on the Loose
(Monogram, 1943)

Released July 30. 63 minutes. Associate Producer: Barney Sarecky. Produced by Sam Katzman and Jack Dietz (Banner Productions). Directed by William Beaudine. Original Screenplay: Kenneth Higgins. Photography: Mack Stengler. Assistant Director: Arthur Hammond. Film Editor: Carl Pierson. Musical Director: Edward J. Kay. Set Designer: Dave Milton. Sound Engineer: Glen Glenn.

   Cast: Leo Gorcey (Mugs McGinnis), Huntz Hall (Glimpy Williams), Bobby Jordan (Danny), Bela Lugosi (Emil), Ava Gardner (Betty Williams Gibson), Rick Vallin (Jack Gibson), Sammy Morrison (Scruno), Billy Benedict (Benny), Stanley Clements (Stash), Bobby Stone (Dave), Minerva Urecal (Hilda), Wheeler Oakman (Tony), Peter Seal (Bruno), Frank Moran (Monk), Jack Mulhall (Police Lt. Brady), Bill Bates (Sleepy), Kay Marvis Gorcey (Bridesmaid), Robert F. Hill (Minister), Blanche Payson, Tom Herbert.

> "Lord knows I'll never make an Academy Award movie, but then I am just as happy to get my achievement plaques from the bank every year." – producer Sam Katzman

> "It's MOIDER! Even the bones in their heads start rattling ... when these roughneck rascals try to mix it with that Dracula man!" – Monogram ad line for *Ghosts on the Loose*

That Dracula man was back, all right, and once again raising hob with the East Side Kids in *Ghosts on the Loose*, Lugosi's seventh and worst Monogram film. Outside of the title and the East Side Kids' tiresome scared-stiff shenanigans, there isn't an ounce of horror in the film. Nor, for all the Kids' misspent energy, an ounce of comedy. It's the sort of film that even makes other East Side Kids pictures, *Spooks Run Wild*, for instance, look awfully good by comparison.

The opening reels get gobbled up by all sorts of silly antics as the East Side Kids prepare for the wedding of Glimpy's (Huntz Hall) sister Betty (Ava Gardner). Gang leader Mugs (Leo Gorcey) leads them in an endless session of choir practice while Danny's (Bobby Jordan) laryngitis gets in the way of his singing and Sleepy (Bill Bates), the organist, keeps nodding off. Later, a few of the boys heist a funeral wreath off a truck for use in the ceremony and others go to a mortuary to borrow a dead gangster's clothes for Glimpy, the best man, to wear.

The bridegroom, Jack (Rick Vallin), has purchased a small cottage on the outskirts of town for Betty and himself, unaware that the big estate next door to it is being used by a Nazi ring of saboteurs. Tony (Wheeler Oakman), a stooge for the enemy agents, is ordered by ringleader Emil (Bela Lugosi) to buy the cottage from the unsuspecting Jack; Emil doesn't want nosy neighbors. Jack hems and haws but Tony gives him a $500 deposit that cinches the deal. Jack decides to use the money to take Betty on a honeymoon.

After the wedding, Jack announces his new plan to take Betty away for a few days instead of repairing to their cottage (which he doesn't mention he's sold). The Kids find a scrap of paper with the Elm Street address of the spy ring's estate on it, and mistakenly believe it's the address of Jack and Betty's little love nest. Armed with brooms, mops and feather dusters, they invade the gloomy old mansion and begin to clean up the place in anticipation of the newlyweds' return. The mansion is sparsely furnished so the Kids decide to "borrow" furniture from the place (Jack's) next door.

Finding their hideout overrun by the East Side Kids, Emil and his henchmen Tony, Bruno (Peter Seal) and Monk (Frank Moran) go to work trying to scare them off with the usual dreary routine of changing portraits and sepulchral laughter; the Kids start to search the house. In the basement they find the Nazi's printing press and pamphlets with titles like *What the New Order Means to You!* and *How to Destroy the Allies*. Still believing that the house is Jack's (and, therefore, the printing press, too), they figure they'd better get the press out of there before it's discovered. Glimpy has the bright idea of taking it next door to the cottage.

The nightmare on Elm Street continues with one silly mixup after another. Two cops arrive, and so do Jack and Betty, and there's a lot of running back and forth between the two houses on everybody's part; even Emil and his men get involved in secretly moving the printing press from one address to the other. One of the cops gets exasperated by the way the press keeps vanishing:

> COP (*sarcastically*): It just got up and walked away, huh?
> GLIMPY: Well, if it can run, I guess a printing press can walk!

Mugs and Glimpy finally bump into Emil and his men in an underground tunnel; the boys are overpowered and dragged back into the Nazi basement. But the rest of the Kids come to the rescue, clobbering Emil, Tony, Bruno and Monk with brooms and mops, and the enemy agents are carted off to jail. The honeymoon of Betty and Jack is delayed because Glimpy contracted German measles (represented by little swastikas) from one of the Nazis, and the newlyweds and the Kids are quarantined together at the cottage for a week.

Interviewed by Lee Server in *Filmfax*, Huntz Hall painted a less than rosy picture of the sort of work that went into the making of East Side Kids films like *Ghosts on the Loose*: "They took six days. But you could work from eight in the morning to twelve at night, and you worked Saturday. So, we actually worked three weeks in one. . . . On Saturday, we might work until four o'clock in the morning. . . . [The budgets] were something like $33,000. The scripts were format. In fact, we used to say it was the same script, they just changed a few names." Billy Benedict, talking about the same subject with *Filmfax*'s Jan Henderson, concurred. "We had a lot of fun, but we really worked hard. They were almost like shooting miniature serials. We did a lot of them in three days and three nights."

The baddies-in-the-haunted-house format was one that the East Side Kids (and later the Bowery Boys) would go back to time and again, and the result was never the rib-tickling time promised on the posters. *Ghosts on the Loose* is particularly dismal, failing to provoke even a single laugh.

Even Bela Lugosi fans are left in the lurch. While Lugosi had plenty of screen time in *Spooks Run Wild*, his appearances in *Ghosts on the Loose* are limited; if what Huntz Hall says about the breakneck shooting schedules is accurate, there isn't any reason to suspect that Lugosi worked on the film for more than a day or so to get all of his footage "in the can." Except for one short scene with Tony (Wheeler Oakman) where the two men are seated in a parked car, Lugosi's Emil doesn't even come on until past the half-hour mark when the film is already more than half over. Grouchy and tired-looking, Lugosi proves once again that his forte isn't gangsters, tough guys *or* enemy agents; he belittles his underlings for the sloppy way they've handled things in his absence, but Lugosi, too, proves himself every inch the bungler. (He gets the billing he deserves, fourth, right underneath Bobby Jordan.)

Talking about Bela Lugosi in *Filmfax*, Huntz Hall had nothing but the highest praise for the actor, calling him "the funniest man I ever worked with. . . . He was always putting everybody on. He had a little midget that went around with him, dressed exactly like him in a cape. He was a beautiful man. I really mean it." Lugosi and Hall only made two films together, but Hall encountered him again years later on the set of *Bela Lugosi Meets a Brooklyn Gorilla*, the 1952 cheapie where Bela contended with Duke Mitchell and Sammy Petrillo, notorious Martin and Lewis imitators:

> I went to the studio where they were shooting to see if my manager was over there. . . . And he said, "Why don't you go in there and say hello to Bela?" I never called him Bela, just Mr. Lugosi. So I went in to see him in his dressing room. He said, "Huntz! My boy! Come in here. . . ."
> . . . I heard that Petrillo and Mitchell were putting him on a lot, trying to make a jerk out of him. So I said, "How are you getting along with the boys?" And he said, "They're *scum!*"*
> You couldn't make a jerk out of Bela Lugosi. He was brilliant. You know, he was a European matinee idol before he came to this country. I loved him. All those guys who play monsters are always nice guys.

Herman Cohen, coproducer of *Meets a Brooklyn Gorilla*, remembers the frail, morphine-addicted Lugosi of the early '50s as being "very, very sick":

> He was an old man and not well, and his wife and son were on the set all the time, the wife giving him shots in the dressing room. I don't know what the hell she was giving him; at that time I didn't know anything about drugs. But I did see syringes occasionally in the dressing room. Lugosi was a nice old guy, and he was happy just to be working. His wife and son would go over his lines with him, he was there when he was supposed to be – but it was sort of like he was "out of it." They brought him there, they told him what to do, he did it for the money – that's my recollection of Bela Lugosi. You couldn't have a personal relationship with him, or a personal conversation, because the minute he was through shooting anything on the sound stage, they would whisk him back to his dressing room.

Everyone else in the *Ghosts on the Loose* cast performs up – or down – to expectations. The East Side Kids themselves (Gorcey, Hall, Jordan, Morrison, Benedict, Clements, et al.) do their shopworn shtick. Reunited from the cast of *The Corpse Vanishes*, enemy agents Minerva Urecal and Frank Moran don't have very much to do, particularly Urecal, who just sits around looking extremely worried; like Lugosi, she appears older and more weatherbeaten here than she does in upcoming pictures, mostly because of the

---

*In a different interview, Hall said that Lugosi once used the word "scum" to describe the East Side Kids! Of course, Hall added, Lugosi was kidding. Yeah, right.

Bela Lugosi and Ava Gardner took back seat billing to the East Side Kids in Monogram's awful *Ghosts on the Loose*.

stripe of white that's been added to her hair. In addition to being a semiregular in the Monogram horrors, onetime pugilist Frank Moran was a fixture in the films of director Preston Sturges (talk about two incompatible sets of movies!). Another Sturges regular, comedian Eddie Bracken, still remembers Moran well:

> Frank was a very intelligent man. When he was a fighter, he was hit in the larynx area, and that's why he talked the way he did. He had the voice of a pretty stupid guy, and so people would come away from him thinking, "My God, where did he get all his intelligence?!" Frank helped Sturges by sitting in on writing sessions quite a few times. In *Hail the Conquering Hero* (1944), it was his idea to put in the marine battles – he knew 'em all, and I put them into the picture with Sturges. That was all Frank Moran. And on the set he was just wonderful – we'd sit around and have so much fun. Conversation with Frank was always very stimulating and pretty wonderful. Frank was around even when he wasn't acting in the movie – he was on the set all the time. Sturges would call in a lot of people; even though they were not working, they would be getting paid for the day. Sturges would make sure of that *[laughs]*!
>
> Sturges loved boxers, and we had a lot of boxers around. So you can understand him loving Frank, because Frank was a fighter, and he was also equal to Sturges in intelligence, in stories, in background. He could have been a great writer also, I guess, but he never got into that. Sturges himself could have written everything there was to know about Frank, 'cause he was extremely interested in Frank's life and his background. In fact, I think that at one time he *was* going to do something about his life – a movie, maybe – because it was very, very interesting. I remember Sturges talking about Frank all the time, because he had a great deal of admiration for him. That "dumb," "punch-drunk" fighter by the name of Frank Moran had more brains than anybody else around him!

Ava Gardner, then at the beginning of her film career, is highly decorative as Huntz Hall's sister(!); the $100 a week MGM contract actress was loaned out to Monogram for the role. In her autobiography *Ava: My Story*, she wrote about Metro's habit of lending her to other studios, "I got sold like a prize hog as often as the studio could manage it, and, honey, I hated that from day one." Surprisingly, she didn't come down on *Ghosts on the Loose* the way one would expect; in fact, she says that *Ghosts* and the Dr. Kildare film *Three Men in White* (1944) were the only two of her early films that made any kind of impact on her, and that being loaned out for *Ghosts* "did have some compensations":

> Bela was a gentle man who wouldn't frighten a nervous kitten, but as Dracula, honey, he'd filled every movie house in the country...

I remember in one scene everyone had swastikas painted all over their faces, so they could say they had German measles; that was our standard of comedy. I don't remember much else about the film because it was shot at such enormous speed. We had one film stage and it took one week. Action–film–print! Even the little experience I'd had with Metro told me that this was not a quality film. In one scene the hero accidentally stumbled over a prop and fell. Nobody cared. No retake. Print it! All part of the glorious fun.... Rick Vallin, the hero, took me out to dinner one night and I liked that. We both knew we were not in the running for the Academy Awards.

Some theater marquees advertised that the film featured Mrs. Mickey Rooney, even though Gardner and the pint-sized actor were already divorced.

To find a future screen goddess like Ava Gardner in *Ghosts on the Loose* makes this Poverty Row film a bit unique. What's also unique about *Ghosts* is the way Bela Lugosi and Huntz Hall both manage to get one by the eagle-eyed (but apparently not eagle-eared) censors of 1943. Lugosi sneezes at one point in the film, but instead of the customary "at-choo!" he quite clearly says "oh, shit!" Later, when Stash (Stanley Clements) wonders out loud whether their friend Jack is mixed up with the Nazis, Huntz Hall unmistakably tells him to "shit your big mouth." (There's also an in-joke moment, rare in horror films, where Hall mentions a gang of tough guys called "the Katzman mob.")

Shot under the title *Ghosts in the Night**, *Ghosts on the Loose* went into production on February 8, 1943. Exactly ten days earlier, coproducer Jack Dietz had been sentenced to seven months in jail following his plea of guilty to evading taxes of $200,237 on income during 1936 and '37. In the '50s, while Sam Katzman was busy at Columbia with a variety of B swashbucklers, crime "exposés," musicals and minibudgeted sci-fi epics, Dietz also kept active, coproducing (among others) *The Beast from 20,000 Fathoms* (1953), *The Black Scorpion* (1957) and his last film *Hannibal* (1959). The independent producer (who was also at one time the operator of Harlem's Cotton Club) died in Boston on January 30, 1969, while undergoing open heart surgery. He was 66.

Variety, often a sucker for the East Side Kids' antics, gave *Ghosts on the Loose* a mildly favorable review, labeling it a "loosely constructed comedy thriller [containing] plenty of laughs despite the long procession of venerable gags.... Bela Lugosi, as the principal menace, is the Nazi chief, but has little to do." *Photoplay* gave it the "phooey" it deserved.

Lugosi biographers Richard Bojarski and Arthur Lennig were unimpressed; the latter commented, "Lugosi gave a routine performance, prob-

---

**Ghosts in the Night* was the film's title in England, "a rare case," noted historian Denis Gifford, "of [the British] trying to make a film sound more horrific than it was." (Its reissue title was the all-explanatory *The East Side Kids Meet Bela Lugosi.)*

ably the result of a justifiable lack of enthusiasm for his role." Monogram expert Don Leifert contended, "The strained excuse for humor consists of Leo Gorcey's tired malapropisms ... and Huntz Hall's uninspired buffoonery.... Even Lugosi, dressed in a pinstriped suit throughout, seems lost amidst the East Side Kids' juvenile antics." Ava Gardner summed the film up as "a piece of sweet, unsophisticated rubbish."

Bela Lugosi's opinion can probably be found within the film itself: "Oh, shit!"

Revenge of the Zombies
(Monogram, 1943)

Released September 17. 61 minutes. Produced by Lindsley Parsons. Directed by Steve Sekely. Original Screenplay: Edmond Kelso and Van Norcross. Director of Photography: Mack Stengler. Production Manager: Richard L'Estrange. Editor: Richard Currier. Technical Director: David Milton. Sound Director: Glen Glenn. Music Director: Edward Kay. Dialogue Director: Jack Linder.

Cast: John Carradine (Dr. Max Heinrich Von Altermann), Gale Storm (Jennifer Rand), Robert Lowery (Larry Adams), Bob Steele (Agent), Mantan Moreland (Jeff), Veda Ann Borg (Lila Von Altermann), Barry McCollum (Dr. Harvey Keating), Mauritz Hugo (Scott Warrington), Madame Sul-Te-Wan (Mammy Beulah), James Baskett (Lazarus), Sybil Lewis (Rosella), Robert Cherry (Pete).

> "I am prepared to supply my country with a new army, numbering as many thousands as are required.... An army that will not need to be fed. That cannot be stopped by bullets. That is, in fact, invincible.... An army of the living dead."—Dr. Max Von Altermann

> "A stunt that has been used to good effect on horror pictures is a search for persons brave enough to view the picture all alone in a completely dark theatre at midnight. To give the gag a fresh twist, make it a search for thirteen people. Work it up with your newspaper editor, with photos of the group being examined by a doctor to make sure their hearts are strong enough to stand the shocks of *Revenge of the Zombies*."—Monogram exploitation idea

Great minds, they say, work alike. While George Zucco plotted to assemble a platoon of werewolves for the Allies in PRC's *The Mad Monster*, over at Monogram John Carradine was endeavoring to put zombies into Axis uniforms in 1943's *Revenge of the Zombies*. The unholy spectacle of these monsters battling helpless soldiers – or, better yet, Zucco's werewolves vs. Carradine's zombies! – went unfilmed, needless to say, as neither Zucco nor Carradine was able to put their fanciful theories into practice. Carradine, a typical Nazi mad scientist, talked one hell of a fight, but his out-of-shape contingent of zombies never got much beyond the boundaries of his swampy Southern estate.

Carradine also shared with Henry (*King of the Zombies*) Victor – *another* great mind! – the ungentlemanly habit of using his own wife in his experiments. While both men had a household full of servants (not to mention a lonely neighborhood stocked with hapless yokels), their baleful hearts were firmly set on bringing a little bit of death into the lives of their better halves. (Which gives us a pretty good idea what *these* marriages must have been like!) Victor used his wife (Patricia Stacey) in a soul-transference ceremony, but the little woman broke under the strain and slipped into a catatonic state. Carradine's Max Von Altermann killed his unsuspecting missus Lila (Veda Ann Borg) with poison and used her as the guinea pig in his zombie experiments. But even in living death, Borg maintained the obstinate streak for which wives are beloved the world over, and the winning habit of always saying *no* at *just* the wrong moment.

Dr. Keating (Barry McCollum), physician of the Warrington family, summons Scott Warrington (Mauritz Hugo), brother of Lila, as a result of her mysterious death at the family mansion in the bayou country of Louisiana. Lila's husband Max pronounced it death by heart attack, but Dr. Keating thinks she was poisoned. To help in his investigation, Scott has hired a private detective, Larry Adams (Robert Lowery), and the pair has concocted a plan to exchange identities when they're introduced to Von Altermann; this will enable Larry to investigate more freely. Dr. Keating accompanies them to the estate of the newly-widowered Von Altermann:

> VON ALTERMANN: You'll remain for the funeral, of course.
> LARRY: If you'll be good enough to have it soon.
> VON ALTERMANN: Tomorrow. Here in the South, it is not wise to waste time. Many things can happen.

Outside, Jeff (Mantan Moreland), Scott's black driver, is approached by the white-haired, big-bellied Lazarus (James Baskett), Von Altermann's zombie servant (the only one with the faculty of speech). "Beautiful car," Lazarus deadpans. "I drove car like this for master . . . when I was alive." Driving away in fear (and in corny fast motion), Jeff next encounters Rosella (Sybil Lewis), a living – and pretty – black domestic in Von Altermann's employ. The sassy Rosella adds to Jeff's unease by talking about "things walkin', ain't got no business walkin'," and leads him into the adjacent graveyard to show him Von Altermann's crew of zombies – some black, some white – busy working amidst the tombstones.

Larry and Scott scoff at Jeff's tales of zombies, but change their tune after walking into the chapel just in time to see Lila, risen from her coffin, exiting through another door. Dr. Keating tells them that although Lila is dead, Von Altermann has been able to make her walk. Von Altermann is confronted with news of what has happened, and he leads his guests back to the chapel, where the quite-dead Lila is once again snugly nestled in her ornate casket. Jennifer Rand (Gale Storm), Von Altermann's unskilled secretary, chides the newcomers for their behavior; obviously not a shrewd judge of character, she's convinced that Von Altermann is guiltless, a position she maintains practically to movie's end. ("Are you being loyal or dumb?" Larry frowns.)

Another unexpected guest, played by Bob Steele, arrives (the character remains stubbornly nameless); a Nazi like Von Altermann, he tells the doctor that transportation back to their fatherland will be arranged now that he (Von Altermann) says his zombie experiments have been successfully completed. Feeling that Steele is unconvinced, Von Altermann pulls out his gun and puts a bullet through Lila, who stands placidly and unfazed.

> VON ALTERMANN: Against an army of zombies, no armies could stand. Why, even blown half to bits – undaunted by fire and gas – zombies would fight on so long as the brain cells which receive and execute commands still remained intact.

Suddenly an echoey "No!" emanates from Lila's dead lips, and Von Altermann realizes that other brain cells that control the will may still need to be paralyzed. He tells Lila to go to her coffin.

More comings and goings ensue, like Lila disappearing from the house (much to Von Altermann's surprise and consternation) and Jeff repeatedly finding (and then losing) a corpse. Searching for Lila, Dr. Keating is beckoned by her unearthly voice into a mausoleum, and is not seen again. Scott insists that Von Altermann call in the sheriff, so to appease him, Von Altermann arranges for his Nazi friend to pose as the local lawman.

Larry discovers a secret radio and overhears an incoming message that makes it obvious Von Altermann is a Nazi. But Von Altermann and Steele catch Larry before he can spread the news; zombies truss him up and toss him into a closet. Freeing himself easily, Larry talks to Mammy Beulah (Madame Sul-Te-Wan), another servant, who wants to help him thwart the evil Von Altermann. By softly imitating a wolf's cry, Beulah summons Lila from her hiding place in the nearby woods, and Larry and the dead woman conspire together against Von Altermann.

Larry startles Von Altermann by showing up and nonchalantly joining him and Scott for dinner. Von Altermann has tainted the meal with the same poison that killed his wife, and Larry and Scott collapse into their plates. Von Altermann hauls the unconscious Scott off to his lab.

But Larry was only feigning illness, having been forewarned by Beulah. He teams up with Steele, who turns out to be a U.S. operative: Steele killed the real Nazi agent (the corpse that Jeff kept finding) and took his place. Smashing open Von Altermann's lab door, they are about to take him into custody when the scientist's zombie bodyguards arrive on the scene. But it's Lila, not the mad doctor, who is now in control of the dead men's minds, and she directs them against her husband. Fleeing into the bayou, Von Altermann is caught by Lila, who embraces her husband as the ground begins to open up beneath them. Begging for his life, Von Altermann is swallowed up, together with Lila, by quicksand.

Cowritten by Edmond Kelso, the solo writer of *King of the Zombies,* *Revenge* is a semiremake of Monogram's earlier zombie film. Once again two men (and servant Mantan Moreland) are guests in a strange house where a mad scientist with a zombie wife is working for the Third Reich. Many minor changes were made, some for the better, and *Revenge* does have the advantage of a stronger cast. But *King of the Zombies,* undistinguished film that it is, distinctly remains the better of the two.

Revenge of the Zombies is awkwardly plotted and unexciting, but then, so was *King of the Zombies.* But *King* made up for it in small ways: some genuinely amusing moments with Mantan Moreland; the interesting character of the Nazi necromancer (well- played by Henry Victor); the eerie-looking zombies; and a bit of action in the finale. For *Revenge,* screenwriter Kelso, abetted by Van Norcross, duplicated many of *King's* plot particulars, but it's this very familiarity that takes much of the fun out of this second picture.

Making his Monogram horror movie debut when *Revenge* began shooting on May 22, 1943, John Carradine underplays the part of the mad Dr. Von Altermann. The actor makes a hammy entrance (the camera dollies into an extreme closeup and thunder rumbles as Carradine, wearing a surgical mask, turns and bulges his eyes at the audience), but for the most part his performance is one of his least vibrant. He saunters around the house, cigarette invariably in hand, schmoozing with his guests and delivering many of his lines in a polite, almost shy murmur. Occasionally he'll treat an outrageous bit of dialogue with the brio it deserves ("What greater destiny could my wife have asked than to serve *me* – and, through me, our country!"), but even his speeches about his planned legion of zombie soldiers are recited as lifelessly as if he were giving directions to the nearest gas station. (He was just as subdued in his next Monogram horror film, *Return of the Ape Man,* although that time around he was playing a good guy, and a fairly insipid one at that.)

Curiously, Carradine is so outnumbered at the end of *Revenge of the Zombies* – not only is he surrounded by the heroes, but then his own wife and zombie corps turn on him – that you almost feel *sorry* for the guy, a reaction Monogram couldn't have counted on. And as he sinks into the bog, pleading

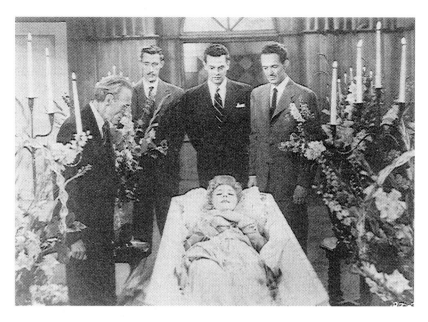

Revenge of the Zombies rehashed the plot of the earlier, better *King of the Zombies*. Here, John Carradine (second from left) looks on casually as Barry McCollum, Robert Lowery and Mauritz Hugo pay their respects. "The departed" is Veda Ann Borg.

frantically with the undead Lila, Carradine allows himself to take in a full mouthful of muck just before he disappears from sight – a noble gesture for such a mediocre movie.

Robert Lowery usually played heroes with a chip on their shoulders in his horror films at Universal (*The Mummy's Ghost*, 1944 – again opposite Carradine – and *House of Horrors*, 1946). Here, if anything, he's a bit too *laid back*, taking everything – including a prearranged midnight meeting with a walking, talking dead woman – completely in stride. Lowery saved the day in lots of B action films of the '40s, not to mention playing the cowled crimefighter in the serial *Batman and Robin* (1949). Middle age, however, brought with it a slightly seedy look and an entirely different set of roles, which had to have come as an unwelcome surprise. He died in 1971 while in the middle of a phone conversation with his mother (*another* unwelcome surprise!).

Carradine and Lowery's low-wattage performances seemed to set the standard for most of the rest of the cast. Gale Storm, much more famous on television than for her handful of B films, takes dictation and follows the men around at a distance whenever anything happens, and that's about it. (Carradine's climactic determination to bring her along when he returns to Germany comes completely out of left field.) Bob Steele and Veda Ann Borg also have very little to do, Borg especially; her echo chamber–type "dead" voice is a nice touch, though, and her occasional slight changes of facial expression speak volumes. Borg's character disappears from her coffin so often that it's surprising no one thinks to put a bell on her.

On the lower half of the castlist, Mauritz Hugo plays a thoroughly obnoxious character; the poisoned meal *doesn't* kill him, but it probably would have been all right with audiences if it had. Madame Sul-Te-Wan, playing much the same part she played in *King of the Zombies*, stands around cackling. An unbilled Robert Cherry, playing zombie Pete, appeared as the derby-wearing comic ghost in Universal's so-so haunted house send-up *Murder in the Blue Room* (1944).

Fifth-billed Mantan Moreland, in the first picture of his new six-picture pact with Monogram, is let down here by witless dialogue and silly situations. He gives it his all, but he's only as good as his low-level material (dumb comments, overdue double-takes, driving and running in fast-motion). Whereas in *King* Moreland interacted with the entire corps of zombies, in *Revenge*, he shares the screen with only one, Lazarus the talking zombie, played by James Baskett (Uncle Remus in Disney's *Song of the South*, 1947). Lazarus feeds straight lines to Moreland in an embarrassing scene or two, and their exchanges are on a grade-school level:

> JEFF: *(scared of Lazarus)*: I got to go home. I forgot somethin'.
> LAZARUS: What...you...forget?
> JEFF: I forgot to *stay* there.

But the most unimpressive players in *Revenge of the Zombies* are the zombies themselves. Some are rail-thin, the rest distressingly flabby; the epitome of 4-F, they're the most unintimidating group of "monsters" ever to show up on the screen. (After seeing them shuffle awkwardly about for half the film, Von Altermann's boast that men like these will comprise his "invincible" army sounds like wishful thinking at best!) Like *King of the Zombies*, *Revenge* doesn't even bother to show or tell us what becomes of them; last seen prowling in the woods after the Von Altermanns have descended into their common quicksand grave, their final disposition is of no importance to our heroes, who talk about other things in the wrap-up while Mantan Moreland gets in one last un-funny bit.

Because *King of the Zombies* had a voodoo setting (a dreary Caribbean island), *Revenge* does as well (the Deep South). But voodoo, which played a large part in Dr. Sangre's experiments in *King*, isn't utilized at all in *Revenge*. Working out of his basement laboratory, Dr. Von Altermann's electro-chemical experiments might just as easily have been conducted in Nazi Germany, where he could have worked without the inconvenience and risk of operating "behind enemy lines." (That's one of the hidden pitfalls of remaking a movie, but changing little things here and there.) World War II was well underway when *Revenge of the Zombies* was made, but again, as

Madame Sul-Te-Wan (center) and Robert Lowery walk with a zombie (Veda Ann Borg) in Monogram's tepid *Revenge of the Zombies*.

in the pre–Pearl Harbor *King of the Zombies*, the film refuses to call a spade a spade: words like "Nazi" are nowhere to be heard, although Bob Steele does call Carradine a heinie – behind his back – in one scene.

First announced nearly a year before it went into production, *Revenge of the Zombies* was originally slated to star Bela Lugosi. But when the film was set to go into production, Lugosi was once again "treading the boards" in yet another stage production of *Dracula*. (One of the places it played was in Buffalo, New York, where a *Variety* reviewer caught it and wrote, "Bela Lugosi's portrayal . . . just doesn't add up to contemporary conceptions of the epitome in fiendishness.") Lugosi also was supposed to be in *King of the Zombies*, that time being replaced by Henry Victor. He finally got to play a zombie-master again in Sam Katzman's *Voodoo Man*, his last Monogram film. Another *Revenge* cast casualty was Lyle Talbot, who was being announced right up until production began; Talbot was probably up for either the Bob Steele or Mauritz Hugo parts.

A few of *Revenge of the Zombies*' latter-day reviews go light on the film's faults, and commend it on its "stylish" direction. There *are* a couple minor touches here and there that one might mistake for style, but again, as in the far *more* stylish *Invisible Ghost*, they're the kind of stuff that would go totally unnoticed in a wholly professional film. Director Steve Sekely lays the atmosphere on thick in the opening scene, which includes wind, storm, a graveyard, a zombie (Baskett) doing the howling bit, and an emaciated zombie (Cherry) rising from his coffin; minutes later, there's a montage and, big deal, even a couple of tilted camera angles. From here on, though, the picture charts a slow but steady course downhill, unimaginatively directed, and further stymied by a slow-paced script filled with fools' errands and dead-end scenes.

Bela Lugosi, Monogram's first choice to star in *Revenge*, might well have enjoyed working with Sekely, a Hungarian like himself. Né Istvan (Stephan) Szekely at the turn of the century, the director arrived in America in 1938 with a long list of Austrian, German and Hungarian films already on his résumé. Here, like many an émigré director, he was relegated at first to Poverty Row; unlike most of the better ones, though, he never rose much above that level of filmmaking. He worked with Carradine again in *Waterfront* and with Lionel Atwill in *Lady in the Death House* (both PRC, 1944); commuted between the U.S. and Europe in the '50s; did lots of television; and directed most but not nearly all of the science fiction thriller *The Day of the Triffids* (1963), probably his best-known credit but still no worldshaker. He died in 1979.

Technically, *Revenge of the Zombies* is a typical Monogram horror film, complete with the usual assortment of not-bad, could-be-better sets and slightly above-average (Monogram's average) cinematography (Mack Stengler on camera). Edward Kay's score is so bad in spots that it calls attention to itself. In England, the country that changed the too-horrific title of Monogram's earlier *The Corpse Vanishes*, *Revenge* was released as *The Corpse Vanished*.

Variety was unimpressed. "Monogram's newest 'Zombie' release is one of the incredibly fantastic yarns that borders on the ludicrous and fails singularly in creating anything near the suggestion of tenseness or suspense that characterizes *I Walked with a Zombie* [1943]. . . . John Carradine as the cracked German scientist is properly villainous as he tries to make the most of an impossible role." *The Hollywood Reporter* actually liked the damn thing: "Well cast and plotted, the yarn has a nice production background, and is neatly paced by director Steve Sekely. . . . The film is interesting fare, with lots of those moments which make for gasps."

The comedy-happy Leonard Maltin (*TV Movies and Video Guide*) thought that Mantan Moreland's comic relief saved the day, which was true in *King of the Zombies* but really not here. *Photon*'s Ron Borst wrote, "The plot for this one made *King of the Zombies*' screenplay seem like a masterpiece of construction, even though it used the same dull formula." In *Filmfax*, Don Leifert examined Carradine's performance and found it wanting: "He lacked Lugosi and Zucco's instincts when performing in Poverty Row productions. Success in these low-budget efforts depended on a strong screen presence, something both Lugosi and Zucco possessed. Their

Nazi dastard John Carradine is about to get his just deserts at the hands of his own corps of zombies in *Revenge of the Zombies.*

charisma was felt the moment they appeared on-screen. Not so with Carradine. When he relied on his abilities as an actor, he was fun to watch and effective; when he underplayed a role and relied on his presence, he was lackluster and ineffective." In *Psychotronic* magazine, Michael Weldon dubbed it "one of Monogram's most entertaining, outrageous and star-filled horror movies." Before it became fashionable to laud Steve Sekely, *Castle of Frankenstein* opined, "Sekely's flat direction keeps it all on sub-serial level."

Voodoo Man
(Monogram, 1944)

Released February 21. 62 minutes. Associate Producer: Barney A. Sarecky. Produced by Sam Katzman and Jack Dietz (Banner Productions). Directed by William Beaudine. Original Story and Screenplay: Robert Charles. Photography: Marcel Le Picard. Assistant Director: Art Hammond. Musical Director: Edward Kay. Film Editor: Carl Pierson. Set Designer: Dave Milton. Sound: Glen Glenn.

Cast: Bela Lugosi (Dr. Richard Marlowe), John Carradine (Toby), George Zucco (Nicholas), Wanda McKay (Betty Benton), Louise Currie (Stella Saunders), Michael Ames [Tod Andrews] (Ralph Dawson), Ellen Hall (Evelyn Marlowe), Terry Walker (Alice), Mary Currier (Mrs. Benton), Henry Hall (Sheriff), Dan White (Elmer, the Deputy), Pat McKee (Grego), Mici Goty (Marie), Ralph Littlefield (Sam), Claire James, Ethelreda Leopold, Dorothy Bailer (Zombies), John Ince (S.K.).

> "It has been obvious for some time that if Bela 'The Mad Doctor' Lugosi, John 'The Mad Scientist' Carradine and George 'The Mad Man' Zucco kept it up long enough, they would eventually be reduced to utter absurdity.... Now the obvious has come to pass. They kept it up." *Voodoo Man* is utterly absurd. — *The New York Post*

> "I hardly think that *Voodoo Man* was designed to tickle the funnybone, but I couldn't help but chuckle over George Zucco, all dressed in robe and feathers with his face marked up; John Carradine, stalking idiotically around bending to his master's will, and as the master himself, Bela Lugosi." — *The New York Daily News*

Here's a description of a movie trio; read it and figure out who we're talking about. The first guy is dark-haired and quite obviously the boss; he gives orders, and the other two jump. He likes to call his underlings by unflattering names and he employs threats and sometimes resorts to violence. The second guy is bald, and doesn't get to do much; he usually stays in the background, engaged in silly stuff, never doing anything right. The third guy is a nitwit, ogles pretty girls and makes the dumbest mistakes. He's the one who's always on the receiving end of the first guy's physical abuse. They're the Three Stooges – right?

In this case, wrong. They're Bela Lugosi, George Zucco and John Carradine, "Joining Icy Hands to Form a Gruesome Threesome" in *Voodoo Man*, Lugosi's final Monogram film (but *not* the last one to be released). Although by no means the best entry in the nine film series, *Voodoo Man* remains a perfect capper in that it's a compendium of everything that went into the Lugosi Monograms: Fun casts; inane, confused plots; lousy dialogue; unintentionally funny scenes; *unfunny intended* comedy; and a stray, fleeting moment or two of not-bad horror.

The production history of *Voodoo Man* is a bit muddled. In March 1943, Monogram announced the purchase of *The Tiger Man* from author Andrew Colvin for production as a Bela Lugosi vehicle, with the starting date given as April 19; according to some sources, *The Tiger Man* and *Voodoo Man* are one and the same, but Colvin gets no on-screen writing credit. In June came announcements of *The Voodoo Man*, with production scheduled for August.

But delays lay ahead, with the next publicity release (in September) stating that *The Voodoo Man* would get underway in October (with William Nigh directing) and be followed by *Return of the Ape Man*. Several days later, Katzman and Dietz announced the formation of a "horror stock company" consisting of Lugosi, Carradine, Zucco and Frieda Inescort (see *Return of the Ape Man* section) which would star in *The Voodoo Man, Return of the Ape Man* and possibly other films.

The plan kept changing, almost on a daily basis. On September 22, *The Hollywood Reporter* announced that Philip Rosen would direct *The Voodoo Man* as soon as Lugosi completed his Hollywood engagement in the stage production of *Arsenic and Old Lace*. Then on September 27, the report came that Rosen had been handed the reins on *Return of the Ape Man*, which would come first and be followed by *Voodoo Man*, with director William Beaudine now presiding over the latter production. *Voodoo Man* finally got underway on October 16.

The plot: Alice (Terry Walker, the murdered maid in *Invisible Ghost*) pulls into an isolated country gas station and gets directions from the owner, Nicholas (George Zucco). After she has driven away, Nicholas makes a phone call, alerting a confederate that a lone female motorist is on the road. A few miles ahead, a tall row of roadside bushes part and reveal two men, the half-witted Toby (John Carradine) and Grego (Pat McKee), who put up a **DETOUR** sign which diverts the unsuspecting Alice into the trap. A futuristic gadget is used to stall her motor; Toby and Grego seize the girl and drag her away.

Alice is the third female motorist that month to have vanished without a trace from lonely Laurel Road. At the headquarters of the Banner Motion Picture Company, executive S.K. (John Ince) asks screenwriter Ralph Dawson (Tod Andrews) to thrash out a horror script with these disappearances as its theme, but Ralph reminds him that he's about to get married and go away on his honeymoon.

Through the type of coincidence on which Monogram films thrive, Ralph's route to his fiancée's house takes him over Laurel Road, where he runs out of gas. Meanwhile, back at the gas station, Nicholas gives directions to Stella Saunders (Louise Currie), then hurries back inside and makes the phone call that puts their evil kidnapping plot into operation once again. Stella picks up the hitchhiking Ralph; through another coincidence, Stella is the cousin of Ralph's fiancée. Their car takes the detour (as planned) and the engine is electronically stalled, but Toby and Grego see Ralph in the car and continue to lie in wait. After Ralph has headed off in the direction of a dark house to use the phone, Toby and Grego move in, abducting Stella.

Through a secret tunnel, Stella is dragged into that same house, where she meets Dr. Richard Marlowe (Bela Lugosi), who has masterminded this entire affair. The mysterious Marlowe ushers Stella into the presence of his wife, Evelyn (Ellen Hall), who appears to be in a catatonic state:

Moonlighting from his gas-pumping duties at the local Mobil service station, Nicholas (George Zucco) casts an evil spell in *Voodoo Man.*

STELLA: Is your wife ill?
MARLOWE: She's dead. . . . She has been dead for 22 years.

Marlowe and Nicholas, abetted by the moronic Toby and Grego, have been abducting girls in hopes that Nicholas, a necromancer and follower of the voodoo god Ramboona, can magically transfer their minds – their wills to live – into the body of the zombie-like Evelyn Marlowe. As Toby and Grego play voodoo drums, and as the other kidnap victims (now zombies themselves) look on, the weird ritual begins. The robed Nicholas, wearing war paint on his face and a feathery hat, chants fervidly over two lengths of rope which move together snake-like and form a knot. The hypnotized Stella sits facing the zombified Evelyn as Marlowe, also in a garish robe, invokes a mystical spell. Evelyn revives, utters a few words, then drops dead again. The experiment has failed. Stella was not the right subject.

Meanwhile, Ralph and his fiancée Betty Benton (Wanda McKay) report Stella's disappearance to the Sheriff (Henry Hall). Investigating, the lawman pays a call on Dr. Marlowe, who serves him sherry and gives him a lot of double-talk. Downstairs, the moronic Toby is visiting with the pretty zombie girls, all of whom are caged in what looks like a row of phone booths (they're probably meant to resemble the glass cases in *The Black Cat*, 1934); Toby likes to touch them and talk to them. The dimwit forgets to lock Stella's cage door, and the entranced girl wanders out of the house into the forest. The Sheriff and his deputy (Dan White) pick her up, driving her to the Benton home where the family puts the girl to bed.

Dr. Marlowe hastens to the Bentons under the pretense of ministering to the afflicted Stella; "I have made a study of these ailments," he claims, before anyone has told him what Stella is suffering from. Ralph and Betty wring their hands over the wide-eyed but comatose Stella:

> BETTY: You know, I've seen people act like that in pictures. What do they call 'em, *zombies* or something?
> RALPH: Now, now, honey, there aren't any such people. That's only a scenario writer's nightmare. I *know*, I wrote them once!

Later, at Marlowe's, the doctor and Nicholas use a long-distance mystical chant to lure Stella back into their evil clutches.

Ralph and Betty call on Marlowe, who is struck by the way Betty reminds him of Evelyn. The doctor points out his wife's picture on the wall, telling his guests that she has passed away. While Marlowe is distracted by an incoming phone call, Ralph and Betty are able to see Evelyn through a doorway, roaming the house in her zombie state.

After Ralph and Betty have left, Marlowe and Nicholas fall back on black magic once again, chanting up a storm to place Betty in their power. Betty, spellbound, drives to Marlowe's, the usual onlookers are rounded up and the ceremony begins again. Ralph has followed and storms into the room, but Grego effortlessly kayoes him and returns to his voodoo drum.

But Ralph had also notified the Sheriff, who arrives with his deputy and breaks into the house. Bursting into the ceremonial room with guns drawn, they are forced to shoot when Marlowe reaches for a weapon. "Evelyn – my darling," the dying Marlowe gasps, "soon vee vill be together . . . !" Marlowe dies, Evelyn dies and the kidnapped girls all come out of their trances. (According to the misinformed pressbook writer, Marlowe "manages to destroy his wife in an explosion"!)

In the final scene, Ralph plops his new script *The Voodoo Man*, an account of their weird adventure, onto the desk of film executive S.K.:

> S.K.: Who do you see playin' the part of the Voodoo Man?
> RALPH: Say, why don't you get that actor, uh-h, Bela Lugosi? It's right up his alley!

John Carradine, in dire need of a haircut and some good career counselling, accepted the role of a comic halfwit in *Voodoo Man.*

Voodoo Man could easily have ranked with some of Lugosi's better Monograms: its eerie plot, which combines futuristic science with black magic, had good possibilities; the device of having a Banner Productions screenwriter as the hero showed some wit; and the teaming of Lugosi, Carradine and Zucco was a natural. Unfortunately, the opportunity is in many ways wasted. The film brims with egregiously poor dialogue, repetitive situations and more than a few dead spots, and Carradine and Zucco play the most demeaning roles of their careers. One of its few real assets is that it's another great "guilty pleasure" film in the vein of *The Ape Man*, although not nearly as lively.

Voodoo Man probably is *the* low point of the long career of John Carradine, which is saying a hell of a lot about an actor who went on to make films with titles like *Blood of Ghastly Horror, Vampire Hookers* and *Demented Death Farm Massacre...The Movie*. In the mid-'40s, Carradine was primarily concerned with forming and maintaining his Shakespearean repertory company, and monies earned appearing in drecky films was going toward that noble cause. He had to know what debasing himself in cheap movies like these would do to his future film career, but apparently this mattered little to the workaholic Carradine; he might appear in a timeless Hollywood classic one day and in a sleazy shoestring horror film the next, but, according to actor Robert Clarke,

> He was a true professional, and he gave every bit as much working for (say) Jerry Warren as he would working for Cecil De Mille or John Ford. He did not stint in the slightest in his performance. He was cooperative, easy to work with and he was not condescending – he was something of a star and we weren't, but he treated us as equals and fellow actors. I had great respect for him.

Producer/director Howard W. Koch reminisces,

> Carradine was always a shifty kind of guy in life, and by "shifty" I definitely do *not* mean that he was dishonest. But he *lived* the make-believe world of the actor. He didn't really believe that he had to pay bills or things like that! When we were making *Desert Sands* [1955], we checked into a hotel in Yuma, and I went to the manager of the hotel and said, "Look, I'm going to warn you up front: *Don't* cash a check for John Carradine. He's the greatest con man in the world, he'll talk you into it, but I'm telling you now, I'm not going to be responsible, *you* are. *Don't cash a check for him.*" He said, "Mr. Koch, I promise."
> About a week later, I came back to the hotel after work, exhausted, and went to the bar to get some beer. The manager sidled up next to me and said, "Mr. Koch, I've got a problem." I said, "Don't tell me you cashed a check for John Carradine." He said, "Yeah, the first night." I cried out, "Right after I *told* you?!" He said Carradine was *so* eloquent, he talked him into it! And the check was a big one, like 200 bucks, which was a fortune in 1955. I said, "Tell you what I'll do. Gimme the check and I'll take it out of his pay." The 200 came out of Carradine's pay, and when he got his money, he didn't say a word. He really lived in a world of his own, in a *dreamworld*, and never faced reality.

This dreamworld was a damn good place for Carradine to be during the making of *Voodoo Man*. His character is a moronic Lennie-like bumpkin, and Carradine – who *under*played his other Monogram horror roles – plays this one to the hilt, spouting the child-like dialogue with little regard for his actor's dignity. Even when his mouth is shut, he's still making a spectacle of himself: His long hair hangs over his face, he runs in short steps and his arms comically dangle and bounce at his sides as he bustles from place to place. Amazingly, even this Carradine performance has its boosters, like Don Leifert, who wrote in *Filmfax*, "Carradine looks as if he's having fun for a change, and *Voodoo Man* remains one of his finest performances in a horror film." For years Carradine used to tell people that *Voodoo Man* was his worst film. Toward the end, he conferred that honor to *Billy the Kid Versus Dracula* (1966). *Both* of these pictures started looking pretty good once

Carradine began appearing in splatter films. Carradine made way-worse films than *Voodoo Man*, but probably never played a more debasing role.

George Zucco comes off just as badly as Carradine; Zucco might have retained more of his dignity had he played the Neanderthal in *Return of the Ape Man*. Except for a few short scenes in his little rural Mobil gas station (where Zucco is teamed with Ralph Littlefield, the nerdy Zippo from *The Ape Man*), all of Zucco's footage finds him in Lugosi's ceremonial chamber, bedizened in silly robe, feathered headgear and voodoo war paint. Staunchly maintaining that "Ramboona is all-powerful" through failure after failure, he belts out the mystical mumbo-jumbo with theatrical aplomb. (Tellingly, when Lugosi's wife is *almost* restored to life following the experiment with Louise Currie, *no* one looks more surprised than Zucco!) At least in *Return of the Ape Man* he would have been unrecognizable; here he makes a horse's ass of himself for all the world to see. Fans generally agree that this is Zucco's all-time worst role as well. (Don Willis wrote that "Zucco, chanting and occasionally glancing up at the camera, looks as if he's as embarrassed as Carradine *should* have been.")

The script is, in fact, dead-set against everyone but Bela Lugosi, who not only does a good job in the lead but is made to look even *better* by the foolish way that everyone around him is forced to behave. Sinister looking in his mustache and short beard, and often eerily lit and photographed, Lugosi gives a good performance as the obsessed (but not unpersonable) Dr. Marlowe.

The role is similar to his Dr. Lorenz in *The Corpse Vanishes*; in fact, *Voodoo Man* is regarded by many as a semiremake of *Corpse*. Like Lorenz, Marlowe is selflessly dedicated to his afflicted wife, and uses a team of co-conspirators to abduct young women for his experiments. In *Corpse*, the wife's (Elizabeth Russell) problem was that she was over the hill; in *Voodoo Man*, Mrs. Marlowe is a zombie. She retains her youthful beauty even though she's been dead 22 years; has the ability to walk around; never speaks; never complains. (Come to think of it, what's wrong with that?) The scenes where Marlowe and Nicholas use voodoo chants and an article of women's clothing to entrance and summon girls over long distances call to mind Lugosi's *White Zombie* (1932); Lugosi's makeup here is in fact a bit reminiscent of that earlier film.

Arthur Lennig, author of *The Count*, rates *Voodoo Man* as the best film in the Lugosi Monogram series, and played up Bela's performance the way only a Lugosiphile could:

> Lugosi ... carries the film. He brings it his demonic intensity and yet also his human warmth, so that the performance is curiously powerful and indeed even touching. He has the opportunity, for a change, to act a more complex character and is convincingly a sympathetic husband, a kindly doctor, a strong-minded villain, and a voodoo mystic.

It may sound like over-praise, but Lennig is on the money. Bela Lugosi gives one of his best '40s performances in *Voodoo Man*. As (too) often happens in Monogram's horror films, the supporting players – "the heroes" – are rather an unlikable bunch. Tod Andrews (Ralph) automatically thinks the worst of everyone. Louise Currie (Stella) is just plain nasty, repeatedly calling Ralph a sap before she's even met him. Wanda McKay (Betty) also has a mean streak. Henry Hall (the Sheriff) is a grumpy old goat whose scenes stop the picture cold; he also gets the all-time worst Monogram horror movie line of dialogue, the deathless "Gosh all fish-hooks!"

Louise Currie scarcely remembers working on *Voodoo Man*, which isn't too surprising considering her limited part and the speed at which it must have been filmed:

> What I remember about *Voodoo Man* was walking around out in the woods with my eyes wide open, wandering around in a trance. . . . I appeared with Bela Lugosi three times; he was so different from the characters he played. He was quiet and unassuming off the screen, very studious and very sedate. Then the cameras would roll and he would be a *horrible* man *[laughs]*! . . . . And poor John Carradine – he played a halfwit in it! (And may I say he played it very *well* – playing a halfwit is *not* the easiest thing to do when you're a good actor!)

Unfortunately, for every scene that plays well in *Voodoo Man*, a like or greater number go awry. There's an early, strikingly well-done sequence where Lugosi confronts the kidnapped Currie for the first time. The lighting is beautifully ominous and there are some great ultra-closeups; it's a neat scene. But minutes later, the film has sunk back into the depths as Henry Hall's Sheriff conducts his investigation and Lugosi plays annoyingly dumb:

> SHERIFF: Was there a **DETOUR** sign lately on the highway?
> MARLOWE: I don't know. Are they repairing the road?
> SHERIFF: No, that's just it. The road's okay.
> MARLOWE: Then why should there be any sign?
> SHERIFF: There shouldn't!
> MARLOWE: This is all very confusing to me, Sheriff!
> SHERIFF: You're telling me!

At the end of the film, when Lugosi dies, his wife also dies and the zombie girls all snap out of their trances, but no one explains why; maybe Ramboona got fed up. (And what made Lugosi think that his still-hot young wife was going to give an old cocker like him a second glance if she *had* recovered?) The gimmick of making the film's hero, Ralph Dawson, a Monogram screenwriter is fun, although more could have been made of it,

perhaps in lieu of the boring scenes of the Sheriff and his complaining deputy. Ralph's boss, producer S. K., is obviously meant to be Sam Katzman (Katzman doesn't play the role, but that *would* have been a great touch!). It's funny, and probably true-to-life, the way S. K. regards Ralph's new script *The Voodoo Man* with more than just a little bit of wariness ("Is it any good...?"); and even funnier that Ralph has to grope for the name of Bela Lugosi, the Banner Motion Picture Company's biggest star!

Voodoo Man is one of those irritating films that could have been good, but through a combination of circumstances, just misses; and the good work of many of the better people involved (e.g., Lugosi) is wasted. Somehow films like these are even *more* disappointing than *worse* films (*Ghosts on the Loose*, for example), which can be dismissed as tripe and written off. Through repeated viewings you try and *make* yourself like *Voodoo Man*, but it's the type of picture that just won't cooperate.

Variety's Sten didn't think much of *Voodoo Man*, calling it "negligible as a chiller ... [Lugosi, Carradine and Zucco] try their best with the material at hand. Rest of the cast gives so-so performances." According to *The Hollywood Reporter*, "The story is no more absurd than the majority of its predecessors, occasionally poking sly fun at the whole scheme of horror pictures." *The New York Post* and *The New York Daily News* both found the picture funny, although neither considered that a plus. It registered a **POOR** on the *Post's* Movie Meter: "Composed of spare parts from previous chillers and thrown together with complete disregard of possibilities, the film induces laughter in what are intended to be tense moments.... It's screwy in a dull, second-hand manner.... This picture isn't content to portray zombies; it gives an impression of having been made by them." The *News* concurred with the rival paper's assessment: "All of this foolery is supposed to be horrendous, to send chills up and down your spine. But, upon this viewer, the effect was a total loss."

Don Leifert, surprisingly impressed, called *Voodoo Man* "director William Beaudine's finest contribution to the horror genre," which is probably true but really isn't saying much. Phil Hardy, unsurprisingly *un*impressed, labeled it "standard Monogram dross." Lugosi biographer Richard Bojarski put it down as "an incredible, but only passably entertaining horror melodrama ... [John Carradine is] woefully miscast as a half-wit whose inefficiency provided unintentional humor during the film's serious moments." *Fangoria's* Alex Gordon thought that it "may not have been one of Lugosi's biggest films but it was possibly the best one in his Monogram series."

Horror films stayed (more or less) in vogue until 1946, but Monogram

Opposite: Long, uneventful scenes of voodoo ceremonies slowed the pace of Monogram's *Voodoo Man.* The men (left to right) are John Carradine, George Zucco (in background), Bela Lugosi and Pat McKee; the ladies seated are Wanda McKay and Ellen Hall. Louise Currie is on the right.

turned their back on them after *Voodoo Man* (made in October, 1943). A few random outings lay ahead, like *The Face of Marble* and a "spooky" Bowery Boys romp or two, but apparently Monogram's confidence in the future of the genre had been dispelled. Occasionally, an additional Monogram horror film was promised, then not delivered:

> In February, 1944, Sam Katzman and Jack Dietz announced their tenth Bela Lugosi film, *The Gold Bug,* based on the Edgar Allan Poe story, with Lugosi as the treasure-hunting Legrand. The film was never made and Bela Lugosi never worked for Monogram again.*
>
> *When Zombies Walked,* announced twice by Monogram (in '42 and again in '44) would have been a third zombie film for producer Lindsley Parsons; when announced in '42, it was slated to star Mantan Moreland. It was based upon a story of the same name by Thorp McCluskey that was published in *Weird Tales.*
>
> *Another* voodoo film, Katzman/Dietz's *Jungle Queen* (later called *Voodoo Queen,* slated to star Acquanetta and scheduled for February, 1945 production) also never got beyond the planning stage. (Acquanetta today recalls, "At Monogram I had approval of my scripts – and I *disap-*proved of every one!")

Fans of Bela Lugosi, a hardy and indefatigible breed, often refer to his Monogram films as the low point of his career, turning a blind eye to the vehicles that now lay ahead for the actor. *The Body Snatcher* (1945, in which Lugosi played a small part), the oft-maligned *Abbott and Costello Meet Frankenstein* (1948, as Dracula) and, way, *way* down the quality scale, *The Black Sleep* (1956, another bit part) are the only post–1944 Lugosi films that can be called worthwhile; most of the rest, from *Scared to Death* (1947) to his transvestite epics *Old Mother Riley Meets the Vampire* (1952) and *Glen or Glenda?* (1953), are really just unwatchable junk. Lugosi always used to talk about Ed Wood as though Wood was the man who was going to put poor Bela back in the forefront of Hollywood stars, but even Lugosi had to know that Wood was driving the final nails into his professional coffin; Lugosi probably spent his spare moments on the sets of pictures like *Glen or Glenda?* pining for the comparatively good old days of Monogram, the East Side Kids, ape men, and William Beaudine calling him (and everybody else) Sam.

He worked as sporadically on television as he did in movies, played Las Vegas in 1954 (his first nightclub appearance, in a *Dragnet*-type spoof at the Silver Slipper) and, of course, made headlines in '55 by committing himself for treatment of his drug addiction. He also married for the fifth time in 1955, but according to Forry Ackerman (interviewed by Mark Voger), his new bride Hope "made him incredibly unhappy":

---

*Several years later, Lugosi and a "gorilla" toured the East Coast with a horror act; their stage show followed the showing of cheaply-rented Monogram movies.

She was really a sadist. She expressed no shame. I remember being in her apartment shortly after Bela had died, and she said, "*I* frightened *him!*"

She was telling us that Bela was very superstitious, and he believed that you should sleep with a glass of water by your bedstand at night to keep away the evil spirits. And she would threaten him: "Now, Bela, if you don't behave, I'm going to take away the water, and the evil spirits are going to *get* you!" The poor old man, I guess, took that pretty seriously. She had him under her thumb.

When he was in our home at one time – he was rather deaf – he didn't realize how loudly his voice was carrying into the next room. And he was kind of singing the Hungarian blues about what a witch she was. And we thought, "Oh my God, wait'll she gets him home!"

Just prior to marrying Hope, Lugosi had left Norwalk, California's Metropolitan State Hospital claiming to have kicked his drug and drinking addictions. Of course, he *hadn't* kicked the drinking habit (in fact, he was drunk at the wedding), and Reginald LeBorg, director of *The Black Sleep*, questioned whether he'd really kicked his drug habit. It all became academic when Lugosi kicked the *oxygen* habit on Thursday, August 16, 1956.

Lugosi's fine performance in *Voodoo Man* had marked the end of his Monogram years and a crude but colorful, maddening yet likable, unmemorable but never-to-be-forgotten series.

The Monster Maker
(PRC, 1944)

Released April 15. 63 minutes. Produced by Sigmund Neufeld. Directed by Sam Newfield. Screenplay: Pierre Gendron and Martin Mooney. Story: Lawrence Williams and (uncredited) Nell O'Day. Director of Photography: Robert Cline. Sound Engineer: Ferol Redd. Set Designer: Paul Palmentola. Set Dressings: Elias H. Reif. Film Editor: Holbrook N. Todd. Assistant Director: Melville DeLay. Music Score: Albert Glasser. Musical Supervisor: David Chudnow. Makeup: Maurice Seiderman. Production Manager: Bert Sternbach.

Cast: J. Carrol Naish (Dr. Igor Markoff), Ralph Morgan (Anthony Lawrence), Tala Birell (Maxine), Wanda McKay (Patricia Lawrence), Terry Frost (Bob Blake), Glenn Strange (Steve), Sam Flint (Dr. Adams), Alexander Pollard (Butler), Ace (by himself).

LAWRENCE: I know you infected me with something that caused acromegaly. But how you made the disease

develop so rapidly, when science has proven that it takes
years to reach this stage, I do not know. But you did!
MARKOFF: You overestimate my control of the disease.
I have made an extensive study of it, yes, that is true,
but, after all, I am only an apprentice.
LAWRENCE: Yes! The devil's apprentice! Markoff, you
have set yourself up as a Frankenstein and created a
monster. I am that monster!—Dialogue from *The
Monster Maker*

Resuming the production of fright films after a hiatus of nearly a year
and a half, PRC returned to the genre with a vengeance with *The Monster
Maker*, a gruesome and slightly unpleasant horror entry. Unlike most of the
other horror films of the period, which focussed on highly fanciful monsters
(vampires, zombies and the like), the ogre in *The Monster Maker* is a victim
of the disease acromegaly, an actual glandular disorder which enlarges and
distorts its victims' faces, hands and feet (and frequently leads to their
death). Obviously, seeing their affliction being treated in this light probably
does very little for the morale of real-life sufferers, just as the film, plodding
and nasty, sizes up as a disappointment for many horror film fanciers.

PRC allowed almost 17 months to pass between the production of *Dead
Men Walk* (in September, 1942) and *The Monster Maker* (which started
shooting Monday, February 7, 1944), perhaps feeling that their release of
the British film *The Night Has Eyes* (retitled *Terror House*, and starring
James Mason) was enough to keep horror fans satiated. Two other PRC
"chillers," *The Black Raven* and *The Ghost and the Guest*, had also bowed in
1943, but horror fans duped in past the box office quickly learned that both
were mundane gangster comedies. Actually, the year 1943 was a busy time
for ambitious little PRC. Aside from their regular roster of murky little
Westerns and other films, PRC was looking to broaden their horizons. They
purchased all the equipment in the Chadwick Studio on Gower (including
electrical fixtures, generators, sets and flats) and installed it in the Fine
Arts studios, another recent acquisition. (PRC bought the studio at a
foreclosure sale for a cash price of $305,000, just topping Columbia's bid of
$300,000. In so doing, PRC also assumed responsibility for $33,000 Fine
Arts owed in back state taxes.)

The Monster Maker was an everything-but-the-kitchen-sink horror
thriller for PRC, incorporating into its screenplay a mad doctor, a monster,
even a sinister henchman (played by horror-star-to-be Glenn Strange) and
a homicidal gorilla.

J. Carrol Naish, the twice Oscar-nominated character actor (for *Sahara*,
1943, and *A Medal for Benny*, 1945), was signed on February 3, 1944, to play
the title role in PRC's newest horror opus, which went into production
under the title *The Devil's Apprentice* four days later. Seasoned devotees of

A heavily made-up Ralph Morgan (center) dominates the lobby card for PRC's *The Monster Maker.*

horror films would find in its plot links to several earlier chillers, the Golden Age classics *The Raven* and *Mad Love* in particular, but perhaps *Monster Maker*'s real distinction is the *later* horror films it might have *inspired.* More on that in a bit.

Anthony Lawrence (Ralph Morgan), a renowned concert pianist, is in the midst of a performance when, in the audience, his daughter Patricia (Wanda McKay) notices that the man in the next theater box (J. Carrol Naish) is staring fixedly at her. She switches seats with her boyfriend Bob Blake (Terry Frost), but the intense stranger is undeterred.

During an intermission, Patricia and Bob are visiting Lawrence backstage in his dressing room when the stranger, Dr. Igor Markoff, enters and introduces himself. The doctor explains his seeming rudeness: Patricia is the living image of his dead wife Lenore.

Patricia accepts Markoff's apology, but continues to be repulsed by the dark little man and the way he ogles her. "Funny people, these foreigners!" Bob complains.

Patricia finds herself being continually harassed at home by Markoff, who messengers to her an unending series of bouquets and notes ("Flowers,

flowers, flowers, morning, noon and night. The man must be crazy!"). When she mentions this to Lawrence, the musician decides to pay a call on Markoff, and tell him that his attentions are unwelcome. Lawrence drives to Markoff's Cliff Drive sanatarium and cools his heels awhile in the doctor's waiting room. Browsing through a medical journal, he finds an article by Markoff, MAN IS WHAT HIS DUCTLESS GLANDS MAKE HIM, an incomprehensible treatise which seems to start in the middle and then, in a different typeface, segues into a love story. (Hopefully Markoff's a better doctor than he is a writer!)

Lawrence confronts Markoff and tells him to leave Patricia alone, but Markoff is unreceptive, even showing Lawrence a photograph of his look-alike dead wife Lenore (Wanda McKay in an old-fashioned dress).

> LAWRENCE: What if there *is* a resemblance? That doesn't give you the privilege of annoying her.
> MARKOFF: But I am going to *marry* her.
> LAWRENCE: Mar–? Heh-heh! I'm *amazed* at your conceit!

Lawrence and Markoff get into a shoving match, with Markoff clubbing his opponent into unconsciousness. An evil scheme now hatches in the doctor's warped mind. Stealing into an adjacent laboratory where his assistant Maxine (Tala Birell) is working, Markoff secretly fills a hypodermic needle with fluid from a bottle less-than-subtly labeled ACROMEGALY. He injects this into the veins of the kayoed Lawrence; once the disease has set in, Markoff will be the only person able to cure Lawrence, and he'll be able to bargain with Lawrence for Patricia's hand in marriage. Unaware of what's happened to him, Lawrence is revived by Markoff and sent on his way.

Markoff has been experimenting to find a cure for acromegaly, but the best he's been able to come up with so far is X-53, a serum which arrests but does not remedy the condition. When he congratulates himself on the progress he's made thus far, Maxine (inexplicably in love with the unreceptive Markoff) is quick to burst his bubble:

> MAXINE: You're not even a doctor. You stole a name and laboratory notes from the man you killed.
> MARKOFF: He deserved to die. And his death made it possible for me to escape from Europe as the real Dr. Markoff.
> MAXINE: And reap the rewards earned by another man with years of work and study!
> MARKOFF: What I took from him was small repayment for what he tried to take from me. The love of Lenore, my wife, the woman I worshipped! But his love cooled, as I knew it would, when he looked at her beautiful face and saw the ravages of the hideous disease acromegaly!
> MAXINE: Did you deliberately inoculate her with that dread–
> MARKOFF: I *did!*. . . . . I knew if she were no longer beautiful, no one

else would want her, then I would have her all for myself!. . . . But – she could not stand the sight of her own face. So she killed herself. . .

At home, the still-unsuspecting Lawrence is coping with the first signs of the disease, restlessness and swollen fingers and feet. When his piano playing suffers, he consults a doctor (Sam Flint) who diagnoses his acromegaly, and suggests that he visit glandular disorder specialist (who else?) Dr. Markoff. Lawrence declines, instead hiding himself away in his bedroom suite at home for weeks on end. When Patricia and Bob finally decide to burst in on him, they get a quick look at him in the shadowy room – his face and hands swollen to ghastly proportions – before Patricia faints and Bob carries her out.

Lawrence finally figures out what Markoff has done to him, and goes to the sanatarium to kill him. But Steve (Glenn Strange), Markoff's attendant, appears just as Lawrence is about to attack Markoff, and Lawrence is subdued and placed under sedation. Maxine, however, has overheard the conversation over a dictagraph and angrily accuses Markoff. After Maxine has gone to bed, Markoff releases a gorilla which he keeps in his laboratory from its cage; the simian hates Maxine, and immediately makes for her bedroom. But Maxine's dog Ace hears her screams, and (off-screen) herds the hairy brute back into the cage.

Markoff lures Patricia to the sanatarium by telling her that her father is there, but when the girl finds her father cruelly strapped to a table, she gets into a fight with Markoff. In a nearby room, adding to this climactic mayhem, Maxine has gotten into a struggle with Steve. Bob Blake arrives on the scene unexpectedly and knocks out Steve, while Lawrence manages to unstrap himself and attack Markoff. The pair fight over Markoff's gun, which discharges, killing the evil scientist. With Markoff's death, Patricia fears that her father will never be cured, but Maxine corrects her: Markoff had indeed developed X-54, a cure for acromegaly, and Lawrence will soon be restored to normal.

Production-wise *The Monster Maker* seems to be a bit above PRC's average, the dialogue is intelligent, and '40s horror film regulars Naish, Morgan, McKay and Strange constitute an appealing B cast. But its grisly theme and lack of action, not to mention Naish's slimy performance, make it one of those unwieldy little numbers which seems to have *most* of the right ingredients, but refuses to gel. Like a cake that won't rise, *The Monster Maker* remains obstinately unpalatable. (Its "excessive gruesomeness" earned it a legion of Decency B.)

Naish's notion that he can force Wanda McKay to marry and love him by blackmailing her father is laughably hokey, practically a throwback to the crude and naive silent films where top-hatted villains lashed leading ladies to the railroad tracks. But added to this hoary framework is the more modern idea of infecting someone with disease via laboratory injection, a

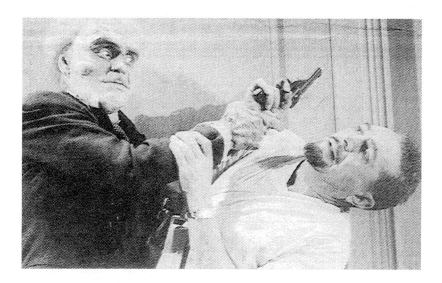

Acromegalic Ralph Morgan in pitched battle with mad medico J. Carrol Naish in
PRC's *The Monster Maker.*

sadistic innovation even by the standards of today's horror films. The
screenplay lingers over this unhappy situation; the film has no subplots and
(except for Naish's scuffles with Ralph Morgan) not a lick of action. *The Monster Maker* is forced to dwell and dawdle over its own unhealthy plot devices.

The introduction of Naish's caged gorilla might have been an attempt
to inject a bit of old-fashioned melodramatic fun into the solemn proceedings. When Naish decides that Tala Birell has outlived her usefulness,
he unleashes the giant brute, which gently upsets a few pieces of patio furniture before making a beeline for Birell's upstairs bedroom. Birell screams
when she awakens to find the gorilla lumbering in her direction, and Ace,
her dog, rushes up toward the room as the screen fades to black; in the next
scene, set the following morning, a disgruntled-looking Naish finds that the
gorilla has been restored to its cage. The sequence, nearly seven minutes
long and containing almost no dialogue, is maddening in its leisurely pacing,
and only adds to the film's lackluster atmosphere.

Here writing in collaboration with action specialist Martin Mooney,
Pierre Gendron was capable of finer work, as witness his scripts for PRC's
later *Bluebeard* and *Fog Island.* (*The Monster Maker*'s script was based on
a story by Lawrence Williams and an uncredited Nell O'Day, an actress best
known for her Westerns; she was the damsel in distress in Universal's semihorror *Mystery of Marie Roget,* 1942.) One of these four, apparently, had a
long memory for horror film plots, as unmistakable elements from Universal's *The Raven* and MGM's *Mad Love* (both 1935) find their way into
Monster Maker's plot.

Ralph Morgan's initial confrontation with J. Carrol Naish used as a blueprint a scene from *The Raven*, where devoted father Samuel S. Hinds tells Poe-obsessed mad doctor Bela Lugosi to keep his mitts off his (Hinds') daughter. Lugosi continues, of course, to pine for his "lost Lenore" – Lenore being also the name of Naish's departed wife – and takes revenge on the father, just as Naish does. *Mad Love*'s influence is seen in the fact that Naish's victim is a pianist; both films feature a scene where this character (Morgan in *Monster Maker*, Colin Clive in *Mad Love*) finds that his hands are losing their touch at the keyboard (not yet realizing that that's the *least* of his troubles!). Another tie to *Mad Love* is a scene where Wanda McKay and Terry Frost listen as the sound of Morgan's masterful piano playing fills the house; rushing to congratulate the off-camera musician on his recovery, they find the piano unattended and the afflicted Morgan merely playing a recording of a past performance.

Perhaps PRC's horror star in residence George Zucco was off working elsewhere, as J. Carrol Naish takes over the horror-man spot in *Monster Maker*. (Zucco played a slightly similar role in Universal's *The Mad Ghoul*, 1943, scientifically turning youthful rival David Bruce into a monster in order to clear his own path to romance with Evelyn Ankers.) Unfortunately, Naish, a fine actor in other genre films (*Dr. Renault's Secret, Calling Dr. Death, House of Frankenstein*), just isn't up to the meager challenge of *The Monster Maker*. While the celebrated character star can't be accused of walking through the role, he lacks the villainous vibes which it requires. Stolid and stiff, silly looking in his pointy goatee and evening clothes (which he wears even around his office and lab!), haughtily waving his cigarette holder, Naish is perhaps Poverty Row's oiliest mad scientist; we share immediately with Wanda McKay a distaste for her unctuous and greasy would-be suitor.

The picture seems to be trying to establish that Naish keeps Tala Birell under hypnotic control, an effect Lugosi could have conveyed with one eyeball tied behind his back. But with Naish in the role, blandly staring at the girl, it's incumbent upon viewers to figure out for themselves that that's what's going on (or, to try and otherwise rationalize Birell's self-contradictory actions). Immediately upon completion of *The Monster Maker*, Naish high-tailed it over to Universal for the horror film *Jungle Woman* (which started shooting February 14), perhaps his all-time worst performance. It's almost as though Naish saw himself getting into a horror rut, and felt that poor acting might turn horror filmmakers off on him. It didn't, and in April, he played a hunchback in *House of Frankenstein* (Universal); he looked silly dressed like an organ grinder's monkey but gave the best performance in the piece and got prominent "and" billing for his efforts. In later years Naish acted in *The Beast with Five Fingers* (Warner Bros., 1946), as a policeman, and in *Dracula vs. Frankenstein* (Independent-International, 1971), where he played a wheelchair-bound mad scientist. Sam Sherman,

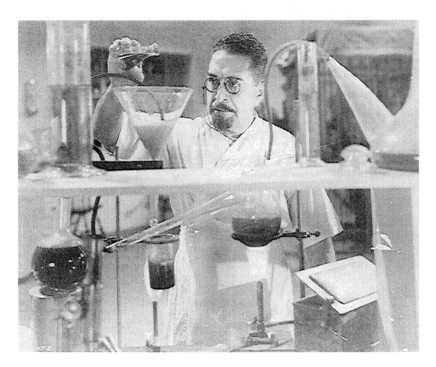

J. Carrol Naish, pretending he knows what he's doing in a posed shot from PRC's *The Monster Maker.*

the latter film's producer and an avid fan of the oldtime horror films, reminisces:

> Naish was a very spunky guy, a tough old codger. I was talking to him one day – I thought he'd have a sense of humor – and I said, "Well, Mr. Naish, I know this is not exactly PRC –." And he snapped, "You bet your *ass* it isn't!" But all his scenes were filmed at Hollywood Stages, which is a nice big commercial studio; he had a nice place to sit; he had food when he wanted it; people were attentive to him; he was courted with probably more respect than he got from big companies. And yet he was not well and he was sort of like *grumpy*, where you couldn't kid around with him. I never felt that moment of informality with him, he was pretty much on the stiff side. But if he didn't need the money at all, maybe he shouldn't have done the picture.

Dracula vs. Frankenstein would be his final film. The New York–born Naish, Irish by descent (a nationality he never played on the screen) and a veteran of the television series *Life with Luigi, The New Adventures of Charlie Chan* and *Guestward Ho!*, died in 1973.

Ralph Morgan, like Naish, managed to pop up in far more than his share of horror thrillers (*Condemned to Live, Night Monster, The Mad Doctor, Weird Woman, The Creeper*, etc.) and serials, yet never became too-closely associated with them in the public eye. As the musician-turned-monster, Morgan effortlessly gives the best performance in *The Monster Maker*, giving his best shot to a sensationalistic role that other actors might have taken far less seriously. The brother of character star Frank Morgan, he died in 1956. Tala Birell and Wanda McKay likewise strive to make their stereotypic characters lifelike, with Birell having the tougher time of it playing a character whose motivation is often more than just a bit hazy. Terry Frost handles his few heroic scenes stalwartly. Glenn Strange, two months from playing the Frankenstein Monster for the first time (in *House of Frankenstein*) and guaranteeing his niche in the Horror Hall of Fame, physically fits the bill as Naish's part-time attendant/full-time henchman (a minuscule part).

Two months after *The Monster Maker* wrapped, Universal put the Sherlock Holmes mystery *The Pearl of Death* (1944) into production, with Rondo Hatton as the spine-snapping Creeper. It is, of course, just an assumption that *The Monster Maker* might have prompted Universal to cast real-life acromegalic Hatton in the murderous role, but stranger things *have* happened; and it *does* seem strange that, after a half-century of filmmaking, the very first film to feature an acromegalic monster should be followed eight weeks later by the second. Hatton was signed for *Pearl* on April 18, three days after *Monster Maker* was released; his Creeper character caught the public's fancy and the Neanderthal-ic actor quickly became a fixture at Universal's B horror unit, showing up in supporting parts in two pictures before becoming the star of his own short-lived series. Hatton died in 1946 – killed by the glandular disorder he had exploited in movies – and, by one of those funny coincidences, his last film *The Brute Man* (1946) ended up being sold by Universal to, of all people, PRC. Interesting, too: That Universal production, based in part on Hatton's own life, is in far worse taste than even *The Monster Maker*.

Acromegaly, inexplicably redubbed "acromegalia," also figured into a subplot of Universal-International's *Tarantula* (1955), with Leo G. Carroll here being subjected to the familiar swollen makeup. *Captive Wild Woman*'s mad scientist in residence (John Carradine) was an expert on acromegaly, but the disease doesn't figure into the plot of that 1943 film. The deformed sailor (stuntman George Sawaya) in *The Black Sleep* (1956) was a victim of acromegaly, according to the script, although this isn't specified in the film itself. Another *real*-life sufferer of acromegaly was the Swedish Angel, a wrestler best-known to fantasy film fans for his brief appearance in *Mighty Joe Young* (1949). Actor Tiny Ron was made up by makeup artist and Rondo Hatton fan Rick Baker to look just like Hatton for his homicidal henchman role in Disney's *The Rocketeer* (1991).

The Monster Maker's musical score was by Albert Glasser, the prolific film composer best-known for his pounding, crescendo-laden scores on '50s sci-fi and horror films. According to Glasser, one week was all the time he was given by PRC for *Monster Maker*, but –

> Luckily there was very little for me to do. Mostly piano work for that. I had to find a concert pianist to record all of the piano stuff and write a couple of cues here and there. Nine times out of ten, all I had was a week. Occasionally two weeks.

Glasser received $250 for his *Monster Maker* score: "I composed, orchestrated, copied, conducted, worked with the music cutter. What the hell? If I didn't want it, they had ten guys waiting. I wanted credit." *Monster Maker* was Glasser's first film as composer, and his first screen credit. His later films include *Rocketship X-M* (1950), *Invasion U.S.A.* (1952), *The Neanderthal Man* (1953), *The Cyclops* (1957), *The Saga of the Viking Women and Their Voyage to the Waters of the Great Sea Serpent* (1957), *Confessions of an Opium Eater* (1962) and, by Glasser's count, over 160 more (credited or uncredited).

Openly appalled by *The Monster Maker*, the reviewer for *The Hollywood Reporter* branded it a "HORROR PIC THAT'S TRULY HORRIBLE": "It attains its extra ounce of nastiness by reason of its definite plausibility.... The results are as stomach-turning as the most ardent neurotic could wish for.... Best performance is turned in by Ralph Morgan, who makes the pianist believable. J. Carrol Naish, considerably below his usual high standard, plays the doctor in the most obvious Bela Lugosi manner, embellished by about 96 points worth of ham. Tala Birell also uses up a few points of same.... Maybe the players aren't to blame for the kind of acting here offered. Maybe it was the direction. And maybe it wasn't the director's fault, either. Maybe it's all just because this is the kind of acting horror film addicts demand." *Variety* wasn't quite as squeamish about it all, but they weren't exactly bowled over either: "The ingredients are there to make this a suspenseful horror film, but somewhere along the line director Sam Newfield got sidetracked. Result is another one of those 'mad scientist' things that wind up on the duals."

The ugliness of the film struck the Phantom of the Movies (*The Phantom's Ultimate Video Guide*) just right: "An authentically creepy flick.... Pretty sick for its time." Denis Gifford (*A Pictorial History of Horror Movies*) branded it "a nasty piece by any standards, even PRC's." In *B Movies*, Don Miller kidded, "*The Monster Maker* had J. Carrol Naish inflicting a distorting disease on Ralph Morgan, who was further victimized by unskilled makeup and looked like he was wearing rubber padding on his face, which was illegal during wartime shortages." William K. Everson wrote that *Monster Maker* "was definitely a cut above the average, perhaps due to better actors than usual and some novelty values in the script."

The Lady and the Monster
(Republic, 1944)

Released April 17. 86 minutes. Associate Producer and Director: George Sherman. Screenplay: Dane Lussier and Frederick Kohner. Based on the novel *Donovan's Brain* by Curt Siodmak. Photography: John Alton, A.S.C. Musical Score: Walter Scharf. Orchestral Arrangements: Marlin Skiles. Film Editor: Arthur Roberts. Sound: Earl Crain, Sr. Art Director: Russell Kimball. Set Decorations: Otto Siegel. Gowns: Adele. Special Effects: Theodore Lydecker. Assistant Director: Bud Springsteen.

Cast: Vera Hruba Ralston (Janice Farell), Richard Arlen (Dr. Patrick Cory), Erich von Stroheim (Prof. Franz Mueller), Helen Vinson (Chloe Donovan), Mary Nash (Mrs. Fame), Sidney Blackmer (Eugene Fulton), Janet Martin (Café Singer), Bill Henry (Roger Collins), Charles Cane (Mr. Grimes), Juanita Quigley (Mary Lou), Josephine Dillon (Mary Lou's Grandmother), Antonio Triana, Lola Montes (Themselves), Tom London (Man Who Tails Cory), Sam Flint (G. Phipps, the Bank Manager), Edward Keane (Manning), Lane Chandler (White, the Ranger), Wallis Clark (Warden), Harry Hayden (Dr. Martin), Maxine Doyle (Receptionist), Billy Benedict (Bellhop), Herbert Clifton (Butler), Harry Depp (Bank Teller), Lee Phelps (Headwaiter), Jack Kirk (The Husky Man), Frank Graham (Narrator).

> "The brain could walk my body in front of a car, throw it out of the window, put a bullet through my head with my own hands. I could only cry out from the despair of my imprisonment, but even the words my mouth formed were those the brain wanted to hear.... It could continue its parasitic life in any other body. A woman's, or a child's. Or, if it chose, a dog's! There was no limit to its polymorphism."—from Curt Siodmak's *Donovan's Brain*

After shying away from the production of horror movies throughout the first eight years of its existence – Republic's only previous horror release was the independent (John H. Auer) production *The Crime of Doctor Crespi* (1935), based on the Poe story *The Premature Burial*, starring Erich Von Stroheim and filmed in eight days at the Biograph Studios in the Bronx – the studio took its first (and only) major plunge with *The Lady and the Monster*, an adaptation of Curt Siodmak's acclaimed 1943 sci-fi novel *Donovan's Brain*. Republic's own publicity releases dubbed it "the most novel picture" they had ever attempted, and the production was given a bigger-than-average budget, indicating that Republic was looking to make the most of Siodmak's macabre story. But the results, unhappily, were something else again.

Try as they did, Republic could just never get the horror film formula nailed down. It was an action studio whose specialty was Westerns and serials, a lot where leading men were signed if they resembled the stunt

men, not vice versa. It's unrealistic and unkind to expect them to be able
to turn out a goosebumpy thriller; Val Lewton probably couldn't have made
a good, kid-pleasing Roy Rogers Western if his life depended on it, but that
doesn't reflect badly on *him*. Maybe Republic shouldn't even have *tried* to
make horror movies; obviously, they themselves knew this for years. These
apologies really don't excuse everything that's wrong with *The Lady and the
Monster*, however. We'll get into that later.

Curt Siodmak's *Donovan's Brain* was an immediate hit with the public
(*and* with literary critics) when it was published by Alfred A. Knopf, Inc.,
in February, 1943 (*"Donovan's Brain* is terrific!" –*New York Times*; "Makes
your blood run cold" –*Baltimore Sun*); according to Siodmak, it's sold five
million copies. But before the thing was even printed in book form, Siodmak
was already trying to peddle the motion picture rights, unsuccessfully; an
executive at Columbia told him it was the most idiotic story he'd ever heard
in his life. Siodmak finally sold the picture rights to Republic president
Herbert J. Yates for $1,900, but as soon as the book began to circulate, peo-
ple like Humphrey Bogart and Laird Cregar were contacting Siodmak,
wanting the property for themselves.

Too late. For better or worse, the ball was already in Republic's court,
and studio screenwriters were adapting *Donovan's Brain*. Siodmak's novel,
done in the form of diary entries, detailed in first-person the activities of
Patrick Cory, a 38-year-old Harvard graduate who married an independently
wealthy New England girl, Janice, at 29, practiced medicine in Los Angeles,
and then retired to arid Washington Junction, Arizona, to carry out his own
experiments, living on the money he had saved and afterwards on Janice's.
Self-absorbed and almost hermit-like, he ignores his loving Janice for weeks
at a time, concentrating on his work. An aging, heavy-drinking European
doctor, Schratt, disapproves of his work but drops by to assist every so
often.

Cory extracts and salvages the brain of plane crash survivor Warren
Horace Donovan, a ruthless tycoon; Cory keeps it alive in his lab through
electrical means, but eventually becomes a slave to the dominating brain.
Traveling to Los Angeles, he intrudes into the lives of Donovan's family and
old acquaintances while living on large sums of money he withdraws from
secret bank accounts which Donovan had opened under the name of Roger
Hinds. Hinds turns out to be the one man that the cold-hearted Donovan
ever regretted swindling (Hinds killed himself as a result), and now Donovan, through Cory, is determined to make amends by securing the release
from prison of young Cyril Hinds, one of Roger's relatives. (Cyril, a ne'er-
do-well, had stolen every last penny from his poor mom, then killed her by
driving over her face!) When Janice tries to reason with him, to get him out
from under Donovan's domination, "Cory" is about to kill her when he unexpectedly becomes himself once again. Returning home a few days later,
Cory and Janice find Dr. Schratt and the brain both dead on the laboratory

floor. Cory pieces together what happened: Schratt had been able to tell by
the brain's encephalogram readings that it was forcing Cory to engage in
violence, so he attacked the brain with his hands, tearing it loose from its
life–sustaining electrical connections. The fiendish and powerful brain in-
duced a coronary thrombosis in Schratt before it expired.

There's a scary touch at the very end of the book, when Cory learns
from a newspaper that Cyril Hinds has been hanged. The newspaper account describes how the lever-activated mechanism controlling the trapdoor beneath Hinds' feet had mysteriously failed – twice. The executioner,
mindful of the ancient law that a man can be hanged only three times,
supported and dropped the door manually on the third try. "Donovan's un-
quenchable energy still roams the mortal world. He had tried again to
push through his will, to save Hinds from hanging!... Energy cannot be
destroyed."

Republic took the expected number of liberties with *Donovan's Brain*;
a talky piece (only partially synopsized above), Siodmak's novel was unsuited for a faithful filmization. The tippling Dr. Schratt fell by the wayside,
replaced by another European doctor, Franz Mueller (played by *Doctor
Crespi* himself, Erich von Stroheim): it's Mueller that's obsessed with the
idea of keeping brains alive after death, while his assistant Patrick Cory is
primarily concerned with testing the potential of his encephalograph (a
word von Stroheim can't pronounce!). In the book, Dr. Cory inherits
Donovan's limp once he becomes the brain's slave; in the film, it's Mueller
who's afflicted right from the picture's start. Janice, Cory's novel-wife, is
his film-sweetheart. Cory/Donovan's adventures in L.A. are also slightly
rewritten, and a tiresome section from the novel (Cory falls into a ditch in
the street, is run over by a steam shovel, and spends time in the hospital!)
is also wisely eliminated. The ending, too, is greatly changed, with the
Republic screenwriters substituting action for the novel's disappointing
denouement.

Herbert Yates wasted little time putting his new screen property into
production. By September 1943, the script (titled *The Monster and the
Lady*) was completed, and George Sherman was confering with Yates about
taking the director's chair for the upcoming film. Erich von Stroheim was
signed on September 25 and the film, still being called *The Monster and the
Lady*, went into production on October 18. During production the title was
shortened to *The Monster*.

At the Castle, "a great, fantastic place" on the edge of the Arizona Desert, Prof. Mueller (von Stroheim) is conducting his maverick experiments
on animal brains. The other occupants of the house are Dr. Cory (Richard
Arlen), his assistant; Janice Farell (Vera Hruba Ralston), his ward; and
Mrs. Fame (Mary Nash), the saturnine housekeeper. Janice also helps out
in the lab, as a nurse; she's in love with Cory, and feels that the gnarled old
Mueller has got his eye on her. (The picture dwells on this angle quite

Erich von Stroheim and Richard Arlen compare their observations of Donovan's brain in Republic's *The Lady and the Monster*. *The Lady,* ice-skating star Vera Ralston, looks on blandly.

a bit, but except for a lecherous look or two, Mueller never makes a move. We even have to wonder if Janice has misjudged him.)

Cory and Janice are at a formal party at the Arizona Palms when they are interrupted by a phone call from Mueller, who tells Cory that a private plane has crashed close to the nearby ranger station; Cory's help is needed. (Mueller can't go, he says, because there's something wrong with the starter of his car, but the camera puts the lie to his statement, pulling back to reveal the little man snug in bed!) At the crash sight, Cory and Ranger White (Lane Chandler) pull from the wreckage the body of a man clinging to life. The man later dies at the Castle, where Mueller suddenly realizes they have an unprecedented opportunity: To remove and preserve his undamaged brain. Cory balks at first but quickly comes around to Mueller's way of thinking, and with Janice's help the brain is extracted and placed in a large serum-filled glass tank, kept alive with electricity and monitored via encephalograph. Only after the dark deed is done do Cory and Mueller realize whose brain it is they stole: "the most illustrious brain in the entire country," that of tycoon William H. Donovan.

The next day, at the Phoenix office of district physician Dr. Martin (Harry Hayden), Cory and Mueller meet Donovan's wife (Helen Vinson) and attorney Eugene Fulton (Sidney Blackmer), who ask whether the financier had made any dying statements. Fulton perceives that Cory is acting suspiciously; at the morgue, the attorney had already noticed that a trepanation of the skull had been performed on Donovan. His curiosity piqued, Fulton steals into the Castle under cover of darkness, finds Donovan's brain and realizes quickly (*too* quickly) what the scientists are up to. Mrs. Donovan is all for calling the police, but Fulton reminds her that Donovan has left her without a cent; all of his money is apparently socked away in secret accounts. Perhaps Cory and Mueller, working with the brain, can be made to lead them to the hidden funds. . .

Janice keeps after Cory to quit his job as Mueller's assistant, which he promises to do, but instead he finds himself becoming increasingly enthusiastic about the experiment. Mueller suggests that they might be able to communicate with the brain through telepathy, using Cory as a medium; the idea works. Cory hears Donovan's voice in his mind's ear that night and, acting on impulse, uses his left hand to sign the left-handed tycoon's name, in Donovan's own handwriting. The next night, the eerie, underwatery voice comes to him again, repeating the words "Federal prison." Acting like an automaton, "Cory" leaves immediately by car for Los Angeles.

In L.A., "Cory," acting under the brain's control, seems to be trying to pick up Donovan's life where the heartless financial wizard left off. At the National Trust Bank, he endorses a $50,000 check to himself using the signature "12531"; Donovan had secretly set up that mysterious account years before. Money in pocket, "Cory" visits Eugene Fulton, hiring him to work to reopen the trial of Roger Collins (Bill Henry), a young man on death row. Collins was convicted of the murder of his stepfather, but maintains his innocence even as he waits to die.

Meanwhile, at the Castle, Janice is sick with worry for Cory; she steals into the laboratory and tampers with the fuse box, cutting off power to Donovan's brain. But the sinister hunk of gray matter is now self-sufficient, continuing to operate independent of electric current.

Successful at reopening the Collins case, lawyer Fulton and his equally crooked associate Grimes (Charles Cane) get $100,000 from "Cory"; they tell him they'll use it to bribe jurors and witnesses, but they're really just keeping the loot for themselves. (Collins is Donovan's son from a secret former marriage, therefore a potential heir, so the Donovan clan wants to keep him on death row.) The one witness that *can't* be influenced, "Cory" is told, is teenager Mary Lou (Juanita Quigley), who saw Collins leaving the murder house.

Now in L.A. herself, Janice catches up with "Cory," who hustles the girl into his car. "Cory" drives to a bus stop near Mary Lou's home and, when the schoolgirl gets off the bus, tries to run her down; Janice grabs the steering wheel and diverts the speeding car at the last second. On a lonely mountain road, the furious "Cory" begins to choke Janice but back at the Castle, through what can only be described as a miraculous coincidence, housekeeper Mrs. Fame has chosen just this moment to anesthetize Donovan's brain by pouring morphine into the tank. Cory becomes himself again, and the two speed by car back to Arizona. En route, the exhausted Cory – whose memory is now apparently one with Donovan's – explains that Roger Collins *is* innocent; Collins was Donovan's son from a marriage nobody but the man who became Collins' foster father knew about. When this man, Donovan's one-time secretary, threatened to publish Donovan's scandalous life story, Donovan killed him himself.

At the Castle, Janice, Cory and Mrs. Fame are conspiring to destroy the brain when the mad Prof. Mueller, wielding a gun, appears. Cory and Mueller get into a fistfight; Mueller gets the upper hand and is about to clobber Cory with a chair when Mrs. Fame scoops up the gun and shoots him. Janice uses a stool to shatter the glass tank, and the brain is swept by a cascade of serum to the laboratory floor. In *Dragnet* style, the film's narrator tells us the results of the upcoming trials: Mrs. Fame is acquitted, Roger Collins is cleared and Patrick Cory serves a short prison stretch while Janice waits for him patiently.

[*The Lady and the Monster*] is not another one of those lurid melodramas designed to throw a scare into moviegoers. It is tense and exciting, but a well-constructed drama, many notches higher than the usual chiller-thriller type of film. – *The Brooklyn Daily Eagle*

The makers of [*The Lady and the Monster*] evidently were not much impressed with what they had done so they labeled their work with a luridly claptrap title. . . . They are altogether wrong in their doubts. Hidden behind this feverish title is a picture worthy of the excellent mystery drama, *Donovan's Brain*, on which it was based. . . . Arlen, newly released from his long series of action melodramas, gives a performance of sustained tenseness that most of us had forgotten he could achieve. The scientific zeal that mounts to ferocious ruthlessness is developed effectively in the performance of Erich von Stroheim. The picture's quality springs largely from the achievements of these two and from the masterful use of eerie lighting and atmosphere by George Sherman as director. – *New York World Telegram*

Given a production quality and a cast far superior to those usually found in pictures of this type, *The Lady and the Monster* comes through as entertainment which grasps the interest at the outset and holds it unflaggingly throughout. . . Miss Ralston. . . shows definite promise. She has a pleasing personality and she meets satisfactorily the limited demands upon her histrionic capabilities. Von Stroheim performs with the brilliance expected of him and Arlen is excellent in his quasi-dual role. . . . The picture as a whole is the best George Sherman has made to date and sends him up another step on his way to the top. John Alton's photography is somewhat uneven, falling short on the star but rising to effective heights on several occasions. – *The Hollywood Reporter*

...one of the most authentic hair-raisers screened this year at
Broadway's horror house, The Rialto. —*New York Herald-Tribune*

Reviews that greeted the release of *The Lady and the Monster* were
largely favorable; most critics appreciated the production gloss and
(especially) the unique plot. Time has a habit of marching on, however: Siodmak's story has been done to death in the nearly 50 years since *The Lady
and the Monster*, and today the film's narrative seems trite and long-in-the-
telling. Of course it's important, in the interests of fairness, to keep in mind
that *Lady and the Monster* preceded the long string of brain- (or head-) on-
the-laboratory-table films that proliferated in the '50s and '60s*; it broke
ground and established many of the conventions that these other films
would follow. Somehow, though, it requires more than an appreciation of
this fact to keep a viewer's eyelids aloft at two in the morning as *Lady and
the Monster* takes its sweet time telling its familiar story on the late, late
show.

A big part of the problem with *Lady and the Monster* is 20-year-old Vera
Hruba Ralston, its (undeservedly) top-billed player. Ralston was the girlfriend of Herbert J. Yates, more than 40 years her senior, and Yates was
anxious to build the Czechoslovakian ice-skating star into one of his studio's
biggest attractions. As Vera Hruba, she had minor figure-skating parts in
her first two Republic films (*Ice-Capades*, 1941, and *Ice-Capades Revue*,
1942) before Yates decided that she was now ready for the Big Time. Her
name was Americanized (Vera retained the Hruba but added Ralston,
selected because she liked that breakfast cereal) and she was placed into her
first nonskating vehicle, *The Lady and the Monster*.

Naturally she got top billing, edging out long-established stars Arlen
and von Stroheim; this type of nepotism is as old as Hollywood itself. The
problem, unfortunately, is that the film makes her work to *earn* her top
spot. Janice Farell is something less than integral to the plot of *The Lady
and the Monster*, yet the picture tries to center itself around this extraneous
character. Every time the film builds up a small head of steam, in steps
Ralston, sick with worry over one thing or another, voicing vague fears at
great length, to put on the brakes. At this early stage in her career, Ralston
was neither a good actress nor overloaded with personality; she was attractive, but no knockout. Her character literally inflicts herself upon the story.
Interviewed by Charles Flynn and Todd McCarthy in *Kings of the Bs*, Joe
Kane (who directed nine of Ralston's 26 pictures) remembered that the
Czech star acted out her role in *The Lady and the Monster* phonetically, not
knowing what she was saying. Kane also told them that George Sher-

*The Thing That Couldn't Die *(1958)*, The Man Without a Body *(1959)*, The Brain That
Wouldn't Die (1962), Madmen of Mandoras *(1964)*, The Frozen Dead *(1967); even Steve Martin's* The Man with Two Brains *(1983)*.

man later quit Republic because he thought he was going to have to direct more Ralston pictures.

Perhaps mostly by contrast, Richard Arlen and Erich von Stroheim both seem to give especially solid performances. Von Stroheim, Hollywood's *homme terrible*, takes every advantage of his stereotypic role, sometimes hamming a bit to compensate for the fact that the film's action frequently strays from the Castle (which *he* almost never leaves). The curmudgeonly, chain-smoking Prof. Mueller is a role made-to-order for the ramrod-spined Prussian actor, billed in silent days as "The Man You Love to Hate." Like Arlen's Patrick Cory, Mueller too becomes something of a Jekyll/Hyde character, pussyfooting and underplaying when it suits his sinister purposes, yet at other times running the Castle like a prisoner of war camp, barking out orders and dressing down anyone who questions his authority. The pit bull of Poverty Row mad scientists, von Stroheim manages even to make such *un*personable movie madmen as George Zucco seem cuddly by comparison. (At one point late in the film, Mrs. Fame [Mary Nash] shares her suspicion that Donovan's brain may have taken possession of Prof. Mueller as well, but at the film's conclusion, the narrator puts the kibosh to that theory, calling Mueller's death "well-deserved. He had tried to distort an experiment of science into a diabolical plot to further his own personal gains.")

Par for von Stroheim's course, the actor shines most brightly when he's making the most out of little "moments." Caught carrying an organ grinder's monkey into the Castle, he explains that he just purchased the little critter, which is ravaged by tuberculosis. "Then why did you buy him?" Ralston's Janice asks innocently – only to have von Stroheim's Mueller shoot her a wordless, knowing look which makes the monkey's impending fate ("Gigli saw!") abundantly clear. Later, at the office of Dr. Martin, (Harry Hayden), this little physician is bubbling excitedly about the events of the previous evening:

> MARTIN: I can't believe it yet. I never thought I'd live to see the day when I'd declare the great W. H. Donovan dead.
> MUELLER *(with faked enthusiasm)*: Yes, you're quite a celebrity, Dr. Martin!

Von Stroheim wasn't particularly enamored of *either* of his Republic excursions into horror. Of *The Crime of Doctor Crespi*, he commented, "[It] was also the crime of Republic, the screenwriter, and the director!" And, on *The Lady and the Monster*: "The story, by Siodmak, was interesting. The film itself – not so good!" Of von Stroheim, Vera Ralston recalled, "He was a little on the hard side to work with; he was very precisioned."

Arlen is effective as Cory, although the actor does strike a few false notes, and may not be entirely the type to play an eager laboratory assistant. The brawny star of many an outdoor action film, he debuted in 1920, worked at Paramount from the '20s through the late '30s, went under contract to Universal for two years and then became a star of low-budget Pine-Thomas attractions (not to mention one of that organization's stockholders) in the early '40s. Among his many films, of course, are the usual mixed bag of horror and science fiction assignments, most notably Paramount's excellent *Island of Lost Souls* (1933) where, as the hero, he took on Charles Laughton's rampaging manimals. It was all downhill for Arlen after that, sci-fi-wise: next came the fair-to-middling *The Lady and the Monster* and *The Phantom Speaks*, then in the '60s the bargain-basement *The Crawling Hand* and *The Human Duplicators*. (Illness, or maybe just common sense, forced him to bow out of *The Slime People*, 1963; Robert Burton replaced him.) Arlen died in 1976.

In *Lady and the Monster*, Arlen is let down by the script in his scenes as Cory/Donovan: Donovan is established in dialogue as a fierce, indomitable character, but in the assumed person of Cory he reveals himself as just a bossy grouch. Lawyer Fulton and his associates are far craftier and more ruthless: They easily discover what Prof. Mueller is up to in his laboratory, and even figure out that Cory is acting under Donovan's telepathic orders. "Cory" hands over to them vast sums of money to use in Roger Collins' defense, but Fulton and his mob laughingly line their own pockets with the loot instead. From beginning to end, despite all of his iron-handed posturing, Cory/Donovan is played for a sucker.

To differentiate between Cory and Cory/Donovan, the latter is harshly lit from below, an ominous but ultimately comical effect. In rooms where all the other characters are evenly bathed in light, and even out in the sunshine, his face remains shadowy and spooky; it's a wonder no one comments on it. It was a neat idea but it's ruined by overuse.

Supporting roles are well played by Helen Vinson (Mrs. Donovan), Mary Nash (the housekeeper, who for some unfathomable reason loves Prof. Mueller), Sidney Blackmer and Charles Cane (Fulton and his even more unscrupulous confederate, the aptly-named Grimes) and Bill Henry (snivelling Collins). Josephine Dillon, Vera Ralston's drama and voice coach (and the ex-wife of Clark Gable), plays a grandmother in the film. Donovan's voice, heard on a recording device in one scene, sounds like actor LeRoy Mason's.

Director George Sherman was a veteran of countless Republic Westerns and maybe not the ideal choice for *The Lady and the Monster*, but he brings a modicum of atmosphere and style to the film; composer Walter Scharf's shrieking violins and noted *film noir* photographer John Alton's efforts also go a long way toward creating the desired mood of eerie tension in some of the laboratory scenes. But Sherman is unable to maintain the proper pace, largely due to the unwieldy script which gives Vera Ralston far too much footage and also introduces such unwanted extras as a dance team

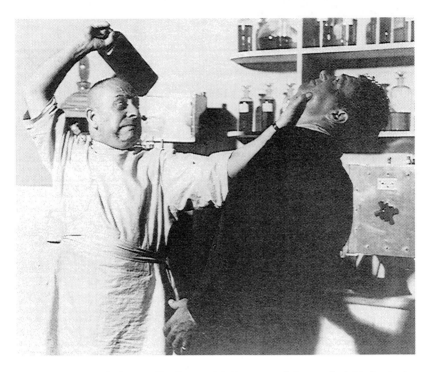

Most every Republic horror film featured at least one elaborate fistfight, beginning with *The Lady and the Monster*. Bloody-lipped Erich von Stroheim seems to have the upper hand over Richard Arlen in this publicity photo.

(Antonio Triana and Lola Montes) and a café thrush (Janet Martin) who sings a Spanish rendition of a song called "Yours."

No Republic horror film would be complete without a fistfight, and *Lady and the Monster* climactically pits Arlen against von Stroheim in a brawl in the Castle laboratory. Von Stroheim, lame and aged, would seem to be no match for Arlen but not only does he hold his own in the battle royale (photographed mostly from a distant high shot, to facilitate the use of stunt doubles), he even *prevails* until housekeeper Mary Nash unsportingly puts a bullet in his back.

The Lady and the Monster finds Republic at their most polished, including spacious sets (Prof. Mueller's Castle would be the pride of any Transylvanian vampire), a plushy nightclub well-stocked with dancing extras, a good cast and an overall look of professionalism that makes the film almost indistinguishable from many major studio productions. But the film's basic idea seems stubbornly uncinematic, and despite the physical mounting, *The Lady and the Monster* fails to impress. A narrator (Frank Graham), who whispers like a golf commentator afraid the players will overhear, describes action that we can see. Characters talk and talk, then talk some more. The brain has its own musical motif, an annoying tick-tock. The script would seem better suited to a radio adaptation of Siodmak's story. (Orson Welles starred as Cory in a two-part airwave presentation of *Donovan's Brain*, heard on CBS' *Suspense* radio series May 18 and 25, 1944. TV's *Studio One* presented it live on February 28, 1955, with Wendell Corey as Cory and E.G. Marshall as Schratt.)

Siodmak, a nice guy but stingy with the compliments, claims never to have seen any of the three official versions of his novel because he disapproves of the way they stray from his novel. Remembering *The Lady and the Monster*, he carps,

> Herbert Yates called me one day and said, "Siodmak, you are crazy!" I said, "Why am I crazy?" He said, "A scientist like Dr. Cory, he doesn't live in a little hut in the desert. He lives in a *castle!*" He put a damn castle in the story, and von Stroheim running around it like a rat. "And," Yates went on, "I have a new title for you – *The Lady and the Monster*. And *The Lady* will be *Vera!*" – Vera Hruba Ralston, the ice-skater, Yates' girlfriend. So I quit. And I never saw the picture.

Actually, although Siodmak may be loath to admit it, *Donovan's Brain*, much vaunted for its uniqueness, begins to seem awfully derivative considering some of the half-alike movies that preceded it. In the English-made *The Man Who Lived Again* (1936), Boris Karloff developed an electronic apparatus to transplant "the consciousness" (the mind) from one subject to another. A physical transplant put the brain of a wrongly executed man (Phillip Terry) into the noggin of an ape (Charles Gemora) in Paramount's *The Monster and the Girl* (1941). Most notably, Universal's *Black Friday* (1940), co-written by Siodmak, saw a portion of a gangster's brain finding a new home in the head of a meek college professor (Stanley Ridges) who becomes a Jekyll-and-Hyde character. Siodmak's novel just seems like a further twist on the SF themes laid out in films like these, additionally introducing the element of long-distance control by mental telepathy. Of course, probably few if *any* of the literary critics who applauded *Donovan's Brain* were aware of these B productions, and Siodmak's not-quite-fully deserved reputation as a sci-fi innovator had its beginnings. (Siodmak later penned a sequel to *Donovan's Brain*, titled *Hauser's Memory*.)

Obviously impressed with Richard Arlen's work in the film, Republic signed him to a three-year contract which called for four "top-budget" productions annually. Herbert Yates instructed his story department to line up "a group of important novels" for Arlen, according to Republic's publicists, but the movies that resulted were strictly grindhouse fodder, including *The Phantom Speaks*, a semiremake of *The Lady and the Monster*. This group of films also included *Storm Over Lisbon* (1944), which teamed him again with Ralston, von Stroheim and director George Sherman.

Republic played up *Lady and the Monster* big, and undoubtedly basked in the glory of its many wholly positive reviews. Only a few dissenting voices were heard. A. Weiler of *The New York Times* complained, "*Donovan's Brain*, the Curt Siodmak horror novel which was published to critical plaudits early last year, lost an intriguing title and a large portion of plausibility and pace in [*The Lady and the Monster*]. . . . Richard Arlen's performance as the possessed assistant is the most credible one. But the truth is *The Lady and the Monster* is a mite too lethargic. In this case, Donovan's brain probably could stand a shot of adrenalin." *Variety*, giving the film the same kind of ultra-terse review they gave Republic's 54-minute horse operas, put their finger right on the problem: "Although title directly implies that this is a thrill-chill melodrama, and tag will catch plenty of customers in spots where such fare is accepted, picture is more of a clinical adventure. . . . Miss Hruba, former ice-skating star, makes bid for dramatic buildup here, but is handicapped by role. Arlen is okay while von Stroheim is most impressive. . . . Story unfolds at a stolid pace, with too few suspenseful episodes."

It's never clear who the *Monster* of the title is, von Stroheim's character or Donovan's brain; who the *Lady* is, of course, is only *too* clear. The British, always quick to look for lewd connotations in every title, redubbed it *The Lady and the Doctor* and released it in a slightly censored version. In 1950, Republic whittled the film's running time down a bit and reissued it as *Tiger Man*, another head-scratcher of a title.

In 1953, Siodmak's story was filmed a second time, remade by producer Tom Gries as *Donovan's Brain*, with Lew Ayres as Cory, Nancy Davis (Reagan) as Janice and Gene Evans as Dr. Schratt (a major character in the novel, missing from *The Lady and the Monster*). This United Artists release followed the novel more closely and is a better film than *Lady and the Monster* all around, but Siodmak disowns it also, *he* says because they changed his ending (in this one, the brain is destroyed when lightning strikes the Cory house). More likely, Siodmak was just miffed because he was slated to direct the film, but got booted off (Felix Feist replaced him). Siodmak recalls,

> Tom Gries . . . didn't like me. He had these advertisements made for the film saying, "Based on the famous book." Period. He didn't want to mention my name! Gries was the producer and he wouldn't let me direct it because of a personal dislike. He was the meanest son of a bitch I had ever seen.

Herbert Strock, film editor on *Donovan's Brain*, later a schlock director of note, remembers a different set of circumstances:

> I was very excited about the fact that Curt was going to direct *Donovan's Brain*, and I wanted him to stay on the picture. But it seems

that in discussions of how things were going to be done, Curt became the stiff, Germanic, immobile person, and would not listen. Gries and the producer, Allan Dowling, became very upset; I pleaded with them to keep Curt on, that I would guide him through, but behind my back they bumped him. And it was too bad, because Curt did feel very badly hurt. I tried to explain to him what had happened, and I also very much wanted to be his friend, but he kept sloughing me off and did not want to discuss it. He was extremely sensitive and extremely hurt. I can't understand his attitude toward Tom, because it wasn't a personal dislike at all. . .

Curt has many negative feelings; he always had a chip on his shoulder because of the fact that he could never follow in the footsteps of Robert, his brother, who *was* a fairly good director. Curt just couldn't get his own projects going the way he wanted to do them.

A third version, a 1962 West German/British production, was called *Vengeance* in England and *Ein Toter sucht seiner Mörder* (A Dead Man Seeks His Murderer) in West Germany. (It was released in the U.S. as *The Brain* in 1965.) Directed by Freddie Francis, it starred Peter van Eyck and Bernard Lee (James Bond's first M) as the scientists who restore the dead tycoon's brain to life. The disagreeable finale left the brain still alive and van Eyck still under its control. Surprise, Siodmak snubs this one, too.

Hollywood in the Forties called *The Lady and the Minister* (sic!) a "cheapie exploitation piece." Bill Warren (*Keep Watching the Skies!*) said that the film was done "very unsatisfactorily" in his writeup on the '53 *Donovan's Brain*, which he much prefers. John Baxter (*Science Fiction in the Cinema*) couldn't have disagreed more: "With Erich von Stroheim contributing a rich portrait of the mad doctor and John Alton's low-key lighting, the film is one of the Forties' most diverting horror films. . . . [George] Sherman's style, slow, detached, inclined to stand back for long shots of lofty Spanish-revival interiors clogged with shadows, gives the trivial plot a Forties ambience that makes it comparable to *The Uninvited* as an exercise in horror. The scene where the brain comes to life in the night-time laboratory and enters the mind of hero Richard Arlen is deservedly a classic of camera-work and direction; in every way, the film far outclasses Felix Feist's 1953 version, best of the remakes."

John Cocchi (*Second Feature: The Best of the "B" Films*) called the film "[o]ne of Republic's infrequent forays into horror and a good one." Leonard Maltin's 2-1/2 star *Movies on TV* writeup rated it a "pretty good chiller." Film historian William K. Everson devoted a whole chapter to it in his *Classics of the Horror Film*: "Despite its title, and undoubtedly horrific content, the film is perhaps only nominally a horror film, though certainly a superior one." Don Willis scoffed, "Too much ground is covered by exposition, not enough by action. Talk tends to slow things up." According to Curt Siodmak, "It was a piece of shit."

Return of the Ape Man
(Monogram, 1944)

Released June 24. 60 minutes. Associate Producer: Barney Sarecky. Produced by Sam Katzman and Jack Dietz (Banner Productions). Directed by Philip Rosen. Screenplay: Robert Charles. Photography: Marcel Le Picard. Set Designer: Dave Milton. Film Editor: Carl Pierson. Musical Director: Edward Kay. Assistant Director: Art Hammond. Special Effects: Ray Mercer. Sound: Glen Glenn.

Cast: Bela Lugosi (Prof. Dexter), John Carradine (Prof. John Gilmore), Frank Moran (The Ape Man), Judith Gibson [Teala Loring] (Anne), Michael Ames [Tod Andrews] (Steve Rogers), Mary Currier (Hilda Gilmore), Ed Chandler (Police Sergeant), Ernie Adams ("Willie the Weasel"), Horace Carpenter (Watchman), Mike Donovan, George Eldredge (Policemen), Frank Leigh (Husband).

> **"They threw away the book when they made [*Return of the Ape Man*], threw it a bit too far. It is one of the wildest, wooliest combination pseudo-scientific and horror films yet, but in its feverish reaching for new sensations and effects, it crosses into the utterly absurd and unacceptable, even for this type of picture."** — *The Hollywood Reporter*

> **"*Return of the Ape Man* ... differs from the usual pseudo-scientific thriller in having a sound basis in modern science."** — Monogram publicity

A busy year for Bela Lugosi was 1943, and not just film-wise. In fact, Bela got a bit of a break from the hustle and bustle of low-budget picture-making that year: after grinding out his scenes for *Ghosts on the Loose* in February (probably in no more than two days), he didn't step in front of the movie cameras again until August. The time in between was spent playing (who else) Count Dracula on stage, with Lugosi leaving California on Sunday, April 11 for the East to start rehearsals on the play (which opened May 3 in Boston). Engagements in Washington and New York followed. The play was also presented at army camps where, for 25 cents a head, recruits watched as Lugosi went through his old-fashioned undead shtick.

Coming home to filmland represented a change of locale, if not of routine: Lugosi's first assignment upon his return was as Armand Tesla, the vindictive vampire of Columbia's *The Return of the Vampire* (1943). Kurt Neumann, the initially-signed director (and author of the film's original story "The Vampires of London") was replaced by Lew Landers, who previously directed Bela in Universal's *The Raven* (1935). Under Landers' guidance, Lugosi gave a strong, malevolent performance in mist-shrouded scenes that reeked with atmosphere. The rest of the picture, unhappily, just reeked.

Monogram, Lugosi's home studio, waited patiently in the wings with plans of their own for the actor they liked to call Mr. Dracula. They had intended to star Lugosi in their spring production of *Revenge of the Zombies*, but with Bela away on tour, that "plum" assignment went to John Carradine. Perhaps to make up for time lost, they now laid plans to star him in two back-to-back horror productions, *Voodoo Man* (to be directed by William Nigh) and *Return of the Ape Man* (to be directed by William Beaudine).

Katzman and Dietz also announced via the Hollywood trades their success in assembling a horror stock company "which will set a new high mark in shivery associates," a threesome who would appear opposite Lugosi in his upcoming thrillers. The terrible trio was comprised of Carradine, George Zucco and – surprise – Frieda Inescort, the stiff-upper-lipped British actress who had played the distaff Van Helsing in *The Return of the Vampire*. The trio was signed for *Voodoo Man* and *Return of the Ape Man*, with the possibility that the deal might be extended to include other pictures. All these plans were modified in the coming weeks: *Return of the Ape Man* preceded *Voodoo Man* onto the Monogram sound stages, Philip Rosen handled its direction rather than Beaudine (as though it made a difference!), and Frieda Inescort dropped from the arrangement entirely. George Zucco we'll discuss later.

The film begins in Prof. Dexter's (Lugosi) basement laboratory, where Dexter (no first name) and his colleague Prof. John Gilmore (Carradine) utilize their newly-developed electro-chemical process to restore life to a tramp (Ernie Adams) they had placed in frozen suspended animation four months before. After sending the unwitting little man on his way (with five of Gilmore's dollars in his pocket for his trouble), Dexter is exultant:

> DEXTER: If I can suspend animation for four months, I can do it for four years, or perhaps 400 years!
> GILMORE: Unfortunately, we couldn't live long enough to prove that, my dear Dexter!

Dexter isn't so sure it can't be proven. His new pet project is to journey to the Arctic and search for prehistoric men imbedded in glaciers; perhaps they, too, are in suspended animation, and can be restored to life under proper conditions.

After a lot of stock footage of ships and polar ice, we find Dexter and Gilmore in furry parkas standing in front of a wall with a snow-covered hill painted on it; behind them, two "Eskimos" are chopping away with pick-axes (obviously being careful not to damage the sound stage floor). Dexter and Gilmore have been traveling around in the Arctic wilderness for ten months, randomly digging holes in hopes that one of them may lead to a frozen body. After nearly a year of this, Gilmore has had enough; he has

responsibilities back home, being a married man. "I'm married, too," Dexter deadpans. "A true scientist is married to his profession." (Behind Dexter's back, a fed-up Gilmore just rolls his eyes.) In what can only be described as a fabulous stroke of luck, part of a glacier crumbles into the sea and the body of a prehistoric man, buried in Arctic ice for 30,000 years, is uncovered. The body, preserved in a block of ice, is secretly shipped to Dexter's lab. Heating lamps and a blowtorch melt the ice, and it isn't long before the body is revealed: a perfect specimen of Pithecanthropus (played by Frank Moran), long-haired, bearded and clad in a ragged animal skin. A dumb, violent brute, the Ape Man starts a fight shortly after reviving; using the blowtorch, Dexter forces him into a nearby cage, which is then closed and securely locked. Dexter's plan now is to transplant a segment of the brain of a present-day man into the skull of the prehistoric creature, endowing him with just enough understanding to make him obey Dexter's orders. This doesn't go over well with Gilmore, who points out that to do so would be to murder the modern man.

Gilmore's home is the scene of a party celebrating the return of Gilmore and Dexter from the Arctic. While Gilmore plays Beethoven's "Moonlight Sonata" on the piano, Dexter is scanning the room for a potential *un*willing brain donor; he eventually sets his little black heart on Steve Rogers (Tod Andrews), a law student and the fiancé of Gilmore's niece Anne (Teala Loring). Dexter imposes on Steve for a lift home, and there he gives him a drugged drink. Steve slips into unconsciousness.

Gilmore notices that Steve is missing from the party and smells a rat. Racing to Dexter's house, he finds Steve on the operating table in the lab and Dexter a split-second away from applying his scalpel to the young man's forehead. Levelling a gun at Dexter, Gilmore forces him to revive Steve, who is made to believe that he passed out on his own.

After Gilmore leaves in an angry huff, the Ape Man bends the bars of his cage and high-tails it out a small window (as he struggles to get his big rear through the opening, you can see the prehistoric man's prehistoric B.V.D.s). Wandering around the city, he spots and accosts a girl but a policeman (George Eldredge) breaks it up. As the girl flees, the Ape Man seizes the cop, effortlessly breaking his neck. Prof. Dexter, searching the city streets toting the lit blowtorch, happens upon the grim scene. At blowtorch-point, he herds the Ape Man back to the house (where the bars of the cage are once again intact).

Dexter telephones Gilmore and tells him he needs help in disposing of the Ape Man; Gilmore, who had read about the murder in the morning paper, is eager to help. But it's a trap: Gilmore finds himself in Dexter's lab

Opposite: Bela Lugosi (third from left) and Frank Moran (in hairy makeup) get "pinched" by the cops; Teala Loring and Tod Andrews seem oblivious to all of it. A fun posed shot with no basis in the plot of *Return of the Ape Man.*

standing on an electrically charged steel plate, paralyzed by the voltage. Soon Dexter is wielding his trusty scalpel once again, transplanting part of Gilmore's brain into the noggin of the Ape Man. The results aren't what Dexter expected: the Ape Man tiresomely repeats "Me...Gil...more...*Gilmore!*" while Dexter argues with him. When Dexter hints that a second operation might be necessary, the Ape Man bolts again, fleeing to Gilmore's house. He climbs an arbor and enters through a second-story window, finds a piano in the room and stands playing the "Moonlight Sonata." After a few stanzas, he strolls into the next room, finds Mrs. Gilmore (Mary Currier) in there, and without provocation chokes the woman to death. In the garden outside the house, he kayoes Steve, then dutifully returns to Dexter's place.

Anne calls the cops, and the usual dumb ones arrive at the house ("Sarge, here's a footprint!" "Aw, that's too big to be real!") Suspecting that Prof. Dexter is somehow behind all of this, Steve leads the cops to Dexter's house, just as the Ape Man comes a-crashing out of his cage; eight point-blank bullets have no effect on the beast. Seizing Dexter, the Ape Man breaks his back and then races out of the house. Slumped uncomfortably across a table, Dexter's last words are to destroy the Ape Man with fire.

The Ape Man, in an obvious rut, goes to Dexter's again and kidnaps Anne ("Very pretty ... you will come with me..."). With the unconscious girl slung over his shoulder, he leads the cops on a merry chase throughout the city, across rooftops, in and out of a theater and then back *again* to Dexter's lab. The Ape Man gets tangled up in some electrical wires which he angrily rips loose, and a fire starts. Police burst in and Steve rescues Anne from the flaming room. As the cops watch the blaze with enthusiasm ("Well, this is one time I hope the fire department lets it get a good start!"), the Ape Man dies in the flames.

Monogram played up *Return* as a "shock-sequel" to *The Ape Man*; behind the opening credits is artwork of a ferocious-looking caged ape. Of course *Return of the Ape Man* is not a sequel, even though the title itself really isn't a misnomer (the film *is* about an ape man who returns to life).

But the title similarity, and Monogram's false advertising, invite comparisons, with the result that it's generally agreed *Return of the Ape Man* is the better of the two. *The Ape Man* is a great "guilty pleasure" film, but *Return* is even more fun. *Return's* action, while small-scale and repetitious beyond belief, is almost nonstop, and there are none of the dreary lulls that we find we find (or, rather, that find *us!* in *The Ape Man*. Also, we get two horror icons for the price of one, even though John Carradine practically

Opposite: **Before "illness" forced him off of the picture, George Zucco actually climbed into the shabby makeup and caveman togs for *Return of the Ape Man*. (Can that *really* be Zucco's nose?) Monogram publicists dubbed Bela Lugosi (left) and John Carradine (right) "Those Two Thrill Boys."**

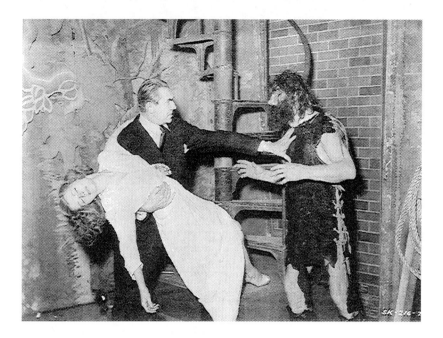

Beauty and the beasts: Teala Loring appears to be the object of some discussion between mad scientist Bela Lugosi and caveman Frank Moran in this *Return of the Ape
Man* publicity photo.

sleepwalks through the picture. *Return of the Ape Man* is yet another
endearingly far-out farrago, the sort that only Monogram was capable of
cooking up.

Doffing his vampire's cape, Bela Lugosi once again dons the cloak of
science in *Return of the Ape Man*, playing the one and only truly full-blooded
mad scientist role of his Monogram career. Unfortunately, it's a rather
snappish and sour one; rather than investing the part with his customary
gusto, Lugosi plays a scowling, sulky misanthrope, perpetually out of
humor, even at his infrequent moments of triumph. He rants that human
lives are unimportant measured against medical progress, and that the
homicidal Missing Link's life must be preserved in the name of science
(outlooks that change drastically after it's his *own* back that gets broken!).

Still, the performance is not without its highpoints and humorous bits.
At Carradine's welcome-home party, Lugosi silently ponders where he's going to get a brain for his next experiment; while guests stand around in
banal chat, Lugosi, sunk deep into an armchair and lost in a swirl of cigar
smoke, smugly looks around him and observes, "You know, some people's
brains would never be missed!" Delicately positioning a heat lamp above the
slab of ice containing the frozen Ape Man, Lugosi insists that the thawing-
out process must be executed with great care, although as soon as Car-

radine leaves the room, Lugosi shoots a dirty look in the direction of his departure, fires up a blowtorch and starts going to town on the thing. Later, after Carradine has thwarted Lugosi's evil plan to carve up Tod Andrews, there's an unintended funny moment when Carradine "tells off" the unfazed Lugosi:

> GILMORE: That was the most contemptible thing a man ever tried to do to his friend. . . . You deliberately tried to murder someone dear to me . . . Dexter, you're a dangerous man . . . I believe you're quite mad!
> DEXTER *(unimpressed)*: I see you and I do not theenk alike!

As in the earlier *Revenge of the Zombies*, Carradine chooses to underplay – *too* much. Like many movie professors, Carradine's character is the absent-minded, inobservant type; after more than a year of working shoulder-to-shoulder with the brooding, obsessive Lugosi, he is slow to notice that the man is certifiably cracked. (Carradine's slightly snobbish wife – Mary Currier, in the role Frieda Inescort probably would have played – picked this up the first time she met the man, and harps on it constantly!) After the first fight in the lab with the Ape Man, a sleepy-looking Carradine wanders up to Lugosi and murmurs, "How will you get him over to the Museum of Natural History?" Carradine remains stubbornly low-key, muttering monotonous platitudes even as Lugosi trusses him up and babbles about removing his brain.

George Zucco was originally lined up to play the Ape Man, which would have been a sight worth paying to see. The British actor was not averse to wearing a bit of gruesome makeup; in *Dead Men Walk* he was a cadaverous vampire, and in Universal's *The Mad Ghoul* (1943), he briefly played a ghoul. But the Ape Man wasn't a role that required a horror star, just a burly type or a stuntman. It would have been completely beneath Zucco to subject himself to the makeup sessions, run around half-naked and give audiences a glimpse of his underpants. On October 6, 1943, the fifth day of production, it was announced in *The Hollywood Reporter* that illness had caused Zucco to withdraw from the cast of *Return of the Ape Man*. Monogram also told the trade paper that Zucco was being replaced by George Moran, apparently confusing Frank Moran with Chicago gangster George "Bugs" Moran. (Even more comically mixed-up, Phil Hardy's *The Encyclopedia of Science Fiction Movies* reports that the beast was played by *The Wizard of Oz*'s Frank Morgan!)

Horror fans have always enjoyed telling themselves that Zucco stalked off the picture when he found out what the role entailed, which very well might have been what happened; actress Helen Hayes once mentioned his "hellish Hellenic temper." Throughout the years, confusion has reigned as to whether Zucco appears briefly in *Return of the Ape Man*. Zucco emphatically told film producer/historian Alex Gordon that he does not, and Frank Moran backed Zucco up, telling Gordon that he alone played the beast; this would seem to settle the question completely. But because Zucco and Moran share billing not only in the pressbook but also in the on-screen credits, and since every so often a fan will insist he's certain it's Zucco in *this* shot or *that* shot, the rumor that Zucco *is* in the picture will always be with us. (He does appear in the Ape Man makeup in at least one still; more than just a few viewers swear that it's Zucco beneath the makeup in the rising-from-the-ice scene. According to *Castle of Frankenstein* magazine, his "one shot" is at the end.)

If Zucco feigned sickness in order to avoid becoming associated with the film, all he missed out on was getting paid: Monogram not only played him up in all publicity, but also concocted stories that centered around him for their pressbook. According to the pressbook, *Return*'s theater scenes were shot at a vacant theater near the Monogram studios, and passersby were horrified when they saw Zucco (in two-and-a-half hours' worth of Ape Man makeup) emerging from the car which delivered him to the location site. Additionally, the item went on, the L.A.P.D. had a busy few minutes reassuring people who phoned in that there really wasn't a monster running loose on city streets.

Another publicity blurb, just as asinine, announced that the two extras who accompany Lugosi and Carradine in the Arctic scenes were played by real Eskimos who worked the swing shift in a local airplane factory. Orientals, the ethnic group that generally played movie Eskimos, were too busy with war films to do *Return of the Ape Man*, according to the blurb. Yet another pressbook item claimed that, in order to create the brutal features of the Ape Man, technicians and research workers studied prehistoric types for several weeks before the picture began. Working with college professors and curators of several museums in the Hollywood area, they traced the various races back to their origins, studied skulls unearthed in archaeological expeditions, pored over texts and examined the theories of noted anthropologists. The sum total of all this work, of course, was Frank Moran's phony beard.

Perhaps the hero and heroine of *Return of the Ape Man* were also a bit embarrassed about being associated with the film; both of them changed their names shortly after the film was made. Judith Gibson, who was also a busy Paramount bit player, became Teala Loring; she's the sister of later screen (and television) stars Debra Paget and Lisa Gaye. Gibson/Loring, also seen in *Bluebeard*, is one of the prettier Poverty Row heroines; the trait ran in the family.

Michael Ames (later known as Tod Andrews) is the usual ineffectual Monogram hero, easily duped by the villain and generally less than useless in moments of crisis. Born in Buffalo, New York, the actor (real name: Ted Anderson) was brought up in L.A. and turned to acting in hopes of overcoming intense bashfulness. After graduation from Washington State College, he joined the Pasadena Playhouse and appeared in more than a dozen productions; a stage role in *My Sister Eileen* won him a Warner Bros. contract. He turned up in a bunch of the studio's early '40s films but often they were the kinds of roles where, if you went to see the movie because *he* was in it, it wasn't a good idea to blink. He had costarring parts in *Return of the Ape Man* and *Voodoo Man* (still using the name Michael Ames) but after the mid-'40s he concentrated on the stage, and appeared in films infrequently.

In later years Andrews never had a kind word to say about his '40s films; he did have much better luck in the theater. He won the Theatre World Award for playing the leading role in the original production of Tennessee Williams' *Summer and Smoke*, and replaced Henry Fonda as *Mister Roberts*, headlining the national company of that play for three years. In 1961 he attempted suicide (he took an overdose of barbiturates in the New York apartment of a Park Avenue socialite); when the story hit the papers, the pretty brunette's photograph dominated the spread, with a little picture of Andrews off in a corner. On television he was *The Gray Ghost* (colorful Confederate hero John Singleton Mosby) in a popular 1957 series; fantasy-wise, he was also the hero in the lousy *From Hell It Came* (1957) and the dying astronaut in *Beneath the Planet of the Apes* (1970). He died of a heart attack in his Beverly Hills home at age 51 on November 7, 1972.

Naturally, *Return of the Ape Man* doesn't make a lot of sense; that would be asking too much. Mostly it's the Ape Man himself who's at the center of the confusion. Once his brain is half-ape, half–Carradine, there's no accounting for the things he does; he can play the "Moonlight Sonata" on the piano one minute, then brutally murder his wife (Mary Currier) the next. (One interesting explanation is that the ape-half of the brain allows Carradine to do all the things he's always wanted to do, like murder his snotty wife and carry off his luscious young niece!)

Ludicrous moments abound, even beyond the spectacle of the rampant Ape Man and that hilarious Arctic scene. The sight of Lugosi calmly searching the streets of the city on foot, dressed in a tux and with a blazing blowtorch in hand, is worth the price of admission all by itself. The climactic chase and fire scene have a lot more action and pizzazz than one learns to expect from Monogram; it's certainly a marked improvement over the conclusion of *The Ape Man*, where Lugosi and gorilla Emil Van Horn just wrestled around on the floor of Lugosi's cramped laboratory. (*Return*'s finale seems a takeoff on Lugosi's *Murders in the Rue Morgue*, 1932, with the ape turning on Bela long before the ending, then toting off the leading lady as the hero and police pursue him across rooftops.)

In addition to the on-screen fun, lucky patrons who paid to see *Return of the Ape Man* in 1944 received a window envelope containing small, harmless sugar-coated pills and the written warning,

FOR YOUR PROTECTION...take these shock-serum pills as an antidote for the shock you are going to get when you see...

RETURN OF THE APE MAN

The Hollywood Reporter didn't find much to recommend, complaining, "The script is bad and the direction matches it, a combination which was just a bit too much for the good cast to overcome." *Variety* liked it a bit better: "*Return of the Ape Man* hits average in the scale of dual horror-thrillers . . . Lugosi and Carradine give okay performances, and Frank Moran is satisfactory as the monster. Michael Ames and Judith Gibson offer stock variations of the romantic duo. Production is satisfactory and direction okay."

Arthur (*The Count*) Lennig enjoyed the film more than many of the other Lugosi Monograms: "The well-performed confrontations between a devoted scientist [Lugosi] and his wishy-washy associate [Carradine] full of middle-class values have a verve beyond the usual character conflicts in such quickie films. The scriptwriters either let out their own resentments or else caught the real essence of Lugosi's dangerous charm." Richard (*The Films of Bela Lugosi*) Bojarski agreed that *Return* was a cut above *The Ape Man*, but had his little quibbles: "The script, after a promising start, meandered into formula situations, rescued only by the menacing unpredictability of the creature, ably acted by Frank Moran . . . Lugosi's performance . . . resembled his earlier Dr. Mirakle role [in *Murders in the Rue Morgue*]–socially detached, hard-working and obsessed with proving his theories, even at the cost of human life. Lugosi gave conviction to this scientific horror tale, excellently assisted by John Carradine." Easy-to-please *Psychotronic* enthusiastically called it "sixty minutes of vintage Monogram nonsense." Don Willis couldn't have disagreed more: "Utterly ridiculous. Probably Monogram's worst."

While not on a par with the better B horror movies that were being made by major studios, *Return of the Ape Man* has an almost professional look and plenty of action, setting it several steps above many of the Monogram Lugosis that preceded it. It's typical of Poor Bela's luck that Monogram seemed on the verge of finally getting the knack of horror moviemaking just as the horror cycle–and his Monogram contract–were expiring.

The Girl Who Dared
(Republic, 1944)

Released August 5. 56 minutes. Associate Producer: Rudolph E. Abel. Directed by Howard Bretherton. Screenplay: John K. Butler. Based on the novel *Blood on*

Her Shoe by Medora Field. Director of Photography: Bud Thackery. Film Editor: Arthur Roberts. Sound: Dick Tyler. Art Director: Gano Chittenden. Set Decorator: Otto Siegel. Costume Supervisor: Adele.

Cast: Lorna Gray (Ann Carroll), Peter Cookson (Rufus Blair), Grant Withers (Homer Norton), Veda Ann Borg (Cynthia Harrison/Sylvia Scott), John Hamilton (Beau Richmond), Willie Best (Woodrow), Vivien Oakland (Chattie Richmond), Roy Barcroft (David Scott), Kirk Alyn (Josh Carroll), Tom London (Old Man).

> "About a hundred years ago, a pirate ship was washed ashore here in a heavy storm.... On the night the ship was wrecked, the beacon in this old lighthouse was blown out by the storm, and the entire crew drowned. Once a year, on the anniversary of that event, the ghost of the ship's captain appears amidst the wreckage—and we're here tonight to see him!"—Beau Richmond (John Hamilton)

Another in the endless string of mysteries that pretend in their advertising to be horror films, *The Girl Who Dared* at least includes more than just a bit of talk about ghosts—and one even makes a brief appearance. It later turns out to be a phony, which is when the film veers suddenly down the well-traveled whodunit lane, but *The Girl Who Dared* remains a not-unwatchable B, and worthy of mention here in this book.

Ann Carroll (Lorna Gray) and her brother Josh (Kirk Alyn) are en route to a party/ghost-hunt at the Georgia island home of their cousin Beau Richmond when their car develops motor trouble. At a remote service station, Blair (Peter Cookson), a man that they mistake for an employee, overhears them talking about their destination and then falsely tells them that their car can go no farther. The Carrolls accept Blair's offer to give them a lift the rest of the way in *his* car.

A long causeway leads out over the ocean to Heron Point, the island whose one house belongs to Richmond (John Hamilton) and his wife Chattie (Vivien Oakland). A number of other guests have already arrived: Cynthia Harrison and her twin sister Sylvia Scott (both played by Veda Ann Borg), Sylvia's fiercely jealous ex-husband David Scott (Roy Barcroft), and a friend, Homer Norton (Grant Withers). As a lightning storm brews, the avuncular Richmond tells his guests that he did not send out the invitations, and doesn't know who did, but that since they've all now gathered together anyway, the mysteriously proposed ghost-hunt party remains a good idea. Richmond turns on a radio just in time for us to hear that Atlanta police are searching for Paul Dexter, a doctor who absconded with $100,000 worth of radium. (The radio voice sounds like actor Kenne Duncan's.)

Braving the cold and wind of the storm, Richmond and his guests hike to the island seashore, where the wreck of the old pirate ship has been beached for 100 years; on this, the anniversary of the date when its entire crew drowned, the ghost of the captain is due to make an appearance. When an eerie figure dressed in pirate's clothes stands up amidst the wreckage, Sylvia cries out and falls to the ground. But the girl hasn't fainted; there's a dagger in her back.

Blair secretly cuts the telephone line and disables all the cars on the island. Tempers flair and accusing fingers are pointed by various guests. Richmond admits that the "ghost" was a phony, operated by wires for the amusement of his guests. Sylvia's body vanishes. Woodrow (Willie Best), the cowardly black butler, discovers the body of radium thief Dexter in the wine cellar. Blair, playing the innocent, offers to walk across the causeway and bring back the police. The next day, when he still hasn't returned, everyone agrees that he's skipped out on them.

That night, Ann finds Blair wandering around in the nearby woods carrying an electroscope, a device used to locate radium. Blair explains that he's an insurance investigator working with the police; he had discovered that Dr. Dexter and Sylvia were in on the radium theft, but now their third partner-in-crime has murdered them both.

The electroscope directs them to a buried trapdoor which in turn leads to a secret cave once used by the pirates to store stolen treasures; in it, Ann and Blair find a protective lead tube used in the storage of radium, as well as Sylvia's missing body. But when Ann realizes that the corpse is wearing a shoe worn by Sylvia's twin Cynthia on the night of the murder – a shoe that isn't Sylvia's size – it becomes obvious that Cynthia and not Sylvia was the victim. Evidently Sylvia had realized that her criminal partner wanted to kill her, and so ruthlessly tricked her twin into changing clothes with her so that the killer would unsuspectingly slay the wrong girl. Unfortunately, the killer is with Ann and Blair in the dark cave, and overhears their conversation. The killer fights with Blair, escapes, and steals back into the Richmond house and now slays the *real* Sylvia.

Blair cooks up a scheme to make the killer expose himself. As police converge on the house, Blair tells the assembled suspects that the killer, having lost the lead safety tube, has been exposed to cancer-causing radium. He adds that the contaminated person cannot pass by a radio without causing static to be heard, and proposes that everyone step one at a time in front of Richmond's radio. Homer Norton accepts the dare confidently, but when Ann secretly monkeys with the radio's ground wire and causes static, he panics. This, together with other evidence, proves him to be the killer.

Dredged up, like the Heron Point pirate ship, from the ocean of forgotten B films, *The Girl Who Dared* emerges as a thoroughly unexceptional time-killer, the 1940s answer to the low-budget, hour-long television detective shows which lay ahead in the Boob Tube era. The mystery is a bit transparent, and the film misleads its audience by pretending to be a chiller; but, clocking in at a fast 56 minutes and populated by a personable cast, *The Girl Who Dared* sizes up as a relatively painless budget whodunit.

The killer can be easily picked out by any fan who's seen his share of mysteries, large- *or* small-screen; it almost becomes similar to a problem in logic. Let's walk this one through: One Veda Ann Borg is murdered by someone who mistook her for her twin, so the killer can't be the other one. The killer's face isn't shown in the scene where he fights with Peter Cookson in the cave, but obviously it's a man; this lets out Vivien Oakland (and, of course, Cookson and Gray). John Hamilton has a loving wife, and Kirk Alyn is the heroine's brother; rare is the B mystery where sympathetic female characters like these are forced to cope with the horror and shame of a killer husband/brother. "Comedy relief" butler Willie Best isn't worth considering. Roy Barcroft's character is a grouch and a troublemaker right from the start, always busy acting suspiciously; this disposes of him as well. Once you've eliminated all of these, the pinkest of red herrings, you're left with only one character, Grant Withers. *Voilà!*

Just about everyone in the cast does a good job, from Western and serial queen Gray (a.k.a. Adrian Booth) and B leading man Cookson to dependable supporting players Withers, Borg, Hamilton and Barcroft; it's fun to see serial Superman Kirk Alyn sharing the screen with television Perry White John Hamilton. Willie Best's bug-eyed, quavery-voiced, scared servant had seen better days. John K. Butler's script, based on Medora Field's novel *Blood on Her Shoe*, tends to keep the lot of them on the go, and Howard Bretherton's direction is what *Variety* (who didn't review the film) liked to call "pacy."

The title is meaningless to the point that you can't even be sure which girl in the film it refers to; one ad line intimates that Lorna Gray is the daring girl in question, while another bestows the title on Veda Ann Borg. Posters featured a black clutching hand and ad lines like, "**Death**...awaits the rash adventurer who dares to discover the chill-filled secret of the screen's most macabre murder!!" (Unfairly, one poster includes an artist's rendition of Grant Withers, the killer of the piece, being hauled off to jail by cops!) *The Girl Who Dared* went into production on Tuesday, March 28, 1944.

Bluebeard
(PRC, 1944)

Released November 11. 71 minutes. Associate Producer: Martin Mooney. Produced by Leon Fromkess. Directed by Edgar G. Ulmer. Screenplay: Pierre Gendron. Original Story: Arnold Phillips and Werner H. Furst. Director of Photography:

Eugen Schufftan.* Operating Cameraman: Jockey A. Feindel, A.S.C. Musical Score Composed and Conducted by Leo Erdody. Supervising Film Editor: Carl Pierson. Production Manager: C. A. Beute. Assistant Director: Raoul E. Pagel. Art Director: Paul Palmentola. Assistant Art Director: Angelo Scibetta. Set Decorator: Glenn P. Thompson. Sound Engineer: John Carter. Master of Properties: Charles Stevens. Wardrobe: James H. Wade. Coiffures: Loretta Francel. Makeup: Milburn Moranti. Marionettes: Barlow & Baker.

Cast: John Carradine (Gaston Morrell), Jean Parker (Lucille), Nils Asther (Insp. Jacques Lefevre), Ludwig Stossel (Jean Lamarte), George Pembroke (Insp. Renard), Teala Loring (Francine), Sonia Sorel (Renee), Henry Kolker (Deschamps), Emmett Lynn (Le Soldat), Iris Adrian (Mimi), Patti McCarty (Bebette), Carrie Devan (Constance), Anne Sterling (Jeanette).

> **"I SEARCH FOR *Beauty* HIDDEN IN A WOMAN'S SOUL ... IN MY ARMS MANY WERE *Beautiful* ... BUT THE FLAME OF *Passion* EXPOSED THEIR SOULS' UGLINESS ... *Ugliness* I DESTROY!"** – from the *Bluebeard* pressbook
> **WARNING! CITIZENS OF PARIS!**
> **A murderer is in your midst! A criminal who strangles young women! Any person having information concerning this Bluebeard, please communicate with the Police at once!**

By 1943, PRC – Hollywood's most notorious bush-league studio – was eagerly laying out its strategy for expansion. "Big" pictures like *Corregidor* and *Isle of Forgotten Sins* were granted "top budgets" (by PRC standards, at any rate). PRC acquired the Fine Arts studios and filled it with newly purchased equipment, sets and flats. A decision was made to place less reliance upon unit producers; the company would be producing films itself rather than allowing the ball to be carried by others. A contract roster would be built up for the first time in the organization's history. The three-legged dog of the movie industry was sitting up and begging to be noticed.

On October 7, 1943, PRC signed Edgar G. Ulmer to a long-term agreement, the veteran director recently having handled the company's "top-budget" musical *Jive Junction* as well as several other 1942–43 PRC pictures. Vienna-born; a set designer and assistant director on the stage productions of Max Reinhardt; assistant to filmland giants like F. W. Murnau; director/designer/co-writer of the horror classic *The Black Cat* (1934) – Ulmer's name brought a touch of class to his minibudgeted productions, and in retrospect his involvement with PRC is one of the few reasons the company is remembered today at all. PRC had to have been proud of the newest addition to their regular roster, but the first assignment they handed him

---

Because Schufftan was never able to break into the cameraman's union, screen credit for director of photography goes to operating cameraman Jockey Feindel. Schufftan gets a Production Designer's credit.

seemed to reflect little of that enthusiasm: Less than a week after Ulmer was signed, PRC loaned him to the R. Wolff Advertising Agency to direct short subject musicals which would be given free of charge to the Army for showing in camps overseas. All costs were assumed by Coca-Cola.

Better things lay ahead, though, and by spring, 1944, one of Ulmer's – and PRC's – most prestigious B films was in the works: *Bluebeard*. Charlie Chaplin had earlier announced that he would produce a film by that title, but it was PRC producer Martin Mooney and not the Little Tramp who was awarded title clearance in April. Mooney was quick to specify that the film would *not* be about Henri Landru, the real-life French lady-killer,* but would center around a 19th century Parisian artist who used his flowing cravat to strangle models.

On May 11, *Bluebeard*'s stars were set. For the title role of the deranged puppeteer/killer: John Carradine, like Ulmer, a Hollywood figure whose career's precipitous ups and downs (mostly downs) have practically become the stuff of legends. Jean Parker, Montana-born beauty, formerly an MGM contractee (and, in the '50s, Mrs. Robert Lowery), was signed to play the female lead, Martin Mooney having been unable to secure the services of actress Marie McDonald from producer Hunt Stromberg. Teala Loring (formerly Judith Gibson, Carradine's niece in Monogram's *Return of the Ape Man*) was loaned to PRC from Paramount for the role of Jean Parker's sister; Patti McCarty, leading lady of PRC Westerns, would play one of Parker's friends. Silent screen heartthrob Nils Asther, character actors Ludwig Stossel, George Pembroke and Henry Kolker and B movie buffoon Emmett Lynn rounded out the cast of the production, which began shooting May 31.

The film opens with police hauling the body of Bluebeard's latest victim from the dark waters of the Seine. All Paris is terrified of the mystery killer save for Lucille (Jean Parker), a poised and beautiful young woman who works in a modiste's shop and discusses the killer with mild indifference. Leaving work with her friends Bebette (Patti McCarty) and Constance (Carrie Devan), she encounters Gaston Morrell (John Carradine), a puppeteer who frequently puts on shows in the park. Morrell, obviously attracted to Lucille, promises to present a show the following night, mainly for Lucille's benefit.

---

*Henri Désiré Landru, an accomplished swindler, murdered at least nine women between 1914 and 1919, when he was caught. Police sifted through the ashes of his stove and examined his outhouse and garden, finding hundreds of human bone and tooth fragments. Landru so loved roses that, as the police dug, his primary concern was for his flowers. People flocked to his sensational trial; the well-mannered Landru volunteered, "If any lady would like my place, I will willingly surrender it." He maintained his innocence in the face of overwhelming evidence; the jury needed 90 minutes to bring in a verdict of guilty. "Ah, well," he commented just before his February 23, 1922, guillotining, "it is not the first time that an innocent man has been condemned."

Stylish and sometimes "artsy," director Edgar G. Ulmer's *Bluebeard* had the "feel" of a film made not to entertain audiences but to impress the critics.

The next night, after the puppeteer-singers Morrell, Le Soldat (Emmett Lynn) and Renee (Sonia Sorel) have staged the puppet opera *Faust*, Lucille visits Morrell backstage and admires the lifelike marionettes:

> MORRELL: They're all likenesses of people I've known.
> LUCILLE: Mephistopheles, too?
> MORRELL: Yes, the Evil One, too. Among other things, he's also my business manager!

The puppet of Faust's Marguerite is the likeness of a girl who met a tragic ending. Lucille discerns that with the puppet, Morrell is keeping that tragedy alive deliberately. She suggests he create a new puppet that will make him think of someone else. Lucille offers to be the model for the new puppet, but when Morrell remembers that he will need to sketch and paint her first, he abruptly declines, and tells Lucille to leave with Bebette and Constance: "You'd better go with them. You'd better stay – *close* to them . . ."

Returning home to his studio, Morrell finds Renee waiting there for him; the girl is obviously in love with Morrell, and has stood by forlornly as he's struck up relationships with other girls, the way he has tonight with Lucille.

RENEE: Gaston – these girls – I've known they didn't mean anything to you, really – because you always came back to me. But, Gaston, what's *happened* to them...?

Renee has her answer when Morrell reaches up to remove his own cravat, and his eyes take on a terrifying, mad look. She screams as she realizes – too late – that Morrell is Bluebeard. Renee's body is later found bobbing in the river. Feigning innocence, Morrell visits the Sûreté Générale and identifies her body as that of his missing employee. Inspector Lefevre (Nils Asther) thanks him for his cooperation.

Morrell sees Lucille again, at his studio, this time telling her that he wants to put on a new puppet ballet and hiring her to create the costumes. Lucille notices the discarded cravat Morrell used to strangle Renee, slightly torn. Over his objection, she quickly puts a few stitches in the damaged cravat. "There we are – all fixed. Now you can use it again!" she beams.

Morrell's business manager Jean Lamarte (Ludwig Stossel) visits him later. Lamarte knows that Morrell is Bluebeard and that the murdered girls were his models; Morrell is unable to paint a girl without killing her immediately afterwards. To cover up for Morrell (and to line his own pockets), Lamarte, greedy and unscrupulous, then "fences" the portraits, lying to Morrell about the price he receives and giving him only a tiny fraction of his due. The portrait of Morrell's fourth victim has been sold to the Duke of Cadignac; Morrell is worried because he knows the duke will publicly exhibit the painting, and the girl might be recognized.

Morrell's fears are confirmed: The resemblance between the girl in the portrait and the murdered girl is perceived by a policeman, and Inspector Lefevre is notified. The duke tells Lefevre that he bought the portrait from Lamarte, so Lefevre goes undercover, visiting Lamarte's shop and telling him he wishes to buy a canvas by the same artist (Morrell uses the pseudonym "Albert Garron"). Lamarte is too cautious to fall into the Inspector's trap. (No one ever explains why the police feel that the man who painted the girl's portrait must also be her murderer.)

Lucille is visited by her younger sister, Sûreté operative Francine (Teala Loring), who is dressing behind a screen and peeking out when Morrell stops by to pay Lucille a short visit. The girlfriend of Inspector Lefevre, Francine visits him at headquarters later that day, and cleverly hatches a plan of her own to ensnare the slippery Lamarte.

Detective Deschamps (Henry Kolker) and Francine visit Lamarte, presenting themselves as father and daughter; Deschamps wants Lamarte to hire "Garron" to paint a portrait of Francine. Lamarte is understandably wary but Deschamps' offer of £150,000 sways the wily art dealer. Lamarte imposes on Morrell to paint the girl but Morrell, sensing a police trap, insists that he will accede only if the sitting takes place in the workroom over Lamarte's shop.

As Deschamps waits in the shop below, Morrell (hiding behind a screen and viewing Francine in a mirror) begins to sketch the girl. Francine tricks Morrell into stepping out where she can see him, and is instantly gripped by terror – the painter, Bluebeard, is her own sister's beau. His secret exposed, Morrell strangles the girl. Downstairs, Deschamps tries to signal a group of policemen secretly stationed outside, but Lamarte catches him at it and clubs him into unconsciousness. Morrell finds Lamarte trying to make a getaway and, feeling that he has been betrayed, kills him, too. Bluebeard escapes through the sewers as police storm the house.

At Francine's wake, Lefevre shows Lucille the cravat that was used to garrote the girl; Lucille recognizes it as the one she repaired for Morrell. Confronting him at his studio, Lucille demands an explanation. Morrell explains (in flashback) that as a starving young art student, one night he saw a girl, Jeanette (Anne Sterling), collapse in the street. Carrying her to his garret, he nursed her back to health and painted her portrait ("There was something in her fever-tormented eyes that was almost spiritual. . . "). The painting, which Morrell titled *Maid of Orléans*, is awarded a prize and hung in the Louvre. Eager to share this great news with Jeanette, who had in the meantime recovered and moved out, Morrell tracked her down and found that in real life his "spiritual" Jeanette was actually a prostitute, "a low, coarse, loathsome creature." Morrell, overtaken by madness, choked her to death.

> MORRELL: Every time I painted again, I painted Jeanette. So I turned to making puppets, because I could make them of wood. Because when they *became* Jeanette, I could take out my fury on them. I couldn't *kill* wood!

Lamarte had learned of Morrell's first murder and forced the artist to continue to paint girls so that he (Lamarte) could sell the canvasses; every time, Morrell killed his model.

Morrell babbles out his love for the frightened Lucille but, involuntarily, he begins to choke her. Suddenly the police arrive; Lefevre had noticed Lucille's suspicious behavior when he showed her the mended cravat, and followed her. Feverishly fighting off Lefevre's gendarmes, Morrell attempts a cross-rooftop escape but the edge of a roof buckles under his feet and Bluebeard plummets into the Seine far below, joining his victims in their watery grave. (In the pressbook synopsis, he purposely jumps to his death.)

In Peter Bogdanovich's legendary 1970 interview with Ulmer, the director seemed to have (understandably) mixed feelings about his association with PRC:

> . . . I drifted into PRC and couldn't get out. I did so many pictures for them. What helped me at PRC was that number 1: I could use my crew,

and I nearly was running the studio from a technical end. The little
Girls in Chains [1943] was such a gigantic money success that we could
have bought the PRC Studio. I wouldn't sign any contract with PRC,
but this was my home and I could operate and bring any ideas immediately to the top echelon. I suffered, of course, from one thing. I was
so tied up that I couldn't take any contracts on the outside. . . . We were
friendly and I kept going there. At that time I was called "the Capra of
PRC." It was a nice family feeling, not too much interference – if there
was interference, it was only that we had no money, that was all. [Leon]
Fromkess became head of the studio; he would listen, and when I would
say I want to make a *Bluebeard*, that's what we would make.

Ulmer also told Bogdanovich that *Bluebeard*, shot in six days, was "a
tremendously challenging picture" and "a very lovely picture," a strange ad-
jective to use to describe a movie about a serial killer.

Although well-received when it was first released, *Bluebeard* remained
a mostly overlooked film until the late '50s when American film critics began
to fall in with the French *auteur* crowd. Seemingly comprised of only the
staff of the influential French film magazine *Cahiers du Cinéma*, these hard-
core Gallic buffs felt that there was far more style and imagination in the
average Hollywood B movie than was generally acknowledged. As this intellectual firestorm swept stateside, programmer directors like Sam Fuller,
Joseph H. Lewis, Budd Boetticher and the like were recognized as ne-
glected artists worthy of full reappraisals. The big winner in the *auteur*
sweepstakes, Edgar Ulmer emerged as a bona fide cult hero, largely on the
basis of *Detour* (1945), a film steeped in a flashy technique (shadowy
photography, doom-laden mock–Raymond Chandler narration and a roster
of down-and-out characters).*

The *auteur* movement now seems a knee-jerk reaction to the cosmopoli-
tan film critics (typified by *The New York Times*' resident stuffed-shirt
Bosley Crowther) who automatically gave a thumbs-down verdict to any
genre movie or programmer-grade Hollywood product that passed their up-
turned noses.

Ulmer's *Bluebeard* is a benchmark example of style on a shoestring,
although it's too easy to be put off by the film's air of cheapness and ar-
tificiality; and on an entertainment level, the picture seems today as creaky
(or creakier) than ever. But, overlooking the glaring shortcomings of
physical production, open-minded viewers of *Bluebeard* can find consolation
in Ulmer's wonderful eye for composition which comes through in even the

*While it became increasingly fashionable to canonize Ulmer and his fellow auteurs, critics
thrashed some of the more respected directors, as if to rectify the slight felt by these under-
appreciated geniuses all those years. Almost overnight, William Wyler, John Huston, Billy
Wilder and others found themselves browbeaten by a small clique of film academics. One
sensed an intellectual conspiracy.

most perfunctory of scenes. For a Poverty Row quickie, the sheer number of camera set-ups is staggering and one can only marvel at the grueling, breakneck pace which the director must have maintained throughout the shooting. *Bluebeard* gives credence to Ulmer's claim that he once made 80 set-ups in one day. The payoff can be seen in the film's remarkable visual richness.

The standard *modus operandi* of shooting a scene in this sort of B picture would be a master two-shot with a few obligatory closeups. Ulmer breaks from this tradition, at least doubling the number of camera angles, always with an eye for the most artful compositions. A case in point is the marionette opera sequence in which the director has a proverbial field day cutting from the puppets to reaction shots of his players to long shots of the audience. But even in far less showy scenes, as in Ludwig Stossel's midnight call to Carradine's house, the director evokes a properly brooding atmosphere with a spate of sinister, dimly lit closeups of the actors. Subjective shots are utilized leading up to Carradine's murder of Sonia Sorel, and tilted camera angles (along with *Caligari*-esque sets complete with painted shadows) are used in Carradine's nightmarish flashbacks.

Of course, Eugen Schufftan, the film's uncredited director of photography, deserves his full share of praise here, too. The genius German cinematographer worked internationally, lending his talents to pictures as diverse as *Metropolis* (1926) and Ulmer's *Menschen am Sonntag* (1929) to *Les Yeux Sans Visage* (a.k.a. *The Horror Chamber of Dr. Faustus*, 1959) and the kiddie fantasy *Captain Sindbad* (1963); he landed an Oscar for his photography of 1961's *The Hustler*. Two years after receiving the Billy Bitzer Award for "outstanding contribution to the motion picture industry," Schufftan died in 1977.

There's no shortage of kudos for *Bluebeard* in film history books, and *auteur*-minded critics are lavish in their priase; it's always been a film that only *audiences* have had a tough time warming up to. It's all well and good to salute Ulmer for the ingenious way he creates a soundstage Paris on a less-than-zero budget, but this doesn't bring an extra ounce of realism to the absurd painted backdrops and papier-mâché sets; in fact, by overreaching, *Bluebeard* is more recognizably an ultra-low budget film than something as drecky as, say, *Dead Men Walk*. Leo Erdody's wall-to-wall music, classically based, calls constant attention to itself, sometimes even drowning out the dialogue. The script is talky, the marionette sequence uncomfortably long, the comedy relief painful. If you're in the market for a creatively-made, old-time, low-budget psychological thriller, *Bluebeard* is nothing short of perfect. But if you want to kick back for an hour of horror film fun, *Bluebeard* can't shine *The Mad Monster*'s shoes.

Some of the gaffes in *Bluebeard* are humorous; *more* humorous, in fact, than the intended comic relief of Emmett Lynn (as Carradine's leering gofer) and camera-conscious Iris Adrian (who puts the brakes to the film as a smirky, Brooklyn-accented Parisian prostitute). The dubbing of the supposedly "singing" actors (Carradine, Lynn and Sonia Sorel) during the marionette scene is hilariously, embarrassingly poor. In the same scene, Carradine puts his eye to a peephole to ogle audience member Jean Parker. In a reverse angle shot (looking *in* at Carradine through the peephole) we see him a good three feet from the opening, his head turned away from it, and looking in exactly the wrong direction anyway! While painting Teala Loring, Carradine can see her in a mirror, but unaccountably, *she* can't see *him*. And Carradine's incriminating portrait of one of his early victims, which is a crucial plot point, looks as if it were executed by a television art school dropout. (Sharp-eyed viewers can catch sight of the very same painting decorating the wall of a beatnik cafe in the 1959 "heist" movie *The Rebel Set.*) The climax of the film is marred by an odd slow-motion shot of Carradine's obvious stunt double falling to his drowning death. (This footage would be used again a year later in PRC's *Fog Island.*)

These reservations certainly did little to impede the flow of favorable critical notices, quite rare for the PRC penny-pinchers. No one was more impressed than *The Hollywood Reporter*, who rained extravagant praise on *Bluebeard* as though it were horror's *Gone with the Wind*:

> [*Bluebeard*] is the kind of picture any company, or any producer, would like to release. It is a class product from start to finish, with every opportunity to entertain, regardless of expense, utilized to the fullest.... [T]hough of the horror variety, [*Bluebeard*] raises this type of entertainment to a new high by combining an intelligent story with psychological overtones and a beautifully-mounted production.... Edgar Ulmer's direction is studied and exact. There is a gentleness and an understanding permeating the entire film that can be attributed to him. Jockey Feindel's photography is always good and, at times, superbly different.

While *Bluebeard* is still on solid ground with dyed-in-the-wool film buffs and the small band of Ulmer cultists, it's a little difficult to imagine a casual viewer getting past PRC's rinky-dink production values and the picture's stodgy pace. More patient viewers should respond to the somewhat dimmed but still suspenseful scenes, like police undercover woman Teala Loring slowly realizing that the notorious strangler is actually her sister's beau. As with most public domain titles, the plethora of poor dupe prints and low-quality videos give the film an even dingier look. Under these conditions, *Bluebeard*'s elevated standing may be in some jeopardy, especially in these days of politically correct, E.R.A.-conscious audiences who might take a dim view of even supposedly sympathetic lady-killers. And the film's atmosphere of failed artistic pretension seems to grow thicker with repeated viewings.

John Carradine plays to perfection the role of the tormented puppeteer;

it's undoubtedly Carradine's finest hour in a horror film (and therefore his best-ever leading movie performance). He's soft-spoken and understated as the haunted Morrell – but not in the meandering, namby-pamby way that he underplayed roles like those in *Return of the Ape Man* and *The Face of Marble*. He enacts the part sensitively and convincingly, and looks almost dashing in his finely tailored period clothes and long haircut; even at the end, when he pours out his heart to Jean Parker, it's with passion and dramatic intensity rather than his accustomed ham. How is it possible that this is the same John Carradine who drooled up a storm in Monogram's *Voodoo Man*, another 1944 release?

The Hollywood Reporter loved Carradine as Bluebeard, although not enough that they resisted the temptation to poke fun at his popular screen image:

> Carradine has never been seen to better advantage. Gone are the familiar, hammish chin-stroking and the leering eye. He gives a sensitive yet virile portrayal of the mad painter that will be marked as one of the finest pieces of acting in a long time.

In a 1980 chat with television's Dick Cavett, Carradine revealed that Ulmer had allowed him to direct one scene in *Bluebeard*: "I had an idea about the scene and [Ulmer] let me direct it, and they shot it and printed it as I directed it, which was very flattering. It's the only time I ever directed in pictures." (In the same interview, Carradine made some of his usual disparaging remarks about horror films in general, claiming to have done only "about 25" of them and reminding Cavett that he had never played a monster, which except for his vampire characters was probably true until 1981's *The Howling*. Carradine also said that Boris Karloff was always sorry that he had played the Monster in *Frankenstein* and become typecast as a horror star. "It typed him for the rest of his career, though it made him a millionaire. But he hated it.")

Talking with *Fangoria*'s Terry Pace, Carradine aired the one major gripe that he had with Ulmer and *Bluebeard*:

> Everything was going fine until we shot one scene. [Ulmer] hired two classic Mack Sennett comedians to play the gendarmes in Paris. They did their same old schtick. I couldn't understand that at all. Ulmer ruined the quality that he had given the picture. Up until then, *Bluebeard* had the feeling of being made in Europe. He was a good director, and it was a *lovely* [italics added] part, but in that scene, he *ruined* the picture.

The problem with Carradine's complaint is that no one knows what he's talking about; except for one leering gendarme that twists the end of his mustache in a brief shot during Iris Adrian's comic relief scene, the gendarmes remain faceless extras throughout the film. He also mentioned to *Filmfax*'s Dennis Fischer that he would like to have done his own singing in the marionette scene.

Oddly, Carradine never again worked with Ulmer, even though the pair appear to have gotten along well enough on *Bluebeard* (and, previously, on *The Black Cat*, in which Carradine played a bit, and *Isle of Forgotten Sins*). Later in 1944, PRC announced that Carradine would play the Count in *The Wife of Monte Cristo*, but that Ulmer production (released in 1946) ended up having Martin Kosleck in the role. Kosleck today shudders at the memory of the film, still appalled by the rock-bottom cheapness of the production and not at all impressed with Ulmer's much-vaunted, back-against-the-wall ingenuity. Ulmer may have thrived on the experience of making movies for next to no money, but it did understandably little for the egos of the actors involved.

Bluebeard's costars are a professional and persuasive lot. Jean Parker fills the bill nicely as the demure Lucille; Parker seemed to specialize in horror pictures that year, turning up also in Universal's Inner Sanctum mystery *Dead Man's Eyes* opposite Lon Chaney, Jr., as well as in the Pine-Thomas semihorror spoof *One Body Too Many* with Bela Lugosi (also filmed at PRC).

Nils Asther, who plays the Inspector, was a handsome silent screen star who, despite being a fine actor, was unaccountably reduced to programmers soon after movies broke the sound barrier. He could always be counted upon to bring a touch of exotic elegance to a film, which is precisely what he does for *Bluebeard*.

Deeper down the castlist, Ludwig Stossel, the frumpy, amiable father of Lou Gehrig (Gary Cooper) in *The Pride of the Yankees* (1942), and the Little Old Winemaker in 1960s television commercials, plays completely against type as the evil Lamarte. Made-up and bizarrely lit to look like something out of a silent horror film, Stossel is a worse fiend than Carradine, remorselessly profiting from the portraits which can only be painted at the cost of their models' lives. George Pembroke is easy-to-miss in a nothing role; Henry Kolker, the head of the French Police in Metro's *Mad Love* (1935), is here demoted to plainclothes detective, and seems strikingly ill-at-ease. As the doomed Renee, Sonia Sorel, then currently "shacked up" with John Carradine (Carradine having left his wife Ardanelle to live with Sorel), gets an on-screen taste of what it's like to be "the woman spurned." Sorel later married him (they announced their engagement during the making of *Bluebeard*) and gave birth to sons Christopher, Keith and Robert before the couple's lurid 1957 divorce.

Production of *Bluebeard* may have been prompted by the huge box office success of 20th Century–Fox's Jack the Ripper film *The Lodger*, shot in 1943 and released in January, 1944 (shortly before PRC announced *Bluebeard*).

Comparisons between the two are almost odious, *The Lodger* being an impressive big-budget production crowded with suspense and breathtaking gaslit sets while *Bluebeard*, small-scale and pedantic, looks like a photographed college stage show. Carradine (Bluebeard) and Laird Cregar (Jack the Ripper) both excelled in their leading roles, fighting to quell homicidal impulses initially brought on by the treachery of a woman, and both films were made with creativity and sincerity. But *Bluebeard* simply isn't in *The Lodger*'s league, or even close.

Ulmer's yen to direct a film version of *Bluebeard* dated back at least as far as April 1934, when in the wake of *The Black Cat* he was reportedly preparing an elaborate Universal production of *Bluebeard* with Boris Karloff tentatively pencilled in as star. Just over a week after this announcement, Ulmer and Universal came to a parting of the ways, with the Hollywood trades reporting that a salary dispute had come between director and studio.

Universal revived the project in 1935, announcing that scenarist Bayard Veiller had been signed to write an original story and screenplay. Although Karloff was to play Bluebeard in the film, its real villain was to have been a woman. According to what Universal told *The Hollywood Reporter*, producer David Diamond and Veiller sought a psychoanalytical treatment that would explain the wife murders in a logical if not sympathetic manner. The horror film was to have been period (1870 France), avoiding both the actual Landru as well as another real-life Bluebeard, the 15th century's Gilles de Rais. Preparations dragged on and on; new writers (Rose Franken and William Brown Maloney) were brought in, the period setting was abandoned in favor of a contemporary milieu, Bela Lugosi was slated to costar with Karloff and the film was finally given a January 1936, starting date. Of course, in 1936 horror films went out of style, and *Bluebeard* (along with *Phantom of the Opera, The Electric Man* and other thrillers Universal was planning) went down the tubes.

Ulmer immodestly claimed that his *Bluebeard* was superior to Charlie Chaplin's 1947 black comedy *Monsieur Verdoux* (Ulmer: "a horrible picture"). There may be some legitimacy to Ulmer's claim if one sees the overrated Chaplin picture for what it is: two hours of comedy genius working at low voltage, capped by the dopiest of self-righteous sermonizing as pacifist Charlie equates wife-killing with nations sending young soldiers off to battle (against Hitler, no less!). The film proved that gallows humor was not Chaplin's forte and was typical of the bone-headed social commentary that got the comedian into so much hot water with the government. Most of the other films that invoked the Bluebeard name were made in the silent days, generally by the French, who filmed it in 1898 (twice), 1901, 1908 and 1910; Edison's company had a go at it in 1909. In 1936 there was an animated puppet short from France and in 1951 a French spoof with separate French and German casts. A French-Italian version came in 1962

Carrie Devan, Patti McCarty and Jean Parker don't realize that the puppeteer (John Carradine) who's just entertained them is actually *Bluebeard.*

(released in France as *Landru*), directed by Claude Chabrol, and in 1972 an international version of *Bluebeard*, with Richard Burton as the killer, was released in the U.S. by Cinerama. Raquel Welch, Virna Lisi and Joey Heatherton were among the damsels in distress in this campy Edward Dmytryk–directed bomb. Uncredited versions and variations are too plentiful to attempt to cite.

Despite racing the clock and having to squeeze every dollar, Ulmer does one of his best jobs of directing in *Bluebeard*, but the film is tainted by its poverty-stricken look, and Pierre Gendron's intelligent but rather garrulous script cries out for pruning and doctoring. *Bluebeard* remains one of Poverty Row's most celebrated diamonds in the rough, a stellar example of brilliance on a minuscule budget, but this dark, moody sleeper has never made much of a splash outside of film cultists' circles.

Sincere, imaginative and artistic, *Bluebeard* is also murky, heavy-handed and more than just occasionally dull. In the classroom of vintage horror films, *Bluebeard* is the overachiever, the teacher's pet, the brown-noser that everyone tends to keep at arm's length. A lot of hard work went into it, but it's one of those alienating films which seems to have been made for the critics instead of the fans.

The Edgar Ulmer "mystique" and his cult director status can be a bit bewildering but there's no denying that the man had a fascinatingly eclectic career, rubbing elbows early on with the cinema's greatest pioneers and then plummeting to the level of grade-Z Westerns, Ukrainian and Yiddish films (shot in New York and New Jersey) and documentary shorts about tuberculosis among blacks; rumor has it he even directed the nudist film 1959 *The Naked Venus.* In fact, even as the French were lauding him in the late '50s, Ulmer was busily putting the lie to their hyberbolic praise with his lackluster handling of horror and science fiction bombs like *Daughter of Dr. Jekyll* (1957), *Beyond the Time Barrier* and *The Amazing Transparent Man* (1960), pictures so indifferently made that they could have been directed by any of Ulmer's Poverty Row compatriots with no discernible difference.

It's unfair, though, to blame Ulmer for the way the *auteur* clique has blown his reputation out of proportion; Ulmer doesn't seem to take himself too terribly seriously in his Bogdanovich chat, and he didn't hesitate to admit that he brought more of "himself" (his style, his "vision," whatever) to some pictures than to others. One of filmland's most colorful characters, he died at the Motion Picture Country Home after a long illness in 1972, at age 68.

PRC was at first unhappy with *Bluebeard* but it eventually made money for the company (probably playing in a far wider assortment of theaters than the usual PRC drivel). Most of *Bluebeard's* contemporary reviews flattered the film and even today it continues to garner complimentary notices, although you have to wonder if maybe just a few of these modern-day writers aren't merely toeing the traditional critical mark.

Fangoria's resident video reviewer Dr. Cyclops played it safe by straddling the fence a bit: "Made in between Ulmer's two best remembered films, *The Black Cat* and *Detour*, *Bluebeard* doesn't measure up to those two underground classics, but it still has more style than most B horror programmers from the '40s. . . . There's not much that is surprising in *Bluebeard*, but the movie has an interesting dark look and mood, and, after a fairly dull first half, moves along quite well. . . . A good bet for B-movie connoisseurs."

Leslie Halliwell did the same thing, uninformatively summing *Bluebeard* up as "possibly the most interesting film ever to come from PRC (which isn't saying *very* much)."

John Cocchi (*Second Feature: The Best of the 'B' Films*) was pretty noncommittal, too: "After *Detour*, this is considered to be PRC's best effort," he wrote, nicely distancing himself from the statement. *Psychotronic* skirted the issue of quality entirely, calling it "a popular B-film from the director of *The Man from Planet X.*"

Others were more opinionated. Leonard Maltin gave it three stars and described it as "surprisingly effective." Don Willis laid it on the line, as usual ("Overrated 'sleeper,' but decent enough"), as did Don Leifert, who complained in *Filmfax*, "[T]he praise heaped upon this mediocre programmer remains a mystery to this author. Carradine's low-key approach to the title role is forgettable, and Ulmer's direction, aside from a few inventive camera angles, is nothing special. Simply put, *Bluebeard* is an overrated disappointment."

A third Don, *B Movies*' Don Miller, seemed genuinely taken with it: "John Carradine gave what remains as one of his best, if not his absolute best, performance. His restraint under conditions that would tempt a Lugosi to overplay was remarkable, and he used his deep, rich voice, one of the best in films, to its fullest advantage. . . . Edgar Ulmer came through with an excellent job of direction, like Carradine's performance restrained and expertly conceived." Peter Bogdanovich said during his Ulmer interview that it was one of his best pictures but, of course, Ulmer was sitting right there. Gregory Mank (*The Hollywood Hissables*) wrote, "Carradine's exquisite performance . . . with Ulmer's unique touch, transforms a low-budget melodrama into a moving tragedy."

Crazy Knights
(Monogram, 1944)

Released December 8. 63 minutes. TV title: *Ghost Crazy*. Associate Producer: Barney Sarecky. Produced by Sam Katzman and Jack Dietz (Banner Pictures). Directed by William Beaudine. Original Screenplay: Tim Ryan. Photography: Marcel Le Picard. Assistant Director: Arthur Hammond. Musical Director: Edward Kay. Special Effects: Ray Mercer. Film Editor: John Fuller. Sound Engineer: Frank Webster.

Cast: Billy Gilbert, Shemp Howard, Maxie Rosenbloom (Themselves), Tim Ryan (Grogan), Jayne Hazard (Joan Gardner), Tay Dunn (Williams), Minerva Urecal (Mrs. Benson), John Hamilton (Mr. Gardner), Bernard Sell (Dave Hammon), Betty Sinclair (Girl), Art Miles (Gorilla).

> **"Make this a travesty on the usual Hollywood opening. Tell the folks that the cashier might refuse their money . . . the ushers might ask you to seat them . . . the picture may run backwards . . . the doorman might match double or nothing . . . and the janitor might be manager for the night. Plaster the town with handbills and plenty of extra advertising. Let 'em know you have the screwiest picture of the year . . . Crazy Knights."** — Monogram exploitation suggestions.

Comedies generally come into this world with two strikes against them already. A horror film doesn't have to be scary to be entertaining; Westerns don't always need a lot of action to be diverting; a transparent mystery can still be worthwhile; and on and on throughout the genres of filmdom. But if a comedy isn't amusing, it usually isn't *anything*. And many (maybe most) of the old programmer comedies–generations removed from what modern audiences find funny–are painful and embarrassing, big round zeroes for the viewer of today.

The fattest, roundest zero of the bunch, *Crazy Knights* is the kind of loutish comedy that raises the blood pressure rather than tickling the funnybone. Producers Sam Katzman and Jack Dietz evidently envisioned stars Billy Gilbert, Shemp Howard and Maxie Rosenbloom as Monogram's answer to Columbia's Three Stooges, with Gilbert as the bossy, quick-to-slap leader (the Moe Howard counterpart), Rosenbloom as the dull-witted middleman (the Larry Fine type) and Shemp as the dimmest of the bunch, perpetually on the receiving end of Gilbert's abuse (just like third Stooge Curly Howard–Shemp's real-life brother). Katzman and Dietz launched a Gilbert-Howard-Rosenbloom series, kicking it off with *Three of a Kind* (1944) and following it up with *Crazy Knights* and yet a third picture, *Trouble Chasers* (1945). None of these films received much in the way of attention from reviewers–even *Variety*, which covered most every new release, managed to miss all three–and ticket sales must have been disappointing, as the witless series was squelched after only these three films. As the late Don Miller points out in his pithy *B Movies*, "No hits, no runs, three errors."

Billy Gilbert (playing himself), a carnival sideshow pitch man, proudly displays Barney from Borneo, the Gorilla with the Human Mind, who counts and shows other mild signs of intelligence. What his audiences don't know is that Gilbert's partner Shemp Howard (as himself) climbs into a gorilla suit, secretly taking Barney's place at one point during each performance. Gilbert and Howard try to decide where they will spend their upcoming vacation, but their carnival co-worker, young barker Dave Hammon (Bernard Sell), reminds them that, with practically no money between the three of them, the only place they're going is to the next town for a new engagement.

Driving on a lonely stretch of road, Gilbert, Howard, Hammon (and, of course, Barney, riding in a special trailer) are passed by a speeding car. In it are Mr. Gardner (John Hamilton), a businessman who fears that attempts are being made on his life; his pretty niece Joan (Jayne Hazard); his secretary Williams (Tay Dunn) and chauffeur Maxie Rosenbloom (as himself). The car's engine catches fire and its occupants pile out just before the explosion. They flag down the carnival performers' car and Hammon offers them a lift to the Gardner family estate. Joan is quite obviously upset over having to return to the Gardner house, which has held unpleasant memories for the girl after the death of her mother.

Weird things begin to happen as soon as the troupe arrives at the estate. Mrs. Benson, the leering housekeeper (Minerva Urecal, who else?), gives

Gilbert and Howard a start; a laughing, disembodied voice throws them into a panic; and a mysterious stranger sneaks up behind Joan and scares her into a faint. Expectedly, Gilbert, Howard and Hammon wind up being invited to spend the night. And, as always happens, there's a romantic attraction between Hammon and Joan.

The film is filled with incidents (none of them scary, none of them funny) which add up to nothing. An electrician skulks around the place looking suspicious, a portrait in Gilbert and Howard's room changes every time they look away, and Gardner is found knocked unconscious. Another fishy character (Tim Ryan) shows up and Mrs. Benson instructs him to hide. Williams the secretary falls under suspicion when the others conjecture that he's out to woo and marry the wealthy Joan.

A ghost-like figure appears outside Gilbert and Howard's window, then turns transparent and levitates down into the adjacent graveyard, where it ducks behind a monument. Gilbert and Howard split up to search the boneyard, with Gilbert finding a monument which slides aside to reveal the entrance to an underground passageway. In it he finds the ghost costume. Later, when Gilbert tries to show the passageway to Hammon and the others, the monument won't budge.

The plot, such as it is, thickens. The mystery stranger played by Tim Ryan turns out to be Grogan, a private eye. Barney the Gorilla gets loose and begins to roam the house while Howard dresses up in his gorilla suit (for no good reason) and does the same. Joan is seized and dragged into a secret passage by the electrician while, elsewhere, the others find the dead body of Williams.

Eventually all parties converge in the underground passageway. The electrician and another accomplice are overpowered and the "ghost" is knocked out by Mrs. Benson. Unmasked, he is Gardner, who wanted his niece out of the way so that he could control her money (the attempts on his life were all phonies); Mrs. Benson hired Grogan because she figured out his scheme. And Barney from Borneo, still on the loose, chases Gilbert, Howard and Rosenbloom around the grounds as the picture fizzles to a halt.

Definitely an acquired taste, comedians like Billy Gilbert, Shemp Howard and Maxie Rosenbloom may not be funny by today's standards, but they still do have small pockets of followers. Leonard Maltin, now a highly-recognizable fixture on television's *Entertainment Tonight* and compiler (since age 17!) of the landmark film guide *TV Movies*, worshipped at the shrine of comics like these within the pages of his now-defunct magazine *Film Fan Monthly*, and apparently a number of other fans also have soft spots in their hearts for this school of screen humor. But while watching something like *Crazy Knights*, a dog from snout to tail, you have to wonder whether these soft spots are cardiovascular or cranial.

Billy Gilbert, famous for his delayed sneeze routine in the days when things like that somehow were funny, was a heavyset (280-pound) veteran of vaudeville and burlesque who went on to appear in over 100 features and scads of comedy short subjects. Gilbert is as swinish as his fans could possibly want in *Crazy Knights*, blustering up a storm but never doing anything that even verges on being faintly amusing. Prizefighter Maxie Rosenbloom, a reform school graduate and onetime holder of the New York State heavyweight amateur title, was a comic whose specialty was punch-drunk characters. Knowing that he was probably exactly the same way in life (he spent his final years in a hospital bed, suffering the cumulative effects of years of punishment in the ring) detracts appreciably from his lowbrow shtick. Shemp Howard, later one-third of the Three Stooges after illness forced brother Curly out of the picture, probably comes off best of the three, the faintest praise you'll find in *this* book.

The script, which is in large part a remake of Monogram's earlier *Boys of the City* with the East Side Kids, is at or below the level of grade-school writing, full of scaredy-cat hijinks and loathsome puns. It's the type of material no comedian could salvage, and certainly not the low-ranking gaggle of goons gathered here.

Even the film's supporting cast is an obnoxious bunch. John Hamilton – Perry White to television's *Superman* – plays his patented grouch; no one tries to explain how (in his "ghost" guise) he manages at one point to become transparent and float through the air. (Perhaps that's meant to be a *real* ghost, pointing the way to Hamilton's secret passage hideout.) Tim Ryan, the minor character player who wrote the *Crazy Knights* script, and many others of equal merit, gets much better-than-deserved billing as the frazzled private eye. Minerva Urecal, Poverty Row's answer to Gale Sondergaard, plays the sinister domestic in the style she was running into the ground. Romantic leads Jayne Hazard and Bernard Sell are so unmemorable as to be almost invisible. Art Miles, who also played apes in *The Gorilla* (1939), *Spook Busters* and the Three Stooges short *A Bird in the Head* (1946), goes unbilled for his simian appearance here.

Crazy Knights was the sort of film that has made director William Beaudine's name mud in all the Hollywood history books. Beaudine began his career as a general helper – i.e., sweeping up the sets – at the Biograph Studios in New York in 1909. ("I started as the lowest guy on [D. W.] Griffith's payroll. I was the assistant to everybody. I painted the properties and cleaned the cuspidors. All for $10 a week," Beaudine told *TV Guide* in 1963.) Arriving in Hollywood in the mid–teens (the century's, not his), Beaudine found work as an assistant director and, during the silent days, directed pictures starring the likes of Pickford, Valentino, Theda Bara and Gloria Swanson. Beaudine was ready to retire by 1928 but the big stock market crash took all his money and it was back to the Hollywood salt mines. Relocating to England in the mid–'30s, he directed more than a dozen films there, but upon his return to California he couldn't get a job for two years:

Everybody had forgotten me. Finally I started working for $500 a picture. Hell, I used to make almost that in a day. Anyway, it took me almost to 1956 to get back on my feet. Every penny I earned would go to pay off debts.

Beaudine probably spent more time at Monogram/Allied Artists than he did at home in the '40s and '50s, directing nearly 80 features, including (in the horror category) *Ghosts on the Loose, Voodoo Man, The Face of Marble* and more; other horror/fantasy credits include the all-black *Condemned Men* (1940) and *Professor Creeps* (1942), and *Billy the Kid versus Dracula* and *Jesse James Meets Frankenstein's Daughter* (both 1966). Even diehard film fans have done a pretty good job of forgetting the "respectable" pictures he directed in the pretalkie days; now his reputation as a director is built around the reckless speed with which he churned out his B-, C- and Z-grade pictures (and which earned him his nickname "One-Shot"). Horror fans in particular hold him in the lowest esteem, Beaudine having dragged Bela Lugosi through the muck of Monogram's *The Ape Man* and Realart's even-worse *Bela Lugosi Meets a Brooklyn Gorilla* (1952).

Crazy Knights went into production on August 7, 1944, at the Chaplin studios in Los Angeles under the working title *Murder in the Family*. Practically no one reviewed the film when it was released. Those few who did, like *The New York Daily News'* Kate Cameron, hated it; she called it a murder mystery "that makes little effort to mystify or interest the audience." *Castle of Frankenstein* magazine called it "typical Monogram nonsense" in a blurb that listed the stars as the East Side Kids.

Crazy Knights is 63 minutes of hog-wallow that deserves all the inattention it gets.

Fog Island
(PRC, 1945)

Released February 15. 72 minutes. Associate Producer and Director: Terry Morse. Screenplay: Pierre Gendron. Based on the play "Angel Island" by Bernadine Angus. Director of Photography: Ira Morgan. Music: Karl Hajos. Film Editor: George McGuire. Assistant Director: William A. Calihan, Jr. Art Director: Paul Palmentola. Set Decorator: Harry Reif. Master of Properties: Charles Stevens. Men's Wardrobe: Larry Judge. Women's Wardrobe: Jean Sharpless. Sound Engineer: Bill Fox.

    Cast: Lionel Atwill (Alec Ritchfield), Jerome Cowan (John Kavanaugh), George Zucco (Leo Grainger), Sharon Douglas (Gail), Veda Ann Borg (Sylvia Jordan), John

Whitney (Jeff Kingsley), Jacqueline de Wit (Emiline Bronson), Ian Keith (Dr. Lake), George Lloyd (Allerton/Al Jenks).

> **"Working at PRC or Monogram was like doing live television. If you made an error, that was it. The first time I made a picture for Monogram, the director told me to enter from outside into a living room. I did. They said, 'Cut!' I said, 'Aren't you going to *rehearse?*'" —**
> **Jacqueline de Wit**

This gloomy, doom-laden melodrama of murder, larceny and revenge could almost be described as Poverty Row's answer to *And Then There Were None.* It's the type of movie that Hollywood used to churn out by the dozen: An old dark house thriller in which nothing remotely supernatural ever occurs. *Fog Island* qualifies as a borderline horror title, if only by a hair. A brief and unmemorable séance scene, a spooky setting (Fog Island's centuries-old stone castle, reputedly built by pirates) and, more importantly, the presence of genre stars Lionel Atwill and George Zucco are enough for it to be included here, but casual readers should be forewarned that only the most hardy, perhaps most foolhardy completists need continue.

The current occupant of the castle on Florida's Fog Island is Leo Grainger (George Zucco), only recently released from prison after serving five years for looting his own company; Grainger has steadfastly maintained his innocence. His return to society has sparked renewed interest in the case, so to escape the glare of publicity, he and his stepdaughter Gail (Sharon Douglas) have sought the solitude of the island fortress.

A mysterious trespasser turns out to be Grainger's ex-accountant (and ex-cellmate) Dr. Lake (Ian Keith), now hiding from the law on a petty larceny charge. Grainger welcomes his old friend, explaining that he is presently expecting a launch from the mainland containing their former business associates whose questionable accounting practices and perjured testimony landed both of them behind bars. Grainger is convinced that one of them is responsible for the murder of his beloved wife Carma, brutally stabbed to death years earlier in a botched attempt to uncover the hiding place of the fortune Grainger supposedly stole.

Coming face to face with the man (Grainger) whom they sent to prison proves disquieting for the newly-arrived guests: Grainger's former secretary Sylvia (Veda Ann Borg), fast-talking con man Kavanaugh (Jerome Cowan), professional spiritualist Emiline (Jacqueline de Wit) and ruthless businessman Ritchfield (Lionel Atwill). They're understandably wary of the embittered Grainger, but all are intrigued by his promise that he'll see that "justice is done," and sense that he is finally going to divide the spoils. Unexpectedly arriving on the same launch is Jeff Kingsley (John Whitney), bearing the invitation intended for his father, who recently died; Gail, Jeff's college girlfriend, has little interest in rekindling the romance.

The poor man's *And Then There Were None, Fog Island* was a trite but likable murder mystery and one of PRC's (slightly) more respectable offerings.

Grainger makes it clear that they are cut off from the outside world until the launch returns the next morning. He further startles his guests by announcing that the murderer of his wife is among them, and likely to strike again in his (her?) quest for the hidden money. Grainger has his butler Allerton (George Lloyd) distribute to each of the group a "clue to retribution" which will help them find the loot's hiding place. Gail finds herself with a key, Jeff a knife, Kavanaugh a book of multiplication tables, Emiline a mechanical pencil, Ritchfield a chisel and Sylvia a miniature human skull.

Unaware that she is being observed by Ritchfield, Emiline unscrews her pencil and finds the scrawled message TOP LEFT MANTLE; examining the fireplace, she discovers a concealed compartment containing a key. In the meantime, Gail plays the large pipe organ for the group. Activating one of the organ plungers, she inadvertently opens the door to a secret passageway, getting the attention of Jeff and Ritchfield. Anxious to do a little discreet treasure-hunting, Ritchfield suggests that Emiline stage a séance, then slips away to explore the castle dungeon.

Emiline's séance proves to be a hit. The medium not only manages to levitate the table, but she succeeds in scaring poor Sylvia out of her wits by predicting that she (Sylvia) will meet a watery death.

The group finally decides to call it a night, but instead of retiring, "Doc" Lake stays behind to spy on Allerton, who is ransacking his employer's desk. Lake confronts the butler, accuses him of being escaped murderer Al Jenks, and the pair get into a brawl. Lake quickly gets the upper hand and knocks the butler off the balcony into the crashing sea below.

Grainger and Ritchfield have it out. After an exchange of barbs, Grainger launches into a tirade, accusing Ritchfield point-blank of murdering Carma. Ritchfield responds by plunging into Grainger's body the same knife he used on Carma. Ritchfield disposes of the corpse in the dungeon, not realizing that Lake has witnessed the crime. Ritchfield also stumbles upon a locked room which he is certain can be opened with Emiline's key.

Ritchfield proposes to Emiline that they pool their resources. Emiline instantly agrees and follows Ritchfield to the cellar; they are shadowed by Kavanaugh, who in turn is tailed by Sylvia, while Lake is spying on the lot of them. While Emiline fits her key into the slot, Ritchfield again makes use of his knife, stabbing her in the back. Later, upstairs, Jeff loses an unprovoked fistfight with Lake.

Kavanaugh, Sylvia and Lake confront Ritchfield and demand a share of the money:

> RITCHFIELD: What makes you think that you're entitled to anything?
> LAKE *(smugly)*: Because *I* know where the bodies are buried!

Now content to split the proceeds four ways, the party rush into the treasure room. A wooden table on which a human skull rests (coinciding with Grainger's clues to Sylvia and Kavanaugh) marks the spot as Ritchfield opens a trap door in the floor, revealing a strongbox. But the box is empty except for a final written message from Grainger: "This represents all I ever stole from Grainger, Inc. – the paper this is written on. Unfortunate investments did the rest. May I suggest you divide it amongst yourselves so that I may feel justice is done." Barely recovering from their shock, the four realize that the removal of the strongbox has activated a concealed mechanism which has not only sealed the room but is now flooding it with sea water.

Jeff and Gail discover a secret desk compartment containing Carma's jewelry box; opening it with the key Grainger gave her, Gail finds a small fortune in gems and a note from Carma explaining that this is all that remains of Grainger's fortune. Their old romance apparently revived, Gail packs her bags while Jeff, acting on a hunch, dashes into the dungeon where he discovers the remains of Grainger and Emiline as well as the drowned bodies of Ritchfield, Kavanaugh, Sylvia and Lake. Rejoining Gail, the couple leaves for the mainland when the launch finally arrives.

It may not be an all-out horror movie, but *Fog Island* is one of the more respectable titles covered in this book; it may rank second, although quite a distant second, to *Bluebeard* and *The Lady and the Monster*. While the look of the movie is as bleak as anything that ever came out of Poverty Row, it is still a pleasant change of pace from that era's usual run of low-budget horrors.

The plot is imitation Agatha Christie and, although it cries out for more intricate development and a fuller measure of wit, it's a decent one. The opening scene, however, offers little promise as George Zucco, looking every inch the heavy, conspires in hushed tones and with sinister aplomb with the mysterious stranger (Ian Keith) stalking the grounds. Though establishing the mood of the movie and conveying essential story points, it's a dead scene that only serves to remind the audience that they're watching a PRC film. From here, the action unfolds most agreeably and by the time the leery guests arrive on Fog Island, the picture is genuinely engaging. There's a nice sense of anticipation and gamesmanship, the reassuring feeling that "something is afoot" in the best tradition of movie thrillers. A dour warning from host Zucco about a killer on the prowl, the dissemination of clues, the disparate characters – it's a stock situation but it works, even in these papier-mâché settings.

Unfortunately, writer Pierre Gendron (who also had his hand in *Bluebeard*) piles on the sort of bromides that wore out their welcome back in the silent days.* Hardly a few minutes go by without someone finding yet another sliding panel or secret drawer, and the way the characters shadow each other down into that dingy dungeon becomes ludicrous. The dialogue is acceptable but the script has a rough-hewn, first-draft quality. There's a lot of just-for-the-sake-of-it action including both of Ian Keith's poorly motivated and perfectly preposterous brawls.

The unveiling of the watery booby-trap comes far too early in the movie in an unnecessary scene where Zucco, in uncharacteristic coveralls, is seen rigging up the deadly contraption. The climactic tank scene is suspenseful as the water mounts higher to consume its victims, who alternately try to crash through the bolted door and struggle amongst themselves. There's a chilling macabre touch in the last shot of the skull bobbing in the water as the candle flame is extinguished, signaling to the audience what it knows already, that all of Zucco's victims have had it. The scene is as disturbing as was intended, but would have packed a greater punch if the audience had not been let in on the surprise earlier.

True to its title, the fog rolls heavily in *Fog Island*. Fortunately, fog effects come cheap but PRC carried this economizing over to every phase of the production. Except for a few stock shots, exterior footage is practically nonexistent.

Gendron, formerly an actor, appeared opposite many top female stars during the early days of pictures, long before turning his hand to the writing of PRC films like The Monster Maker, Bluebeard *and* Fog Island. *He died in Hollywood on November 27, 1956.*

Lionel Atwill, once again up to his mustache in malicious mischief, this time in PRC's
Fog Island.

The lack of exteriors is gratingly underscored as characters peer
through out windows to comment on outdoor action which the audience cannot share. The producers, unwilling to furnish a boat mock-up nor even a
single dock set, have George Zucco's guests arrive on the island off-camera,
to be met by Zucco who stubbornly holds his position at the front door. The
shot of the island is the same one seen in Universal's *Horror Island* (1941).
This is one Poverty Row movie where a somewhat bigger budget would
have paid off to produce a better and more handsome product, unlike a
hopeless stiff like *Devil Bat's Daughter*, which no amount of enhanced production values could have made bearable. Watching *Fog Island*, one aches
for the relative lavishness of the worse Universal horror movies of the same
period – pictures like *She-Wolf of London* and *The Cat Creeps* (both 1946),
which squandered their slickly atmospheric ambience and well-appointed
sets on inferior scripts and no-name casts. (The script of *The Cat Creeps* is,
in fact, reminiscent of *Fog Island* with its long-ago murder/robbery and the
reunion of all suspects in a lonely island mansion.)

Karl Hajos contributed an original and relatively lush score that is a vast improvement over the PRC usual. Horror fans best remember Hajos for his score for *WereWolf of London* (1935); the composer obligingly reminds us of his earlier work by pilfering the melancholy theme from that pioneering lycanthropic romp as John Whitney conducts his body count in the last reel.

Director Terry Morse, who also takes an associate producer credit, doesn't bring much style or pizzazz to *Fog Island*, even though this is the kind of spooky material that an interested director could have had fun with. Morse takes the simplest, most time-efficient way out every time, compounding the claustrophobic cheapness that pervades the film. Years earlier, he worked his "magic" in the Warner Bros. *British Intelligence* (1940), presenting Boris Karloff with one of the more resounding duds of his career; his first science fiction credit was the even-duller *Unknown World* (1951). Moore's most offbeat credit is the English-language version footage of Toho's mighty *Godzilla, King of the Monsters!* (1956), directing Raymond Burr as a persevering newsman whose footage was edited into the action. Morse's trickery proved adequate for the Saturday matinee crowd, and the picture was staggeringly successful, but he went on to more conventional assignments.

Lionel Atwill heads up the cast of *Fog Island* but third-billed George Zucco has a more legitimate claim to the top spot (even though he's dispatched a trifle more than halfway through the film). Zucco bitterly complained of being endlessly typed as a villain but, as luck would have it, even the supposedly sympathetic role of Leo Grainger isn't *all* that sympathetic. You can't help feeling the loss of his cruelly butchered wife but even so, the character comes off so cold and mean-spirited that his claim of moral superiority to the crooks and shysters he targets for death seems dubious. His ugly little booby-trap is designed to kill the innocent along with the guilty and the character doesn't bother to take precautions that his own stepdaughter isn't among the casualties. Perhaps sensing this, Zucco doesn't strain to give his character much in the way of pathos and plays the part in his usual heavy fashion. Zucco was a far more beguiling semihero in PRC's *The Black Raven* (1943).

Zucco comes on like gangbusters in his big confrontation scene with Atwill. His high-flown theatrics aren't too far removed from his ravings in *The Mad Monster*, laying it on thick with bulging eyes, calculated gestures and a near-cackling voice. As hard as he tries, Zucco is too aloof an actor to make it all work although it's great fun watching him try. It would have been a more entertaining scene all around if Zucco switched roles with the far heartier ham, Atwill.

Leaving his familiar mad scientist smock and police inspector uniform behind him, a relatively restrained Lionel Atwill proves he could convey white-collar arrogance with the best of them. Atwill was a more personable but no less lethal villain than Zucco, but one could always detect a jolly fat man quality even in his nastiest roles. He even manages to get off one near-comic line in his first exchange with Zucco, asking if his colleague George ever received the gift box of cigars he sent while Zucco was in prison. When the ever-suspicious Zucco replies he passed them along to a cellmate who not only smoked them, but actually *survived* the experience, Atwill retorts with deadpan sarcasm, "Lucky!"

We view *Fog Island* with sadness and a little awe as Atwill, looking visibly tired, "drowns" in the studio tank like a trouper for what could have been only a pittance of a paycheck. A tragic end to a career wrecked by scandal, *Fog Island* (filmed beginning Wednesday, October 25, 1944) would be one of his last roles before succumbing to throat cancer in April, 1946.

Most of the less flashy roles are well-handled. Jerome Cowan, who spent most of his Hollywood days playing acerbic second (or third) bananas, does well in the made-to-order role of Kavanaugh. Cowan is best remembered for supporting roles in top-grade Warners features, playing Humphrey Bogart's partner who gets knocked off early in *The Maltese Falcon* (1941) and the weakling husband of Jimmy Cagney's girlfriend in *Torrid Zone* (1940). In the horror menagerie, he killed off Universal's Ape Woman in *The Jungle Captive* (1945); the animal kingdom got back at him when he was mauled to death by a tiger in producer Herman Cohen's *Black Zoo* (1963). Our most endearing image of Cowan is his uncavalierly pushing a screaming Veda Ann Borg off the floating wooden table in *Fog Island*'s climactic flood scene.

Veda Ann Borg, previously seen sinking into the muck in *Revenge of the Zombies*, and who drowns again here, likewise does a thoroughly professional job. Indeed, she's the only character in *Fog Island* who senses disaster, but is far too greedy to keep her nose out of further mischief. It's a relatively small part but Ms. Borg vests it with a believable tension.

Jacqueline de Wit's puffed-up, turban-topped Emiline character lends a pseudo-occult touch to the movie and the actress plays her as if she were understudying Gale Sondergaard. She does have *one* good line – assuring Zucco that a spiritualist's gifts are such that she can't predict her own future – later proving it by falling victim to Atwill's knife. Curiously, de Wit played a half-alike character and met an almost identical fate in United Artists' horrific Hawthorne anthology *Twice Told Tales* (1963). Schmoozing about *Fog Island* with writer Don Leifert, de Wit tended mostly to remember the problems that were associated with the film:

> I was mainly concerned over how they were going to make the fog. I wanted to know the answer before I signed. They burned some kind of oil to make the fog, and it was awful. At the time, we provided our own wardrobes and received no money for cleaning. When they burned the oil, a haze filled the studio. It even got on the camera lenses. We could hardly breathe.

Originally, they told me I didn't look sufficiently mysterious for the role. I said, "I can't grow fangs!" They decided on having me wear a turban.

I remember that Lionel Atwill had a very avid interest in *The Wall Street Journal*. He would peruse it during each break. In the film's climax, his character and some others were drowned. I told them that I wasn't well, so I didn't have to get in the water. I didn't want my clothes to shrink, so I argued that I might get pneumonia. I told them they should provide a nurse, and they changed the script for my character. I knew there would be foibles. The others were in that swimming pool for two days and two nights!

I wasn't particularly proud of being in *Fog Island*. I didn't say anything to my friends about it, but the stations ran it forever on television. Everyone said, "What were you doing telling fortunes on *Fog Island*?" Such are the vagaries of life!

Ian Keith seems to get into the spirit of the movie and plays "Doc" Lake in a bemused, tongue-in-cheek fashion. The actor, a matinee idol gone to seed, could be counted on to bring a theatrical bearing to almost everything he played, except for perhaps his best role, as a down-and-out carnival performer in *Nightmare Alley* (1947). It wouldn't be unfair to suggest that Keith walks through the part, but at least he brings the right tone to the character. (While *Fog Island* was in release in February 1945, Keith and Bela Lugosi were costarring in the mystery play *No Traveler Returns*, which broke in at Santa Barbara's Lobero Theater on February 24 and opened in San Francisco two days later. Keith had been considered for the role of Dracula in the 1931 Universal film before Lugosi won out.)

Fog Island's seasoned players, unfortunately, leave the less experienced juvenile leads floundering. Sharon Douglas as Gail is no better than ordinary, but she's still ahead of the hero, John Whitney, exactly the sort of performer who got most of his breaks during the war years when most all the *good* young actors were out of town. The couple's initial scenes of cat-and-mouse romance are awkward and things don't improve much after that.

The play upon which *Fog Island* was based, *Angel Island*, began its Broadway run October 20, 1937, at the National Theatre on Manhattan's 41st Street. A mystery comedy in three acts and nine scenes, it starred Betty Field, Lea Penman, Arlene Francis, Morgan Conway, Maidel Turner, David Hoffman, Doro Merande and ten others, for a total of 17 characters (including Carma Grainger); *Fog Island*, a streamlined version of it, features only nine. The play, directed by George Abbott, received mixed first night notices, mostly negative; the *New York Journal-American* called *Angel Island* "a large body of dialogue entirely surrounded by dullness." Two days after the play's opening, the *New York World-Telegram* reported that $30,000 had been bid for the film rights by an unnamed movie company (twice the sum spent to produce the play), but this unconfirmable report sounds like wishful thinking on someone's part; the play lasted less than three weeks. Playwright Bernadine de Tuvache Angus, who was also an actress, died in New York in 1948, at age 48.

Wanda Hale of *The New York Daily News* gave *Fog Island* a two-and-a-half star rating, describing it as a "murder thriller guaranteed to give you the creeps.... While *Fog Island* [and its co-feature, PRC's *Hollywood and Vine*] aren't anything you'd go out of your way to see, each in its own way is as agreeably entertaining as the other." *Variety*'s unsigned critique was also mildly favorable: "A chiller with strictly stock situations, this picture is nevertheless done well throughout.... Good acting is supplemented by smooth production, combining to lift a murder story that's not too subtle into a picture that's above the mediocre." *The Hollywood Reporter*'s reviewer sounded as though he *tried* to like the picture, but couldn't: "The production values are undeniably fine, with lots of set space and furniture in evidence. The cast is good for the most part. But the plot seems like something that might have been stolen from Pearl White's tomb.... The thing gets gory — but gory. Everybody begins killing everybody else, without the slightest apparent motivation or profit. It goes into a 'Perils of Pauline' climax with four actors in a basement room ready to cut up an old mortgage they have found in a drain. Then these four actors begin killing one another over a floating table. The leading man finds all the bodies, goes upstairs, straightens his tie, packs the girl's bag and — clinch.... For the fans who keep on patronizing horror stuff season after season, to usually record grosses, *Fog Island* certainly will fill the bill."

More style and a more generous budget could have gone a long way in putting *Fog Island* over the top as a Poverty Row miniclassic. As it is, we can still enjoy it for its moments of intrigue and full-throttle performances of horror standbys Zucco and Atwill.

The Phantom Speaks
(Republic, 1945)

Released May 10. 69 minutes. Associate Producer: Donald H. Brown. Executive Producer: Armand Schaefer. Directed by John English. Original Screenplay: John K. Butler. Photography: William Bradford. Film Editor: Arthur Roberts. Sound: Earl Crain, Sr. Art Director: Russell Kimball. Musical Director: Richard Cherwin. Set Decorator: George Milo. Costume Supervisor: Adele Palmer. Assistant Director: Johnny Grubbs.

Cast: Richard Arlen (Matt Fraser), Stanley Ridges (Dr. Paul Renwick), Lynne Roberts (Joan Renwick), Tom Powers (Harvey Bogardus), Charlotte Wynters (Cornelia Willmont), Jonathan Hale (District Attorney Owen McAllister), Pierre Watkin (Charlie Davis), Marian Martin (Betty Hanzel), Garry Owen (Louis Fabian), Ralf Harolde (Frankie Teel), Doreen McCann (Mary Fabian), Joseph Granby (James J. Kennerley), Frank Fanning, Eddie Parker (Policemen), Charles Sullivan (Cab Driver), Robert Homans (Dan [Guard]), Tom Chatterton (Prison Chaplain), Ed Cassidy (Prison Doctor), Edmund Cobb (Warden), Nolan Leary (Watchman), Jack Perrin (Policeman), Bob Alden (Newsboy), Jack Ingram (Detective), Robert Malcolm (Fingerprint Man), Walter Shumway (Deputy), Roy Barcroft (Voice of Taxi Dispatcher).

"Man exists on the physical plane with a body and a brain. Those of us who follow any religion believe that he has something else—a spirit, a *soul*. Now, I contend that the body and brain are not merely composed of physical cells that decay after death. They're allied with the *spirit*. An intangible energy, a force that cannot *possibly* die!"—Dr. Paul Renwick

No one ever accused Republic of being particularly original in their basic horror plots, but neither could anyone have suspected that they would turn out a film as baldly derivative as *The Phantom Speaks*. A mélange of plot ideas from numerous previous horror films, it owes its most considerable debts to Republic's own *The Lady and the Monster* and to Universal's *Black Friday*; such a debt to *Black Friday*, in fact, that it's surprising Universal never went after Republic and "original" screenplay writer John K. Butler in court. The piracy even extended to hiring Stanley Ridges, who played the Jekyll-and-Hyde-ish professor/gangster in *Black Friday*, to play precisely the same role here. It's one of the gutsier instances of plagiarism in horror film history.

The film gives several early indications that it's going to be directed with some style, but doesn't quite live up to this initial promise. It begins with a shadowy figure walking down an office building corridor, bringing his handheld gun into closeup and then firing it toward the camera, at which point the titles come up.

After the credits, a man in a park (Ralf Harolde) comes up to the camera, stares into it and begins adjusting his tie. Now the camera pivots and we see that we've been looking at his reflection in the mirror pane of a cigarette machine.

The man is Frankie Teel, and he's come to Lincoln Park at the written request of his girlfriend Betty Hanzel, wife of mobster Harvey Bogardus. But it turns out that it was Bogardus (Tom Powers) who wrote the note in order to lure Teel into this trap: confronting Teel in a remote section of the park, the gun-waving Bogardus takes from Teel the note along with a photo of Betty that Teel liked to carry.

Bogardus then shoots and kills Teel. Leaving the scene of the crime, he is spotted by Louis Fabian (Garry Owen) and his little daughter Mary

(Doreen McCann). Fabian recognizes the dangerous mobster and promises to keep his mouth shut.

But Bogardus had accidentally dropped Betty's photo at the scene of the crime; he's arrested and brought to trial. The Fabians testify that they saw him at the park and Betty lies that she wasn't having an affair with Teel. Bogardus's lawyer isn't able to get him off the hook. Bogardus is sentenced to death. (No part of the trial is shown.)

At the offices of the newspaper *The Daily Globe*, editor Davis (Pierre Watkin) has his nose buried in the book *Contact with the World Beyond* by Dr. Paul Renwick: Davis has found out that Renwick has made an appointment to visit Bogardus in his cell exactly one hour before the execution. One of Davis's reporters, Matt Fraser (Richard Arlen), is the sweetheart of Renwick's daughter Joan (Lynne Roberts), so Davis assigns Fraser to find out what the noted psychic scientist intends to talk to Bogardus about.

Fraser goes to Renwick's and, while he's waiting for an audience with the doctor, kills a minute or two by presenting Joan with a diamond ring and obnoxiously proposing marriage. Joan accepts.

> FRASER: How'd you like to go out tonight and celebrate? I can get an extra ticket.
> JOAN *(eagerly)*: An extra ticket to *what?*
> FRASER: To the execution of a guy named Harvey Bogardus!

(Some joke.) Fraser and Dr. Renwick (Stanley Ridges) talk awhile; Renwick seems on the level and sincere about his work, but Fraser isn't sure he buys any of it.

That night, at State Prison, Renwick gets the same reaction from Bogardus, although the doomed mobster certainly *wants* to believe that it's possible to come back after death; he has a few scores to settle. Renwick knows Bogardus's life story and the reputation of his iron will; if *any*one can return from beyond the grave, Renwick feels that it's Bogardus. "It's not hard to die. It's the coming-back that's hard!" Renwick says encouragingly. "Yer a crackpot. Get outta here!" Bogardus snarls, unimpressed. Bogardus walks the last mile an hour later, pausing to tell a roomful of reporters and spectators (and Renwick):

> Okay, so I killed a rat. He got what was coming to him. And I know some others that'll get the same thing. I'm not through yet—hear me? Not yet!

Led through "that little green door," Bogardus pays for his crime in the electric chair.

Renwick holes himself up in his library for days; in a curtained-off section of the room, light- and sound-proof, he waits for Bogardus to return.

Which he does: Renwick first hears his voice, and then Bogardus materializes in a chair. "There are some things I can't do without you," he tells Renwick. "I've got hands – but I can't pick anything up with 'em. I've got legs – but I can't walk around on 'em. These eyes – all I can see is *you*, Renwick. But I've got a *mi-i-i-ind*."

Somehow, Renwick manages not to detect the ominous tone in Bogardus' voice as Bogardus "offers" to take over his mind.

> RENWICK: That's a fact I've sought all my life to prove! That a spirit from the dead could take possession of the living. If we can conduct a successful experiment along those lines, we can prove that there's no such thing as insanity. It's a case of a spirit from the beyond, crowding out the mind and spirit of the living.
> BOGARDUS *(leering)*: Wanna *try* it, doctor?

Renwick falls into Bogardus' clutches: Now possessed by the dead killer's spirit, "Renwick" hurries to the office of Bogardus' defense attorney (Joseph Granby), threatens him ("Renwick" talks with Bogardus' voice) and then shoots him to death. Always the sloppy killer, he fails to notice that the attorney's recording device is operating. Investigating the scene of murder, D. A. McAllister (Jonathan Hale) and Fraser play back the recording and recognize Bogardus' voice.

After a brief stint as himself again, Renwick is possessed by Bogardus once more. This time he kills Betty (Marian Martin), Bogardus' wife, who betrayed him in court; Betty is shot to death in an alley behind the night club where she sings. When Renwick reawakens as himself again, Bogardus' disembodied voice tells him that they'll kill Louis and Mary Fabian next. Renwick gets in a cab, asking to be taken to police headquarters (he intends to turn himself in), but Bogardus takes over and the cabby is now instructed to drive to Lincoln Park. There "Renwick" kills Fabian as he snoozes on a park bench. He's about to snuff out Mary's life when he hears Fraser's approach (Fraser had followed him) and flees. Cornelia (Charlotte Wynters), Renwick's housekeeper, shows up and takes him home; she also had tailed him there. (She's in love with Renwick, although he doesn't know it, and has somehow managed to figure out exactly what's going on.)

Cornelia tips Fraser that "Renwick" will go after D. A. McAllister next, so Fraser rushes to McAllister's office to warn him. As Fraser and McAllister drive off together, "Renwick," gun in hand, sits up in the back seat; Fraser swerves the car, overpowering "Renwick."

Renwick is tried for the three murders, judged guilty and condemned to die; Renwick awaits his impending execution serenely, pleased that "Bogardus" will claim no more victims. Fraser watches as Renwick walks the last mile. Before he is killed in the electric chair, Renwick addresses the observers – in Bogardus' voice:

Okay, so I killed a rat. He got what was coming to him. And I know some others that'll get the same thing. I'm not through yet – hear me? Not yet!

Reference books list *The Phantom Speaks* as a pirated remake of *Black Friday*, but writer John K. Butler actually lifts plot devices from numerous earlier films. Certainly *Black Friday* is the main source. In that film, Boris Karloff transplanted a portion of a dying gangster's brain into the skull of a mild college professor (Stanley Ridges again); at odd moments, the professor now takes on the identity of the gangster, and kills members of the criminal gang that had betrayed him (including Bela Lugosi). A nightclub singer in on the treachery (Anne Nagel in *Black Friday*, Marian Martin in *The Phantom Speaks*) is among the victims. In both films, the gangster half of Ridges' personality leaves broken cigarettes around, a trait that he had in life (and a tipoff to other characters that he's come back). Both films have early *and* climactic scenes in a prison death house. The audacious casting of Ridges again in *Phantom Speaks* made Republic's duplication unmistakable. (Similarly, in the '50s, Patricia Neal, leading lady of *The Day the Earth Stood Still* [1955], also starred in an unauthorized semiremake, England's *Immediate Disaster* [1955].)

But *Black Friday* wasn't the only property being ripped off. The return of the gangster in *Phantom Speaks* comes about not scientifically but supernaturally, calling to mind the Halperin Brothers' *Supernatural* (1933), in which Carole Lombard is possessed by the spirit of an executed murderess (and continues to go about her old dirty work). The business of an executed man returning to settle scores with old associates (or with the judge and jurors who had condemned him) also turns up in *The Walking Dead* (1936), *The Man They Could Not Hang* (1939) and *The Monster and the Girl* (1941). Of course Republic's own *The Lady and the Monster* is represented, too; the stories, again, are half-alike, and we even find in both movies Richard Arlen as well as a gloomy housekeeper unaccountably in love with the older professor. Both Donovan (*The Lady and the Monster*) and Bogardus (*The Phantom Speaks*) make an unsuccessful attempt on the life of a child who was a witness at a crime scene.

Of course, it's maddening to find that *Phantom Speaks* is such a derivative movie, but it can also be fun to try and pick out all the pictures from which it pilfers. Interestingly, *Phantom Speaks* does manage to *pioneer* at least one idea, that of the killer left "alive" at the conclusion of the movie; this foreshadows many horror films of the past 20 years in which, seemingly as often as not, hints that the monster/killer/whatever is alive and well and primed for a sequel are climactically dropped.

In the '40s, the Breen Office, watchdogs of Hollywood morality, of course demanded that killers (real *and* supernatural) pay for their crimes, but Republic gets around this obstacle in an interesting way. As Stanley

Ridges is being marched toward the electric chair, the camera moves toward the Bible being held by the prison chaplain (Tom Chatterton), and a block of text is highlighted: "For as he thinketh in his heart so *is* he." This intimates that Ridges has gone mad and killed people under the *delusion* that the gangster (Tom Powers) was guiding his actions. The *Phantom Speaks* pressbook also points out at the end of their synopsis that the entire thing *may* have been a figment of Ridges' troubled mind. The picture, of course, is at odds with this: Ridges talks with Powers' voice when he's under the gangster's influence, and several characters give the impression that they somehow visually recognize Ridges' scientist character as the gangster (Powers). It may have been a cheat, and it leaves viewers a bit up in the air, but it *was* a clever way to get by the censors.

They might be in bad taste, but there *are* ghoulish moments in *The Phantom Speaks* that linger in the memory, like the tearful little girl (Doreen McCann) trying to wake up her father (Ridges murdered the man while he slept), a hysterical Marian Martin being cold-bloodedly pumped full of lead, and a midnight cemetery scene where police dig up Tom Powers' coffin in order to take the corpse's fingerprints. (The date of death on the tombstone is October 27, 1944, the seventh day of production on *Phantom Speaks*, and possibly the day the scene was shot.) The ending of the film, unhappily, lacks any sort of pizzazz, with killer Ridges effortlessly out-wrestled by Richard Arlen, arrested, tried and executed. It's as though everyone involved ran plum out of ideas, and wrapped the thing up in the most mundane manner possible.

The performances in *The Phantom Speaks* are good, with Stanley Ridges once again coming off well in a dual role. In fact, he's *more* convincing as Dr. Renwick in *The Phantom Speaks* than he was as the impossibly meek and milquetoasty college professor in *Black Friday*. This, unfortunately, is offset by the fact that he was better as the *killer* in *Black Friday*.

In *The Phantom Speaks*, Tom Powers overdubs Ridges' dialogue when he's in his gangster mode, and the result is off-puttingly unrealistic. Tom Powers, a Broadway actor who had film-debuted as Barbara Stanwyck's doomed husband in *Double Indemnity* (1944), is good as the vicious Bogardus but his footage, naturally, is brief.

Richard Arlen does his best but again, as in *The Lady and the Monster*, the script calls for a much younger actor. In *The Phantom Speaks*, Arlen's newsman character is boyishly glib and frisky, and the scenes where he romances Lynne Roberts are embarrassing (Arlen was making pictures under his real name, Van Mattimore, before Roberts was even born).

After singing her one song ("Who Took Me Home Last Night" by Jule Stein and Harold Adamson, formerly heard in Republic's *Hit Parade of 1943*), former Ziegfeld girl Marian Martin gets exactly 30 seconds of screen time before Ridges drills her.

Like Marian Martin, Lynne Roberts also doesn't get a chance to do much in the way of acting, but it's always a pleasure to find the button-cute actress in *any* genre film, whether it be *The Phantom Speaks, Dr. Renault's Secret* (1942) or *Port Sinister* (1953, her last film, throughout most of which she showed off her legs in the '50s equivalent of '70s hot pants). Her father, a sales executive, had a lingering illness which kept the family purse fairly well drained, so at age four the Texas-born Roberts (real name: Theda May Roberts) and her six-year-old brother were put to work in the theater. She signed with Republic when she was 13 and was playing romantic leads only two years later. There was more money in freelancing so in 1939 when her father's medical expenses began to soar, she branched out and worked at a variety of studios. She also acted extensively in television during the medium's early years (*Daily Variety* dubbed her the Queen of Video) but little has been heard about her in the decades since, except for the fact that in 1961 she divorced her brassiere-manufacturing husband (he made fun of her acting when her movies were shown on television, and then would fall asleep during them). According to *rumor*, she passed away several years ago.

The Phantom Speaks played on the bottom of a double-bill with the lesser film *The Vampire's Ghost. Variety*'s Sten, who apparently thought that the plot was innovative, was understandably taken with the movie ("This one is a spine-tingling sadistic chiller that has its odd moments, and on the whole does not test the credulity of the audience. . . . Entire cast enact their parts in fairly good fashion. Settings and camerawork, too, are above par"). *The Hollywood Reporter* felt that *Phantom* was "lifted above the average entry in the thriller bracket by virtue of a showmanly production, cleverly restrained direction and an uncommonly good cast. . . . The imaginative, tightly-knit screenplay manages to pose an almost believable plot . . . [The producers] have given the film the kind of supervision and thoughtful casting that stretch a medium budget to the point where it spells quality." The Legion of Decency gave it a "B": "The film misinterprets the nature and power of the human will; suggestive song." Whenever it comes up in film books today, which is seldom, it's just blasted as a rip-off movie and quickly dismissed.

The Phantom Speaks is a well-made picture and director John English supplies a few imaginative touches, and if the ideas in it had been more original, it might rank as Republic's best horror movie. But more likely than not, fans still wouldn't have much use for it. Republic's big "mistake" (if it should be called that) during their horror film period was in never using established horror stars; the people Republic *did* put into these pictures might be fine and capable character actors, but horror buffs don't give two hoots in a barn about the likes of John Abbott, Douglass Dumbrille, Ian Keith, Stanley Ridges or even Erich von Stroheim.

It's interesting to conjecture how much different the reputations of the

Republic horror films would be if, say, George Zucco played the mad doctor in *The Lady and the Monster*; if Bela Lugosi played the madman in *Valley of the Zombies*; if John Carradine were *The Vampire's Ghost*; or Lionel Atwill *The Catman of Paris*. Or if, say, Boris Karloff were in *The Phantom Speaks*. Then also, conversely, how much *less* appeal pictures like *The Ape Man*, *The Mad Monster*, etc., would have if they starred the *Republic* people. It proves that the average horror fan isn't as interested in the basic quality of the movies as he is in seeing his favorite horror stars strut their shopworn stuff. Maybe the only sin these much-maligned Republic horror pictures really committed was to be more original in their casting than Monogram and PRC and even Universal, who slavishly used the same small band of horror actors time and again, until the public became sick to death of them and horror films drifted out of vogue.

It's a mighty poor distinction, but like a good "fence," *The Phantom Speaks* does a nice job of repackaging and reselling stolen goods.

The Vampire's Ghost
(Republic, 1945)

Released May 21. 59 minutes. Associate Producer: Rudolph E. Abel. Executive Producer: Armand Schaefer. Directed by Lesley Selander. Screenplay: John K. Butler and Leigh Brackett. Original Story: Leigh Brackett. Photography: Bud Thackery and Robert Pittack. Film Editor: Tony Martinelli. Sound: Dick Tyler. Art Director: Russell Kimball. Musical Director: Richard Cherwin. Set Decorations: Earl Wooden. Dance Director: Jerry Jarrette.

Cast: John Abbott (Webb Fallon), Charles Gordon (Roy), Peggy Stewart (Julie Vance), Grant Withers (Father Gilchrist), Emmett Vogan (Thomas Vance), Adele Mara (Lisa), Roy Barcroft (Jim Barrat), Martin Wilkins (Simon Peter), Frank Jacquet (The Doctor), Jimmy Aubrey (The Bum), Zack Williams (Taba), Floyd Shackelford (Native), George Carleton (Commissioner), Fred Howard (Inspector), Constantine Romanoff (Kibitzer), Jim Thorpe (Gambler), Tom Steele, Charles Sullivan (Sailors), Pedro Regas (Waiter).

"Africa! The dark land where voodoo drums beat in the night. Where the jungles are deep and full of secrets. And the moon that lights them is still a mystic moon. Africa! Where men have not forgotten the evil they learned in the dawn of time. I always come back to Africa, but even here there is no rest for me. The path of time is curved upon itself like a circle, without beginning, without end. I must follow it forever. I cannot die! I cannot rest! I cannot rest! I cannot rest!"—John Abbott's opening narration

In the mid-'40s, when the second great horror film cycle was petering out, writers at nearly all the studios were beginning to run low on inspiration. The classic monsters had been squeezed dry of practically all their screen potential, and variations on their plots were difficult to dream up. Universal hoped that a change of locale would be enough to dispel the air of déjà vu. From the ancient tombs of Egypt they transplanted the Mummy (Lon Chaney), first to a small town in Massachusetts (*The Mummy's Tomb*, 1942, and *The Mummy's Ghost*, 1944) and later to the swamps of Louisiana (*The Mummy's Curse*, 1944). Dracula, too, packed his bags: The Count (Chaney again) took up residence in the Deep South in *Son of Dracula* (1943). The idea of relocating these "old world" bogeymen into our own backyards seemed sound; the results were mixed. Fifties filmmakers tried it, too: stateside werewolves (*The Werewolf*, 1956, *I Was a Teenage Werewolf*, 1957), Dracula in California (*The Return of Dracula*, 1958)–even the Abominable Snowman in the back alleys of Los Angeles (*The Snow Creature*, 1954)!

Another globe-trotting ghoul was the protagonist of Republic's *The Vampire's Ghost*, which went into production on October 2, 1944. Writers John K. Butler and Leigh Brackett obviously realized that the bloodsucker's bag of tricks had been pretty well exhausted, and sought to–pardon the pun–revamp the classic character almost completely. Rewriting much of Hollywood's vampire lore, they conceived a vampire whose undead existence is the result of a curse. He roams freely about in the daylight, his victims remain dead, and his destruction can be effected only by fire. (Other elements of the vampire mythos, like its craving for human blood, invisibility in mirrors and aversion to crosses, remained intact.)

And, instead of placing their vampire in its usual European haunts, Butler and Brackett set their story in an African village where the monster chooses its victims from among the natives. In Universal's Dracula movies, it was the Transylvanian peasantry who believed in vampires, warding them off with crucifixes and wolfsbane, much to the amusement of unbelieving tourists; in *The Vampire's Ghost* it's the jungle tribesmen of the Dark Continent that are up on vampire lore, the white bwana who refuses to accept the supernatural creature.

The opening sequence is narrated by the vampire himself (see introductory quote above) as the camera roams the darkened streets of an African village. The camera moves up to the door of one of the small native houses and the vampire's hand, a large and distinctive ring on one finger, lifts the latch. A frightened dog backs into a hiding place in a corner of the room. A native girl awakens from a light slumber and her eyes widen in terror as the vampire's shadow falls upon her body. . . .

This killing is just the latest in a series which has plagued the plantation town of Bakunda, and ascribed by the local natives to a vampire; the leading (white) members of the community–merchant Thomas Vance

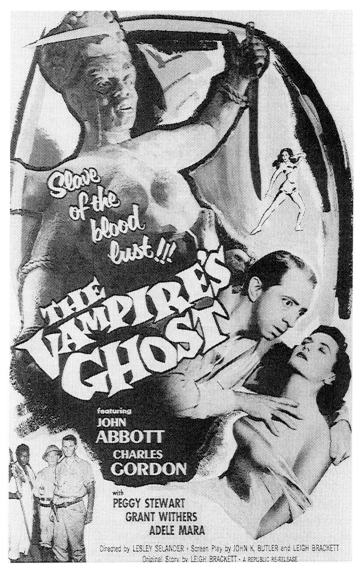

Voodoo and vampirism made for an unlikely combination in the plot of Republic's *The Vampire's Ghost*. Leading lady Peggy Stewart (lower right) wears nothing so provocative in the film.

(Emmett Vogan), rubber plantation official Roy* (Charles Gordon) and missionary Father Gilchrist (Grant Withers)–have gathered to discuss a

*The character's last name is alternately spelled Hendrick and Kendrick in the pressbook, and never mentioned in the film.

course of action. Young Roy, who is engaged to Vance's daughter Julie (Peggy Stewart), is hopeful that Webb Fallon, operator of a waterfront dive and an expert on the Bakunda underworld, can provide a clue to the killer's identity.

Roy drops in at Fallon's Place, where the saturnine Fallon (John Abbott)–who wears the ring we saw on the vampire's hand in the opener–is shooting craps, rolling natural after natural, and beating the pants off of Jim Barrat (Roy Barcroft), skipper of the trader boat *Bakunda Queen.* "The Devil himself couldn't have such luck!" Barrat scowls after Fallon wins the man's share of the boat. Barrat returns with two of his men a few moments later, insisting that Fallon cheated. Roy stands up for Fallon and a fistfight begins. Roy is blackjacked into unconsciousness and is about to be knifed by Barrat when Fallon intercedes, transfixing the skipper with a wide-eyed glare.

Fallon is that night's dinner guest at the Vance home, where Father Gilchrist comments that the urbane Fallon is an odd type to find setting up shop in the jungle. "Sometimes things drive a man, regardless of his will," Fallon mutters. "Things that may even tear his soul. . . ." As Simon Peter (Martin Wilkins), a servant, pours coffee, he notices Fallon's reflection in a nearby mirror: An empty suit of clothes, the cup and saucer he's holding seemingly suspended in mid–air. Fallon, following the direction of Simon Peter's stare, looks into the mirror, which shatters. For no apparent reason, Simon Peter keeps the news of his discovery to himself.

Continuing his investigation, Roy decides to safari to the neighboring village of Molongo, and Fallon invites himself along. Tramping through the jungle, Roy accidently trips a booby-trapped gun, with the bullet passing harmlessly through Fallon and striking Taba (Zack Williams), one of the native carriers. When the troupe beds down for the night, Simon Peter and Taba–both rightly convinced that Fallon is the vampire–dip a spear into molten silver, planning to kill Fallon with it (the weapon would seem better-suited for werewolf hunters). Suddenly a hostile band of natives attacks, killing Taba; in the mêlée, Simon Peter lances Fallon with the spear before he too is wounded.

After the angry natives have been driven off, Roy is attending to the dazed Fallon when he finds that there is no blood on the spear nor any mark on Fallon's body. Mesmerizing Roy, Fallon explains that, 400 years ago, he caused a young woman's death and has been under the curse of the vampire ever since. Acting on Fallon's direction, the entranced Roy carries the injured vampire up a mountain, along with a small box of earth from Fallon's original grave. As Roy returns to camp to lead his carriers back to Bakunda, the light of the rising moon bathes Fallon and restores him to full strength.

Diagnosed as having fever and confined to bed, Roy–still in Fallon's power–is unable to tell what he knows about the undead fiend. Fallon, in the meantime, has his saucer eyes on Julie, much to the chagrin of Lisa

(Adele Mara), an entertainer who dances at Fallon's Place. A woman scorned, Lisa introduces a marked deck into a card game, enabling Jim Barrat to win a large sum of money from Fallon. Fallon realizes what Lisa and Barrat have done, and later stalks and kills the pair of them.

The natives realize that Fallon is the killer and they beat out the message on their native drums. Father Gilchrist, deducing what is happening, takes Roy to church, and through prayer, Fallon's dominating power is dispelled. But before Roy and Father Gilchrist can act, Fallon flees Bakunda – taking the hypnotized Julie along with him. All of the local villages are alerted to the vampire's presence, and news of Fallon's whereabouts is constantly relayed via native drums. Roy, Father Gilchrist, Vance and a recovered Simon Peter dog Fallon's trail, eventually tracking him down to a deserted village where, on an altar in a crude Temple of Death dominated by a fearsome four-armed idol, Fallon is about to finally put the bite on Julie. Father Gilchrist uses his cross to ward off the vampire while Roy strikes him down with a spear and Simon Peter sets fire to the temple. As our heroes flee, the flames spread and the wounded Fallon is pinned to the floor by the toppled idol.

It seems unkind, when the charge of familiarity is leveled against so many B movies, to come down on a film (like *The Vampire's Ghost*) which modifies the standard horror film recipe. But the idea behind *The Vampire's Ghost* was probably to churn out a cheapie chiller on Republic's existing jungle and Western sets, with the change in vampiric milieu merely the result of that economic decision. *The Vampire's Ghost*'s mix of vampire, voodoo and jungle film elements is offbeat enough to be almost appealing, but the film generates so few thrills and so little atmosphere that even at a scant 59 minutes, it nearly succeeds in wearing out its welcome.

An unconventional vampire to say the least, Webb Fallon shoots craps with criminals, fights like a featherweight champ and safaris in the burning African sun with only minor eye irritation resulting (he wears dark glasses while out of doors). It's tough enough to accept a two-fisted, sun-loving vampire with underworld connections, but Republic stacked the deck against themselves from the outset by casting John Abbott in the role. A reedy, bug-eyed British character actor, Abbott was best-suited to play bookworms, snooty academics and creepy red herrings. The role of Fallon required an actor with considerable physical presence, and the wispy Abbott – capable actor though he is – is distinctly unsuited. But Abbott carries himself with self-assurance throughout *The Vampire's Ghost* as he did through most all of his 80-plus films during a long and formidable career.

The son of a London stockbroker, Abbott readied himself for a career in commercial art before deciding to "tread the boards" (first at the semi-amateur St. Pancras People's Theatre and later at the prestigious Old Vic), appearing on stage opposite luminaries like Laurence Olivier, Vivien Leigh, Dame Sybil Thorndike and Alec Guinness. He made his first films in

England in the mid–'30s and later emigrated to America, where he bopped back and forth between films both major (*Mrs. Miniver, Mission to Moscow, Jane Eyre, Gigi*) and unspeakably minor (*Rubber Racketeers, Get Hep to Love, Cry of the Werewolf*). His bio in the playbill of the 1949 Broadway play *Monserrat* concludes, "In Hollywood he has appeared in some forty films, but cares to cite only" – no, not *The Vampire's Ghost* – "Wilkie Collins' *The Woman in White* [1948]." Other Abbott credits include *The Bandit of Sherwood Forest* (as Will Scarlet!), *Humoresque* (both 1946), *Madame Bovary* (1949), *The Merry Widow* (1952), *The Greatest Story Ever Told* (1965), *Gambit* (1966), *The Black Bird* (1975) and *Slapstick (Of Another Kind)* (1984).

There's a mild effort to portray Fallon in a slightly sympathetic light. The ornate box in which he dutifully totes around earth from his original grave was given to him in 1588 by Elizabeth Regina for services rendered to the Crown, indicating some sort of noble past, and Fallon occasionally makes an oblique and world-weary reference to his unfortunate lot. But not enough is made of this side of the Fallon character, and these off-handed references are easily dismissed. (Female fans of vampire films make quite a learned fuss over the angst and tragic qualities of vampires like this – but only when the bloodsucker in question is played by beefcake like Frank Langella or Ben Cross. Vampires like goony John Abbott aren't "tragic" enough to get their undies in a knot over.)

Almost everyone else in the film looks as though they'd be more at home in a Western or serial. Heroine Peggy Stewart was, in fact, a regular in Republic Westerns, and is now a fixture at Western nostalgia conventions. She's just The Girl in *The Vampire's Ghost*, a too-conventional role in a too-unconventional picture. Adele Mara, whose suggestive dance earned the film a Legion of Decency "B," spent nearly half of her career at Republic, in B's like *The Vampire's Ghost* and *The Catman of Paris* and an occasional A like the John Wayne actioners *Wake of the Red Witch* (1948) and *Sands of Iwo Jima* (1949). She's married to television producer Roy Huggins (*The Fugitive, Run for Your Life*). A stage and radio actor (and a cousin of Clara Bow), Charles Gordon (Roy) acts pretty much the same in or out of trance. Supporting players like Grant Withers and Emmett Vogan are just around to give the stars someone to bounce lines off of.

The main flaw in *The Vampire's Ghost* is that director Lesley Selander never succeeds in creating any sort of menacing atmosphere. Too much of the film is overlit, and even segments set after dark, like the scene of Abbott stalking Roy Barcroft through the empty streets of midnight, have the look of daytime. The interior jungle sets are phony-looking, almost claustrophobic; although the film is set near the west coast of Africa, with plenty of talk of waterfronts and boats, we never see as much as a drop of water, and the village looks almost Mexican. The tattoo of native drums, heard nearly from one end of the film to the other, becomes irritating. The mood which *The Vampire's Ghost* best evokes is one of heat and oppression.

British character actor John Abbott was distinctly unsuited to play the title role in Republic's jungle/voodoo/action mishmash *The Vampire's Ghost.*

But there are also more than the usual number of unintentionally humorous moments. The idea of 98-lb. weakling John Abbott going toe-to-toe with waterfront mugs and burly tough guy Roy Barcroft is mildly comical, as are the daylight scenes in which he wears his mod sunglasses. Grant Withers' missionary character looks thoroughly overheated in his heavy black clerical frock as he slogs around beneath the Equatorial sun. Martin Wilkins, who plays Simon Peter, is easily the worst actor in the film, and both his dialogue and the actor's delivery are ludicrous. Possibly the unintended comic highlight is a dinner scene where Abbott shrinks from Withers (there's a large cross embroidered on Withers' frock), only to have Withers follow, *re*-retreats, as Withers follows *again* – Abbott playing the scene with the pained expression of a man who's detected an unpleasant odor.

A slightly similar, much-better film than *The Vampire's Ghost,* Universal-International's *Curse of the Undead* (1959) starred Australian-born actor Michael Pate as Drake Robey, a vampire who earns a living as a hired gun in the Old West. Like Webb Fallon, Robey became a vampire as a result of a curse, frequents a saloon, tangles with secondary (human) baddies, moves about in broad daylight, lusts after the leading lady (Kathleen Crowley) and contends with a preacher (Eric Fleming) dedicated to his destruction. One of Universal's cheapest-looking '50s chillers, *Curse of the Undead* nevertheless earns points for its novel plotting and a strong performance by Pate; for all its faults, it's still probably the best-ever horror/Western, a hybrid genre doomed right from the start.

Watching Republic films like *The Vampire's Ghost* and *Valley of the Zombies*, you have to wonder whether the studio's writers even bothered to acquaint themselves with the legends and traditions of the monsters involved. In *The Vampire's Ghost*, writers Butler and Brackett get almost every aspect of the vampire mythos wrong, voodoo plays a role in the film and it's set, jarringly, in Africa; what *Ghost* is doing in the title is anybody's guess. Then in *Valley of the Zombies*, whose title promises a voodoo film, fans are thrown a curve once again when voodoo, valleys and zombies are nowhere in sight and the "monster" turns out to be another semi-vampire! (*The Vampire's Ghost* uses several minor plot elements from Dr. John Polidori's 1819 story *The Vampyre*. Polidori receives no screen credit; the *The Vampire's Ghost* pressbook makes a brief reference to an early vampire tale on which the film was based, but here again story and author go unnamed.)

Leigh Brackett, who also furnished the original story for *The Vampire's Ghost*, was a screenwriter and novelist whose movie-writing career later took a step-up: she wrote or co-wrote the classic Howard Hawks films *The Big Sleep* (1946), *Rio Bravo* (1959) and *El Dorado* (1967), lesser Hawks films like *Hatari!* (1962) and *Rio Lobo* (1970), director Robert Altman's *Big Sleep* remake *The Long Goodbye* (1973) and the *Star Wars* sequel *The Empire Strikes Back* (1979). Blasé Brackett told Steve Swires (*Films in Review*) how she happened to receive *The Vampire's Ghost* assignment: "[Republic] decided to cash in on the Universal monster school, and I had been doing science fiction, and to them it all looked the same—bug-eyed monsters. It made no difference." Also known for her mystery novels, she died in 1978.

While Brackett and John Butler touch upon some offbeat notions in *The Vampire's Ghost*, the picture comes across as bleak and silly despite one or two semi-memorable moments (the mirror scene, for instance) and John Abbott's sincere but ineffective performance. Giving the film all the inattention it deserved, *Variety*'s three-paragraph writeup (by Sten) began, "Republic endeavored to wrap this one up as economically as possible, and encase within the 59 minutes enough thrills to give the picture some semblance of respectability. Whether [they] succeeded is another matter entirely. . . . [The actors] go through their paces in stilted fashion. Script, settings and camerawork just so-so." *The Hollywood Reporter* found *The Vampire's Ghost* much inferior to its cofeature, *The Phantom Speaks*: "[It's] a routine, formula chiller—one that will get by in its division solely on the strength of its title . . . [John Abbott's] own competence as an actor almost succeeds in making plausible the poorly-defined vampire role. . . . There is little quality to the routine production, and Lesley Selander's direction reflects the confusion of the shabbily constructed screenplay."

More recently, *The Psychotronic Encyclopedia* dubbed the film "slow horror," and Don Willis (in *Horror and Science Fiction Films*) called it "Republic's most honorable attempt at a horror film, yet still very much a failure." Phil Hardy (*The Encyclopedia of Horror Movies*) described it as "a real shoestring shocker, which is quite unable to make anything out of a potentially intriguing story. . . . John Abbott [stands] out in a more than indifferent cast."

Strangler of the Swamp
(PRC, 1945)

Released January 1, 1946. 60 minutes. Associate Producer: Raoul Pagel. Screenplay and Direction: Frank Wisbar. Original Story: Frank Wisbar and Leo McCarthy. Additional Dialogue and Dialogue Direction: Harold Erickson. Musical Director: Alexander Steinert. Director of Photography: James S. Brown, Jr., A.S.C. Assistant Director: Harold Knox. Art Director: Edward C. Jewell. Set Decorator: Glenn P. Thompson. Director of Makeup: Bud Westmore. Sound Engineer: Frank Webster. Film Editor: Hugh Winn.

Cast: Rosemary LaPlanche (Maria), Robert Barrat (Christian Sanders, Sr.), Blake Edwards (Chris Sanders, Jr.), Charles Middleton (Douglass), Effie Parnell (Martina Sanders), Nolan Leary (Pete Jeffers), Frank Conlan (Joseph Hart), Therese Lyon (Bertha), Virginia Farmer (Anna Jeffers).

> "Old legends—strange tales—never die in the lonely swamp land. Villages and hamlets lie remote and almost forgotten. Small ferryboats glide between the shores, and the ferryman is a very important person. Day and night he is at the command of his passengers. On his little barge ride the good and the evil; the friendly and the hostile; the superstitious and the enlightened; the living and—sometimes—the dead."

This evocative opener prefaces writer/director Frank Wisbar's *Strangler of the Swamp*, Poverty Row's "other" alleged diamond in the rough (the first supposedly being *Bluebeard*). A remake of Wisbar's 1935 German film *Fährmann Maria* (literal translation, Ferryboat Woman Maria), and based on the legend of "Death and the Maiden," it's a cheaply made, quasiartsy little B, done in the heavy-handed style that only a foreign director (like Wisbar) would take pains to achieve. Today this PRC film is sometimes called a B picture that manages to step out of its class—a reputation that the film itself has never quite affirmed. Mostly it's just silly and dull. Its "classic" attributes, and the directorial qualities that make Frank Wisbar a name to conjure with in some film books, remain evasive at best.

Strangler of the Swamp's inflated reputation may have begun with film historian William K. Everson's inclusion of the film in his landmark 1974 book *Classics of the Horror Film*. There, amidst writeups of *Frankenstein, The Old Dark House, King Kong, Cat People* and the like (plus, of course, a number of more esoteric gems), Everson devoted a full chapter to *Strangler*, praising director Wisbar and describing "stylish" touches within this film; Everson's writing was customarily informed and level-headed, and in his summation he freely conceded that overall *Strangler* was "*far from a classic.*" But in the years since, perhaps as a result of Everson's temperate recommendation, *Strangler* has acquired the reputation of "sleeper," of "cult classic."

Following Everson's lead, many subsequent writers have extolled the virtues of director Wisbar, but you have to wonder whether they're writing from the heart or merely parroting Everson's initial writeup (and, latterly, each other's); you have to wonder, too, whether these self-styled Wisbar "fans" have even seen more than just one of his pictures (*Strangler*). A list of Wisbar's American credits makes for desultory reading: His other directing credits include *Lighthouse* (PRC, 1947), a romantic triangle; *The Prairie* (Screen Guild, 1948), a Lenore Aubert Western based on a James Fenimore Cooper novel; and, of course, the atrocious *Devil Bat's Daughter*, one of the worst horror films of the '40s. Writing-wise, he contributed to *Women in Bondage* (a.k.a. *Hitler's Women*, Monogram, 1943), a propaganda piece directed by Steve Sekely; *Madonna of the Desert* (Republic, 1948), a melodrama; and *Rimfire* (Lippert, 1949), another oater.

So is it his *overseas* career that makes Wisbar everything he's cracked up to be? Maybe, but none of these foreign jobs seem to be written or talked about, either; perhaps the only one that ever made it to these shores was *Commando* (1962), an obscure Italian-Spanish-Belgian-German action film that Wisbar directed and co-wrote (AIP, the Monogram of the '60s, released it in the United States two years later). All-inclusive film reference books (*The Filmgoers Companion, The Film Encyclopedia*, etc.) list countless directors, even abject hacks like Jean Yarbrough, Lesley Selander, *et al.* But Frank Wisbar? Nowhere to be found; he hasn't yet elbowed his way even into the footnotes! So who *is* Frank Wisbar, and why are some people saying such nice things about him?

Strangler of the Swamp has few traits in common with the other PRC horrors, except for the fact that it's up and running just as soon as the credits fade (a proud PRC tradition). The camera moves in on a noose hanging from a tree branch at the edge of a body of swamp water; next we see a small boat operated by a ferryman (Joseph Hart, played by Frank Conlan) who maneuvers the raft from one side of the swamp to the other, using a pull-rope that extends from bank to bank. This time, the ferry has three passengers: Christian Sanders (Robert Barrat), the swamp community's leading citizen; Jeffers (Nolan Leary), a grizzled ne'er-do-well local; and the body of a young swimmer. His body had been discovered in the swamp near the ferry, only the legs extending up out of the water; vines and roots are still tangled about his neck.

The locals are certain that the lad was killed by Douglass, the Strangler of the Swamp. Douglass, a card sharp and a drunken no-good, was accused of the murder of Berkley, a farmer, and Hart's testimony got him hanged; Hart then assumed Douglass' duties as ferryman. Just before he was strung up, Douglass cursed his hangmen, vowing to return from the grave and strike down them *and* their descendants. (From the pressbook: "Strangely, the curse works.") Since then, one local has been thrown from his horse and choked to death by the reins; a second was strangled by a pulley rope after falling from his hayloft; yet another was throttled by a fishnet; and now tonight's victim has been choked by weeds. Sanders (one of the marked men) scoffs at the townsfolk who believe that the curse is at work, although (tellingly) he's sent his own son Chris to live in the city, away from the swamp and the curse.

A trio of townswomen (Effie Parnell, Therese Lyon, Virginia Farmer) are determined to take down the noose with which Douglass was hanged; they have Hart ferry them across the swamp to the hanging tree. Hart objects to the idea of removing the noose; "Since that's been there, there hasn't been any more trouble!" he sputters, betraying his poor memory for recent events. As he chides them for their superstitious behavior, the noose falls from the tree and lands around his neck, scaring him into conniptions. The women try to convince him to give himself willingly into the hands of the strangler; only a sacrifice like that will break the curse. Hart balks. ("I'm only 70. That's not old for a man. I've plans for the future!")

Later that night, as Hart broods in his swamp's-edge hut, he hears the clang of the plowshare ferry signal, sounded on the far shore. He pulls the ferry across but the opposite shore seems deserted. Suddenly the Strangler (Charles Middleton) materializes; "whenever the heart and soul of a cursed one are filled with anguish to the brim," he appears. Hart, frantically pulling the ferry back across, tries to convince himself that the Strangler is a figment of his imagination, but according to the phantom, "Tonight, it is *your* soul that calls me!" In a panic, Hart throws the rotted noose up in the air, but one end loops around a high tree limb and the noose catches Hart around the neck. He's pulled from the ferryboat and chokes to death.

Days later, Sanders and Jeffers are at the ferry hut inventorying the late Hart's few belongings when they notice a girl (Rosemary LaPlanche) on the opposite bank, climbing aboard the ferry and pulling it across (how did the ferry get on the *far* side?). She's Maria, Hart's granddaughter;

Sanders tells her that her granddad committed suicide (the popular belief), and extends an invitation for her to stay at his home. Maria decides to take on the job of ferryman, even though it means living in the lonely hut.

Going through Hart's effects, Sanders finds a written confession; it was Hart who killed the farmer and gave wrong testimony so that Douglass would hang and *he'd* get the ferry job. Meanwhile, Mrs. Sanders (Effie Parnell) takes the strangler's noose to a battered mission chapel deep in the swamp and hangs it from the bell. In the ruins of that sacred place, she feels that the Strangler will be unable to retrieve it. (So what? He doesn't need it.)

Sanders' son Chris (Blake Edwards), returned home for a visit, is smitten with Maria, and after a (short) time he proposes and she accepts. Sanders disapproves of the announced marriage, objecting on the grounds that her grandfather was a murderer.* Chris angrily barks that there's a murderer in *his* family, too (Sanders himself, for helping hang the innocent Douglass). Father and son have a big row and Chris stalks out.

Hurrying through the swamp toward Maria's hut, Chris is caught in a noose-like deer trap; only Maria's fast action saves him from hanging. Chris is near death so Maria ferries herself across to fetch the local doctor, but before she can disembark, the Strangler appears and pulls the boat back again. Now she races to the Sanders house, telling Sanders what has happened; Sanders rushes out to find and help his son. Maria tries to alert the other townspeople, but the Strangler supernaturally causes their doors and windows to shut tight and their ears to be deafened to Maria's cries.

Maria and Sanders (carrying the dying Chris) take refuge in the chapel, whose sacred threshold the Strangler cannot cross, but they realize that Chris will die without a doctor. Maria decides to make the ultimate sacrifice: to offer herself willingly to the Strangler, ending the curse so that Sanders might save his son's life. As the girl stands before the Strangler, the phantom bows his head and backs away, almost sheepishly. "Give up the fight! Leave vengeance to the Almighty! Make peace with Him!" Maria pleads. A huge cloud of swamp mist envelopes the Strangler as he kneels praying. Chris begins breathing again. The curse is ended.

Perhaps *Strangler of the Swamp* would have been a classic if it had been made by a major studio, with a truly imaginative director, and with a better script, and better actors, and better *this*, and better *that*. (And if I only had some ham, and if I only had some cheese, I could make myself a ham and cheese sandwich, if I only had some bread.) But *Strangler* is so cheaply made, and has such a heavy and peculiar "Alice in Bogeyland" netherworld flavor, that the film becomes too unreal and off-putting.

PRC publicity made much over the fact that the filmmakers converted an acre of California soil into a patch of swamp, but this press blurb is as

---

*Coincidentally (?), in Wisbar's *Devil Bat's Daughter*, *audiences are* again *told to believe that criminal traits are hereditary. Maybe Wisbar believed it himself.*

Charles Middleton (in Bud Westmore makeup) and Miss America of 1941, Rosemary LaPlanche in *Strangler of the Swamp,* a mood-crusted cheapie with a minor "cult" reputation.

phony as the interior sets on which *Strangler'*s marsh scenes were actually filmed. *Strangler of the Swamp* is so small-time and contrived that our credulity is strained just pretending that there's as much as a drop of water in PRC's soundstage swamp; forget about believing in ghosts and curses.

There *are* a number of minor touches worth mentioning in *Strangler of the Swamp;* this type of pseudostylish exploitation entry, one seasoned with a bit of Germanic flavoring, is obviously a worthier *object of study* than the average Poverty Row horror film, even if it can't muster up a fraction of the entertainment value of a sleazy fan favorite like, say, *The Corpse Vanishes.* James S. Brown's photography is a plus factor throughout, adding to the mood and compensating for some of the other deficiencies of production. While the swampland sets obstinately remain phony-looking, Brown's lens captures a few arresting images which might have sent a tingle or two up the spines of '40s audiences.

The staging and photography of some of the Strangler's manifestations are mildly impressive, even though they're achieved with only the most rudimentary special effects. After the murder of Hart, the spirit captains the ferry himself, disappearing from sight in a fog bank; at the end, as the Strangler prays on bended knee outside the ruined chapel, a great billowing cloud of mist closes around him (signaling his ascension). They're moments that have long since lost their ability to chill the blood or inspire wonder, but they're also the type of aesthetically pleasing touches that you just don't get in movies like *The Monster Maker* or *King of the Zombies*. (Or even in the Universal horror films of that period.)

But the Strangler is only a (very) supporting character; he turns up at the beginning and then comes in and out during the film's final third. The rest of the film's 60 minute running time is gobbled up by the comings and goings of the mangy swamp hicks, who bicker amongst themselves, point accusatory fingers, and argue at length whether there *are* such things as ghosts (the kind of talk we shouldn't have to put up with in a movie that's already *shown* us the spook). The swamp sets, which crawl with ground mist even in daylit scenes, aren't very convincing, and only contribute to an antsy sense of claustrophobia. (Note to budding film historians: When an American director makes a movie on cheap sets like these, they're just cheap sets. When a *foreign* director does it, it's *stylization*. It's an important distinction that you must remember to make in order to be "correct.")

Some writers complain that the ghostly Strangler is seen too indistinctly, while others feel that he ought not to have been seen at all. The one thing PRC *definitely* did wrong was to vary the appearance of the Strangler: sometimes he's matted amidst a great dark splotch, sometimes he's transparent, and sometimes he's standing there just like any other character. The one thing *every*one agrees upon is that he shouldn't have talked; his appearances are almost eerie until he opens his mouth and begins chatting, which practically ruins the whole effect. The fact that his lips don't move is a nice touch, as are his whiteface makeup and blacked-out eyes, but the effect just isn't what it should and could have been.

Charles Middleton was probably a good choice to play the ghost, what with his gaunt but commanding appearance and sepulchral voice (not to mention his long history of appearing in villainous or stone-hearted roles). Middleton turns up the "spooky" timbre of his voice perhaps a bit too much, as though he's trying to match the time-honored cliché of what a ghost sounds like, but overall he does a good job, "voice of doom" and all.

Rosemary LaPlanche, 1941's Miss America, has the same problem here that she does in her later *Devil Bat's Daughter*: being trapped in a nearly impossible role. She isn't much good in *Strangler*, which has given her the reputation of being a bad actress, but she plays such an odd character that you have to wonder if *any* actress could have acquitted herself with honors. Dreamy-eyed and preoccupied, quietly obsessed with her meaningless ferry

duties and enraptured with her empty life of poverty and loneliness, Maria
is a character right out of the pages of a children's storybook, an earthbound
angel complete with halo (her white hairband); LaPlanche contends with the
fanciful turns of the plot the best she can. The fact that she's one hell of a
looker doesn't hurt either; even at the end, after sprinting hither and yon
through swamp country, she still looks as though she'd give the other girls
in that Atlantic City pageant a run for their money. After giving up on
features in the late '40s, LaPlanche went on to do much TV, including Geri-
tol commercials on *The Lawrence Welk Show*.

Blake Edwards (yes, *the* Blake Edwards) is faced with the same dilemma,
coping with an absurd role that (among other things) calls for him to pro-
pose marriage to LaPlanche even before he's shown her any sign of affec-
tion. He doesn't give a *bad* performance, but he's a typical mid-'40s leading
man, one who probably got his break only because there was a war on and
producers would hire anybody who didn't have two heads. (It was just a few
years after the war ended that he switched careers.) Robert Barrat, playing
Edwards' father, provided good, solid character support in many major
films; as the stolid, skeptical leader of the unnamed community (one of the
movie's few sensible characters), he comes off perhaps better than any other
actor in the piece. Certainly better than Nolan Leary, whose over-the-top
performance as the blubbering good-for-nothing Jeffers is probably the low
point of the film, but again through no fault of the actor's. (Leary, too, turned
up in *Devil Bat's Daughter*; later he played the deaf-and-dumb Pa Chaney
in the 1957 biopic *Man of a Thousand Faces*.)

Dom Salemi's mini article on *Strangler* in the fanzine *Ecco* sounded a
bit like Everson's 1974 writeup, rerun courtesy of thesaurus (with a generous helping of Don Miller's *B Movies* tossed in, too), but Salemi made a few
highly interesting points in his examination of the characters in *Strangler
of the Swamp*:

> The town magistrate [Robert Barrat], a symbol of justice, is an impo-
> tent liar. The town church cannot provide spiritual guidance; its minis-
> ters are dead and its grounds are in ruins. What's more, the sons of the
> patriarchy offer little promise for the future. Although they exercise
> control of the swamp, the film's male characters achieve nothing be-
> cause they are fools, knaves and cowards. It is the women who prove
> to be the source of strength and wisdom needed to overcome the
> strangler's threat. When the magistrate's son seeks counsel, he ap-
> proaches his mother instead of his father. While the men bewail the fate
> under which the town is laboring, the women attempt to end the curse
> by taking down the noose. And finally it is a woman, Maria, who is will-
> ing to give up her life for love and community.

Wisbar's approach in both his script and his direction is recognizably
"foreign"; no American would have thought to make a film owing to Old

World mythology and German fantasy/romanticism the way this one does. In Everson's book, he writes learnedly and very readably about Wisbar's debt to the old school of German fantasies, comparing *Strangler* to the original *Fährmann Maria* and also drawing parallels between it and even *earlier* German cinema (e.g., Fritz Lang's *Destiny*, 1921), all worthy and productive pursuits for the Serious Film Historian.

But the more casual film fan finds no such rewards in *Strangler of the Swamp*; in *their* book, it may rate an E for Effort and an A for Atmosphere, but after a promising start it's mostly good just for Zzzzz's. Unevenly paced and awkwardly plotted, *Strangler* takes more than a bit of patience to sit through. It might be a well-made movie in light of the economics involved, but this too is of no consequence to the average viewer. *Strangler of the Swamp* may be unique but it probably wasn't what audiences expected or wanted to find in a movie with such a lurid title, either in 1946 or in the present Video Age. Between its ersatz swamp scenery, "make-believe" flavor and frequent lapses into total tedium, it has few of the qualities that would bring viewers back for a second look..

The stories of *Fährmann Maria* and *Strangler of the Swamp* have the same basics but are otherwise quite different. In the German film, the "phantom" is Death personified (Peter Voss), claiming his victims not out of vengeance but only because their time has come. An elderly ferryman is the first casualty, and his replacement is Maria (*Vampyr's* Sybille Schmitz), a girl who takes the job out of desperation. A handsome young man, on the losing side in a revolution in a neighboring country, is saved from mounted pursuers by Maria, and the two fall in love while he rests up in her ferry hut. When he's stricken with fever, Death turns up again but Maria decoys him, first into the nearby village where she dances with him at a festival, and then into the swamp, where he sinks in quicksand. An infinitely better-made film than *Strangler*, *Fährmann Maria* has flaws of its own. The basically realistic story of Maria and the soldier collides rather than converges with the outré angle of the Death character; the actual exteriors also make too natural a backdrop for such a bizarre tale. *Strangler of the Swamp*, on the other hand, is just so artificial and phony from beginning to end that it's tough to take *any* of it seriously.

Frank Wisbar was born in East Prussia (Poland today) and was a German officer before entering the picture business in 1927. He started out with jobs like production manager and assistant director (he worked on the German lesbian drama *Mäedchen in Uniform*, 1931) before directing films of his own. In a protest against the cultural politics of the then–Nazi rulers, he left Germany in 1938, became active as a political writer and lecturer upon his arrival in the U.S. in '39, and came to Hollywood in '43. There he found a niche for himself on Poverty Row, working at studios on the level of PRC and Republic on the handful of ignominious films listed earlier.

When television came in, Wisbar jumped in with both feet, doing lots

STRANGLER OF THE SWAMP

of directing and even heading his own company which at one point had 125 people on the payroll. He went back to West Germany in 1957 and made "message pictures" that centered around World War II or on topical subjects. The decline of that country's film industry put the kibosh on a number of projects Wisbar had in mind during the last years of his life, and after a long illness he died in Mainz on March 17, 1967, at age 64. The Wisbar films which will justify the praise that has occasionally been heaped on him, generally in the oddest places, continue to lurk just around the *next* corner. And probably always will.

Wisbar was signed to direct *Strangler of the Swamp* on May 30, 1945; it started shooting August 23 and was released on New Year's Day, 1946. Long before *Strangler* became the modest cult item it is today, before people told us why we *had* to respect it, reviewer Jim Henaghan capably applied the critical hatchet to it for *The Hollywood Reporter*:

> If the thing had been made with a modicum of subtlety, somebody might have emerged as a genius. . . . However, situations of this kind, precedent has dictated, must only be hinted to educated audiences. When you dress the ghost up in a suit of starched levis and give him that emaciated make-up, you've got to believe in Santa Claus to believe in the spirit. This ghost looks pretty sick, as though he could do with some "bicarb," and yet get the feeling somebody with a heavy hand is joshing you. . . . Rosemary LaPlanche, the star, is attractive to a degree, but not attractive enough to make up for her lack of acting ability here. That, however, might be due in a measure to her direction, which is nothing to get excited about unless you paid for it – then you have a complaint.

William Everson wrote in *Classics of the Horror Film*, "Like so many horror films, this one never quite sustains the tension of its opening sections – but it is too brief for that tension ever to evaporate entirely, and the closing reels re-establish much of it. Make no mistake about it, *Strangler of the Swamp* is a Grade 'B' movie, and not an unsung masterpiece." Dom Salemi echoed pretty closely: "Artful as it is, *Strangler of the Swamp* falls considerably short of being a masterpiece." He went on to call it PRC's best film – as though he'd seen them all – and said that it was "one of the most somber and atmospheric horror films of its decade."

The Motion Picture Guide opined, "[T]hough Wisbar didn't come close to re-creating the excellence of the original, his inventive use of lighting, camera, and sets certainly covered over the usual production deficiencies that accompanied the low-budget films made by PRC." Jeffrey Richards of *Focus on Film* is another writer taken with *Strangler*'s heavy German flavor and portentous aura of doom. According to Richards, *Strangler* "symbolises the fusion of the German fantasy influence of mood and atmosphere with the American thriller tradition of pace and violence. . . . The whole film is an excellent demonstration of how to make on a low budget a consistently compelling and marvellously atmospheric film."

Filmfax's Don Leifert liked *Strangler*'s mixture of horror and "religious allegory," "a unique combo that works well under Frank Wisbar's direction." Like Leifert, the mysterious Phantom of the Movies raved about the film's murky ambience, although neither explained why the *Strangler of the Swamp* bog had a leg up on, say, *The Mad Monster* or *Night Monster* swamps; a better class of mosquito, perhaps. The Phantom wrote, "Slow pacing and PRC's no-budget production values hinder the pic's progress, but *Strangler* remains well worth seeing"; he didn't say why. Don Willis, always ready to burst a "classic's" bubble, wrote, "The film, supposedly a sleeper, is, in the wrong way. It's a little better (maybe) than Wisbar's *Devil Bat's Daughter*, but less interesting." (*Nothing* is less interesting than *Devil Bat's Daughter!*) Phil Hardy said it was "probably PRC's finest hour," and the one Hollywood film "that gave some measure of Wisbar's talent." Film buff extraordinaire John Cocchi saw *Fährmann Maria* and *Strangler of the Swamp* on a modern-day double-bill and commented, "When run back to back . . . the lowly PRC proved to be more exciting than the stylish but slow original." Ivan Butler, Denis Gifford, Carlos Clarens and most other comprehensive chroniclers of the horror film scene overlooked the film entirely.

It's a nice change of pace to find a horror film that has a different approach, and it's all well and good for schlocksters to attempt to penetrate a little beyond the narrow exploitation sphere. Like *Bluebeard*, *Strangler of the Swamp* is a film that seems sincere, that gives an impression of honest effort having gone into it. You try hard *not* to detect that the swamp ferry is on wheels, rolling across the misty floor of a soundstage; try not to judge the film by its halting, old-fashioned direction, or by the long stretches of useless dialogue that slow the plot. You try *not* to notice that everything everyone does in this boggy never-never land defies all laws of normal human behavior; you work valiantly to overlook the absurd story, poor acting and rock-bottom production. In fact, if you can ignore *everything* that goes on in *Strangler of the Swamp* for the full 60 minutes, it's probably one hell of a picture. But watch it with even one eye open and the cat jumps right out of the bag.

The Face of Marble
(Monogram, 1946)

Released January 19. 70 minutes. Produced by Jeffrey Bernard. Directed by William Beaudine. Screenplay: Michel Jacoby. Original Story: William Thiele and Edmund Hartmann. Director of Photography: Harry Neumann, A.S.C. Production Manager: Glenn Cook. Film Editor: William Austin. Assistant Director: Theodore Joos. Musical Director: Edward Kay. Technical Director: David Milton. Sound Recording: Tom Lambert. Set Decorations: Vin Taylor. Special Effects: Robert Clark.

    Cast: John Carradine (Prof. Charles Randolph), Claudia Drake (Elaine Randolph), Robert Shayne (Dr. David Cochran), Maris Wrixon (Linda Sinclair), Willie Best (Shadrach), Thomas E. Jackson (Police Insp. Norton), Rosa Rey (Maria), Neal Barns (Jeff), Donald Kerr, Allan Ray (Photographers).

> "I'll never quit the stage or the films. I'd go out of my skull!"—John Carradine
>
> "John Carradine definitely will die with his boots on—that's the way he would have it."—Anthony Eisley
>
> "John Carradine . . . seemed like he was just not in good health, and he should have stayed home and taken care of himself, and relaxed, and been a human being for a while. It was really uncomfortable for him. I don't think he got much out of the film."—Karen Witter, star of Carradine's last film, *Buried Alive* (1990)

    Monogram's horror cycle of the '40s had seemed to end with the wrap-up of Sam Katzman's Bela Lugosi series at the close of 1943, but the studio still had one ace up its sleeve. Well, actually, more like a joker. *The Face of Marble* has a bit more going for it production-wise than most of the other Monograms, and even John Carradine, the movie's star, puts forth a (slightly) more genuine effort than he did in the last two Lugosi films, *Return of the Ape Man* and *Voodoo Man*. The trouble, as always, was with the script, this time a truly bizarre and unfathomable jumble of science and the supernatural. In fact, for sheer, unadulterated poppycock, *Face of Marble* may rank second—a *close* second—to Lugosi's unbeatably balmy *Invisible Ghost*.

    The Face of Marble gets off to an interesting start—for horror film trivia nuts, at any rate. After the credits, it begins in a darkened room, on a shot of a Great Dane snoozing by a blazing fireplace. Now the camera pans to show us a woman sleeping on a nearby couch. A second person enters the scene, only the legs seen, walking toward the sleeping woman. It turns out to be a servant who, after accidentally waking the woman, worries her by telling her that her husband has gone out—and it's a bad night to *be* out. The scene is an unmistakable carbon copy of the opener of 20th Century–Fox's *The Undying Monster* (1942); the two films had the same writer, Michel Jacoby. (In *Undying Monster*, it was the woman's *brother* who had picked the wrong night for walking.)

    The woman is Elaine Randolph (Claudia Drake), and her husband, eminent brain surgeon Prof. Charles Randolph, strolled off into the stormy

The last gasp of the Monogram horror film cycle, *The Face of Marble* was an indecipherable mess about life-restoring experiments.

night hours before, according to the servant, the Haitian Maria (Rosa Rey). Suddenly a second servant, Shadrach (Willie Best), bursts into the room, babbling that he's seen a monster carrying a body ("It must be the devil collectin' the dead!").

It's no monster, just Prof. Randolph (John Carradine), lugging back to his laboratory the dead body of a drowned fisherman that had washed ashore while he strolled along the nearby beach. Randolph and his assistant Dr. David Cochran (Robert Shayne) have been working to perfect an electro-chemical process which will return life to the recently dead, and the waterlogged sailor is a perfect guinea pig. Stretched out on an operating table, the cadaver is subjected to the injection and to a giant dose of electricity. His face goes white and his eyelids begin to flutter. "He's alive, sir, but look at that *face* – it's a face of marble!" David sputters.

The fisherman rises from the table but suddenly lightning strikes nearby, shorting out Prof. Randolph's equipment; the fisherman (unaccountably) falls to the floor, dead again. Randolph totes the body back to the beach and dumps it where he found it. (Nothing ventured, nothing gained.) Meanwhile Elaine, who has a pretty good idea what's going on and doesn't like it, begs David not to put his career in danger by dabbling in such illegal experimentation. She's sweet on him but, except for Maria, no one else (including the rather dense David) knows it.

Maria puts a *fetich* (voodoo doll) under David's pillow so that *he'll* fall in love with Elaine; instead of having the desired effect, it only seems to annoy David, who drops it in a container of acid. Elsewhere in the house, Maria, somehow sensing what he has done, swoons and does a nice header down a flight of stairs. This breaks up a conversation between Randolph and Police Insp. Norton (Thomas E. Jackson), a dogged detective who suspects that Randolph monkeyed with the dead fisherman's body. Revived, Maria angrily tells David that the voodoo gods will not forgive him for destroying the fetich, and that violent death will take place in the house.

Randolph kills his wife's faithful Great Dane, Brutus, confident that he can bring it back to life via his process. But Brutus returns to life a snarling, vicious killer; Randolph puts four bullets into the beast, with no effect. Suddenly turning semitransparent *and* intangible, Brutus casually hops out through the closed laboratory window and disappears into the night.

The next day is David's birthday; at the breakfast table, Elaine gives him a long, lingering kiss right in front of Randolph (who for some unexplained reason doesn't share a bedroom with his wife). To David's surprise, his hometown sweetheart Linda Sinclair (Maris Wrixon) comes walking in; as a birthday present, Randolph had signed David's name to a telegram inviting her to come and visit. Linda's arrival turns Elaine green with jealousy. That night, the ghostly Brutus walks through a closed door into Linda's room, badly frightening the girl. Between visits to his old stomping grounds, busy Brutus has also been tearing out the throats of local livestock.

John Carradine (right) brings a drowned fisherman back from the dead, and gets a working-over for his trouble. (From *The Face of Marble.*)

The next day, Linda convinces David to pack up and leave for good, something he's been wanting to do anyway; Randolph takes the news well. That night, Elaine, anxious to see Brutus again, switches bedrooms with Linda – picking exactly the *wrong* night to make the exchange. Maria, who wants David unattached and available for her mistress's sake, has decided to kill Linda, and places in the shadowy guest room an urn filled with exotic roots used in voodoo ceremonies. Lethal fumes from the smoldering roots of course kill Elaine instead. Maria faints and takes another nice fall when she realizes her boo-boo.

While Randolph weeps over his wife's body, Cochran realizes that they can restore her to life. Randolph refuses, picking *now* of all times to get religion ("There's more to it than anyone knows – than any man is *given* to know..."), but Cochran persists and soon Elaine is in the lab getting the full treatment. Randolph mopes and whines while Cochran does all the work and revives Elaine, who returns to consciousness muttering David's name. David *still* doesn't get the message.

Randolph finds the urn, realizes that Maria was responsible for Elaine's death, and decides to kill the servant with a knife; Cochran stops him, taking the knife away. Later, Elaine goes into a trance and, joined by Brutus, wanders about the house, walking ectoplasmically through doors the same way the dog does. Maria puts the knife in Elaine's hand and Elaine, acting under Maria's influence, stabs Randolph in the back, killing him.

"Fingered" by Maria, David is arrested by Insp. Norton and taken in for questioning; while at the station house, he suddenly realizes what danger Linda is in with Maria still at large. Slugging Norton, he escapes. Meanwhile, Elaine has slipped into trance again; together with Brutus, they've trapped Linda in her bedroom and are closing in. David arrives on the scene, tackling and fighting with the dog while Elaine chokes the unconscious Linda. When Norton rushes in and turns on the light, both phantoms vanish.

In a hasty wrap-up, Shadrach, an eyewitness to Randolph's murder, tells Norton what he saw, clearing David; Maria kills herself by burning and sniffing her own deadly roots; and two sets of footprints, a woman's and a dog's, are shown in the sand leading into the ocean, indicating that Elaine and Brutus, for no apparent reason, have committed suicide. (A *dog*, committing suicide. . . ?)

Part of the problem with *Face of Marble* is that it doesn't know what it wants to be. Early scenes of Carradine and Shayne working in the lab are science fiction. The notion of dead bodies coming back to half-life qualify it as a zombie film. But the bodies, for no imaginable reason, can become semitransparent and intangible, as though the bodies had somehow *become* their own ghosts; this is fantasy. Brutus drinks blood—which is why *Face of Marble* turns up on vampire checklists. As if all this wasn't enough, we also get a four-way romantic entanglement, a murder and a frameup. None of this fits together. *Face of Marble* is one of the unwieldiest films, horror or otherwise, of the 1940s.

The film was first announced almost two years before it was made, perhaps indicating that someone recognized the original story as malarkey and put it on the back burner. In January 1944, Monogram told the Hollywood trades that it had bought the original story of *The Face of Marble* from writers William Thiele and Edmund L. Hartmann, and that producer Lindsley Parsons would soon be supervising its production. All was quiet again until September of '45, when Monogram proclaimed the purchase a second time and listed the producer as Jeffrey Bernard. The film finally rolled on Friday, October 5, 1945.

There really isn't much worth recommending in *Face of Marble*; the story is so maddeningly mixed-up that the few things the film *does* have going for it don't even begin to compensate. Some of the sets are large and well-appointed, far better than the sets seen in the Bela Lugosi films; and the chalky "marble" makeup is actually creepy, even though neither Claudia Drake nor the unlucky fisherman get to chance to do more than just briefly wear it. (Referring back to the brief resuscitation of the fisherman at a point later in the film, Carradine says, "He was insane—his actions proved it," when all the fellow did was quietly get up from the table. Perhaps an action scene was cut from the script. The film could have used one.)

John Carradine gives a not-bad performance as Prof. Randolph, but because *Face of Marble* is a horror film and because Carradine is . . . well,

Carradine, it's a disappointment to find him playing an ordinary doctor, and a rather mealy-mouthed one at that. The script seems almost determined to keep the actor in check; his character isn't even confident enough about the success of his experiments that Carradine can do a bit of enthusiastic overplaying in his lab scenes. Of course, Carradine is in low gear anyway, which was the way he acted in most of his Monogram horror films. Once Carradine became inescapably established as a horror star, he brought a bit more to his low-budget horror roles; there are few later horror films where he is as lacking in screen presence as he is in *Face of Marble*. But in 1945 he probably still thought that different, better things lay ahead.

Robert Shayne is decidedly miscast as Carradine's assistant. Throughout the film, there are several references to Shayne's ingenuous, bow-tied character as a "young" assistant, and Shayne is just too old for the part; Maris Wrixon, his film sweetheart, is probably young enough to be Shayne's real-life daughter. Even Carradine treats Shayne as though he were little more than a kid, calling him "my boy" in seemingly every other line (Shayne calls *him* "sir"), while actually Shayne is several years *older* than his "fatherly" costar. In interviews, Robert Shayne remembers *The Face of Marble* as the first freelance picture he did after leaving his "home studio" Warner Bros., but it wasn't; he was in PRC's *I Ring Doorbells* (1946) first. It always feels odd to me when I find out that I know things about an actor's career that he himself has forgotten; in fact, when the actors and pictures involved are on the level of Robert Shayne, *The Face of Marble* and *I Ring Doorbells*, it can be downright scary. Shayne recalls,

> We broke for lunch one day, and I came back early, onto the semi-darkened stage. John Carradine was on the dark stage spouting the dialogue of some character from Shakespeare, I forget which one, and I started to laugh, and poked fun at him. I said, "What the hell are you doing? Are you spouting Shakespeare?" He didn't like that, he didn't like my kidding him, and he got mad as hell *[laughs]*!

Neither of the film's leading ladies add much to the picture, both being handicapped by the senseless screenplay the same way Carradine and Shayne are; it's a nice touch that Maris Wrixon should be in Monogram's last "straight" '40s horror film, being that she was also in their first (*The Ape*). Willie Best does his scared black servant shtick in the familiar style that tickled the funnybones of '40s audiences but today gives the N.A.A.C.P. conniptions. Thomas E. Jackson plays his usual irascible detective; Jackson's long career as a supporting (or bit) player took him from classic '30s horror (*Doctor X, Mystery of the Wax Museum*) to bread-and-butter '40s horror (*Valley of the Zombies, The Face of Marble*) and classic '50s sci-fi schlock (*It Conquered the World, Attack of the 50 Foot Woman*). Rosa Rey, seventh- and last-billed, doesn't bring much oomph or menace to her pivotal sinister role although, again, that might be more the script's fault than the actress's.

Like most horror movie scientists, Carradine and Shayne never profited from past mistakes; in the movies, life-restoring experiments are usually just about the quickest and surest way for a well-meaning scientist to permanently kill off a roomful or two of people. Carradine's *Face of Marble* experiments are almost identical to the ones he and Lugosi were conducting in *Return of the Ape Man*, with only tragedy resulting in both instances. Robert Shayne gave it another go in *Indestructible Man* (1956), bringing executed killer Lon Chaney, Jr., back from the dead via a staggering electrical charge. In that one, Shayne was the brains and Joe Flynn the bow-tied, slightly mousy junior assistant. Chaney choked them both to death (simultaneously!) before going out on a new killing binge.

The Face of Marble got better reviews when it came out than it does today. *The Hollywood Reporter* opined, "Because, no doubt, audiences halfway want to believe such nightmares, and aided considerably by director William Beaudine's in-mood pace, Jeffrey Bernard's little property will find it okay going in the chiller market. No work of art or beauty, the film nevertheless succeeds pretty well in achieving what it sets out to do – thrill and scare you. . . . In a sympathetic role, Carradine proves the most competently restful character in the melee, underplaying and not once shaking his Shakespearean locks. For his pains, he is murdered. As the jungle version of Mrs. Danvers, Rosa Rey's delivery of lines is not quite up to her beautifully baleful glare." *Variety*'s Bron also found it a painless 70 minutes: "Typical horror film has a confusing story but a plausible, serious treatment to make it acceptable. Good camerawork, a well-chosen cast and a lot of pseudoscientific and medical gadgets and palaver give pic more solid substance than it rates." The Legion of Decency gave it a "B": "Encourages credence in voodooism and superstitious practices; suicide in plot solution."

Robert Shayne was more critical:

> After we had finished it, I went to see a preview of it over in South Los Angeles somewhere, with my wife and another couple. We were near the back of the house, and as this picture went along I hung my head, I was so embarrassed by it! Finally, when the thing was over, I got out into the lobby before anybody else did, and I was standing against a wall with my wife and this other couple. Two young ladies came out and stood against an opposite wall, and they did a double-take when they saw who I was. And one of them came over to me and said *[wagging a finger]*, "Mr. Shayne, you ought to be ashamed to be in a picture like that!"

Michael Weldon (*Psychotronic*), usually a pushover for Monogram movies, called *The Face of Marble* "bad as only a Monogram movie can be." Don

Willis, in seeming agreement, designated it "one of the weirdest horror movies ever." "Anemic chiller" and "cinema rot" were the descriptions used by Ron Borst (*Photon*) and Greg Mank (*The Hollywood Hissables*), respectively. A euphemistic Don Leifert wrote in *Filmfax*, "The melodramatic storyline was in keeping with Monogram's tendency towards colorful plots."

It really isn't surprising that *The Face of Marble* is poor, because by 1946, studios had either given up on horror films or made them on the most meager of budgets. But *The Face of Marble* stands out as a dreadful film even in this year of decline. And even on Poverty Row, a horror film where a big dog and a crabby housekeeper represent the "menace" was quite obviously sadly lacking.

The Flying Serpent
(PRC, 1946)

Released February 20. 59 minutes. Produced by Sigmund Neufeld. Directed by Sherman Scott [Sam Newfield]. Original Story and Screenplay: John Thomas Neville. Production Manager: Burt Sternbach. Director of Photography: Jack Greenhalgh, A.S.C. Musical Director: Leo Erdody. Sound Engineer: Frank McWhorter. Film Editor: Holbrook N. Todd. Art Director: Edward C. Jewell. Set Dresser: Syd Moore. Director of Makeup: Bud Westmore. Master of Properties: Eugene C. Stone.

Cast: George Zucco (Prof. Andrew Forbes), Ralph Lewis (Richard Thorpe), Hope Kramer (Mary Forbes), Eddie Acuff (Jerry "Jonesey" Jones), Wheaton Chambers (Prof. Lewis Havener), James Metcalfe (Dr. John Lambert), Henry Hall (Sheriff Bill Hayes), Milton Kibbee (Superintendent Hastings), Budd Buster (Coroner), Terry Frost (Vance Bennett).

> Near the little city of San Juan, New Mexico, stand the Aztec ruins. Archeologists tell us they are the remains of a once-great temple, abandoned by the Aztecs when they migrated south to the Valley of Mexico, where they founded a rich empire.
>
> To defeat the greed of Cortez and his Spanish adventurers who had inaugurated a campaign of loot and murder, the wiley Emperor Montezuma hid his fabulous treasure far to the North and implored his native gods to guard it.
>
> Among these gods was the feathered serpent QUETZALCOATL.

The basic plot of *The Devil Bat* got its *third* workout via *The Flying Serpent*, George Zucco's fourth and final PRC production. The film has the traditional strengths and weaknesses of the average PRC horror title. To its credit, it stars fan favorite Zucco playing one of his trademark mad-at-the-world characters (and doing the carried-away, eye-bulging shtick that went with it); it features yet another bizarre airborne monster (a prehistoric creature, half-bird, half-reptile, that lives on blood); and, best of all, it clocks in at just under an hour, which is about all the running time its slim story rated. Unfortunately, the physical mounting tends to be a bit on the shabby side and some of the dialogue is laughable; also, the thrice-told story, appealingly lurid the first time around in *The Devil Bat*, had lost a bit of its edge through repetition.

According to the movieland trade papers, producer Sigmund Neufeld bought the "original" story for *The Flying Serpent* from writer John Neville on January 10, 1945; this initial announcement claimed that the film's action would be set amidst the Aztec tribes at the time of Montezuma. You have to doubt whether that ever was *really* the plan; when production got underway in mid–August, Neville's screenplay was an unabashed rehash of his earlier script *The Devil Bat* (the film even features some reorchestrated *Devil Bat* music). Maybe even PRC knew that they had gone to the proverbial well once too often with this plot; the film went into release without a press or trade preview, which is Hollywood's way of trying to foist a film they *know* is bad onto the public. *The Flying Serpent isn't* bad, but it's certainly no classic, not even on a B level.

Prof. Andrew Forbes (George Zucco), authority on the ancient Aztecs, drives past the Azteca National Monument in San Juan County, into the rugged country beyond. Clambering up a rocky hillside, he opens a secret stone door and enters a great dark chamber he had discovered five years ago; numerous trunks filled with the treasures of Emperor Montezuma are hidden therein. Elsewhere in the cave is a caged-off altar where Quetzalcoatl, an eagle-sized winged reptile, lurks. Forbes feels that the treasure is his by right of discovery, and is happy to have Quetzalcoatl there protecting the loot for him. Years before, Forbes had given one of the winged serpent's feathers to his wife; the monster got out, tracked down the feather by its scent, tore out the wife's throat and drank her blood. Now armed with this knowledge, the professor knows that he can dispose of his enemies by planting a Quetzalcoatl feather upon them.

The latest unfortunate to incur Forbes' wrath is Dr. John Lambert (James Metcalfe), a noted ornithologist whose most recent article *Birds of the Southwest* mentions the legendary treasures of Azteca and is bound to draw unwanted treasure-hunters. Forbes' stepdaughter Mary (Hope Kramer) drops in on Lambert (without knocking), looking for advice; she's worried about her stepfather.

> Dr. Lambert, I wish there had never been any such *thing* as Aztec Indians. Father does nothing but think, dream and talk Aztecs!

Lambert feels that perhaps Forbes is on the trail of the treasure, but Mary scoffs that one off, telling Lambert that he doesn't know Forbes as well as she does. "Finding Montezuma's treasure wouldn't mean nearly as much to him as digging up the key to some old Azteca picture-writings!" she tells him confidently (betraying to the audience how damn little about the guy *she* knows!). Forbes storms in, also without knocking (doesn't Lambert have a door?), and reads the ornithologist the riot act for publicizing the treasures of Azteca. On the way out, he surreptitiously drops one of Quetzalcoatl's feathers.

Intrigued by the unusual plume, Lambert drives out to Azteca to ask a superintendent there about it. By the time he's making his return trip, Forbes has unleased Quetzalcoatl; the flying monster catches Lambert's eye, and he steps out of his car for a better look. The feathered serpent power-dives at Lambert, who plunges into a bush for cover. The monster bird tears out his throat and drains the blood from his body.

Richard Thorpe (Ralph Lewis), a mystery writer who broadcasts his fictional whodunits over New York radio network XOR, talks about the killing coast-to-coast on XOR; one possibility he mentions is that the crime was committed by a mad mortician (paging Ormand Murks!). He also talks about "supernatural" monsters of the sort that might be involved. Over Mary's objection, Forbes snaps off the radio. "Next thing you know, *you'll* be believing in werewolves and devil worshipers!" he chides her. (In-joke dialogue, perhaps? A werewolf and a devil worshiper were the monsters in Zucco's two previous PRC horrors, *The Mad Monster* and *Dead Men Walk*, respectively.)

Engaged by XOR to investigate the mystery in-person, Thorpe and his broadcast technician "Jonesey" (comedy relief "specialist" Eddie Acuff) go to San Juan to begin their probe. Thorpe is allowed to cross-examine people at Lambert's inquest, including Forbes. (After killing Lambert for mentioning Montezuma's treasure in a stupid little bird article that nobody was going to read anyway, Forbes enthusiastically talks all about the treasure on the radio!) Thorpe becomes convinced that the mystery feather is an important clue, and that the killer was winged.

Sensing that Thorpe may stumble onto the truth, Forbes accompanies him to the spot where Lambert was killed, drops another feather and departs. Bill Hays (Henry Hall), Sheriff of San Juan, arrives on the scene and *he* finds the feather; he sends Thorpe to get some back-up while he stands guard over the plume. Quetzalcoatl, set loose by Forbes, attacks and kills the Sheriff.

Forbes is determined to try, try again, plucking *another* feather (Quetzalcoatl ought to be snatched bald by now!) and getting it into Thorpe's hands again. Thorpe's ornithologist friend Lewis Havener (Wheaton Chambers) doesn't know what to make of it; "It resembles a feather from the meat-eating species of the Bird of Paradise, yet it's somewhat different," he

The Flying Serpent was one of the 1940s' most unique and colorful monsters, even if the film itself occasionally left something to be desired. Getting his jugular vein severed here is slow-on-the-draw lawman Henry Hall. The Legion of Decency cited the film for its "excessive gruesomeness."

tells Thorpe less-than-helpfully. On his daily broadcast from a San Juan radio studio, Thorpe talks about Quetzalcoatl and his theory that a human fiend has sufficient control over the monster to use it as an instrument of murder. Havener, examining the feather while waiting in an adjoining room to join Thorpe "on the air," is killed when Quetzalcoatl flies in through a window and attacks his throat.

Another one of Thorpe's associates, Bennett (Terry Frost), arrives in San Juan posing as a treasure-hunter; he brings along with him his *own* Quetzalcoatl feather, borrowed from the collection of a Honduran bird-lover. Thorpe, who now suspects Forbes, arranges for Bennett to show Forbes that he (Bennett) has "found" a feather; Forbes hurries off to unleash Quetzalcoatl. Thorpe tails Forbes to the secret cave and watches as he sets the flying monster free. Bennett, anticipating the attack, hides with "Jonesey" behind the barred entrance to a small cave, where Quetzalcoatl can't get at them.

Later, in a great bit of showmanship, Thorpe broadcasts from *inside* the

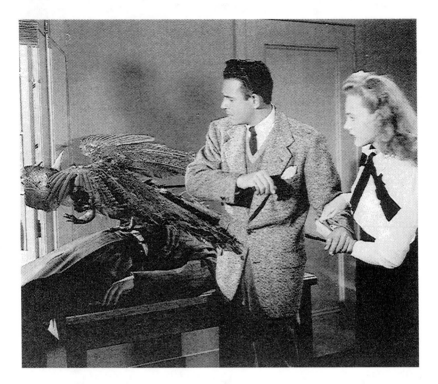

Ralph Lewis and Hope Kramer recoil as *The Flying Serpent* **prepares for liftoff. The launching pad is actor Wheaton Chambers.**

Aztec secret chamber, describing to the nation the fabulous treasure as well as the caged-up Quetzalcoatl. Meanwhile, Forbes has discovered that stepdaughter Mary knows far too much, and he lures her to the cave with the intention of killing her. Thorpe and Forbes fight, and Forbes is knocked back against the lever that releases Quetzalcoatl. Carrying one of the bird's feathers in his hand, Forbes makes a dash across a field but Quetzalcoatl swoops down and kills him. Thorpe shoots and kills the flying serpent as it attempts to get away.

Like *The Devil Bat*, *The Flying Serpent* is a fun but flawed production. It's temptingly easy to write the whole thing off as rubbish, but the serpent itself is a colorful monster character, more interesting even than the Devil Bat, and Zucco hams it up aggressively. The reliable "murder-a-reel" formula (four in 59 minutes, plus an extra unsuccessful attack) also keeps the interest up. The flying effects are nicely done and there are even a few matte shots of Aztec ruins, an ambitious touch for a PRC movie.

Of course, *The Flying Serpent* is one of those sloppy little B films that can be picked apart endlessly. It's notorious already for its absurd ending – why doesn't Zucco drop the feather, instead of trying to outdistance the bird? – but above and beyond that bit of egregious stupidity, there are any number of additional plot points that defy analysis. The entrance to the treasure chamber, sought by fortune-hunters for hundreds of years, is a conspicuous door-shaped opening in a stone wall near the Aztec temple. Quetzalcoatl doesn't always bother to retrieve the feathers it kills for. By using the bird to kill everyone who rubs him the wrong way, Zucco does nothing but draw attention to the area (just what he's trying to avoid). In his final broadcast, Ralph Lewis forgets to mention that the flying serpent is dead. "Yet," as Don Leifert cogently points out in *Filmfax*, "it is precisely this wonderful absence of logical human behavior that gives these crazy little programmers their charm. Leave the logic to the majors. The independents couldn't care less."

The flying serpent itself was generally mocked out by contemporary reviewers, but it deserves a few points just for its *uniqueness* as a movie monster (dinosaurish face and horned head, birdlike beak, exotically plumed wings and reptilian claws); it even breathes smoke at one point, another nice touch. The scenes where it soars along on wires, wings a-flapping, are well-executed; in fact, they so much resemble the flying effects in Republic serials like *Adventures of Captain Marvel* (1941) and *King of the Rocket Men* (1949) that you have to wonder if Howard and Theodore Lydecker, Republic's ace special effects men, might not have been doing a bit of uncredited moonlighting at PRC. In a neat split-second shot, Quetzalcoatl has its oversized beak clamped around Henry Hall's throat and is rocking the head as it tears the flesh (bloodlessly, of course). It may not be great, but it's a hell of a lot better than anything Universal, who supposedly led the horror field, contributed to horror history in 1946.

It might seem like an odd quibble, but once again George Zucco isn't colorfully insane (like a Lugosi), or flamboyantly insane (like a Carradine), or good-naturedly insane (like an Atwill); he's just bitchily, disagreeably insane. His whole life revolves around the treasure ("No other human eye shall see it and live!" he rants at Quetzalcoatl), but he never spends a cent of it; in fact, the one time he pores over it, he couldn't seem less interested, expressionlessly picking up a trinket or two and then nonchalantly letting them fall back into the box. People like Prof. Lambert, who pose no threat whatsoever, wind up on his hit list; he even tries to kill his own stepdaughter. In *The Devil Bat*, Bela Lugosi marks for death two families that (*he* thinks) cheated him; some writers – Lugosi fans, of course – even try to make it sound like he's in the right(!). In *The Flying Serpent*, Zucco sics the bird on someone if he doesn't like the way they part their hair. Zucco is one movie madman you never find yourself rooting for, especially in something like *The Flying Serpent* where his character *isn't* even insane – just the world's meanest s.o.b. This is not to say he's *bad* at these kitschy crackpot roles; just that, among the major oldtime horror stars, he might have been the least *good* at it.

The ancient Aztecs considered Quetzalcoatl the patron of saints and the inventor of calendars and books. (Ah, those wacky Mexicans!) A great closeup peek (wires and all) at *The Flying Serpent.*

But even if he *isn't* the most huggable of screen heavies, Zucco played all his horror roles to the hilt, even minute ones like the palsied priest in *The Mummy's Tomb* (1942) or the bombastic showman in *House of Frankenstein* (1944); this is meant as no small compliment. Greg Mank wrote in *Filmfax,*

> Zucco always played with aplomb, color and an impeccable taste which saved many a movie melodrama. No matter how he turned on that vibrant, purring-cat voice, no matter how he lit up those glorious, pin-ball eyes, this superb British stage actor exuded a sophistication, an intelligence, and a professionalism which assured one that the "guilty pleasure" in watching a horror show was legitimate – all worthy make-believe in the grand tradition of theater.

Greek/English, Zucco was born in Manchester, England, completed his studies at Kent and even played on the cricket and soccer teams. After working in a Winnipeg bank as a teenager, he joined a touring company and played stage roles throughout Canada and the United States. Returning to England to join the army at the outbreak of World War I, he had his right arm shot up in a 1916 battle; he permanently lost the use of two of the fingers of his right hand (occasionally visible flopping around in his movies). He worked in films first in England and later in America; his stateside movie career started at MGM where he acted opposite Harlow, Gable and Garbo, and ended up in places like PRC, where he acted opposite mad monsters, flying serpents and (in *Dead Men Walk*) himself.

Zucco had a leg up on some of the other actors that toiled in these B-grade '40s thrillers: He wasn't restricted to horror films (or even B films) the way people like Atwill and Lugosi were. For just about every *Voodoo Man* or *The Mad Ghoul* on his résumé, there were also (smaller) parts in films like *Joan of Arc, A Woman's Face* or *The Black Swan* – the kind of pictures Atwill and Lugosi went home and dreamed about (or went out and paid to see!). By the early '50s, however, it was obvious that something was wrong. Richard Denning, who combatted Zucco's evil in the Columbia potboiler *Flame of Stamboul* (1951), recalls,

> Dear George! That's when he was really losing his memory; I remember this one scene in particular, and the poor guy, I just died for him, because he couldn't remember *any*thing. And it got worse and worse and *worse* and the sweat was coming off him and he just couldn't do it.

Zucco was signed up for a role in *The Desert Fox*, 20th Century–Fox's 1951 Rommel biopic, when his co-workers discovered that not only couldn't he remember his lines, he didn't even know where he was. Zucco had suffered a stroke; and after two years of being cared for by his family, his condition worsened to the point where his wife Stella was forced to put him into a nursing home. Mrs. Zucco told Greg Mank, "He always knew me, and our daughter Frances, but he didn't know other people, his friends."

Alex Gordon, lifelong film enthusiast and fan of character stars like Zucco, always wanted to have him in one of his American International Pictures; the AIP producer decided to offer him the villainous role in the company's *Voodoo Woman* (1957). Gordon, luckily, caught Zucco in one of his more lucid moods:

> We thought that Zucco might be very good in *Voodoo Woman*. His agent said that I could meet Zucco at his [the agent's] office; he added that, unfortunately, Zucco was not able to remember lines anymore, but that it would boost Zucco's morale tremendously if we at least went through the motions of having an interview and *offered* him the part. Zucco's wife was with him, and he was very frail, a little shaky – very weak and so on. But his mind was all there. He sat there and I told him

that I had always admired his work, particularly in some of the bigger pictures he'd been in. He was very pleased to hear that, especially when I mentioned some of the titles and players he'd been with.

Then I explained to him what *Voodoo Woman* was all about. He was very, very polite, very nice; he said, well, he appreciated very much being offered the role, but he had done so *many* low-budget horror films that what he would really like to do was something a little more in the classical vein; maybe go back to England and do something more classical or some famous kind of story. I told him that my brother Richard had been involved with the company [Renown Pictures] that had made Charles Dickens' *Pickwick Papers* [1954]; Richard represented them in New York, and knew they were hoping to do more Dickens-type pictures. I told Zucco that if he was interested in something like that, maybe we could talk again when they did the *next* one. He was *very*, very pleased with that, thought that would be just wonderful; he said we should think of him if something like that came along, and he would be most interested.*

Zucco lived quietly at the home until his May 17, 1960, death (from pneumonia). His daughter Frances, who had had a spotty career in pictures, died of throat cancer less than two years later. The account of George and Frances Zucco's final years found in the contemptible Kenneth Anger's *Hollywood Babylon II* is pure fiction. (According to Anger, even *Mrs.* Zucco – interviewed by Greg Mank in 1991 – died in 1960!)

Further down the *Flying Serpent* castlist, Ralph Lewis carries himself well as the radio sleuth, although the pipe upon which he pensively puffs becomes an annoying prop. Hope Kramer may not be a bad actress but she plays an irritatingly woebegone character, and has a single pained expression for all occasions. Wheaton Chambers, Henry Hall and Terry Frost are all okay in smallish assignments. Eddie Acuff isn't funny, but at least he isn't offensive.

Just as Bela Lugosi addressed the giant bat in the first scene of *The Devil Bat*, Zucco makes a long-winded speech to Quetzalcoatl at the opening of *Flying Serpent* (hopefully the poor bird didn't have to listen to *that* whole spiel every time Zucco swung by!). PRC wasn't much for buildup and usually got their horror films into gear as quickly as possible, even if it meant kicking off the movies with scenes of grown men talking to bats and birds (or, in *The Mad Monster*, to themselves). But again, as with *The Devil Bat*, the filmmakers go to this ludicrous extent in order to get the picture off to a running start, then later allow the pace to falter in spots (for instance, barrages of headlines and Ralph Lewis's extended radio speeches, describing at length events we've seen).

The next one to be offered the Voodoo Woman *role was John Carradine, who also wanted to do no more low-budget horror films. The role eventually went to Tom Conway, who wore a voodoo headdress almost identical to the get-up worn by Zucco in* Voodoo Man.

Quetzalcoatl was worshiped as far back as the third century, when the Teotihuacán civilization regarded the feathered serpent as a vegetation god. In later centuries, the conception changed drastically. The Toltec culture (the 9th through 12th centuries) honored gods like Quetzalcoatl via war and human sacrifice; the later Aztecs (14th through 16th centuries) revered the plumed reptile as "the patron of priests, the inventor of the calendar and of books, and the protector of goldsmiths and other craftsmen" (*Encyclopedia Britannica*). In addition to his guise as a feathered serpent, Quetzalcoatl was also pictured as a man with a beard (among other conceptions); there's a photo of an ancient limestone figure of Quetzalcoatl in the *Britannica* that looks a lot like *The Wizard of Oz*'s Tin Woodsman in a raincoat. Quetzalcoatl buffs will also want to know that Teotihuacán, the ancient city where the deity was first worshiped, was the scene of location shooting for *Tarzan and the Valley of Gold* (1966), with Mike Henry and Nancy Kovack. After giving the filmmakers permission to shoot there, the Mexican government suddenly felt that their monuments were being desecrated and tried to boot the film company out. Shooting continued amidst many difficulties and the exposed film had to be smuggled out of the country.

Quetzalcoatl flew again in *Q* (a.k.a. *The Winged Serpent*, 1982), this time depicted as a pterodactyl-sized monster nesting at the top of Manhattan's Chrysler Building; a string of construction workers, window washers and sunbathers are killed by the giant bird, but only small-time crook Michael Moriarty discovers its hiding place (and intends to cash in on it). The film's conception of Q owed a lot more to '50s sci-fi pictures like *Rodan* and *The Giant Claw* than it did to *The Flying Serpent*, but the results were entertainingly campy and animator David Allen's effects were well-done. Larry Cohen wrote, produced and directed this minor cult item.

The New York Daily News gave *The Flying Serpent* a two-star rating, but their writeup sounded more like a pan: "[It's] a thriller that is just too obvious to create the desired effect. If you want to see this 'flying serpent,' you can . . . but you will be disillusioned." *The Hollywood Reporter* rapped it as well; they also weren't fooled by director Sam Newfield's use of his "Sherman Scott" pseudonym: "It must have been anticipated that the serpent itself would be a mighty important actor in the proceedings. What was mounted on wires – wires that not even the best photographic tricks of Jack Greenhalgh could hide – has all the reality of an infuriated feather duster. Even PRC can't hope to scare audiences with a thing like this. . . . Sam Newfield is a better director than the circumstances confronting him in *The Flying Serpent* permit him to show. The same is to be said of the acting of George Zucco who headlines the unfortunate cast."

Variety sang the next chorus of critical doom. Its unsigned review carped, "This picture could have been the curdling meller it set out to be if its instrument of horror, a winged serpent, did not resemble an oversized hawk rather than the lethal, blood-sucking monster intended. As it is, *The Flying Serpent* may provide a few uneasy moments for the kids but will fail to garner thrills from the incredulous adult. Suspense, fatally lacking, could well have been used to spike the picture. It's headed for minor biz. . . . Zucco physically fills his part well and performs satisfactorily in poorly motivated role. . . . Sherman Scott's direction is only so-so with several good opportunities for dramatic buildup badly muffed." The *Motion Picture Exhibitor* wrote of the serpent, "Its ability to chill anything is to be questioned."

It's been open season on *The Flying Serpent* in more recent writeups as well. Phil Hardy wrote, "Accompanied in flight by what sounds absurdly like a revving engine and all too clearly a prop slung about on wires, the creature occasions more giggles than chills." Even *Psychotronic*, who usually went easy on Poverty Row pictures, felt like sniping: "The monster bird was an interesting idea, but you know that at a studio like PRC the wires will show and uncontrolled acting will do in any attempt at seriousness." According to Maltin's *Movies on TV*, "Zucco sole interest in B movie reminiscent of serials." *Midnight Marquee*'s Jim Coughlin called it Zucco's "most outlandish" PRC effort.

Devil Bat's Daughter
(PRC, 1946)

Released April 15. 66 minutes. Associate Producer: Carl Pierson. Produced and Directed by Frank Wisbar. Screenplay: Griffin Jay. Original Story: Leo J. McCarthy and Ernst Jaeger. Director of Photography: James S. Brown, Jr., A.S.C. Musical Score: Alexander Steinert. Film Editor: Douglas W. Bagier. Special Effects: Ray Mercer. Production Manager: Norman Cook. Dialogue Director: Harold Erickson. Assistant Director: Louis Germonprez. Art Director: Edward C. Jewell. Set Decorator: Glenn P. Thompson. Wardrobe Designer: Karlice. Sound Engineer: Earl Sitar. Makeup: Bud Westmore.

Cast: Rosemary LaPlanche (Nina MacCarron), John James (Ted Masters), Michael Hale (Dr. Clifton Morris), Molly Lamont (Ellen Morris), Nolan Leary (Dr. Elliot), Monica Mars (Myra Arnold), Edward Cassidy (Sheriff), Eddie Kane (George).

"Bats! Bats! My *father!*"—Nina MacCarron (Rosemary LaPlanche)

Universal remained the standard-bearer for horror filmmakers throughout the late 1930s and the '40s. When Universal started making monster movies again, so did everybody else; and when Universal stopped, that represented the end of the whole cycle. But the other Hollywood studios —

even those located on Poverty Row – deserve a small tip of the hat for not being as sequel-happy as the folks at Universal, who invariably went to the well a few times too often per monster character. It takes a bit more imagination to concoct a new menace and new situations each and every time than to just keep trundling out the same old characters. Many of Universal's latter-day horror plots were staler than last year's bread, their once-proud monsters disgraced in sequel after sequel. Monogram, Republic and PRC certainly recycled a plot or two each, but in the 1940s only one sequel would roll off of Poverty Row's horror movie assembly line.

PRC's first horror movie, *The Devil Bat*, was apparently a big favorite with *some*one at the company: The film was semiremade twice in the five years following its release, first as *The Mad Monster* and then, more recognizably, as *The Flying Serpent*. So somehow it seems fitting that the *last* PRC horror film, *Devil Bat's Daughter*, should be a sequel to the first. It's only unfortunate that this follow-up is a lifeless mystery – and one that makes a mockery of the first film, to boot. The plot of that original is reworked to suit the purposes of *Devil Bat's Daughter*, to the ludicrous extent of exonerating mad killer Bela Lugosi of all responsibility for the Devil Bat murders.

A pretty brunette (Rosemary LaPlanche) is found lying in the road near the Westchester County, New York town of Wardsley, and brought to the office of the Sheriff (Edward Cassidy). (In *The Devil Bat,* the town was called Heathville.) As Dr. Elliot (Nolan Leary) works unsuccessfully to restore the dazed girl to consciousness, the sheriff interrogates a cab driver who reveals that, earlier in the day, she had hailed him at the local train station and asked to be driven to the home of Dr. Paul W. Carruthers – even *after* the cabbie told her that Carruthers was dead and his house deserted. She wasn't seen again until she was found in the road.

Searching the empty Carruthers home for a clue that might lead them to the girl's identity, Dr. Elliot and the sheriff find her traveling bag. Her passport indicates that her name is Nina MacCarron, and that she came to the U.S. from Scotland via Canada. Another document divulges that her father was the late Dr. Carruthers. "Paul Carruthers? Then the girl's the Devil Bat's daughter!" Elliot exclaims, getting a big reaction out of the musical track if not the sheriff.

Dr. Elliot, unable to revive Nina and at his wits' end, consults with Wardsley resident Dr. Clifton Morris (Michael Hale), a respected psychiatrist who practices in Manhattan. Morris has never heard of Dr. Carruthers, so Elliot relates the whole sordid story: Carruthers was a scientist who came to Wardsley to conduct experiments in cell growth stimulation. He experimented on bats, enlarging them to gigantic size; several local people became victims of the giant marauders, and then Carruthers himself. Since then, a rumor has spread that Carruthers was a vampire. (Nina had found newspaper accounts of this tragic episode in her father's house;

reading them for the first time put her into her present state of mental shock.)

Morris is able to bring Nina out of her strange trance, but the girl remains hospitalized; when she dreams of bats, she runs hysterically to Morris' home (how did she find it?), collapsing at the feet of Morris' wife Ellen (Molly Lamont). (As in *Bowery at Midnight*, there's a portrait of Mary Shelley in the house.) Ellen puts Nina into a guest room and telephones her husband in Manhattan. Morris isn't pleased to hear that the disturbed Nina will be staying under his roof; and even *less* happy that Ellen's call interrupted a tryst with his fur-clad, Hungarian-accented girlfriend Myra Arnold (Monica Mars). Myra (and Ellen) knows that Morris married Ellen for her money and position, and now she wants him to ask Ellen for his freedom.

Morris begins to psychoanalyze Nina at his home; the girl makes slow progress over the next few weeks, but freezes up every time he asks what her father was like. During one head-shrinking session, held outdoors, a bird flies overhead and Nina is panicked ("Bats! Bats! My *father!*"). Everything comes back to Nina in a flash: Her father, a Romanian, married her mother in Scotland, but left his wife and daughter when Nina was four. Soon afterwards, her mother died of anemia, and superstitious locals (who *also* thought Carruthers was a vampire!) started the rumor that he had killed her. "For a long time, I believed those stories, too," Nina continues. "I used to dream of him as a bat, and I would be flying beside him...."

Dr. Elliot has tea with Morris and Ellen; Ellen asks what a vampire is. Elliot tells her and mentions that it's possible for a person to *think* he is possessed by a vampire and to commit murder while suffering under that delusion. As Elliot talks, Morris' face takes on the look of a man who's up to no good; the only thing missing is cartoon art of a lightbulb above his head.

Not unexpectedly, strange things now start happening to Nina. For three nights in a row, she fails to drink a tonic that Morris prepares for her, but the glass is always half-empty the next morning; the fact that she can never remember having drunk it upsets her (a *lot*), and she makes a big deal over it. (Why doesn't she just *drink* the damn stuff the night before, like she's supposed to?) Ellen's son Ted Masters (John James), who greatly mistrusts his stepfather Dr. Morris, has started falling for Nina, even though she obviously doesn't have all her marbles. Before leaving home again to take a job at a Boston law office, Ted even proposes to her.

Another glassful of tonic mysteriously disappears (y-a-w-n), and Ted's dog is found dead in Nina's room, killed with scissors. (Nina goes to bed, *and* wakes up, looking like she just stepped off an Atlantic City runway—lipstick, eye shadow, the works.) The next night, Nina awakens not in her bed but on the floor in the downstairs hallway. Nearby, Ellen Morris lies dead, stabbed with scissors. Convinced that she must have done it, Nina even confesses to the crime, which makes lurid headlines from coast to coast (*The Chicago Star*: NINA MACCARRON—VAMPIRE?).

It's PRC's version of the Bat-Signal, with Miss America of 1941 Rosemary LaPlanche caught in the glare. (From *Devil Bat's Daughter.*)

Ted is convinced that Morris, not Nina, killed his mother, and that somehow Dr. Carruthers' missing notes are tied in. He gets Dr. Elliot to help him search the Carruthers place again, but all they find is a rifled safe.

> TED (*flustered*): I don't get it, Doctor. *Who* would be interested in learning the secret of – enlarging *bats? Who?!*
> ELLIOT: Well, to speak for myself, Ted, I'd be *very* interested!

Ted's investigations take him to Morris' New York apartment and even to Myra Arnold's; long-suffering Myra, too, thinks Morris might be guilty. Ted finds Carruthers' notes at Myra's, and rounds up Morris, Dr. Elliot and the sheriff at the Morris home for a showdown. The evidence against Morris becomes overwhelming: Dr. Carruthers' notes, which prove that he was a great scientist, not a vampire or even a killer, were discovered by Morris but kept from Nina, which proves that Morris wanted to keep her mentally off-balance. Secondly, the dream-stimulating pills that Morris gave Nina each night would render her incapable of movement, so that she *couldn't* have killed Ellen. Caught with his pants down, Morris whips out a gun, blazes away and tries to make a getaway, but the sheriff plugs him in the back, killing him. Ted and Nina look forward to a bright future.

Devil Bat's Daughter easily ranks as one of the dullest horror films of the '40s; it isn't even fractionally as good as *The Devil Bat*, the film it's purportedly a sequel to. In fact, some optically blurred and distorted clips from *Devil Bat*,* shown to depict Rosemary LaPlanche's nightmares, represent the only action in the film right up until villain Michael Hale's climactic getaway attempt. The rest of it is just talk, talk, talk.

The film is really more of a whodunit than a horror film but, oddly, there isn't even the slightest effort to create an atmosphere of mystery. Michael Hale's Dr. Morris is a cold fish, a social climber and a disloyal husband, and even though these qualities tend to make him *too* obvious a suspect, we never take our eyes off him; even the greenest armchair sleuth should have him pegged right from the start. Some of *Daughter*'s contemporary reviews even single out Hale as the murderer; it was so obvious, the critics evidently didn't even realize that the film was *meant* to be a mystery, and that they were giving the game away.

Devil Bat's Daughter ought to be required viewing for horror aficionados who routinely praise Frank Wisbar to the skies based on his direction of *Strangler of the Swamp*. In *Devil Bat's Daughter*, the *real* Frank Wisbar takes his more rightful place in Hollywood history – behind the eight ball. Dialogue scenes are long and dull, and Wisbar fails to breathe any life into these desultory goings-on. Whole sequences are shot in one camera take, with the actors moving around a bit to break up the visual monotony. Not one scene has an ounce of pace. It's almost as though the film didn't even *have* a director.

There's a trend in some film fan circles to automatically heap kudos on European directors who emigrate to Hollywood, and a proclivity even to try to make their fairly lousy horror films like Wisbar's *Strangler of the Swamp* and Steve Sekely's *Revenge of the Zombies* sound (much) better than they really are; even Edgar Ulmer's *Bluebeard*, a good but not great picture, is a major beneficiary. Minor stylistic touches are fussed over like mad, and everything that's indefensibly *wrong* with these films either becomes the fault of someone *else*, or is embraced as yet another facet of that pet filmmaker's elusive "genius." ("Ulmer employed absurd scripts and monotonal acting to reach the kind of controlled expression he felt compelled to create" – writer Myron Meisel.) This inexplicable elevation of lowly hacks like Sekely and Wisbar, and maybe even Ulmer, must be as bewildering to Europeans as their doting on people like Jerry Lewis is to us.

Of course, in this case it should be pointed out that on *Devil Bat's Daughter* Wisbar was stuck with one of Poverty Row's lamest horror scripts, the work of Universal alumnus Griffin Jay. A veteran of that studio's Mummy series (*Hand, Tomb* and *Ghost*), Jay also worked on their *Captive Wild Woman* (1943) as well as Columbia's *The Return of the Vam-*

---

*Dave O'Brien, Hal Price, John Ellis and Alan Baldwin are the Devil Bat actors hazily visible in these clips.

pire (1943), which was a derivative hack job, and *Cry of the Werewolf* (1944), which was worse. Jay's probably at his all-time worst in *Devil Bat's Daughter*, trying to wring suspense out of ridiculous situations; the business about the glasses of tonic being half-empty each morning is just plain stupid, but Jay means it to be frightening. Michael Hale is constantly tossing a walnut in the air, so self-consciously that you just *know* it'll eventually become some kind of a clue (John James finds it on the floor at Carruthers'). Psychoanalysis plays a large role in the film, but Jay isn't being hifalutin, just imitative; films using this as a theme flourished around the time of World War II, all of them (three were *Spellbound, The Dark Mirror* and *Possessed*) infinitely better than *Devil Bat's Daughter*. Indeed, Hale's nefarious plan to pin his wife's murder on LaPlanche, which confidently hinges on a jury's willingness to condemn her on the basis of "inherited criminal tendencies," is almost comically naive.

Daughter's drab cast further limits the film's already minuscule appeal. John James, a not-particularly-good-looking leading man, was a veteran of B Westerns and serials in which he sometimes played minor baddies. His first love scene with Rosemary LaPlanche is an embarrassment, but he's much better later as he investigates his mother's death. Michael Hale and Nolan Leary are both quite capable, as is Molly Lamont, who went on to play the dead woman who narrates *Scared to Death* (1947). Monica Mars, who talks like Zsa Zsa Gabor, is playing an angst-ridden "other woman" type, but comes off funny instead.

The fetching Rosemary LaPlanche is again a pleasant treat for the eyes, although her acting as Nina leaves much to be desired. Breathy and wide-eyed, she does her darnedest to seem overwrought, but it isn't much of a performance. Spirited away to a sanatarium after the murder of Molly Lamont, she's missing from most of the film's final third.

It's easy, of course, to make fun of this type of acting, and probably also not fair; how well would Katharine Hepburn, Bette Davis or even today's much-vaunted Meryl Streep come off belting out lines like "Bats! Bats! My *father!*", on a too-tight schedule, and under the direction of a Frank Wisbar? Maybe Rosemary LaPlanche isn't so bad after all. The daughter of a telephone company employee, the hazel-eyed, "dream-figured" (34-24-36) LaPlanche grew up taking ballet, tap dance and singing lessons, acting in school plays and winning dozens of local and national beauty contests, culminating in her crowning as Miss America of 1941. This achievement finally opened some Hollywood doors for LaPlanche, who worked under contract to Hal Roach and to RKO in the early '40s, all the while keeping up her business skills (80 words a minute typewriting, 140 dictation; "It's a good thing to know, just in case my acting career doesn't jell, " she explained). She dropped out of pictures when she became a Los Angeles television personality (she had three local shows, and also appeared in commercials); her husband was television producer Harry Koplan. In 1973, while scouting New Mexico locations for a new television series, Koplan suffered a heart attack while dancing with LaPlanche, and died an hour later, at age 63. LaPlanche died even younger, at 56, of cancer in 1979.

Devil Bat's Daughter's plot was more than just a little reminiscent of the storyline of Universal's *She-Wolf of London* (1946), made only a month earlier. In *She-Wolf*, it's June Lockhart who thinks she's some sort of supernatural killer; the film's climax reveals the true culprit as her phony "aunt" (Sara Haden), who drugged Lockhart's nightly glasses of milk before committing the murders herself. The plot got even more of a workout in the '50s: Louis Hayward was tricked through similar means into believing himself a Mr. Hyde in *The Son of Dr. Jekyll* (1951); like *Daughter*, this film also saw fit to clear its protagonist's father – the original Dr. Jekyll – of all blame for the earlier crimes. Back on the distaff side, Gloria Talbott fancied herself a nocturnal she-monster in *Daughter of Dr. Jekyll* (1957) – again the victim of nightly doses of drugged milk and an avaricious guardian.

Devil Bat's Daughter went into production on Wednesday, January 9, 1946. On the second day of production, according to the Hollywood trades, PRC reportedly had bats in their own belfry: six flying rodents being used in the picture escaped from their cage and lodged in a prop tower. The film was released in mid–April, garnering several reviews that, surprisingly, were somewhat favorable. Wanda Hale of *The New York Daily News* was one of the critics who didn't bother to withhold the fact that Michael Hale was the killer, but she liked the picture overall, and gave it two-and-a-half stars: "*Devil Bat's Daughter* is one of those murder thrillers that keeps no secrets from the audience. . . . Despite a story that is basically artificial, the picture manages, through capable acting and Frank Wisbar's direction, to be diverting." *Variety* liked it, too: "*Devil Bat's Daughter* is never quite as lurid as its title, [but] is well weighted with suspense and will give the horror fans enough gasps to satisfy 'em. . . . Sprinting off to a good start, pace is maintained and suspense tightly built most of footage save for sag midway when time-out is called so romantic angle can be inserted. . . . Rosemary LaPlanche doesn't accomplish any miracles of character-delineation, but at bottom it's a tough part. John James [is] a brisk, forthright fellow who helps keep pace driving. Michael Hale's psychiatrist tops the cast; in great measure his acting lends film much of its credulity and interest." *The Hollywood Reporter* called Wisbar's direction "never better than third-rate."

The Phantom of the Movies (*The Phantom's Ultimate Video Guide*) enjoyed the film a bit, too, but wished Lugosi had been in it: "Far from a classic, [but] it does offer more atmospheric touches than most PRC quickies." (*Does* it?) Denis Gifford (*A Pictorial History of Horror Movies*) called the exoneration of Bela Lugosi's *Devil Bat* character "as blatant a whitewash job as was ever conceived by Tom Sawyer." *Psychotronic* brushed the film off as "a cheat sequel." Don Willis wrote, "The cast does some hilariously exaggerated double takes, and there are some double-take lines too."

Don Leifert (*Filmfax*) called it "a predictable murder mystery with few horror elements and too much talk . . . just another routine melodrama." *Photon*'s Ron Borst, plainly appalled, called it an "incredibly awful sequel."

The Catman of Paris
(Republic, 1946)

Released April 20. 65 minutes. Associate Producer: Marek M. Libkov. Directed by Lesley Selander. Original Screenplay: Sherman L. Lowe. Photography: Reggie Lanning. Film Editor: Harry Keller. Musical Director: Richard Cherwin. Music Score: Dale Butts. Sound: Fred Stahl. Art Director: Gano Chittenden. Costumes: Adele Palmer. Set Decorators: John McCarthy, Jr. and James Redd. Special Effects: Howard Lydecker and Theodore Lydecker. Dance Director: Larry Ceballos. Makeup Supervisor: Bob Mark.

Cast: Carl Esmond (Charles Regnier), Lenore Aubert (Marie Audet), Adele Mara (Marguerite Duval), Douglass Dumbrille (Henry Borchard), Gerald Mohr (Police Insp. Severen), Fritz Feld (Prefect of Police), Francis Pierlot (Paul Audet), George Renavent (Guillard), Francis McDonald (Devereaux), Maurice Cass (Paul deRoche), Alphonse Martell (Maurice Cavaignac), Paul Marion (Jules), John Dehner (Georges), Anthony Caruso (Raoul), Carl Neubert (Philippe), Elaine Lange (Blanche de Clermont), Tanis Chandler (Yvette), George Davis (Concierge), Albert Petit (Paris Policeman), Jean De Briac (Butler), Gino Corrado (Policeman), Louis Mercier (Old Man), Eugene Borden (Porter), Steve Darrell (Driver), Armand Roland (André), Bob Wilke (The Catman), Claire Du Brey (Woman Servant), Hector Sarno (Farmer).

"BLOODSTAINED HANDS OF HORROR!—a sinister shriek . . . a cry of pain . . . then death to another "cat" victim!"—*Catman* publicity

"Many charming people are tied up with the film of this absurdity. It is an experience that cannot fail to be embarrassing to all, but they can take consolance in the shortness of memories where such low-budget product is concerned. . . . Oddly enough, it never occurs to anyone to yell, "Scat.'"—*The Hollywood Reporter*

Republic was nothing if not efficient. One day after *Valley of the Zombies* wrapped, its planned cofeature, *The Catman of Paris*, was already in production on the San Fernando Valley lot. The setting was turn-of-the-century Paris and the story a variation on the tried-and-true werewolf theme, a combination which might have had possibilities. The result was again, however, a distinct disappointment—par for Republic's horror course. There's a shock moment or two, and even a scene that's halfway suspenseful, but the plot is so muddled, almost self-contradictory, that the film becomes bewildering.

Author Charles Regnier (Carl Esmond), newly returned from an extended trip to the Orient, comes home to Paris a hero: His book *Fraudulent Justice* is the rage of France, even though it's made him unpopular with the French government. ("It is the courage to risk official persecution that makes an author like you important!" an admirer tells him at the Café duBois.) Regnier maintains that the book *is* fiction, but by some weird coincidence it also happens to be a wholly accurate reflection of what went on at the real-life trial of one Louis Chambre, held in strict secrecy in 1871. The people have recognized *Fraudulent Justice* as an account of that trial, and the scandalous nature of what Regnier has revealed is causing a public reaction that threatens the government.

Suffering from a strange headache, Regnier begs the forgiveness of his patron (and companion on the Far East trip) Henry Borchard (Douglass Dumbrille) and leaves the café in a daze. Elsewhere that night, Devereaux (Francis McDonald), a librarian at the Ministry of Justice archives, is leaving work with a portfolio containing the secret Chambre file. Walking through the dark and lonely streets, Devereaux is attacked by a Catman (Bob Wilke) who leaps down at him from out of a tree, strangles and claws him to ribbons. The Catman escapes with the file.

Police Inspector Severen (Gerald Mohr) is convinced that Regnier is the killer; Severen's theory is that Regnier gained access to the secret documents through Devereaux, and has now murdered him and stolen the papers in order to stay out of jail. Severen's boss, the prefect of police (Fritz Feld), disagrees; he believes in werewolves and cat people, and is confident that Devereaux was killed by a supernatural being. Regnier is brought in and questioned, but maintains his innocence even though he had suffered a blackout the night before, and remembers nothing between the time he left the café and the moment he was picked up by the police. (Each of Regnier's amnesia attacks is preceded by the same poorly selected montage of filmclips from the stock footage library: shots, shown in negative, of Arctic ice, lightning, a buoy, and then a wide-eyed black cat.)

Fraudulent Justice continues to sell well, but the publisher, Paul Audet (Francis Pierlot), worries that Regnier *did* gain illegal access to the trial records, and that all copies of the book will be confiscated. Audet's daughter Marie (Lenore Aubert) is clearly smitten with Regnier, and he with her, but Regnier is engaged to marry heiress Marguerite Duval (Adele Mara).

During a dinner party given by the Duvals in his honor, Regnier squabbles with Marguerite on the veranda: He feels that they became engaged in haste, isn't sure he loves her, and wants to break it off. Marguerite, who is quite obviously a schemer and a social climber, won't hear of it. Regnier wanders off, afflicted again by a headache. Later that night, while enjoying a carriage ride through the park, Marguerite spots a man she *thinks* is

A production pose more striking than anything in the movie itself: Carl Esmond, Lenore Aubert and (above) Robert Wilke as *The Catman of Paris*.

Regnier and has her driver stop while the man, his face unseen by Marguerite (or by the audience), climbs into the closed carriage. When Marguerite finally faces him, she screams as the intruder closes in with a bestial *meow*, snuffing out her life.

Later, Regnier recovers from a blackout that began after his quarrel with Marguerite and finds himself outside the Audet home. He and Marie go to the Café duBois for a midnight snack, but through a coincidence a newspaperman arrives with the news that Regnier is being sought by the police for Marguerite's murder. The newsman and his friends recognize Regnier and attempt to detain him for the police, but the author bests the four of them in a wild brawl and leaves with Marie.

Borchard arranges for Regnier and Marie to hide out at the chateau of a friend while he (Borchard) makes arrangements to smuggle the author over the border into Spain. By now, the distraught Regnier is convinced he *is* the Catman; Borchard says he thinks so, too, and gives Marie a gun to protect herself from Regnier just in case.

Back at police HQ, the prefect has called in Paul deRoche (Maurice Cass), an obsessive little man whose life is dedicated to proving the existence of the Catman. According to research done by deRoche's grandfather, the Catman appears when Jupiter and a certain constellation are juxtaposed; he made his first appearance back in the days of Christians and lions, and later turned up in the Balkans, Alexandria, Cairo and even Moscow, where he was responsible for scores of murders that were blamed on Ivan the Terrible(!). This newest incarnation will be his ninth and last, according to deRoche. The prefect listens raptly. Severen thinks they're both nuts.

That night, the Catman bursts into Marie's room and chases her through the house and across the grounds. Marie empties her gun into her pursuer to no effect, but as he closes in on her, police arrive, shooting and mortally wounding the Catman. Everyone assumes the captured Catman is Regnier until Regnier wearily wanders into the scene; he slept through the whole thing.

The injured Catman reveals that he is Borchard, and that he had attended the closed trial of Chambre in cat form, then psychically conveyed the information to Regnier, who used it in what *he* thought was a work of fiction. Borchard killed Devereaux because he was a menace to Regnier's career, and Marguerite because she threatened his happiness. Dying, the Catman transforms one last time into Borchard.

Catman is one of those pictures that just doesn't make a whole lot of sense, even *after* you swallow its fantastic premise. The film establishes the fact that the Catman is a mystical type of monster, brought into existence by the juxtaposition of planets and stars; in a scene that was probably designed to inspire wonder, the crotchety old deRoche details for the prefect the various incarnations of the Catman over the past 2000 years. But the film doesn't bother to explain why this deathless fiend, responsible for perhaps hundreds of murders, suddenly takes a paternal interest in the career and personal happiness of a struggling French writer. You *try* to accept that premise – maybe the Catman's getting soft in his old age! – but now you have to figure out why the Catman then proceeds to *frame* this fellow for the murders he himself committed! Regardless of how it's sliced, it just can't be worked out.

The Catman's about to tear out Adele Mara's throat, but she doesn't look like she minds. An odd posed shot from *The Catman of Paris*.

The silliness of the story blunts the impact of some of the film's horror episodes. In *Catman*'s best scene, Marguerite unsuspectingly invites the Catman to ride in her carriage; she's assumed, without seeing his face, that the man is her fiancé, with whom she had just argued. As the carriage continues through the park, the girl demurely makes her apologies, her eyes still averted; the audience *knows* he's the Catman, and the filmmakers *know* we know, so it's drawn out rather suspensefully. The *absence* of background music here adds to the creepy mood and the air of anticipation.

The Catman's proclivity for pouncing on his victims from high places is also a nice surprise: He leaps unexpectedly onto Devereaux the librarian from the branches of a tree, and in the climax he drops onto Marie's darkened veranda from a point above. Unfortunately, the ensuing chase is a disappointment, with neither party in much of a hurry as the killer follows the frightened girl through the shadowy chateau and out onto the grounds.

Another script innovation which doesn't play well is the way the prefect of police (an unusually subdued, and white-haired, Fritz Feld) believes in monsters and the supernatural, and his subordinate (Gerald Mohr) remains unconvinced. Generally in werewolf movies, it's the detective or some lowly bobby who thinks that monsters are involved, and the higher-ups who scoff at their childish notions (*The Wolf Man, The Return of the Vampire, She-Wolf of London*, etc.). Here for once the situation is reversed, but the scenes, again, are absurd. If the prefect is so convinced that a supernatural creature is at large, why does he entrust the investigation to a man who dismisses that theory and continues to badger an innocent writer? "It *is* a Catman after all," Inspector Severen grumbles disappointedly as lantern-light illuminates the face of the killer (doubting thomas Severen now believes in monsters without checking to see if the Catman is just wearing a mask!). The prefect, annoying beyond belief, quietly simpers, "I *told* you there are cat people . . ." with the patronizing attitude of a parent addressing a child.

   The Catman of Paris underlines once more the fact that Republic was far more at home with action than with suspense or horror films. As if they doubted their own ability to produce a horror film that would entertain audiences, they again insert elements that they themselves are more comfortable with. Charles Regnier isn't able to learn that he's a wanted man in a dialogue exchange, he has to find out when four men try to detain him in a closed café, and a room-wrecking fistfight begins (with the little bookworm prevailing!). Later, the fugitive boldly rides through the countryside in an open(!) carriage, and is of course promptly spotted by the police. A chase over hill and dale ensues, with the inspector's gun blazing away, the horses running at full gallop and the police carriage eventually overturning.

   These were, of course, the same hills, guns and stunts that were employed whether a catman was on the prowl, the Comanches on the warpath or the rustlers herding stolen cattle through the valley; in other words, the same brand of film action with which Republic had built itself up from a lowly B studio to the MGM of Poverty Row. The sort of fisticuffs and fast-paced excitement that enhance a John Wayne or Roy Rogers outdoor show do remarkably little for horror films like *The Vampire's Ghost* and *The Catman of Paris*, but Republic didn't want to realize that. (Similarly, in the '30s, Warner Bros. muddied up their horror flicks with the sort of underworld and newsroom scenes *they* excelled at.)

   The performances in *Catman* are okay, although most of the people concerned look more than a bit uncomfortable in their stuffed shirts and frilly get-ups. Carl Esmond gets suitably worked up as the anguished Regnier, but we never feel for him the way we would for a Larry Talbot; maybe it's *Catman's* foreign milieu, but it's tough to associate and empathize with its characters. Vienna-born, Esmond worked on the stage there and in Berlin, fled Nazi persecution by relocating to London, came to Hollywood in the late '30s and has made dozens of movies here, specializing in suave, sometimes arrogant portrayals. In the fantasy and horror vein, he also played Jules Verne in *From the Earth to the Moon* (1958), and was in the added American scenes for Hammer's *The Kiss of the Vampire* (1963).

Lenore Aubert, the sinister but sexy Sandra of *Abbott and Costello Meet Frankenstein* (1948), does all the girlish things expected of a B horror film leading lady. Just as in *The Vampire's Ghost*, Adele Mara has a knack for falling for the wrong man (and paying with her life). Douglass Dumbrille is earnest and sincere as Esmond's loyal friend Borchard; his transformation from Catman to human form is lazily achieved through a single lap dissolve. Gerald Mohr and Fritz Feld, as minions of the law, spend more time debating with one another over the existence of the supernatural than in looking for the killer. Francis Pierlot, George Renavent, Francis McDonald and all the rest contribute professional performances. Some of the actors employ a French accent while others don't; some bit players even speak in French, with the stars answering back in English. The sign for the Ministry of Justice is in French; a newspaper seen at one point has a French masthead, but the *headlines* are in English!

Bob (later Robert J.) Wilke, a busy utility player at the time, plays the Catman complete with widow's peak, pointed ears, vampire teeth and fancy evening clothes (including opera hat!); he's easily the screen's best-dressed werewolf (or, more accurately, a were*cat*) since Henry Hull in *WereWolf of London* (1935). Wilke went on to juicy supporting roles in many memorable Westerns, including *High Noon* (1952), as one of the outlaws (the one shot by Grace Kelly), and *The Magnificent Seven* (1960), as the trouble-maker killed by James Coburn.

Often the problem with Republic horror films is that the writers didn't know how monsters behave; *Valley of the Zombies* didn't see much difference between vampires and zombies, and *The Vampire's Ghost* (John Abbott) walked around in the daylight and went on safaris. *Catman of Paris* featured an original monster, so Republic was safe on that count, but the problem this time was that no one seemed to realize how *people* behave. When told that his "fictional" book *Fraudulent Justice* mirrored exactly *all* the particulars of a trial held in close secrecy and under the tightest security, Regnier merrily shrugs it off as the type of coincidence that happens every day. The book has the French people up in arms over what went on at that secret trial, but no one explains how they were able to make the connection between supposed fiction and a trial no one knows anything about. Regnier and Marguerite spat and have nothing in common, but are engaged to be married. The prefect of police believes in the boogie man.

Nuts and bolts: Marek Libkov, associate producer of *Catman*, got the assignment from supervisor William O'Sullivan along with a starting date of September 20, 1945. John Alton, later the Oscar-winning cinematographer of *An American in Paris* (1951), was originally assigned as director of photography, but was replaced with Reggie Lanning. Shooting got underway a day late, on September 21, and the production "wrapped" on the evening of October 10 with the shooting of exterior scenes on the Republic backlot.

"Werecat" Bob Wilke behind-the-scenes with makeup artist Bob Mark on Republic's
The Catman of Paris.

In *The Hollywood Reporter*'s opinion, *Catman*'s period setting and
foreign locale contributed to a stilted feeling, adding, "Associate producer
Marek M. Libkov erred in okaying a wordy script, its every character utter-
ing editorials instead of dialogue." *The New York Times* felt that "even a
mouse should be able to watch it without too great alarm. The cat in this

case is permitted such infrequent appearances on the screen and is such a decrepit looking monster that it is more to be pitied than feared. Harder, by far, on the audience are the stretches of dull and dreary talk indulged in by several pompous actors dressed up in musty costumes."

Variety's unnamed reviewer was favorable, although he (she?) admitted that the film's mix of Jekyll-and-Hyde horror and a whodunit atmosphere "taxes belief to the breaking point. But customers preferring to check credulity at the box office will okay this film for its rolling pace, sustained tension and competent cast. Neat direction succeeds in focussing interest on the Catman's homicidal urges, while the makeup can be expected to earn balcony shrieks at the denouement. . . . Settings have solid mahogany look but the script only has a literate veneer. . . . Carl Esmond turns in a distraught and sympathetic, although occasionally stiff performance. Esmond especially suffers by comparison alongside Douglass Dumbrille who, as the hero's patron devil, goes through his paces in polished and eloquent form."

Phil Hardy didn't much care for it ("Although the cast all turn in reasonable performances, all the sinister hocus-pocus goes for very little, given leaden direction and a ridiculous pantomime makeup for the werecat"). Michael Weldon (*Psychotronic*) mocked the film out as well: "[The Catman] basically looks like an unshaven guy with vampire teeth and Spock ears who went wild with an eyebrow pencil." Don Willis called *Catman* "derivative, especially from *Cat People*, *The Leopard Man* and *The Wolf Man.*"

Again, as in *The Vampire's Ghost*, Republic took a monster that was fairly well played-out (in this case, the werewolf, done to death at Universal) and dared to try to do something different with it: Turn-of-the-century Paris was a new film setting for this type of tale, a political subplot was introduced, Republic's were*cat* had mystical qualities, there was a whodunit twist and even a jolt or two of two-fisted action. These elements, unfortunately, are not cleverly interwoven, just tossed together; and Douglass Dumbrille has **killer** written all over him right from the get-go. *The Catman of Paris* builds up a bit of suspense here and there, but the plotline is foolish and the Catman looks more like an overdressed hobo than a hobgoblin. Republic's final horror production of the '40s is, once again, a bust.

Valley of the Zombies
(Republic, 1946)

Released May 24. 56 minutes. Associate Producers: Dorrell McGowan and Stuart McGowan. Directed by Philip Ford. Screenplay: Dorrell McGowan and Stuart

McGowan. Story: Royal K. Cole and Sherman L. Lowe. Photography: Reggie Lanning. Art Director: Hilyard Brown. Music Director: Richard Cherwin. Special Effects: Howard Lydecker and Theodore Lydecker. Film Editor: William P. Thompson. Set Decorators: John McCarthy, Jr. and Allan Alperin. Costumes: Adele Palmer. Sound: Fred Stahl. Makeup: Bob Mark. Assistant Director: Joe Dill.

Cast: Robert Livingston (Dr. Terry Evans), Adrian Booth (Susan Drake), Ian Keith (Ormand Murks), Thomas E. Jackson (Blair), Charles Trowbridge (Dr. Rufus Maynard), Earle Hodgins (Fred Mays), LeRoy Mason (Hendricks), William Haade (Tiny), Wilton Graff (Dr. Lucifer Garland), Charles Cane (Police Insp. Ryan), Russ Clark (Lacy), Charles Hamilton (The Driver).

> **"In my former profession, death was an everyday occurrence. I began to wonder, would it be possible for a man to *appear* to be dead, and still be *alive?* The thought fascinated me, it became an obsession. I gave up everything to find the answer. And at last I found it, in the land of voodoo rites and devil potions — the Valley of the Zombies!" — Ormand Murks (Ian Keith)**

A mad undertaker with a fixation for blood transfusions furnished the goosebumps in Republic's next-to-last horror thriller, *Valley of the Zombies.* The title, of course, is actually a misnomer; the sinister Ormand Murks behaves like a vampire, not a zombie, even taking tips on dressing and grooming from classic screen bloodsuckers (his long black coat could easily pass for a vampire's cloak). While this minor film adds less than nothing to the classic horror canon, it's a bit of a historical curiosity in that it gives us a glimpse of the way actor Ian Keith *might* have played Count Dracula — a role he was up for twice.

The camera prowls around a darkened, mist-shrouded big city skyscraper as a bell chimes out the hour and a caped man (Keith) skulks on the rooftop. On the sixteenth floor we find the office of brain specialist Rufus Maynard (Charles Trowbridge), a noted physician perplexed by the way his office supply of blood keeps disappearing; just this night, twelve more pints have turned up missing, according to Dr. Maynard's employee, chemist Fred Mays (Earle Hodgins). Two other associates of Maynard's, Dr. Terry Evans (Robert Livingston) and nurse Susan Drake (Adrian Booth), are also at a loss to explain the thefts.

After everyone but Maynard has gone, the lurking stranger steals into the shadowy office and confronts the surprised physician.

> STRANGER: My wants are simple, Dr. Maynard — very simple. Blood!
> MAYNARD: Blood? *That's* a strange request.
> STRANGER: I'm a strange man, doctor!

The enigmatic visitor rummages in one of Maynard's file drawers, pulls out a single case-history card and graciously hands it to the doctor ("My card...!"). Maynard now realizes that the man is a former patient, Ormand Murks, an undertaker whom he had committed to the Brookdale Mental Institute in 1939 for manic depressive insanity. Pathologically disturbed, Murks had been convinced that periodic transfusions would give him a kind of immortality. (In a flashback, we see Maynard explain Murks' foolish delusion to a Dr. Garland [Wilton Graff], who eagerly asks, "Do you think there's anything *in* it?") Maynard was also present in 1943 when Murks *died* at the Institute; Murks now tells Maynard that he had only *simulated* the appearance of death through a mystic process.

Murks feels, however, that this temporary death-in-life state has placed him in greater need of blood than ever; his brother, Mays the chemist, has been secretly stealing it for him from Maynard's stockpile. When Maynard explains that the supply has been completely depleted, the ghoulish Murks moves in for the kill....

Mays shows up back at the office to filch some additional bottles of blood which he had purposely mislabeled and hidden from Dr. Maynard; Murks shocks his brother by showing him the dead body of his employer. "I'm not going to be a party to murder," Mays declares, dialing the local police station. "I'll put you back in the grave where you belong!" But Murks' hypnotic stare transfixes the poor man, who is unable to complete the call. "*You're* going to put *me* in *my* grave?" Murks leers as he closes in on his new victim.

Later that night, a pair of cops spot Murks as he is preparing to bury the bloodless and embalmed body of Dr. Maynard in a secluded spot. Murks gets away, and detectives from the homicide bureau are called to the scene. Identifying the corpse, the lawmen, led by Blair (Thomas E. Jackson), pay a visit to Maynard's office, where Terry and Susan have returned to complete some work. (Doesn't *any*body in this movie have a home life?) When the body of Mays is found in a freezer, the cops drag Terry and Susan downtown for questioning.

Blair and his men grill their suspects all night before Police Inspector Ryan (Charles Cane) tells Blair that a cab driver was killed and embalmed while Terry and Susan were in custody. Blair still feels they are responsible, and that an accomplice has committed this third murder. Terry and Susan are released, but police are following them.

Terry realizes that they are still the cops' number one suspects, and feels that it behooves them to try and solve the case themselves. Back at the office, they find Murks' card; even though it specifies that Murks is dead, they still feel there might be a connection. That night, they head out to the deserted Murks estate at Greenwood Knolls, pausing to ask questions from a man working under a car at a service station; the estate turns out to be within walking distance. After Terry and Susan have left, the man shows himself to us, and it's Murks.

Terry and Susan enter the Murks family crypt and open Ormand's casket; the box is empty. Now searching the house, they find the body of Dr.

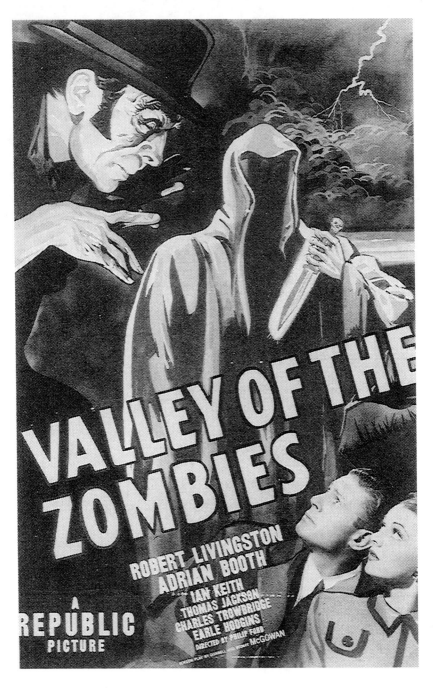

Republic's *Valley of the Zombies* poster art promised more than the film—an often lightweight blend of horror and wisecracks—could deliver.

Garland, the other physician against whom Murks held a grudge, in an embalming room. The police arrive, and a series of mix-ups begins. The cops found the dead body of the *real* service station attendant stuffed into Terry's car, which makes Terry and Susan look guiltier than ever. The body of Dr. Garland has disappeared. Terry decides to show the cops Ormand Murks' empty coffin, but now *Garland* is in it.

Susan is handcuffed to a cabinet by Tiny (William Haade), one of the police officers who now stands guard over the detained girl. But Murks knocks out Tiny and kidnaps Susan, escaping from the scene in one of the policemen's own squad cars. Through a silly, Hollywood-y coincidence, the stolen police car has a broken transmitter which is always broadcasting. Terry and the other policemen tune in on that wavelength and listen keenly as Murks drives past railroad crossings, a power station and other aural landmarks; finally the clock bell of Dr. Maynard's office building is overheard. Terry and the police rush to the scene.

When they arrive, Susan, hypnotized, has just finished giving Murks a transfusion; she and Murks now escape to the roof of the building. When Terry comes bursting onto the scene, Murks orders the entranced girl to shoot him. She is about to when Blair finally appears and puts two bullets into Murks, who plummets from the foggy rooftop. Susan snaps out of her spell and she and Terry agree that they need a drink. "Let's get a zombie!" he jokes.

Valley of the Zombies' story harkens back to the earlier *The Return of Doctor X* (1939), the Warner Bros. film with which that studio tentatively returned to horror moviemaking after the mid–'30s drought. *Return* also centered around a madman (Humphrey Bogart) returning to life following the simulation of death, and now requiring occasional "fixes" of human blood to sustain his existence. Other elements in common include *Return*'s metropolitan (New York) setting, much hospital talk of blood and blood types, drained corpses, bilious city cops, a graveyard scene with empty coffins, a doctor hero (Dennis Morgan) and his put-upon nurse (Rosemary Lane) and the "vampire's" spooky suburban lair. With his marble-white face and what could be mistaken for a hairpiece made from a skunk, the unhappy looking Bogart is a sorry spectacle; singer Morgan and professional oaf Wayne Morris are likewise out of place as monster hunters. But *The Return of Doctor X* plays surprisingly well despite the unsuited cast and the characteristic WB hurry-hurry! pacing, achieving an air of mystery that *Zombies* never tries to muster, a mood of menace that *Zombies* frequently works to dispel.

Withal, *Valley of the Zombies* is a tough film to dislike. At only 56 minutes, it scarcely has an opportunity to wear out its welcome, and there are a number of minor macabre highlights. Of course, it's Ian Keith who "makes" the film with his ghoulish portrayal of the mad Ormand Murks. Director Philip Ford and cinematographer Reggie Lanning add solid

Ormand smirks! Ian Keith as the blood-obsessed mortician in Republic's *Valley of the Zombies.*

contributions to the ominous atmosphere, frequently keeping Keith in shadows, taking numerous subjective shots of the saturnine actor, using selective focus and other tricks of the horror filmmaker's trade. But it's Keith who carries the ball: leering, glowering and leaving no piece of scenery unchewed, his voice alternately dripping with honey and venom. The performance is pure ham, but it adds hugely to the film's entertainment value.

In 1930, Keith had been among the contenders to play the title role in Universal's *Dracula*; other actors mentioned included Lon Chaney, Sr. (who died that year), Paul Muni, William Courtenay and Conrad Veidt. (John Carradine, a bit player then and for years afterward, also *claimed* to have been considered by Universal.) It's fun, after a viewing of *Valley of the Zombies*, to contemplate what Keith would have been like as Dracula: You can easily envision Ormand Murks skulking about the Transylvanian castle and Carfax Abbey. It's tougher, of course, to picture him as the suave, urbane Count that inveigles his way into Dr. and Mina Seward's inner circle; Ormand Murks had few of the social graces. (Needless to say, Bela Lugosi won the role.)

Probably none of this hypothesizing is very productive. The Ian Keith of 1930 was a romantic leading man–type while the Keith of 1945 (*Valley of the Zombies* was shot in mid–September) was a dissipated, hammy character actor; there's no reason to think that his *Zombies* performance would be any sort of indicator of what he would have done in *Dracula*. It *might*, however, give us a pretty good idea how he would have played it in *Abbott and Costello Meet Frankenstein* (1948), the other time that Universal pencilled him in for the Dracula role. (Again it was Lugosi who got the part.)

Keith, a one-time Broadway matinee idol, played in many '40s Bs, but worked less steadily in the '50s. He played the historical characters Henry IV and Ramses I in *The Black Shield of Falworth* (1954) and *The Ten Commandments* (1956), respectively, as well as the King in the "Hamlet" sequence of *Prince of Players* (1955); genre-wise, he popped up as an admiral in Sam Katzman's *It Came from Beneath the Sea* (1955) and on television's *Captain Midnight, Inner Sanctum* and *Rocky Jones, Space Ranger*. Ian Keith stepped off life's curb in 1960.

Robert Livingston and Adrian Booth are both ingratiating players, but the screenplay works too hard to make them glib and funny; hardly a straight line passes between them, and their endless "whistling-in-the-dark" puns and wisecracks become more than tedious.

That, in fact, is the major problem with *Valley of the Zombies*, the way the script works overtime to make Livingston and Booth clever and "cute"; there's very little that's legitimately clever (*or* funny) about their unending witticisms.

Even the irascible, suspicious Detective Blair (Thomas E. Jackson) is hung with awful dialogue. Over the body of the embalmed Dr. Maynard, he deadpans, "Let's go over to Dr. Maynard's office and see if we can pick up a clue that will lead us to this peculiar party that has a passion for pickling!"

What makes these silly moments even more regrettable is the fact that, between them, director Ford, photographer Lanning and actor Keith do a good job of building up a hokey but enjoyable horror film "mood" – one that's constantly being spoiled by other players' penchant for light badinage and

Booth's "scared" antics. It's just another case of Republic not knowing what horror fans wanted from a movie.

Some notes on Adrian Booth: Alternately known by that name and as Lorna Gray, the actress (real name: Virginia Pound) was born in Grand Rapids, Michigan, where her father operated a chain of hat stores. During her high school years she wanted to become a writer, but lack of funds prevented her from attending college. After stints as a singer, she went to Hollywood to break into pictures, but it was a slow process during which she accepted modeling jobs to keep the wolf from the door ("He was on the doorstep, howling, though," she admitted). She finally landed a berth at Columbia where (among many other roles) she played Boris Karloff's daughter in the first of his "Mad Doctor" films, *The Man They Could Not Hang* (1939). She's best-known today for her long run in Republic features and serials: She was the capable, gun-wielding leading lady of the 15-chapter *Captain America* (1944), and dished out dastardly deeds as the leggy high priestess Vultura in the chapterplay *Perils of Nyoka* (1942). In 1949 she told interviewer Myrtle Gebhart,

> Ever since humanity began, woman has contributed 75 percent of progress, man 25. I think I'm being generous to the man, at that.

Booth retired from the business in 1951 (her last film was *The Sea Hornet*, where she was a baddie again), and she's long been married to actor David Brian. She's a good, personable, "game" actress, even if she *doesn't* know anything about the history of human progress.

Supporting players in *Valley of the Zombies* are a mixed bag. Charles Trowbridge was ideally suited to play a physician, Republic publicists averred, coming from a long line of doctors and having attended Harvard Medical School. The silver-haired, distinguished looking actor was another one of filmland's Old Reliables, generally playing doctors, politicians, judges, grouches or doting father-figures. His was a familiar face to horror/serial fans, appearing as it does in *Valley of the Zombies, Mad Love* (1935), *The Man They Could Not Hang* and the additional "Mad Doctor" Karloffilms *Before I Hang* and *The Man with Nine Lives* (both 1940), *The Mummy's Hand, Mysterious Dr. Satan* (also 1940), *Captain America* and more. Thomas E. Jackson, another busy oldtime veteran, is too harried and petulant as the head detective; his sidekick LeRoy Mason, the erstwhile Western and serial baddie, looks out of place on the *right* side of the law. Earle Hodgins, Wilton Graff and Charles Cane do well what little they do.

Technically, everything is up to the usual fairly high Republic B standards; the photography, lighting and music are all a bit *above* average. *Zombies* was only the second film for director Philip Ford, a former A.D. who made his directorial debut (and won a seven-year contract) with Republic's *The Tiger Woman* (1945), a murder story with Adele Mara. The son of actor

Francis Ford (and the nephew of legendary director John), Ford stayed busy in B films and with television work, and died at the Motion Picture Country Hospital in 1976.

Variety saw *Valley of the Zombies* for *just* what it was. "[*Valley*], which will never get out of the twin-bill B league, features an unzombie-like zombie and a fairly horrorless story, despite half a dozen murders. However, it's pretty fair Saturday matinee stuff.... Ian Keith plays a big-city zombie on a lost weekend for blood.... Photography is better than fair, and the inclusion of Ian Keith and a group of experienced supports brings thesping up to a good B level.... Scripting features all the horror-whodunit cliches."

Phil Hardy wrote, "Wearily predictable, the script seems to have exhausted its supply of wit in finding the name Ormand Murks for its mad undertaker." Ronald Borst (*Photon*) liked it a whole lot better: "[This] low-budgeted quickie had a thoroughly engaging plot throughout its brief running time.... On the plus side is its darkly photographed settings, its musical score, and the surprisingly well-played performance by Ian Keith. Keith combined the melodramatic suaveness of Lugosi with the softly subtle and smilingly macabre voice of Karloff, and it is quite sad that he never had another opportunity to create a macabre role.... The film is neither a gem nor a bomb, but is enjoyable, even today." *Psychotronic* felt gypped ("Non-thrills with Robert Livingston, Adrian Booth, and a total lack of zombies"), as did Don Willis ("Always cliched, sometimes cloddish dialogues.... No thrills"), although Willis felt that the leads were "mildly amusing."

Just another old B movie in a world overfilled with them, *Valley of the Zombies* was probably a bit corny and dated even by 1940s standards; Ian Keith's smirky performance, left over from the days of twirling mustaches, is old-fashioned by *talking picture* standards. But it's silly, harmless oldtime horror fun, a trifling 56 minute investment that no open-minded fan could call a total loss.

Spook Busters
(Monogram, 1946)

Released August 24. 68 minutes. Produced by Jan Grippo. Directed by William Beaudine. Original Screenplay: Edmond Seward and Tim Ryan. Photography: Harry Neumann, A.S.C. Supervising Film Editor: Richard Currier. Film Editor: William Austin. Production Manager: Glenn Cook. Technical Director: Dave Milton. Musical Director: Edward J. Kay. Sound Recorder: Tom Lambert. Makeup: Harry Ross.

Cast: Leo Gorcey ("Slip" Mahoney), Huntz Hall ("Sach" Jones), Douglass Dumbrille (Dr. Coslow), Bobby Jordan (Bobby), Gabriel Dell (Gabe), Billy Benedict (Whitey),

David Gorcey (Chuck), Tanis Chandler (Mignon), Maurice Cass (Dr. Bender), Vera Lewis (Mrs. Grimm), Charles Middleton (Stiles), Chester Clute (Mr. Brown), Richard Alexander (Ivan), Bernard Gorcey (Louie), Charles Millsfield (Dean Pettyboff), Arthur Miles (Herman the Gorilla), Tom Coleman (Police Capt. Ryan).

> "LOADED WITH SCREAMY-MEANIES! Those mad doctors have ganged up on Leo's gang for the funniest chiller of the year!" — Monogram ad lines

In the fall of 1945, in keeping with Steve Broidy's plan to upgrade the Monogram product, it was announced that the budgets of many Monogram series would be upped 50 percent. Among the series affected were the Johnny Mack Brown, Jimmy Wakely and Cisco Kid Westerns, the Charlie Chans and, of course, the Bowery Boys, those lovable ragamuffins from New York's Lower East Side. Practically overnight, the entire complexion of the series changed: While most of the early-'40s East Side Kids "comedies" are crudely made, some almost squalid in look and tone, the Bowery Boys films from 1946 on are considerably slicker, better-written and better-directed. Miracle of miracles, a couple of them are even funny in spots.

Spook Busters really isn't one of them. The picture is amiable enough, but the situations are so hackneyed that the average first-time viewer probably gets the impression of having seen the film before – repeatedly. In fact, some of the movie's best elements – the Boys contending with "magic" props in an eerie old house, and an assortment of baddies working overtime to scare them away – are right out of the Boys' old Lugosi films *Spooks Run Wild* and *Ghosts on the Loose*. (All of these tired shenanigans would be dusted off and reused yet again in '50s Bowery Boys flicks like *Ghost Chasers*, 1951, and *Spook Chasers*, 1957.)

In this one, the Bowery Boys are pest exterminators, but their newly-formed business is already on the brink of what group leader "Slip" (Leo Gorcey) calls "acute bankrupture." Mr. Brown (Chester Clute), a realtor, offers them a job cleaning out a deserted old house which once belonged to a magician – and which now is supposedly haunted. "Slip" and his Boys – "Sach" (Huntz Hall), Bobby (Bobby Jordan), Whitey (Billy Benedict) and Chuck (David Gorcey) – drive to the house (at night, naturally) to begin their work.

Ghostly stuff starts happening at once, although it isn't the work of spirits: In secret rooms beneath the cobwebby mansion, Stiles (Charles Middleton), Mrs. Grimm (Vera Lewis) and muscular giant Ivan (Richard Alexander) are monitoring the Boys on a television screen and working to frighten them out of the house. Their employer, psychiatric researcher Dr. Coslow (Douglass Dumbrille), also has a caged gorilla (Arthur Miles) in his subterranean lab, and (like all mad scientists in comedies) he's looking for just-the-right-subject for his upcoming experiment – someone whose brain he can transplant into the noggin of his simian pet. "Sach," the dimmest member of the gang, is (of course) ideal, so now instead of trying to scare off the Boys, the ruthless Coslow determines not to let them leave:

> DR. COSLOW: I intend to transplant part of ["Sach's" brain] to that of the gorilla.
> "SLIP": *That* wouldn't be fair to the gorilla!

"Slip" and "Sach" brawl with Coslow, Stiles and Ivan, even though all of them have been doused with ether (the fight is in slow motion). The gorilla escapes from its cage and chases Coslow through a cave-like tunnel just as the police finally arrive on the scene. The gorilla is shot to death, Coslow and his cronies are rounded up and the Boys go back to doing whatever it is they do between pictures.

The Bowery Boys give *Spook Busters* their best shot, but they're stuck with the tritest of material and the movie bogs down quickly. There isn't a thing original about the Edmond Seward-Tim Ryan "original screenplay"; it's the sort of dreary plot that wears out its welcome in a Three Stooges two-reeler, even in a Disney cartoon short like *Lonesome Ghosts* (1940), much less in a 68 minute feature. *Spook Busters'* villains, veterans Douglass Dumbrille, Charles Middleton, Vera Lewis and Richard Alexander, play their roles straight, but for the most part they act in a low key and their stock characters are colorless. Even man-mountain Alexander, who played Prince Barin in the Flash Gordon serials and the brain-damaged henchman of Bela Lugosi in Republic's 1937 serial *S O S Coast Guard*, comes across as an unmenacing oaf (Leo Gorcey bests him in the climactic fistfight!). Edward J. Kay's placid music is strikingly unsuited to the goings-on, be they comedic or melodramatic, throughout.

More on director William Beaudine: Apparently never saying no to any offer of work, "One-Shot" worked constantly (and consistently!) throughout the '50s, directing films for Monogram, Allied Artists, Republic, Lippert and even a half-dozen for the Protestant Film Commission. Of course, television was the ideal medium for Beaudine and he jumped in feet-first, directing scores of television episodes (*Racket Squad, Wild Bill Hickok, Rin-Tin-Tin, Circus Boy, Naked City, The Green Hornet*, ad infinitum) while twisting and smoothing his handlebar mustache, calling everybody Sam and bellowing instructions to actors all the time they were in front of the camera; "He still thinks he's directing silent movies," actor Peter Graves remarked. (While directing television's *Lassie*, Beaudine regularly aggravated trainer Rudd Weatherwax by referring to the famous collie as "the meat-hound" or "the mutt.") In 1969 he boasted to interviewer Philiph K. Scheuer, "I'll live to be 100," the quickest and surest way for someone to put the whammy on himself. The patron saint of hurry-up filmmakers went belly-up in life's aquarium on March 18, 1970.

Irascible as he may have been, however, Beaudine was also careful to keep in regular contact with many of his old pals, and nearly every week he trouped off to the Motion Picture Country Hospital, smuggling in fifths of bourbon for his oldtime cronies. Director Bobby Gordon told *TV Guide,*

> No matter what set you're on in this town, if you mention Bill Beaudine's name, half the faces will light up. If he didn't teach the director or the cameraman or one of the actors, he taught the director who taught him. He's the heavyweight champion of the world.

The champion's *Spook Busters* got kayoed by critics like *Variety*'s Wit: "Entire story . . . reeks of gleanings from past productions long gone into the limbo of unremembered celluloid. . . . Even the old business of two people, searching for something in the wall, and answering each other's knocks, is used. Overall, the film drags and is repetitious. It hasn't much appeal except to the grammar school level and weekend matinee business."

Spook Busters is the type of haunted house comedy where the baddies go boo and the audience boos right back.

Opposite: The Bowery Boys (represented here by Gabriel Dell, Bobby Jordan and Billy Benedict) brought their usual high-spiritedness to *Spook Busters,* but the trite haunted house pic was beyond rescue. Douglass Dumbrille (with glasses) and Charles Middleton are the baddies being corralled.

Appendix I:
The Music of Poverty Row

by Bill Littman

They waxed lyrical about ape men, devil bats and voodoo men. Armed only with a handful of music sheets, a modest band of musicians and a willing desire to labor in the field they loved, they dared to embellish the histrionics of Bela Lugosi and George Zucco, while divining the proper way to musically interpret "Death by Mad Monster."

Who were they? They were the poor, overworked, underpaid "Toscaninis" of Gower Gulch, the men who churned out musical scores for the Monogram and PRC movies of the 1940s.

Appointed as musical director for Monogram Pictures around 1939, Edward Kay began his career by graduating from the College of Dental and Oral Surgery in New York. (He probably realized much later the advantage of a second career when working for Monogram Pictures.) After years of private musical study prior to his stint at Monogram, Kay had been a conductor and arranger of vaudeville shows, musicals and operettas as well as musical supervisor for various radio programs. Once hired by Monogram, he immediately found himself composing, arranging and conducting music for most of the studio's features. Whether Western, musical, horror or tenpenny war film, Kay either scored or supervised background melodies for them all.

In the horror field, Kay was tunesmith for zombies, ape guys and East Side Kids alike in titles such as *The Ape, The Ape Man, Return of the Ape Man, Voodoo Man, King of the Zombies, Revenge of the Zombies* and *Ghosts on the Loose*. As can be imagined, such movies often contained scores amounting to little more than a 12-bar exercise in primitive mood-making. With little budget, time or imagination to provide only the simplest and most basic of musical scores, these one-trick themes were repeated endlessly throughout each picture.

For example, *The Ape Man*, one of Monogram's classic Lugosi scenarios, had a frenetic little action theme played during the main title and climax, with dour-sounding woodwind wallpaper music in-between. *Voodoo Man* employed a score of harp arpeggios and woodwinds, along with a flute trilling out a theme that might have been more appropriate in a Charlie Chan picture. In this case "Oriental" seemed to equal "voodoo." Ah so. . .

The Ape had a pounding circus theme during the credits, interspersed with splashes of some ham-fisted trombone playing. Unfortunately, the overall effect was more that of noise than music. The biggest surprise to anyone researching Eddie Kay's career might be that in 1941 he was nominated for an Academy Award for a Monogram picture – a Monogram *horror* picture, no less. Along with Bernard Herrmann's scores for *Citizen Kane* and *All That Money Can Buy*, Alfred Newman's *How Green Was My Valley*, Max Steiner's *Sergeant York* and Franz Waxman's *Suspicion*, Kay had been nominated for . . . *King of the Zombies!* Where else but in Hollywood could a poor Brooklyn dentist get an Academy Award nomination for composing music about zombies? Eddie didn't take home the statuette.

A few Monogram movie scores, *The Corpse Vanishes* and *Spooks Run Wild* to be specific, are listed on-screen as the work of Lange and Porter. Johnny Lange and Lew Porter were a couple of songwriters working for Monogram at that time (Lew composed the immortal "In Elk Valley") and may have contributed something musical to the films, but for the most part, those scores arrived courtesy of Abe Meyer Synchronizing Service, an outfit that provided recorded music tracks to studios that simply couldn't afford a 45-picture-a-year battery of original scores. Lange and Porter's names may have been listed simply for A.S.C.A.P. registration or for financial purposes. At any rate, Meyer's group provided themes that should be quite familiar to Monogram fanatics.

In *The Corpse Vanishes*, the well-worn "mysterioso" of Charles Dunworth tests its dulcet tones as Frank Moran's idiot character goes about busily sulking. The main title music to *Corpse* sounds like someone's idea of a diabolical Charleston, while the short, staccato pieces connecting several opening scenes show up elsewhere in no less than five Monogram and PRC mystery features. No musical director worth his salt at these studios would dare let a good track go to waste. In addition, the music for the credit sequence and climax of *Spooks Run Wild* was lifted directly from the chase finale of Columbia's 1935 Boris Karloff thriller *The Black Room*. One thing you can say about all of this *ex post facto* is that it does manage to give the various attempts toward musical backing a somewhat perverse and off-kilter sense of variety, if nothing else.

PRC's musical director without portfolio was David Chudnow, former head of scoring at Grand National Pictures during the late '30s. Chudnow is listed as composer for *The Devil Bat* and *The Mad Monster*, but again it's difficult at times to ascertain where Chudnow leaves off and Abe Meyer begins, or vice versa. If anything is original in *Devil Bat*, it's that strange, lopsided saxophone-orchestra main title theme. The sax calmly plays a five-note introduction and the orchestra answers it with a musical shriek. The two repeat, then play a nice, bouncy bridge that leads to more shrieking until the whole piece collapses in a pile of organ codas. Lots of sound and fury signifying cacophony.

PRC's other resident music man was Leo Erdody, a former Chicago native whose musical education and expertise as violinist came about via training under masters in Berlin. Erdody was probably the best of the lot of composers on Poverty Row chiefly because his material was developed with a little more variety and complexity than the others. Most of Leo's musical sequences, however, were very brief, probably due to pinchpenny underscoring, and were repeated as many times as possible to musically fill out the running time of the picture.

But familiarity breeds listener exasperation. *Dead Men Walk*'s score employed skittery, somewhat formless violin, organ and flute sections that were eerie and interesting once or twice, but could easily drive the listener up the wall when repeated for the twentieth time. Similar problems were inherent in Erdody's scores for *White Pongo* (1945) and *Bluebeard*. The latter, in fact, bases several of its musical sequences on sections of Mussorgsky's "Pictures at an Exhibition." But the high tones must have swelled Leo's head a bit, as he is billed in *Bluebeard* as just Erdody.

Like those who labor in other types of factories, the composers at Monogram and PRC did their jobs simply and directly, then went on to the next assignment, expending about as much effort as was needed to complete their less-than-hifalutin tasks. Musically, the pictures ended up pretty much with what they deserved, a crude but distinctive tonal personality to match their visuals. Bravo, nonetheless, to all!

Appendix II:
Exclusions, Borderline Inclusions,
a Few Late '40s Films

The following is a list of (a) movies which readers may have expected to find in the main section, and the reason for their exclusion; (b) movies which include some minor science fiction or fantasy elements (nonhorror films which nonetheless fall into the category of "cinema of the fantastic"); and (c) a few late '40s films that just missed the boat. They are in one alphabetical sequence, for convenience.

The Black Raven (PRC, 1943) Directed by Sam Newfield. Cast: George Zucco, Wanda McKay, Noel Madison, Robert Randall [Robert Livingston], Byron Foulger, Charlie [sic!] Middleton, Robert Middlemass, Glenn Strange, I. Stanford Jolley. Often listed as a horror film by people who would like it to be one, this is just a murder mystery with a cast of horror movie semi-regulars. Zucco, proprietor of the Black Raven country inn, has a sideline of smuggling lawbreakers up into Canada; murder occurs beneath his roof one rainy night. Zucco and Glenn Strange (as Zucco's dimwitted handyman) are reteamed after *The Mad Monster*. Fans partial to the cast should enjoy it.

The Brute Man (PRC, 1946) Directed by Jean Yarbrough. Cast: Rondo Hatton, Tom Neal, Jan Wiley, Jane Adams, Donald MacBride, Peter Whitney, Fred Coby, Beatrice Roberts, John Hamilton, Tristram Coffin. Made by Universal, but sold to PRC in the face of Universal's impending merger with International Pictures and its new policy of no-more-B-pics. Hatton, real-life victim of acromegaly, gives his worst-ever performance as a deranged killer in this unbelievably tacky film which even weaves into its story details from Hatton's personal life! Hatton died from the cumulative effects of acromegaly ten months before the film's release.

Chamber of Horrors (Monogram, 1940) Directed by Norman Lee. Cast: Lilli Palmer, Leslie Banks, Gina Malo, R. Montgomery, Richard Bird, Romill Lange, David Horne, Cathleen Nesbitt, J. H. Roberts, Harry Hutchinson, Phil Ray, Ross Landon. A sadistic doctor (Banks) kills off the heirs to an English estate and kidnaps an heiress (Palmer). Co-written by director Lee (from a story by Edgar Wallace), this is the Monogram release of

A police trap snares mad killer Rondo Hatton in the incredibly dull wrap-up of *The Brute Man,* a Universal film peddled to PRC for release. The plainclothes cops are Peter Whitney and Donald MacBride; the girl, Jane Adams.

the British-made *The Door with Seven Locks.* "There's about enough in the picture for an hour's thriller. Rest is waste." – *Variety.*

The Enchanted Forest (PRC, 1945) Directed by Lew Landers. Cast: Edmund Lowe, Brenda Joyce, Billy Severn, Harry Davenport, John Litel, Clancy Cooper. An old forest hermit (Davenport) seems to talk with woodland critters and hear the music of the trees in a Disney-esque "prestige" picture for PRC. Shot in Cinecolor.

The Ghost and the Guest (PRC, 1943) Directed by William Nigh. Cast: James Dunn, Florence Rice, Mabel Todd, Sam McDaniel, Robert Dudley, Eddie Chandler, Robert Bice, Tony Warde, Anthony Caruso. No ghost; lotsa guests. A newly-married Manhattan couple (Dunn, Rice) move into an old country house overrun by gangsters, dumb cops and other zany characters. Scripted by Morey Amsterdam, and enthusiastically acted by Dunn (two years away from his *A Tree Grows in Brooklyn* Oscar), it's a fun and lively 59 minutes, but having "ghost" in the title is a definite cheat.

The Ghost Goes Wild (Republic, 1947) Directed by George Blair. Cast: James Ellison, Anne Gwynne, Edward Everett Horton, Ruth Donnelly, Stephanie Bachelor, Grant Withers, Lloyd Corrigan, Charles Halton, Holmes Herbert, Olaf Hytten, Pierre Watkin. A ghost comedy, about as funny as a cry for help. Taking advantage of the false report of his death, artist James Ellison poses as a spook (for reasons not worth going into). A real ghost (Lloyd Corrigan) adds to "the fun." Loaded with ham actors, endless contrivances, boy-girl stuff and an irritating whimsical score. Anne Gwynne recently reminisced, "Yuck...I thought it was embarrassing."

Ghost Town Law (Monogram, 1942) Directed by Howard Bretherton. Cast: Buck Jones, Tim McCoy, Raymond Hatton, Virginia Carpenter, Murdock McQuarrie, Charles King. A gang of desperadoes try to scare people away from their hideout with fake ghosts. "An attempt to combine a Western with a mystery story has not fared too well in this Mono meller.... Masked riders prowling in black shadows, and sudden attempts at killings are all tossed into the melting plot without much rhyme or reason."— *Variety.*

Haunted House (Monogram, 1940) Directed by Robert McGowan. Cast: Jackie Moran, Marcia Mae Jones, George Cleveland, Henry Hall, John St. Polis, Jessie Arnold, Henry Roquemore. The first of many thoroughly mundane Poverty Row films of the '40s with unsuited, horrific-sounding titles. There's not a bit of horror content in this story of teenage sleuths (Moran, Jones) working to clear a friend accused of murder. Released in England as *The Blake Murder Mystery.*

His Brother's Ghost (PRC, 1945) Directed by Sam Newfield. Cast: Buster Crabbe, Al "Fuzzy" St. John, Charles King, Karl Hackett, Archie Hall. A gang of outlaws tries to drive out the local sharecroppers; hero Crabbe has the brother of a murdered man (both played by St. John) pose as his brother's ghost to scare the baddies. Only 52 minutes, and way too long at that. A number of other B- and Z-grade Westerns of the '40s have "supernatural"-sounding titles—*The Phantom Cowboy* (Republic, 1941), *Spook Town* (PRC, 1944), *Ghost of Hidden Valley* (PRC, 1946), on and on— but none of them has the least bit of horror or fantasy element.

How DOoo You Do (PRC, 1946) Directed by Ralph Murphy. Cast: Bert Gordon, Harry Von Zell, Cheryl Walker, Frank Albertson, Ella Mae Morse, Claire Windsor, Keye Luke, Charles Middleton, Thomas Jackson. When a much-hated radio agent dies mysteriously at a desert resort, airwave star Bert Gordon wires his screen detective friends to come out and solve the case. The dead man comes back to life—but only because his earlier appearance of death had been caused by an experimental drug.

The Human Monster (Monogram, 1940) Directed by Walter Summers. Cast: Bela Lugosi, Hugh Williams, Greta Gynt, Edmon Ryan, Wilfred Walter, Alexander Field, Arthur E. Owne. The best horror film released by Monogram in the '40s; too bad they had nothing to do with the making of it. In this British-made chiller, based on an Edgar Wallace novel and released in the U.K. as *The Dark Eyes of London*, Lugosi is an insurance swindler who sends his brutish blind henchman (Walter) out to kill people whose insurance policies have been signed over to him. The horror scenes

EXCLUSIONS AND BORDERLINE INCLUSIONS

are strong and the picture appealingly unpleasant. The plot was faintly echoed in Monogram's *Bowery at Midnight* in 1942; the Wallace novel was filmed a second time, in West Germany in 1961 (*Dead Eyes of London*). In December, 1939, *Dark Eyes* producer John Argyle tried to induce Lugosi to return to England to make another film for him; possibly Bela declined because of the way the war was developing.

The Invisible Killer (Producers Distributing Corp. [PRC], 1940) Directed by Sherman Scott [Sam Newfield]. Cast: Grace Bradley, Roland Drew, William Newell, Boyd Irwin, Jeanne Kelly [Jean Brooks], Crane Whitley, Harry Worth. A police crackdown on a gambling syndicate is punctuated by several mysterious murders, apparently the work of an invisible killer. Deadly gas emanating from the mouthpieces of telephones is the actual cause of death, and a girl reporter helps her detective boyfriend land the culprit. Neither horror nor SF. Based on the novel *Murder for Millions;* shot in November 1939.

The Jade Mask (Monogram, 1945) Directed by Phil Rosen. Cast: Sidney Toler (as Charlie Chan), Mantan Moreland, Edwin Luke (Keye's brother), Hardie Albright, Frank Reicher, Janet Warren, Cyril Delevanti, Alan Bridge, Joe Whitehead. At his isolated country home, a scientist (Reicher) develops a gas process that hardens wood to the toughness and durability of steel; there's no shortage of suspects when the nasty old coot is killed. This ludicrous Chan entry briefly features a "walking" corpse (seen only minutes after one of the suspects gives their occupation as puppeteer – enough said?). And why the hell, after all these years, does Chan still talk like he just got off the boat? Shot in September 1944, as *Mystery Mansion*.

Johnny Doesn't Live Here Anymore (Monogram, 1944) Directed by Joe May. Cast: Simone Simon, James Ellison, William Terry, Minna Gombell, Chick Chandler, Alan Dinehart, Gladys Blake, Robert Mitchum, Janet Shaw. Bedroom comedy about a defense plant worker (Simon) who must choose between Marine Terry and his sailor-buddy Ellison. Midget Jerry Maren, a regular on television's *The Gong Show*, has a bit part as a bad-luck gremlin, as does Rondo Hatton (as an undertaker). Reissued as *And So They Were Married*.

The Living Ghost (Monogram, 1942) Directed by William Beaudine. Cast: James Dunn, Joan Woodbury, Jan Wiley, Paul McVey, Minerva Urecal, George Eldredge, Lawrence Grant, Forrest Taylor. Monogram really played this one up as though it was a horror film, with ad lines like "Is He Man or Zombie?" and "The Nightmare of the Month!... A mad killer who transforms his victims into white ZOMBIES!" It's really just a trite whodunit, further dampened by lots of idiot comedy. A wealthy man (Gus Glassmire) vanishes, then turns up again later in a sleepwalker-like state due to a brain injury; sleuth James Dunn unravels the mystery. The misleading title and a short scene in a spooky rainswept house (mostly played for laughs, and featuring an unbilled Frank Moran) hardly qualify it

for inclusion here. Dunn later starred in PRC's *The Ghost and the Guest*, also non-horror despite the title.

London Blackout Murders (Republic, 1942) Directed by George Sherman. Cast: John Abbott, Mary McLeod, Lloyd Corrigan, Lester Matthews, Anita Bolster, Billy Bevan, Lumsden Hare, Keith Hitchcock, Tom Stevenson. A series of murders takes place under cover of the London blackouts. À la *Black Dragons*, the victims turn out to have been men engaged in sabotaging Britain's war effort. The film also includes talk about Jack the Ripper, and the rumor that the scene of one of his murders is now haunted. Screenplay by Curt Siodmak.

Macbeth (Republic, 1948) Directed by Orson Welles. Cast: Orson Welles, Jeanette Nolan, Dan O'Herlihy, Edgar Barrier, Roddy McDowall, Robert Coote, Erskine Sanford, Alan Napier, John Dierkes, William Alland. Witches, prophecies, ghosts and all that other good stuff in Welles' intriguing but bizarre adaptation of Shakespeare's enduring tale. A big part of the reason this book cuts off in 1946 instead of tackling the entire decade of the '40s is because this author had no intention of taking flak for shoehorning this Welles classic in with *Dead Men Walk* and *Spooks Run Wild*!

The Main Street Kid (Republic, 1948) Directed by R. G. Springsteen. Cast: Al Pearce, Janet Martin, Alan Mowbray, Adele Mara, Arlene Harris, Emil Rameau, Byron S. Barr, Douglas Evans, Roy Barcroft, Dick Elliott. Pearce, a small town print shop owner, finds he is able to

Left: In the 1940s, ads like this sometimes lured thriller fans into theaters showing whodunits or comedies with few (or no) horror elements. *The Living Ghost* was a lightweight mystery.

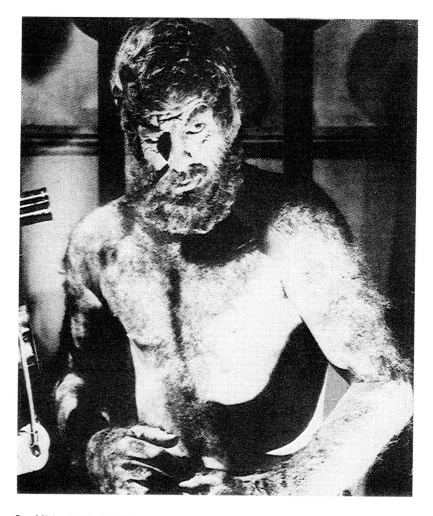

In addition to his *Mad Monster* and Frankenstein roles, burly Glenn Strange was also an imposing presence as the monstrous Atlas in the Bowery Boys' *Master Minds* (pictured).

read other people's minds after receiving a blow on the head. Based on a radio play by Caryl Coleman.

The Mask of Diijon (PRC, 1946) Directed by Lew Landers. Cast: Erich von Stroheim, Jeanne Bates, William Wright, Edward Van Sloan, Mauritz Hugo, Denise Varnac, Anthony Warde. Somber melodrama about a magician (von Stroheim) using his newly-developed powers of mesmerism in an attempt to force his wife (Bates) to commit murder. In an implausible and morbid final touch, von Stroheim, fleeing from the law, manages to accidentally throw himself onto a guillotine which lops off his head!

Master Minds (Monogram, 1949) Directed by Jean Yarbrough. Cast: Leo Gorcey, Huntz Hall, Gabriel Dell, Alan Napier, Jane Adams, Billy Benedict, Bernard Gorcey, Glenn Strange, Skelton Knaggs, Minerva Urecal. When a toothache turns Sach (Hall) into a fortune teller, the rest of the Bowery Boys put him in a carnival (promoting him as Ali Ben Sachmo, the Bowery Prophet). Catching wind of this, kooky scientist Alan Napier kidnaps Hall with the intention of electronically switching Hall's brain into the head of Atlas (Glenn Strange), a primitive *Island of Lost Souls*-style man-monster. It's fun (but not funny), after the switch is made, to watch Strange's impersonation of Hall, complete with Hall's (dubbed-in) voice, fluttering hands and mildly effeminate gestures. The makeup on Strange, applied by Jack P. Pierce (hair from the waist up, a bushy beard and dark facial makeup) took three hours to apply and one to remove. Whoever wrote the film's pressbook apparently thought Strange played the Wolf Man at Universal. A not-bad cast for a picture of this sort (Strange, Adams and Knaggs reunited four years after *House of Dracula!*), but it's just another one of the Bowery Boys' umpteen haunted house movies and it gets real tiresome, real quick.

Mr. Hex (Monogram, 1946) Directed by (who else?) William Beaudine. Cast: Leo Gorcey, Huntz Hall, Bobby Jordan, Gabriel Dell, Billy Benedict, David Gorcey, Gale Robbins, Ben Welden, Ian Keith, Bernard Gorcey, Gene Stutenroth (Roth). Not-bad Bowery Boys extravaganza with Hall, hypnotized into believing he's as strong as ten men, going into an amateur boxing contest. Written and associate-produced by Cyril Endfield, director of *Zulu* (1964) and *De Sade* (1969), and inventor of the computerized pocket-sized typewriter.

Mystery of the 13th Guest (Monogram, 1943) Directed by William Beaudine. Cast: Dick Purcell, Helen Parrish, Tim Ryan, Frank Faylen, John Duncan, Paul McKay, Jacqueline Dalya, Addison Richards, Lester Dorr, Donald Kerr. "13 guests assembled in a ghostly mansion ... one of them a fiendish killer!" the poster promised; but horror fans thusly lured into the theater got a hackneyed, draggy whodunit: A killer in a *Halloween*-style mask uses an electrified phone to zap visitors to an abandoned house. Based on the novel by Armitage (*Scarface*) Trail, and previously filmed as *The Thirteenth Guest* (1932) with Ginger Rogers and Lyle Talbot. *Mystery*'s musical score was lifted from *Revenge of the Zombies*.

Nabonga (PRC, 1944) Directed by Sam Newfield. Cast: Buster Crabbe, Fifi D'Orsay, Barton MacLane, Julie London, Bryant Washburn, Herbert Rawlinson, Jackie Newfield. In the Belgian Congo, a "nabonga" (native for "gorilla") protects and raises a young girl who grows up to be Julie London. "London, in her first film, hasn't much to do except slink around in a modified sarong and mouth an occasional phrase in pidgin English."– *Variety*. Shooting title: *Jungle Terror*.

Phantom Killer (Monogram, 1942) Directed by William Beaudine.

Monkey business with Fifi D'Orsay and simian friend on the set of PRC's *Nabonga.*

Cast: Dick Purcell, Joan Woodbury, John Hamilton, Warren Hymer, Kenneth Harlan, J. Farrell MacDonald, Mantan Moreland, George Lewis. A great lurid title squandered on a B mystery. The stars of *King of the Zombies* – Purcell, Woodbury and Moreland – are reunited in this remake of Lionel Atwill's *The Sphinx* (1933), with Purcell as an ambitious D. A. who's convinced that the deaf-and-dumb Hamilton (Perry White on television's *Adventures of Superman*) is guilty of murder.

The Phantom of 42nd Street (PRC, 1945) Directed by Albert Herman. Cast: Dave O'Brien, Kay Aldridge, Alan Mowbray, Frank Jenks, Jack Mulhall, Stanley Price, John Crawford, Cyril Delevanti. Murder at a Broadway theater is investigated and solved by a drama critic (Dave O'Brien) turned detective.

The Spell of Amy Nugent (PRC, 1945) Directed by John Harlow. Cast: Derek Farr, Vera Lindsay, Frederick Leister, Hay Petrie, Felix Aylmer, Joyce Redman, Diana King. A 1940 British fantasy/horror film called *Spellbound,* reaching U.S. shores five years later. A young university student (Farr) grieving over the death of his girlfriend turns to spiritualism and materializes her at a séance. The movie was banned in England on the grounds that it would offend spiritualists(!) until one (Hannen Swaffer) came forward pleading for its release, and even agreeing to appear in a foreword. Screenplay by Miles Malleson, based on the novel *The Necromancers* by Hugh Benson.

Strange Holiday (PRC, 1946) Directed by Arch Oboler. Cast: Claude Rains, Barbara Bates, Paul Hilton, Gloria Holden, Milton Kibbee, Bobbie Stebbins, Martin Kosleck. Released in England as *The Day After Tomorrow*. An "it-was-all-a-dream!" ending caps this account of an American businessman (Rains) who returns home from a long vacation to discover that a Fascist dictatorship has replaced democracy. Originally a commercial film, shot in 1940 to boost the morale of General Motors workers; G.M. shelved it, then it was sold by Oboler to MGM, who did the same thing! A later short, *Red Nightmare* (Warner Bros., ca. 1960), starring Jack Kelly and Jeanne Cooper and "hosted" by Jack Webb, was pretty much the same thing all over again, but with Russkies instead of Nazis.

Strange Illusion (PRC, 1945) Directed by Edgar G. Ulmer. Cast: James Lydon, Warren William, Sally Eilers, Regis Toomey, Charles Arnt, George H. Reed, Pierre Watkin, John Hamilton, Sonia Sorel. Also released as *Out of the Night*, this one combines elements from *Hamlet* with a mild fantasy element as a youth (Lydon) seeks to prove that his father was murdered.

The Strange Mr. Gregory (Monogram, 1945) Directed by Phil Rosen. Cast: Edmund Lowe, Jean Rogers, Don Douglas, Frank Reicher, Marjorie Hoshelle, Robert Emmett Keane, Jonathan Hale, Fred Kelsey, Jack Norton. A magician (Lowe) who's supposedly been murdered poses as his own nonexistent brother and tries to pin the nonexistent killing on a romantic rival. Nonexistent thrills. Shooting title: *Gregory*.

The Strangler (PRC, 1942) Directed by Harold Huth. Cast: Judy Campbell, Sebastian Shaw, Niall MacGinnis, Henry Edwards, George Pughe, Martita Hunt. In the Soho quarter of London, a killer uses silk stockings to strangle wayward women; a girl crime reporter (Campbell) fingers an innocent man (Pughe). PRC release of an English mystery (their title: *East of Piccadilly*).

Terror House (PRC, 1943) Directed by Leslie Arliss. Cast: James Mason, Wilfred Lawson, Mary Clare, Joyce Howard, Tucker McGuire, John Fernald. Living the life of a recluse in a great house on the swampy moors, Mason is a music composer who fears that he's committed a murder during a mental blackout. English-made (as *The Night Has Eyes*), it's stagey and slow, but the finale lifts it up out of the rut a bit. In his autobiography, James Mason called it "an effective and rather original thriller."

Tower of Terror (Monogram, 1942) Directed by Lawrence Huntington. Cast: Wilfred Lawson, Movita, Michael Rennie, Morland Graham, George

Woodbridge, Edward Sinclair, Richard George. A few minor horror touches in a confused English-made World War II tale of strange goings-on at a lighthouse on a German island. "When the British make a horror picture, it usually is either god-awful or excellent," wrote *Variety*'s Wear. "This is the former."

White Pongo (PRC, 1945) Directed by Sam Newfield. Cast: Richard Fraser, Maris Wrixon, Lionel Royce, Al Eben, Gordon Richards, Michael Dyne, George Lloyd, Egon Brecher. A safari adventure segues into a *Kong*-type Beauty and the Beast story when a white gorilla (the Missing Link) abducts the daughter (Maris Wrixon) of the expedition leader. Occasionally bogged down by antique wildlife footage and comedy relief, and a bit overlong (77 minutes), it still dishes up some good, hokey fun. Richard Fraser later played the Quaker in Val Lewton's *Bedlam* (1946). "Excepting Fraser and Wrixon, rest of the cast constitutes some of the most wooden-faced actors seen on the screen."–*Variety* Shooting title: *Congo Pongo*.

The Woman Who Came Back (Republic, 1945) Directed by Walter Colmes. Cast: Nancy Kelly, John Loder, Otto Kruger, Ruth Ford, J. Farrell MacDonald, Harry Tyler, Almira Sessions. An independent production released through Republic, this imitation-Lewton chiller is probably Republic's best horror film. A descendant (Nancy Kelly) of a witch-hanging judge becomes obsessed with fears that she is possessed by a witch's vengeful spirit. After a great start, the film winds down into a lot of anxiety attacks, mumbo-jumbo and small town spook-talk. But as a minor-league Lewton homage, it rates an A for effort.

Appendix III: Filmographies
Compiled by Tom Weaver, John Cocchi and Jack Dukesbery

Following are complete filmographies for 35 actors and actresses who worked in B-grade horror films at Monogram, PRC and Republic and in the horror films made by the B units at other '40s studios. Karloff, Lugosi, Atwill and Carradine, their lists of credits done to death in many other books and magazines, have been excluded.

John Abbott (1905–)

Conquest of the Air (United Artists, 1936)
Mademoiselle Docteur (United Artists, 1937; U.S.: *Under Secret Orders* [Guaranteed, 1943])
The Saint in London (RKO, 1939)
Ten Days in Paris (British: Columbia, 1939; U.S.: *Missing Ten Days* [Columbia, 1941])
The Shanghai Gesture (United Artists, 1941)
This Above All (20th Century–Fox, 1942)
Joan of Paris (RKO, 1942)
Rubber Racketeers (Monogram, 1942)
London Blackout Murders (Secret Motive) (Republic, 1942)
Mrs. Miniver (MGM, 1942)
Get Hep to Love (Universal, 1942)
Nightmare (Universal, 1942)
Dangerous Blondes (Columbia, 1943)
The Gorilla Man (Warner Bros., 1943)
They Got Me Covered (RKO, 1943)
Mission to Moscow (Warner Bros., 1943)
Once Upon a Time (Columbia, 1944)
Cry of the Werewolf (Columbia, 1944)
Jane Eyre (20th Century–Fox, 1944)
The Mask of Dimitrios (Warner Bros., 1944)
Summer Storm (United Artists, 1944)
Abroad with Two Yanks (United Artists, 1944)

The Falcon in Hollywood (RKO, 1944)
Secrets of Scotland Yard (Republic, 1944)
U-Boat Prisoner (Columbia, 1944)
End of the Road (Republic, 1944)
Honeymoon Ahead (Universal, 1945)
A Thousand and One Nights (Columbia, 1945)
Saratoga Trunk (Warner Bros., 1945)
The Vampire's Ghost (Republic, 1945)
Pursuit to Algiers (Universal, 1945)
Crime Doctor's Warning (Columbia, 1945)
Scotland Yard Investigator (Republic, 1945)
The Power of the Whistler (Columbia, 1945)
Deception (Warner Bros., 1946)
Anna and the King of Siam (20th Century–Fox, 1946)
The Bandit of Sherwood Forest (Columbia, 1946)
One More Tomorrow (Warner Bros., 1946)
Humoresque (Warner Bros., 1946)
The Notorious Lone Wolf (Columbia, 1946)
Time Out of Mind (Universal, 1947)
The Web (Universal, 1947)
Adventure Island (Paramount, 1947)
If Winter Comes (MGM, 1947)
The Woman in White (Warner Bros., 1948)

Bug-eyed vampire John Abbott bares the throat of swooned leading lady Peggy Stewart in the anemic *The Vampire's Ghost.*

Madame Bovary (MGM, 1949)
Her Wonderful Lie (Columbia, 1950)
Sideshow (Monogram, 1950)
Navy Bound (Monogram, 1951)
Thunder on the Hill (Universal, 1951)
Crosswinds (Paramount, 1951)
The Merry Widow (MGM, 1952)
Rogue's March (MGM, 1952)
The Steel Lady (United Artists, 1953)
Thunder in the East (Paramount, 1953)
Sombrero (MGM, 1953)
Public Pigeon No. One (Universal, 1957)

Omar Khayyam (Paramount, 1957)
Gigi (MGM, 1958)
Who's Minding the Store? (Paramount, 1963)
The Greatest Story Ever Told (United Artists, 1965)
Gambit (Universal, 1966)
The Jungle Book (voice only; Buena Vista, 1967)
Three Guns for Texas (Universal, 1968)
2000 Years Later (Warner Bros., 1969)

The Black Bird (Columbia, 1975)
Slapstick (Of Another Kind) (Entertainment Releasing/International Film Marketing, 1984)

Tod Andrews (1920–1972)

As Michael Ames

International Squadron (Warner bros., 1941)
Dive Bomber (Warner Bros., 1941)
They Died with Their Boots On (Warner Bros., 1941)
The Body Disappears (Warner Bros., 1941)
Dangerously They Live (Warner Bros., 1941)
Spy Ship (Warner Bros., 1942)
Bullet Scars (Warner Bros., 1942)
Men of the Sky (Warner Bros. short, 1942)
The Male Animal (Warner Bros., 1942)
Captains of the Clouds (Warner Bros., 1942)
Murder in the Big House (Born for Trouble) (Warner Bros., 1942)
I Was Framed (Warner Bros., 1942)
Now, Voyager (Warner Bros., 1942)
Truck Busters (Warner Bros., 1943)
Action in the North Atlantic (Warner Bros., 1943)
Heaven Can Wait (20th Century-Fox, 1943)
The Last Ride (Warner Bros., 1944)
Return of the Ape Man (Monogram, 1944)
Voodoo Man (Monogram, 1944)

As Tod Andrews

Outrage (RKO, 1950)
Between Heaven and Hell (20th Century-Fox, 1956)
From Hell It Came (Allied Artists, 1957)
In Harm's Way (Paramount, 1965)
Hang 'Em High (United Artists, 1968)
Beneath the Planet of the Apes (20th Century-Fox, 1970)

John Archer (1915–)

As Ralph Bowman

Flaming Frontiers (Universal serial, 1938)

Letter of Introduction (Universal, 1938)
Overland Stage Raiders (Republic, 1938)
Dick Tracy Returns (Republic serial, 1938)
Spring Madness (MGM, 1938)
Barnyard Follies (Republic, 1940)
Cheers for Miss Bishop (United Artists, 1941)

As John Archer

Career (RKO, 1939)
Curtain Call (RKO, 1940)
City of Missing Girls (Select, 1941)
Mountain Moonlight (Republic, 1941)
King of the Zombies (Monogram, 1941)
Scattergood Baines (RKO, 1941)
Paper Bullets (Gangs Incorporated) (PRC, 1941)
Highway West (Warner Bros., 1941)
Sucker List (MGM short, 1941)
Hi, Neighbor (Republic, 1942)
Bowery at Midnight (Monogram, 1942)
Mrs. Wiggs of the Cabbage Patch (Paramount, 1942)
Scattergood Survives a Murder (RKO, 1942)
Police Bullets (Monogram, 1942)
Shantytown (Republic, 1943)
The Purple V (Republic, 1943)
Crash Dive (20th Century-Fox, 1943)
Guadalcanal Diary (20th Century-Fox, 1943)
Hello Frisco, Hello (20th Century-Fox, 1943)
Sherlock Holmes in Washington (Universal, 1943)
The Eve of St. Mark (20th Century-Fox, 1944)
Roger Touhy, Gangster (20th Century-Fox, 1944)
No Exceptions (20th Century-Fox/Office of War Information short, 1944)
I'll Remember April (Universal, 1945)
The Lost Moment (Universal, 1947)
Colorado Territory (Warner Bros., 1949)
White Heat (Warner Bros., 1949)
Destination Moon (Eagle-Lion, 1950)
The Great Jewel Robber (Warner Bros., 1950)

High Lonesome (Eagle-Lion, 1950)
My Favorite Spy (Paramount, 1951)
Best of the Badmen (RKO, 1951)
Santa Fe (Columbia, 1951)
Rodeo (Monogram, 1951)
The Big Trees (Warner Bros., 1952)
Sea Tiger (Monogram, 1952)
A Yank in Indo-China (Columbia, 1952)
Sound Off (Columbia, 1952)
The Stars Are Singing (Paramount, 1953)
Dragon's Gold (United Artists, 1954)
No Man's Woman (Republic, 1955)
Emergency Hospital (United Artists, 1956)
Rock Around the Clock (Columbia, 1956)
Three Brave Men (20th Century-Fox, 1957)
Affair in Reno (Republic, 1957)
She Devil (20th Century-Fox, 1957)
Decision at Sundown (Columbia, 1957)
Ten Thousand Bedrooms (MGM, 1957)
City of Fear (Columbia, 1959)
Blue Hawaii (Paramount, 1961)
Apache Rifles (20th Century-Fox, 1964)
I Saw What You Did (Universal, 1965)
How to Frame a Figg (Universal, 1971)

Joan Barclay

As **Geraine Greear** (her real name; sometimes misspelled **Grear**)

The Gaucho (United Artists, 1927
I Am a Fugitive from a Chain Gang (Warner Bros., 1932)
42nd Street (Warner Bros., 1933)
The Little Giant (Warner Bros., 1933)
The Life of Jimmy Dolan (Warner Bros., 1933)
Gold Diggers of 1933 (Warner Bros., 1933)
Baby Face (Warner Bros., 1933)
Private Detective 62 (Man Killer) (Warner Bros., 1933)
Dames (Warner Bros., 1934)
Finishing School (RKO, 1934)

Madame Du Barry (Warner Bros., 1934)
The St. Louis Kid (Warner Bros., 1934)
Harold Teen (Warner Bros., 1934)
The Firebird (Warner Bros., 1934)
Sweet Music (Warner Bros., 1935)
Gold Diggers of 1935 (Warner Bros., 1935)
Moonlight on the Prairie (Warner Bros., 1935)
Broadway Hostess (Warner Bros., 1935)
Stranded (Warner Bros., 1935)
Shipmates Forever (Warner Bros., 1935)
The Murder of Dr. Harrigan (Warner Bros., 1935)
In Caliente (Warner Bros., 1935)
Strike Me Pink (United Artists, 1936)
Ridin' On (Reliable/William Steiner, 1936)
Carnival Day (Warner Bros./Vitaphone short, 1936)

As **Joan Clayton**

Convict's Code (Monogram, 1939)

As **Mary Douglas**

Riding the Wind (RKO, 1941)

As **Joan Barclay**

Feud of the West (Division, 1936)
Prison Shadows (Mercury/Puritan, 1936)
The Glory Trail (Crescent, 1936)
The Dancing Pirate (RKO, 1936)
Missing Girls (Chesterfield, 1936)
Dodsworth (United Artists, 1936)
West of Nevada (Colony, 1936)
The Kid Ranger (Supreme/William Steiner, 1936)
Phantom Patrol (Ambassador, 1936)
Men of the Plains (Colony, 1936)
Colleen (Warner Bros., 1936)
Shadow of Chinatown (Victory serial, 1936)
Follow Your Heart (Republic, 1936)
Island Captives (Principal, 1937)
The Trusted Outlaw (Republic, 1937)
Million Dollar Racket (Victory, 1937)
Harris in the Spring (RKO short, 1937)

Beauty and the beast: Joan Barclay seems intent on catching the eye of Bela Lugosi in a behind-the-scenes shot from *Black Dragons*.

Sky Racket (Victory, 1937)
Blake of Scotland Yard (Victory serial, 1937)
The Singing Outlaw (Universal, 1938)
Lightning Carson Rides Again (Victory, 1938)
Pioneer Trail (Columbia, 1938)
The Purple Vigilantes (Republic, 1938)
Whirlwind Horseman (Grand National, 1938)
Two Gun Justice (Monogram, 1938)
Sweethearts (MGM, 1938)
Outlaw's Paradise (Victory, 1939)
Texas Wildcats (Victory, 1939)

Six-Gun Rhythm (Grand National, 1939)
Billy the Kid's Range War (PRC, 1941)
Flying Wild (Monogram, 1941)
Ziegfeld Girl (MGM, 1941)
Love Crazy (MGM, 1941)
The Trial of Mary Dugan (MGM, 1941)
Man I Cured (RKO short, 1941)
Bandit Ranger (RKO, 1942)
Mr. Wise Guy (Monogram, 1942)
Black Dragons (Monogram, 1942)
Pretty Dolly (RKO short, 1942)
The Corpse Vanishes (Monogram, 1942)

Ladies' Day (RKO, 1943)
Rookies in Burma (RKO, 1943)
Sagebrush Law (RKO, 1943)
This Land Is Mine (RKO, 1943)
Bombardier (RKO, 1943)
The Falcon in Danger (RKO, 1943)
Gildersleeve's Bad Day (RKO, 1943)
Mexican Spitfire's Blessed Event (RKO, 1943)
The Seventh Victim (RKO, 1943)
The Falcon Strikes Back (RKO, 1943)
Around the World (RKO, 1943)
My Pal, Wolf (RKO, 1944)
Girls, Girls, Girls (RKO short, 1944)
Step Lively (RKO, 1944)
Music in Manhattan (RKO, 1944)
Youth Runs Wild (RKO, 1944)
The Falcon Out West (RKO, 1944)
The Shanghai Cobra (Monogram, 1945)
The poster for *The Corpse Vanishes*, prominently featuring Barclay, is on display outside a theater during a street scene in *Bowery at Midnight* (Monogram, 1942).

Billy Benedict (1917–   )

$10 Raise (Fox, 1935)
The Farmer Takes a Wife (Fox, 1935)
Steamboat 'Round the Bend (Fox, 1935)
Doubting Thomas (Fox, 1935)
Ladies Love Danger (Fox, 1935)
College Scandal (Paramount, 1935)
Silk Hat Kid (Fox, 1935)
Way Down East (Fox, 1935)
Welcome Home (20th Century–Fox, 1935)
Your Uncle Dudley (Fox, 1935)
Show Them No Mercy (Fox, 1935)
Three Kids and a Queen (Universal, 1935)
Can This Be Dixie (20th Century–Fox, 1936)
Meet Nero Wolfe (Columbia, 1936)
The Country Doctor (20th Century–Fox, 1936)
Theodora Goes Wild (Columbia, 1936)
Adventure in Manhattan (Columbia, 1936)
Crack-Up (20th Century–Fox, 1936)

After the Thin Man (MGM, 1936)
Ramona (20th Century–Fox, 1936)
M'Liss (RKO, 1936)
The Witness Chair (RKO, 1936)
Libeled Lady (MGM, 1936)
Captain January (20th Century–Fox, 1936)
They Wanted to Marry (RKO, 1937)
The Last Gangster (MGM, 1937)
Jim Hanvey–Detective (Republic, 1937)
Rhythm in the Clouds (Republic, 1937)
That I May Live (20th Century–Fox, 1937)
Love in a Bungalow (Universal, 1937)
Tim Tyler's Luck (Universal serial, 1937)
Laughing at Trouble (20th Century–Fox, 1937)
The Road Back (Universal, 1937)
Tramp Trouble (RKO short, 1937)
There's Always a Woman (Columbia, 1938)
Hold That Co-ed (20th Century–Fox, 1938)
Bringing Up Baby (RKO, 1938)
Say It in French (Paramount, 1938)
Walking Down Broadway (20th Century–Fox, 1938)
Young Fugitives (Universal, 1938)
King of the Newsboys (Republic, 1938)
Little Tough Guys in Society (Universal, 1938)
I Met My Love Again (United Artists, 1938)
Pack Up Your Troubles (20th Century–Fox, 1939)
Newsboys' Home (Universal, 1939)
Timber Stampede (RKO, 1939)
Code of the Streets (Universal, 1939)
Call a Messenger (Universal, 1939)
Man of Conquest (Republic, 1939)
Hollywood Hobbies (MGM short, 1939)
The Bowery Boy (Republic, 1940)
Legion of the Lawless (RKO, 1940)
My Little Chickadee (Universal, 1940)
Adventures of Red Ryder (Republic serial, 1940)
Lucky Partners (RKO, 1940)
Rhythm on the River (Paramount, 1940)
Grand Ole Opry (Republic, 1940)
Second Chorus (Paramount, 1940)

Young People (20th Century-Fox, 1940)

Melody Ranch (Republic, 1940)

Give Us Wings (Universal, 1940)

Chicken Feed (RKO short, 1940)

And One Was Beautiful (MGM, 1940)

Citadel of Crime (Republic, 1941)

In Old Cheyenne (Republic, 1941)

The Richest Man in Town (Columbia, 1941)

Jesse James at Bay (Republic, 1941)

She Knew All the Answers (Columbia, 1941)

Unholy Partners (MGM, 1941)

The Man Who Lost Himself (Universal, 1941)

Variety Reels (Meet the Stars series) (Republic short, 1941)

Mr. District Attorney (Republic, 1941)

Bad Man of Deadwood (Republic, 1941)

Great Guns (20th Century-Fox, 1941)

Adventures of Captain Marvel (Return of Captain Marvel) (Republic serial, 1941)

The Great Mr. Nobody (Warner Bros., 1941)

The Mad Doctor (Paramount, 1941)

Tuxedo Junction (Republic, 1941)

Time Out for Rhythm (Columbia, 1941)

Confessions of Boston Blackie (Columbia, 1941)

Dressed to Kill (20th Century-Fox, 1941)

Home in Wyomin' (Republic, 1942)

Talk of the Town (Columbia, 1942)

A Night to Remember (Columbia, 1942)

Valley of Hunted Men (Republic, 1942)

Right to the Heart (20th Century-Fox, 1942)

A Tragedy at Midnight (Republic, 1942)

On the Sunny Side (20th Century-Fox, 1942)

Junior "G" Men of the Air (Universal serial, 1942)

Get Hep to Love (Universal, 1942)

Perils of Nyoka (Nyoka and the Tigermen) (Republic serial, 1942)

Rings on Her Fingers (20th Century-Fox, 1942)

Lady in a Jam (Universal, 1942)

The Glass Key (Paramount, 1942)

Wildcat (Paramount, 1942)

Two Yanks in Trinidad (Columbia, 1942)

Mrs. Wiggs of the Cabbage Patch (Paramount, 1942)

Almost Married (Universal, 1942)

Heart of the Golden West (Republic, 1942)

Affairs of Jimmy Valentine (Unforgotten Crime) (Republic, 1942)

Thank Your Lucky Stars (Warner Bros., 1943)

Clancy Street Boys (Monogram, 1943)

Aerial Gunner (Paramount, 1943)

Hangmen Also Die! (United Artists, 1943)

Mr. Muggs Steps Out (Monogram, 1943)

Whispering Footsteps (Republic, 1943)

Adventures of the Flying Cadets (Universal serial, 1943)

Ghosts on the Loose (Monogram, 1943)

The Ox-Bow Incident (20th Century-Fox, 1943)

Moonlight in Vermont (Universal, 1943)

Nobody's Darling (Republic, 1943)

All By Myself (Universal, 1943)

Million Dollar Kid (Monogram, 1944)

The Lady and the Monster (Republic, 1944)

Janie (Warner Bros., 1944)

The Whistler (Columbia, 1944)

My Gal Loves Music (Universal, 1944)

Follow the Leader (Monogram, 1944)

Goodnight Sweetheart (Republic, 1944)

The Merry Monahans (Universal, 1944)

Block Busters (Monogram, 1944)

That's My Baby (Republic, 1944)

They Live in Fear (Columbia, 1944)

Cover Girl (Columbia, 1944)

Follow the Boys (Universal, 1944)

Bowery Champs (Monogram, 1944)

Night Club Girl (Universal, 1944)

Brenda Starr, Reporter (Columbia serial, 1945)

The Story of G.I. Joe (G.I. Joe) (United Artists, 1945)

Docks of New York (Monogram, 1945)

Mr. Muggs Rides Again (Monogram, 1945)

Patrick the Great (Universal, 1945)

Come Out Fighting (Monogram, 1945)

Road to Utopia (Paramount, 1945)

Hollywood and Vine (PRC, 1945)

A Boy, a Girl and a Dog (Film Classics, 1946)

Apart from his East Side Kids/Bowery Boys roles, Billy Benedict (right) played hero's-sidekick in serials like *Perils of Nyoka* (1942). His chimp friend is played by Professor.

One More Tomorrow (Warner Bros., 1946)
Live Wires (Monogram, 1946)
In Fast Company (Monogram, 1946)
Without Reservations (RKO, 1946)
Bowery Bombshell (Monogram, 1946)
Spook Busters (Monogram, 1946)

Mr. Hex (Monogram, 1946)
Gay Blades (Tournament Tempo) (Republic, 1946)
Do You Love Me? (20th Century-Fox, 1946)
Never Say Goodbye (Warner Bros., 1946)

The Kid from Brooklyn (RKO, 1946)
Hard Boiled Mahoney (Monogram, 1947)
The Hucksters (MGM, 1947)
Fun on a Weekend (United Artists, 1947)
Bowery Buckaroos (Monogram, 1947)
The Pilgrim Lady (Republic, 1947)
News Hounds (Monogram, 1947)
Merton of the Movies (MGM, 1947)
Jinx Money (Monogram, 1948)
Smugglers' Cove (Monogram, 1948)
Angels' Alley (Monogram, 1948)
Trouble Makers (Monogram, 1948)
Secret Service Investigator (Republic, 1948)
Night Wind (20th Century-Fox, 1948)
Fighting Fools (Monogram, 1949)
Hold That Baby! (Monogram, 1949)
Master Minds (Monogram, 1949)
Riders of the Pony Express (Kayson/Screencraft, 1949)
Angels in Disguise (Monogram, 1949)
Blonde Dynamite (Monogram, 1950)
Lucky Losers (Monogram, 1950)
Triple Trouble (Monogram, 1950)
Blues Busters (Monogram, 1950)
Bowery Battalion (Monogram, 1951)
Ghost Chasers (Monogram, 1951)
Let's Go Navy! (Monogram, 1951)
Crazy Over Horses (Monogram, 1951)
The Magnetic Monster (United Artists, 1953)
Bride of the Monster (Banner, 1956)
The Killing (United Artists, 1956)
Rally 'Round the Flag, Boys! (20th Century-Fox, 1958)
Last Train from Gun Hill (Paramount, 1959)
Lover Come Back (Universal, 1961)
Dear Heart (Warner Bros., 1964)
Harlow (Paramount, 1965)
Zebra in the Kitchen (MGM, 1965)
The Hallelujah Trail (United Artists, 1965)
Frankie and Johnny (United Artists, 1966)
What Am I Bid? (Emerson, 1967)
Funny Girl (Columbia, 1968)
Big Daddy (Paradise Road) (Syzygy/United, 1969)
Hello, Dolly (20th Century-Fox, 1969)
The Dirt Gang (AIP, 1972)

The Sting (Universal, 1973)
Homebodies (Embassy, 1974)
Farewell, My Lovely (Embassy, 1975)
Won Ton Ton, the Dog Who Saved Hollywood (Paramount, 1976)
Born Again (Embassy, 1978)
Benedict's footage was deleted from *Metropolitan* (20th Century-Fox, 1935).

Adrian Booth (1924–   )

As Virginia Pound

Hold 'Em Navy (Paramount, 1937)
Thrill of a Lifetime (Paramount, 1937)
The Buccaneer (Paramount, 1938)
Scandal Street (Paramount, 1938)
The Big Broadcast of 1938 (Paramount, 1938)
Mad About Music (Universal, 1938)

As Lorna Gray

Red River Range (Republic, 1938)
Adventure in Sahara (Columbia, 1938)
Good Girls Go to Paris (Columbia, 1939)
Flying G-Men (Columbia serial, 1939)
The Lone Wolf Spy Hunt (Columbia, 1939)
Outside These Walls (Columbia, 1939)
Missing Daughters (Columbia, 1939)
Pest from the West (Columbia short, 1939)
Skinny the Moocher (Columbia short, 1939)
Coast Guard (Columbia, 1939)
Those High Grey Walls (Columbia, 1939)
Oily to Bed, Oily to Rise (Columbia short, 1939)
Cafe Hostess (Columbia, 1939)
Three Sappy People (Columbia short, 1939)
Andy Clyde Gets Spring Chicken (Columbia short, 1939)
The Amazing Mr. Williams (Columbia, 1939)
The Man They Could Not Hang (Columbia, 1939)
Smashing the Spy Ring (Columbia, 1939)

Being equally adept at heroine *and* villainess roles, Adrian Booth had a leg up on most
B movie and serial actresses. Maybe *two* legs. She's seen here as the ruthless Vultura
in Republic's 15-episode *Perils of Nyoka* (1942).

Mr. Smith Goes to Washington (Columbia, 1939)
The Stranger from Texas (Columbia, 1939)
Convicted Woman (Columbia, 1940)
Deadwood Dick (Columbia serial, 1940)
Bullets for Rustlers (Columbia, 1940)
You Nazty Spy! (Columbia short, 1940)
Rockin' Thru the Rockies (Columbia short, 1940)
Drums of the Desert (Monogram, 1940)
Up in the Air (Monogram, 1940)
City Limits (Monogram, 1941)
Tuxedo Junction (Republic, 1941)
Father Steps Out (Monogram, 1941)
Perils of Nyoka (Nyoka and the Tigermen) (Republic serial, 1942)
Ridin' Down the Canyon (Republic, 1942)
O, My Darling Clementine (Republic, 1943)
So Proudly We Hail! (Paramount, 1943)
Captain America (Return of Captain America) (Republic serial, 1944)
The Adventures of Kitty O'Day (Monogram, 1944)
The Girl Who Dared (Republic, 1944)
Federal Operator 99 (Republic serial, 1945)
Fashion Model (Monogram, 1945)

As Adrian Booth

Dakota (Republic, 1945)
Tell It to a Star (Republic, 1945)
Daughter of Don Q (Republic serial, 1946)
Out California Way (Republic, 1946)
The Man from Rainbow Valley (Republic, 1946)
Valley of the Zombies (Republic, 1946)
Home on the Range (Republic, 1946)
Last Frontier Uprising (Republic, 1946)
Exposed (Republic, 1947)
Spoilers of the North (Republic, 1947)
Under Colorado Skies (Republic, 1947)
Along the Oregon Trail (Republic, 1947)

The Gallant Legion (Republic, 1948)
The Plunderers (Republic, 1948)
Lightnin' in the Forest (Republic, 1948)
California Firebrand (Republic, 1948)
Hideout (Republic, 1949)
The Last Bandit (Republic, 1949)
Brimstone (Republic, 1949)
Rock Island Trail (Republic, 1950)
The Savage Horde (Republic, 1950)
Oh! Susanna (Republic, 1951)
The Sea Hornet (Republic, 1951)
Yellow Fin (Monogram, 1951)
Stock footage of Booth from *Andy Clyde Gets Spring Chicken* can be seen in *Love's A-Poppin'* (Columbia short, 1953). Her short *You Nazty Spy!* is included in the compilation film *3 Stooges Follies* (Columbia, 1974).

Tristram Coffin (1909–1990)

The Saint Strikes Back (RKO, 1939)
Overland Mail (Monogram, 1939)
Irish Luck (Monogram, 1939)
Oklahoma Terror (Monogram, 1939)
Dick Tracy's G-Men (Republic serial, 1939)
The Fatal Hour (Mr. Wong at Headquarters) (Monogram, 1940)
Melody and Moonlight (Republic, 1940)
The Cowboy from Sundown (Monogram, 1940)
Hidden Enemy (Monogram, 1940)
On the Spot (Monogram, 1940)
The Bowery Boy (Republic, 1940)
Doomed to Die (Monogram, 1940)
Meet the Wildcat (Universal, 1940)
The Green Hornet Strikes Again (Universal serial, 1940)
Mysterious Dr. Satan (Republic serial, 1940)
Chasing Trouble (Monogram, 1940)
Rhythm of the Rio Grande (Monogram, 1940)
Arizona Frontier (Monogram, 1940)
Queen of the Yukon (Monogram, 1940)
West of Pinto Basin (Monogram, 1940)
Up in the Air (Monogram, 1940)
Holt of the Secret Service (Columbia serial, 1941)
Father Steps Out (Monogram, 1941)
King of Dodge City (Columbia, 1941)
They Met in Bombay (MGM, 1941)

Tonto Basin Outlaws (Monogram, 1941)
Appointment for Love (Universal, 1941)
Roaring Frontiers (Columbia, 1941)
Hard Guy (PRC, 1941)
Forbidden Trails (Monogram, 1941)
No Greater Sin (Social Enemy No. 1) (University Films, 1941)
Sky Raiders (Universal serial, 1941)
Arizona Bound (Monogram, 1941)
A Man Betrayed (Wheel of Fortune) (Republic, 1941)
You're Out of Luck (Monogram, 1941)
Let's Go Collegiate (Monogram, 1941)
Blossoms in the Dust (MGM, 1941)
Top Sergeant Mulligan (Monogram, 1941)
Sailors on Leave (Republic, 1941)
Tuxedo Junction (Republic, 1941)
Man with Two Faces (voice only; Monogram, 1942)
A Tragedy at Midnight (Republic, 1942)
Police Bullets (Monogram, 1942)
Cowboy Serenade (Republic, 1942)
The Corpse Vanishes (Monogram, 1942)
Perils of Nyoka (Nyoka and the Tigermen) (Republic serial, 1942)
Spy Smasher (Republic serial, 1942)
Meet the Mob (So's Your Aunt Emma) (Monogram, 1942)
Bells of Capistrano (Republic, 1942)
Dawn on the Great Divide (Monogram, 1942)
Lure of the Islands (Monogram, 1942)
The Devil's Trail (Columbia, 1942)
Prairie Gunsmoke (Columbia, 1942)
Not a Ladies' Man (Columbia, 1942)
A Tornado in the Saddle (Columbia, 1942)
You Can't Beat the Law (Prison Mutiny) (Monogram, 1943)
Cosmo Jones in Crime Smasher (Monogram, 1943)
Idaho (Republic, 1943)
Destroyer (Columbia, 1943)
Silver Skates (Monogram, 1943)
Bombardier (RKO, 1943)
The Vigilantes Ride (Columbia, 1944)
Wyoming Hurricane (Columbia, 1944)
Lady in the Dark (Paramount, 1944)
The Purple Monster Strikes (voice only; Republic serial, 1945)

Sioux City Sue (Republic, 1946)
The Brute Man (PRC, 1946)
Dangerous Money (Monogram, 1946)
Two Guys from Milwaukee (Warner Bros., 1946)
The Gentleman from Texas (Monogram, 1946)
G. I. War Brides (Republic, 1946)
The Invisible Informer (Republic, 1946)
Rendezvous with Annie (Corporal Dolan Goes A.W.O.L.) (Republic, 1946)
The Mysterious Mr. Valentine (Republic, 1946)
Rio Grande Raiders (Republic, 1946)
Under Nevada Skies (Republic, 1946)
Under Arizona Skies (Monogram, 1946)
The Gay Cavalier (Monogram, 1946)
Shadows Over Chinatown (voice only; Monogram, 1946)
Land of the Lawless (Monogram, 1947)
Valley of Fear (Monogram, 1947)
Blackmail (Republic, 1947)
Louisiana (Monogram, 1947)
Trail to San Antone (Republic, 1947)
Jesse James Rides Again (Republic serial, 1947)
The Fabulous Texan (Republic, 1947)
The Unfaithful (Warner Bros., 1947)
The Voice of the Turtle (One for the Book) (Warner Bros., 1947)
Possessed (Warner Bros., 1947)
Swing the Western Way (Columbia, 1947)
Where the North Begins (Screen Guild, 1947)
The Hunted (Allied Artists, 1948)
Romance on the High Seas (Warner Bros., 1948)
The Gallant Blade (Columbia, 1948)
California Firebrand (Republic, 1948)
The Shanghai Chest (Monogram, 1948)
Desperadoes of Dodge City (Republic, 1948)
Range Justice (Monogram, 1948)
Crashing Thru (Monogram, 1949)
Bruce Gentry – Daredevil of the Skies (Columbia serial, 1949)
Federal Agents vs. Underworld, Inc. (Republic serial, 1949)
King of the Rocket Men (Republic serial, 1949)

Tristram Coffin operated on the right side of the law in most of his horror and SF films, but moviemakers generally capitalized on his shady looks and cast him in "heavy" roles.

Duke of Chicago (Republic, 1949)
Flamingo Road (Warner Bros., 1949)
Homicide (Warner Bros., 1949)
Lawless Code (Monogram, 1949)
Riders of the Dusk (Monogram, 1949)
The Fountainhead (Warner Bros., 1949)

My Dream Is Yours (Warner Bros., 1949)
Angels in Disguise (Monogram, 1949)
Desert Vigilante (Columbia, 1949)
The Baron of Arizona (Lippert, 1950)
Outrage (RKO, 1950)

Radar Secret Service (Lippert, 1950)
Square Dance Katy (Monogram, 1950)
The Old Frontier (Republic, 1950)
Pygmy Island (Columbia, 1950)
Undercover Girl (Universal, 1950)
Short Grass (Allied Artists, 1950)
The Big Hangover (MGM, 1950)
Pirates of the High Seas (Columbia serial, 1950)
Radar Patrol vs. Spy King (Republic serial, 1950)
The Damned Don't Cry (Warner Bros., 1950)
Cactus Caravan (Universal short, 1950)
The Lady Pays Off (Universal, 1951)
Queen for a Day (United Artists, 1951)
Buckaroo Sheriff of Texas (Republic, 1951)
Mask of the Avenger (Columbia, 1951)
Rhubarb (Paramount, 1951)
Sirocco (Columbia, 1951)
The Cimarron Kid (Universal, 1951)
Captain Video (Columbia serial, 1951)
The Fat Man (Universal, 1951)
Disk Jockey (Allied Artists, 1951)
According to Mrs. Hoyle (Monogram, 1951)
Indian Uprising (Columbia, 1951)
Rodeo King and the Senorita (Republic, 1951)
On the Loose (RKO, 1951)
Northwest Territory (Monogram, 1951)
Flight to Mars (voice only; Monogram, 1951)
Painting the Clouds with Sunshine (Warner Bros., 1951)
Smoky Canyon (Columbia, 1952)
The Kid from Broken Gun (Columbia, 1952)
My Man and I (MGM, 1952)
At Sword's Point (RKo, 1952)
So This Is Love (Warner Bros., 1953)
I Love Melvin (MGM, 1953)
Outlaw Territory (Hannah Lee) (Realart, 1953)
Law and Order (Universal, 1953)
Salome (Columbia, 1953)
City of Bad Men (20th Century–Fox, 1953)
Latin Lovers (MGM, 1953)
Clipped Wings (Allied Artists, 1953)
Torpedo Alley (voice only; Allied Artists, 1953)
Combat Squad (Columbia, 1953)

The Eddie Cantor Story (Warner Bros., 1953)
Fireman Save My Child (Universal, 1954)
Dawn at Socorro (Universal, 1954)
A Star Is Born (Warner Bros., 1954)
The Scarlet Coat (MGM, 1955)
Creature with the Atom Brain (Columbia, 1955)
The Man in the Gray Flannel Suit (20th Century–Fox, 1956)
Back from Eternity (RKO, 1956)
Three for Jamie Dawn (Allied Artists, 1956)
The First Traveling Saleslady (RKO, 1956)
The Maverick Queen (Republic, 1956)
The Night the World Exploded (Columbia, 1957)
Last Stagecoach West (Republic, 1957)
Kathy O' (Universal, 1958)
Ma Barker's Killer Brood (Filmservice Distributors Corp., 1960)
The Silent Witness (Emerson, 1962)
The Crawling Hand (Hansen Enterprises, 1963)
Good Neighbor Sam (Columbia, 1964)
Iron Angel (Ken Kennedy Productions, 1964)
Zebra in the Kitchen (MGM, 1965)
The Barefoot Executive (BV, 1971)
The Resurrection of Zachary Wheeler (Vidtronics, 1971)
Kino, the Padre on Horseback (Key International, 1977)
Coffin's 1950 short Cactus Caravan was incorporated into the 55 minute feature Tales of the West #1 (Universal, 1950). Coffin's footage was deleted from Sideshow (Monogram, 1950).

Louise Currie

Billy the Kid Outlawed (PRC, 1940)
Billy the Kid's Gun Justice (PRC, 1940)
The Green Hornet Strikes Again (Universal serial, 1940)
You'll Find Out (RKO, 1940)
Citizen Kane (RKO, 1941)
Dude Cowboy (RKO, 1941)
Orchids to Charlie (Elizabeth Arden–Fine Arts Studios featurette, 1941)

Lovely Louise Currie screamed her way through a long line of '40s horror films, mysteries and serials.

The Pinto Kid (Columbia, 1941)
The Reluctant Dragon (RKO, 1941)
Look Who's Laughing (RKO, 1941)
Adventures of Captain Marvel (Return of Captain Marvel) (Republic serial, 1941)

Hello, Sucker (Universal, 1941)
Tillie the Toiler (Columbia, 1941)
Double Trouble (Monogram, 1941)
Bedtime Story (Columbia, 1941)
Call Out the Marines (RKO, 1942)
The Bashful Bachelor (RKO, 1942)

Stardust on the Sage (Republic, 1942)
Tireman, Spare My Tires (Columbia short, 1942)
Around the World (RKO, 1943)
The Masked Marvel (Republic serial, 1943)
A Blitz on the Fritz (Columbia short, 1943)
His Wedding Scare (Columbia short, 1943)
The Ape Man (Monogram, 1943)
Forty Thieves (United Artists, 1944)
Million Dollar Kid (Monogram, 1944)
Voodoo Man (Monogram, 1944)
Christmas Holiday (Universal, 1944)
Practically Yours (Paramount, 1944)
Sensations of 1945 (United Artists, 1944)
Love Letters (Paramount, 1945)
Wild West (Prairie Outlaws) (PRC, 1946)
Gun Town (Universal, 1946)
The Bachelor's Daughters (United Artists, 1946)
Three on a Ticket (PRC, 1947)
The Chinese Ring (Monogram, 1947)
Backlash (20th Century–Fox, 1947)
Second Chance (20th Century–Fox, 1947)
The Crimson Key (20th Century–Fox, 1947)
This Is Nylon (Nylon/Apex Film Corp., 1948)
And Baby Makes Three (Columbia, 1949)
Queen for a Day (United Artists, 1951)

John Davidson (1886–1969)

Danger Signal (Edison-Kleine, 1915)
The Green Cloak (Edison-Kleine, 1915)
Sentimental Lady (Edison-Kleine, 1915)
The Wall Between (Metro, 1916)
The Brand of Cowardice (Metro, 1916)
A Million a Minute (Metro, 1916)
Pawn of Fate (World, 1916)
Romeo and Juliet (Metro, 1916)
The Awakening (World, 1917)
The Power of Decision (Metro, 1917)
Souls Adrift (Peerless-World, 1917)
The Spurs of Sybil (Peerless-World, 1918)

Through the Toils (World, 1919)
Black Circle (World, 1919)
Forest Rivals (World, 1919)
The Genius Pierre (World, 1919)
The Great Lover (Goldwyn, 1920)
The Tiger's Cub (Fox, 1920)
Cheated Love (Universal, 1921)
No Woman Knows (Universal, 1921)
The Bronze Bell (Paramount, 1921)
The Idle Rich (Metro, 1921)
Fool's Paradise (Paramount, 1921)
Saturday Night (Paramount, 1922)
The Woman Who Walked Alone (Paramount, 1922)
Under Two Flags (Universal, 1922)
His Children's Children (Paramount, 1923)
Monsieur Beaucaire (Paramount, 1924)
Ramshackle House (PDC, 1924)
Skin Deep (Warner Bros., 1929)
The Thirteenth Chair (MGM, 1929)
The Time, the Place and the Girl (Warner Bros., 1929)
Kid Gloves (Pathé, 1929)
Queen of the Night Clubs (Warner Bros., 1929)
The Rescue (United Artists, 1929)
The Life of the Party (Warner Bros., 1930)
Arsene Lupin (MGM, 1932)
Docks of San Francisco (Mayfair, 1932)
Behind Jury Doors (Mayfair, 1932)
6 Hours to Live (Fox, 1932)
Grand Hotel (MGM, 1932)
The Devil's in Love (Fox, 1933)
Broadway Bad (Fox, 1933)
The Mad Game (Fox, 1933)
Dinner at Eight (MGM, 1933)
Gabriel Over the White House (MGM, 1933)
Oliver Twist (Monogram, 1933)
Viva Villa! (MGM, 1934)
Murder in Trinidad (Fox, 1934)
Hollywood Hoodlum (Hollywood Mystery) (Regal, 1934)
Bombay Mail (Universal, 1934)
Hold That Girl (Fox, 1934)
The Scarlet Empress (Paramount, 1934)
Burn-'Em-Up Barnes (Mascot serial, 1934)
Perils of Pauline (Universal serial, 1934)

John Davidson (right) had some of his best film roles in Republic serials like *Dick Tracy vs. Crime, Inc.* (1941), where he played right-hand man to the masked arch-villain The Ghost.

Stand Up and Cheer! (Fox, 1934)
The Moonstone (Monogram, 1934)
Tailspin Tommy (Universal serial, 1934)
Lightning Strikes Twice (RKO, 1934)
The Call of the Savage (Universal serial, 1935)
Charlie Chan in Egypt (Fox, 1935)
Reckless (MGM, 1935)
A Shot in the Dark (Chesterfield, 1935)
Behind the Green Lights (Mascot, 1935)
A Tale of Two Cities (MGM, 1935)
The Last Days of Pompeii (RKO, 1935)
Death from a Distance (Invincible, 1935)

Live, Love and Learn (MGM, 1937)
The Fighting Devil Dogs (Republic serial, 1938)
Storm Over Bengal (Republic, 1938)
Arrest Bulldog Drummond! (Paramount, 1938)
Mr. Moto Takes a Vacation (20th Century-Fox, 1939)
Mr. Moto's Last Warning (20th Century-Fox, 1939)
Miracles for Sale (voice only; MGM, 1939)
The Devil Bat (PRC, 1940)
King of the Royal Mounted (Republic serial, 1940)
Adventures of Captain Marvel (Return

of Captain Marvel) (Republic serial, 1941)

Dick Tracy vs. Crime, Inc. (Dick Tracy vs. Phantom Empire) (Republic serial, 1941)

Perils of Nyoka (Nyoka and the Tigermen) (Republic serial, 1942)

Secret Service in Darkest Africa (Manhunt in the African Jungles) (Republic serial, 1943)

Captain America (Return of Captain America) (Republic serial, 1944)

Call of the Jungle (Monogram, 1944)

The Chinese Cat (Monogram, 1944)

Where Do We Go from Here? (20th Century–Fox, 1945)

The Purple Monster Strikes (Republic serial, 1945)

Sentimental Journey (20th Century–Fox, 1946)

Shock (20th Century–Fox, 1946)

Daisy Kenyon (20th Century–Fox, 1947)

Bungalow 13 (20th Century–Fox, 1948)

The Luck of the Irish (20th Century–Fox, 1948)

A Letter to Three Wives (20th Century–Fox, 1948)

That Wonderful Urge (20th Century–Fox, 1948)

The Iron Curtain (20th Century–Fox, 1948)

Dancing in the Dark (20th Century–Fox, 1949)

Slattery's Hurricane (20th Century–Fox, 1949)

Oh, You Beautiful Doll (20th Century–Fox, 1949)

You're My Everything (20th Century–Fox, 1949)

The Sword of Monte Cristo (20th Century–Fox, 1951)

Thunder in the East (Paramount, 1953)

Prince Valiant (20th Century–Fox, 1954)

A Gathering of Eagles (Universal, 1963)

Wallace Ford (1897–1966)

X Marks the Spot (Tiffany, 1931)

Possessed (MGM, 1931)

Hypnotized (World Wide, 1932)

Are You Listening? (MGM, 1932)

Skyscraper Souls (MGM, 1932)

The Beast of the City (MGM, 1932)

The Wet Parade (MGM, 1932)

Freaks (MGM, 1932)

Central Park (Warner Bros., 1932)

Employees Entrance (Warner Bros., 1933)

The Big Cage (Universal, 1933)

Goodbye Again (Warner Bros., 1933)

Headline Shooter (RKO, 1933)

Night of Terror (Columbia, 1933)

My Woman (Columbia, 1933)

East of Fifth Avenue (Columbia, 1933)

Three-Cornered Moon (Paramount, 1933)

The Lost Patrol (RKO, 1934)

A Woman's Man (Monogram, 1934)

Money Means Nothing (Monogram, 1934)

The Man Who Reclaimed His Head (Universal, 1934)

Men in White (MGM, 1934)

I Hate Women (Framed for Murder) (Goldsmith, 1934)

The Informer (RKO, 1935)

Swell-Head (Called on Account of Darkness) (Columbia, 1935)

The Nut Farm (Monogram, 1935)

The Whole Town's Talking (Columbia, 1935)

In Spite of Danger (Columbia, 1935)

Men of the Hour (Columbia, 1935)

She Couldn't Take It (Columbia, 1935)

One Frightened Night (Mascot, 1935)

The Mysterious Mr. Wong (Monogram, 1935)

Get That Man (Empire, 1935)

Mary Burns, Fugitive (Paramount, 1935)

Another Face (RKO, 1935)

Absolute Quiet (MGM, 1936)

Two in the Dark (RKO, 1936)

A Son Comes Home (Paramount, 1936)

The Rogues Tavern (Puritan, 1936)

You're in the Army Now (O.H.M.S.) (Gaumont-British, 1937)

Swing It Sailor (Grand National, 1937)

Exiled to Shanghai (Republic, 1937)

Jericho (General Film Distributors, 1937; U.S.: *Dark Sands* [Record, 1938])

Mad About Money (British Lion, 1938;
U.S.: *He Loved an Actress* [Grand
National, 1938])
*Back Door to Heaven (Hell Bent for
Murder)* (Paramount, 1939)
Two Girls on Broadway (MGM, 1940)
Isle of Destiny (RKO, 1940)
Scatterbrain (Republic, 1940)
The Mummy's Hand (Universal, 1940)
Love, Honor and Oh, Baby! (Universal, 1940)
Give Us Wings (Universal, 1940)
A Man Betrayed (Wheel of Fortune)
(Republic, 1941)
Roar of the Press (Monogram, 1941)
Murder by Invitation (Monogram,
1941)
Blues in the Night (Warner Bros.,
1941)
All Through the Night (Warner Bros.,
1942)
Inside the Law (PRC, 1942)
*Scattergood Survives a Murder (Cat's-
Claw Murder Mystery)* (RKO, 1942)
Seven Days' Leave (RKO, 1942)
The Mummy's Tomb (Universal, 1942)
Shadow of a Doubt (Universal, 1943)
The Ape Man (Monogram, 1943)
The Marines Come Through (Astor,
1943)
The Cross of Lorraine (MGM, 1943)
Secret Command (Columbia, 1944)
Machine Gun Mama (Tropical Fury)
(PRC, 1944)
Spellbound (United Artists, 1945)
Blood on the Sun (United Artists, 1945)
The Great John L. (United Artists,
1945)
On Stage Everybody (Universal, 1945)
A Guy Could Change (Republic, 1946)
The Green Years (MGM, 1946)
Lover Come Back (Universal, 1946)
Crack-Up (RKO, 1946)
Black Angel (Universal, 1946)
*Rendezvous with Annie (Corporal
Dolan Goes A.W.O.L.)* (Republic,
1946)
Magic Town (RKO, 1947)
Dead Reckoning (Columbia, 1947)
T-Men (Eagle-Lion, 1947)
Shed No Tears (Eagle-Lion, 1948)
Coroner Creek (Columbia, 1948)
The Man from Texas (Eagle-Lion, 1948)
Embraceable You (Warner Bros., 1948)

Belle Starr's Daughter (20th Century–Fox, 1948)
Red Stallion in the Rockies (Eagle-
Lion, 1949)
The Set-Up (RKO, 1949)
The Breaking Point (Warner Bros.,
1950)
The Furies (Paramount, 1950)
Dakota Lil (20th Century–Fox, 1950)
Harvey (Universal, 1950)
Painting the Clouds with Sunshine
(Warner Bros., 1951)
Warpath (Paramount, 1951)
He Ran All the Way (United Artists,
1951)
Rodeo (Monogram, 1951)
Flesh and Fury (Universal, 1952)
The Great Jesse James Raid (Lippert,
1953)
The Nebraskan (Columbia, 1953)
Destry (Universal, 1954)
She Couldn't Say No (RKO, 1954)
The Boy from Oklahoma (Warner
Bros., 1954)
3 Ring Circus (Paramount, 1954)
The Man from Laramie (Columbia,
1955)
Wichita (Allied Artists, 1955)
The Spoilers (Universal, 1955)
A Lawless Street (Columbia, 1955)
Lucy Gallant (Paramount, 1955)
The Maverick Queen (Republic, 1956)
Thunder Over Arizona (Republic,
1956)
Stagecoach to Fury (20th Century–
Fox, 1956)
Johnny Concho (United Artists, 1956)
The First Texan (Allied Artists, 1956)
The Rainmaker (Paramount, 1956)
Twilight for the Gods (Universal, 1958)
The Matchmaker (Paramount, 1958)
The Last Hurrah (Columbia, 1958)
Warlock (20th Century–Fox, 1959)
Tess of the Storm Country (20th Century–Fox, 1961)
A Patch of Blue (MGM, 1965)
Ford's footage was cut from the
release version of *They Were Expendable* (MGM, 1945).

Robert Frazer (1891–1944)

Robin Hood (Eclair, 1912)
All on Account of a Ring (Eclair, 1912)

Bela Lugosi tries to stare down one of his most frequent on-screen antagonists, Wallace Ford, this time in *Night of Terror* (1933).

Rob Roy (Eclair, 1913)
The Witch (Eclair, 1913)
The Holy City (1913)
The Squatter (Eclair, 1914)
The Lone Star Rush (Eclair-Alliance, 1915)
The Ballet Girl (Brady-World, 1916)

The Feast of Life (World, 1916)
The Decoy (World, 1916)
The Light at Dusk (Lubin, 1916)
The Dawn of Love (Metro, 1916)
Her Code of Honor (World, 1919)
Bolshevism on Trial (Select, 1919)
Without Limit (Metro, 1921)

Love, Hate and a Woman (Arrow, 1921)
Partners of the Sunset (Lubin, 1922)
Fascination (Metro, 1922)
The Faithless Sex (Signet, 1922)
How Women Love (B. B. Features, 1922)
When the Desert Calls (American, 1922)
My Friend, the Devil (Fox, 1922)
As a Man Lives (American, 1923)
Jazzmania (Metro, 1923)
The Love Piker (Goldwyn, 1923)
A Chapter in Her Life (Universal, 1923)
After the Ball (FBO, 1924)
When a Man's a Man (Associated First National, 1924)
Women Who Give (MG, 1924)
Men (Paramount, 1924)
Traffic in Hearts (Columbia, 1924)
The Foolish Virgin (Columbia, 1924)
Broken Barriers (MG, 1924)
Bread (MG, 1924)
The Mine with the Iron Door (Principle, 1924)
Miss Bluebeard (Paramount, 1925)
The White Desert (MG, 1925)
The Charmer (Paramount, 1925)
The Scarlet West (First National, 1925)
The Love Gamble (Banner, 1925)
The Keeper of the Bees (FBO, 1925)
Why Women Love (First National, 1925)
The Other Woman's Story (B. P. Shulberg, 1925)
The Golden Strain (Fox, 1925)
The Splendid Road (First National, 1925)
Secret Orders (FBO, 1926)
Desert Gold (Paramount, 1926)
The Isle of Retribution (FBO, 1926)
The Speeding Venus (PDC, 1926)
Dame Chance (American Cinema Associates, 1926)
The City (Fox, 1926)
Sin Cargo (Tiffany, 1926)
One Hour of Love (Tiffany, 1927) ˙
Wanted—A Coward (Banner, 1927)
The Silent Hero (Rayart, 1927)
Back to God's Country (Universal, 1927)
Out of the Past (Peerless, 1927)
Burning Up Broadway (Sterling, 1928)

The Scarlet Dove (Tiffany, 1928)
Out of the Ruins (First National, 1928)
City of Purple Dreams (Rayart, 1928)
Black Butterflies (Quality, 1928)
Sioux Blood (MGM, 1929)
Careers (First National, 1929)
The Drake Case (Universal, 1929)
The Woman I Love (FBO, 1929)
Frozen Justice (Fox, 1929)
The King of the Kongo (Mascot serial, 1929)
Beyond the Law (Syndicate, 1930)
Ten Nights in a Barroom (Roadshow Productions, 1931)
The Wide Open Spaces (RKO short, 1931)
Two Gun Caballero (Imperial, 1931)
The Rainbow Trail (Fox, 1932)
The Bride's Bereavement or The Snake in the Grass (RKO short, 1932)
The Saddle Buster (RKO, 1932)
Discarded Lovers (Tower, 1932)
Arm of the Law (Monogram, 1932)
The King Murder (Chesterfield, 1932)
White Zombie (United Artists, 1932)
The Crooked Circle (World Wide, 1932)
The Vampire Bat (Majestic, 1933)
Justice Takes a Holiday (Majestic, 1933)
Notorious But Nice (Chesterfield, 1933)
The Three Musketeers (Mascot serial, 1933)
The Fighting Parson (Allied Pictures, 1933)
The Mystery Squadron (Mascot serial, 1933)
Found Alive (Ideal, 1933)
Love Past Thirty (Freuler Film Associates, 1934)
Guilty Parents (Syndicate, 1934)
Men in White (MGM, 1934)
Green Eyes (Chesterfield, 1934)
Monte Carlo Nights (Monogram, 1934)
Fifteen Wives (Invincible, 1934)
The Trail Beyond (Monogram, 1934)
Counsel on De Fence (Columbia short, 1934)
The Fighting Trooper (Ambassador, 1934)
One in a Million (Dangerous Appointment) (Invincible, 1934)

Robert Frazer (right) played his most memorable role as the plantation owner in the creaky horror epic *White Zombie* (1932).

Million Dollar Haul (Stage & Screen/First Division, 1935)
The World Accuses (Chesterfield, 1935)
Circumstantial Evidence (Chesterfield, 1935)
Trails of the Wild (Ambassador, 1935)
Public Opinion (Chesterfield, 1935)
The Fighting Pilot (Ajax, 1935)
Fighting Marines (Mascot serial, 1935)
Ladies Crave Excitement (Mascot, 1935)
Condemned to Live (Chesterfield, 1935)
Never Too Late (Reliable, 1935)
Death from a Distance (Invincible, 1935)
Murder Man (MGM, 1935)
The Miracle Rider (Mascot serial, 1935)

Murder at Glen Athol (Invincible, 1935)
The Clutching Hand (Stage & Screen serial, 1936)
What Becomes of the Children? (Puritan, 1936)
The Black Coin (Weiss-Mintz/Stage & Screen serial, 1936)
It Couldn't Have Happened – But It Did (Invincible, 1936)
Easy Money (Invincible, 1936)
The Garden of Allah (United Artists, 1936)
Below the Deadline (Chesterfield, 1936)
Ellis Island (Invincible, 1936)
Gambling with Souls (Jay Dee Kay Productions, 1936)
We're in the Legion Now (The Rest Cure) (Grand National/Hirliman/ Regal, 1936)

Left-Handed Law (Universal, 1937)
Vice Racket (State Rights, 1937)
Black Aces (Universal, 1937)
The Toast of New York (RKO, 1937)
Religious Racketeers (Mystic Circle Murder) (Fanchon Royer/Merit, 1938)
Delinquent Parents (Progressive Pictures, 1938)
Cipher Bureau (Grand National, 1938)
Smashing the Rackets (RKO, 1938)
On the Great White Trail (Renfrew on the Great White Trail) (Grand National, 1938)
Navy Secrets (Monogram, 1939)
Hotel Imperial (Paramount, 1939)
Six-Gun Rhythm (Grand National, 1939)
Disbarred (Paramount, 1939)
Riders of the Frontier (Monogram, 1939)
Daughter of the Tong (Times Pictures/Metropolitan, 1939)
Crashing Thru (Monogram, 1939)
The Mad Empress (Juarez and Maximillian) (Warner Bros., 1939)
Love, Honor and Oh, Baby! (Universal, 1940)
One Man's Law (Republic, 1940)
Forgotten Girls (Republic, 1940)
The Crooked Road (Republic, 1940)
Grand Ole Opry (Republic, 1940)
Criminals Within (PRC, 1941)
Pals of the Pecos (Republic, 1941)
Law of the Wild (Law of the Wolf (Arthur Zeihm Productions, 1941)
Roar of the Press (Monogram, 1941)
Gangs of Sonora (Republic, 1941)
The Gunman from Bodie (Monogram, 1941)
Dick Tracy vs. Crime, Inc. (Dick Tracy vs. Phantom Empire) (Republic serial, 1941)
Bad Man of Deadwood (Republic, 1941)
The Devil Pays Off (Republic, 1941)
Code of the Outlaw (Republic, 1942)
Black Dragons (Monogram, 1942)
Flight Lieutenant (Columbia, 1942)
Riders of the West (Monogram, 1942)
A Night for Crime (PRC, 1942)
Dawn on the Great Divide (Monogram, 1942)
Dead Man's Gulch (Republic, 1943)
Wagon Tracks West (Republic, 1943)

The Stranger from Pecos (Monogram, 1943)
Daredevils of the West (Republic serial, 1943)
Forty Thieves (United Artists, 1944)
Law Men (Monogram, 1944)
Partners of the Trail (Monogram, 1944)
Captain America (Return of Captain America) (Republic serial, 1944)
The Tiger Woman (Perils of the Darkest Jungle) (Republic serial, 1944)
Frazer's footage from *Come On Danger!* (RKO, 1932) wound up on the cutting room floor.

Dwight Frye (1899–1943)

The Doorway to Hell (Warner Bros., 1930)
Man to Man (Warner Bros., 1930)
Dracula (Universal, 1931)
The Black Camel (Fox, 1931)
The Maltese Falcon (Dangerous Female) (Warner Bros., 1931)
Frankenstein (Universal, 1931)
Attorney for the Defense (Columbia, 1932)
By Whose Hand? (Murder Express) (Columbia, 1932)
A Strange Adventure (The Wayne Murder Case; A Strange Case of Murder) (Monogram, 1932)
The Western Code (Columbia, 1932)
The Invisible Man (Universal, 1933)
The Vampire Bat (Majestic, 1933)
The Circus Queen Murder (Columbia, 1933)
Bride of Frankenstein (Universal, 1935)
The Great Impersonation (Universal, 1935)
The Crime of Doctor Crespi (Liberty/Republic, 1935)
Atlantic Adventure (Columbia, 1935)
Alibi for Murder (Columbia, 1936)
Tough Guy (MGM, 1936)
Florida Special (Paramount, 1936)
Beware of Ladies (Republic, 1936)
The Man Who Found Himself (RKO, 1937)
Sea Devils (RKO, 1937)

His pants are too long and his cane too short, but the mad gleam in his eyes is *just right*. Dwight Frye in a typical pose from *Frankenstein* (1931).

The Road Back (Universal, 1937)
Renfrew of the Royal Mounted (Grand National, 1937)
The Shadow (Columbia, 1937)
Something to Sing About (Battling Hoofer) (Grand National, 1937)
The Invisible Enemy (Republic, 1938)

Fast Company (The Rare Book Murder) (MGM, 1938)
Adventure in Sahara (Columbia, 1938)
The Night Hawk (Republic, 1938)
Think It Over (MGM short, 1938)
Who Killed Gail Preston? (Columbia, 1938)

Sinners in Paradise (Universal, 1938)
Son of Frankenstein (Universal, 1939)
The Man in the Iron Mask (United Artists, 1939)
Conspiracy (RKO, 1939)
Mickey the Kid (Republic, 1939)
Sky Bandits (Monogram, 1940)
Drums of Fu Manchu (Republic serial, 1940)
The Son of Monte Cristo (United Artists, 1940)
Gangs of Chicago (Republic, 1940)
Phantom Raiders (MGM, 1940)
The People vs. Dr. Kildare (MGM, 1941)
Flying Blind (Paramount, 1941)
The Blonde from Singapore (Columbia, 1941)
The Devil Pays Off (Republic, 1941)
Mystery Ship (Columbia, 1941)
Sleepytime Gal (Republic, 1942)
Don't Talk (MGM short, 1942)
Danger in the Pacific (Universal, 1942)
The Ghost of Frankenstein (Universal, 1942)
Dangerous Blondes (Columbia, 1943)
Dead Men Walk (PRC, 1943)
Submarine Alert (Paramount, 1943)
Hangmen Also Die! (United Artists, 1943)
Frankenstein Meets the Wolf Man (Universal, 1943)
According to the rumor mill, Frye also appeared in the silent film *The Night Bird* (Universal, 1928), played the "cat-man" in *The Cat and the Canary* (Paramount, 1939) and starred in a nudist colony film in the late '30s. He also appeared in the unreleased version of MGM's *I Take This Woman* (shot in 1939).

I. Stanford Jolley (1900–1978)

Luck (C. C. Burr, 1923)
Ghost Town Gold (Republic, 1936)
The Gentleman from Louisiana (Republic, 1936)
The Big Show (Republic, 1936)
The Old Corral (Republic, 1936)
They Won't Forget (Warner Bros., 1937)
Boy of the Streets (Monogram, 1937)
Kid Galahad (Warner Bros., 1937)

A Bride for Henry (Monogram, 1937)
Dick Tracy (Republic serial, 1937)
A Star Is Born (United Artists, 1937)
Kentucky (20th Century–Fox, 1938)
Woman Against Woman (MGM, 1938)
A Christmas Carol (MGM, 1938)
Over the Wall (Warner Bros., 1938)
Woman Against Woman (MGM, 1938)
Street of Missing Men (Republic, 1939)
S.O.S. Tidal Wave (Republic, 1939)
The Lone Wolf Spy Hunt (Columbia, 1939)
The Mystery of Mr. Wong (Monogram, 1939)
Mr. Wong in Chinatown (Monogram, 1939)
The Private Lives of Elizabeth and Essex (Elizabeth the Queen) (Warner Bros., 1939)
The Fatal Hour (Monogram, 1940)
Hidden Enemy (incorrectly billed as Stanley Jolley; Monogram, 1940)
Chasing Trouble (Monogram, 1940)
Midnight Limited (Monogram, 1940)
Rollin' Home to Texas (Monogram, 1940)
The Ape (Monogram, 1940)
Queen of the Yukon (Monogram, 1940)
Trail of the Silver Spurs (Monogram, 1941)
Arizona Bound (Monogram, 1941)
Emergency Landing (PRC, 1941)
Gentleman from Dixie (Monogram, 1941)
Desperate Cargo (PRC, 1941)
Criminals Within (PRC, 1941)
Black Dragons (Monogram, 1942)
The Sombrero Kid (Republic, 1942)
The Valley of Vanishing Men (Columbia serial, 1942)
Arizona Roundup (Monogram, 1942)
Boot Hill Bandits (Monogram, 1942)
Prairie Pals (PRC, 1942)
Border Roundup (PRC, 1942)
Outlaws of Boulder Pass (PRC, 1942)
Dawn on the Great Divide (Monogram, 1942)
Perils of the Royal Mounted (Columbia serial, 1942)
Road to Happiness (Monogram, 1942)
The Rangers Take Over (PRC, 1942)
The Black Raven (PRC, 1943)
Corregidor (PRC, 1943)

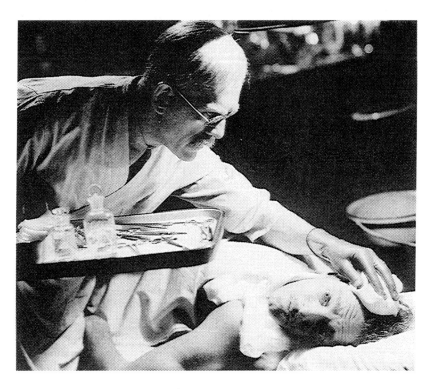

The baddie in countless Westerns and serials, I. Stanford Jolley (on table) is about to find out from Boris Karloff what it's like to be on the *receiving* end. (From *The Ape.*)

Frontier Fury (Columbia, 1943)
The Kid Rides Again (PRC, 1943)
Bad Men of Thunder Gap (PRC, 1943)
Wild Horse Stampede (Monogram, 1943)
Death Rides the Plains (PRC, 1943)
Wolves of the Range (PRC, 1943)
Blazing Frontier (PRC, 1943)
Batman (Columbia serial, 1943)
Trail of Terror (PRC, 1943)
Isle of Forgotten Sins (Monsoon) (PRC, 1943)
The Return of the Rangers (PRC, 1943)
The Phantom (Columbia serial, 1943)
Man from Music Mountain (Republic, 1943)
Frontier Law (Universal, 1943)
What a Man! (Monogram, 1943)
Brand of the Devil (PRC, 1944)
Call of the Jungle (Monogram, 1944)
The Chinese Cat (Monogram, 1944)

Cyclone Prairie Rangers (Columbia, 1944)
Oklahoma Raiders (Universal, 1944)
Gangsters of the Frontier (PRC, 1944)
Shake Hands with Murder (PRC, 1944)
The Desert Hawk (Columbia serial, 1944)
Black Arrow (Columbia serial, 1944)
Swing, Cowboy, Swing (Bad Man from Big Bend) (Three Crown, 1944)
The Whispering Skull (PRC, 1944)
Outlaw Roundup (PRC, 1944)
Crime, Inc. (PRC, 1945)
The Fighting Guardsman (Columbia, 1945)
The Power of the Whistler (Columbia, 1945)
Fighting Bill Carson (PRC, 1945)
The Scarlet Clue (Monogram, 1945)
Mr. Muggs Rides Again (Monogram, 1945)

Gangster's Den (PRC, 1945)
Outlaws of the Rockies (Columbia, 1945)
Springtime in Texas (Monogram, 1945)
Stagecoach Outlaws (PRC, 1945)
Jungle Raiders (Columbia serial, 1945)
Prairie Rustlers (PRC, 1945)
Frontier Fugitives (PRC, 1945)
Secret Agent X-9 (Universal serial, 1945)
Flaming Bullets (PRC, 1945)
The Navajo Kid (PRC, 1945)
Swamp Fire (Paramount, 1946)
Ambush Trail (PRC, 1946)
Lightning Raiders (PRC, 1946)
Silver Range (Monogram, 1946)
The Crimson Ghost (Republic serial, 1946)
Daughter of Don Q (Republic serial, 1946)
Son of the Guardsman (Columbia serial, 1946)
Border Bandits (Monogram, 1946)
Six Gun Man (PRC, 1946)
Terrors on Horseback (PRC, 1946)
Two-Fisted Stranger (Columbia, 1946)
'Neath Canadian Skies (Screen Guild, 1946)
North of the Border (Screen Guild, 1946)
Land of the Lawless (Monogram, 1947)
West of Dodge City (Columbia, 1947)
Prairie Express (Monogram, 1947)
The Romance of Rosy Ridge (MGM, 1947)
The Black Widow (Republic serial, 1947)
Wild Country (PRC, 1947)
The Prince of Thieves (Columbia, 1948)
Whiplash (Warner Bros., 1948)
Feudin', Fussin' and A-Fightin' (Universal, 1948)
Adventures of Frank and Jesse James (Republic serial, 1948)
Congo Bill – King of the Jungle (Columbia serial, 1948)
Dangers of the Canadian Mounted (Republic serial, 1948)
The Fighting Ranger (Monogram, 1948)
Gunning for Justice (Monogram, 1948)
Tex Granger (Columbia serial, 1948)

Joan of Arc (RKO, 1948)
Check Your Guns (PRC/Eagle-Lion, 1948)
Oklahoma Blues (Monogram, 1948)
Sands of Iwo Jima (Republic, 1949)
Desert Vigilante (Columbia, 1949)
Son of Billy the Kid (Screen Guild, 1949)
Stampede (Monogram, 1949)
Roll, Thunder, Roll (Eagle-Lion, 1949)
Bandit King of Texas (Republic, 1949)
King of the Rocket Men (Republic serial, 1949)
Trouble at Melody Mesa (Three Crown/Astor, 1949)
Calamity Jane and Sam Bass (Universal, 1949)
Gun Law Justice (Monogram, 1949)
Haunted Trails (Monogram, 1949)
Rimfire (Lippert, 1949)
Ghost of Zorro (Republic serial, 1949)
Bodyhold (Columbia, 1949)
The Baron of Arizona (Lippert, 1950)
Rock Island Trail (Republic, 1950)
Sierra (Universal, 1950)
The Return of Jesse James (Lippert, 1950)
Curtain Call at Cactus Creek (Universal, 1950)
Hostile Country (Outlaw Fury) (Lippert, 1950)
Trigger, Jr. (Republic, 1950)
Fast on the Draw (Sudden Death) (Lippert, 1950)
Colorado Ranger (Guns of Justice) (Lippert, 1950)
Desperadoes of the West (Republic serial, 1950)
Pirates of the High Seas (Columbia serial, 1950)
California Passage (Republic, 1950)
Comanche Territory (Universal, 1950)
The Longhorn (Monogram, 1951)
Cattle Queen (Queen of the West) (United Artists, 1951)
Oklahoma Justice (Monogram, 1951)
I Want You (RKO, 1951)
Texans Never Cry (Columbia, 1951)
Westward the Women (MGM, 1951)
Nevada Badmen (Monogram, 1951)
Canyon Raiders (Monogram, 1951)
Whistling Hills (Monogram, 1951)
Stage to Blue River (Monogram, 1951)
Texas Lawmen (Monogram, 1951)

The Red Badge of Courage (MGM, 1951)
Lawless Cowboys (Monogram, 1951)
Rodeo (Monogram, 1951)
Don Daredevil Rides Again (Republic serial, 1951)
Captain Video (Columbia serial, 1951)
The Thundering Trail (Realart, 1951)
Wagons West (Monogram, 1952)
The Raiders (Riders of Vengeance) (Universal, 1952)
The Lawless Breed (Universal, 1952)
Rancho Notorious (RKO, 1952)
Fargo (Monogram, 1952)
Leadville Gunslinger (Republic, 1952)
Waco (Monogram, 1952)
Man from the Black Hills (Monogram, 1952)
Kansas Territory (Monogram, 1952)
Wild Stallion (Monogram, 1952)
Wyoming Roundup (Monogram, 1952)
Yukon Gold (Monogram, 1952)
The Gunman (Monogram, 1952)
Dead Man's Trail (Monogram, 1952)
Fort Osage (Monogram, 1952)
Hired Gun (Monogram, 1952)
Topeka (Monogram, 1953)
Count the Hours (RKO, 1953)
Rebel City (Allied Artists, 1953)
Tumbleweed (Universal, 1953)
The Marksman (Allied Artists, 1953)
Son of Belle Starr (Allied Artists, 1953)
Vigilante Terror (Allied Artists, 1953)
City of Bad Men (20th Century-Fox, 1953)
Kansas Pacific (Allied Artists, 1953)
Calamity Jane (Warner Bros., 1953)
Silver Lode (RKO, 1954)
Seven Brides for Seven Brothers (MGM, 1954)
The Desperado (Allied Artists, 1954)
Two Guns and a Badge (Allied Artists, 1954)
The Forty-Niners (Allied Artists, 1954)
Man with the Steel Whip (Republic serial, 1954)
White Christmas (Paramount, 1954)
Seven Angry Men (God's Angry Man) (Allied Artists, 1955)
Wichita (Allied Artists, 1955)
The Young Guns (Allied Artists, 1956)
The Violent Years (Female) (Headliner Productions, 1956)

Outlaw Queen (Globe Releasing Corp., 1956)
Backlash (Universal, 1956)
Perils of the Wilderness (Gun Emperor of the Northwest!) (Columbia serial, 1956)
Fury at Gunsight Pass (Columbia, 1956)
The Rawhide Years (Universal, 1956)
Kentucky Rifle (Howco, 1956)
Three for Jamie Dawn (Allied Artists, 1956)
The Wild Dakotas (Associated, 1956)
The Proud Ones (20th Century-Fox, 1956)
I Killed Wild Bill Hickok (Wheeler Co. Productions, 1956)
The Iron Sheriff (United Artists, 1957)
Gunsight Ridge (United Artists, 1957)
Gun Battle at Monterey (Allied Artists, 1957)
The Halliday Brand (United Artists, 1957)
The Storm Rider (20th Century-Fox, 1957)
The Oklahoman (Allied Artists, 1957)
Man from God's Country (New Day at Sundown) (Allied Artists, 1958)
The Long, Hot Summer (20th Century-Fox, 1958)
Day of the Bad Man (Universal, 1958)
The Saga of Hemp Brown (Universal, 1958)
Gunsmoke in Tucson (Allied Artists, 1958)
The Rebel Set (Allied Artists, 1959)
Lone Texan (20th Century-Fox, 1959)
Alias Jesse James (United Artists, 1959)
The Miracle of the Hills (20th Century-Fox, 1959)
Here Come the Jets (20th Century-Fox, 1959)
Thirteen Fighting Men (20th Century-Fox, 1960)
The Story of Ruth (20th Century-Fox, 1960)
Ice Palace (Warner Bros., 1960)
One Foot in Hell (20th Century-Fox, 1960)
Little Shepherd of Kingdom Come (20th Century-Fox, 1961)
Atlantis, the Lost Continent (MGM, 1961)

Valley of the Dragons (Columbia, 1961)
Posse from Hell (Universal, 1961)
The Firebrand (20th Century–Fox, 1962)
Terror at Black Falls (Beckman Films, 1962)
The Haunted Palace (AIP, 1963)
The Bounty Killer (Embassy, 1965)
The Restless Ones (World Wide, 1965)
The Shakiest Gun in the West (Universal, 1968)
The Phynx (Warner Bros., 1970)
Night of the Lepus (MGM, 1972)
Jolley is frequently credited with appearing in *The Lost Planet* (Columbia serial, 1953), but was replaced by Lee Roberts.

Ian Keith (1899–1960)

Manhandled (Paramount, 1924)
Christine of the Hungry Heart (First National, 1924)
Her Love Story (Paramount, 1924)
Love's Wilderness (First National, 1924)
Enticement (First National, 1925)
My Son (First National, 1925)
The Talker (First National, 1925)
The Tower of Lies (MGM, 1925)
The Greater Glory (First National, 1926)
The Lily (Fox, 1926)
The Prince of Tempters (First National, 1926)
The Truthful Sex (Columbia, 1926)
Convoy (First National, 1927)
The Love of Sunya (United Artists, 1927)
A Man's Past (Universal, 1927)
Two Arabian Knights (United Artists, 1927)
What Every Girl Should Know (Warner Bros., 1927)
The Look Out Girl (Quality Pictures, 1928)
The Street of Illusion (Columbia, 1928)
The Great Divide (Warner Bros., 1929)
Light Fingers (Columbia, 1929)
The Divine Lady (First National, 1929)
Prisoners (First National, 1929)
The Big Trail (Fox, 1930)

Boudoir Diplomat (Universal, 1930)
Prince of Diamonds (Columbia, 1930)
Abraham Lincoln (United Artists, 1930)
A Tailor-Made Man (MGM, 1931)
Sin Ship (RKO, 1931)
Susan Lenox: Her Fall and Rise (MGM, 1931)
The Phantom of Paris (MGM, 1931)
The Deceiver (Columbia, 1931)
The Sign of the Cross (Paramount, 1932)
Queen Christina (MGM, 1933)
Dangerous Corner (RKO, 1934)
Cleopatra (Paramount, 1934)
The Crusades (Paramount, 1935)
The Three Musketeers (RKO, 1935)
The White Legion (Grand National, 1936)
The Preview Murder Mystery (Paramount, 1936)
Don't Gamble with Love (Columbia, 1936)
Mary of Scotland (RKO, 1936)
The Buccaneer (Paramount, 1938)
Comet Over Broadway (Warner Bros., 1938)
All This, and Heaven Too (Warner Bros., 1940)
The Sea Hawk (Warner Bros., 1940)
The Sundown Kid (Republic, 1942)
The Payoff (PRC, 1942)
Remember Pearl Harbor (Republic, 1942)
I Escaped from the Gestapo (No Escape) (Monogram, 1943)
Wild Horse Stampede (Monogram, 1943)
Here Comes Kelly (Monogram, 1943)
Five Graves to Cairo (Paramount, 1943)
The Man from Thunder River (Republic, 1943)
Bordertown Gunfighters (Republic, 1943)
Corregidor (PRC, 1943)
That Nazty Nuisance (United Artists, 1943)
The Chinese Cat (Monogram, 1944)
Casanova in Burlesque (Republic, 1944)
Arizona Whirlwind (Monogram, 1944)
Cowboy from Lonesome River (Columbia, 1944)
Bowery Champs (Monogram, 1944)

Both times that Bela Lugosi played Dracula on film (in *Dracula* and *Abbott and Costello Meet Frankenstein*), he beat out Ian Keith for the role. Here they are working together in a stageplay, presumably *No Traveler Returns* (1945).

The Spanish Main (RKO, 1945)
Northwest Trail (Action Pictures/Lippert, 1945)
She Gets Her Man (Universal, 1945)
Song of Old Wyoming (PRC, 1945)
Under Western Skies (Universal, 1945)

Identity Unknown (Republic, 1945)
Fog Island (PRC, 1945)
Phantom of the Plains (Republic, 1945)
Captain Kidd (United Artists, 1945)
Valley of the Zombies (Republic, 1946)
Singing on the Trail (Columbia, 1946)

Mr. Hex (Monogram, 1946)
Dick Tracy vs. Cueball (RKO, 1946)
The Strange Woman (United Artists, 1946)
Border Feud (PRC, 1947)
Forever Amber (20th Century-Fox, 1947)
Dick Tracy's Dilemma (RKO, 1947)
Nightmare Alley (20th Century-Fox, 1947)
The Three Musketeers (MGM, 1948)
The Black Shield of Falworth (Universal, 1954)
Prince of Players (20th Century-Fox, 1955)
It Came from Beneath the Sea (Columbia, 1955)
New York Confidential (Warner Bros., 1955)
Duel on the Mississippi (Columbia, 1955)
The Ten Commandments (Paramount, 1956)

Skelton Knaggs (1911–1955)

Strangers on a Honeymoon (Gaumont-British, 1937)
The High Command (Associated British/Grand National, 1937)
South Riding (United Artists, 1938)
The Spy in Black (U-Boat 29) (Columbia, 1939)
Torture Ship (PDC [PRC], 1939)
Diamond Frontier (Universal, 1940)
The Ghost Ship (RKO, 1943)
Headin' for God's Country (Republic, 1943)
Thumbs Up (Republic, 1943)
The Lodger (20th Century-Fox, 1944)
The Invisible Man's Revenge (Universal, 1944)
None But the Lonely Heart (RKO, 1944)
Isle of the Dead (RKO, 1945)
The Picture of Dorian Gray (MGM, 1945)
House of Dracula (Universal, 1945)
Night and Day (Warner Bros., 1946)
Bedlam (RKO, 1946)
Terror by Night (Universal, 1946)
Dick Tracy vs. Cueball (RKO, 1946)
Just Before Dawn (Columbia, 1946)
A Scandal in Paris (Thieves' Holiday) (United Artists, 1946)

Forever Amber (20th Century-Fox, 1947)
Dick Tracy Meets Gruesome (RKO, 1947)
The Paleface (Paramount, 1948)
Master Minds (Monogram, 1949)
Captain Video (Columbia serial, 1951)
Million Dollar Mermaid (MGM, 1952)
Blackbeard, the Pirate (RKO, 1952)
Rogue's March (MGM, 1952)
Botany Bay (Paramount, 1953)
Casanova's Big Night (Paramount, 1954)
Moonfleet (MGM, 1955)

Rosemary LaPlanche (1922–1979)

The Bearded Lady (Paramount short, 1930)
100 Men and a Girl (Universal, 1937)
Mad About Music (Universal, 1938)
Irene (RKO, 1940)
Two Weeks to Live (RKO, 1943)
Gildersleeve on Broadway (RKO, 1943)
Around the World (RKO, 1943)
The Falcon and the Co-Eds (RKO, 1943)
Swing Your Partner (Republic, 1943)
The Falcon in Danger (RKO, 1943)
Mexican Spitfire's Blessed Event (RKO, 1943)
Prairie Chickens (United Artists, 1943)
None But the Lonely Heart (RKO, 1944)
The Falcon Out West (RKO, 1944)
Heavenly Days (RKO, 1944)
Youth Runs Wild (RKO, 1944)
Mademoiselle Fifi (RKO, 1944)
Girl Rush (RKO, 1944)
Step Lively (RKO, 1944)
Johnny Angel (RKO, 1945)
Zombies on Broadway (RKO, 1945)
Pan-Americana (RKO, 1945)
Strangler of the Swamp (PRC, 1945)
What a Blonde (RKO, 1945)
Devil Bat's Daughter (PRC, 1946)
Betty Co-Ed (Columbia, 1946)
Jack Armstrong (Columbia serial, 1947)
Angels' Alley (Monogram, 1948)
An Old-Fashioned Girl (Eagle-Lion, 1948)
Federal Agents vs. Underworld, Inc. (Republic serial, 1949)

Baddies Bela Lugosi and Frank Moran team up against lovely Teala Loring in a
publicity photo from *Return of the Ape Man.*

Teala Loring

As Judith Gibson

The Fleet's In (Paramount, 1942)
Holiday Inn (Paramount, 1942)
Bombs Over Burma (PRC, 1942)
My Favorite Blonde (Paramount,
  1942)
Young and Willing (United Artists,
  1943)
Double Indemnity (Paramount, 1944)
Henry Aldrich's Little Secret (Para-
  mount, 1944)
I Love a Soldier (Paramount, 1944)
Halfway to Heaven (Paramount short,
  1944)
Standing Room Only (Paramount,
  1944)
*Sweethearts of the U.S.A. (Sweethearts
  on Parade)* (Monogram, 1944)
Return of the Ape Man (Monogram,
  1944)

As Teala Loring

Bluebeard (PRC, 1944)
Delinquent Daughters (PRC, 1944)
Allotment Wives (Woman in the Case)
  (Monogram, 1945)
You Hit the Spot (Paramount short,
  1945)
The Affairs of Susan (Paramount,
  1945)
Bowery Bombshell (Monogram, 1946)
Dark Alibi (Monogram, 1946)
Partners in Time (RKO, 1946)
Wife Wanted (Monogram, 1946)
Gas House Kids (PRC, 1946)
Black Market Babies (Monogram, 1946)
Hard Boiled Mahoney (Monogram,
  1947)
Riding the California Trail (Mono-
  gram, 1947)
Fall Guy (Monogram, 1947)
The Arizona Cowboy (Republic, 1950)

Robert Lowery (1916–1971)

Come and Get It (United Artists, 1936)

Great Guy (Grand National, 1936)

Wake Up and Live (20th Century-Fox, 1937)

Big Town Girl (20th Century-Fox, 1937)

Life Begins in College (20th Century-Fox, 1937)

The Lady Escapes (20th Century-Fox, 1937)

You Can't Have Everything (20th Century-Fox, 1937)

The Jones Family in Hot Water (20th Century-Fox, 1937)

Wife, Doctor and Nurse (20th Century-Fox, 1937)

Charlie Chan on Broadway (20th Century-Fox, 1937)

Second Honeymoon (20th Century-Fox, 1937)

City Girl (20th Century-Fox, 1937)

Passport Husband (20th Century-Fox, 1938)

Island in the Sky (20th Century-Fox, 1938)

Always Goodbye (20th Century-Fox, 1938)

Keep Smiling (20th Century-Fox, 1938)

Submarine Patrol (20th Century-Fox, 1938)

Kentucky Moonshine (20th Century-Fox, 1938)

Happy Landing (20th Century-Fox, 1938)

One Wild Night (20th Century-Fox, 1938)

Alexander's Ragtime Band (20th Century-Fox, 1938)

Four Men and a Prayer (20th Century-Fox, 1938)

Safety in Numbers (20th Century-Fox, 1938)

Josette (20th Century-Fox, 1938)

A Trip to Paris (20th Century-Fox, 1938)

Kentucky (20th Century-Fox, 1938)

Gateway (20th Century-Fox, 1938)

Everybody's Baby (20th Century-Fox, 1939)

Young Mr. Lincoln (20th Century-Fox, 1939)

The Escape (20th Century-Fox, 1939)

The Baroness and the Butler (20th Century-Fox, 1938)

Charlie Chan in Reno (20th Century-Fox, 1939)

Hollywood Cavalcade (20th Century-Fox, 1939)

Drums Along the Mohawk (20th Century-Fox, 1939)

Danger Island (Mr. Moto in Danger Island) (20th Century-Fox, 1939)

Wife, Husband, and Friend (20th Century-Fox, 1939)

Irving Berlin's Second Fiddle (20th Century-Fox, 1939)

Day-Time Wife (20th Century-Fox, 1939)

Tail Spin (20th Century-Fox, 1939)

City of Chance (20th Century-Fox, 1940)

Free, Blonde and 21 (20th Century-Fox, 1940)

Shooting High (20th Century-Fox, 1940)

Charlie Chan's Murder Cruise (20th Century-Fox, 1940)

Star Dust (20th Century-Fox, 1940)

The Mark of Zorro (20th Century-Fox, 1940)

Maryland (20th Century-Fox, 1940)

Murder Over New York (20th Century-Fox, 1940)

Four Sons (20th Century-Fox, 1940)

Ride On, Vaquero (20th Century-Fox, 1941)

Private Nurse (20th Century-Fox, 1941)

Cadet Girl (20th Century-Fox, 1941)

Remember the Day (voice only; 20th Century-Fox, 1941)

Great Guns (20th Century-Fox, 1941)

Sex Hygiene (Audio Productions/U.S. Navy short, 1942)

My Gal Sal (20th Century-Fox, 1942)

Who Is Hope Schuyler? (20th Century-Fox, 1942)

Dawn on the Great Divide (Monogram, 1942)

Lure of the Islands (Monogram, 1942)

She's in the Army (Monogram, 1942)

Criminal Investigator (Monogram, 1942)

Rhythm Parade (Monogram, 1943)

A Scream in the Dark (Republic, 1943)

What did Robert Lowery expect to find with those skeleton keys? A gag shot from *Revenge of the Zombies.*

The North Star (Armored Attack) (RKO, 1943)
Tarzan's Desert Mystery (RKO, 1943)
So's Your Uncle (Universal, 1943)
Revenge of the Zombies (Monogram, 1943)
Campus Rhythm (Monogram, 1943)
The Mummy's Ghost (Universal, 1944)
Hot Rhythm (Monogram, 1944)
Dark Mountain (Paramount, 1944)
Dangerous Passage (Paramount, 1944)
The Navy Way (Paramount, 1944)
The Mystery of the Riverboat (Universal serial, 1944)
High Powered (Paramount, 1945)
Fashion Model (Monogram, 1945)
Road to Alcatraz (Republic, 1945)
Prison Ship (Columbia, 1945)
Sensation Hunters (Club Paradise) (Monogram, 1945)
The Monster and the Ape (Columbia serial, 1945)
House of Horrors (Universal, 1946)
They Made Me a Killer (Paramount, 1946)

Gas House Kids (PRC, 1946)
Lady Chaser (PRC, 1946)
Death Valley (Screen Guild, 1946)
God's Country (Screen Guild, 1946)
Big Town (Paramount, 1947)
I Cover Big Town (I Cover the Underworld) (Paramount, 1947)
Queen of the Amazons (Screen Guild, 1947)
Jungle Flight (Paramount, 1947)
Danger Street (Paramount, 1947)
Killer at Large (PRC, 1947)
Shep Comes Home (Screen Guild, 1948)
Heart of Virginia (Pride of Virginia) (Republic, 1948)
Highway 13 (Lippert/Screen Guild, 1948)
Mary Lou (Columbia, 1948)
Batman and Robin (Columbia serial, 1949)
The Dalton Gang (The Outlaw Gang) (Lippert, 1949)
Arson, Inc. (Lippert, 1949)
Call of the Forest (Lippert, 1949)
Western Pacific Agent (Lippert, 1950)

Gunfire (Lippert, 1950)
Border Rangers (Lippert, 1950)
Train to Tombstone (Lippert, 1950)
Everybody's Dancin' (Lippert, 1950)
I Shot Billy the Kid (Lippert, 1950)
Crosswinds (Paramount, 1951)
Cow Country (Allied Artists, 1953)
Jalopy (Allied Artists, 1953)
The Homesteaders (Allied Artists, 1953)
Lay That Rifle Down (Republic, 1955)
Two Gun Lady (Associated Film Releasing, 1955)
The Parson and the Outlaw (Columbia, 1957)
The Rise and Fall of Legs Diamond (Warner Bros., 1960)
When the Girls Take Over (Parade Films, 1962)
Young Guns of Texas (20th Century-Fox, 1962)
Deadly Duo (United Artists, 1962)
McLintock! (United Artists, 1963)
Stage to Thunder Rock (Paramount, 1964)
Zebra in the Kitchen (MGM, 1965)
Johnny Reno (Paramount, 1966)
Waco (Paramount, 1966)
The Undertaker and His Pals (Howco, 1967)
The Ballad of Josie (Universal, 1968)
Lowery's footage was cut from *Rebecca of Sunnybrook Farm* (20th Century-Fox, 1938).

Wanda McKay (1923–   )

$1,000 a Touchdown (Paramount, 1939)
Our Neighbors – The Carters (Paramount, 1939)
The Great McGinty (Paramount, 1940)
Those Were the Days (Paramount, 1940)
The Quarterback (Paramount, 1940)
The Farmer's Daughter (Paramount, 1940)
Mystery Sea Raider (Paramount, 1940)
Dancing on a Dime (Paramount, 1940)
A Night at Earl Carroll's (Paramount, 1940)
The Way of All Flesh (Paramount, 1940)
Las Vegas Nights (The Gay City) (Paramount, 1941)

New York Town (Paramount, 1941)
Life with Henry (Paramount, 1941)
You're the One (Paramount, 1941)
Virginia (Paramount, 1941)
The Lady Eve (Paramount, 1941)
The Mad Doctor (Paramount, 1941)
The Royal Mounted Patrol (Columbia, 1941)
The Pioneers (Monogram, 1941)
Twilight on the Trail (Paramount, 1941)
Stars Past and Present (Meet the Stars series) (Republic short, 1941)
Rolling Down the Great Divide (PRC, 1942)
The Lone Rider in Texas Justice (PRC, 1942)
One Thrilling Night (Horace Takes Over) (Monogram, 1942)
Bowery at Midnight (Monogram, 1942)
Billy the Kid's Law and Order (PRC, 1942)
Corregidor (PRC, 1943)
Danger! Women at Work (PRC, 1943)
The Deerslayer (Republic, 1943)
Let's Face It (Paramount, 1943)
The Black Raven (PRC, 1943)
What a Man! (Monogram, 1943)
Smart Guy (You Can't Beat the Law) (Monogram, 1943)
Belle of the Yukon (RKO, 1944)
Leave It to the Irish (Monogram, 1944)
Raiders of Ghost City (Universal serial, 1944)
The Monster Maker (PRC, 1944)
Voodoo Man (Monogram, 1944)
Hollywood and Vine (PRC, 1945)
Sensation Hunters (Club Paradise) (Monogram, 1945)
There Goes Kelly (Monogram, 1945)
Kilroy Was Here (Monogram, 1947)
Jiggs and Maggie in Society (Monogram, 1948)
Stage Struck (Monogram, 1948)
Because of Eve (The Story of Life) (Crusade Productions/International Pictures, 1948)
The Golden Eye (The Mystery of the Golden Eye) (Monogram, 1948)
Jinx Money (Monogram, 1948)
Jungle Goddess (Lippert/Screen Guild, 1948)
A Woman of Distinction (Columbia, 1950)

Roaring City (Lippert, 1951)
Hollywood Honeymoon (RKO short, 1951)
Fast and Foolish (RKO short, 1951)
The Merry Widow (MGM, 1952)
Ten Thousand Bedrooms (MGM, 1957)
A scene from *Because of Eve (The Story of Life)* is included in the campy compilation film *It Came from Hollywood* (Paramount, 1982).

Charles Middleton (1874–1949)

Hobart Bosworth in "A Man of Peace" (Warner Bros./Vitaphone short, 1928)
The Farmer's Daughter (Fox, 1928)
The Bellamy Trial (MGM, 1929)
Welcome Danger (Paramount, 1929)
The Far Call (Fox, 1929)
Beau Bandit (RKO, 1930)
Way Out West (MGM, 1930)
More Sinned Against Than Sinners (Warner Bros./Vitaphone short, 1930)
William Boyd in "The Frame" (Warner Bros./Vitaphone short, 1930)
Christmas Knight (Warner Bros./Vitaphone short, 1930)
Framed (RKO, 1930)
East Is West (Universal, 1930)
An American Tragedy (Paramount, 1931)
Ships of Hate (Monogram, 1931)
Caught Plastered (Full of Notions) (RKO, 1931)
Palmy Days (United Artists, 1931)
The Miracle Woman (Columbia, 1931)
Alexander Hamilton (Warner Bros., 1931)
A Dangerous Affair (Columbia, 1931)
Sob Sister (Fox, 1931)
Safe in Hell (Warner Bros., 1931)
Beau Hunks (MGM featurette, 1931)
A House Divided (Universal, 1931)
Manhattan Parade (Warner Bros., 1931)
The Ruling Voice (Warner Bros., 1931)
X Marks the Spot (Tiffany, 1931)
High Pressure (Warner Bros., 1932)

The Sign of the Cross (Paramount, 1932)
The Hatchet Man (Warner Bros., 1932)
I Am a Fugitive from a Chain Gang (Warner Bros., 1932)
The Strange Love of Molly Louvain (Warner Bros., 1932)
Mystery Ranch (Fox, 1932)
Kongo (MGM, 1932)
The Phantom President (Paramount, 1932)
Pack Up Your Troubles (MGM, 1932)
Hell's Highway (RKO, 1932)
Silver Dollar (Warner Bros., 1932)
Breach of Promise (World Wide, 1932)
Rockabye (RKO, 1932)
Tomorrow at Seven (RKO, 1933)
Sunset Pass (Paramount, 1933)
The Bowery (United Artists, 1933)
Pick Up (Paramount, 1933)
Destination Unknown (Universal, 1933)
Disgraced (Paramount, 1933)
This Day and Age (Paramount, 1933)
Big Executive (Paramount, 1933)
White Woman (Paramount, 1933)
Duck Soup (Paramount, 1933)
Doctor Bull (Fox, 1933)
The Road Is Open Again (Warner Bros./Vitaphone short, 1933)
The Lone Cowboy (Paramount, 1933)
Broadway Bill (Columbia, 1934)
The Last Roundup (Paramount, 1934)
Whom the Gods Destroy (Columbia, 1934)
Murder at the Vanities (Paramount, 1934)
Massacre (Warner Bros., 1934)
David Harum (Fox, 1934)
The Mystic Hour (Progressive Pictures, 1934)
Nana (United Artists, 1934)
The St. Louis Kid (Warner Bros., 1934)
Private Scandal (Paramount, 1934)
Mrs. Wiggs of the Cabbage Patch (Paramount, 1934)
When Strangers Meet (Liberty, 1934)
Behold My Wife! (Paramount, 1934)
Red Morning (RKO, 1934)
The County Chairman (Fox, 1935)
Reckless (MGM, 1935)
Hop-A-Long Cassidy (Hopalong Cassidy Enters) (Paramount, 1935)

Square Shooter (Columbia, 1935)
In Spite of Danger (Columbia, 1935)
Frisco Kid (Warner Bros., 1935)
The Virginia Judge (Paramount, 1935)
Special Agent (Warner Bros., 1935)
Steamboat 'Round the Bend (Fox, 1935)
The Fixer Uppers (MGM short, 1935)
The Miracle Rider (Mascot serial, 1935)
The Trail of the Lonesome Pine (Paramount, 1936)
Road Gang (Warner Bros., 1936)
Sunset of Power (Universal, 1936)
Flash Gordon (Universal serial, 1936)
Ramona (20th Century-Fox, 1936)
Empty Saddles (Universal, 1936)
Show Boat (Universal, 1936)
Song of the Saddle (Warner Bros., 1936)
Jailbreak (Warner Bros., 1936)
A Son Comes Home (Paramount, 1936)
Wedding Present (Paramount, 1936)
Career Woman (20th Century-Fox, 1936)
The Texas Rangers (Paramount, 1936)
Rose of the Rancho (Paramount, 1936)
The Last Train from Madrid (Paramount, 1937)
The Good Earth (MGM, 1937)
John Meade's Woman (Paramount, 1937)
We're on the Jury (RKO, 1937)
Stand-In (United Artists, 1937)
Souls at Sea (Paramount, 1937)
Two Gun Law (Columbia, 1937)
Hollywood Cowboy (Wings Over Wyoming) (RKO, 1937)
Yodelin' Kid from Pine Ridge (Republic, 1937)
Slave Ship (20th Century-Fox, 1937)
Flash Gordon's Trip to Mars (Universal serial, 1938)
Flaming Frontiers (Universal serial, 1938)
Strange Faces (Universal, 1938)
Dick Tracy Returns (Republic serial, 1938)
Outside the Law (Universal, 1938)
Kentucky (20th Century-Fox, 1938)
Jesse James (20th Century-Fox, 1939)
One Against the World (MGM short, 1939)
Captain Fury (United Artists, 1939)

The Oklahoma Kid (Warner Bros., 1939)
Blackmail (MGM, 1939)
Daredevils of the Red Circle (Republic serial, 1939)
Wyoming Outlaw (Republic, 1939)
Cowboys from Texas (Republic, 1939)
Thou Shalt Not Kill (Republic, 1939)
Way Down South (RKO, 1939)
The Flying Deuces (RKO, 1939)
Allegheny Uprising (RKO, 1939)
$1,000 a Touchdown (Paramount, 1939)
Juarez (Warner Bros., 1939)
Abe Lincoln in Illinois (RKO, 1940)
The Grapes of Wrath (20th Century-Fox, 1940)
Brigham Young–Frontiersman (20th Century-Fox, 1940)
Virginia City (Warner Bros., 1940)
Island of Doomed Men (Columbia, 1940)
Shooting High (20th Century-Fox, 1940)
Charlie Chan's Murder Cruise (20th Century-Fox, 1940)
Flash Gordon Conquers the Universe (Universal serial, 1940)
Chad Hanna (20th Century-Fox, 1940)
Santa Fe Trail (Warner Bros., 1940)
Rangers of Fortune (Paramount, 1940)
Gold Rush Maisie (MGM, 1940)
Jungle Man (PRC, 1941)
Western Union (20th Century-Fox, 1941)
Wild Geese Calling (20th Century-Fox, 1941)
Belle Starr (20th Century-Fox, 1941)
Wild Bill Hickok Rides (Warner Bros., 1941)
The Shepherd of the Hills (Paramount, 1941)
Sergeant York (Warner Bros., 1941)
Bad Men of Missouri (Warner Bros., 1941)
Ride, Kelly, Ride (20th Century-Fox, 1941)
Mystery of Marie Roget (Universal, 1942)
Tombstone, the Town Too Tough to Die (Paramount, 1942)
Men of San Quentin (PRC, 1942)
Perils of Nyoka (Nyoka and the Tigermen) (Republic serial, 1942)

Sing Your Worries Away (RKO, 1942)
Oklahoma Outlaws (Warner Bros.
short, 1943)
Wagon Wheels West (Warner Bros.
short, 1943)
Two Weeks to Live (RKO, 1943)
Hangmen Also Die! (United Artists,
1943)
Crazy House (Universal, 1943)
Spook Louder (Columbia short, 1943)
Boobs in the Night (Columbia short,
1943)
The Black Raven (PRC, 1943)
Batman (Columbia serial, 1943)
Black Arrow (Columbia serial, 1944)
The Town Went Wild (PRC, 1944)
Kismet (Oriental Dream) (MGM, 1944)
The Desert Hawk (Columbia serial,
1944)
Our Vines Have Tender Grapes (MGM,
1945)
Strangler of the Swamp (PRC, 1945)
Watchtower Over Tomorrow
(WAC/Office of War Information
short, 1945)
Hollywood and Vine (PRC, 1945)
Captain Kidd (United Artists, 1945)
Who's Guilty? (Columbia serial, 1945)
Northwest Trail (Action Pictures/Lip-
pert, 1945)
How DOoo You Do (PRC, 1946)
Spook Busters (Monogram, 1946)
The Killers (Universal, 1946)
The Pretender (Republic, 1947)
Welcome Stranger (Paramount,
1947)
Unconquered (Paramount, 1947)
Gunfighters (Columbia, 1947)
Jack Armstrong (Columbia serial,
1947)
Wyoming (Republic, 1947)
Road to Rio (Paramount, 1947)
The Sea of Grass (MGM, 1947)
Station West (RKO, 1948)
Feudin', Fussin' and A-Fightin'
(Universal, 1948)
*Mr. Blandings Builds His Dream
House* (RKO, 1948)
My Girl Tisa (Warner Bros., 1948)
*Here Comes Trouble (Laff-Time Part
I)* (Hal Roach/United Artists, 1948)
Jiggs and Maggie in Court (Mono-
gram, 1948)
The Last Bandit (Republic, 1949)

Dennis Moore (1908–1964)

As **Denny Meadows**

The Red Rider (Universal serial, 1934)
Coming Out Party (Fox, 1934)
West on Parade (B'n'B/Reliable/Astor
short, 1934)
The Dawn Rider (Monogram, 1935)
Sagebrush Troubador (Republic, 1935)
Valley of the Lawless (Supreme, 1936)
Desert Justice (Atlantic, 1936)
Hair Trigger Casey (Atlantic, 1936)
The Lonely Trail (Republic, 1936)
Too Much Beef (First Division/Grand
National, 1936)

As **Dennis Moore**

Sing Me a Love Song (Warner Bros.,
1936)
China Clipper (Warner Bros., 1936)
Down the Stretch (Warner Bros., 1936)
Here Comes Carter (Warner Bros.,
1936)
King of Hockey (Warner Bros., 1936)
Black Legion (Warner Bros., 1936)
Smart Blonde (Warner Bros., 1936)
Mountain Justice (Warner Bros.,
1937)
Fugitive in the Sky (Warner Bros.,
1937)
Under Southern Stars (Warner Bros.
short, 1937)
San Quentin (Warner Bros., 1937)
Ready, Willing and Able (Warner
Bros., 1937)
Rebellious Daughters (Progressive/
Times, 1938)
Across the Plains (Monogram, 1939)
The Girl from Rio (Monogram, 1939)
Danger Flight (Monogram, 1939)
Overland Mail (Monogram, 1939)
Irish Luck (Monogram, 1939)
Wild Horse Canyon (Monogram, 1939)
Trigger Smith (Monogram, 1939)
Mutiny in the Big House (Monogram,
1939)
*Fugitive from a Prison Camp (Prison
Camp)* (Columbia, 1940)
East Side Kids (Monogram, 1940)
Rainbow Over the Range (Monogram,
1940)

Rocky Mountain Rangers (Republic, 1940)

Boys of the City (The Ghost Creeps) (Monogram, 1940)

Up in the Air (Monogram, 1940)

Know Your Money (MGM short, 1940)

Spooks Run Wild (Monogram, 1941)

Arizona Bound (Monogram, 1941)

Billy the Kid in Santa Fe (PRC, 1941)

Cyclone on Horseback (RKO, 1941)

Law of the Wild (Law of the Wolf) (Arthur Ziehm Productions, 1941)

Dude Cowboy (RKO, 1941)

Ellery Queen and the Murder Ring (Columbia, 1941)

Flying Wild (Monogram, 1941)

Fangs of the Wild (Astor/Metropolitan, 1941)

The Lone Rider Fights Back (PRC, 1941)

Pals of the Pecos (Republic, 1941)

Criminals Within (PRC, 1941)

Pirates on Horseback (Paramount, 1941)

Roar of the Press (Monogram, 1941)

Below the Border (Monogram, 1942)

Riders of the West (Monogram, 1942)

Border Roundup (PRC, 1942)

Bombs Over Burma (PRC, 1942)

Outlaws of Boulder Pass (PRC, 1942)

Bandit Ranger (RKO, 1942)

The Lone Rider in Texas Justice (PRC, 1942)

Dawn on the Great Divide (Monogram, 1942)

The Lone Rider and the Bandit (PRC, 1942)

Rolling Down the Great Divide (PRC, 1942)

The Lone Rider in Cheyenne (PRC, 1942)

Raiders of the Range (Republic, 1942)

Texas Man Hunt (PRC, 1942)

Arizona Trail (Universal, 1943)

Hitler's Madman (Hitler's Hangman) (MGM, 1943)

Black Market Rustlers (Monogram, 1943)

Cowboy Commandos (Monogram, 1943)

Frontier Law (Universal, 1943)

Land of Hunted Men (Monogram, 1943)

Bullets and Saddles (Monogram, 1943)

Tenting Tonight on the Old Camp Ground (Universal, 1943)

Destroyer (Columbia, 1943)

Adventures of a Rookie (RKO, 1943)

Action in the North Atlantic (Warner Bros., 1943)

Can't Help Singing (Universal, 1944)

Follow the Boys (Universal, 1944)

Lady in the Dark (Paramount, 1944)

The Imposter (Bayonet Charge; Strange Confession) (Universal, 1944)

West of the Rio Grande (Monogram, 1944)

Thirty Seconds Over Tokyo (voice only; MGM, 1944)

Song of the Range (Monogram, 1944)

Mr. Winkle Goes to War (Columbia, 1944)

See Here, Private Hargrove (MGM, 1944)

Wells Fargo Days (Warner Bros. short, 1944 [originally released independently as *Man from Tascosa*, 1940])

Twilight on the Prairie (Universal, 1944)

Weekend Pass (Universal, 1944)

Oklahoma Raiders (Universal, 1944)

Ladies Courageous (Fury in the Skys) (Universal, 1944)

The Mummy's Curse (Universal, 1944)

Raiders of Ghost City (Universal serial, 1944)

Springtime in Texas (Monogram, 1945)

The Master Key (Universal serial, 1945)

The Frozen Ghost (Universal, 1945)

The Crime Doctor's Courage (Columbia, 1945)

The Purple Monster Strikes (Republic serial, 1945)

Frontier Feud (Monogram, 1945)

Colorado Serenade (PRC, 1946)

Driftin' River (PRC, 1946)

The Mysterious Mr. M (Universal serial, 1946)

Rainbow Over the Rockies (Monogram, 1947)

Frontier Agent (Monogram, 1948)

Million Dollar Weekend (Eagle-Lion, 1948)

The Gay Ranchero (Republic, 1948)

Range Renegades (Monogram, 1948)

The Tioga Kid (PRC/Eagle-Lion, 1948)

Riders in the Sky (Columbia, 1949)
Haunted Trails (Monogram, 1949)
Roaring Westward (Boom Town Badmen) (Monogram, 1949)
Navajo Trail Raiders (Republic, 1949)
Across the Rio Grande (Monogram, 1949)
Silver Raiders (Monogram, 1950)
West of the Brazos (Rangeland Empire) (Lippert, 1950)
Colorado Ranger (Guns of Justice) (Lippert, 1950)
Crooked River (Blazing Guns) (Lippert, 1950)
Fast on the Draw (Sudden Death) (Lippert, 1950)
Arizona Territory (Monogram, 1950)
Hostile Country (Outlaw Fury) (Lippert, 1950)
Hot Rod (Monogram, 1950)
Marshal of Heldorado (The Last Bullet) (Lippert, 1950)
Gunslingers (Monogram, 1950)
Federal Man (Eagle-Lion, 1950)
Snow Dog (Monogram, 1950)
Desperadoes of the West (Republic serial, 1950)
I Killed Geronimo (Eagle-Lion, 1950)
King of the Bullwhip (Western Adventure/Realart, 1950)
Singing Guns (Republic, 1950)
Buccaneer's Girl (Universal, 1950)
West of Wyoming (Monogram, 1950)
Fort Defiance (United Artists, 1951)
Abilene Trail (Monogram, 1951)
Man from Sonora (Monogram, 1951)
Blazing Bullets (Monogram, 1951)
I Was an American Spy (Allied Artists, 1951)
Canyon Ambush (Monogram, 1952)
The Lusty Men (RKO, 1952)
Montana Belle (RKO, 1952)
Guns Along the Border (Monogram, 1952)
I Died a Thousand Times (Warner Bros., 1955)
The Shrike (Universal, 1955)
One Desire (Universal, 1955)
The Square Jungle (Universal, 1955)
The Man from Bitter Ridge (voice only; Universal, 1955)
The Gun That Won the West (Columbia, 1955)

Rage at Dawn (RKO, 1955)
A Day of Fury (Universal, 1956)
Don't Knock the Rock (Columbia, 1956)
The Harder They Fall (Columbia, 1956)
Hot Shots (Allied Artists, 1956)
The White Squaw (Columbia, 1956)
Tribute to a Bad Man (MGM, 1956)
Friendly Persuasion (Allied Artists, 1956)
Blazing the Overland Trail (Columbia serial, 1956)
Perils of the Wilderness (Columbia serial, 1956)
Great Day in the Morning (RKO, 1956)
The Phantom Stagecoach (Columbia, 1957)
Gunfight at the O.K. Corral (Paramount, 1957)
Domino Kid (Columbia, 1957)
Chicago Confidential (United Artists, 1957)
Utah Blaine (Columbia, 1957)
Beginning of the End (Republic, 1957)
God Is My Partner (20th Century-Fox, 1957)
The Night the World Exploded (Columbia, 1957)
Stock footage of Moore from *Destroyer* (1943) appears in *It Came from Beneath the Sea* (Columbia, 1955).

Frank Moran

Me and My Gal (Fox, 1932)
She Done Him Wrong (Paramount, 1933)
Hooks and Jabs (Educational short, 1933)
The Bowery (United Artists, 1933)
Sailor's Luck (Fox, 1933)
Gambling Ship (Paramount, 1933)
Her First Mate (Universal, 1933)
Pilgrimage (Fox, 1933)
Song of the Eagle (Paramount, 1933)
The Man Who Dared (Fox, 1933)
Mr. Skitch (Fox, 1933)
Flaming Gold (RKO, 1933)
Sensation Hunters (Monogram, 1933)
Jealousy (Columbia, 1933)
The Little Giant (Warner Bros., 1933)
Have a Heart (MGM, 1934)
Coming Out Party (Fox, 1934)
Bright Eyes (Fox, 1934)

Helldorado (Fox, 1934)
Looking for Trouble (United Artists, 1934)
The Mighty Barnum (United Artists, 1934)
Judge Priest (Fox, 1934)
Change of Heart (Fox, 1934)
No More Women (Paramount, 1934)
The World Moves On (Fox, 1934)
Six Gun Justice (Spectrum, 1935)
We're in the Money (Warner Bros., 1935)
Dante's Inferno (Fox, 1935)
Sylvia Scarlett (RKO, 1935)
Swell-Head (Called on Account of Darkness) (Columbia, 1935)
Stars Over Broadway (Warner Bros., 1935)
The Informer (RKO, 1935)
Public Hero No. 1 (MGM, 1935)
Don't Bet on Blondes (Warner Bros., 1935)
The Winning Ticket (MGM, 1935)
Princess O'Hara (Universal, 1935)
The Good Fairy (MGM, 1935)
The Rainmakers (RKO, 1935)
Let 'Em Have It (United Artists, 1935)
Bad Boy (20th Century-Fox, 1935)
Gold Diggers of 1935 (Warner Bros., 1935)
Baby Face Harrington (MGM, 1935)
The Call of the Wild (United Artists, 1935)
Navy Wife (20th Century-Fox, 1935)
Counterfeit (Columbia, 1936)
Mummy's Boys (RKO, 1936)
End of the Trail (Columbia, 1936)
It Had to Happen (20th Century-Fox, 1936)
Follow the Fleet (RKO, 1936)
Modern Times (United Artists, 1936)
This Is My Affair (20th Century-Fox, 1937)
Angel's Holiday (20th Century-Fox, 1937)
Shall We Dance? (RKO, 1937)
Super-Sleuth (RKO, 1937)
The Last Gangster (MGM, 1937)
They Gave Him a Gun (MGM, 1937)
Wise Girl (RKO, 1937)
Sea Devils (RKO, 1937)
The Law West of Tombstone (RKO, 1938)
The Higgins Family (Republic, 1938)

Passport Husband (20th Century-Fox, 1938)
The Battle of Broadway (20th Century-Fox, 1938)
Submarine Patrol (20th Century-Fox, 1938)
Time Out for Murder (20th Century-Fox, 1938)
Joy of Living (RKO, 1938)
Carefree (RKO, 1938)
Captain Fury (United Artists, 1939)
Beware Spooks (Columbia, 1939)
Boy Friend (20th Century-Fox, 1939)
Everybody's Baby (20th Century-Fox, 1939)
Inside Story (20th Century-Fox, 1939)
The Big Guy (Warden of the Big House) (Universal, 1939)
East Side of Heaven (Universal, 1939)
Another Thin Man (MGM, 1939)
Torchy Plays with Dynamite (Warner Bros., 1939)
Ex-Champ (Universal, 1939)
The Lady's from Kentucky (Paramount, 1939)
6,000 Enemies (MGM, 1939)
Christmas in July (Paramount, 1940)
Brother Orchid (Warner Bros., 1940)
Honeymoon Deferred (Universal, 1940)
Behind the News (Republic, 1940)
Love Thy Neighbor (Paramount, 1940)
A Night at Earl Carroll's (Paramount, 1940)
The Great McGinty (Paramount, 1940)
Federal Fugitives (PRC, 1941)
Double Cross (PRC, 1941)
Knockout (Warner Bros., 1941)
High Sierra (Warner Bros., 1941)
A Date with the Falcon (RKO, 1941)
The Man Who Came to Dinner (Warner Bros., 1941)
Sullivan's Travels (Paramount, 1941)
The Lady Eve (Paramount, 1941)
Penny Serenade (Columbia, 1941)
Meet John Doe (Warner Bros., 1941)
Footlight Fever (RKO, 1941)
The Flame of New Orleans (Universal, 1941)
Pacific Blackout (Midnight Angel) (Paramount, 1941)
Gentleman Jim (Warner Bros., 1942)
Grand Central Murder (MGM, 1942)
'Neath Brooklyn Bridge (Monogram, 1942)

Butch Minds the Baby (Universal, 1942)
Star Spangled Rhythm (Paramount, 1942)
Dudes Are Pretty People (United Artists, 1942)
The Corpse Vanishes (Monogram, 1942)
The Big Street (RKO, 1942)
The Living Ghost (Monogram, 1942)
The Palm Beach Story (Paramount, 1942)
No Time for Love (Paramount, 1943)
Salute for Three (Paramount, 1943)
Ghosts on the Loose (Monogram, 1943)
Government Girl (RKO, 1943)
Cowboy in Manhattan (Universal, 1943)
Lady of Burlesque (United Artists, 1943)
The Great Moment (Paramount, 1944)
I Love a Soldier (Paramount, 1944)
Belle of the Yukon (RKO, 1944)
Hail the Conquering Hero (Paramount, 1944)
The Man in Half-Moon Street (Paramount, 1944)
The Princess and the Pirate (RKO, 1944)
The Miracle of Morgan's Creek (Paramount, 1944)
Return of the Ape Man (Monogram, 1944)
Man from Frisco (Republic, 1944)
Over the Wall (Warner Bros. short, 1944)
Pardon My Past (Columbia, 1945)
Salty O'Rourke (Paramount, 1945)
Road to Utopia (Paramount, 1945)
Crack-Up (RKO, 1946)
No Leave, No Love (voice only: MGM, 1946)
The Kid from Brooklyn (RKO, 1946)
Wild Harvest (Paramount, 1947)
Unconquered (Paramount, 1947)
Mad Wednesday (The Sin of Harold Diddlebock) (United Artists, 1947)
On Our Merry Way (A Miracle Can Happen) (United Artists, 1948)
Unfaithfully Yours (20th Century-Fox, 1948)
The Lady Gambles (Universal, 1949)
Fighting Fools (Monogram, 1949)
The Beautiful Blonde from Bashful Bend (20th Century-Fox, 1949)

Stage to Tucson (Columbia, 1950)
Iron Man (Universal, 1951)
The Square Jungle (Universal, 1955)

Mantan Moreland (1901–1973)

Spirit of Youth (Grand National, 1937)
Shall We Dance? (RKO, 1937)
Gun Moll (Toddy Pictures, 1938)
Next Time I Marry (RKO, 1938)
There's That Woman Again (Columbia, 1938)
Frontier Scout (Grand National, 1938)
Gang Smashers (Million Dollar Productions, 1938)
Harlem on the Prairie (Associated Features, 1938)
Two-Gun Man from Harlem (Hollywood Productions, 1938)
One Dark Night (Million Dollar Productions/Sack Amusement, 1939)
Irish Luck (Monogram, 1939)
Tell No Tales (MGM, 1939)
Riders of the Frontier (Monogram, 1939)
The City of Chance (20th Century-Fox, 1940)
Pier 13 (20th Century-Fox, 1940)
Chasing Trouble (Monogram, 1940)
Millionaire Playboy (RKO, 1940)
Drums of the Desert (Monogram, 1940)
Laughing at Danger (Monogram, 1940)
On the Spot (Monogram, 1940)
Viva Cisco Kid (20th Century-Fox, 1940)
Maryland (20th Century-Fox, 1940)
Star Dust (20th Century-Fox, 1940)
Condemned Men (Toddy, 1940)
The Man Who Wouldn't Talk (20th Century-Fox, 1940)
The Girl in 313 (20th Century-Fox, 1940)
Four Shall Die (Million Dollar Productions, 1940)
Lady Luck (Dixie National, 1940)
While Thousands Cheer (Million Dollar Productions, 1940)
Mr. Washington Goes to Town (Dixie National, 1940)
The Bowery Boy (Republic, 1940)
Up Jumped the Devil (Dixie National/Toddy Pictures, 1941)

Up in the Air (Monogram, 1940)
Ellery Queen's Penthouse Mystery (Columbia, 1941)
Bachelor Daddy (Universal, 1941)
Cracked Nuts (Universal, 1941)
It Started with Eve (Universal, 1941)
Accent on Love (20th Century-Fox, 1941)
The Gang's All Here (Monogram, 1941)
Birth of the Blues (Paramount, 1941)
King of the Zombies (Monogram, 1941)
Hello, Sucker (Universal, 1941)
Dressed to Kill (20th Century-Fox, 1941)
Footlight Fever (RKO, 1941)
Four Jacks and a Jill (RKO, 1941)
Sign of the Wolf (Monogram, 1941)
You're Out of Luck (Monogram, 1941)
Let's Go Collegiate (Monogram, 1941)
Sleepers West (20th Century-Fox, 1941)
Marry the Boss's Daughter (20th Century-Fox, 1941)
World Premiere (Paramount, 1941)
Professor Creeps (Dixie National, 1942)
Andy Hardy's Double Life (MGM, 1942)
Law of the Jungle (Monogram, 1942)
A-Haunting We Will Go (20th Century-Fox, 1942)
Freckles Comes Home (Monogram, 1942)
Mexican Spitfire Sees a Ghost (RKO, 1942)
Treat 'Em Rough (Universal, 1942)
The Strange Case of Doctor Rx (Universal, 1942)
Footlight Serenade (20th Century-Fox, 1942)
The Palm Beach Story (Paramount, 1942)
Phantom Killer (Monogram, 1942)
Eyes in the Night (MGM, 1942)
Tarzan's New York Adventure (MGM, 1942)
Girl Trouble (20th Century-Fox, 1942)
Cabin in the Sky (MGM, 1943)
Hi'Ya, Sailor (Universal, 1943)
Hit the Ice (Universal, 1943)
Cosmo Jones in Crime Smasher (Monogram, 1943)
Sarong Girl (Monogram, 1943)
Melody Parade (Monogram, 1943)

Revenge of the Zombies (Monogram, 1943)
It Comes Up Love (Universal, 1943)
She's for Me (Universal, 1943)
He Hired the Boss (20th Century-Fox, 1943)
My Kingdom for a Cook (Columbia, 1943)
Slightly Dangerous (MGM, 1943)
We've Never Been Licked (Fighting Command) (Universal, 1943)
You're a Lucky Fellow, Mr. Smith (Universal, 1943)
This Is the Life (Universal, 1944)
Swing Fever (MGM, 1944)
The Mystery of the Riverboat (Universal serial, 1944)
Moon Over Las Vegas (Kid from Las Vegas) (Universal, 1944)
The Chinese Cat (Monogram, 1944)
Chip Off the Old Block (Universal, 1944)
Pin-Up Girl (20th Century-Fox, 1944)
South of Dixie (Universal, 1944)
Black Magic (Meeting at Midnight) (Monogram, 1944)
Bowery to Broadway (Universal, 1944)
Charlie Chan in the Secret Service (Monogram, 1944)
See Here, Private Hargrove (MGM, 1944)
She Wouldn't Say Yes (Columbia, 1945)
The Scarlet Clue (Monogram, 1945)
The Jade Mask (Monogram, 1945)
The Spider (20th Century-Fox, 1945)
The Shanghai Cobra (Monogram, 1945)
Captain Tugboat Annie (Republic, 1945)
Mantan Messes Up (Toddy, 1946)
Mantan Runs for Mayor (Toddy, 1946)
Dark Alibi (Monogram, 1946)
Shadows Over Chinatown (Monogram, 1946)
The Trap (Monogram, 1946)
Riverboat Rhythm (RKO, 1946)
Tall, Tan and Terrific (Astor, 1946)
What a Guy (Lucky Star Productions/Toddy, 1947)
Ebony Parade (Astor, 1947)
The Chinese Ring (The Red Hornet) (Monogram, 1947)
Docks of New Orleans (Monogram, 1948)

The Golden Eye (The Mystery of the Golden Eye) (Monogram, 1948)
The Feathered Serpent (Monogram, 1948)
The Shanghai Chest (Monogram, 1948)
Best Man Wins (Columbia, 1948)
Come On, Cowboy (Goldmax, 1948)
The Dreamer (Astor, 1948)
She's Too Mean to Me (Goldmax, 1948)
Return of Mandy's Husband (Lucky Star/Toddy, 1948)
Sky Dragon (Monogram, 1949)
Rockin' the Blues (Fritz Pollard Associates, 1956)
Rock'n'Roll Revue (Studio Films, 1956)
Rock'n'Roll Jamboree (Studio Films, 1957)
The Patsy (Paramount, 1964)
Alvarez Kelly (Columbia, 1966)
Enter Laughing (Columbia, 1967)
The Comic (Columbia, 1969)
Spider Baby; or: The Maddest Story Ever Told (Cannibal Orgy; The Liver Eaters) (American General, 1970)
Watermelon Man (Columbia, 1970)
The Biscuit Eater (BV, 1972)
The Young Nurses (New World, 1973)

Ralph Morgan (1882–1956)

The Master of the House (Triumph/Equitable, 1915)
Madame X (Pathé, 1915)
The Penny Philanthropist (Wholesome Films, 1917)
The Man Who Found Himself (Paramount, 1925)
Excuse the Pardon (Warner Bros./Vitaphone short, 1930)
Honor Among Lovers (Paramount, 1931)
Cheaters at Play (Fox, 1932)
Charlie Chan's Chance (Fox, 1932)
Dance Team (Fox, 1932)
After Tomorrow (Fox, 1932)
Disorderly Conduct (Fox, 1932)
Devil's Lottery (Fox, 1932)
Strange Interlude (MGM, 1932)
Rasputin and the Empress (MGM, 1932)
The Son-Daughter (MGM, 1932)
Humanity (Fox, 1933)
Trick for Trick (Fox, 1933)
Shanghai Madness (Fox, 1933)
The Power and the Glory (Fox, 1933)

Doctor Bull (Fox, 1933)
Walls of Gold (Fox, 1933)
The Kennel Murder Case (Warner Bros., 1933)
The Mad Game (Fox, 1933)
Orient Express (Fox, 1934)
No Greater Glory (Columbia, 1934)
The Last Gentleman (United Artists, 1934)
Stand Up and Cheer! (Fox, 1934)
She Was a Lady (Fox, 1934)
Their Big Moment (RKO, 1934)
Girl of the Limberlost (Monogram, 1934)
Hell in the Heavens (Fox, 1934)
Transatlantic Merry-Go-Round (United Artists, 1934)
Little Men (Mascot, 1934)
I've Been Around (Universal, 1934)
Unwelcome Stranger (Columbia, 1935)
Star of Midnight (RKO, 1935)
Calm Yourself (MGM, 1935)
Condemned to Live (Chesterfield, 1935)
Magnificent Obsession (Universal, 1935)
Muss 'Em Up (RKO, 1936)
Little Miss Nobody (20th Century-Fox, 1936)
Human Cargo (20th Century-Fox, 1936)
The Ex-Mrs. Bradford (RKO, 1936)
Anthony Adverse (Warner Bros., 1936)
Speed (MGM, 1936)
Yellowstone (Universal, 1936)
General Spanky (MGM, 1936)
Crack-Up (20th Century-Fox, 1936)
The Man in Blue (Universal, 1937)
The Life of Emile Zola (Warner Bros., 1937)
The Outer Gate (Behind Prison Bars) (Monogram, 1937)
Exclusive (Paramount, 1937)
That's My Story (Universal, 1937)
Mannequin (MGM, 1937)
Wells Fargo (Paramount, 1937)
Love Is a Headache (MGM, 1938)
Wives Under Suspicion (Universal, 1938)
Army Girl (Republic, 1938)
Mother Carey's Chickens (RKO, 1938)
Barefoot Boy (Monogram, 1938)
Shadows Over Shanghai (Grand National, 1938)

In addition to his many horror movie roles, Ralph Morgan also made a number of appearances in serials. Here, as the villain in Universal's *Gang Busters* (1942), his climactic getaway attempt through a subway tunnel has been grossly mis-timed.

Orphans of the Street (Republic, 1938)
Out West with the Hardys (MGM, 1938)
Trapped in the Sky (Columbia, 1939)
Fast and Loose (MGM, 1939)
The Lone Wolf Spy Hunt (Columbia, 1939)

Man of Conquest (Republic, 1939)
Smuggled Cargo (Republic, 1939)
Way Down South (RKO, 1939)
Geronimo (Paramount, 1939)
Forty Little Mothers (MGM, 1940)
Soak the Old (MGM short, 1940)
I'm Still Alive (RKO, 1940)

Dick Tracy vs. Crime, Inc. (Dick Tracy vs. Phantom Empire) (Republic serial, 1941)
Adventure in Washington (Columbia, 1941)
The Mad Doctor (Paramount, 1941)
Gang Busters (Universal serial, 1942)
Klondike Fury (Monogram, 1942)
Keeping Fit (Universal short, 1942)
A Close Call for Ellery Queen (Columbia, 1942)
Night Monster (Universal, 1942)
A Gentleman After Dark (United Artists, 1942)
The Traitor Within (Republic, 1942)
Stage Door Canteen (United Artists, 1943)
Hitler's Madman (Hitler's Hangman) (MGM, 1943)
Jack London (United Artists, 1943)
The Great Alaskan Mystery (Universal serial, 1944)
Weird Woman (Universal, 1944)
Trocadero (Republic, 1944)
Enemy of Women (Mad Lover; The Secret Life of Paul Joseph Goebbels) (Monogram, 1944)
The Imposter (Bayonet Charge; Strange Confession) (Universal, 1944)
The Monster Maker (PRC, 1944)
The Monster and the Ape (Columbia serial, 1945)
This Love of Ours (Universal, 1945)
Hollywood and Vine (PRC, 1945)
Black Market Babies (Monogram, 1946)
Mr. District Attorney (Columbia, 1947)
Song of the Thin Man (MGM, 1947)
The Last Round-Up (Columbia, 1947)
Sleep, My Love (United Artists, 1948)
Sword of the Avenger (Eagle-Lion, 1948)
The Creeper (20th Century–Fox, 1948)
Blue Grass of Kentucky (Monogram, 1950)
Heart of the Rockies (Republic, 1951)
Gold Fever (Monogram, 1952)

Anne Nagel (1912–1966)

College Humor (Paramount, 1933)
Sitting Pretty (Paramount, 1933)
I Loved You Wednesday (Fox, 1933)

Stand Up and Cheer! (Fox, 1934)
Search for Beauty (Paramount, 1934)
Coming Out Party (Fox, 1934)
She Learned About Sailors (Fox, 1934)
George White's 1935 Scandals (Fox, 1935)
Redheads on Parade (20th Century–Fox, 1935)
Doubting Thomas (Fox, 1935)
Music Is Magic (20th Century–Fox, 1935)
Reckless Roads (Majestic, 1935)
Everybody's Old Man (20th Century–Fox, 1936)
Hot Money (Warner Bros., 1936)
Bullets or Ballots (Warner Bros., 1936)
Polo Joe (Warner Bros., 1936)
China Clipper (Warner Bros., 1936)
King of Hockey (Warner Bros., 1936)
Down the Stretch (Warner Bros., 1936)
Here Comes Carter (Warner Bros., 1936)
Love Begins at Twenty (Warner Bros., 1936)
Here Comes Trouble (20th Century–Fox, 1936)
Three Legionnaires (Three Crazy Legionnaires) (General, 1937)
Devil's Saddle Legion (Warner Bros., 1937)
The Adventurous Blonde (Warner Bros., 1937)
The Footloose Heiress (Warner Bros., 1937)
The Case of the Stuttering Bishop (Warner Bros., 1937)
Romance Road (Warner Bros. short, 1937)
Escape by Night (Republic, 1937)
Hoosier Schoolboy (Forgotten Hero) (Monogram, 1937)
A Bride for Henry (Monogram, 1937)
Guns of the Pecos (Warner Bros., 1937)
Saleslady (Monogram, 1938)
Under the Big Top (Monogram, 1938)
Gang Bullets (Monogram, 1938)
Mystery House (Warner Bros., 1938)
Convict's Code (Monogram, 1939)
Unexpected Father (Sandy Takes a Bow) (Universal, 1939)

Lovely Anne Nagel cowers from a midnight menace in Universal's *Man Made Monster* (1941).

Call a Messenger (Universal, 1939)
Legion of Lost Flyers (Universal, 1939)
The Witness Vanishes (Universal, 1939)
Should a Girl Marry? (Monogram, 1939)
Black Friday (Universal, 1940)
Ma, He's Making Eyes at Me (Universal, 1940)
Winners of the West (Universal serial, 1940)
The Green Hornet (Universal serial, 1940)
Hot Steel (Universal, 1940)
My Little Chickadee (Universal, 1940)
Argentine Nights (Universal, 1940)
Diamond Frontier (Universal, 1940)
The Green Hornet Strikes Again (Universal serial, 1940)
The Invisible Woman (Universal, 1940)
Meet the Chump (Universal, 1941)

Man Made Monster (Universal, 1941)
Mutiny in the Arctic (Universal, 1941)
Sealed Lips (Universal, 1941)
Never Give a Sucker an Even Break (Universal, 1941)
Road Agent (Texas Road Agent) (Universal, 1941)
Hollywood Meets the Navy (Meet the Star series) (Republic short, 1941)
The Mad Doctor of Market Street (Universal, 1942)
Don Winslow of the Navy (Universal serial, 1942)
The Dawn Express (Nazi Spy Ring) (PRC, 1942)
Stagecoach Buckaroo (Universal, 1942)
The Secret Code (Columbia serial, 1942)
The Mad Monster (PRC, 1942)
Women in Bondage (Monogram, 1943)
Murder in the Music Hall (Midnight Melody) (Republic, 1946)
Traffic in Crime (Republic, 1946)

FILMOGRAPHIES

335

The Spirit of West Point (Film
Classics, 1947)
The Trap (Monogram, 1947)
Blondie's Holiday (Columbia, 1947)
The Hucksters (MGM, 1947)
Homecoming (MGM, 1948)
Every Girl Should Be Married (RKO,
1948)
Family Honeymoon (Universal, 1948)
One Touch of Venus (Universal, 1948)
Don't Trust Your Husband (An Inno-
cent Affair) (United Artists, 1948)
Pal's Return (RKO short, 1948)
Prejudice (New World/Motion Picture
Sales, 1949)
The Stratton Story (MGM, 1949)
Armored Car Robbery (RKO, 1950)

J. Carrol Naish (1900–1973)

What Price Glory? (Fox, 1926)
Good Intentions (Fox, 1930)
Cheer Up and Smile (Fox, 1930)
Double Cross Roads (Fox, 1930)
The Royal Bed (The Queen's Husband)
(RKO, 1931)
The Finger Points (voice only; Warner
Bros., 1931)
Tonight or Never (United Artists, 1931)
Gun Smoke (Paramount, 1931)
Ladies of the Big House (Paramount,
1931)
Kick In (Paramount, 1931)
Homicide Squad (Lost Men) (Univer-
sal, 1931)
The Hatchet Man (Warner Bros., 1932)
The Beast of the City (MGM, 1932)
Two Seconds (Warner Bros., 1932)
It's Tough to Be Famous (Warner
Bros., 1932)
Washington Merry-Go-Round (Colum-
bia, 1932)
The Famous Ferguson Case (Warner
Bros., 1932)
Crooner (Warner Bros., 1932)
Week-End Marriage (Warner Bros.,
1932)
The Mouthpiece (Warner Bros., 1932)
Tiger Shark (Warner Bros., 1932)
No Living Witness (A Gangster Talks)
(Mayfair, 1932)
The Kid from Spain (United Artists,
1932)
Big City Blues (Warner Bros., 1932)

The Conquerors (RKO, 1932)
Cabin in the Cotton (Warner Bros.,
1932)
The Mystery Squadron (Mascot serial,
1933)
No Other Woman (RKO, 1933)
Frisco Jenny (Warner Bros., 1933)
Ann Vickers (RKO, 1933)
The Infernal Machine (Fox, 1933)
Central Airport (Warner Bros., 1933)
The World Gone Mad (Public Be
Damned) (Majestic, 1933)
The Past of Mary Holmes (RKO, 1933)
Elmer the Great (Warner Bros., 1933)
The Avenger (Monogram, 1933)
Arizona to Broadway (Fox, 1933)
The Devil's in Love (Fox, 1933)
The Whirlwind (Columbia, 1933)
Captured! (Warner Bros., 1933)
The Big Chance (Arthur Greenblatt,
1933)
The Last Trail (Fox, 1933)
The Mad Game (Fox, 1933)
Silent Men (Columbia, 1933)
Gabriel Over the White House (MGM,
1933)
Notorious But Nice (Chesterfield,
1933)
Sleepers East (Fox, 1934)
British Agent (Warner Bros., 1934)
Bachelor of Arts (Fox, 1934)
What's Your Racket? (Mayfair, 1934)
Murder in Trinidad (Fox, 1934)
One Is Guilty (Columbia, 1934)
Upper World (Warner Bros., 1934)
The Return of the Terror (Warner
Bros., 1934)
Hell Cat (Columbia, 1934)
Girl in Danger (Columbia, 1934)
The Defense Rests (Columbia, 1934)
Hell in the Heavens (Fox, 1934)
The President Vanishes (Paramount,
1934)
Marie Galante (Fox, 1934)
The Lives of a Bengal Lancer (Para-
mount, 1935)
Behind the Green Lights (Mascot, 1935)
Black Fury (Warner Bros., 1935)
Under the Pampas Moon (Fox, 1935)
Little Big Shot (Warner Bros., 1935)
Front Page Woman (Warner Bros.,
1935)
The Crusades (Paramount, 1935)
Special Agent (Warner Bros., 1935)

Confidential (Mascot, 1935)
Captain Blood (Warner Bros., 1935)
The Leathernecks Have Landed (Republic, 1936)
Moonlight Murder (MGM, 1936)
The Return of Jimmy Valentine (Republic, 1936)
Exclusive Story (MGM, 1936)
Robin Hood of El Dorado (MGM, 1936)
Two in the Dark (RKO, 1936)
Absolute Quiet (MGM, 1936)
Charlie Chan at the Circus (20th Century-Fox, 1936)
Special Investigator (RKO, 1936)
Anthony Adverse (Warner Bros., 1936)
Ramona (20th Century-Fox, 1936)
We Who Are About to Die (RKO, 1936)
The Charge of the Light Brigade (Warner Bros., 1936)
Crack-Up (20th Century-Fox, 1936)
Think Fast, Mr. Moto (20th Century-Fox, 1937)
Song of the City (MGM, 1937)
Border Cafe (RKO, 1937)
Hideaway (RKO, 1937)
Bulldog Drummond Comes Back (Paramount, 1937)
Sea Racketeers (Republic, 1937)
Thunder Trail (Thunder Pass) (Paramount, 1937)
Night Club Scandal (Paramount, 1937)
Daughter of Shanghai (Paramount, 1937)
Her Jungle Love (Paramount, 1938)
Tip-Off Girls (Paramount, 1938)
Hunted Men (Paramount, 1938)
Prison Farm (Paramount, 1938)
Bulldog Drummond in Africa (Paramount, 1938)
Illegal Traffic (Paramount, 1938)
King of Alcatraz (Paramount, 1938)
Persons in Hiding (Paramount, 1939)
Hotel Imperial (Paramount, 1939)
Undercover Doctor (Paramount, 1939)
Beau Geste (Paramount, 1939)
Island of Lost Men (Paramount, 1939)
King of Chinatown (Paramount, 1939)
Typhoon (Paramount, 1940)
Queen of the Mob (Paramount, 1940)
Golden Gloves (Paramount, 1940)
Down Argentine Way (20th Century-Fox, 1940)
A Night at Earl Carroll's (Paramount, 1940)

Mr. Dynamite (Universal, 1941)
That Night in Rio (20th Century-Fox, 1941)
Blood and Sand (20th Century-Fox, 1941)
Forced Landing (Paramount, 1941)
Accent on Love (20th Century-Fox, 1941)
Birth of the Blues (Paramount, 1941)
The Corsican Brothers (United Artists, 1941)
Stars at Play (Meet the Stars series) (Republic short, 1941)
Sunday Punch (MGM, 1942)
Dr. Broadway (Paramount, 1942)
Jackass Mail (MGM, 1942)
The Pied Piper (20th Century-Fox, 1942)
A Gentleman at Heart (20th Century-Fox, 1942)
Tales of Manhattan (20th Century-Fox, 1942)
The Man in the Trunk (20th Century-Fox, 1942)
Dr. Renault's Secret (20th Century-Fox, 1942)
Batman (Columbia serial, 1943)
Harrigan's Kid (MGM, 1943)
Good Morning, Judge (Universal, 1943)
Behind the Rising Sun (RKO, 1943)
Sahara (Columbia, 1943)
Gung Ho! (Universal, 1943)
Calling Dr. Death (Universal, 1943)
Voice in the Wind (United Artists, 1944)
The Monster Maker (PRC, 1944)
Two-Man Submarine (Columbia, 1944)
Waterfront (PRC, 1944)
The Whistler (Columbia, 1944)
Jungle Woman (Universal, 1944)
Know for Sure! (Office of War Information short, circa 1944)
Dragon Seed (MGM, 1944)
Enter Arsene Lupin (Universal, 1944)
House of Frankenstein (Universal, 1944)
A Medal for Benny (Paramount, 1945)
The Southerner (United Artists, 1945)
Getting Gertie's Garter (United Artists, 1945)
Strange Confession (The Missing Head) (Universal, 1945)
Bad Bascomb (MGM, 1946)
The Beast with Five Fingers (Warner Bros., 1946)

Horror stars at their lowest ebb: Lon Chaney, Jr., and J. Carrol Naish as the menaces in Independent-International's *Dracula vs. Frankenstein* **(1971).**

Humoresque (Warner Bros., 1946)
Carnival in Costa Rica (20th Century–Fox, 1947)
The Fugitive (RKO, 1947)
Joan of Arc (RKO, 1948)
The Kissing Bandit (MGM, 1948)

Canadian Pacific (20th Century–Fox, 1949)
Vacation at Del Mar (Columbia short, 1949)
That Midnight Kiss (MGM, 1949)
Black Hand (MGM, 1950)

Please Believe Me (MGM, 1950)
Annie Get Your Gun (MGM, 1950)
The Toast of New Orleans (MGM, 1950)
Rio Grande (Republic, 1950)
Mark of the Renegade (Universal, 1951)
Bannerline (MGM, 1951)
Across the Wide Missouri (MGM, 1951)
Denver and Rio Grande (Paramount, 1952)
Clash by Night (RKO, 1952)
Woman of the North Country (Republic, 1952)
Ride the Man Down (Republic, 1952)
Beneath the 12-Mile Reef (20th Century-Fox, 1953)
Fighter Attack (Allied Artists, 1953)
Saskatchewan (Universal, 1954)
Sitting Bull (United Artists, 1954)
Hit the Deck (MGM, 1955)
Rage at Dawn (RKO, 1955)
Violent Saturday (20th Century-Fox, 1955)
New York Confidential (Warner Bros., 1955)
The Last Command (Republic, 1955)
Desert Sands (United Artists, 1955)
Rebel in Town (United Artists, 1956)
Yaqui Drums (Allied Artists, 1956)
This Could Be the Night (MGM, 1957)
The Young Don't Cry (Columbia, 1957)
Force of Impulse (Sutton, 1961)
Dracula vs. Frankenstein (Independent-International, 1971)
Chapter 1 of Naish's serial *Batman* is included in the compilation film *3 Stooges Follies* (Columbia, 1974). He was cut out of *Scotland Yard* (Fox, 1930).

George Pembroke (1901–1972)

Counsel on De Fence (Columbia short, 1934)
Irish and Proud of It (British: Paramount, 1936; U.S.: Guaranteed, 1938)
The Stars Can't Be Wrong (Warner Bros./Vitaphone short, 1936)
False Evidence (Paramount, 1937)
Darts Are Trumps (RKO, 1938)
Merely Mr. Hawkins (RKO, 1938)
Buried Alive (PDC [PRC], 1939)
Calling All Marines (Republic, 1939)

Smuggled Cargo (Republic, 1939)
The Last Alarm (Monogram, 1940)
The Cowboy from Sundown (Monogram, 1940)
Drums of Fu Manchu (Republic serial, 1940)
Meet John Doe (Warner Bros., 1941)
Paper Bullets (PRC, 1941)
Flying Wild (Monogram, 1941)
Adventures of Captain Marvel (Return of Captain Marvel) (Republic serial, 1941)
Invisible Ghost (Monogram, 1941)
I Killed That Man (Monogram, 1941)
The Dawn Express (PRC, 1942)
Captain Midnight (Columbia serial, 1942)
Black Dragons (Monogram, 1942)
Perils of Nyoka (Nyoka and the Tigermen) (Republic serial, 1942)
They All Kissed the Bride (Columbia, 1942)
A Night to Remember (Columbia, 1942)
The Daring Young Man (Columbia, 1942)
Daredevils of the West (Republic serial, 1943)
The Masked Marvel (Republic serial, 1943)
Bluebeard (PRC, 1944)
That's My Man (Republic, 1947)
Call Northside 777 (Calling Northside 777) (20th Century-Fox, 1948)
Red Snow (Columbia, 1952)
Carbine Williams (MGM, 1952)
So You Want to Get It Wholesale (Warner Bros. short, 1952)
Count the Hours (RKO, 1953)
Scotched in Scotland (Columbia short, 1954)
The Girl Rush (Paramount, 1955)
I'll Cry Tomorrow (MGM, 1955)
Shoot-Out at Medicine Bend (Warner Bros., 1957)
Fear Strikes Out (Paramount, 1957)
Hell Canyon Outlaws (Republic, 1957)
Outlaw's Son (United Artists, 1957)
Showdown at Boot Hill (20th Century-Fox, 1958)

Angelo Rossitto (1908–1991)

The Beloved Rogue (United Artists, 1927)

FILMOGRAPHIES **339**

Old San Francisco (Warner Bros., 1927)
While the City Sleeps (MGM, 1928)
Seven Footprints to Satan (First National, 1929)
The Mysterious Island (MGM, 1929)
One Stolen Night (Warner Bros., 1929)
Freaks (MGM, 1932)
The Sign of the Cross (Paramount, 1932)
Babes in Toyland (MGM, 1934)
Carnival (Columbia, 1935)
Charlie Chan at the Circus (20th Century-Fox, 1936)
The Wizard of Oz (MGM, 1939)
Mr. Wong in Chinatown (Monogram, 1939)
Doomed to Die (Monogram, 1940)
Spooks Run Wild (Monogram, 1941)
Hellzapoppin' (Universal, 1941)
The Corpse Vanishes (Monogram, 1942)
A clip of Rossitto from *Dementia* appears in *The Blob* (Paramount, 1958).
Take It Big (Paramount, 1944)
The Spider Woman (Universal, 1944)
Lady in the Dark (Paramount, 1944)
Ali Baba and the Forty Thieves (Universal, 1944)
Scared to Death (Screen Guild, 1947)
Mad Wednesday (United Artists, 1947)
Samson and Delilah (Paramount, 1949)
The Baron of Arizona (Lippert, 1950)
Bandit Queen (Lippert, 1950)
The Greatest Show on Earth (Paramount, 1952)
The Mesa of Lost Women (Howco, 1953)
Jungle Moon Men (Columbia, 1955)
Dementia (Van Wolf-API, 1956)
Carousel (20th Century-Fox, 1956)
The Story of Mankind (Warner Bros., 1957)
Invasion of the Saucer Men (AIP, 1957)
The Wild and the Innocent (Universal, 1959)
The Big Circus (Allied Artists, 1959)
Pocketful of Miracles (United Artists, 1961)
The Magic Sword (United Artists, 1962)

Confessions of an Opium Eater (Allied Artists, 1962)
The Wonderful World of the Brothers Grimm (MGM, 1962)
The Trip (AIP, 1967)
Dr. Dolittle (20th Century-Fox, 1967)
Pufnstuf (Universal, 1970)
Dracula vs. Frankenstein (Independent-International, 1971)
Brain of Blood (Hemisphere Pictures, 1971)
The Stone Killer (Columbia, 1973)
The Clones (Clones) (Film Makers International, 1973)
Little Cigars (AIP, 1973)
The Master Gunfighter (Taylor-Laughlin/Billy Jack, 1975)
Lord of the Rings (voice only; United Artists, 1978)
Galaxina (Crown International, 1980)
Something Wicked This Way Comes (Buena Vista, 1983)
Mad Max Beyond Thunderdome (Warner Bros., 1985)
The Offspring (Conquest Entertainment, 1987)

As **Don Barrett**

Child Bride (Stern Fisher-Raymond Friedgen, 1938)

Elizabeth Russell (1916–)

Girl of the Ozarks (Paramount, 1936)
My American Wife (Paramount, 1936)
Lady Be Careful (Paramount, 1936)
Forgotten Faces (Paramount, 1936)
Hideaway Girl (Paramount, 1937)
Annapolis Salute (RKO, 1937)
A Date with the Falcon (RKO, 1941)
Miss Polly (United Artists, 1941)
Cat People (RKO, 1942)
Meet the Mob (Monogram, 1942)
The Corpse Vanishes (Monogram, 1942)
Stand by for Action (MGM, 1942)
The Seventh Victim (RKO, 1943)
Hitler's Madman (MGM, 1943)
A Scream in the Dark (Republic, 1943)
She Has What It Takes (Columbia, 1943)
Summer Storm (United Artists, 1944)
The Curse of the Cat People (RKO, 1944)

Elizabeth Russell had a forbidding screen personality that she turned on not only in *The Corpse Vanishes* and the Val Lewton chillers, but also in Universal's *Weird Woman* (pictured).

The Uninvited (Paramount, 1944)
Youth Runs Wild (RKO, 1944)
Weird Woman (Universal, 1944)
Keep Your Powder Dry (MGM, 1944)

Our Vines Have Tender Grapes (MGM, 1945)
Adventure (MGM,1945)
Bedlam (RKO, 1946)

Opposite: One of Angelo Rossitto's best-known roles was as the circus dwarf in Tod Browning's grotesque *Freaks* (1932).

Wild Stallion (Monogram, 1952)
Feudin' Fools (Monogram, 1952)
So Big (Warner Bros., 1953)
From the Terrace (20th Century–Fox, 1960)

Glenn Strange (1899–1973)

Wild Horse (Silver Devil) (Allied, 1931)
The Deadline (Columbia, 1931)
Border Law (Columbia, 1931)
The Hard Hombre (Allied Artists, 1931)
Range Feud (Columbia, 1931)
The Fighting Marshal (Columbia, 1931)
The Guilty Generation (Columbia, 1931)
Ride Him, Cowboy (Warner Bros., 1932)
The Hurricane Express (Mascot serial, 1932)
His Royal Shyness (Sennett-Educational short, 1932)
McKenna of the Mounted (Columbia, 1932)
The Cowboy Counsellor (Allied, 1932)
The Whirlwind (Columbia, 1933)
The Thrill Hunter (Columbia, 1933)
Somewhere in Sonora (Warner Bros., 1933)
The Law of the Wild (Mascot serial, 1934)
His Fighting Blood (Ambassador, 1935)
Cyclone of the Saddle (First Division, 1935)
Moonlight on the Prairie (Warner Bros., 1935)
Hard Rock Harrigan (Sol Lesser/20th Century–Fox, 1935)
Gallant Defender (Columbia, 1935)
The Law of 45's (Normandy/First Division, 1935)
Border Vengeance (Willis Kent/Marcy, 1935)
Westward Ho (Republic, 1935)
Stormy (Universal, 1935)
The New Frontier (Republic, 1935)
The Lawless Range (Republic, 1935)
Suicide Squad (Puritan, 1935)
Flash Gordon (Universal serial, 1936)
Sunset of Power (Universal, 1936)
Conflict (Universal, 1936)

The Cattle Thief (Columbia, 1936)
Avenging Waters (Columbia, 1936)
Trailin' West (Warner Bros., 1936)
The Fugitive Sheriff (Columbia, 1936)
Song of the Gringo (Grand National, 1936)
The California Mail (Warner Bros., 1936)
The Lonely Trail (Republic, 1936)
Adventure's End (Universal, 1937)
Guns of the Pecos (Warner Bros., 1937)
Trouble in Texas (Grand National, 1937)
Danger Valley (Monogram, 1937)
Courage of the West (Universal, 1937)
A Tenderfoot Goes West (Hoffberg, 1937)
Arizona Days (Grand National, 1937)
Stars Over Arizona (Monogram, 1937)
Empty Holsters (Warner Bros., 1937)
The Californian (Gentleman from California) (Principal/20th Century–Fox, 1937)
Land Beyond the Law (Warner Bros., 1937)
The Sunday Round-Up (Warner Bros./Vitaphone short, 1937)
Blazing Sixes (Warner Bros., 1937)
The Devil's Saddle Legion (Warner Bros., 1937)
The Cherokee Strip (Warner Bros., 1937)
The Singing Outlaw (Universal, 1938)
Whirlwind Horseman (Grand National, 1938)
Six-Shootin' Sheriff (Grand National, 1938)
Gunsmoke Trail (Monogram, 1938)
Ghost Town Riders (Universal, 1938)
Forbidden Valley (Universal, 1938)
California Frontier (Columbia, 1938)
Guilty Trails (Universal, 1938)
Prairie Justice (Universal, 1938)
The Frontiersman (Paramount, 1938)
Prison Break (Universal, 1938)
In Old Mexico (Paramount, 1938)
State Police (Universal, 1938)
The Painted Trail (Monogram, 1938)
The Mysterious Rider (Mark of the Avenger) (Paramount, 1938)
Border Wolves (Universal, 1938)
The Spy Ring (Universal, 1938)
The Last Stand (Universal, 1938)

Black Bandit (Universal, 1938)
Cull of the Rockies (Columbia, 1938)
Gun Packer (Monogram, 1938)
Honor of the West (Universal, 1938)
Pride of the West (Paramount, 1938)
Cupid Rides the Range (RKO short, 1939)
The Lone Ranger Rides Again (Republic serial, 1939)
The Llano Kid (Paramount, 1939)
Sunset Trail (Paramount, 1939)
Across the Plains (Monogram, 1939)
Oklahoma Terror (Monogram, 1939)
Range War (Paramount, 1939)
Arizona Legion (RKO, 1939)
The Night Riders (Republic, 1939)
Ride, Cowboy, Ride (Warner Bros./Vitaphone short, 1939)
Blue Montana Skies (Republic, 1939)
Law of the Pampas (Paramount, 1939)
Rough Riders' Round-Up (Republic, 1939)
Overland Mail (Monogram, 1939)
Flying G-Men (Columbia serial, 1939)
The Fighting Gringo (RKO, 1939)
Days of Jesse James (Republic, 1939)
The Phantom Stage (Universal, 1939)
Dark Command (Republic, 1940)
Bar Buckaroos (RKO short, 1940)
The Fargo Kid (RKO, 1940)
Three Men from Texas (Paramount, 1940)
Pioneer Days (Monogram, 1940)
Rhythm of the Rio Grande (Monogram, 1940)
Pals of the Silver Sage (Monogram, 1940)
Covered Wagon Trails (Monogram, 1940)
Land of the Six Guns (Monogram, 1940)
Stage to Chino (RKO, 1940)
Teddy, the Rough Rider (Warner Bros./Vitaphone short, 1940)
Triple Justice (RKO, 1940)
Wyoming (MGM, 1940)
Wagon Train (RKO, 1940)
San Francisco Docks (Universal, 1940)
The Cowboy from Sundown (Monogram, 1940)
Wide Open Town (Paramount, 1941)
California or Bust (RKO short, 1941)
Lone Star Law Men (Monogram, 1941)

Billy the Kid Wanted (PRC, 1941)
Forbidden Trails (Monogram, 1941)
Riders of Death Valley (Universal serial, 1941)
In Old Colorado (Paramount, 1941)
Saddlemates (Republic, 1941)
The Kid's Last Ride (Monogram, 1941)
Dude Cowboy (RKO, 1941)
The Bandit Trail (RKO, 1941)
Badlands of Dakota (Universal, 1941)
Fugitive Valley (Monogram, 1941)
The Driftin' Kid (Monogram, 1941)
Westward Ho-Hum (RKO short, 1941)
Billy the Kid's Roundup (PRC, 1941)
Arizona Cyclone (Universal, 1941)
The Mummy's Tomb (Universal, 1942)
The Lone Rider and the Bandit (PRC, 1942)
Western Mail (Monogram, 1942)
Army Surgeon (RKO, 1942)
Sundown Jim (20th Century–Fox, 1942)
Raiders of the West (PRC, 1942)
Boot Hill Bandits (Monogram, 1942)
Rolling Down the Great Divide (PRC, 1942)
Texas Trouble Shooters (Monogram, 1942)
Overland Stagecoach (PRC, 1942)
Sunset on the Desert (Republic, 1942)
Juke Girl (Warner Bros., 1942)
Billy the Kid Trapped (PRC, 1942)
Romance on the Range (Republic, 1942)
Come On, Danger! (RKO, 1942)
Stagecoach Buckaroo (Ghost Town Buckaroo) (Universal, 1942)
Little Joe, the Wrangler (Universal, 1942)
Bandit Ranger (RKO, 1942)
Down Texas Way (Monogram, 1942)
The Mad Monster (PRC, 1942)
Action in the North Atlantic (Warner Bros., 1943)
Western Cyclone (Frontier Fighters) (PRC, 1943)
Bullets and Saddles (Monogram, 1943)
Death Valley Rangers (Monogram, 1943)
Cattle Stampede (PRC, 1943)
The Kansan (United Artists, 1943)
The Desperadoes (Columbia, 1943)

The Woman of the Town (United Artists, 1943)
The Return of the Rangers (PRC, 1943)
The Black Raven (PRC, 1943)
False Colors (United Artists, 1943)
Mission to Moscow (Warner Bros., 1943)
The Kid Rides Again (PRC, 1943)
Haunted Ranch (Monogram, 1943)
Wild Horse Stampede (Monogram, 1943)
Black Market Rustlers (Monogram, 1943)
Arizona Trail (Universal, 1943)
Forty Thieves (United Artists, 1944)
Harmony Trail (White Stallion) (Mattox Productions, 1944)
Silver City Kid (Republic, 1944)
Can't Help Singing (Universal, 1944)
The Contender (PRC, 1944)
Valley of Vengeance (PRC, 1944)
Trail to Gunsight (Universal, 1944)
The San Antonio Kid (Republic, 1944)
Knickerbocker Holiday (United Artists, 1944)
The Monster Maker (PRC, 1944)
Sonora Stagecoach (Monogram, 1944)
Alaska (Monogram, 1944)
House of Frankenstein (Universal, 1944)
Bad Men of the Border (Universal, 1945)
Saratoga Trunk (Warner Bros., 1945)
Blazing the Western Trail (Columbia, 1945)
Renegades of the Rio Grande (Universal, 1945)
House of Dracula (Universal, 1945)
Beauty and the Bandit (Monogram, 1946)
Up Goes Maisie (MGM, 1946)
The Sea of Grass (MGM, 1947)
The Fabulous Texan (Republic, 1947)
Sinbad the Sailor (RKO, 1947)
The Wistful Widow of Wagon Gap (Universal, 1947)
Heaven Only Knows (Montana Mike) (United Artists, 1947)
Brute Force (Universal, 1947)
Wyoming (Republic, 1947)
Northwest Outpost (Republic, 1947)
Abbott and Costello Meet Frankenstein (Universal, 1948)
Red River (United Artists, 1948)
The Gallant Legion (Republic, 1948)

A Southern Yankee (MGM, 1948)
Silver Trails (Monogram, 1948)
California Firebrand (Republic, 1948)
The Gal Who Took the West (Universal, 1949)
Master Minds (Monogram, 1949)
Rimfire (Lippert, 1949)
Roll, Thunder, Roll (Eagle-Lion, 1949)
Comanche Territory (Universal, 1950)
Double Crossbones (Universal, 1950)
Surrender (Republic, 1950)
Vengeance Valley (MGM, 1951)
Callaway Went Thataway (MGM, 1951)
Texas Carnival (MGM, 1951)
The Red Badge of Courage (MGM, 1951)
Comin' Round the Mountain (Universal, 1951)
Wagons West (Monogram, 1952)
The Lawless Breed (Universal, 1952)
I Dream of Jeanie (Republic, 1952)
The Lusty Men (RKO, 1952)
Montana Belle (RKO, 1952)
All the Brothers Were Valiant (MGM, 1953)
Escape from Fort Bravo (MGM, 1953)
Calamity Jane (Warner Bros., 1953)
Born to the Saddle (Astor, 1953)
The Great Sioux Uprising (Universal, 1953)
Devil's Canyon (RKO, 1953)
The Veils of Bagdad (Universal, 1953)
Jubilee Trail (Republic, 1954)
Gypsy Colt (MGM, 1954)
The Road to Denver (Republic, 1955)
The Vanishing American (Republic, 1955)
Treasure of Ruby Hills (Allied Artists, 1955)
Backlash (Universal, 1956)
The Fastest Gun Alive (MGM, 1956)
Last Stagecoach West (Republic, 1957)
The Halliday Brand (United Artists, 1957)
Jailhouse Rock (MGM, 1957)
Gunfire at Indian Gap (Republic, 1957)
Quantrill's Raiders (Allied Artists, 1958)
Terror in a Texas Town (United Artists, 1958)
Alias Jesse James (United Artists, 1959)
Last Train from Gun Hill (Paramount, 1959)

The Jayhawkers! (Paramount, 1959)
Clips of Strange in: *Flash Gordon* appear in *Flash Gordon's Trip to Mars* (Universal serial, 1938); *Abbott and Costello Meet Frankenstein* appear in *The World of Abbott and Costello* (Universal, 1965); *Red River* appear in *The Last Picture Show* (Columbia, 1971). He was cut out of *The Spoilers* (Universal, 1942) *Playmates* (RKO, 1941) features him in a clip from an unidentified Western.

Robert Strange (1881–1952)

The Smiling Lieutenant (Paramount, 1931)
The Cheat (Paramount, 1931)
The Misleading Lady (Paramount, 1932)
The Crane Poison Case (Warner Bros./Vitaphone short, 1932)
These Thirty Years (Caravel, 1934)
Gambling (Fox, 1934)
Frisco Kid (Warner Bros., 1935)
Special Agent (Warner Bros., 1935)
The Story of Louis Pasteur (Warner Bros., 1935)
I Found Stella Parish (Warner Bros., 1935)
The Walking Dead (Warner Bros., 1936)
The Murder of Dr. Harrigan (Warner Bros., 1936)
The Leathernecks Have Landed (Republic, 1936)
Beware of Ladies (Republic, 1936)
Trapped by Television (Columbia, 1936)
Beloved Enemy (United Artists, 1936)
Stolen Holiday (Warner Bros., 1936)
Roaming Lady (Columbia, 1936)
John Meade's Woman (Paramount, 1937)
Marked Woman (Warner Bros., 1937)
Partners in Crime (Paramount, 1937)
Racket Busters (Warner Bros., 1938)
Sky Giant (RKO, 1938)
I Stand Accused (Republic, 1938)
Made for Each Other (United Artists, 1939)
Hell's Kitchen (Warner Bros., 1939)
The Story of Vernon and Irene Castle (RKO, 1939)
They Made Me a Criminal (Warner Bros., 1939)

Missing Evidence (Universal, 1939)
The Saint Strikes Back (RKO, 1939)
The Spellbinder (RKO, 1939)
You Can't Get Away with Murder (Warner Bros., 1939)
In Name Only (RKO, 1939)
The Angels Wash Their Faces (Warner Bros., 1939)
The Great Man Votes (RKO, 1939)
Flag of Humanity (Warner Bros. short, 1940)
Dr. Ehrlich's Magic Bullet (Warner Bros., 1940)
Castle on the Hudson (Warner Bros., 1940)
Gambling on the High Seas (Warner Bros., 1940)
King of the Royal Mounted (Republic serial, 1940)
Invisible Ghost (Monogram, 1941)
All That Money Can Buy (The Devil and Daniel Webster) (RKO, 1941)
Arizona Cyclone (Universal, 1941)
Paper Bullets (Gangs Incorporated) (PRC, 1941)
High Sierra (Warner Bros., 1941)
Desert Bandit (Republic, 1941)
Robin Hood of the Pecos (Republic, 1941)
Adventures of Captain Marvel (Republic serial, 1941)
Manpower (Warner Bros., 1941)
Wild Bill Hickok Rides (Warner Bros., 1941)
Mr. District Attorney (Republic, 1941)
Blondie in Society (Columbia, 1941)
South of Santa Fe (Republic, 1942)
Perils of Nyoka (Republic serial, 1942)
The Mad Monster (PRC, 1942)
Law of the Jungle (Monogram, 1942)
Mission to Moscow (Warner Bros., 1942)
Dead Men Walk (PRC, 1943)
Mr. Lucky (RKO, 1943)
Captain America (Return of Captain America) (Republic serial, 1944)
Rosie, the Riveter (Republic, 1944)
Your Weapons (Navy training/Republic short, 1944)
Thoroughbreds (Republic, 1945)
A Tree Grows in Brooklyn (20th Century–Fox, 1945)
The Phantom of 42nd Street (PRC, 1945)
Gangs of the Waterfront (Republic, 1945)

Silver Trails (Monogram, 1948)
The Far Frontier (Republic, 1948)
Flamingo Road (Warner Bros., 1949)
Stock footage of Strange in a submarine (taken from *King of the Royal Mounted*) is utilized in *G-Men vs. the Black Dragon* (Republic serial, 1942) and in *Zombies of the Stratosphere* (Republic serial, 1952)
He was cut out of *Spendthrift* (Paramount, 1936).

Charles Trowbridge (1882–1967)

The Fight (World, 1915)
The Siren's Song (World, 1915)
Sunday (World, 1915)
Prohibition (Prohibition Films, 1915)
Thais (Goldwyn, 1916)
The Eternal Magdalene (Goldwyn, 1919)
The Fortune Hunter (Vitagraph, 1920)
Island Wives (Vitagraph, 1922)
Damaged Love (Superior/Sono Art-World Wide, 1930)
24 Hours (Paramount, 1931)
Silence (Paramount, 1931)
Honor Among Lovers (Paramount, 1931)
The Secret Call (Paramount, 1931)
I Take This Woman (Paramount, 1931)
Rendezvous (MGM, 1935)
Mad Love (MGM, 1935)
Calm Yourself (MGM, 1935)
Murder Man (MGM, 1935)
It's in the Air (MGM, 1935)
I Live My Life (MGM, 1935)
Exclusive Story (MGM, 1936)
Born to Dance (MGM, 1936)
Wife Versus Secretary (MGM, 1936)
The Devil Is a Sissy (MGM, 1936)
Love on the Run (MGM, 1936)
Speed (MGM, 1936)
The Garden Murder Case (MGM, 1936)
Moonlight Murder (MGM, 1936)
After the Thin Man (MGM, 1936)
We Went to College (MGM, 1936)
Robin Hood of El Dorado (MGM, 1936)
The Gorgeous Hussy (MGM, 1936)
The Great Ziegfeld (MGM, 1936)
Important News (MGM short, 1936)
Libeled Lady (MGM, 1936)
Man of the People (MGM, 1936)
Captains Courageous (MGM, 1937)

The Thirteenth Chair (MGM, 1937)
Dangerous Number (MGM, 1937)
A Day at the Races (MGM, 1937)
They Gave Him a Gun (MGM, 1937)
Espionage (MGM, 1937)
That Certain Woman (Warner Bros., 1937)
That's My Story (Universal, 1937)
Ever Since Eve (Warner Bros., 1937)
Sea Racketeers (Republic, 1937)
Reported Missing (Universal, 1937)
Fit for a King (RKO, 1937)
Saturday's Heroes (RKO, 1937)
Servant of the People (MGM short, 1937)
Exiled to Shanghai (Republic, 1937)
City Girl (20th Century-Fox, 1937)
Alcatraz Island (Warner Bros., 1937)
Angels with Dirty Faces (Warner Bros, 1938)
Racket Busters (Warner Bros., 1938)
Nancy Drew, Detective (Warner Bros., 1938)
Gang Bullets (Monogram, 1938)
College Swing (Paramount, 1938)
Men with Wings (Paramount, 1938)
Little Tough Guy (Universal, 1938)
The Invisible Menace (Warner Bros., 1938)
The Patient in Room 18 (Warner Bros., 1938)
Smashing the Rackets (RKO, 1938)
Holiday (Columbia, 1938)
Crime Ring (RKO, 1938)
The Last Express (Universal, 1938)
Thanks for Everything (20th Century-Fox, 1938)
Kentucky (20th Century-Fox, 1938)
Gangs of New York (Republic, 1938)
Four's a Crowd (Warner Bros., 1938)
The Buccaneer (Paramount, 1938)
Submarine Patrol (20th Century-Fox, 1938)
Crime School (Warner Bros., 1938)
Swanee River (20th Century-Fox, 1939)
Undercover Doctor (Paramount, 1939)
Boy Trouble (Paramount, 1939)
The Story of Alexander Graham Bell (20th Century-Fox, 1939)
The Lady's from Kentucky (Paramount, 1939)
King of the Underworld (Warner Bros., 1939)
Each Dawn I Die (Warner Bros., 1939)

Confessions of a Nazi Spy (Warner Bros., 1939)
The Man They Could Not Hang (Columbia, 1939)
Cafe Society (Paramount, 1939)
King of Chinatown (Paramount, 1939)
Sergeant Madden (MGM, 1939)
Risky Business (Universal, 1939)
Mutiny on the Blackhawk (Universal, 1939)
Lady of the Tropics (MGM, 1939)
Tropic Fury (Universal, 1939)
The Angels Wash Their Faces (Warner Bros., 1939)
Pride of the Navy (Republic, 1939)
On Trial (Warner Bros., 1939)
Elsa Maxwell's Hotel for Women (20th Century-Fox, 1939)
Joe and Ethel Turp Call on the President (MGM, 1939)
While America Sleeps (MGM short, 1939)
Disputed Passage (Paramount, 1939)
Let Us Live! (Columbia, 1939)
Homicide Bureau (Columbia, 1939)
Mysterious Dr. Satan (Republic serial, 1940)
The Fatal Hour (Mr. Wong at Headquarters) (Monogram, 1940)
Dr. Kildare Goes Home (MGM, 1940)
The Man Who Wouldn't Talk (20th Century-Fox, 1940)
Sailor's Lady (20th Century-Fox, 1940)
Before I Hang (Columbia, 1940)
Edison, the Man (MGM, 1940)
I Take This Woman (MGM, 1940)
Cherokee Strip (Paramount, 1940)
The Mummy's Hand (Universal, 1940)
Virginia City (Warner Bros., 1940)
Andy Hardy Meets Debutante (MGM, 1940)
The Fighting 69th (Warner Bros., 1940)
The Man with Nine Lives (Columbia, 1940)
Our Town (United Artists, 1940)
Knute Rockne – All American (Warner Bros., 1940)
My Love Came Back (Warner Bros., 1940)
The House of the Seven Gables (Universal, 1940)
Trail of the Vigilantes (Universal, 1940)

Charlie Chan at the Wax Museum (20th Century-Fox, 1940)
Johnny Apollo (20th Century-Fox, 1940)
The Son of Monte Cristo (United Artists, 1940)
Let's Make Music (RKO, 1940)
Dr. Kildare's Victory (MGM, 1941)
Dressed to Kill (20th Century-Fox, 1941)
Sergeant York (Warner Bros., 1941)
Design for Scandal (MGM, 1941)
The Great Lie (Warner Bros., 1941)
The Nurse's Secret (Warner Bros., 1941)
Strange Alibi (Warner Bros., 1941)
Belle Starr (20th Century-Fox, 1941)
Cadet Girl (20th Century-Fox, 1941)
Great Guns (20th Century-Fox, 1941)
Too Many Blondes (Universal, 1941)
King of the Texas Rangers (Republic serial, 1941)
Rags to Riches (Republic, 1941)
Hurricane Smith (Republic, 1941)
We Go Fast (20th Century-Fox, 1941)
The Great Mr. Nobody (Warner Bros., 1941)
Blue, White and Perfect (20th Century-Fox, 1941)
They Met in Bombay (MGM, 1941)
Sex Hygiene (Audio Productions/U.S. Navy short, 1942)
The Magnificent Dope (20th Century-Fox, 1942)
Sweetheart of the Fleet (Columbia, 1942)
That Other Woman (20th Century-Fox, 1942)
Wake Island (Paramount, 1942)
Ten Gentlemen from West Point (20th Century-Fox, 1942)
Thunder Birds (20th Century-Fox, 1942)
Who Is Hope Schuyler? (20th Century-Fox, 1942)
Tennessee Johnson (MGM, 1942)
Over My Dead Body (20th Century-Fox, 1942)
Meet the Stewarts (Columbia, 1942)
Sweet Rosie O'Grady (20th Century-Fox, 1943)
Mission to Moscow (Warner Bros., 1943)
Madame Curie (MGM, 1943)

She's for Me (Universal, 1943)
Action in the North Atlantic (Warner Bros., 1943)
Salute to the Marines (MGM, 1943)
Adventures of the Flying Cadets (Universal serial, 1943)
Wintertime (20th Century–Fox, 1943)
The Amazing Mrs. Holliday (Universal, 1943)
The Falcon in Danger (RKO, 1943)
The Story of Dr. Wassell (Paramount, 1944)
Summer Storm (United Artists, 1944)
Captain America (Return of Captain America) (Republic serial, 1944)
Faces in the Fog (Republic, 1944)
Wing and a Prayer (20th Century–Fox, 1944)
The Fighting Seabees (Republic, 1944)
Hey, Rookie (Columbia, 1944)
Heavenly Days (RKO, 1944)
Mildred Pierce (Warner Bros., 1945)
The Red Dragon (Monogram, 1945)
Within These Walls (20th Century–Fox, 1945)
Colonel Effingham's Raid (20th Century–Fox, 1945)
They Were Expendable (MGM, 1945)
Valley of the Zombies (Republic, 1946)
Smooth as Silk (Universal, 1946)
Shock (20th Century–Fox, 1946)
Don't Gamble with Strangers (Monogram, 1946)
Secret of the Whistler (Columbia, 1946)
The Hoodlum Saint (MGM, 1946)
Undercurrent (MGM, 1946)
Honeymoon (RKO, 1947)
Shoot to Kill (Police Reporter) (Screen Guild, 1947)
The Beginning or the End (MGM, 1947)
The Secret Life of Walter Mitty (RKO, 1947)
The Private Affairs of Bel Ami (United Artists, 1947)
Her Husband's Affairs (Columbia, 1947)
Key Witness (Columbia, 1947)
Mr. District Attorney (Columbia, 1947)
Buck Privates Come Home (Universal, 1947)
Michigan Kid (Universal, 1947)
Tarzan and the Huntress (RKO, 1947)
Tycoon (RKO, 1947)

Black Gold (Allied Artists, 1947)
Song of My Heart (Allied Artists, 1947)
The Sea of Grass (MGM, 1947)
The Paleface (Paramount, 1948)
Stage Struck (Monogram, 1948)
Hollow Triumph (The Scar; The Man Who Murdered Himself) (Eagle-Lion, 1948)
Mr. Soft Touch (Columbia, 1949)
The Fountainhead (Warner Bros., 1949)
The Sun Comes Up (MGM, 1949)
Bad Boy (Allied Artists, 1949)
A Woman of Distinction (Columbia, 1950)
When Willie Comes Marching Home (20th Century–Fox, 1950)
Unmasked (Republic, 1950)
Peggy (Universal, 1950)
Hoodlum Empire (Republic, 1952)
The Bushwhackers (Realart, 1952)
The Wings of Eagles (MGM, 1957)
The Last Hurrah (Columbia, 1958)
Scenes of Trowbridge in *The Mummy's Hand* are seen in flashbacks in *The Mummy's Tomb* (Universal, 1942).

Minerva Urecal (1896–1966)

Meet the Baron (MGM, 1933)
You Can't Buy Everything (MGM, 1934)
Sadie McKee (MGM, 1934)
Straight Is the Way (MGM, 1934)
Student Tour (MGM, 1934)
Bonnie Scotland (MGM, 1935)
It Happened in New York (Universal, 1935)
His Bridal Sweet (Columbia short, 1935)
Here Comes the Band (MGM, 1935)
Man on the Flying Trapeze (Paramount, 1935)
God's Country and the Woman (Warner Bros., 1936)
Fury (MGM, 1936)
Bulldog Edition (Republic, 1936)
Love on a Bet (RKO, 1936)
The Three Godfathers (Miracle in the Sand) (MGM, 1936)
Oh, Doctor (Universal, 1937)
Mountain Justice (Warner Bros., 1937)

Minerva Urecal provided memorable support in six of Monogram's horror (or horror/comedy) films, most notably *The Ape Man* with Bela Lugosi.

Ever Since Eve (Warner Bros., 1937)
Her Husband's Secretary (Warner Bros., 1937)
Live, Love and Learn (MGM, 1937)
The Go-Getter (Warner Bros., 1937)
Behind the Mike (Universal, 1937)
Love in a Bungalow (Universal, 1937)
Charlie Chan at the Olympics (20th Century-Fox, 1937)
Life Begins with Love (Columbia, 1937)
She Loved a Fireman (Warner Bros., 1937)
Exiled to Shanghai (Republic, 1937)
Portia on Trial (Republic, 1937)
Wives Under Suspicion (Universal, 1938)
The Devil's Party (Universal, 1938)
In Old Chicago (20th Century-Fox, 1938)
The Lady in the Morgue (Universal, 1938)

Start Cheering (Columbia, 1938)
Thanks for Everything (20th Century-Fox, 1938)
Dramatic School (MGM, 1938)
Prison Nurse (Republic, 1938)
Frontier Scout (Grand National, 1938)
Air Devils (Universal, 1938)
City Streets (Columbia, 1938)
Should Husbands Work? (Republic, 1939)
Sabotage (Republic, 1939)
Four Girls in White (MGM, 1939)
Little Accident (Universal, 1939)
She Married a Cop (Republic, 1939)
Dancing Co-Ed (voice only; MGM, 1939)
No Place to Go (Warner Bros., 1939)
You Can't Cheat an Honest Man (Universal, 1939)
The Unexpected Father (Universal, 1939)
Destry Rides Again (Universal, 1939)
S.O.S. Tidal Wave (Republic, 1939)
Maid to Order (RKO short, 1939)

Missing Evidence (Universal, 1939)
Golden Boy (Columbia, 1939)
Irving Berlin's Second Fiddle (20th
Century-Fox, 1939)
The Sagebrush Family Trails West
(PDC [PRC], 1940)
Wildcat Bus (RKO, 1940)
Boys of the City (The Ghost Creeps)
(Monogram, 1940)
You Can't Fool Your Wife (RKO, 1940)
No, No Nanette (RKO, 1940)
San Francisco Docks (Universal, 1940)
Never Give a Sucker an Even Break
(Universal, 1941)
A Man Betrayed (Wheel of Fortune)
(Republic, 1941)
Man at Large (20th Century-Fox,
1941)
Marry the Boss's Daughter (20th Cen-
tury-Fox, 1941)
Skylark (Paramount, 1941)
The Wild Man of Borneo (MGM, 1941)
Murder by Invitation (Monogram,
1941)
Murder Among Friends (20th Cen-
tury-Fox, 1941)
Arkansas Judge (Republic, 1941)
The Trial of Mary Dugan (MGM, 1941)
They Died with Their Boots On
(Warner Bros., 1941)
Six Lessons from Madame La Zonga
(Universal, 1941)
The Cowboy and the Blonde (20th Cen-
tury-Fox, 1941)
Golden Hoofs (20th Century-Fox,
1941)
Lady for a Night (Republic, 1941)
Bowery Blitzkrieg (Monogram, 1941)
Accent on Love (20th Century-Fox,
1941)
Moon Over Her Shoulder (20th Cen-
tury-Fox, 1941)
Sailors on Leave (Republic, 1941)
Dressed to Kill (20th Century-Fox,
1941)
In Old California (Republic, 1942)
The Man in the Trunk (20th Cen-
tury-Fox, 1942)
Beyond the Blue Horizon (Paramount,
1942)
Henry Aldrich, Editor (Paramount,
1942)
Almost Married (Universal, 1942)
Sweater Girl (Paramount, 1942)

Sons of the Pioneers (Republic, 1942)
That Other Woman (20th Century-
Fox, 1942)
Quiet Please, Murder! (20th Cen-
tury-Fox, 1942)
Riding Through Nevada (Columbia,
1942)
Henry and Dizzy (Paramount, 1942)
The Powers Girl (United Artists,
1942)
The Living Ghost (Monogram, 1942)
The Corpse Vanishes (Monogram,
1942)
The Daring Young Man (Columbia,
1942)
My Favorite Blonde (Paramount,
1942)
A Tragedy at Midnight (Republic,
1942)
The Ape Man (Monogram, 1943)
Dangerous Blondes (Columbia, 1943)
Wagon Tracks West (Republic, 1943)
My Kingdom for a Cook (Columbia,
1943)
So This Is Washington (RKO, 1943)
White Savage (Universal, 1943)
The Song of Bernadette (20th Cen-
tury-Fox, 1943)
A Stranger in Town (MGM, 1943)
Ghosts on the Loose (Monogram, 1943)
Pitchin' in the Kitchen (Columbia
short, 1943)
Klondike Kate (Columbia, 1943)
You Dear Boy (Columbia short, 1943)
Here Comes Elmer (Republic, 1943)
Hit the Ice (Universal, 1943)
Keep 'Em Slugging (Universal, 1943)
Shadow of a Doubt (Universal, 1943)
Kid Dynamite (Monogram, 1943)
Dixie Dugan (20th Century-Fox, 1943)
Man from Frisco (Republic, 1944)
Mr. Skeffington (Warner Bros., 1944)
Louisiana Hayride (Columbia, 1944)
The Doughgirls (Warner Bros., 1944)
Irish Eyes Are Smiling (20th Cen-
tury-Fox, 1944)
And Now Tomorrow (Paramount,
1944)
Kismet (Oriental Dream) (MGM, 1944)
The Mark of the Whistler (Columbia,
1944)
Music in Manhattan (RKO, 1944)
Moonlight and Cactus (Universal,
1944)

One Mysterious Night (Columbia, 1944)
The Bridge of San Luis Rey (United Artists, 1944)
Bachelor Daze (Columbia short, 1944)
Block Busters (Monogram, 1944)
When Strangers Marry (Betrayed) (Monogram, 1944)
Crazy Knights (Ghost Crazy) (Monogram, 1944)
State Fair (It Happened One Summer) (20th Century-Fox, 1945)
The Kid Sister (PRC, 1945)
Sensation Hunters (Club Paradise) (Monogram, 1945)
Men in Her Diary (Universal, 1945)
George White's Scandals (RKO, 1945)
The Bells of St. Mary's (RKO, 1945)
Out of This World (Paramount, 1945)
Wanderer of the Wasteland (RKO, 1945)
Salty O'Rourke (Paramount, 1945)
Mr. Muggs Rides Again (Monogram, 1945)
Alibi Baby (RKO short, 1945)
Colonel Effingham's Raid (20th Century-Fox, 1945)
A Medal for Benny (Paramount, 1945)
A Bell for Adano (20th Century-Fox, 1945)
Who's Guilty? (Columbia serial, 1945)
No Leave, No Love (MGM, 1946)
The Virginian (Paramount, 1946)
Little Miss Big (Universal, 1946)
Crime Doctor's Man Hunt (Columbia, 1946)
Andy Plays Hookey (Columbia short, 1946)
The Bride Wore Boots (Paramount, 1946)
Sioux City Sue (Republic, 1946)
Rainbow Over Texas (Republic, 1946)
Wake Up and Dream (20th Century-Fox, 1946)
The Dark Corner (20th Century-Fox, 1946)
The Well Groomed Bride (Paramount, 1946)
Swell Guy (Universal, 1946)
Without Reservations (RKO, 1946)
California (Paramount, 1946)
Voice of the Whistler (Columbia, 1946)
Saddle Pals (Republic, 1947)
Ladies' Man (Paramount, 1947)

Undercover Maisie (MGM, 1947)
Apache Rose (Republic, 1947)
Cynthia (MGM, 1947)
The Trap (Monogram, 1947)
The Devil Thumbs a Ride (RKO, 1947)
Blaze of Noon (Paramount, 1947)
The Secret Life of Walter Mitty (RKO, 1947)
Bowery Buckaroos (Monogram, 1947)
Hired Husband (RKO short, 1947)
The Lost Moment (Universal, 1947)
Heartaches (PRC, 1947)
The Noose Hangs High (Eagle-Lion, 1948)
Sitting Pretty (20th Century-Fox, 1948)
Fury at Furnace Creek (20th Century-Fox, 1948)
Night Has a Thousand Eyes (Paramount, 1948)
Family Honeymoon (Universal, 1948)
Marshal of Amarillo (Republic, 1948)
The Strange Mrs. Crane (Eagle-Lion, 1948)
The Snake Pit (20th Century-Fox, 1948)
Joan of Arc (RKO, 1948)
April Showers (Warner Bros., 1948)
Secret Service Investigator (Republic, 1948)
Good Sam (RKO, 1948)
Sundown in Santa Fe (Republic, 1948)
Song of Surrender (Paramount, 1949)
Big Jack (MGM, 1949)
The Lovable Cheat (Film Classics, 1949)
Outcasts of the Trail (Republic, 1949)
Down to the Sea in Ships (20th Century-Fox, 1949)
Holiday in Havana (Columbia, 1949)
Side Street (MGM, 1949)
Take One False Step (Universal, 1949)
Master Minds (Monogram, 1949)
Scene of the Crime (MGM, 1949)
The Jackpot (20th Century-Fox, 1950)
Traveling Saleswoman (Columbia, 1950)
A Slip and a Miss (Columbia short, 1950)
His Baiting Beauty (Columbia short, 1950)
The Arizona Cowboy (Republic, 1950)
Mister 880 (20th Century-Fox, 1950)
Quicksand (United Artists, 1950)

My Blue Heaven (20th Century–Fox, 1950)
Harvey (Universal, 1950)
The Milkman (Universal, 1950)
The Awful Sleuth (Columbia short, 1951)
The Raging Tide (Universal, 1951)
Dear Brat (Paramount, 1951)
Stop That Cab (Lippert, 1951)
Blonde Atom Bomb (Columbia short, 1951)
Mask of the Avenger (Columbia, 1951)
Texans Never Cry (Columbia, 1951)
The Great Caruso (MGM, 1951)
Harem Girl (Columbia, 1952)
Anything Can Happen (Paramount, 1952)
Lost in Alaska (Universal, 1952)
Fearless Fagan (MGM, 1952)
Aaron Slick from Punkin Crick (Paramount, 1952)
Oklahoma Annie (Republic, 1952)
Gobs and Gals (Republic, 1952)
Niagara (20th Century–Fox, 1953)
She's Back on Broadway (Warner Bros., 1953)
Woman They Almost Lynched (Republic, 1953)
Two-Gun Marshal (Newhall/Allied Artists, 1953)
By the Light of the Silvery Moon (Warner Bros., 1953)
Marty (United Artists, 1955)
Double Jeopardy (Republic, 1955)
A Man Alone (Republic, 1955)
So You Want to Be a V.P. (Warner Bros. short, 1955)
Sudden Danger (Allied Artists, 1955)
Crashing Las Vegas (Allied Artists, 1956)
Miracle in the Rain (Warner Bros., 1956)
Death of a Scoundrel (RKO, 1956)
Footsteps in the Night (Allied Artists, 1957)
The Adventures of Huckleberry Finn (MGM, 1960)
Mr. Hobbs Takes a Vacation (20th Century–Fox, 1962)
7 Faces of Dr. Lao (MGM, 1964)
That Funny Feeling (Universal, 1965)
Urecal's footage was deleted from *Blondes at Work* (Warner Bros., 1938). Urecal footage from the shorts *You Dear Boy* and *Hired Husband* appear in *Happy Go Wacky* (Columbia short, 1952) and the compilation film *Variety Time* (RKO, 1948), respectively. She's frequently credited with a role in *High Conquest* (Monogram, 1947) actually played by Mary Field.

Luana Walters

Reaching for the Moon (United Artists, 1930)
Miss Pinkerton (Warner Bros., 1932)
Two Seconds (Warner Bros., 1932)
End of the Trail (Columbia, 1932)
Fighting Texans (Monogram, 1933)
The Merry Widow (The Lady Dances) (MGM, 1934)
Broadway Melody of 1936 (MGM, 1935)
Suzy (MGM, 1936)
Aces and Eights (Puritan, 1936)
Ride 'em Cowboy (Cowboy Roundup) (Universal, 1936)
The Speed Reporter (Dead Line) (Reliable, 1936)
Shadow of Chinatown (Victory serial, 1936)
Souls at Sea (Paramount, 1937)
Assassin of Youth (BCM Productions, 1937)
Under Strange Flags (Crescent/States Rights, 1937)
Youth on Parole (Republic, 1937)
Marie Antoinette (MGM, 1938)
Where the West Begins (Monogram, 1938)
Algiers (United Artists, 1938)
The Buccaneer (Paramount, 1938)
Say It in French (Paramount, 1938)
Honeymoon in Bali (My Love for Yours) (Paramount, 1939)
Thanks for the Memory (Paramount, 1938)
Mutiny on the Blackhawk (Universal, 1939)
Hotel Imperial (Paramount, 1939)
Cafe Society (Paramount, 1939)
Paris Honeymoon (Paramount, 1939)
Eternally Yours (United Artists, 1939)
Mexicali Rose (Republic, 1939)
The Magnificent Fraud (Paramount, 1939)

King of Chinatown (Paramount, 1939)

St. Louis Blues (Best of the Blues) (Paramount, 1939)

The Return of Wild Bill (Columbia, 1940)

The Durango Kid (Columbia, 1940)

The Tulsa Kid (Republic, 1940)

The Range Busters (Monogram, 1940)

Blondie Plays Cupid (Columbia, 1940)

Drums of Fu Manchu (Republic serial, 1940)

Misbehaving Husbands (PRC, 1940)

Road Agent (Texas Road Agent) (Universal, 1941)

Lovable Trouble (Columbia short, 1941)

Law of the Wild (Law of the Wolf) (Arthur Ziehm Productions, 1941)

Fangs of the Wild (Astor/Metropolitan, 1941)

No Greater Sin (Social Enemy No. 1) (University Films, 1941)

Arizona Bound (Monogram, 1941)

Across the Sierras (Columbia, 1941)

The Kid's Last Ride (Monogram, 1941)

The Lone Star Vigilantes (Columbia, 1941)

Thundering Hoofs (RKO, 1942)

The Corpse Vanishes (Monogram, 1942)

Lawless Plainsmen (Columbia, 1942)

Down Texas Way (Monogram, 1942)

Inside the Law (PRC, 1942)

Bad Men of the Hills (Columbia, 1942)

Captain Midnight (Columbia serial, 1942)

Bells of San Angelo (Republic, 1947)

Arthur Takes Over (20th Century–Fox, 1948)

Superman (Columbia serial, 1948)

Mighty Joe Young (RKO, 1949)

Girls in Prison (AIP, 1956)

The She-Creature (AIP, 1956)

As Susan Walters

Shoot to Kill (Police Reporter) (Screen Guild, 1947)

As June Walters

Secrets of Hollywood (Lester F. Scott, 1933).

George Zucco (1886–1960)

Dreyfus (The Dreyfus Case) (Wardour/Columbia, 1931)

There Goes the Bride (Ideal/Gaumont-British, 1932)

The Midshipmaid (Midshipmaid Gob) (W&F/Gaumont-British, 1932)

The Roof (Radio/Gaumont-British, 1933)

The Good Companions (Ideal/Gaumont-British, 1933)

The Man from Toronto (Ideal/Gaumont-British/Gainsborough, 1933)

What Happened Then? (Wardour/British International Pictures, 1934)

What's in a Name? (First National/British International Pictures, 1934)

Autumn Crocus (Associated British Film Distributors, 1934)

It's a Bet (Wardour/British International Pictures, 1935)

Abdul the Damned (Wardour/British International Pictures, 1935)

After the Thin Man (MGM, 1936)

Sinner Take All (MGM, 1936)

The Man Who Could Work Miracles (United Artists, 1937)

The Bride Wore Red (MGM, 1937)

Conquest (MGM, 1937)

The Firefly (MGM, 1937)

London by Night (MGM, 1937)

Madame X (MGM, 1937)

Parnell (MGM, 1937)

Rosalie (MGM, 1937)

Saratoga (MGM, 1937)

Souls at Sea (Paramount, 1937)

Suez (20th Century–Fox, 1938)

Arsene Lupin Returns (MGM, 1938)

Charlie Chan in Honolulu (20th Century–Fox, 1938)

Fast Company (The Rare Book Murder) (MGM, 1938)

Lord Jeff (MGM, 1938)

Marie Antoinette (MGM, 1938)

Three Comrades (MGM, 1938)

Vacation from Love (MGM, 1938)

Arrest Bulldog Drummond! (Paramount, 1938)

Captain Fury (United Artists, 1939)

The Adventures of Sherlock Holmes (20th Century–Fox, 1939)

No one gave "the evil eye" better than George Zucco, the veteran British actor who provided Grade A villainy in many a Grade B production.

The Cat and the Canary (Paramount, 1939)

Here I Am a Stranger (20th Century-Fox, 1939)

The Hunchback of Notre Dame (RKO, 1939)

The Magnificent Fraud (Paramount, 1939)

Arise, My Love (Paramount, 1940)

Dark Streets of Cairo (Universal, 1940)

The Mummy's Hand (Universal, 1940)

New Moon (MGM, 1940)

International Lady (United Artists, 1941)

The Monster and the Girl (Paramount, 1941)

Ellery Queen and the Murder Ring (Columbia, 1941)

Topper Returns (United Artists, 1941)

A Woman's Face (MGM, 1941)

The Black Swan (20th Century-Fox, 1942)

Dr. Renault's Secret (20th Century-Fox, 1942)

Halfway to Shanghai (Universal, 1942)

The Mad Monster (PRC, 1942)

The Mummy's Tomb (Universal, 1942)

My Favorite Blonde (Paramount, 1942)

Sherlock Holmes in Washington (Universal, 1943)

The Black Raven (PRC, 1943)

Dead Men Walk (PRC, 1943)

Holy Matrimony (20th Century-Fox, 1943)

Song of Russia (MGM, 1943)

Never a Dull Moment (Universal, 1943)

The Mad Ghoul (Universal, 1943)

The Mummy's Ghost (Universal, 1944)

House of Frankenstein (Universal, 1944)

The Seventh Cross (MGM, 1944)

Shadows in the Night (Columbia, 1944)

Voodoo Man (Monogram, 1944)

One Exciting Night (Midnight Manhunt) (Paramount, 1945)

Confidential Agent (Warner Bros., 1945)

Fog Island (PRC, 1945)

Watchtower Over Tomorrow (WAC/Office of War Information short, 1945)

Having Wonderful Crime (RKO, 1945)

Hold That Blonde! (Paramount, 1945)

Sudan (Universal, 1945)

Week-End at the Waldorf (MGM, 1945)

The Flying Serpent (PRC, 1946)

Captain from Castile (20th Century-Fox, 1947)

Lured (United Artists, 1947)

Desire Me (MGM, 1947)

The Imperfect Lady (Paramount, 1947)

Moss Rose (20th Century-Fox, 1947)

Scared to Death (Screen Guild, 1947)

Where There's Life (Paramount, 1947)

The Pirate (MGM, 1948)

Joan of Arc (RKO, 1948)

Secret Service Investigator (Republic, 1948)

Tarzan and the Mermaids (RKO, 1948)

Who Killed Doc Robbin? (The Adventures of Curley and His Gang) (United Artists, 1948)

The Barkleys of Broadway (MGM, 1949)

Madame Bovary (MGM, 1949)

The Secret Garden (MGM, 1949)

Harbor of Missing Men (Republic, 1950)

Let's Dance (Paramount, 1950)

Flame of Stamboul (Columbia, 1951)

The First Legion (United Artists, 1951)

David and Bathsheba (20th Century-Fox, 1951)

Zucco may or may not play the Ape Man in the first few shots of *Return of the Ape Man* (Monogram, 1944).

Appendix IV

Apparently cursed—*à la* Bela Lugosi's many mad scientist characters—with the burning desire to delve into Things Man Is Not Meant to Know, I conducted a survey among a select group of die-hard Lugosi fans/collectors/chroniclers to determine which of the actor's notorious Monogram films of the 1940s size up best according to the experts. (Also humbly included is my own list.) The participants were asked to rank these nine films in order of preference, from number 1 (favorite) to number 9.

The blue-ribbon panel of Lugosiphiles consists of:

Forrest J Ackerman, editor of *Famous Monsters of Filmland* magazine;

Buddy Barnett, manager of Hollywood's Cinema Collectors Shop and coauthor of the underground book *Lugosi—Then and Now!*;

Richard Bojarski, author of *The Films of Bela Lugosi*;

Ronald V. Borst, writer/historian/collector-dealer, specializing in horror and science fiction;

John and **Mike Brunas**, research associates on *Poverty Row HORRORS!*;

John Cocchi, one of America's most respected film researchers;

Mike Copner, host of the home video tribute *Bela Lugosi—Then and Now*;

Glenn Damato, prominent Lugosi fan and convention figure, and a collector-dealer in Lugosi memorabilia;

Joe Dante, the Fan Who Made Good, rising from editorial associate of *Castle of Frankenstein* magazine to director of Hollywood hits like *The Howling* and *Gremlins*;

Marta Dobrovitz, coeditor of *Cult Movies and Video* magazine;

William K. Everson, noted film archivist, teacher and author;

Alex Gordon, friend to Lugosi, film historian, movie producer (*Day the World Ended, Voodoo Woman, The Atomic Submarine*, many more); brother of...

Richard Gordon, friend to Lugosi, film historian, movie producer (*The Haunted Strangler, Fiend Without a Face, The Projected Man*, more); brother of Alex;

Don Leifert, whose *Filmfax* articles on Poverty Row horror films spawned this book;

Arthur Lennig, author of the Lugosi biography *The Count*;

Greg Luce, impresario of Sinister Cinema, "The leading source of horror, mystery, and science fiction on video";

Scott MacQueen, film historian/writer whose articles have appeared in *American Cinematographer*;

Greg Mank, author of the landmark horror film book *It's Alive! The Classic Cinema Saga of Frankenstein* and McFarland's *Karloff and Lugosi*;

Sam Sherman, editor of *Screen Thrills Illustrated*; more recently, the head of the New Jersey-based Independent-International Pictures;

Gary Svehla, whose fanzine *Midnight Marquee* (formerly *Gore Creatures*) has now entered its *fourth*(!) decade of publication;

Maurice Terenzio, a teacher of cinema for ten years, now with Northeastern Illinois University;

Tom Weaver, myself;

Michael Weldon, author of *The Psychotronic Encyclopedia of Film* and editor of the *Psychotronic* fanzine;

Don Willis, author of the *Horror and Science Fiction Films* book series;

and **Del Winans**, writer for *The Monster Times, Midnight Marquee, Cinemacabre*; publisher of *Fantasy Magazine Index*.

Some survey-related nuts and bolts: One of the few things our voters could agree on was to *dis*agree. Four films received votes that ranged the whole way from 1 to 9 and several others came close. Buddy Barnett and Mike Copner both rated *Bowery at Midnight* number 1; Barnett commented, *"Bowery* had the best script, a lot of that enjoyable Monogram skid row atmosphere, and Lugosi in an interesting part." But no one liked it so little as John and Mike Brunas, who rated it 8 and 9, respectively ("It's stupid, plodding and dull, dull, dull!"). A *much*-echoed sentiment was that if Lugosi's PRC film *The Devil Bat* had been a Monogram film, it would have been number 1.

Greg Luce insists that *Spooks Run Wild* and *Return of the Ape Man* are exactly equal in quality, and lists them in a tie for seventh place; *Return*, he feels, has "one of the worst music scores in the history of film." Apropos of nothing, he also provided his Top Ten list of Poverty Row horror films of the '40; in reverse order, they are *The Face of Marble, Voodoo Man, Revenge of the Zombies, The Devil Bat, The Monster Maker, The Ape, The Amazing Mr. X* (1948), *The Woman Who Came Back* (1945), *Fear in the Night* (1947) and – his favorite – *Strangler of the Swamp*. He rated *Voodoo Man* as number 1 in this survey because he "likes its rural feel"; Greg Mank also put it in his top spot ("Fine showcase for Bela, who looks distinguished in his goatee and robes, and acts with a winning – dare we say Karloffian? – melancholy"). But Richard Bojarski apparently liked nothing about it, slotting it dead last. Of *The Corpse Vanishes*, Scott MacQueen asks, "What other movie from the World War II period – or any period – dares to have a Charleston for its main title music?"

Return of the Ape Man – my favorite – got off to a strong start in the survey with several votes for number 1 but eventually slipped several rungs, partly thanks to Alex Gordon, who kiddingly rated it tenth out of nine films. Alex was the only one of the 26 voters whose top four coincided *in order* with the compendium survey's top four; at the race track, that would have earned him some money, but not here. Maurice Terenzio wants us all to know that, where his list is concerned, "The distance between numbers 1 and 9 is thinner than a hair." The two Lugosi/East Side Kids films, *Spooks Run Wild* and *Ghosts on the Loose*, battled tooth and nail for the bottom spot, with *Ghosts* eventually winning it by a huge margin; it raked in 20 out of 26 votes for 9th place.

Screwy idea, wasn't it?

Survey Results

1. Invisible Ghost
2. The Corpse Vanishes
3. Voodoo Man

4. Bowery at Midnight
5. Return of the Ape Man
6. Black Dragons
7. The Ape Man
8. Spooks Run Wild
9. Ghosts on the Loose

	Invisible Ghost	Spooks Run Wild	Black Dragons	The Corpse Vanishes	Bowery at Midnight	The Ape Man	Ghosts on the Loose	Voodoo Man	Return of the Ape Man
Forrest J Ackerman	1	7	5	2	8	3	9	6	4
Buddy Barnett	2	6	3	5	1	8	9	4	7
Richard Bojarski	7	5	2	6	3	1	8	9	4
Ronald V. Borst	5	8	6	2	3	7	9	1	4
John Brunas	2	7	3	1	8	6	9	4	5
Mike Brunas	2	4	5	1	9	7	8	3	6
John Cocchi	1	9	5	3	2	6	4	7	8
Mike Copner	2	7	3	6	1	9	8	5	4
Glenn Damato	6	8	7	5	4	3	9	2	1
Joe Dante	1	8	4	2	3	7	9	5	6
Marta Dobrovitz	4	6	1	3	2	5	9	7	8
William K. Everson	1	3	6	2	5	8	9	4	7
Alex Gordon	1	7	5	2	4	6	8	3	9
Richard Gordon	1	8	3	6	2	7	9	4	5
Don Leifert	3	8	6	7	5	4	9	2	1
Arthur Lennig	4	6	7	3	5	8	9	1	2
Greg Luce	4	7	5	3	2	6	9	1	7
Scott MacQueen	5	7	8	1	2	3	9	4	6
Greg Mank	5	8	6	3	7	2	9	1	4
Sam Sherman	1	4	6	2	7	8	9	5	3
Gary Svehla	1	8	7	2	6	5	9	4	3
Maurice Terenzio	1	8	6	2	3	5	9	7	4
Tom Weaver	4	8	7	2	6	3	9	5	1
Michael Weldon	4	8	3	5	7	2	9	1	6
Don Willis	7	2	5	1	6	4	8	3	9
Del Winans	1	8	7	5	6	3	9	2	4

Index

Bold numbers indicate photographs

Abbott, Bud 24
Abbott, George 203
Abbott, John 94, 210, 214, 215–16, 217, **217**, 218–9, 259, 288–89, **289**
Abbott and Costello Meet Frankenstein (1948) 79–80, 140, 259, 267
The Abbott and Costello Show (TV) 24
Ackerman, Forrest J 111, 140–41, 356
Acquanetta 104, 140
Acuff, Eddie 238, 244
Adams, Ernie 27, 165
Adams, Jane **279**, 284
Adamson, Al 69–71
Adamson, Harold 209
Adrian, Iris 184–85, 187
Adventures of Captain Marvel (1941 serial) 99, 110, 241
Adventures of Superman (TV) 194, 285
Adventures of Tugboat Annie (TV) 4
Alexander, Richard 270, 271
Alexander, Ross 82
All That Money Can Buy (1941) 44, 45, 276
Allen, David 245
Altman, Robert 218
Alton, John xv, 156, 159, 163, 259
Alyn, Kirk 175, 177
The Amazing Transparent Man (1960) 190
An American in Paris (1951) 259
Ames, Michael *see* Andrews, Tod
Amsterdam, Morey 279
And So They Were Married see *Johnny Doesn't Live Here Anymore*
And Then There Were None (1945) 196
Anders, Rudolph 72
Andrews, Tod 131, 137, **166**, 167, 171, 172–73, 174, 290
Angel Island (stage) 203–04
Angels with Dirty Faces (1938) 4

Anger, Kenneth 244
Angus, Bernadine 204
Ankers, Evelyn 147
Antosiewicz, John 100
The Ape (1940) 5–14, **8**, **13**, 22, 31, 72, 79, 104, 234, 275, 276, **313**
The Ape Man (1943) **ii**, xiv, 3, 10, 27, 82, 85, 102–14, **105**, **108**, **112**, 134, 136, 169, 173, 195, 275–76, **349**
Archer, Anne 42
Archer, John 37, 42, **42**, 86, 89, 290–91
Argyle, John 15, 281
Arlen, Richard 153, **154**, 156, 157, 158–59, 160, **160**, 161, 162, 163, 206, 208, 209
Arsenic and Old Lace (stage) 26, 112, 131
Asther, Nils 179, 181, 187 Astor, Mary 82
Atom Age Vampire (1960) 73
Atomic Monster see *Man Made Monster*
Attack of the 50 Foot Woman (1958) 234
Atwill, Lionel xi, xiv, 42, 80, 128, 196, **200**, 201–02, 203, 204, 243, 285
Aubert, Lenore 220, 254, **255**, 259
Auer, John H. 151
"Ava: My Story" 119
Ayres, Lew 162

Babes in Toyland (1934) 69
Baker, Rick 149
Baldwin, Alan 17, **19**, 22, 250
Banks, Leslie 278
Barclay, Joan 55, 60, 64, 73, 91, 291–93, **292**
Barcroft, Roy 175, 177, 214, 216, 217
Barlow, Reginald 81
Barnett, Buddy 356, 357

Barnett, Vince xii, 2, 3, 43, 64, 68, **72**, 85, **87**, 89
Barrat, Robert 221, 225
Barrymore, John 69
Baskett, James 122, 126, 128
Bates, Bill 115
Batman and Robin (1949 serial) 125
Battle Stripe see *The Men*
The Beast from 20, 000 Fathoms (1953) 4, 120
The Beast with Five Fingers (1946) 147
Beaudine, William 5, 111, 113, 131, 139, 140, 165, 194–95, 235, 271–72
Beck, Calvin 109
Bedlam (1946) 68, 287
Before I Hang (1940) 10, 112, 268
Beginning of the End (1957) xv
Bela Lugosi Meets a Brooklyn Gorilla (1952) 112, 117, 195
Beneath the Planet of the Apes (1970) 173
Benedict, Billy 116, 117, 270, **272**, 293–96, **295**
Berkes, John 85, **87**, 89, 92
Bernard, Jeffrey 233, 235
Bernds, Edward xv, 4
Best, Willie 43, 176, 177, 231, 234
Beware Spooks (1939) 99
Beyond the Time Barrier (1960) 190
The Big Sleep (1946) xv, 218
Billy the Kid (1941) 25
Billy the Kid Versus Dracula (1966) 135, 195
A Bird in the Head (1946 short) 194
Birell, Tala 144, 146, 147, 149, 150
The Black Cat (1934) 63, 133, 178, 187, 188, 190; (1941) 24, 26, 27
Black Dragons (1942) xii, xiii, 12, 19, 27, 35, 36, 37, 52–63, **56**, **59**, 64, 72, 91, 282, **292**
Black Friday (1940) 7, 10, 15, 81, 161, 205, 208, 209
The Black Raven (1943) 80, 90, 98, 142, 201, 278
The Black Room (1935) 51, 276
The Black Scorpion (1957) 120
The Black Shield of Falworth (1954) 267
The Black Sleep (1956) 72, 140, 141, 149
Black Zoo (1963) 202
Blackmer, Sidney 22, 62, 154, 159
The Blake Murder Mystery see *Haunted House*

Blazing the Overland Trail (1956 serial) 51
The Blob (1958) 3
Blood of Frankenstein see *Dracula vs. Frankenstein*
"Blood on Her Shoe" 177
The Blood Seekers see *Dracula vs. Frankenstein*
Bluebeard (unmade Karloff film) 188; (1944) xi, xiv, xvi, 146, 172, 177–91, **180**, **189**, 199, 219, 228, 250, 277; (1962) 188–89; (1972) 189
The Body Snatcher (1945) 11, 140
Boetticher, Budd 183
Bogart, Humphrey 152, 202, 265
Bogdanovich, Peter 182, 183, 190, 191
Bojarski, Richard 356, 357; *see also* "The Films of Bela Lugosi"
Booth, Adrian 109, 175, 177, 262, 267, 268, 269, 296–98, **297**
Borg, Veda Ann 122, 125–26, **125**, **127**, 175, 177, 196, 202
Born Yesterday (stage) 22
Borst, Ron 102, 128, 236, 253, 269, 356
Bow, Clara 216
Bowery at Midnight (1942) xii, 27, 35, 36, 42, 73, 84–93, **87**, **90**, 109, 281, 358
The Bowery Boys xv, 24, 32, 48, 116, 270, 271, 284
The Bowery Boys Meet the Monsters (1954) 1
Bowery to Bagdad (1955) 1
The Boys from Brooklyn see *Bela Lugosi Meets a Brooklyn Gorilla*
Boys of the City (1940) 1–5, 30, 46, 67, 194
Bracken, Eddie xv, 119
Brackett, Leigh xv, 212, 218
The Brain (1965) 163
The Brain That Wouldn't Die (1961) 73, 157
Bretherton, Howard 37, 177
Brian, David 268
Bricker, George 20
Bride of Frankenstein (1935) 43, 81
Bride of the Monster (1956) 58, 67, 71
The Bridge on the River Kwai (1957) xv, 51
The Brighton Strangler (1945) 37
British Intelligence (1940) 201
Broidy, Steve 270
Brown, James S., Jr. 223–24

Brown, Joe E. 90 Brown, Karl 112
Browning, Tod 44, 110
Bruce, David 147
Brunas, Ruth xv
The Brute Man (1946) 20, 24, 79, 149, 278, **279**
Bryan, Arthur Q. 18, 22
Burbank, Luther 20
Burke, Frankie 4
The Burning Question see *Reefer Madness*
Burr, Raymond 201
Burton, Richard 189
Burton, Robert 159
Busch, Mae 79, 81
Butler, John K. 177, 205, 208, 212, 218

Cagney, James 4, 202
"Cahiers du Cinéma" 183
Calling Dr. Death (1943) 147
Calvert, Steve 109, 112
Cameron, Rod 61
Cane, Charles 155, 159, 263, 268
The Canterville Ghost (1944) ix, 37
Captain America (1944 serial) 42, 60, 268
Captain Midnight (TV) 267
Captain Sindbad (1963) 184
Captive Wild Woman (1943) 104, 149, 250
Carlisle, Mary 94, 98-9, **100**, 102
Carpenter, John (actor) 67
Carradine, Ardanelle 187
Carradine, Christopher 187
Carradine, John ix, xi, xii, xiv, 80, 104, 121, 122, 124–25, **125**, 127, 128–29, **129**, 130, 131, 134–36, **134**, 137, **138**, 139, 149, 165, **168**, 169, 170–71, 172, 173, 174, 179, 184, 185–87, 188, **189**, 191, 229, 231, **232**, 233–34, 235, 244, 267
Carradine, Keith 187
Carradine, Robert 187
Carroll, Leo G. 149
Carroll, Richard 7, 10
The Case of the Missing Brides see *The Corpse Vanishes*
Cass, Maurice 256
Cassidy, Edward 76, 81, 247
Castle, William 34
"Castle of Frankenstein" 129, 172, 195, 356

The Cat Creeps (1946) 200
Cat People (1942) 67, 261
The Catman of Paris (1946) xv, 80, 216, 253–61, **255**, **257**, **260**
Cavett, Dick 186
Chabrol, Claude 189
Chamber of Horrors (1940) 278-79
Chambers, Wheaton 238, **240**, 244
Champion (1949) xv, 51
Chandler, Lane 154
Chaney, Lon, Jr. 20, 25, 26, 69, 79, 92, 187, 212, **337**
Chaney, Lon, Sr. 12, 14, 25, 32, 267
Change of Heart see *Hit Parade of 1943*
Chaplin, Charlie 179, 188
Charlie Chan at the Opera (1936) 6
Chase, Alden *see* Chase, Stephen
Chase, Stephen 2, 3
Chatterton, Tom 209
Cherry, Robert 126, 128
Chester, Hal E. 4
Chudnow, David 82-83, 276
The Cisco Kid (TV) 90
Citizen Kane (1941) 44, 276
Clarke, Robert xv, 135
Clements, Stanley 117, 120
Cleveland, George 9
The Climax (1944) ix, 10, 12
Clive, Colin 147
The Clutching Hand (1936 serial) 60
Clute, Chester 270
Coburn, James 259
Cocchi, John xvi, 43, 102, 163, 190, 228, 356
Coffin, Tristram 66, 71–72, 73, **73**, 74, 298–301, **300**
Cohen, Herman 117, 202
Cohen, Larry 245
"Collier's" 6
Colvin, Andrew 130
Commando (1964) 220
Compson, Betty 27, **30**, 32
Condemned Men (1940) 195
Condemned to Live (1935) 60, 149
Confessions of a Nazi Spy (1939) 44
Confessions of an Opium Eater (1962) 150
Conlan, Frank 220
Conway, Morgan 203
Conway, Tom 244
Cookson, Peter 175, 177
Cooper, Gary 187
Cooper, James Fenimore 220

Copner, Mike 356, 357
Corey, Wendell 161
The Corpse Vanished see *Revenge of the Zombies*
The Corpse Vanishes (1942) xii–xiii, 3, 27, 61, 63–74, **65**, **70**, **72**, **73**, 85, 89, 91, 117, 128, 136, 276, 357
Corregidor (1943) 178
Corrigan, Lloyd 280
Corrigan, Ray 9, 11, 12
Corruption (1968) 73
Costello, Lou 24, 89
Costello, Pat 89 Coughlin, Jim 246
"The Count" 25, 74, 92-93, 113, 120–21, 136–37, 174
Courtenay, William 267
Cowan, Jerome 196, 202
Crawford, Broderick 79
The Crawling Hand (1963) 159
Crazy Knights (1944) 5, 191-95
Creature of the Devil see *Dead Men Walk*
Creature with the Atom Brain (1955) 33
The Creeper (1948) 24, 149
Cregar, Laird 152, 188
The Crime of Doctor Crespi (1935) 151, 153, 158
Criner, Lawrence 39
Crowley, Kathleen 218
Cry of the Werewolf (1944) ix, 216, 251
"Cult Movies and Video" 356
Currie, Louise xv, 103, 104, 106, 110, 111, 113–14, 131, 136, 137, **138**, 301–03, **302**
Currier, Mary 169, 171, 173
Curse of Dracula see *The Return of Dracula*
The Curse of the Cat People (1944) ix, 68
Curse of the Demon (1958) 4
Curse of the Undead (1959) 217–18
The Cyclops (1957) 150
Cyrano de Bergerac (1950) 51

Damato, Glenn 356
Daniel and the Devil see *All That Money Can Buy*
Dante, Joe 84, 356
The Dark Eyes of London see *The Human Monster*
The Dark Mirror (1946) 251

Daughter of Dr. Jekyll (1957) 190, 252
Davenport, Harry 279
Davidson, John 303–05, **304**
Davis, Bette 82
Davis, Jimmy 40, 41
Davis, Nancy 162
The Day After Tomorrow see *Strange Holiday*
The Day of the Triffids (1963) 128
The Day the Earth Stood Still (1951) 208
The Dead End Kids 4, 48
Dead Eyes of London (1965) 281
Dead Man's Eyes (1944) ix, 20, 187
Dead Men Walk (1943) xiv, 79, 80, 84, 93–102, **94**, **97**, **100**, 142, 171, 238, 243, 277
The Defiant Ones (1958) 98
Del Vecchio, Carl xv
Dell, Gabriel **272**
Demain, Gordon 77
The Demon Doctor see *Juggernaut*
Denning, Richard 243
The Deputy (TV) 111
De Sade (1969) 284
The Desert Fox (1951) 243
Desert Sands (1955) 135
Desperate Journey (1942) 44
Destination Moon (1950) 42
Destiny (1921) 226
Detour (1945) 183, 190
Devan, Carrie 179, **189**
The Devil and Daniel Webster see *All That Money Can Buy*
The Devil Bat (1940) 11, 14–25, **16**, **19**, **23**, 82, 236, 237, 240, 241, 244, 247, 250, 252, 276–77, 357
Devil Bat's Daughter (1946) 24, 94, 220, 222, 224, 225, 228, 246–53, **249**
The Devil Commands (1941) 10
The Devil's Apprentice see *The Monster Maker*
de Wit, Jacqueline 196, 202–03
Diamond, David 188
Dick Tracy vs. Crime, Inc. (1941 serial) 60, **304**
Dick Tracy vs. the Phantom Empire see *Dick Tracy vs. Crime, Inc.*
Dickens, Charles 244
Dietz, Jack 63, 85, 104, **112**, 120, 131, 140, 165, 192
Dillon, Josephine 159
Dmytryk, Edward 189
Dobrovitz, Marta 356

Dr. Cadman's Secret see *The Black Sleep*
Dr. Renault's Secret (1942) xi, 80, 147, 210
Doctor X (1932) 234
The Doctor's Secret see *The Return of Doctor X*
Donlan, Yolande xv, **19**, 21, 22–23
Donovan's Brain (1953) 162–63
"Donovan's Brain" xi, xiv, 152-53, 156, 161, 162
Doomed to Die (1940) 6
The Door with Seven Locks see *Chamber of Horrors*
D'Orsay, Fifi **285**
Double Indemnity (1944) 209
Douglas, Nathan E. *see* Young, Ned
Douglas, Sharon 196, 203
Dowling, Allan 163
Downs, Johnny 76, **78**, 81, 84
Dracula (1931) 22, 24, 46, 50, 71, 98, 100, 102, 104, 203, 267; (stage) 91, 92, 127, 164
Dracula vs. Frankenstein (1971) 69–71, 147–48, **337**
Drake, Claudia 229, 234
Dukesbery, Jack xvi
Dumbrille, Douglass 80, 210, 254, 259, 261, 270, 271, **272**
Dunn, Harvey B. 67
Dunn, James 279, 281, 282
Dunn, Tay 192

Earth vs. the Flying Saucers (1956) 33
East of Piccadilly see *The Strangler*
The East Side Kids xii, 1, 2, 3, 4, 5, 46, 48, 49, 50, 51, 52, 88, 91, 115, 116, 117, 120, 121, 194, 270
East Side Kids (1940) 2, 46
The East Side Kids Meet Bela Lugosi see *Ghosts on the Loose*
"Ecco" 225
Edwards, Blake xv, 222, 225
Eggenton, Joseph 54
El Dorado (1967) 218
Eldredge, George 66, 167
Ellis, John 17, **19**, 21, 22, 250
Ellison, James 280, 281
Emerson, Hope 4
Emmett, Fern 95, 99
The Empire Strikes Back (1980) xv, 218

The Enchanted Forest (1945) 279
Endfield, Cyril 284
English, John 210
Erdody, Leo 101, 184, 277
Esmond, Carl 254, **255**, 258, 259, 261
Evans, Gene 162
Everson, William K. 25, 84, 102, 150, 163, 220, 225, 226, 227, 356

The Face of Marble (1946) 140, 186, 195, 228–36, **230**, **232**
Faceless (1988) 73
Fährmann Maria (1935) 219, 226, 228
"Famous Monsters of Filmland" 84, 111, 356
"Fangoria" xv, 48, 52, 93, 102, 113, 139, 186, 190
Farmer, Virginia 221
Fatal Attraction (1987) 42
The Fatal Hour (1940) 6
Feindel, Jockey A. 178, 185
Feist, Felix 162, 163
Feld, Fritz 254, 257, 259
Feltenstein, George xv
Field, Betty 203
Field, Medora 177
"Films in Review" 218
"The Films of Bela Lugosi" 25, 48, 51, 60, 74, 93, 120, 139, 174, 356
Fine, Larry 192
Fischer, Dennis 187
Fiske, Robert 54, 60
Flame of Stamboul (1951) 243
Fleming, Eric 218
Flint, Sam 95, 145
The Flying Serpent (1946) 20, 21, 23, 80, 82, 236–46, **239**, **240**, **242**, 247
Flynn, Charles 157
Flynn, Joe 235
"Focus on Film" 227
Fog Island (1945) xvi, 80, 146, 185, 195–204, **197**, **200**
Fonda, Henry 111, 173
For Whom the Bell Tolls (1943) 53
Ford, Francis 269
Ford, John xiv, 269
Ford, Philip 265, 267, 268–69
Ford, Wallace (actor) 22, 104, 106, 110–11, 113, 305–06, **307**
Ford, Wallace (bum) 111
Foreman, Carl xv, 51
4D Man (1959) 79

Fox, Wallace 67, 92
Francis, Arlene 203
Francis, Freddie 163
Franken, Rose 188
Frankenstein (1931) 79, 92, 100, 186, **311**
Frankenstein Meets the Wolf Man (1943) 79, 99–100, 103, 104
Fraser, Richard 287
Frazer, Robert 54, 60, 306–10, **309**
Freaks (1932) 44, 69, 110, **340**
From a Whisper to a Scream see *The Offspring*
From Hell It Came (1957) 173
From the Earth to the Moon (1958) 258 Fromkess, Leon 183
Frost, Terry xv, 143, 147, 149, 239, 244
The Frozen Dead (1967) 157
Frye, Dwight 95, 98, 99–101, **100**, 102, 310–12, **311**
Frye, Dwight, Jr. 100-01
The Fugitive (TV) 216
Fuller, Sam 183
Fulton, John P. 80

G-Men vs. the Black Dragon (1942 serial) 616–62
Gable, Clark 159
Gang Busters (1942 serial) 332
Gardner, Ava xv, 115, 119–20, 121
Gates, Harvey 54, 57, 58, 64, 67
Gaye, Lisa 172
Gemora, Charles 80, 109, 161
Gendron, Pierre 146, 189, 199
Gest, Inna 2
The Ghost and the Guest (1943) 142, 279, 282
The Ghost Breakers (1940) 37, 41
Ghost Catchers (1944) ix
Ghost Chasers (1951) 1, 270
Ghost Crazy see *Crazy Knights*
The Ghost Creeps see *Boys of the City*
The Ghost Goes Wild (1947) 279-80
The Ghost of Frankenstein (1942) 26, 58
The Ghost Ship (1943) 99
Ghost Town Law (1942) 280
Ghostbusters (1984) xv
Ghosts in the Night see *Ghosts on the Loose*
Ghosts on the Loose (1943) xii, 1, 3, 27, 37, 52, 114–21, **118**, 164, 195, 270, 275, 357

The Giant Claw (1957) 33, 245
Gibson, Judith see Loring, Teala
Gifford, Denis see "A Pictorial History of the Horror Film"
Gilbert, Billy 192, 193–94
The Girl Who Dared (1944) 174–77
Girls in Chains (1943) 183
Girls in Prison (1956) 71
Glasser, Albert xv, 83, 149–50
Glen or Glenda? (1953) 67, 114, 140
Glut, Don 79
Godzilla, King of the Monsters! (1956) 201
The Gold Bug (unmade Lugosi film) 140
Goldstein, Bruce xv
Gollomb, Joseph 53
Gorcey, Bernard **56**, 89
Gorcey, David 47, 50, 270
Gorcey, Leo 1, 46, 50, 115, 117, 121, 270, 271
Gordon, Alex xv, 71, 139, 172, 243–44, 356, 357
Gordon, Bobby 273
Gordon, Charles 213, 216
Gordon, Richard 244, 356
The Gorilla (1939) 15, 112, 194
Gorilla at Large (1954) 12
The Gorilla Man (1943) 37
The Gorilla Strikes see *The Ape Man*
Gould, Harvey 30
Graff, Wilton 263, 268
Graham, Frank 160
Granby, Joseph 207
Grave Robbers from Outer Space see *Plan 9 from Outer Space*
Graves, Peter 271
Gray, Lorna see Booth, Adrian
The Gray Ghost (TV) 173
The Great Gabbo (1929) 32
Greenhalgh, Jack 101, 245
Gries, Tom 162, 163
Griffith, Billy 21
Griffith, D. W. 194
Guest, Ina 3
Guest, Val 22
Guestward Ho! (TV) 148
Gun Crazy (1949) 2
The Guns of Navarone (1961) 51

Haade, William 265
Haden, Sara 252
Hail the Conquering Hero (1944) 119

Haines, Donald 47
Hajos, Karl 201
Hale, Jonathan 207
Hale, Michael 247, 250, 251, 252
Hall, Ellen 131, 136, **138**
Hall, Henry 9, 11, 81, 104, 133, 137, 238, **239**, 241, 244
Hall, Huntz xv, 46, 48, 50, 115, 116–77, 119, 120, 121, 270, 284
Halliwell, Leslie 25, 113, 190
Hamilton, John 175, 177, 192, 194, 285
Hannibal (1959) 120
Harem Scarum (1965) 34
Harlan, Kenneth 55, 66, 67
Harlem on the Prairie (1938) 98
Harolde, Ralf 205
Harris, Marilyn 79
Hartmann, Edmund L. 233
Hatari! (1962) 218
Hatton, Rondo xiv, 149, 278, **279**, 281
Haunted House (1940) 280
"Hauser's Memory" 161
Hawks, Howard 218
Hazard, Jayne 192, 194
Hayden, Harry 154, 158
Hayes, "Gabby" 80 Hayes, Helen 171
Hayward, Louis 252
He or She see *Glen or Glenda?*
Heatherton, Joey 189
Henderson, Jan 116
Henry, Bill 155, 159
Henry, Mike 245
Here Is a Man see *All That Money Can Buy*
Herrmann, Bernard 44, 45, 276
High Noon (1952) xv, 51, 259
Hillbillys in a Haunted House (1967) 24
Hinds, Samuel S. 147
His Brother's Ghost (1945) 280
His Private Secretary (1933) 33
Hit Parade of 1943 (1943) 209
Hitchcock, Alfred 99
Hitler's Women see *Women in Bondage*
Hodgins, Earle 262, 268
Hoffman, David 203
Hoffman, Max, Jr. 54, 60
Hold That Hypnotist (1957) 1
Holden, Eddie 76
Hollywood and Vine (1945) 204
"Hollywood Babylon II" 244
"Hollywood in the Forties" 163

Home of the Brave (1949) 51
Hope, Anna 86 Hope, Bob 37, 41
The Horror Chamber of Dr. Faustus (1962) 72–73, 184
Horror Island (1941) 200
Hotel (1967) 110
House of Dracula (1945) 79, 284
House of Frankenstein (1944) 10, 79, 147, 149, 242
House of Horrors (1946) 20, 24, 125
The House of Mystery (1934) 12
House of Wax (1953) 98
House on Haunted Hill (1959) 34
How DOoo You Do (1946) 280
How Green Was My Valley (1941) 44, 276
Howard, Curly 192, 194
Howard, Moe 192
Howard, Shemp 43, 192, 193, 194
The Howling (1981) 186, 356
Huggins, Roy 216
Hugo, Mauritz 122, **125**, 126, 127
Hull, Henry 259
The Human Duplicators (1965) 159
The Human Monster (1940) 15, 26, 92, 112, 280–81
The Hunchback of Notre Dame (1939) 15
The Hustler (1961) 184

I Changed My Sex see *Glen or Glenda?*
I Eat Your Skin (1970) 41
I Led Two Lives see *Glen or Glenda?*
I Ring Doorbells (1946) 234
I Walked with a Zombie (1943) 12, 40, 128
I Was a Teenage Werewolf (1957) 212
Ice-Capades (1941) 157
Ice-Capades Revue (1942) 109, 157
Immediate Disaster (1955) 208
In Old New Mexico (1945) 83
In the Money (1958) 32
Ince, John 131
Indestructible Man (1956) 235
Inescort, Frieda 131, 165, 171
Inherit the Wind (1960) 98
Inner Sanctum (TV) 267
Invasion of the Saucer Men (1957) 31
Invasion U.S.A. (1952) 150
Invisible Agent (1942) 37
Invisible Ghost (1941) xiii, 26–35, **28**, **30**, 37, 46, 51, 58, 63, 127, 131, 229

The Invisible Killer (1940) 281
The Invisible Man Returns (1940) 15
Island of Lost Souls (1933) 82, 104,
  113, 159
Isle of Forgotten Sins (1943) 178, 187
Isle of the Snake People see *Snake
  People*
It Came from Beneath the Sea (1955)
  33, 267
It Conquered the World (1956) 234

Jackson, Selmer 11 Jackson, Thomas
  E. 231, 234, 263, 267, 268
Jacoby, Michel 229
The Jade Mask (1945) 281
James, John 248, 251, 252
Jay, Griffin 250–51
*Jesse James Meets Frankenstein's
  Daughter* (1966) 195
Jive Junction (1943) 178
Joan Medford Is Missing see *House of
  Horrors*
The Joe Franklin Show (TV) 22
Johnny Doesn't Live Here Anymore
  (1944) 281
Johnny Guitar (1954) xiv
Johnson, Noble 37
Johnson, Tom xv
Jolley, I. Stanford 9, 60, 312–16, **313**
Jordan, Bobby 1, 46, 115, 116, 117,
  270, **272**
Juggernaut (1936) 10
The Jungle Captive (1945) 104, 202
Jungle Queen (unmade Monogram
  film) 140
Jungle Woman (1944) 147
Junior G-Men (1940 serial) 1
Junior "G" Men of the Air (1942
  serial) 1
Juran, Nathan 111

Kaaren, Suzanne 17, **19**, 20, 22
Kaminsky, Stuart 62
Kane, Joe 157-58
Karloff, Boris xi, 6–7, 10–11, 12, 13,
  13, 14, 15, 16, 22, 24, 26, 41, 79, 80,
  81, 92, 103, 104, 111, 112, 161, 186,
  188, 201, 208, 268, 276
Katzman, Sam xii, **xiii**, 27, 33–34, 46,
  48, 49, 53–54, 57, 63, 67, 69, 74, 85,
  93, 104, 120, 127, 131, 139, 140, 165,
  192, 229, 267

Kay, Edward 44–45, 128, 271, 275,
  276
Keep 'Em Flying (1941) 109
"Keep Watching the Skies!" 163
Keith, Ian 94, 196, 199, 203, 210, 262,
  265, **266**, 266, 267, 269, 316–18, **317**
Kelley, P. J. 46
Kelly, Grace 259
Kelly, Lew 86, **87**, 89
Kelsey, Fred 27, 29
Kelso, Edmond 44, 124
Kenyon, Gwen 66
Kerr, Donald 17, 20, 22
Killer Bats see *The Devil Bat*
King, Loretta 67
King of the Rocket Men (1949
  serial) 241
King of the Zombies (1941) xii, xv, 24,
  35–45, **38**, **42**, 89, 122, 124, 126,
  127, 128, 275, 276, 285
"Kings of the Bs" 157
Kirby, George 106
Kiss of Evil see *The Kiss of the
  Vampire*
The Kiss of the Vampire (1963) 258
Knaggs, Skelton 99, 284, 318
Koch, Howard W. xv, 135
Kohner, Frederick 157
Kolker, Henry 179, 181, 187
Koplan, Harry 251-2
Kosleck, Martin xv, 187
Kovack, Nancy 245
Kramer, Hope 237, **240**, 244
Kramer, Stanley 98
Kyser, Kay 24

The Lady and the Doctor see *The
  Lady and the Monster*
The Lady and the Monster (1944) xi,
  xiv, 82, 151–63, **154**, **160**, 205, 208,
  209
Lady in the Death House (1944) 128
Lamont, Molly 248, 251
Landers, Lew 164
Landru, Henri 179
Landru see *Bluebeard* (1962)
Lane, Rosemary 265
Lang, Fritz 226
Lange, Johnny 51, 276
Lanning, Reggie 259, 265, 267
LaPlanche, Rosemary 24, 221, **223**,
  224–25, 227, 247, **249**, 250, 251–52,
  318

Lassie (TV) 271
Late Night with David Letterman (TV) 92 Laughton, Charles 82, 159
The Lawrence Welk Show (TV) 225
Leary, Nolan 221, 225, 247, 251
LeBorg, Reginald 141
Lee, Bernard 163
Lee, Norman 278
Leifert, Don xv, 11, 25, 43, 60, 84, 99, 113, 121, 128–29, 135, 139, 190–91, 202, 228, 236, 241, 253, 356
Lennig, Arthur 356; *see also* "The Count"
The Leopard Man (1943) 79, 261
Le Picard, Marcel 30
Letterman, David 92
Lewis, Jerry 117, 250
Lewis, Joseph H. xi, xv, 1–2, 3, 4–5, 30, 31, 34, 35, 46, 67, 183
Lewis, Ralph 238, **240**, 241, 244
Lewis, Sybil 122
Lewis, Vera 270, 271
Lewton, Val ix, 40, 67, 93, 99
Libkov, Marek M. 259, 260
Life with Luigi (TV) 148
Lighthouse (1947) 220
Lisi, Virna 189
The Little Tough Guys 48
Littlefield, Ralph 106, 136
Littman, Bill xvi, 45
The Living Dead (1936) 44
The Living Ghost (1942) 281–82, **282**
Livingston, Robert 262, 267, 269
Lloyd, George 197
Lock Your Doors see *The Ape Man*
Lockhart, June 252
The Lodger (1944) xi, 187–88
Lombard, Carole 208
London Blackout Murders (1942) 282
The Lone Ranger (TV) 60, 90
The Long Goodbye (1973) 218
Loring, Teala **166**, 167, **170**, 174, 179, 181, 185, 319, **319**
Lorre, Peter 15, 24, 37
Lowery, Robert 122, 125, **125**, **127**, 179, 320–22, **321**
Luce, Greg 356, 357
Lugosi, Bela **ii**, ix, xi, xii, xiv, xvi, 6, 7, 11, 12, 15–17, **19**, 19, 20, 21, 22, 23, **23**, 24–25, 26–27, **28**, **30**, 31, 32, 33, 34, 35, 37, 40, 41, 42, 43, 46, 48, 49, **49**, 50, 51, 52, 53, 54, 56, **56**, 57, 58–60, 61, 62, 63, 64, **65**, 67, 68, 69, **70**, 71, 72, **72**, 73, **73**, 74, 79, 80, 82,

85, 86, **87**, 88, 89, **90**, 91–92, 93, 103–04, 107–09, **108**, 110, 111, 112–13, **112**, 113, 114, 115, 116–17, 119, 120, 121, 127, 130, 131, 134, 136–37, **138**, 139, 140–41, 147, 164, 165, **166**, **168**, 170–71, **170**, 171, 172, 173, 174, 187, 188, 195, 203, 208, 229, 235, 241, 243, 244, 247, 252, 267, 270, 271, 280, 281, **292**, **307**, **317**, **319**, **349**, 356, 357
Lugosi, Bela, Jr. 48, 117
Lugosi, Hope 63, 140, 141
Lugosi, Lillian 103, 117
Luke, Keye 7
Lydecker, Howard 241
Lydecker, Theodore 241
Lynn, Emmett 179, 180, 184, 185
Lyon, Therese 221

Macbeth (1948) xiv, 282
MacBride, Donald **279**
McCann, Doreen 206, 209
McCarthy, Todd 157
McCarty, Patti 179, **189**
McCluskey, Thorp 140
McCollum, Barry 122, **125**
McDonald, Francis 254, 259
McDonald, Marie 179
McDonnell, Dave xv
McGuire, John 27, 28–29, 32, 35
McKay, Wanda **87**, 88, 89, 90-91, 133, 137, **138**, 143, 145, 147, 149, 322–23
McKee, Pat 131, **138**
MacQueen, Scott xv, 356, 357
The Mad Doctor (1941) 149
The Mad Doctor of Market Street (1942) 31 *The Mad Ghoul* (1943) 147, 171
Mad Love (1935) 143, 146, 147, 187, 268
Mad Max Beyond Thunderdome (1985) 69
The Mad Monster (1942) xiv, 20, 23, 74–84, **76**, **78**, **81**, 98, 99, 121, 201, 238, 244, 247, 276, 278
Madmen of Mandoras (1964) 157
Madonna of the Desert (1948) 220
Maëdchen in Uniform (1931) 226
The Magic Sword (1962) 69
The Magnificent Seven (1960) 259
The Main Street Kid (1948) 282–83
Mallott, Yolande *see* Donlan, Yolande
Maloney, William Brown 188

The Maltese Falcon (1941) 202
The Man from Planet X (1951) 190
The Man in Half Moon Street (1944) ix
Man Made Monster (1941) 81, **334**
Man of a Thousand Faces (1957) 225
The Man They Could Not Hang (1939)
    112, 208, 268
The Man Who Changed His Mind see
    The Man Who Lived Again
The Man Who Knew Too Much (1956)
    99
The Man Who Lived Again (1936) 161
The Man Who Turned to Stone (1957)
    33
The Man with Nine Lives (1940) 10,
    112, 268 *The Man with Two Brains*
    (1983) 157
The Man Without a Body (1959) 157
The Manchurian Candidate (1962) 62
Mank, Greg xv, 191, 236, 242, 243,
    244, 356, 357
Mansion of the Doomed (1977) 73
Mara, Adele 215, 216, 254, **257**, 259,
    268
March of the Wooden Soldiers see
    Babes in Toyland
Marion, Charles 51
Mark, Bob **260**
Mark of the Vampire (1935) 50
Mars, Monica 248, 251
Marshall, E. G. 161
Martin, Al 31–32, 34
Martin, Dean 117
Martin, Helen 34
Martin, Marian 207, 208, 209
Martin, Steve 157
Martucci, Mark xvi
The Mask of Diijon (1946) 283
The Masked Marvel (1943 serial) 110
Mason, James 142, 286
Mason, LeRoy 159, 268
Master Minds (1949) 1, 24, **283**, 284
A Medal for Benny (1945) 142
Melman, Larry (Bud) 92
The Men (1950) 51
Men Must Fight (1933) 98
Menschen am Sonntag (1929) 184
Merande, Doro 203
Metcalfe, James 237
Metropolis (1926) 184
Middleton, Charles 221, **223**, 224,
    270, 271, **272**, 323–25
"Midnight Marquee" 100, 246
Mighty Joe Young (1949) 71, 149

Miles, Art 112, 194, 270
Miller, Don 150, 191, 192, 225
Miller, Ray 86, 92, 106
The Miracle Man (1919) 32
Mr. Hex (1946) 284
Mister Roberts (stage) 173
Mr. Wise Guy (1942) 91
Mr. Wong at Headquarters see *The
    Fatal Hour*
Mr. Wong, Detective (1938) 6
Mr. Wong in Chinatown (1939) 6
Mr. Wu (1927) 12
Mitchell, Duke 117
Mitchell, Irving 54, 60
Mohr, Gerald 254, 257, 259
Monserrat (stage) 216
Monsieur Verdoux (1947) 188
Monsoon see *Isle of Forgotten Sins*
The Monster see *The Lady and the
    Monster The Monster and the Girl*
    (1941) xi, 80, 161, 208
The Monster and the Lady see *The
    Lady and the Monster*
The Monster Maker (1944) ix, xiv, 90,
    141–50, **143**, **146**, **148**, 199
Mooney, Martin 146, 179
Moore, Clayton 55, 60–61
Moore, Dennis 2, 3, 46, 51, 325–27
Moran, Frank 65, 68, 112, 115, 117,
    119, **166**, 167, **170**, 171, 172, 174,
    276, 281, **319**, 327–29
Moreland, Mantan xii, 36, 37, 41, 42,
    42, 43, 44, 45, 122, 124, 126, 128,
    140, 285, 329–31
Morgan, Dennis 265
Morgan, Frank 149
Morgan, Ralph ix, xiv, 143, 145, 146,
    146, 147, 148–49, 150, 331–33, **332**
Moriarty, Michael 245
Morris, Wayne 265
Morrison, Sunshine Sammy 47, 50–
    51, 117
Morse, Terry 201
The Mortal Storm (1940) 44
Mortimer, Edward 17, **19**, 22
Mother Riley Meets the Vampire
    (1952) 140
La Muerte Viviente see *Snake People*
Mulhall, Jack 27
The Mummy's Curse (1944) 51, 212
The Mummy's Ghost (1944) 125, 212,
    250
The Mummy's Hand (1940) 110, 250,
    268

The Mummy's Tomb (1942) 110, 212, 242, 250
Muni, Paul 267
Murder by Television (1935) 58, 114
Murder by the Stars& see Invisible Ghost
Murder in the Blue Room (1944) ix, 126
Murder in the Family see *Crazy Knights*
Murders in the Rue Morgue (1932) 32, 71, 109, 112, 173, 174
Murnau, F. W. 178
Muse, Clarence 27, 32
My Name Is Julia Ross (1945) 2
My Son, the Vampire see *Mother Riley Meets the Vampire*
The Mysterious Doctor (1943) 37
Mysterious Dr. Satan (1940 serial) 268
The Mysterious Island (1929) 69
The Mysterious Mr. M (1946 serial) 51
The Mysterious Mr. Wong (1935) 12, 26, 110
Mystery of Marie Roget (1942) 50, 146
The Mystery of Mr. Wong (1939) 6
Mystery of the 13th Guest (1943) 42, 284
Mystery of the Wax Museum (1933) 234
Myton, Fred 98

Nabonga (1944) 98, 284, **285**
Nagel, Anne 75, **78**, 81–82, **81**, 83, 84, 208, 333–35, **334**
Naish, J. Carrol 69, 80, 142, 143, 145, 146, **146**, 147–48, **148**, 149, 150, 335–38, **337**
The Naked Venus (1959) 190
Nalder, Reggie 99
Napier, Alan 284
Narrow Margin (1990) 42
Nash, Mary 153, 158, 159, 160
Neal, Patricia 208
Neal, Tom 86, **87**, 89
The Neanderthal Man (1953) 150
Nelson, Sam 4
Nesmith, Ottola 29
Neufeld, Sigmund 16, 237
Neumann, Kurt 164
"Never Cross a Vampire" 62–63
Never Give a Sucker an Even Break (1941) 109

Neville, John 237
The New Adventures of Charlie Chan (TV) 148
Newfield, Sam 83, 101, 102, 150, 245, 246
Newman, Alfred 44, 276
Nigh, William 11–12, 14, 60–61, 131, 165
The Night Has Eyes see *Terror House*
Night Key (1937) 6
Night Monster (1942) 26, 85, 149
Night of Terror (1933) 110, **307**
Night of the Demon see *Curse of the Demon*
Night of the Ghouls (1959) 67
Night of the Living Dead (1968) 41
Night Star – Goddess of Electra see *War of the Zombies*
Nightmare Alley (1947) 203
Ninotchka (1939) 15
No Traveler Returns (stage) 203, **317**
Norcross, Van 124
Nyoka and the Tigermen see *Perils of Nyoka*

Oakland, Vivien 175, 177
Oakman, Wheeler 86, 115, 116
O'Brien, Dave 2, 3, 5, 17, 20, 22, **23**, 46, **49**, 50, 51, 86, 89, 250, 285
O'Day, Nell xv, 146
O'Donnell, Gene xv, 9, 11, 18, **19**, 22
Of Mice and Men (1939) 44; (stage) 44, 79, 111
The Offspring (1987) 69
The Old Dark House (1932) 3
Old Mother Riley Meets the Vampire see *Mother Riley Meets the Vampire*
One Body Too Many (1944) 187
One Frightened Night (1935) 98–99
$1,000 a Touchdown (1939) 90
O'Sullivan, William 259 Ouspenskaya, Maria 104
Out of the Night see *Strange Illusion*
The Outer Limits (TV) xiii, 62, 63
Owen, Garry 205
The Ox-Bow Incident (1943) 44

Pace, Terry 186
Padden, Sarah 77
Paget, Debra 172
Palmer, Lilli 278
Parker, Jean 179, 185, 186, 187, **189**

Parnell, Effie 221, 222
Parsons, Lindsley xii, 37, 140, 233
Pate, Michael 217, 218
Patton, George 69
The Pearl of Death (1944) 149
Peil, Edward, Sr. 54, 60
Pembroke, George 27, 28, 51, 54, 60, 179, 187, 338
Pendleton, Nat 43
Penman, Lea 203
Perils of Nyoka (1942 serial) 99, 109, 268, **295**, **297**
Perils of the Darkest Jungle see *The Tiger Woman*
Perils of the Wilderness (1956 serial) 51
Peter Gunn (TV) 4
Petrillo, Sammy 117
The Phantom Creeps (1939 serial) 15
Phantom Killer (1942) 42, 284–85
The Phantom Killer see *Invisible Ghost*
Phantom Monster see *Invisible Ghost*
Phantom of Chinatown (1940) 7
The Phantom of 42nd Street (1945) 285
Phantom of Paris see *Mystery of Marie Roget*
The Phantom Speaks (1945) 159, 161, 204–11, 218
"The Phantom's Ultimate Video Guide" 102, 150, 228, 252
"Photon" 102
Pickwick Papers (1954) 244
"A Pictorial History of the Horror Film" 25, 26, 36, 150, 252
The Picture of Dorian Gray (1945) 44
Pierce, Jack P. 80, 284
Pierlot, Francis 254, 259
Pillow of Death (1945) 20, 31
Pipitone, Nino 62
The Plague of the Zombies (1966) 40
Plan 9 from Outer Space (1959) 67
Poe, Edgar Allan 140, 151
Polidori, John 218
Port Sinister (1953) 210
Porter, Lew 51, 276
Portia, Rosemary 46
Possessed (1947) 251
Powers, Tom 205, 209 *The Prairie* (1948) 220
Preble, Fred 101
"The Premature Burial" 151
Presley, Elvis 34

Price, Hal 17, 96, 250
Price, Vincent 98
Pride of the Bowery (1941) 5
The Pride of the Yankees (1942) 187
Prince of Players (1955) 267
Professor Creeps (1942) 195
"The Psychotronic Encyclopedia of Film" 14, 25, 43, 74, 84, 93, 113, 174, 190, 219, 235, 246, 252, 261, 269
Purcell, Dick 36, 37, 41, 42, 285

Q (1982) 245
The Quiet Man (1952) xiv
Quigley, Juanita 155

Ralston, Vera xv, 153, **154**, 156, 157-58, 159, 161, 162
The Range Rider (TV) 90
Rathbone, Basil 72
The Raven (1935) 19, 71, 143, 146, 147, 164
Ray, Nicholas xiv
The Ray Milland Show (TV) 4
Raye, Martha 90
The RCA Victor Show (TV) 4
The Rebel Set (1959) 185
Reefer Madness (1936) 51
Reinhardt, Max 178
Renavent, George 259
Return of Captain America see *Captain America*
Return of Captain Marvel see *Adventures of Captain Marvel*
The Return of Doctor X (1939) 15, 265
The Return of Dracula (1958) 98, 212
Return of the Ape Man (1944) ix, xiv, xvi, 27, 50, 68, 112, 124, 131, 136, 164–74, **166**, **168**, **170**, 179, 186, 229, 235, 275, **319**, 357
The Return of the Vampire (1943) 37, 80, 94, 164, 165, 250-51, 258
Revenge of the Dead see *Night of the Ghouls*
Revenge of the Zombies (1943) xii, 37, 40, 41, 43, 73, 79, 121-29, **125**, **127**, **129**, 165, 171, 202, 250, 275, 284, **321**
Revolt of the Zombies (1936) x, 41
Rey, Rosa 230, 234–35
Rice, Florence 279
Ridges, Stanley 161, 205, 206, 208, 209, 210

Rimfire (1949) 220
Rio Bravo (1959) xv, 218
Rio Grande (1950) xiv
Rio Lobo (1970) 218
The Ritz Brothers 15
Rizzo, Charlie 100
Roach, Hal 251
Roberts, Lynne 206, 209, 210
Robot Monster (1953) 79
The Rocketeer (1991) 149
Rocketship X-M (1950) 150
Rocky Jones, Space Ranger (TV) 267
Rodan (1957) 245
The Rogues Tavern (1936) 31
Roma Contro Roma see *War of the Zombies*
Rooney, Mickey 120
Rosen, Phil 5, 50, 131, 165
Rosenbloom, Maxie 192, 193, 194
Ross, Harry 80
Rossitto, Angelo 46, 48–49, **49**, 52, 65, 67, 68–71, **70**, 338–39, **340**
Run for Your Life (TV) 216
Runser, Mary xv
Russell, Elizabeth xv, 2, 65, **65**, 66, 67–68, 72, **73**, 136, 339–41, **343**
Ryan, Tim 193, 194, 271

S O S Coast Guard (1937 serial) 92, 271
The Saga of the Viking Women and Their Voyage to the Waters of the Great Sea Serpent (1957) 150
Sahara (1943) 142
St. John, Al "Fuzzy" 99, 280
The Saint's Double Trouble (1940) 15
Salemi, Dom 225, 227
Sands of Iwo Jima (1949) 216
Sarecky, Barney 104 Sawaya, George 149
Scared to Death (1947) 69, 114, 140, 251
Scharf, Walter 159
Schmitz, Sybille 226
Schnitzer, Gerald 91
Schufftan, Eugen xv, 178, 184
"Science Fiction in the Cinema" 163
Scott, Sherman see Newfield, Sam
"Scream Queens" 109
The Sea Hornet (1951) 268
Seal, Peter 115
Seddok, l'Erede di Satana see *Atom Age Vampire*

Sekely, Steve xv, 127–28, 129, 220, 250
Selander, Lesley 216, 219
Sell, Bernard 192, 194
Sergeant York (1941) 45, 276
Server, Lee 116
Seven Footprints to Satan (1929) 69
Seward, Edmond 271
The Seventh Victim (1943) 67–68
Sh! The Octopus (1938) 20
Shadow of Chinatown (1936 serial) 60, 64, 114
Shadow Over Chinatown see *Doomed to Die*
Sharpe, Dave 109
Shayne, Robert xv, 231, 233, 234, 235
She (1916) 44
The She-Creature (1956) 71
She Demons (1958) 72
She Devil (1957) 42
She-Wolf of London (1946) 20, 24, 200, 252, 258
Sherlock Holmes and the Secret Weapon (1942) 44
Sherman, George 153, 156, 157–58, 159, 161, 163
Sherman, Sam xv, 69–71, 148, 356
Shirk, Adam Hull 12
Short, Dorothy 47, **49**, 51
Silent Death see *Voodoo Island*
Siodmak, Curt xi, xiv, xv, 7, 10, 12, 151, 152, 153, 157, 158, 161, 162–63, 282
Siodmak, Robert 163
Sleepy Lagoon (1943) 109
The Slime People (1963) 159
Smith, Harold Jacob 98
Snake People (1968) 41
The Snow Creature (1954) 212
So Dark the Night (1946) 2
The Son of Dr. Jekyll (1951) 252
Son of Dracula (1943) xi, 98, 104, 212
Son of Frankenstein (1939) 7, 15, 19
Song of the South (1947) 126
Sorel, Sonia 180, 184, 185, 187
The Soul of a Monster (1944) ix *The Spell of Amy Nugent* (1945) 285–86
Spellbound (1940) see *The Spell of Amy Nugent*
Spellbound (1945) 251
The Sphinx (1933) 285
The Spider Woman (1944) 69
Spook Busters (1946) 194, 269–73, **272**
Spook Chasers (1957) 270

Spooks Run Wild (1941) xv, 1, 5, 27, 35, 45–52, **49**, 58, 71, 94, 115, 116, 270, 276, 357
Stacey, Patricia 39, 122
Stanwyck, Barbara 209
Star Wars (1977) 218
"Starlog" xv
Steele, Bob 123, 125, 127
Stein, Jule 209
Steiner, Max 45, 276
Stengler, Mack 44, 128
Sterling, Anne 182
Stewart, Peggy 214, 216, **289**
Storm, Gale xv, 123, 125
Storm Over Lisbon (1944) 161
Stossel, Ludwig 179, 181, 184, 187, 284
Strange, Glenn xi, xv, 75, **76**, **78**, 79–80, 81, **81**, 82, 83, 84, 142, 145, 149, 278, **283**, 284, 341–45
Strange, Robert 29, 76, 80, 97, 99, 345–46
The Strange Case of Dr. Rx (1942) 12
Strange Holiday (1946) 286
Strange Illusion (1945) 286
The Strange Mr. Gregory (1945) 286
Stranger from Venus see *Immediate Disaster*
Stranger on the Third Floor (1940) 32
The Strangler (1942) 286
Strangler of the Swamp (1945) xiv, 20, 79, 219–28, 223, 250
Strock, Herbert L. xv, 162–63
Stromberg, Hunt 179
Student Tour (1934) 51
Studio One (TV) 161
Sturges, Preston 119
Sul-Te-Wan, Madame 39, 123, 126, **127**
Summer and Smoke (stage) 173
Supernatural (1933) 208
Suspicion (1941) 45, 276
Svehla, Gary xv, 357
The Swedish Angel 149
Swires, Steve xv, 218

Talbot, Lyle 127, 284
Talbott, Gloria 252
Tarantula (1955) 149
Tarzan and the Valley of Gold (1966) 245
Taylor, Forrest 2, 3, 98
Teenage Zombies (1960) 41

Tell Your Children see *Reefer Madness*
Temple, Shirley 69
The Ten Commandments (1956) 267
Terenzio, Maurice xvi, 357
Terror House (1943) 142, 286
The Terror of Tiny Town (1939) 98
Terry, Phillip 80, 161
That Gang of Mine (1940) 5
They Saved Hitler's Brain see *Madmen of Mandoras*
Thiele, William 233
The Thing That Couldn't Die (1958) 157
The Thirteenth Guest (1932) 284
Three Men in White (1944) 119
Three of a Kind (1944) 192
The Three Stooges 192, 194
Tiger Man see *The Lady and the Monster*
The Tiger Woman (1944 serial) 60; (1945) 268
The Time Travelers (1964) 43
Timpone, Tony xv, 48, 52, 67, 69
The Tingler (1959) 34
Tiny Ron 149
To Be or Not to Be (1942) 44
Torrid Zone (1940) 202
Ein Toter sucht seiner Morder see *The Brain*
Tower of Terror (1942) 286–87
Toyama, Mitsuru 60
Trail, Armitage 284
The Transvestite see *Glen or Glenda?*
Trapped by Television (1936) 31
A Tree Grows in Brooklyn (1945) 279
Trouble Chasers (1945) 192
Trowbridge, Charles 262, 268, 346–48
Turner, Maidel 203
Twice Told Tales (1963) 202

Ulmer, Edgar G. xi, xv, 2, 178–79, 182–83, 184, 185, 186, 187, 188, 189, 190, 191, 250
The Undercover Man (1949) 2
The Undying Monster (1942) 75, 80, 229
The Unearthly (1957) xv
The Uninvited (1944) xi
Unknown World (1951) 201
Up in Smoke (1957) 1
Urecal, Minerva 2, 3–4, 65, 71, 104, 110, 117–19, 192, 194, 348–52, **349**
Usher, Guy 17, **19**, 21–22, 40

Valley of the Zombies (1946) 94, 218, 234, 253, 259, 261–69, **264**, **266**
Vallin, Rick 115, 120
The Vampire Bat (1933) 60, 99
The Vampire's Ghost (1945) xv, 94, 210, 211–19, **213**, **217**, 258, 259, 261, **289**
"The Vampires of London" 164 *Vampyr* (1932) 226
"The Vampyre" 218
Vance, Lucille 89
van Eyck, Peter 163
Van Horn, Emil 106, 109–10, **112**, 173
Van Sloan, Edward 92
The Vanishing Body see *The Black Cat*
Vaughan, Dorothy 7
Veidt, Conrad 267
Veiller, Bayard 188
Vengeance see *The Brain*
Victor, Henry 37, 39, 43–44, 122, 124, 127
Vinson, Helen 154, 159
Visaroff, Michael 71
Vogan, Emmett 213, 216
Voger, Mark 140
von Stroheim, Erich 32, 151, 153, **154**, 156, 157, 158, 160, **160**, 161, 162, 163, 210, 283
Voodoo Blood Bath see *I Eat Your Skin*
Voodoo Island (1957) 41
Voodoo Man (1944) xii, xiii, xvi, 27, 32, 63, 71, 72, 90, 110, 127, 129–41, **132**, **134**, **138**, 165, 173, 186, 195, 229, 244, 275, 276, 357
Voodoo Queen see *Jungle Queen*
Voodoo Woman (1957) 243, 244
Voss, Peter 226

Wake of the Red Witch (1948) 216
Walker, Terry 27, **28**, 32, 131
The Walking Dead (1936) 99, 208
Wallace, Edgar 278, 280, 281
Walter, Wilfred 112, 280
Walters, Luana 3, 64, 66, 67, 68, 71, 73, **73**, 74, 352–53
War of the Zombies (1965) 41
Ward, Amelita 104
Warner, Harry 53
Warner, Jack 53
Waterfront (1944) 128
Watkin, Pierre 206
Waxman, Franz 44, 276

Wayne, John 33, 216
Weatherwax, Rudd 271
"Weird Tales" 140
Weird Woman (1944) ix, 68, 149, **343**
Welch, Raquel 189
Weldon, Michael 357; *see also* "The Psychotronic Encyclopedia of Film"
Welles, Orson xiv, 282
The Werewolf (1956) 212
WereWolf of London (1935) 201, 259
Whale, James 3
"When Zombies Walked" 140
Whipper, Leigh 39, 44
White, Dan 133 *White Pongo* (1945) 11, 277, 287
White Zombie (1932) 32, 40, 60, 136, **309**
Whitney, John 196, 201, 203
Whitney, Peter **279**
Whitten, Marguerite 39, 45
The Wife of Monte Cristo (1946) 187
Wiley, Hugh 6
Wilke, Robert 254, **255**, 259, **260**
Wilkins, Martin 214, 217
Williams, Lawrence 146
Williams, Tennessee 173
Williams, Zack 214
Willis, Don 25, 43, 74, 102, 136, 163, 174, 190, 219, 228, 235–56, 252–53, 261, 269, 357
Winans, Del 357
The Winged Serpent see *Q*
Wisbar, Frank xv, 219, 220, 222, 226–27, 228, 250, 252
Withers, Grant 175, 177, 213, 216, 217
The Wizard of Oz (1939) 171
The Wolf Man (1941) 20, 25, 26, 58, 75, 82, 258, 261
The Woman in White (1948) 216
The Woman Who Came Back (1945) 287
Women in Bondage (1943) 220
Wood, Edward D. 64, 67, 140
Woodbury, Joan 36, 39, 42, 43, 285
Wrixon, Maris 6, 7, 11, 12, 104, 231, 234, 287
Wynters, Charlotte 207

X the Unknown (1956) 79

Yarbrough, Jean 24, 25, 36, 37, 44
Yates, Herbert J. 152, 153, 157, 161

The Yellow Menace see *Black Dragons*
Les Yeux Sans Visage see *The Horror
  Chamber of Dr. Faustus*
You'll Find Out (1940) 12, 24, 110
Young, Ned xv, 95, 98
Young, Polly Ann 27, 32, 35, 51

Zombies of Mora Tau (1957) 33, 41
Zombies on Broadway (1945) 41, 112–13

Zucco, Frances 243, 244
Zucco, George xi, xiv, 23, 75, 80, 81,
  82, 83, 84, 94, 95, **97**, 98, 99, 101,
  102, 121, 122, 128–29, 130, 131, **132**,
  134, 136, **138**, 139, 165, **168**, 171-72,
  196, 199, 200, 201, 202, 204, 236,
  237, 240, 241–44, 245, 246, 278,
  353–55, **354**
Zucco, Stella 243, 244
Zulu (1964) 284